CW01522704

AN ILLUSTRATED HISTORY OF THE WORLD FROM THE MOST IMPORTANT MAGAZINE IN HOLLYWOOD

VAR

IETY®

AN ILLUSTRATED HISTORY OF THE WORLD FROM THE MOST IMPORTANT MAGAZINE IN HOLLYWOOD

Written by TIM GRAY
Foreword by MARTIN SCORSESE
Introduction by BRIAN GOTT

RIZZOLI
NEW YORK
New York · Paris · London · Milan

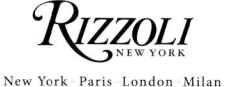

Gab
BY ALTA DURANT

DAVID NIVEN admits he is not above a bit of graceful strutting on occasion but just now he regrets it . . . he lives in one of the Marion Davies beach cottages at Santa Monica . . . while surf fishing the other afternoon, he glimpsed a movie struck bunch of girls eyeing him a short distance away . . . Niven thought he would give them a bit of he-man stuff, and show them how far he could cast . . . he made a tremendous heave . . . the line fouled, jerked, he took a step forward, stumbled and fell flat on his face just in time to be covered by an incoming wave . . . he was fully clothed.

> *Clark Gable and Vivien Leigh started that super romantic sequence for 'Gone With the Wind.' Action takes place in the Scarlett O'Hara home and probably will continue through Monday.*

THE JOHN GILBERT bungalow at Metro, long unused, has been turned into a sound stage . . . Charlie Peterson is doing his billiard stuff there for a Pete Smith short . . . Nancy Kelly giving her dad a birthday party at B-Bar-H ranch . . . Jerry Shelton passing around stogies on account of new daughter . . . Joe E. Brown made his broadcast over CBS in a photo finish Thursday . . . arrived late by plane from Washington and beat the traffic to the studio with the aid of a sheriff's car . . . Jane Withers has given that cow which disturbed Bel-Air neighbors' sleep to Henry Wilcoxon for his ranch with the promise that bossy never must visit a barbecue pit . . . Alice Faye back from east, hosted mother and friends at a Hollywood Tropics homecoming party . . . Old Doc Baker planed in yesterday ready for action at Hollywood park . . . just phoned that he has nothing but winners.

> *Groucho Marx hopes rain sequences in 'A Day at the Circus' don't last too long. He's wasting away to a whisper. Wears rubber union suit in sequence which already has cost him five pounds.*

BRUCE CABOT Sky Chiefed for Washington with a one way passage . . . his parting message: 'I don't know when I'll be back' . . . the 'Pattie Cake' is latest dance to hit Hollywood . . . Duke Daly's ork will play it for Los Angeles Junior College dance, next Thursday night . . . James Cawthorn and wife off for summer in Connecticut home . . . Oscar Oldknow tossed stag birthday party for Charles P. Skouras at his Bel-Air home with 40 guests and plenty of gag gifts . . . Patricia Ziegfeld and William Robert Stephenson filed intention to wed yesterday.

Left: May 27, 1939.

Right: The Muppets take a look at *Variety*.

Editor: Robb Pearlman
Designer: Chris McDonnell

This edition published in the United States of America in 2012 by Rizzoli International Publications, Inc.
300 Park Avenue South
New York, NY 10010
www.rizzoliusa.com

Copyright © Variety, Inc. All rights reserved.

No part of this publication may be reproduced, stored in a retreival system, or transmitted in any form or by any means, electronic, mechanical, photocopying, recording, or otherwise, without prior consent of the publishers.

2012 2013 2014 2015 / 10 9 8 7 6 5 4 3 2 1

Printed in China

ISBN: 978-0-8478-3880-6

Library of Congress Control Number: 2012932479

Left: Cary Grant.

Contents

Foreword	**8**
Introduction	**10**
1905	**12**
1920s	**42**
1930s	**64**
1940s	**104**
1950s	**132**
1960s	**164**
1970s	**210**
1980s	**248**
1990s	**272**
2000s	**292**
The Future	**310**
Photo Credits	**316**
Thanks and Acknowledgments	**320**

Foreword

By Martin Scorsese

James Cagney introduced me to *Variety*. Maybe he did the same for you.

When I was growing up, getting my first movie education on the black and white DuMont TV in our apartment, and in the neighborhood theaters, I'd hear many references in musicals to something called *Variety*, but I had only a vague understanding of what it was. It seemed like theatrical news central, something Dennis Morgan and Jack Carson referred to and fretted about and yearned to be in while they rounded the fleapit vaudeville circuit, looking for a big break. Or any break at all. I couldn't work out whether it was a newspaper, a gossip tabloid, or a tip sheet.

Mr. Cagney cleared all that up in *Yankee Doodle Dandy*, in a scene (one of many from that wonderful movie) that's become a touchstone: reclining in a hammock, as George M. Cohan, he translates *Variety*'s most famous headline— STICKS NIX HICK PIX— for a group of jive-mad kids passing by his country house. I have to admit, I thought the kids were a little silly, but I was transported by the *Variety* language. So this was *Variety*. The bible of show business. Got it.

And I got it even before I fully understood that show business— the making of magic in so many forms—was a business. Making a life and a living doing one of the things that *Variety* covered so thoroughly and indelibly—acting, writing plays, creating music, and, of course, most of all, making movies—seemed like a goal that was almost out of reach. Almost. But maybe not quite. Reaching for it was something between a calling and a compulsion. The breezy energy on every page of the paper didn't just reflect my own excitement at the idea of trying. It added to it, even if it was almost too dangerous to dream that one day I could be a part of this world too. It was inconceivable that I would be written about in those pages.

Variety may have covered all the news and gossip of show business, but for me it was something more important: an introduction to the mysterious mechanics that actually backstop wonders—the deals, the money, the rivalries, and, at the end of it all, the tough realities of the box office. It made show business seem like a pretty risky undertaking, but also— even more—impossibly challenging

Right: Martin Scorsese and Ben Kingsley on the set of *Hugo*.

and strange, seductive and, in the end, totally irresistible.

Part of this seduction was *Variety*'s language, which was slangy, brash, respectful, but always a little irreverent too, whether the subject under discussion was Eugene O'Neill or Topo Gigio. The whole paper seemed to be written by a gang of Damon Runyon characters, who took nothing too hard or too seriously, and who made up their own slang, which, once you started to understand it, made you think you were part of the big party. Once I figured out what an "ozoner" was, I felt like I'd started to crack a code, although part of my difficulty may have simply been the nearest ozoner was miles away from my neighborhood.

But *Variety* opened up the whole of show business, made it seem tough and unforgiving, and, despite all the numbers and pitiless tallying of the grosses, wildly glamorous. The centrifugal verve of the writing and reporting was intoxicating, like the buckshot dialogue in *His Girl Friday*. It seemed to reflect the high stakes and high energy of the business you had to learn and come to terms with, just the way you learned your craft.

Looking through these pages that represent a century of the single most formidable trade publication ever, I'm also struck by how immediately *Variety* makes you feel not only like a witness to history, but part of it, too, whether as a spectator or a participant. You are front row center here for plenty of folly across the century, more than a fair share of grandeur, a heaping portion of nostalgia and the creation and ascension of a great popular, populist culture—never, of course, forgetting about the wickets.

Introduction

By Brian Gott, Publisher

Since 1905, *Variety* has been situated at the epicenter of Hollywood. Not on the outside, looking in, but on the inside, looking out. Intimately woven into the fabric of the culture of a tight-knit community, *Variety* has enjoyed a unique perspective on the evolution of the entertainment industry in Los Angeles, New York, and around the globe. Note the difference between Hollywood and Los Angeles. Los Angeles is a place. Hollywood is a business. And *Variety* has been there, virtually from day one, chronicling the highs and lows, the ups and downs, the breakthroughs and breakdowns. And through it all, we've been able to literally witness and document the creation of, by a relatively small number of hugely creative and influential minds, popular culture.

Over the past century, *Variety* has also been able to provide a fascinating perspective on the people, places, and events outside of Hollywood—the very force that has shaped the world as we know it—for those within showbiz. From the sinking of the *Titanic* to man landing on the moon, from Hitler and Capone to Princess Diana and Mother Teresa, *Variety* has viewed global issues and events through a uniquely Hollywood prism. The driving force behind these stories is simple: What does it mean for showbiz? How can we learn from it? How should we respond? How will we respond? How will it look on camera?

I joined *Variety* in 1999. Not that long ago, that is, in any world other than entertainment. In that time, I've seen the dotcom boom (and the dotcom bust), the rise of (and decline of) DVD, the "re-imagining" of the music industry, and the explosion of mobile, digital, 3-D, and multi-platform content (just to name a few). Frankly, there is probably no other time I'd want to be a part of this business. Every day is different, and *Variety* is at the bleeding edge, deciphering what all of these constant changes mean for the future of our business. Of course, this is nothing new for *Variety*; the same could have been said when the industry and audiences migrated from vaudeville houses to movie theaters showing silent films, and then again shifting from the silent films to "talkies." Or the evolution of family entertainment going from clustering around the radio to clustering around the television. It's what we

Clockwise from left: Frank Sinatra, Penelope Cruz, Oliver Stone, Ben Affleck, David Furnish and Elton John, Jerry Bruckheimer, Melissa Leo, Kermit the Frog, Baz Luhrmann, Jeff Bridges, Ian McKellen, Alec Baldwin, and Helen Mirren.

 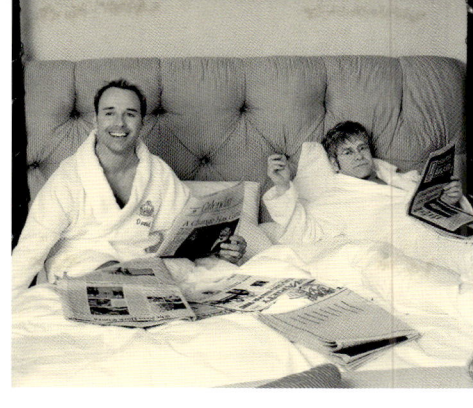 

do. It's who we are. We talk about the changes and teach our industry how to cope with them, before they actually happen. It's why we are a trusted friend (albeit a critical one much of the time) and confidant of showbiz.

Once, the head of a major motion picture studio told me that "*Variety* has always been behind the velvet rope." I respectfully corrected him, saying, "*Variety created* the velvet rope." To have your name appear in *Variety* means you've made it, you're in an exclusive club, and you belong to an extraordinarily vibrant, creative, artistic, and special community. We take great pride in having been bestowed the role as curators.

It's taken a long time to earn the level of trust, access, respect, authority, confidence, and admiration that we enjoy in showbiz. And we do not take it for granted. If we did, even if it were just for one day, the more than one hundred years of hard work and dedication that thousands of *Variety* staffers have contributed would be for naught. And that is something we simply will never compromise.

The entertainment industry may be glamorous, exciting, frustrating, and tragic, but the community is built on a single concept: telling a story. Within the pages of this book, you'll read but some of the great stories *Variety* has told.

1905

(MISS) SYDNEY SHIELDS.

Ever since Sime Silverman began *Variety* in 1905, its mandate was clear: to bring people in the entertainment business the news of the world. But initially, that world was very small.

The pages of *Variety* were filled with news and reviews of vaudeville, touring companies, burlesque, minstrel shows, the music hall, and the still-new concept of "Broadway." Most performers made their living touring, sometimes with plays but usually on a vaudeville bill with other specialty acts. In an era before mass communication, *Variety* was like a bulletin board, keeping the folks in "showbiz" abreast of what was going on.

Many *Variety* stories were only a few paragraphs long, due, in part, to the era's technology (or lack thereof). The paper was based in New York and stories from out of town were filed via pay-per-word cablegrams. Other stories were brief because, well, that was the nature of the news in those days.

News fell into several categories back then. Here are examples of four reports, repeated in their entirety:

Business deals: August 10, 1907
"Cook's Opera House, Rochester, opens Sept. 2."

Announcements: August 22, 1908
"A mass meeting will be held by the White Rats' Political League to-morrow (Sunday) at 8 P.M."

Gossip: December 3, 1910, page 10
"Big excitement around the American [theater] early this week. New carpets."

Personal info: August 22, 1908
"Tom Fitzpatrick, Al Sutherland's office guardian, is away on his vacation."

News stories were the early twentieth-century equivalent of Twitter feeds.

A key part of *Variety* was the reviews, such as this October 8, 1910, critique of a vaudeville show at New York's Colonial:

"Chaplin is typically English, the sort of comedian that the American audiences seem to like, although unaccustomed to. His manner is quiet and easy and he goes about his work in a devil-may-care manner. . . . Chaplin will do all right for America, but it is too bad that he didn't first appear In New York with something with more in it than this piece."

Yes. That was Charlie Chaplin, newly imported from the U.K. in his

Above: Sydney Shields, 1910.

Right: It's no illusion, *Variety* cost 5 cents.

KNOX and ALION
Presenting fifteen minutes of effervescent comedy in "one."
Not a dull moment between the laughs. A lively act that is away from everything else in vaudeville.
They have been booked over the UNITED TIME by NORMAN JEFFERIES.

Left: Meet Dolores, Concheta, Lucia, Cartouche, and . . . Tom.

Above: The comedy team of Knox and Alion show their best sides.

Following Spread: Alice Lloyd toasts *Variety*'s original statement of intent.

first U.S. appearance, a year before he started making films.

According to industry lore, Sime Silverman left his post at the *New York Morning Telegraph* in 1905 after his boss told him he should be more positive when reviewing shows that were buying ads. An indignant Silverman borrowed $2,500 from his father-in-law, Alderman George Freeman of Syracuse, to start up a weekly paper of his own. There is the further legend that the flying *V* in the title on the masthead was a result of Sime liking one of the doodlings of his wife Hattie.

The first issue contained a statement of intent. The paper's foremost principle would be fairness:

> "'All the news all the time' and 'absolutely fair' are the watchwords. . . . We aim to make this an artists' paper; a medium; a complete directory; a paper to which anyone connected with or interested in the theatrical world may read with the thorough knowledge and belief that what is printed is not dictated by any motive other than the policy above outlined."

The earliest issues carried a condensed version of the policies, including the fact—emphasized in capital letters—that it would not be influenced by advertising, clearly reflecting Silverman's earlier trauma. Even in subsequent issues, the statement emphasized: "The reviews are written in a strictly impartial manner and for the benefit of the artists. . . . [*Variety*] will not be influenced by advertising; it will be honest from the first page to the last." In retrospect, this may sound like a rather obvious statement, but *Variety* was then, and is now, unlike consumer newspapers. The *Variety* readers, the advertisers, and the people being written about were all parts of the same group. And in the days of "yellow journalism," many newspapers let ad money influence content, so the temptation must have been even stronger for a trade paper.

Folks in the entertainment industry responded positively to Silverman's new publication. It felt and read like a small-town newspaper, except the "town" was the entire United States and some foreign countries as well.

Variety gave readers their own paper and their own lingo. The paper quickly became known for its sassy headlines and its unique "slanguage," which, for the first time in print, utilized vocabulary commonly used within the industry. A show had "legs," which was shorthand for saying it had the potential for a long run. If business was terrible, the show "laid an egg." Burlesque was a "wiggle opera." Most so-called respectable papers avoided street lingo, but *Variety* embraced it.

The Chaplin act was reviewed by someone under the name of "Dash." *Variety* lore says reviewers were given four-letter monikers to protect their identity from gangsters who may have invested in the show. That's possible, but when you have a masthead every week that lists Sime Silverman as editor and proprietor, and you see a review signature "Sime," it's not hard to guess the identity of the writer. Those four-letter "sig" lines were also consistent with the era of pseudonyms and journalistic anonymity. H. H. Munro wrote short stories for various newspapers under the name Saki; Lois Long used the byline Lipstick for the *New Yorker*, starting in the 1920s; the first *Tintin* book debuted in 1929, by Hergé, the pen name of Georges Prosper Remi. *Variety* had a Paris correspondent named Jolo (long before J-Lo), while men's fashion was covered by Longaquer. But the vast majority of *Variety* stories were unsigned; it wasn't until much later, in the twentieth century, that bylines became common.

Like any startup, *Variety* took a while to find its voice. In the paper's first decade of existence, Henry Ford introduced the Model T and created an assembly line, three-year-old Pu Yi became emperor of China, the National Association for the Advancement of Colored People was founded, Machu

VARIETY

A Variety Paper for Variety People.
Published every Saturday by
THE VARIETY PUBLISIHING COMPANY,
Knickerbocker Theatre Building, New York City.

SUBSCRIPTION RATES
Annual....................$2
Foreign..................... 3
Six and three months in proportion.
Single copies five cents.

VARIETY in its initial issue desires to announce the policy governing the paper.

We want you to read it. It will be interesting if for no other reason than that it will be conducted on original lines for a theatrical newspaper.

The first, foremost and most extraordinary feature of it will be FAIRNESS. Whatever there is to be printed of interest to the professional world WILL BE PRINTED WITHOUT REGARD TO WHOSE NAME IS MENTIONED OR THE ADVERTISING COLUMNS.

"ALL THE NEWS ALL THE TIME" and "ABSOLUTELY FAIR" are the watchwords.

The news part of the paper will be given over to such items as may be obtained, and nothing will be suppressed which is considered of interest. WE PROMISE YOU THIS AND SHALL NOT DEVIATE.

The reviews will be written conscientiously, and the truth only told. If it hurts it is at least said in fairness and impartiality.

We aim to make this an artists' paper; a medium; a complete directory; a paper to wich anyone connected with or interested in the theatrical world may read with the thorough knowledge and belief that what is printed is not dictated by any motive other that the policy above outlined.

WE WANT YOU FOR A SUBSCRIBER. If you don't read VARIETY you are missing something.

Do you want to read a paper that's honest from the ttitle page to its last line? That will keep its columns clean of "wash notices." That WILL NOT BE INFLUENCED BY ADVERTISING? That's VARIETY.

To insure you receiving VARIETY REGULARLY, send in your subscription now. You will find it coming to you regularly to any permanent address given, or "as per route."

The only positive way to get VARIETY is to subscribe for it NOW.

This paper is for variety and variety only in the broadest sense that term implies.

When answering advertisements kindly mention VARIETY.

Picchu was discovered, and Roald Amundsen reached the South Pole. None of these were about showbiz, so none were reported. Neither was the start of World War I, certainly big news but barely covered.

But on occasion, *Variety* began to recognize that world events were closely tied to the world of showbiz.

On April 28, 1906, after the San Francisco earthquake, *Variety* reported: "Freeman Bernstein, one of the New York representatives of the Sullivan-Considine circuit, received a wire from the Western headquarters a day or two ago, saying that the circuit's house, the Lyceum in San Francisco, is the only theatre left standing in that city."

On April 20, 1912, under the headline "Paralyzing Titanic Terror Casts Pall," the paper reported that the deaths on the sinking ship had created a pervasive sense of mourning, so that audiences seemed to be in a funereal mood even for musical and comedy shows. But because news reporting was so slow in those days, many thought the *Titanic* was safely being towed into Halifax. Among the passengers was Benjamin Guggenheim, one of the heirs to his father's mining fortune. His sister, convinced that her brother was safe, attended a performance at the Winter Garden. But a male companion who had stepped into the lobby for a drink heard the facts of the sinking and "with almost unpardonable stupidity," relayed them to Ms. Guggenheim.

> "As almost anybody else might have foreseen, she promptly dropped into a dead faint, almost precipitating a panic in the music hall." The unnamed author concluded, "With the stories of the survivors and other harrowing accounts of grief that will be constantly in the papers for the next week, it is expected theater will continue to suffer in attendance and appreciation until the frightful Titanic Terror commences to dim."

On May 4, 1912, the Philadelphia police were warning theater managers not to screen "several reels of pictures showing the wreck of the steamer *Titanic*, the rescue of survivors and other scenes attending the recent calamity." The pictures were fakes, according to the cops, and were being circulated throughout the country. Shortly thereafter, some audiences began the recovery process, as evidenced by this item, quoted in its entirety on May 25:

> "TITANIC IN VAUDEVILLE. [special cable to *Variety*.] London, May 22. The Titanic disaster, reproduced by the Diorama with all realistic details, opens in vaudeville next week by Poole at Gloucester."

So the world went from mourning to being duped to being entertained, all within six weeks. But that's life. And that's showbiz. Even the *Titanic* was fair game for a vaudeville act.

Vaudeville is generally conceded to have begun in 1881, when producer Tony Pastor presented a touring-show-style entertainment in New York. B. F. Keith then started building theaters and showing vaude-type shows. Later, E. F. Albee managed the chain, which became the Keith-Albee circuit, handling "polite" vaudeville in the 1880s. In 1906, they established the United Booking Office, booking acts for nationwide tours, rather than the chaotic one-off bookings.

Martin Beck started the Orpheum Circuit, which eventually incorporated in 1919 and united forty-five vaudeville theaters in thirty-six North American cities. Alexander Pantages also had about thirty theaters in his chain.

These circuits were considered "the big time." Almost anything else was "the small time." Then, as now, audiences' tastes changed, regionally and economically, and Peoria was considered a test site, which led to the rhetorical "Yeah, but will it play in Peoria?"

Variety featured regular roundups of news about "Summer Parks."

Below: Don't be fooled by imitators, these are the Original Tossing Austins.

Right: Only some staffers earned nicknames.

ORIGINAL TOSSING AUSTINS
Merry Christmas to All.
On the UNITED TIME.
Direction ALF. T. WILTON.

THAT "BLACKLIST"

It needs some convincing to make any one believe men who have made thousands, hundreds of thousands, and some with millions, from playing vaudeville, do not understand their business. It's so impossible that the

KINGSTON and THOMAS.

Are presenting a piano act and singing specialty in the middle west. They style their interlude "AFTER THE MATINEE," and therein MISS THOMAS, conceded to be the queen of "rag-time," introduces solo selections on the instrument and plays the accompaniment for MR. KINGSTON'S songs.

Vaudeville has yet to produce MISS THOMAS' equal as a lady "rag-time" pianist.

HAIGHT ST. THEATRE.

Messrs. HALLAHAN & GETZ, sole proprietors and managers of the AUTOMATIC VAUDEVILLE CO., owning and controlling three of SAN FRANCISCO'S best paying vaudeville and picture houses which have adopted the continuous policy, have made rapid and envious strides since entering the field and are deserving of the more credit for the faith and confidence displayed in the future of this city, at the time they decided to become an important factor in its amusement enterprises.

Both are pioneers in the Nickleodeon business of the city, having opened their first

matter of the "blacklist" has reached, in the minds of many people, a plain case of "pride."

The United Booking Offices managers, who, with Martin Beck, of the Orpheum Circuit, first decided that a "blacklist" should be maintained, have upheld the theory that to bar acts (which play "opposition") from appearing in the vast majorty of the largest variety theatres in the country must, in time, crush that opposition.

The "blacklist" was not created—as some may believe—to intimidate. It was a business proposition. When E. F. Albee, general manager of the United Booking Offices, laid in an Albany (N. Y.) hospital recovering from broken limbs resulting from an automobile accident on election day, 1908, he may have utilized a portion of his restful waking moments to theorize out the ultimate accomplishment of a

ROSE SYDELL

The statuesque and attractive star of "THE LONDO front rank among the best dressed women in burlesque. taste and wears gowns or tights with becoming grace. dence with this season's production, she fills the eye effe is typical of the dash and verve which makes burles actresses, and her fame is as wide as the realm she ad

can tell. For over a year back it has been the heighth of folly for the United Booking Offices to maintain that list. It has been continued nevertheless. While not always strictly lived up to, the exceptions (outside of two or three large bookings) have been the engagement by United managers of minor "blacklisted" turns. There are numberless instances of "blacklisted acts" appearing in United managers' houses under assumed names or titles. Also there are numberless instances of "United acts" playing "opposition houses" under a nom de plume. These individual exceptions were a matter of "taking chances" by the act and the manager.

"The blacklist" is known "officially" as the "opposition sheet." Wher-

At a time when electricity was still a novelty, the May 25, 1907, edition announced the openings of three "electric parks": in Waterloo, Iowa; Newark, New Jersey; and Kansas City, Missouri, reps of which bragged-complained they were spending eleven dollars an hour to illuminate the place.

An item on the same page said Resisto, "a new electric act," had received verification of his claim that he could indeed have received one million volts of electricity, or "juice," pass through his body, from no other than Thomas Edison and Nikola Tesla.

There was also much talk of a blacklist concerning rival booking groups refusing to hire anyone who worked for their competition.

"The blacklist was not created—as some may believe—to intimidate. It was a business proposition." E. F. Albee, general manager of United Booking Office, met with Beck, Percy G. Williams, William Hammerstein, and A. Paul Keith. They would bar acts that play the "opposition," but there were many instances of people using aliases to get around this.

In the first issue of *Variety*, Silverman said,

> "*Variety* is to be an artists' paper, we want you to take an interest in it and its columns. You are traveling around the country, if not the world. Why not be a traveling correspondent for *Variety*?"

The readers accepted his offer. The Artists Forum was a regular feature, where performers could weigh in. (A note on the page tells would-be contributors, "Confine your letters to 150 words and write on one side of paper only.")

One of the recurring themes in the early days was of artists asserting their copyrights. Edgar Foreman in the October 26, 1907, issue on page ten wrote to complain about Lo Miers, who presented an act at Pastor's called *The First Quarrel*. Foreman said he'd been presenting that act since 1899.

> "I have been advertising 'The First Quarrel' in *Variety* for the past six months, warning unprincipled people to respect my rights. . . ."

On August 28, 1909, a performer claimed that the Barber-Palmer Trio had stolen his song "Pie, Pie, Pie"; on December 21, 1907, Bert Dell questioned H. M. Lorrette's claim to be the "Original Dancing Juggler." Dell acknowledged that a certain Mr. Weston had done a clog dance while juggling ten to fifteen years ago, but that Dell and his partner Fonda had originated "a double routine of buck dancing while juggling and passing clubs."

And what was life like for these traveling performers? In the December 3, 1910, edition, a letter to the editor carried the headline "Getting a Start in Vaudeville." It was written by J. A. Murphy from Michigan, who wrote about life on the road and details the telegrams from the Jasbo Agency alerting him to his upcoming bookings: "It cost me $3.60 to confirm messages. I'm only getting $25."

He adds that arriving in new cities,

> "I had some trouble getting a place to board. The first place I went to, the lady asked me where I was working and when I told her at the Happy Hour, she said she didn't harbor show folks and slammed the door."

Left: Labor pains.

Below: Miss Shaw keeps her head up.

Following Spread: Say hello, gorgeous, to Fannie Brice and other vaudevillians.

LILLIAN SHAW
Vaudeville's newest headliner. Just finishing a tour of P. G. WILLIAMS' houses as star attraction. Offered return dates this season from Mr. Williams. Preparing an entirely new specialty for next season.

This is the girl that became an over-night sensation in Ziegfeld's Revue "Follies of 1910" singing "Lovie Joe."

FANNIE BRICE

Miss Brice is one of the most promising character comediennes we have. Her rendition of "Lovie Joe" is really one of the few real treats of the year, and she has easily placed that song in a class by itself as a "coon" number.

"Lovie Joe" is probably the most talked of song amongst vaudeville top-liners, and to **Miss Brice** great credit is due for its popularity.

MOUNTFORD'S RISE AND FALL

The rise and fall of Harry Mountford, and all that happened in between, constitutes a peculiar epoch in the annals of American vaudeville. In England, however, there was a somewhat similar period, again with Mr. Mountford as the centre.

JEAN IRWIN
THE CAPTIVATING GIRL.
Equipped with a well trained voice of exceptional quality, JEAN IRWIN is a mistress of the art of "putting 'em over." This is due to her lively personality and genial style. In baseball parlance she has a sure fire delivery.
Direction of NORMAN JEFFERIES.

As the recognized, if not the authorized, leader of the White Rats Actors' Union of America, the fall of Harry Mountford came more quickly even than his ascension to the captaincy of the largest body of vaudeville artists in the world.

In July, last, Mr. Mountford, directing and ordering the White Rats and its affairs, with the autocracy of a dictator, left New York for Paris, to attend the International Conference of Artists' Societies. Late in the following month, he returned to New York, to find himself stripped of all power, shorn of even the lightest responsibilities, and placed in a position that forced his resignation within one month after.

Just why this complete reversal of attitude by the White Rats occurred as it did has never been made public. The facts seem to be though, that for some time previously, there had been making itself manifest among the principal members and advisers of the Rats an unsettled feeling regarding Mountford. This feeling probably found its culmination during Mountford's absence. To hold his leadership required his presence. Mountford always had to be on the ground, to offset the antagonism rising against him. More than once his persuasive powers of argument calmed down an impending storm within the order. Members who railed against him and his methods outside the lodge rooms, and went into the club house prepared to repeat the statements to the International Secretary (as Mountford termed himself) learned Mountford could controvert anything said. He found no difficulty in convincing his "constituency."

While away for several weeks, Rats had the opportunity to coldly consider what Mountford had done. What he had done was evident upon the face. A great number of new members had been added, the surplus of the White Rats had piled up into a formidable amount, the organization stood where it had never stood before in point of numbers and finances, and several other items that would have been very material in estimating Mountford's importance were more than offset by the conditions created by the agitator.

These things went into the credit side of his accounting. On the charge page stood a long list of indictments against Mountford. These were all headed by the not-to-be-denied entry, "Mountford doesn't make good." Following that line came proof upon proof that although Mr. Mountford promised many things, started as many others, told what he would and could do, he never finished. And there were other items connected with Mountford's disappearance from the White Rats that may never see print.

The net balance was a large organization against a bad standing, and this standing caused by their leader-agitator, who had theoretical ideas only, holding them strongly enough to inaugurate or bring about the inception, then abandoning them to the society itself to do as best it could.

Members were dissatisfied, the profession at large, including managers and agents with whom White Rats have to do business, were displeased.

History with Mr. Mountford had repeated itself. He reached the same ending in America he had in England.

Though it seems incredible, Mountford's staunchest supporters appear to have found out more reasons why he

HARRY TSUDA
The popular Japanese equilibrist who has been playing for over two years without a break. Harry is booked solid in this country until next September, when he will leave for Europe to fulfill a year's booking in England and on the Continent.

should not be their leader in one week after he resigned, than had ever suggested itself to them in the three or four years he was in control of the order.

The fault was not altogether with the White Rats, however. They had permitted a man to gain influence in the lodge, who spent all his time thinking how to increase his hold. Though in this country but comparatively a short while, Harry Mountford within a few months after landing here, gained a foothold with the American vaudeville artist, such as no one else has ever had. He worked upon this, and improved his opportunities until he thought himself intrenched so strongly nothing could dislodge him.

Mountford proceeded in his reign much as a Minister of Affairs in a foreign court. It was all intrigue, but

(Continued on page 122.)

"THOSE PICKANINNIES."
ETHEL WHITESIDE
"FOLLIES OF COONTOWN."

Why such a warm reception? Well, show folks had a reputation (unfair or not) for having loose morals—and for skipping out of town without paying.

Two stories from that same issue offer insights into the moral question.

From Chicago:

> "Monday at the American, Lee Kohlmer, a female impersonator, did not appear, having been requested by the management (following a suggestion by the police) to leave the program. Geo. W. Day stepped in. Kohlmer had a monolog at the Monday matinee that was voted the limit, without a dissenting voice."

There was no explanation as to what "the limit" might be.

An item out of Pittsburgh recounted the tale of Elinor Gray, also known as Mrs. Grace Burnett,

> "a chorister with the burlesque company," who charged comedian Joseph K. Watson with disorderly conduct. "She said he 'was not a gentleman' when addressing the girls in the troupe, continually found fault with them and fined her $5 for 'not stepping high enough.' Furthermore, on Thanksgiving Day, he hurled epithets at her 'which even a chorus girl could not stand.' The Alderman hearing the case gave Watson a choice of 10 days in jail or a fine of $6.89. He paid the money. The court said 'Do not use any bulldog tactics on chorus girls. Remember they are not rats, and only trying to earn an honest living.' Immediately afterwards, Miss Gray was given two weeks salary by the company manager and dismissed."

If that angry landlady thought show folk were second-class citizens, evidently chorus girls were third-class. "Remember they are not rats" has to be one of the most poignant attempts at chivalry in history.

As for fiscal irresponsibility, there was a letter of July 13, 1917, to Artists Forum: "I would like it known I am not the Ben Harrison whose act, wardrobe, music, trunks and unpaid bills were left in Newport, R.I. This has been a source of annoyance to me and I am quite sure I can prove prior claim to the name, Ben Harrison, as it has been mine since birth. Ben Harrison (Formerly of Shirli Rives and Ben Harrison)."

In addition to insights on the business, *Variety* offered stats. Each stage show review indicated the production costs associated with the show. The October 29, 1910, issue pegged the price tag at the Colonial at $5,400; American $4,400; The Bronx, $3,550; and Hammerstein's, $3,250.

The December 10, 1910, issue touted the opening of the Liberty Theatre in Philadelphia, built by J. Fred Zimmerman Sr. at a cost of $250,000.

> "Mr. Zimmerman has given to the Quaker City one of the costliest, largest and most beautiful theatres in America devoted to high class vaudeville at popular prices. . . ."

In the late nineteenth century, theaters in New York were located

Above: Four Ziegfeld Girls strike a sultry pose.

Right: Six Kirksmith Sisters study.

Left: Theda Bara.

Above: Collars were popular in *The Follies*.

between Union Square and 24th Street. But when legit impresario Rudolph Aronson wanted to build a theater, he got a good deal on some property "uptown," at Broadway and 39th Street, where he built in 1882, the Casino. The area really started to take off a decade later when operettas, vaudevilles, and melodramas were staged in Charles Frohman's Empire and Abbey's Theater and venues by Oscar Hammerstein and the Shuberts. In 1905, James M. Barrie's London import *Peter Pan* was a big hit, as was Sarah Bernhardt's farewell tour in *Camille*, entertainments like *The Belle of New York*, and more serious fare from Ibsen and George Bernard Shaw.

After a dozen long-forgotten Broadway shows, Florenz Ziegfeld Jr. debuted his *Follies of 1907*. Though first appearing in the summer on the New York Roof, the revue was "slated to play at the Broadway theatre the last of this month, with a revised edition suitable for winter patronage." Ziegfeld was one of the key figures in the growth of theater, staging spectacles with elaborate sets and costumes, gorgeous chorus girls, and stars including Will Rogers, Fanny Brice, W. C. Fields, Bert Williams, and Eddie Cantor. Ziegfeld's *Follies* became an annual event that lasted through 1931.

Even in its early days, *Variety* saw the need to expand beyond stage entertainment, and the *Weekly* of January 19, 1907, carried what are considered the world's first movie reviews, for *The Exciting Honeymoon*, *The End*, and others.

Reviews quickly became a staple of the paper, such as the brief review of *Caught* (1915), which centered on an attempted bank robbery. Sime said that it "holds interest easily." This was apparently a major accomplishment, even for a film that was only seven minutes long.

Though audiences liked certain on-screen personalities, films had no billing, so Biograph Studio's Florence Lawrence was simply known as "The Biograph Girl." But in 1909 she joined Carl Laemmle's Independent Moving Pictures Company of America and received billing with her name. As a result, Laemmle made Lawrence the world's first movie star.

Above: A scene from *The Birth of a Nation*.

Oh, Mr. Laemmle. Look what you started.

In 1910, a year after Charlie Chaplin's stage comedy got him noticed, he was making films, and he was already a movie veteran by 1914 when he debuted "the Little Tramp" character (or "the Little Fellow," as Chaplin called him). Directors Mack Sennett, Cecil B. DeMille, John Ford, and D. W. Griffith, and actors such as the Gish sisters, Lillian and Dorothy, all started their prolific and heralded careers in *Variety*'s nascent days.

From Italy came *Cabiria* (1914), the mother of all toga spectacles—and indeed, of all film spectacles, which included scenes of Mount Etna erupting and Hannibal crossing the Alps. On May 15, 1914, Sime wrote that "the audience realized it was looking at one of the greatest spectacular productions yet placed on the screen." He estimates its cost between $80,000 and $100,000 "and that is high enough in these times when a very big feature can be put on under $30,000." Sime noted that some in the audience laughed when told that the film they were about to see was in twelve reels, which meant it was going to run more than two hours. In those days, films were measured in reels rather than running times, since there was no uniform projector speed and, equally important, no uniform print. Individuals (distributors, censors, theater operators) would sometimes cut a film as they saw fit, resulting in multiple versions. A twenty-first-century restored version of *Cabiria* runs nearly three hours. The large-scale Italian storytelling of *Cabiria* directly inspired D. W. Griffith's very American *The Birth of a Nation* (1915). Reviewer Mark (probably *Variety* staffer Mark Vance) hailed Griffith as "the world's best film director" and said he "has been responsible for so many of the innovations in picture making, doing more to make filming an art than any one person." Mark concluded that the film was inaugurating "a great epoch in picture making; it's great for pictures and it's great for the name and fame of David Wark Griffith."

Before this, film going was casual and cheap, starting in nickelodeon "peep machines," broadening into makeshift storefronts with uncomfortable seats and then further into theaters. Griffith made film going an event by booking *Nation* into high-class legitimate theaters, charging higher ticket prices, emphasizing the huge budget (estimated by some at $300,000), commissioning a special music score to be written for the film, and drumming up plenty of publicity.

But Mark was off the mark with one key premise:

> "One may find some flaws in the general running of the picture, but they are so small and insignificant that the bigness and greatness of the entire film production itself completely crowds out any little defects that might be singled out."

Well, except for the fact that one of the film's "little defects" was its overt racism.

In citing the film's scope, Mark said it covered Civil War battles, the assassination of Lincoln, and

> "the terrorizing of the southern whites by the newly freed blacks and the rise of the Ku Klux Klan that later overpowers the negroes and gives the white men the authority rightfully theirs. . . ."

VARIETY 205
FOREMOST PICTURE DIRECTORS

Compliments of the Season
D. W. GRIFFITH

D. W. GRIFFITH ATTRACTIONS

Above: Lillian Gish seems shocked at a scene from *The Birth of a Nation*.

Right: D.W. doesn't seem shocked at a scene from *The Birth of a Nation*.

BELLA DOYLE and EARL GOFORTH
In their COMEDY MINSTREL SKIT in "ONE," with special scenery,
Wishes all a Merry Xmas and Happy New Year.

Left: One assumes Doyle and Goforth wish you a Happy Kwanzaa, too.

Above: P.T. Barnum surprises no one.

To contemporary eyes, the film is jaw-dropping, with blacks smacking their lips in delight at the prospect of killing, raping, or merely harassing whites. But in 1915, many people, including Mark, were content just to watch the spectacle without ever questioning the implications.

The relatively new National Association for the Advancement of Colored People was outraged at such negative portrayals and were, along with other organizations, thrust into the spotlight. Founded in 1909, the NAACP received an international profile due to its battle against *Birth of a Nation*, and membership grew from around 9,000 in 1917 to around 90,000 in 1919.

In a time when a ticket topped out at fifty cents, the review pointed out that skeptics were incredulous that Griffith had planned to charge a whopping two dollars. However, on October 25, 1918, *Variety* said the Liberty in New York had indeed set some tickets at the two-dollar level, but demand was so great that the theater started charging that amount for all orchestra seats and portions of the balcony. In three years, the film had earned $3 million, repaying investors 800 percent.

In 1915, there was no such thing as a nationwide release. A distributor made a few prints and slowly opened them across the country. Though *Nation* bowed in '15, as late as September 23, 1921, *Variety* ran a story that the film's scheduled opening at San Francisco's Savoy was delayed after two hundred people gathered to protest. The theater withdrew the film and showed *The Cabinet of Dr. Caligari* (1920) instead.

Few American films are as problematic as *Birth*. Griffith's storytelling and showmanship made it a landmark film, but as for content? Oy-yoy-yoy. In fact, the material becomes even more outrageous because the film was so expertly made. If the film was created with a combination of bad storytelling, poor production values, and no marketing, people would have forgotten it long ago.

To modern audiences, one of the many (very, very) shocking elements of *Birth* was that some of the black characters were played by Caucasians in blackface. But, back then, audiences used to America's long tradition of minstrel shows were hardly shocked.

For centuries, the word "minstrel" had referred to an entertainer, as in Gilbert & Sullivan's "A Wand'ring Minstrel, I." But it eventually became synonymous with blackface entertainment, first as Caucasians using burnt cork as crude makeup and eventually being "liberated" to include black performers with blackened faces.

A December 10, 1910, guest column by minstrel-show veteran George Primrose lamented the fast fading of the genre. Recalling such performers as Lew Rattler, who performed as "Camille" in blackface; someone known as "The Watermelon Man"; and John Stuart, aka Fatty Stuart. Primrose related that Stuart had started in showbiz as a "fat boy" at P. T. Barnum's American Museum in New York. However, "he graduated from the freak class, put on burnt cork and amused the public as a fat minstrel." Wow. There's a real American success story for ya.

As minstrel shows were being replaced by vaudeville (and its saucier offshoot, burlesque), there were plenty of other new entertainment options. An April 7, 1906, story reported that "roller skating rinks are seriously cutting into the business of variety houses in many cities in the West and Southwest." And, of course, there were those moving pictures.

In 1912, Carl Laemmle merged his Independent Motion Picture Company with other indies and created Universal Pictures, and Adolph Zukor established Famous Players Film Company, bringing actors like Sarah Bernhardt to

Above: A scene from *Tarzan*.

Right: Miss Heath's hat steals attention.

the screen. Two years later, Famous Players and Jesse L. Lasky's Feature Play Company signed a distribution deal with W. W. Hodkinson's Paramount Pictures Corporation—a theater chain established in 1907—for distribution of its pics. When Zukor merged Famous and Lasky in 1916 and quickly added other small indies and small theater chains, he was credited with the first "vertical integration," as it came to be called, by merging production with exhibition. Further studio building continued into 1916, when William Fox moved his Fox to the West Coast and, in 1917, First National was formed.

It's hard to imagine a time when readers had to be told the basic premise of *Tarzan*. But just a few years after Edgar Rice Burroughs's 1912 novel first appeared, the August 3, 1917, issue said the National Film Corporation in Hollywood intended tackling *Tarzan of the Apes* for a feature film:

"The tale is of the African jungles and an English baby boy brought up among the apes until he became King of them. The first volume was so fascinatingly absorbing in its weirdness two sequels have been published by the author, almost as interesting as his first flight of fancy. . . . It will require jungle scenes, and a large number of animal impersonators to play the apes necessary to the picture."

Animal impersonators. As they said: "fascinatingly absorbing in its weirdness."

Director Scott Sidney had begun filming the project for First National, though the concept was still new enough that *Variety* at that point erroneously called it *Tarzan of the Alps*. But yodeling aside, *Variety*'s style of reporting was becoming more worldly,

PRINCIPALS
—WITH—
HENRY P. DIXON'S
BIG REVIEW

Miss May Wiley — Miss Florrie Brooks — Chas. Saxon — Miss Will Nell Lavender — Henry P. Dixon — Russell Simpson — Harry Loraine — Miss Frankie Heath — George Howard — Harry LeVan — Miss Billie Davis

Above: Audiences were drawn to the theater.

Above Right: Nice feathers.

Below Right: Nice feathers.

even as the paper maintained its mandate of giving need-to-know info to show folk.

On December 10, 1910, Edward G. Kendrew wrote advice for any entertainer heading overseas: "As Russia is fast becoming a music hall country where, particularly during the summer, large numbers of performers are engaged, a few remarks on the subject may be interesting." He pointed out that there are numerous legal holidays in Russia, for which no salary is paid, "so an artist should negotiate such holidays in the contract ahead of time." He also pointed out that

"Passports are necessary for Russia, and must be vised by the Russian consul. . . . An American passport is good for two years, but the visa for Russia is only available for six months. While on this subject I will say that it is an excellent precaution to carry a passport. It may not be needed in England and France, but is often useful in Germany and other European countries, while it is obligatory for Russia, Turkey and the Orient."

Variety covered World War I strictly from showbiz's POV.

November 21, 1914:

"The suggestion that the theatre landlords be made to bear a share of the war burden by reducing their rent has been followed by a howl of protest."

June 16, 1916:

"The new Drury Lane revue, scheduled to open this week, will be extremely shy of men. There are 240 girls in the show and only 30 chorus men, all of the latter being over the age of service. . . ."

Other news in that issue was direct: "The Great Lorraine, the ventriloquist, is reported to have been killed while serving with the French Army on May 13, at Verdun."

April 27, 1917:

"The declaration of war did not materially change business to any great extent and no radical change is looked for unless it is necessary to declare martial law. In France and England on account of the scarcity of coal and the fear of Zeppelins, outside illumination was completely curtailed, which considerably affected business, but no such situation is expected to develop here."

The story added that the lobbies of many theaters in New York and Philadelphia were doubling as recruiting stations.

November 7, 1917:

"The German Secret Service, diplomatic and consular departments have been furthering the propaganda of Hun Kultur via the theatre and its artists. Since the execution of Mata Hari, the dance queen of Holland, by the French after she was tried and convicted of being a spy in the pay of Berlin, further secrets of the workings of the methods employed by the Germans have come to light. . . . That a number of France and English officers are prone to spend short furloughs in Switzerland after having had their nerves shattered at the front has been taken under notice by the Germans and that men in this condition are extraordinarily susceptible to the charms of women has led them to employ the women of the stage in furthering their lines of information."

October 11, 1918:

"[that] pictures showing the atrocities of the Hun are helping to convert the 'Conscientious Objectors' has been proven recently at a number of the camps. This statement was made by E. L. Hyman, Director of Pictures for War Department's Commission on Training Camp Activities. 'To Hell with the Kaiser' was recently shown at Camp Pike and 15 objectors, after seeing the picture, stated their willingness to fight, some of these men having even refused to don the uniform previously."

December 6, 1918:

"Free shows were offered during the afternoon of Tuesday, Nov. 12, to celebrate the signing of the armistice and consequent end of the war. The enthusiastic scenes witnessed in the theaters and music halls during the week were unique. The Marseillaise was repeatedly sung during the performances, soldiers getting on to the stage in some resorts to lead the measure."

Soldiers returning from World War I and their loved ones had another horror to face: Spanish influenza, which killed 3 percent of the world's population.

The October 11, 1918, issue included a rundown of twenty-three U.S. cities where theaters were closed:

"Nothing in the annals of American theatricals has so disastrously affected such a complete shut-down of theatres in so wide a territory as the epidemic of Spanish influenza. News of the blight in foreign lands

BUY BONDS

VARIETY

VOL. LII, No. 7   NEW YORK CITY, FRIDAY, OCTOBER 11, 1918   PRICE FIFTEEN CENTS

EPIDEMIC SHOWS NO SIGNS OF IMMEDIATE ABATEMENT

Wholesale Closing of Theatres All Over the Country. Only Sparse Sections Remain Open. New York Held Open by City's Health Commissioner. Theatrical Business Paralyzed.

Boston, Oct. 9.
Postponement of all theatre openings for at least a third week is now apparently inevitable. The city is absolutely dead.

Contrary to expectations, the closing of everything else did not benefit either the bottled goods side of the liquor industry nor the cafes where so-called cabarets are allowed. These cabarets are in reality mere quartets or soloists singing in designated spots in the restaurant. Both the cafes and the liquor stores are doing very little business, the answer being that without the theatres, the general public decided to go home and the danger of catching the new form of grippe aids them in deciding that home isn't such a sad place after all.

The theatre men are naturally blue and for the estimated closing period, which will probably end a week from next Monday (Oct. 21), they estimate their gross loss throughout Massachusetts in receipts to be in excess of $3,000,000.

There is but slight, if any, improvement in the influenza epidemic here. On Tuesday there were more than 7,000 new cases, but the health authorities augmented by many nurses who were rushed to the Hub, feel that the situation is under control.

Ayer, Mass., Oct. 9.
Conditions at Camp Devens were considerably improved by Wednesday. It was even hoped that the quarantine would be removed next week and the Liberty Theatre resume operations. That, however, was unofficial. Devens is some distance from Boston, which is the centre of the epidemic, but it was in this camp that the disease was first discovered.

Pittsburgh, Oct. 9.
With a slight check in the spread of the epidemic the local health board would hold out no hope for lifting the closing order on the theatres.

John P. Harris, manager of the local managers' association, left yesterday for Harrisburgh to attempt to persuade the State authorities to give Pittsburgh local option in the matter. This city has been the least affected of any in the State.

The closing order has been extended to include gatherings of all sorts, including churches.

Moving picture exchange men protested to the city officials, but were informed the matter was wholly in the hands of the State health department and no action could be taken excepting through orders from it.

Denver, Oct. 9.
The epidemic will keep this city closed for at least three weeks, said City Health Commissioner W. H. Sharpley last night. The closing rule is effective throughout Colorado.

The epidemic here is increasing daily. Health officials yesterday started an investigation of the Sells-Floto Circus, which has winter quarters here. It is thought the circus may have brought the influenza germ into the city.

Vaudeville artists laying off this week through the closing order gave a big Liberty Loan show on the capital grounds yesterday, witnessed by the largest crowd ever attending a theatrical performance in this city.

Seattle, Oct. 9.
The city health department closed all places of gathering Saturday last. Many civilian deaths so far, but none reported among professionals.

First time this city has ever been closed tight.

Washington, D. C., Oct. 9.
All theatres are closed because of the epidemic. Poli's (C. J. Harris, manager) was confident the order would be recalled by Monday, and had billed the incoming attraction; also selling tickets, which had to be refunded.

Among the attractions booked were: "The Kiss Burglar," at Poli's; "The
(Continued on page 6.)

IMPORTANT NOTICE to VAUDEVILLE ARTISTS

(The following notice was issued this week at the United Booking Offices, New York City)

Vaudeville managers, circuits and booking managers generally have a difficult problem in handling the routing of vaudeville acts, due to the influenza epidemic in various parts of the country. They are endeavoring to do their best to keep theatres open, artists working, and to bring order out of chaos.

AS IT IS INDEFINITE WHEN THE CLOSED THEATRES WILL OPEN, IT IS OF THE UTMOST IMPORTANCE THAT EVERY VAUDEVILLE ARTIST, AND ESPECIALLY THE MANAGERS OF ACTS, SHOULD KEEP IN CLOSE AND CONSTANT COMMUNICATION WITH THEIR BOOKING MANAGERS. DON'T TAKE ANYTHING FOR GRANTED. CALL UP YOUR BOOKING MANAGER ON THE 'PHONE, OR, BETTER STILL, GO TO THE BOOKING OFFICES FOR INFORMATION.

Be sure the booking offices or your representative has your home address and telephone number, and if you go out, leave word where you can be reached, and when you will be back again

---

SOLDIER PLAY ON ROOF.

Oswego, N. Y., Oct. 9.
The epidemic permitting the Fort Ontario soldier play, "Carry On," will be given on the 44th Street Theatre Roof, New York, for a week commencing Oct. 21.

After New York the show expects to go to Washington.

The show was to have opened at Fulton, N. Y., Monday, but owing to illness among the cast had to be postponed.

Makes a fiddle talk. CHAS. ALTHOFF.

MME. BERNHARDT GOING HOME.

Cleveland, O., Oct. 9.
Sarah Bernhardt will close her American vaudeville tour here Saturday night at the Hippodrome, immediately leaving for New York, from which point she will sail for France.

Mme. Bernhardt has found it imperative to undergo another operation. She wishes to have it performed at her home abroad.

Mme. Bernhardt had 12 more weeks in vaudeville over here at $5,500 weekly as salary.

CAMP SHOWS IN OPEN.

Washington, D. C., Oct. 9.
In order to permit the men in quarantine and those who are too ill to attend the Liberty theatres the Commission on Training Camp Activities announces that dates are being set aside in each camp for the appearance of traveling companies in the base hospitals. When the weather permits these performances will be given in the open air.

The Commission has also directed the Liberty theatre managers to set aside a night each week for the benefit of the men in quarantine.

ENGLISH SUBJECT TO DRAFT.

All English subjects in the United States between the ages of 18 and 45 are now subject to conscription by the U. S. as the time limit for their enlistment in the British armies has expired.

There are thousands of Englishmen on this side who come under the new army service pact. Among them are many actors now required to accept service by the draft over here when called.

TEN YEARS' ALIMONY DUE.

San Francisco, Oct. 9.
Harry Davis, manager of the Will King Co. at the Hippodrome, was ordered to appear in the Superior Court, to show cause why he should not pay back alimony amounting to $3,000.

His former wife, Mrs. May F. Davis, was given a divorce in 1907 and $25 a month alimony.

CUTTING COST OF BILLS.

To be forearmed against an anticipated drop in patronage, gauged by that of this week and since the epidemic became prevalent, several of the small-time vaudeville theatres around New York have arranged for much cheaper programs next week.

had but partially reached here. One news item was that there had been 150,000 cases in Madrid, Spain. The amazing speed with which the epidemic spread through many of our most populous states astonished officials and many municipalities quickly closed all places where people foregather as a preventative. It was estimated early this week that communities holding over half the population of the country were under quarantine. Mounting casualty lists, with many sudden deaths roused health boards to instant action."

Unions came to prominence after the war, both internationally and domestically, but also in show business.

In 1919, the four-year-old Actors' Equity Association called a strike against stage theaters and was soon joined by other unions in sympathy. Most people

"never believed the players would go through with it. For 30 days—starting Aug. 7 and stopping Sept. 6, 1919—the theatre of New York felt the might of the actor, in combination with the stage hands and musicians. By degrees the houses were closed. . . . The strikes in Chicago, Boston and several other cities were just as effective. Coming in the midst of Broadway's greatest summer season the losses were enormous."

Equity was seeking limits of eight performances a week, plus guarantees

Previous Spread: October 11, 1918.

Above: The founders of United Artists: Mary Pickford, Douglas Fairbanks, Charlie Chaplin, and D.W. Griffith.

Right: A "Joy-Thriller," indeed!

Following Spread: You can do so many things with lattice.

GETTING A START IN VAUDEVILLE
By J. A. MURPHY.

Wetwater, Mich., Dec. 6.

Dear Ed:

I came mighty near not getting here on account of such heavy expense last week. I had to stay at the hotel in Waupaso all day Sunday as there was no train for this town until night and my board bill was $14. When I got my salary from the manager he only gave me $19. I said there was some mistake about it and I should have $23.75. He took a little book out of his vest pocket and showed me where he had written Newcom Pyker 20. "There," he said, "that's what you are down for and that's what you will get, less five per cent. I don't often pay that much for an act, but the Jasbo people said you were good and I took their word for it."

I had nothing to show that I was to get any more. The telegram did not mention the price it just said "Waupaso rush photos confirm." I took the $19 and after paying the baggage man, laundry, hotel and other expenses I only had $4.90 left. Then I paid 60 cents express charges on a bundle of photos returned from one of the towns I had rushed them to. When I opened the bundle they were not mine at all but belonged to some trained dogs. This left me with $4.30, the exact fare to Wetwater.

I arrived here at 2 a. m. and not knowing where to go I stayed in the depot until day light and then found the Hippodrome, an old skating rink turned into a theatre.

There were several bills pasted on the outside, but I couldn't find my name.

I was cold and hungry but had no money to buy breakfast with so I went back to the depot to get warm. A train came in about eight o'clock and one man got off. I thought I would see where he went so I followed him up town. He turned down a side street and stopped at a house that had a sign on the door "Mrs. Patton.

ALF. CAMM and THEIRA
Introducing a new "Joy-Thriller," intermingled with real ventriloquism and artistic dramatics, inaugurating a vast departure and aptly termed
VENTRILO-DRAMA.
S.-C. Circuit.
Direction
NORMAN JEFFERIES.

Theatrical Boarding House." He opened the door and went in. So did I. A big woman in an apron came up from the basement and said, "I can't give you any rooms till some of last week's people get out. Every room is full and there is a sketch team in the parlor. You can set in the kitchen till breakfast time and after that I can fix a room for you."

After breakfast I went to the Hippodrome and found the manager. He said he never did any business with the Jasbo Agency and had not engaged me through any other agency. He didn't know what they meant by sending me. His bill was full. He was very sorry but that settled it.

While he was telling me this a messenger boy handed him a telegram. He read it quickly and said, "I have a disappointment, and if you can work in one I will give you $30 for the week. I confirmed at once.

Newcom Pyker.

about pay, work hours, and time off. The Producing Managers' Association refused to sit down with the org so in August, actors refused to appear in twelve shows. In the next month, other shows joined in. On August 29, 1919, *Variety* carried a story that Samuel Gompers, president of the American Federation of Labor, declared his org "unqualifiedly with the Actors' Equity until the end in their battle with the managers. . ." Later that year, *Variety* carried the page-one headline that a settlement was expected just before the issue went to press, and that the remaining concern was a stagehands and musicians agreement. "The strike broke up a hundred or more rehearsals, closed or stopped 44 attractions from appearing and left but one Broadway show open after a strike had been called upon it."

The decade ended with a bang. The year 1919 saw the signing of the Treaty of Versailles, the founding of the Weimar Republic, ratification of the 18th Amendment, and, most significant for Hollywood, the creation of Columbia Pictures and United Artists.

Charlie Chaplin, Mary Pickford, Douglas Fairbanks, and D. W. Griffith formed UA. For the first time, rather than be paid salaries by producers, stars became their own employers. They had control over their output and took the producer's share of the profits. It was a concept that wasn't widely imitated until the decline of the studio system in the 1950s.

In its first fifteen years of existence, *Variety* had chronicled the changing tastes and times.

The innocence of vaudeville performer Toots Paka and Her Hawaiians were replaced by Mata Hari. The world of P. T. Barnum was replaced by Broadway (both with and without labor unrest). Seven-minute moving pictures were replaced by two-hour storytelling.

But, to quote a line of dialogue from the next decade, you ain't heard nothin' yet.

EVA TANGUAY

Here Is a Headliner Who Made Her Reputation In Vaudeville and Who Has Remained a Vaudeville Headliner 10 Years

Can You Name Three Others?

THE MARVELOUS CE'DORA

Sole Management of **CHAS. HADFIELD**

PAT CASEY

CE DORA

PAT CASEY

1920s

If you'd seen the entire planet turned upside down by World War I and the flu pandemic, you would either become thoughtful and introspective, or you'd go wild. In the 1920s, people did both.

Introspection led to remarkable creativity. George Gershwin wrote *Rhapsody in Blue* (1924) and *An American in Paris* (1928) while Giacomo Puccini was working on *Turandot*. On Broadway, 1927's *Show Boat* revolutionized musical theater while Eugene O'Neill electrified drama throughout the decade. On the screen, silent movies evolved from a novelty into an art form with such films as *Nanook of the North* (1922), *Greed* (1924), 1925's *The Big Parade*, Buster Keaton's *Seven Chances*, and Charlie Chaplin's *The Gold Rush*, and *Sunrise* (1927). Sinclair Lewis's *Main Street*, F. Scott Fitzgerald's *The Great Gatsby*, Theodore Dreiser's *An American Tragedy*, Ernest Hemingway's *The Sun Also Rises*, and William Faulkner's *The Sound and the Fury* hit bookshelves between 1920 and 1929. But introspection led to repression, and the 1920s were also a decade of prohibition, moral crusades, and legal debates over religious teachings.

And on the wild side, the 1920s were filled with bootleggers, gangsters, jazz, wriggle dancing, Hollywood scandals, traveling carnivals, and flappers.

In other words, the decade had something for everyone. During that ten-year period, the average person's definition of entertainment was revolutionized by the radio and Vitaphone's talking-pictures technology.

The year 1920 was the blossoming of radio, as the *Detroit News* started radio station WWJ; Westinghouse Electric Corporation was given a commercial license for KDKA of Pittsburgh; and Argentina, Sri Lanka, and other countries started national radio stations, the most famous of which may be Great Britain's BBC.

Radio audiences were small in the early days. Few listened to the "wireless" or to "the ether," via homemade crystal sets or battery-powered sets.

According to a 1922 article,

"The wireless telephony 'concerts' which have become the national rage the past few months under the exploitation of the Westinghouse Electric Co. have progressed to the state where the music publishers

Above: Dancers kick up their heels.

VARIETY

Vol. LVII. No. 6   NEW YORK CITY, JANUARY 2, 1920

ALL VAUDEVILLE BOX OFFICE RECORDS SMASHED BY PALACE

Christmas Week's Palace Gross Approximated $40,000. Indications Point to Current Week's Business Topping Last Week's High Mark. State Lake, Chicago, Also Establishes New Record by Playing to 11,000 Admissions Day After Christmas.

All vaudeville box office records went by the board last week in the gross business done by the Palace, New York. The Palace's gross is reported to have approximated $40,000, with the holiday scale continuously in effect.

The opening attendance Monday at the same house indicated this week with the same scale in effect the Palace will beat last week's mark.

Early last week in the three days before Christmas, when every house in town was suffering from the pre-Christmas droop, the Palace played to capacity at each performance.

What started off as the biggest week, theatrically, of this season is the current one. Managers around New York of all policies anticipated banner business.

Next week is expected to be a follow up with the Auto Show in the metropolis. The hotels commenced filling up as early as Tuesday, with visitors attracted by the automobile exhibit.

Chicago, Dec. 30.
If any records remained to be broken at the State-Lake Theatre they perished the day after Christmas, when 5,800 admissions were recorded at the morning and matinee show and 5,760 at the supper show and night performance, making more than 11,000 on the day. On Christmas day the management supplied luncheon in the restroom, back stage, to the performers and house staff, feeding 160 persons. The collation was served by Pete Soteros from his Thirteenth Chair Cafe, and consisted of turkey, chicken and other seasonable dainties.

HOUDINI'S ENGLISH SALARY.

The Mauretania, Tuesday, carried away Mr. and Mrs. Harry Houdini. Houdini is to start a tour of 20 weeks on the other side, opening on the Moss time. His contracts, made about eight years ago, call for a salary of £400 weekly, believed at the time of execution to equal $2,000 in American money. At the present rate of exchange Houdini will receive the equivalent of about $1,550 weekly while in England.

Another item of Houdini's English contract is the income tax he will be subjected to, also foreign in the calculations of years ago. The contracts have been extended from time to time, with the foreign managers now insisting they be played.

JOLSON AT AUDITORIUM.

Chicago, Dec. 30.
An engagement for Al Jolson and "Sinbad" to play here at the Auditorium, opening Jan. 24 has been entered into by the Shuberts.

The Jolson run will be set for four weeks, perhaps longer. The show will be able to play to slightly over $63,000 on the week if drawing capacity at its scale.

Jolson has appeared at the Auditorium before, in other Shubert productions.

Las week, Jolson's first at the Crescent, Brooklyn, with that house initialing its big production policy, Jolson did $24,000. "Sinbad" remains at the Crescent this week.

LONG HAIRED JAZZERS.

Ernie Young dug 'em up somewhere and has a picture to prove it. The photo shows about 30 jazz-playing musicians from "The House of David" at Benton Harbor, Mich. The House of David represents a religious sect and the members of the band look it. Nearly all have long hair and they are elderly.

Mr. Young believes the long-haired jazzers could become a vaudeville act and he has obtained their consent, it is said.

TO FINE CHORUS.

The Chorus Equity Association and Producing Managers' Association are working out the details of an agreement, which will call for the imposition of certain money penalties on any member of the Chorus association guilty of breaking managerial rules, such as tardiness, careless performance or any deliberate action calculated to injure a show. The plan now formulating embraces a system of fines, to be imposed by the show manager and remitted to the Chorus Equity, which will in turn place the penalties thus received in a sick benefit fund to be created by the organization.

It is illegal in New York state and most of the other states now for an employer, theatrical or otherwise, to fine an employee, according to a law enacted several years ago. The proposed arrangement, of the managers turning over fines to the Chorus Equity, would come within the law, according to legal opinion, and at the same time provide a measure of discipline for rule,breaking chorus people which would be satisfactory to both managerial and actors' associations.

Prior to the passage of the above-mentioned law regarding fines all penalties inflicted on show people were retained by the management. A meeting between committees representing the C. E. A. and P. M. A. is scheduled for Friday (Jan. 2) to put the proposed new plan in execution.

ERLANGER CLOSES MAYFLOWER.

Providence, R. I., Dec. 30.
Providence is not yet big enough to support three legitimate houses. This is the conclusion drawn from the announcement this week that the Mayflower, opened this season nder the management of A. L. Erlanger as the city's third legitimate house, will abandon legitimate after next week and after two weeks of pictures, go into stock.

The house has been competing against the Shubert Majestic and the Opera house, the houses of the Shuberts and Col. Felix R. Wendleschaefer.

The Mayflower was formerly the Colonial, where burlesque failed to bring returns last season. Erlanger leased the place. Considerable money was spent on an attractive lobby, but the interior of the house was changed little and apparently did not appeal to the class of theatregoers who support legitimate productions.

This, rather than the productions that have been seen, it is said, caused the downfall and the resultant closing of the Mayflower as a legitimate house.

DRAMA LEAGUE SELLS STOCK.

Chicago, Dec. 30.
Stock is being hawked about for a proposed monthly magazine to be called "The Drama," to be edited by Prof. Hinckley, head of the dramatic art department of the University of Chicago. "The Drama" has been issued from time to time, irregularly, as a highbrow pamphlet discussing altruistic and academic topics related to the stage. It was never classed as a commercial proposition.

Now it appears the Drama League, claiming it can start the paper off with a subscription of 10,000 by attaching the subscription charge as a compulsory addition to membership dues of the organization and give space to its "bulletins."

Prof. Hinckley, though still attached to the university staff, is soliciting money for stock in person. There is to be common and preferred, and a prospectus sets forth in glowing potentialities the financial possibilities. An advance copy says it is "Published by the Drama League." The headquarters of that body are supposed to be in New York, but the place of publication is given as Chicago. The stock is being offered as an investment and as supporting "the uplift of the theatre." Prof. Hinckley argues either way.

WOODS IN WITH SELZNICK.

A. H. Woods has bought an interest in the Lewis J. Selznick stage production, "Bucking the Tiger." The piece according to the present plans will be booked through the Woods office. Selznick completed the arrangement with Woods shortly after signing the contract for the play with the author Achmed Abdullah.

Allan Rock represented the author in placing the play.

"VARIETY'S" HIGH SELLING MARK.

Chicago, Dec. 30.
The highest mark known locally in sales of VARIETY was reached last Saturday, when one dealer, Universal News Co., Randolph and Clark streets, sold 700 copies of VARIETY's Anniversary number.

14TH STREET BEHIND IN RENT.

Justice Sampson Friedlander gave Joseph S. Klein, manager of the 14th Street Theatre, until today to pay $1,800 back rent for the theatre or vacate the property.

The proceedings were brought by Jerome Rosenberg, from whom the house is sub-leased, for the payment of December rent.

Above: Clara Bow.

Left: January 2, 1920.

> are investigating the matter on the theory the corporation is conducting public performances for profit and performing copyrighted music for similar purposes."

a reporter from London said the phenomenon of the "listening-in boom" was making everyone grumpy. Workers and the post office complained of being underpaid by the Marconi company, with its alleged radio monopoly, while artists were unhappy at not being paid at all. And the public criticized the clergy "who have managed to get 'broadcasting' prohibited during the hours of Divine service on Sunday, just the time when most people are desirous of using the instruments." (March 8, 1923)

By 1925, *Variety* was regularly reporting growth. Secretary of Commerce Herbert Hoover said there were 563 radio stations in the United States and, as an example,

> "Michigan's radio boom is on . . . . [Lansing] claims to have 184 dealers in radio business and more than 6,000 actual fans with sets."

> In addition, "not to be outdone by the rest of the world," Hongkong [as *Variety* spelled it on February 11, 1925] announced its own radio station. And final tallies showed that the Union of South Africa "imported radio equipment valued at approximately $900,000 in 1924," a huge jump from $137,000 in 1923.

Japan had received 818 applications for receiving sets through February 20, 1925, and a headline boasted "First Radio Show in China Proves Success" on July 1, 1925.

That year, *Variety* estimated that the newfangled radio business was raking in $150 million a week (December 2, 1925), even though (per a July 22, 1925, article)

> "the broadcasters and radio manufacturers continue to tell the Department of Commerce officials that no broadcasting station in the country is making money."

The March 18, 1925, page of radio news was filled with oddities. By that point, manufacturers were creating attractive wooden structures in order to make radio a central piece of home furnishings, and "the great majority of the radio cabinets come from Latvia, where they are made by the school boys of that country. . . ."

The village of Theresa, New York, planned to cancel its summer band concerts and would instead have radio concerts, using "the latest type of radio with the strongest loud speaker obtainable . . ." and from D.C., a report that Federal Trade Commission hearings on an alleged radio monopoly had been postponed yet again, now scheduled for sixteen months after the original target date, had the author wondering if they would ever take place.

On that same page, *Variety*'s New Orleans correspondent, O. M. Samuel, reviewed various radio shows "through the courtesy of Dr. W. A. Love, in whose home this dandy radio instrument is located."

And, of course, on July 22, 1925, the money issue again:

> "With time radio will be forced to pay for its talent. This becomes manifest from week to week as more and more people are added to the permanent studio staffs by the various broadcasters throughout the country. Radio is finding gratis talent dwindling."

Just a few years after its widespread acceptance, radio was being hailed as a political conduit. On September 21, 1927, *Variety* reported Radio Corporation of America president General James G. Harbor as saying, "The radio will form an important fight in the next presidential campaign" and vowing that the leading candidates would be allowed equal time.

On June 22, 1927, *Variety* reported "the supreme accomplishment in the history of radio's progress," a fifty-station broadcast on the NBC network of Washington, D.C.'s salute to Charles Lindbergh for flying solo across the Atlantic. The item estimated fifteen million North Americans heard the broadcast, and it was likely that some folks in New Zealand, Australia, and Europe had picked it up as well. The story concluded, "It is but a matter of a few years—much less before transatlantic aviation becomes a passenger service—when the Singapore Syncopaters will broadcast from India and be picked up in St. Louis." It's not clear if the Syncopaters ever made radio history, but the predictions of imminent international broadcasts and commercial transatlantic flights became a fact.

By 1930, the census estimated that 40.3 percent of the nation's households owned radios, a group that grew to 83 percent in 1940 and topped 95 percent by 1950.

In the June 22, 1927, issue, Harry Crull, manager of the Branford movie theater in Newark, New Jersey, said he "will turn the show off and the radio on" during the Chicago boxing match between Gene Tunney and Jack Dempsey (aka "the million-dollar scrappers"). There you have it: in one evening, you could enjoy the two newest and most dominant entertainment forms of the decade.

The 1920s saw the birth, and rebirth, of the major studios. In 1924, Metro Pictures, Goldwyn Pictures, and Louis B. Mayer's company merged to form MGM, owned by Loew's, Inc. Radio-Keith-Orpheum, more familiarly known as RKO, was created with the January 28, 1928, incorporation of the Keith-Albee-Orpheum live-theater chain with Joseph Kennedy's Radio Corp. of America and the fledgling Pathé Studios. But it was the veteran Warner Brothers who made a quantum leap forward. On the heels of opening of a studio and flush with newfound success from *The Jazz Singer*, they made a major expansion in 1928 by buying majority interest in First National, one of the biggest theater chains that also produced films. The goal was to combine distribution with exhibition—in other words, create a company that could not only make the films but exhibit them as well.

By the end of the decade, Fox, Loew's, Paramount, RKO, and Warner Brothers all had production, distribution, and exhibition capabilities.

But nobody would go to see their films were it not for the actors. On January 4, 1928, *Variety* printed its annual rundown of breakthrough actors. Most of the names are long forgotten, but among the laundry list of now-obscure names were

> "Gilbert Roland, Mexican lad [who] started as an extra two years ago" [and who went on to a long career] and "Gary Cooper, an extra little more than a year ago who got his break in 'Barbara Worth,' with a Paramount contract following . . ."

and Charles Chaplin, Buster Keaton, Harold Lloyd, Ben Blue, and Roscoe (Fatty) Arbuckle; Clara Bow (labeled "the It Girl"), Lon Chaney ("The man of a thousand faces"), and Mary Pickford ("America's sweetheart"); romantic onscreen pairs Janet Gaynor and Charles Farrell, and Greta Garbo and John Gilbert; and exotic sex symbols Rudolph Valentino, Theda Bara, and Ramon Navarro; plus Marlene Dietrich, Gloria Swanson, Francis X. Bushman, Joan Crawford, Norma Shearer, Ronald Colman, the Talmadge sisters (Norma and Constance), and the Gish sisters (Lillian and Dorothy).

The two biggest stars of the decade were a German Shepherd named Rin Tin Tin, and a mouse named Mickey. Mickey's creator, Walt Disney, created the entertainment icon and his debut 1928 short "Steamboat Willie," shortly after a dispute with his previous employer, Charles Mintz, for whom he created Oswald the Lucky Rabbit.

Among comedy's star producers were Mack Sennett and Hal Roach, with the latter producing Harold Lloyd comedies, and shorts with Laurel & Hardy, Charlie Chase, and *Our Gang* (which became known as *The Little Rascals* when it went into TV syndication in the 1950s).

A remarkable group of directors were turning the once-jerky novelty of films into art. That list included Tod Browning, Cecil B. DeMille, John Ford, Howard Hawks, Sergei Eisenstein, Erich von Stroheim, Josef von Sternberg, and Robert Wiene.

According to the August 27, 1920, issue, D. W. Griffith kicked off the decade by again setting a new high for ticket prices, charging ten dollars for the opening night of his screen adaptation of the play *Way Down East* at the 44th Street Theatre. After that evening, tickets would range from fifty cents to two dollars. The nearest, the story said, was the ten-dollar top for *Ravished Armenia* at the Plaza, but that was for a fund-raiser performance.

Movies were big bucks.

In the December 2, 1925, issue, MGM expressed glee that King Vidor's *The Big Parade* had done $20,000 in one week, with an advance of $5,000. In those days, films opened at one or two screens; *Parade* proved such a hit that it played ninety-six weeks at one Gotham screen. MGM considered the film the studio's biggest success until *Gone with the Wind*, in 1939.

According to a May 12, 1926, story, the country had an estimated twenty thousand theaters, 97 percent of which were devoted to movies, with the remaining fraction split among legit, vaudeville, and burlesque.

Amid the artistic growth came a tech breakthrough: Warner Brothers' 1926 *Don Juan*, directed by Alan Crossland and starring John Barrymore, was released with sound. There was no dialogue, but sound effects and the music were synchronized in the print that went out. The audience members asked, "How do they do it?" after they

Above Left: Joan Crawford.

Below Left: Harold Lloyd.

Above: Buster Keaton.

"had awakened to the fact that the entrancing symphony music that accompanied the film was actually being reproduced and was not being played from behind the screen by a cleverly hidden orchestra. . . . First-nighters became conscious that they were listening to a revolutionary instrument, and one that would be far-reaching in its effect. . . . It is believed that the Vitaphone will revolutionize the presentation of moving pictures in the largest metropolitan theatres as well as in the smallest theatres in the smallest towns. It is intended to bring to audiences in every corner of the world the music of the greatest symphony orchestras and the vocal entertainment of the most popular stars of the operatic and theatrical fields."

The following year, on June 1, 1927, an item about *The Jazz Singer* barely hinted at the revolution to come. It said vaudeville star Al Jolson would "begin work on the picture, which will take at least eight or nine weeks to complete, as it will be experimental in a good many ways with the Vitaphone adjustment with it."

On September 21, 1927, a few weeks before the film's October 6 premiere, Jolson wrote a guest column justifying his move to films. He wrote that he'd been doing eight shows a week for eighteen years in vaudeville and saw pictures as a way to attract new audiences, "people who were dyed-in-the-wool picture theatre addicts and who never paid the $4.40 top which I was getting with my own show. . . . My drawing power in the musical comedy field has been limited. In the picture houses it is not."

The birth of talkies was spoofed in George Kaufman and Moss Hart's 1930 play (and subsequent film) *Once in a Lifetime*, the classic 1952 musical *Singin' in the Rain*, and the 2011 Michel Hazanavicius–directed *The*

Artist. All of them addressed the adjustments that filmmakers, actors, and technicians had to make when talkies came in, but the advent of talkies wreaked havoc on musicians who depended on performing with movies for their income. And while talking was all the rage, some filmgoers were calling for silence and censorship, thanks to then-shocking films such as the Valentino star maker *The Sheik* (1921), Cecil B. DeMille's *Manslaughter* (1922), and the Greta Garbo–John Gilbert film *Flesh and the Devil* (1926).

Some in the public saw the wicked film industry as the depths of immorality, thanks to scandals like the 1921 Roscoe "Fatty" Arbuckle case. Arbuckle and his friends had thrown a prolonged Labor Day weekend party at San Francisco's St. Francis hotel, a lot of liquor was consumed, and starlet Virginia Rappe died. Charged with her murder, Arbuckle went through three trials in five months. Finally acquitted on all charges, the jury wrote a note saying, among other things, "Acquittal is not enough for Roscoe Arbuckle. We feel that a great injustice has been done him." His fate, however, was sealed in the court of public opinion. Since the day of the murder, tabloid newspapers had printed "facts" about his role in Rappe's death, so in the public's mind, he was permanently cast as the villain. Also in the court of public opinion, the film industry was cited for the general decline in morals, as the public chewed gum, smoked, were raucous, danced the Charleston, and found inventive ways of circumventing prohibition: bootleggers, bathtub gin, and speakeasies. It was the Roaring Twenties all right. To counter morality claims, the studios formed the Motion Picture Producers and Distributors of America (MPPDA) and in 1922 hired U.S. Postmaster General Will H. Hays as president. Hays saw Arbuckle as one of his favorite scapegoats and so banned Arbuckle from filmmaking. And though Hays later quietly rescinded the ban, by the end of 1922, the actor's career was all but over. On March 3, 1926, *Variety* reported that William Randolph Hearst, whose newspapers had carried stories about Arbuckle's "guilt," had signed Arbuckle (billed as William Goodrich) to direct Marion Davies in *The Red Mill*. Arbuckle continued to direct under that name until his death in 1933, at age forty-six.

A November 9, 1927, article reported that the American Association for the Advancement of Atheism had asked Hays to keep God out of films,

Previous Spread: Lon Chaney as *The Hunchback of Notre Dame*; Al Jolson as *The Jazz Singer*.

Left: Rudolph Valentino as *The Sheik*.

Following Spread: "Fatty" Arbuckle; Theda Bara.

but he gave a lengthy rebuttal, saying,

> "We could not do it even if we wanted to. God is in every art, in every laudable ambition, in every worthy achievement. . . . God is in our wholesome pleasures and our wholesome entertainment."

Hays was just beginning to taste his power. On August 29, 1928, *Variety* published the list of eleven taboos "which must be observed by all producers to avoid international complications and general censorship throughout the world." There were also twenty-six rules "where special care must be exercised."

Also in 1927, the Academy of Motion Picture Arts and Sciences was formed. Like the MPPDA, the Academy wanted to mediate labor disputes and, crucially, to present a good image of industry. Buried on page seven of the February 20, 1929, issue, *Variety* reported that the organization gave out a set of awards. The Academy Awards were nice, but not an immediate sensation, and they weren't the primary goal of the organization.

The demand for moral reform was reflected by Billy Sunday, an "old-time religion" advocate who preached against vice, alcohol, and greed and was the inspiration for Sinclair Lewis's *Elmer Gantry*. He pushed for prohibition and fought against the theory of evolution. Naturally, he was wildly popular. But his powers started fading in the 1920s as numerous imitators, including Aimee Semple McPherson, aka Sister Aimee, gained popularity. An October 28, 1921, item talked about Dr. John Roach Straton, "the stage-denouncing pastor of Calvary Church." Showbizzers disliked him but took the bait. Dancers Maurice and Leonora Hughes invited him to see their wholesome dance exhibit; Straton didn't respond directly, but instead told newspapermen that "dancing must be fundamentally wrong in that it necessitated the hugging of both sexes."

There were other taboos. A June 25, 1920, column by Ivan P. Gore from London noted that theater managers, or those who had leased concession rights from them, were demanding the right to sell chocolates in theaters after 8:00 p.m. "Crowds of chocolate sellers have demonstrated with banners, etc., all complete in true trade union style. Questions are being asked in Parliament. . . ."

In Boston, Isadora Duncan was causing a sensation. The dancer "brought to the stage the novelty of bared-leg dancing," *Variety* wrote on September 21, 1927, and her freeform dancing, often in thin tunics to mimic ancient Greek style, earned her as many fans as it did detractors. She was also a shocker for having children out of wedlock and for her political beliefs. An October 27, 1922, article said that Mayor Curley had banned her from Boston:

> "The trouble started when Isadora, in one of her dances, had an accident to her flimsy garb which allowed more to show than even the most liberal person believes permissible on the stage. Isadora, in commenting on the accident, later chided Bostonians for their narrow views on such a matter, especially roasting those who had left the hall when it occurred. Not content with this, Isadora, at the Saturday afternoon performance, made a speech in which she said that America needed a revolution, and that it was up to the women to start it. She avowed herself a 'red' and made it clear that she gloried in the distinction."

So what have we learned from this: not only was a "wardrobe malfunction" not a twenty-first-century invention, but the phrase "banned in Boston" is not just a vague expression.

A letter to *Variety* from Broadway actress Irene Franklin on February 10, 1922, suggested the problem was not

STARS OF THE SCREEN

"FATTY"
(ROSCOE)
ARBUCKLE

A
HAPPY
NEW YEAR
TO ALL
MY FRIENDS
AND
EVERYBODY

"Fatty" Arbuckle
Comedy Company
Long Beach, California

with showbiz, but with the audience. She complained about "the young bloods and the flappers" who "spooned shamelessly" and showed no respect for the performers or for others in the audience:

> "Prattlers against 'the morals of the stage' always sit outside looking in, don't they? I wish they'd come in now and then, and look out. The reformers might then contemplate the result of their own fondest endeavor and accomplishment—prohibition.
> "I have a daughter of my own and I shudder to think of the environment that fanatical 'puritanism' has created for the youth of this generation."

John T. Scopes was put on trial in Tennessee for teaching his high school biology class about evolution and Charles Darwin's *On the Evolution of Species*. This was a violation of Tennessee's Butler Act, which was backed by the World's Christian Fundamentals Association. The trial created great hoopla and was broadcast on the then-innovative medium of radio. (It also inspired the Jerome Lawrence and Robert Edwin Lee 1955 play and 1960 film *Inherit the Wind*.). *Variety*, on July 29, 1925, had a unique angle: Scopes defied predictions and announced he would not capitalize on his fame by hitting the lecture circuit. "Modest Evolutionist Scopes Scorns Money; Wants Post-Graduate Course"

Left: Josephine Baker.

Following Spread: August 31, 1927; March 13, 1929.

said the headline, while a smaller headline read:

> "Biggest current 'name' for any kind of show business declining all theatrical offers. Willing to write for newspaper syndicate if given $5,000 to pay three years' more schooling—figures at $111 monthly—Lee Ochs amused Southerner with wired offer and comment—Prof. Scopes has no job in sight for next season."

Duncan wasn't the only dancer under scrutiny. A September 8, 1926, rundown of Paris nightclubs said America's Josephine Baker was "a substantial success at the revue at the Folies Bergere." However, in the June 12, 1929, issue,

> "Josephine Baker, colored American wriggle dancer, started a riot here [Buenos Aires]. . . . Colored girl's reported marriage to an Italian count is held responsible for public hostility. Audience here stampeded upon her appearance . . . and a general fight developed all over the auditorium. . . . Colored girl was driven to South America after being expelled from several of the European countries. . . ."

The story never explained whether the hostility was due to the fact that she was a wriggle dancer, a commoner marrying a count, or a black woman marrying a white man, but it's not hard to guess.

STAGE BROADWAY SCREEN

Variety

PRICE 20 CENTS

Published Weekly at 154 West 46th St., New York, N. Y., by Variety, Inc. Annual subscription, $7. Single copies, 20 cents.
Entered as second class matter December 22, 1905, at the Post Office at New York, N. Y., under the act of March 3, 1879.

VOL. LXXXVIII. No. 7   NEW YORK CITY, WEDNESDAY, AUGUST 31, 1927   64 PAGES

COPS NO BOOZE SMELLERS

'STEALING DATES' FOR LARCENY CHARGE IN BILLING BATTLE

Sells-Floto Circus Starts $50,000 Damage Suit and Secures Injunction Against Miller Bros.' 101 Ranch Show in Topeka—Billers Arrested

Topeka, Aug. 30.
County attorney Ed Rooney found a new charge for larceny in swearing out warrants for "stealing dates" against billposters in the advance "wrecking crew" of Miller Brothers' 101 Ranch show.
Complaint was entered by the Sells-Floto Circus through the opposition billing forces of the two outfits having gone into the usual savage processes of tearing down paper, pasting up and over when dates clash.
S-F attorneys commenced an action for $50,000 damages against Joe, Jack and George Miller, with
(Continued on page 41)

Mary Pickford as Joan Of Arc With Reinhardt

Los Angeles, Aug. 30.
Though Douglas Fairbanks refuses to comment upon the report that his wife, Mary Pickford, will play Joan of Arc in a super picture of that title, it is understood that the rumor is virtually correct.
As her director Miss Pickford will have Max Reinhardt, the eminent German stager. Reinhardt is under contract to also make another picture for United Artists, the distributor that will handle the Joan film.
Morris Revenes is said to have sold Fairbanks on the Joan of Arc idea.
Reinhardt when out here will produce "Everybody" for the Hollywood Bowl, under a separate agreement.

Brains with Beauty

Watertown, N. Y., Aug. 30.
One beautiful girl in northern New York showed that she had good sense as well as beauty. At a recent beauty contest, held in connection with the Greater Carthage Exposition, Gwendolyn Smith of Lowville, N. Y., was named Miss Exposition.
The management gave her the option of attending the Atlantic City Beauty contest for a week or taking the cash. Miss Smith, graduate of Lowville, N. Y., high school this June, and intending to enter Potsdam Normal school next term, took the $100 in cash.

Homely Bronxites

Bronx swains may be bashful, and again may realize they are just homely.
A male beauty contest announced by the Metropolitan Swimming Pool, known as an "Adonis of the Beach" contest, failed to get a single entry, although the lists were held open for a month.

JOLSON IN FILM HOUSE SEPT. 8 AT $17,500

Playing 1 Week at Met, L. A., for West Coast— 3 Days of 5 Shows

Los Angeles, Aug. 30.
Al Jolson makes his debut in the picture theatres opening at the local Metropolitan the week of Sept. 8 at $17,500 net.
Jolson will appear with one of the Fanchon and Marco "Ideas" for one week plus the possibility of excepting 30 weeks more in the film houses out of the following 52 weeks.
All bookings are going through the William Morris Agency in New York, the local week having been arranged with Harold B. Franklin.
(Continued on page 36)

COM'R WARREN TELLS INSPECTORS

Only Exception Where Police Find Gambling or Prostitution in Connection With Liquor Selling— Prohibition for Federal Agents, Says Commissioner, and There Are Enough of Them

TIMES SQ. AFFECTED

New York cops are not booze detectors and need not use their smellers for that purpose, said Police Commissioner Warren to his inspectors at a special meeting called of the cops' commanders at headquarters.
The Commissioner's only exceptions to his new ruling were that if the police discovered liquor selling in conjunction with gambling or prostitution, they were to take cognizance of the Volstead violation or to act upon specific instruction from headquarters.
According to the account of the conference, Commission Warren informed the inspectors that he considered Prohibition a federal matter, that New York State has no enforcement law, as the Mullen
(Continued on page 36)

16 B'WAY MUSICALS ON AIR AS CIGARET ADV.

P. Lorillard to Radio Only First Act—Showmen See B. O. Trade in Piqued Interest

"Old Gold on Broadway" is a showmanly tie-up with 16 Broadway musical shows by P. Lorillard & Co., tobacconists and producers of their new Old Gold cigaret brand, which calls for the first act
(Continued on page 36)

PETTING PARTIES IN THEATRES BLUSHINGLY AWFUL—SHE SAYS

Speaking, However, Only for K. C.—Combined Women Forces on Drive Against Indecent Shows and Pictures, Too—Women's Societies in On It

Bernie's New Record

Ben Bernie claims a world's record.
More people passed the Strand on Broadway Sunday, claims Bernie, than any other house on earth.
Bernie is the featured attraction at the Strand this week.

U. S. D. A. SAYS FIGHT FILMS CAN SHOW

Stops All Talk of Federal Warrants in Milwaukee —Transportation

Milwaukee, Aug. 30.
Fight films may come and go in the state of Wisconsin and not fear serious action from the United States attorney's office here, it was learned after a federal investigator finished a probe on the showing of the Tunney-Dempsey and Dempsey-Sharkey fight films in local houses.
Senator Levi H. Bancroft, U. S. attorney here, informed Variety's correspondent he had been approached by the federal agents who sought to make arrests for the showing of the fight films in Mil-
(Continued on page 44)

Kansas City, Aug. 30.
Combined forces of Kansas City Women's clubs, Society for the Prevention of Commercialized Vice and the recreation department of the city government are planning a concerted drive against indecent shows, suggestive pictures and motion house petting parties, to be started as soon as details can be worked out.
Letters asking for help in uplifting the morals of the shows and the conduct of the young people attending them have been sent to eight women's organizations — Kansas City Athenaeum, the Parent-Teachers Association, district, state and national bodies of the Federation of Women's Clubs, Women's City Club, P. E. O. Sisterhood, and the state club magazine, Missouri Club Woman.
"We are working as much to improve the behavior of young boys and girls attending the picture shows as for the character of the shows themselves," Mrs. Mason C.
(Continued on page 31)

ROGER KAHN RETIRING FROM DANCE B'D FIELD

Fed Up On Temperament and Bickering—Leaves Hotel Penn and Closing Office

"The millionaire maestro," Roger Wolfe Kahn, who went from riches to rags, has decided he has had enough of the jazz band racket and is retiring from that field of endeavor. His new professional pursuit of composition, and the new hobby of airplane operation, prompted young Kahn against further bothering with jazz bands, and
(Continued on page 2)

An Announcement of World Wide Interest:
Un Communique d'un Interet Mondial:
Eine Anzeige von Welt Interesse:
Un Aviso de Interes Mundial:
In Sept. 7 Issue of Variety

BROOKS
THE NAME YOU GO BY WHEN YOU GO TO BUY
COSTUMES
GOWNS AND UNIFORMS
1437 B'WAY, N.Y.   TEL. 5580 PENN.
ALSO 25,000 COSTUMES TO...

STAGE **BROADWAY** **SCREEN**

Variety

PRICE 25¢

Published Weekly at 154 West 46th St., New York, N. Y., by Variety, Inc. Annual subscription, $10. Single copies, 25 cents.
Entered as second-class matter December 22, 1905, at the Post Office at New York, N. Y., under the act of March 3, 1879.

VOL. XCIV. No. 9   NEW YORK, WEDNESDAY, MARCH 13, 1929   64 PAGES

WHAT SOUND HAS DONE

Reformers in Panic as Hoover Starts Ignoring Their Job Claims

Washington, March 12.
Anti-everything and paid reformer contingents are getting panicky. Actually looks like a riot ahead. As Canon Chase put it at his $3.50 gate party last November, "Herbert Hoover gives us the greatest chance we've had in ten years," and the promise does not seem to be materializing. The new President has not run to the form the reformers thought he would, in the picking of his aides in the big jobs.

In his appointments to date he has turned his back on the politically inclined parsons that did the bush-beating down South for votes during the campaign.

The squawk is already beginning to be heard even though there are still plenty of jobs to be handed out.

Antis Blocked Donovan

Hoover's cabinet looks okay. It was there that the reformer contingent hoped to place the "right" man. They did win out in getting Col. William J. Donovan out of the Attorney General berth, but to balance this Mr. Hoover appoints a founder of the Association Against the Prohibition Amendment.

If the Canon Chases and the others do pull a lesser plum it is not going to satisfy the reformer workers. This is clearly evidenced by the quitting of Col. Horace A. Mann who was credited with having been the guiding head of the political parsons in the South.

Col. Mann has been at the White House many times. He is known to have put up a strong fight to have his helpers taken care of. When they were not he walked out.
(Continued on page 59)

Snake Oil Spieler's Refuge for Outcasts

Chicago, March 12.
Buffalo Cody, cousin of Buffalo Bill, is "pastor" of a Harrison street mission house for down and outs. Cody is a disciple of Rev. Benjamin Mickle who runs a similar place on Lake street. When the Harrison street spot, then a cafe, was padlocked for liquor violations, Rev. Mickle secured it rent free and turned it over to Cody.

The long-haired Cody previously was one-nighting with snake oil.

Chain Books College Musical; 7 One-Nighters

Chicago, March 12.
"Brazil Nuts," University of Illinois' Pierrot Club all male musical, has been booked for seven one night stands by Great States for a total of $6,000. This follows a regular presentation at the university.

Great States gave the youngsters a one night test with their last year production and regarded it favorably. Route includes Decatur, Joliet, Galesburg, Aurora, Bloomington, Quincy and Peoria.

Cantor's $5,000

Eddie Cantor demanded and received $5,000 from the Lucky Strike people for his published endorsement of that cigaret. It's the highest price paid to date by any cigaret manufacturer. Next top was the $2,500 paid to Al Jolson.

Many of the stars of both sexes, who gave their names as endorsers for the bull of the national publicity are grieving.

Direct NBC-RKO Air Tieup at the Palace

The first of a series of direct tieups between the National Broadcasting Co. artists and RKO starts at the RKO Palace, New York, shortly after Easter when "A Night at the NBC" becomes a feature act. This will comprise Phillips Carlin, the announcer, who will m.c., Gladys Rice, Billy Jones and Ernest Hare, to be billed as the Inter-Woven Pair (formerly the Happiness Boys) and a name radio band yet to be selected.

The act will be a broadcasting studio counterpart with all the authentic trimmings and may actually be broadcast on a several special days direct from the stage.

The success of Rudy Vallee's band, strictly a radio product, for personal appearances, prompted this experimental innovation to test the same stunt with a succession of radio-famed artists.

Keith agents have been advised by the booking office that Keith's expects first call on radio and club services of all acts playing in Keith's vaude, and restrained by contract from radio, club and film work outside the RKO subsidiaries.

Clause in the Keith artists' contract bans all forms of outside engagements, including the above three.

However, as the radio broadcasts for Keith's (RKO) by vaude acts is without financial compensation, acts have a chance at extra income through other work elsewhere. Keith's does not object to alien radio work by acts not needed for radio by Keith's, but the circuit demands first call and final say.

GLASS BALCONY

London, Ont., March 12.
Crying infants will no longer be a nuisance to local theatre audiences. Both babe and mother may now view the performances and no one will hear the squawk if the tot goes critic and audibly protests.

New Palace theatre has sound proofed the east section of its balcony in glass with comfortable chairs for the elders and such offspring as they want to share the entertainment.

LIST OF CHANGES IN EIGHT MONTHS

$24,000,000 Spent So Far in Revising Studios and $3,000,000 to Go on Experiments—Opinions Differ Over Sound Costs—90 Systems at Present—Negative Film Stock Increase—Sets Reduced One-Third—Figures Show Public Will Attend Bad Talkies, but Not Just Sound Films

ACOUSTICS BIG PROBLEM

Los Angeles, March 12.
During the past eight months the picture industry has spent around $24,000,000 in shaping up studios for the making of sound product and $3,000,000, or more will be laid on the line for experimentation this year. This is the financial sidelight on the sound revolution within the picture making business.

Producers, in some instances, have gone ahead blindly. Others have been more discreet in trying to adapt themselves and their organizations to this new wrinkle. With sound still an infant, figures obtainable demonstrate a marked dislike for sound and musical synchronization of pictures, while those of the all dialog type have at least been fairly successful at the box-office.

The heavy expenditure has been for building and equipment, also experimentation. Latter item is an expensive one, with studio paying large amounts to improve recording, etc., which in some instances has been totally lost, but in others have proven highly successful.

Not Sure

And producers are not yet sure of just what they want in sound. Result has been that product is considerably curtailed and the so-called promised number of pictures is not coming from any one company. During the first six months of 1928, when silent pictures held the field to themselves, production was normal. Today, on account of the new era and its handicaps in getting equipment, space, etc., none of the companies are up to a normal production schedule.

Though it took the industry 15 years to be able to create a production structure valued at $65,000,000, in eight months this same industry has expended another $20,000,000 and more, and still lacks what can be construed as a definite and stable
(Continued on page 56)

BOX SCORES

Dramatic Critics' box score will be found on page 51.

Film critics' box score will be found on page 4.

$1,000,000 in Free Talent Donated Yearly on Coast by Film Colony

Jazz for Speaks

Most radio stations devote set periods to orchestral stuff. The wise boys among speak proprietors have the schedule down pat. Periodical dial turnings bring consecutive band music.

They say orchestras are most desirable as bar room entertainment, helping to brighten up the surroundings more than sopranos, pianists and lecturers.

Chicago's Canned Applause Making 'Em Warm Up

Chicago, March 12.
"Canned" applause as an inducement to the real thing is reported successful at the Harding, wired Balaban and Katz de luxe stand here.

House is being used for experiments in sound with horns installed in the auditorium as well as behind the screen. An applause record was put on the wire equipment following the regular organ solo, and is said to have induced considerably more than the customary reception by power of suggestion. Few in the audience are apparently aware of the phoney angle.

For talking pictures, however, horns any place other than near the screen tend to destroy the dialog illusion.

SEX LECTURER IGNORED IN BROADWAY THEATRE

Dr. M. Sayle Taylor, the sex "authority" lecturing at the National, is not the same exponent of the old racket who appeared recently in Brooklyn. L. M. Gordon, former assistant to Dr. M. Davidson, once teamed with Taylor, worked in Brooklyn until enjoined by Taylor. Prior to the present date Taylor, who is a doctor of philosophy, lectured in Pittsburgh and Philadelphia where he remained 10 weeks at the Earle. At the National he's losing money.

He was formerly city bacteriologist in Seattle, Wash., assigned to the red light district. Taylor is quite a debater. In a verbal contest on the topic of companionate marriage, he bested Judge Lindsay in Chicago, Clarence Darrow being the judge. Dr. Davidson, a practicing physician, is a member of the British Royal Academy of Medicine.

"Incompatibility," which Taylor titles his lecture and question hour, restricted to women, has not done well here, but in Philly it was a clean-up.

Los Angeles, March 12.
More than $1,000,000 worth of free talent is donated annually in Los Angeles by the film colony. Charity benefits, theatres, radio broadcasts and night clubs get the bulk of it. Screen actors generally respond to these affairs not because they like to do it, but because they are so ordered by their employer. Producers are careful in ordering their players to make personals and will only do so where actor's appearance in connection with the showing of a picture on a percentage basis will help.

Present popularity for midnight shows has drawn heavily on the players to make a bow on stage in act, but the theatre is by no means the largest user of free talent. There are countless dancehalls, beach clubs, skating rinks and night clubs who set aside one night a week as "Movie Night." They emphasize this in all advertising, and despite that only one or two may show up, the public, regardless of disappointment, continues to fall.

Big Names Dodge

Exclusive cafes with dance floor connections also use the "Movie Night" thing to lure the tourist as well as the old time residents. These places exact a stiff cover charge for the privilege of mingling with the free talent who are spotted for a
(Continued on page 3)

Wall Paper Faces

Los Angeles, March 12.
A promoter has approached a number of studios for permission to photograph film stars and use the pictures for wall paper prints. Plan is to create a vogue for homes. Special combinations are being arranged for many moods and fancies. The Shebas may have a John Gilbert room, or a group of panels carrying portraits of many screen idols. Movie struck sheik can have his selection of screen flaps. Hoot Gibson is being sought to fill the demands of the kid lovers of westerns, and the prominent child players are being sought for decorating the nurseries. Chaney will look after the bad little boys and girls.

Sound for 1,000

Laurens, Ia., March 12.
This Pocahontas town of 1,000 claims distinction of being the smallest Iowa community with sound pictures.

Elite theatre opened Sunday with the new policy.

However, of all the 1920s crackdowns, nothing matches Prohibition. One of the stranger reports of the time was about "Booze robbers who prey on 'legitimate' bootleggers," which is a long tale about an elaborate and successful scam to steal a load of illicit hooch from professional bootleggers, whom *Variety* sometimes called "'leggers."

Over the years, there were many anecdotes about showbiz people using their wiles to get around the law. But as the decade progressed, the anecdotes indicate that the pressures were easing up. By 1927, an unnamed columnist was openly recommending scotch highballs made with the new-to-the-U.S. Perrier water.

The decade was called the Jazz Age, and the word "jazz" became synonymous with "progressive" people having a wild time. But even today, "jazz" is a vague term, encompassing everything from Dixieland to Big Band music of the 1930s and '40s, and later used more to define the later be-bop and free jazz styles. In a 1917 item, *Variety* tried to define the genre in writing about the Jazz Band at New York City's Reisenweber's cabaret:

> "Late in the morning the Jazzers go to work and the dancers hit the floor, to remain there until they topple over. . . . If the dancers see someone they know at the tables, it's common to hear 'Oh, boy!' as they roll their eyes while floating past, and the 'Oh, boy!' expression probably describes the Jazz Band music better than anything else could."

Well. That doesn't exactly clarify things. A month later (April 27, 1917), a story, in its entirety, said "New Orleans is being depleted of its jazz bands, about 20 of them having left there recently. Several negro jazz bands remain. Negro bands were the original jazz bands, and their expressions of 'jazzing it' and 'put a little jazz on it' are still very popular at their picturesque balls."

In music and nightclubs, whether in Paris or the United States, Caucasians were fascinated with black performers. Catering to this trend, the Cotton Club opened in Harlem and featured performances by entertainers who, by virtue of their skin color, were forbidden to be in the audience. Duke Ellington led the house band from 1927 to 1931, and the long list of performers appearing there included Louis Armstrong, Count Basie, Cab Calloway, Ella Fitzgerald, the Nicholas Brothers, Bessie Smith, Fats Waller, and Lena Horne. It was considered hip to go "slumming" in Harlem. In those days, few people thought segregation was a problem. And in truth, not many people worried about things like fascism—yet.

A September 21, 1927, page one headline read "Mussolini's Hope in Screen" with the subhead "Duce hails world mediator. 'This can bring world together and end war,' says Italian dictator upon viewing own image and hearing record of Movietone—Sheehan planning on non-partisan political uses."

The story details how the Italian premier was speaking to the Fox Movietone newsreel people and requested two retakes until he was happy with the results. That final take "will be the Movietone reproduction shown at the opening Friday night [September 16] at the Times Square theatre, New York, along with Fox's special picture "Sunrise." In light of this, *Variety* asked Winfield R. Sheehan if Movietone would make "individual records for political campaigns." 'Movietone will be strictly neutral in politics,' answered Fox's production chief. 'If it presents a candidate of one party, his opponent will be on in the same viewing. It suggests to me,' said Mr. Sheehan, 'that the politicians will soon be looking after their teeth, for, in my opinion, the best looking candidate on the Movietone sheet will be the winner.' "

Political leaders had learned the value of the new media. Meanwhile, the "old media" were surprisingly robust in the 1920s.

Right: September 21, 1927.

STAGE · BROADWAY · SCREEN

Variety

PRICE 20 CENTS

Published Weekly at 154 West 46th St., New York, N. Y., by Variety, Inc. Annual subscription, $7. Single copies, 20 cents.
Entered as second class matter December 22, 1905, at the Post Office at New York, N. Y., under the act of March 3, 1879.

VOL. LXXXVIII. No. 10 — NEW YORK CITY, WEDNESDAY, SEPTEMBER 21, 1927 — 64 PAGES

MUSSOLINI'S HOPE IN SCREEN

3 B'WAY SHOWS IN 'RED' TROUBLES; TEX'S 'PADLOCKS,' $120,000 IN BOX

"Half a Widow" Turns Back Audience for Leblang Refund—"Footlights" Moves Its Struggles Across 42d St.—2 Shows Still Playing on Slim Prospects

Last week-end saw three musical shows in financial difficulties. Two managed to continue this week, while the other passed out of the picture after seven performances.

"Padlocks of 1927," at the Shubert, reported having bankroll trouble from time to time, came near winding up Friday night. Texas Guinan, starred in the revue, called for a showdown on the coin owed her, but was persuaded to go on after holding the curtain 15 minutes.

Miss Guinan claimed something like $26,000 due. Her contract called for $3,500 weekly, but she had accepted $2,000 until business picked up, thereby receiving the cut figure for 10 weeks. It appears that she got nothing for two weeks, and it is only with that part of the claim that Equity became concerned. According to Equity Miss Guinan was owed $5,100 up to Saturday.

A bond guaranteeing two weeks' salaries is on deposit at Equity. When it was reported to Equity last
(Continued on page 43)

FARMER HIT FLIER FOR FLYING LOW

Davenport, Ia., Sept. 20.
Ben Kahl, a farmer residing near the landing field of the Davenport Airport, became as frightened as the chickens and cows on his farm last week when planes operated from the airport flew low over his property. One of them swooped down until it nearly crashed his windmill.

Ben's ire flamed, and although he made prior protests against the practice, he wasted no time on words on this occasion. He met Alfred Sporrer, one of the aviators, and smacked him down. Sporrer has filed information charging assault and battery against the farmer.

Case is to be heard later in the week. Meantime Kahl has consulted his lawyers about getting an injunction to protect rights to the air over his farm fields.

Average Burlesque Age, 32

In one of the 37 shows on the Mutual burlesque wheel the average age among its feminine contingent is 32 years.

Radio Lined Up for Presidential Fight

Kansas City, Sept. 20.
The radio will form an important fight in the next presidential campaign. Gen. James G. Harboard, president Radio Corporation of America, while here, stated that the leading candidates in the forthcoming national scrap would have an equal number of hours on the air.

The national party committees will select the speakers for the "mike."

NON-KOSHER CHORINES MAY GO YIDDISH

East Side Demand for B'way Fine Lookers—Needed for Musical Shows

Broadway chorus girls may find themselves more and more in demand in the downtown Yiddish musical comedy theatres. Keen competition this fall in the Ghetto show business foretells a battle of
(Continued on page 39)

"ON THE CUFF" FOR FILM HOUSE TRADE

Picture patronage on the cuff is the latest business stimulus adopted by small house operators in towns where competition is keen.

These small houses, many operating with a daily change system, are issuing credit coupon books, with the coupons good for admission and payable weekly or semi-monthly.

Those working the racket claim it to be successful as a business builder. They figure that families short on ready cash would otherwise remain away but now come more frequently since the credit system has been installed.

DUCE HAILS WORLD MEDIATOR

"This Can Bring World Together and End War," Says Italian Dictator Upon Viewing Own Image and Hearing Record of Movietone — Sheehan Planning on Non-Partisan Political Uses

CONNOLLY'S MISSION

"This can bring the world together; it can settle all differences; it can become the international medium, educator and adjuster; it can prevent war," said Mussolini, Italy's dictator, when seeing himself pictured as he delivered through Movietone his message to the United States, taken in Rome.

The Italian Premiere gave concrete evidence of faith in his statements when requesting the Fox people to retake him, and for the second time spoke before the camera in English. The second record not pleasing him, Mussolini suggested that he repeat, and again called at the studio in Rome, making his third talk, once more in English. It will be the Movietone reproduction shown at the opening Friday night (Sept. 16) at the Times Square theatre, New
(Continued from page 23)

$1,000 Weekly and Bonus For M.-G.-M. Scenarist

Los Angeles, Sept. 20.
Metro-Goldwyn-Mayer has renewed its contract with A. P. Younger, scenario writer, at $1,000 weekly and $5,000 as a bonus for each story accepted.
Younger has had an average of 10 stories a year accepted by the company.

Radioed Fight as Show

Newark, N. J., Sept. 20.
Thursday night during the little muss in Chicago, Harry Crull, manager of the Branford (pictures) will turn the show off and the radio on.
If the boys go the limit at Soldier's Field that will wind up the night's final performance. Otherwise the show will resume after the million-dollar scrappers decide who's what.

MY WEEK IN A PICTURE HOUSE
By AL JOLSON

Los Angeles, Sept. 13.
Appearing in picture theatres, I believe, is to the advantage of any star, regardless of how big as a box office attraction.

For the past 18 years I have been appearing in legit productions doing eight performances a week. When

HOSPITAL RYE AT $96

Hospital liquor, genuinely labeled as legitimately assigned to the institutions, has recently flooded the Manhattan market in quantities. It is all rye and is peddled at $4 the pint, $15 for four.

It is genuine aged goods, and the original hospital names to which allowed are not scratched off.

'Leggers handling this product offer to make regular weekly deliveries in small lots. The price, totaling $96 a case, is not regarded as high for bona fide rye, which is scarce as hair on the chest of a chorusman around Times Square.

CHI CASHING IN ON FIGHT CROWD

Theatres and Hotels Raising Rates—"Scandals" from $4.40 to $7.70

Chicago, Sept. 20.
To "accommodate" the many persons who may or may not arrive tomorrow (Wednesday) to get a load of the big quarrel, six of the 10 legits in the Loop will boost the scale.

"Scandals" is chancing the heaviest increase, going from the regular $4.40 to $7.70 for the one night. Those trudging along without balloon rates are "Chicago," Harris; "Tommy," Cort; "The Barker," Blackstone, and "Broadway," Selwyn.

The jumpers are: "The Spider," $3.30 to $4.40; "Crime," $3.30 to $3.85; "Yours Truly," $4.40 to $5.50; "American Tragedy," $3.30 to $3.85; "Desert Song," $3.85 to $5.50, and "Scandals."

Hotels have already cashed in on advance reservations, many operating at raised rates.

It appears to be a general cash-in, with the railroads, Rickard, Dempsey, Tunney et al. getting most of the gravy.

the opportunity presented itself for me to go into picture houses I looked at it from the angle of a following I never had before; people who were dyed-in-the-wool picture theatre addicts and who never paid the $4.40 top which I was getting with my own shows.

Then again, the engagement at the Metropolitan here for a week gave me an opportunity to play to volume. There were somewhere around 80,000 admissions on the week.

My drawing power in the musical comedy field has been limited. In the picture houses it is not.

Therefore, when I appeared for the first time in a picture theatre after my legit career I felt that I was creating a following which will be loyal to me in my screen career.

Of course, my motive may have been selfish in going with the picture houses, naturally, otherwise I would not have been doing' four, five and six performances a day as I did here.

However, I found the audiences here in the picture houses more wholesome and more appreciative than those who put the $4.40 over the ticket office ledge. These are the people also who would be my loyal rooters in the picture theatres whenever there is a screen offering with me in it.

At this time I don't know whether
(Continued on page 10)

Jeanne Eagels Too Difficult In M-G-M Film—Let Out

Los Angeles, Sept. 20.
Jeanne Eagels, in Hollywood for several weeks, playing opposite John Gilbert in "Fires of Youth," now in production at the M-G-M studios, has been let out by that organization due to squawks by Monta Bell, director of the picture.

Bell complained he could not put up with Miss Eagels' temperament and found her too difficult to handle.

The legit actress is said to have arrived at the studio at any and all times, provoking scenes upon her arrival.

Miss Eagels was let out by Paramount once before for the same reasons.

AMUSEMENTS | PRICE 20c | TIMES SQUARE

VARIETY

Published Weekly at 154 West 46th St., New York, N. Y., by Variety, Inc. Annual subscription $7. Single copies 20 cents.
Entered as second class matter December 22, 1905, at the Post Office at New York, N. Y., under the act of March 3, 1879.

VOL. LXXXII. No. 13 — NEW YORK CITY, WEDNESDAY, MAY 12, 1926 — 64 PAGES

THEATRES 97% PICTURES

"ABIE'S IRISH ROSE" 5TH YEAR; EVERY RUN RECORD TAKEN

4th Year Ends May 22—No Prediction Possible at End of Unprecedented Consecutive Engagement on Broadway—"Abie's Children" as Sequel

"Abie's Irish Rose," with every run record for non-musical plays in her cap, establishes a new mark in theatrical history when Saturday of next week Anne Nichols' world's champion comedy enters a fifth year on Broadway at the Republic. "Abie" is technically in the
(Continued on page 38)

OVER $160,000 SUNK IN TWIN OAKS FLOP

B'way's Elaborate Cellar Cabaret in Receivership—48 "Founders" Lost $3,500

With "too many bosses," a common complaint from the performers and musicians at the Twin Oaks restaurant, in the basement of 1560 Broadway, New York, cornering 46th street, the place has run into business difficulties and is in receivership. It suspended suddenly last week.
The room was founded by 48 investors with $2,500 each, from reports, including H. H. Frazee, Col. Jacob Ruppert, one of the Ward baking people, and others. A Mr. Zelcer who runs the White Horse Tavern on 45th street, opposite the Piccadilly-Rendezvous where the White Horse people were formerly affiliated, was also chief executive
(Continued on page 62)

LEAGUE OF NATIONS PICTURE CONGRESS

Paris, May 7.
An international convention of the moving picture industry is being organized in Paris, Sept. 27-Oct. 3, by the International Institute of Intellectual Co-operation, under the auspices of the League of Nations.
Fred Cornelissen, Institut International de Co-operation Intellectuellede la Societe des Nations, 2 Rue de Montpensier, Paris, is the organizing secretary, who will on application mail printed details as soon as published.
The use of pictures in education will be an important item to be studied by the Congress, but all subjects pertaining to the industry will be discussed by various committees to be formed later.

RADIO FAN LETTERS FALL DOWN 75%

Gratis Entertainers Expecting Glory Get Little of It—Spring Laziness

Fan mail to radio entertainers has dropped off 75 per cent these balmy days, with the result the gratis performer is somewhat disappointed.
Some looked upon it as a serious indication of their fall from public grace as popular entertainers, but when the general apathy toward writing the entertainers became known it was dismissed as natural spring laziness.
Broadcasting officials are phased by this turn. Insistent calls for public response to the acts, to "let them know how they pleased" is propaganda to stimulate and maintain interest from the free talent, that has but the glory as a reward.

Airdomes About Through; Several Good Reasons

The outdoor picture places in and around New York will not be numerous this summer. It's due to the increase in building, installation of cooling plants in the regular film houses and the passing of many "airdomes" through other interests acquiring the sites.
Not many summers ago one could find an outdoor picture show on almost every corner in the residential districts. A few are still getting primed for warm weather, but proximity to the bigger houses with the "cooler than the street" slogans and tied-up film services are expected to eventually eliminate them.

Elephants by Express

Monmouth, Ill., May 11.
Robbins Bros. circus officials wore out several pencils in the American Express company office here trying to figure transportation for a couple of untrained elephants, shipped from New Orleans to join the show on its western Illinois itinerary.
The animals are reputed to have cost $6,000; express bill between $900 and $1,000.

UNDER 500 IN U. S. WHOLLY AWAY FROM FILMS

3% Remaining Includes Legit, Straight Vaudeville and Burlesque—Not 100 Picture Houses in This Country Charging Above 85c. Top Admission—Little Building Nowadays for Anything but Films—All Theatrical Managers Are Dubious About Future in Raging Picture Craze

20,000 THEATRES

Of the estimated 20,000 theatres in this country 97 per cent. are devoted to pictures to a greater or minor extent. The remaining 3 per cent. are wholly divorced from the films. The latter comprise the legitimate, straight vaudeville and burlesque theatres.
In the estimate of 20,000 theatres are included 17,000 houses admittedly for pictures, 2,500 playing a combination entertainment policy in
(Continued on page 14)

Longest Boardwalk

At Coney Island work is under way to extend the board walk to Manhattan Beach. Coney claims it will then be the world's longest boardwalk.
There has been a decided increase for walk space, with the majority running to something in the eats or soft drink line.

Marion Davies' "Miracle"

Los Angeles, May 11.
Marion Davies wants it known that she has purchased "The Miracle" for pictures and that when it goes into production she will play the role created on the stage by Lady Diana Manners, that of the Nun.

Absent-Minded 'Legger

A bootlegger backing one of the Broadway shows is picking up most of his knowledge of the show business hanging around the box office.
He was inside the other afternoon, when a woman walked up, saying, "I want two. How much?"
With the bootlegger answering:
"$55 a case."

CHINESE RESTAURANT ON B'WAY DOING $25,000 WEEKLY TRADE

Insight on Chinese Operation—Many Failed American-Managed Restaurants in New York Turned Into Winners by Chinamen—Low Food Cost

FIELDS FOUND SUMMONS LYING ON HIS CHEST

Comedian Served in Bed at Home in $150,000 Contract Breach Action

W. C. Fields, the comedian, now making pictures for Famous Players-Lasky Corp., woke up the other morning at his Bayside, L. I., home and found a summons in a $150,000 suit pinned on his chest like a lily, as a final and, this time, successful effort by O'Brien, Malevinsky & Driscoll, Charles Walton's lawyers.
(Continued on page 58)

DeWolf Hopper's Debut; Radio Paying Him

DeWolf Hopper joins the ranks of the commercial radio advertisers as a paid artist via WEAF with the Eveready Carbon Co.'s weekly program, starting May 18. This marks Hopper's debut on the radio.

Bucky Harris Marrying Miss Sutherland of W. Va.

Washington, May 11.
It is well authenticated here that Bucky (Stanley) Harris, manager of the champion Washington baseball team, is to wed the daughter of former U. S. Senator Sutherland of West Virginia.
Senator Sutherland is the present Alien Property Custodian.

Musical "3 Weeks"

Elinor Glyn's "Three Weeks" will be converted into an operetta with score by Rudolf Friml and produced in San Francisco in August. The librettist and lyricist have not been decided upon.
The production will be financed by a California syndicate with Ross Mobley in charge. The company will be assembled in New York and taken to California for rehearsals.

A Chinese restaurant on Broadway doing $100,000 gross business monthly, with 55c. lunch, $1.50 dinner and cabaret, without couvert charge.
Vaguely, the American cabaret and restaurant men, particularly in New York, have been decrying the
(Continued on page 29)

NON-EQUITY CAST FOR 'FRENCH MODEL' SHOW

Revival with 45 People—Paying Off Weekly with Certified Checks

"The French Model," running for a single performance at the Cort, New York, last season is to be revived and spotted at the Frolic, New York, after a preliminary week at the Metropolis, Bronx, May 17. The cast will be 100 per cent non-Equity, making the first non-Equity musical coming into Broadway since the actor-managers strike six years ago. Alessandra Baccari, author-sponsor of the piece has rounded up a
(Continued on page 53)

RAN $1,000 CONTRACTED SALARY UP TO $5,000

Los Angeles, May 11.
A four-year agreement was made between Jean Hersholt and Universal, after the character actor threatened to break his contract. Hersholt complained he had to battle to get the right stories and recognition and that he was getting $1,000 a week from Universal who were farming him out as high as $3,500.
By the terms of the new agreement, Hersholt will get $3,000 weekly for the first year, $2,500 during the next and on a sliding scale up to $5,000 for seven days.

IF IT'S
COSTUMES
GOWNS OR UNIFORMS
LEARN TO SAY
"BROOKS"
1437 BROADWAY – TEL. 5580 PEN.
ALSO 25,000 COSTUMES TO RENT

Left: May 12, 1926.

Above: Florenz "Don't call me *Flo*" Ziegfeld.

Aside from *Rhapsody in Blue* and *An American in Paris*, between 1924 and 1927, Gershwin and his lyricist brother, Ira, wrote for the stage *Lady Be Good*, *Oh, Kay*, *Funny Face*, and *Strike Up the Band*. Impressive output by any standard, but to modern eyes it seems astonishingly prolific. And if you talk about prolific, nobody deserves that term more than George S. Kaufman. Between 1918 and 1948, he was represented on Broadway, either as a writer or director, with about seventy productions. But as *Variety* reported in the December 2, 1925, issue, everybody was prolific: two hundred shows were expected to open during the 1924–25 Broadway season (compared to an average of forty during each season of the twenty-first century).

In its December 27, 1923, Broadway listings, *Variety* casually mentions a production at the Garrick presented by the Theatre Guild: "New play is by G. Bernard Shaw and due to open Friday night." The play was *Saint Joan*, and the paper later announced an extension for "the presentation, which is regarded as one of the most interesting of the season, despite the need for excision."

Now it's astonishing to think of a new play by Shaw or a slew of Eugene O'Neill debuts including *Anna Christie* and *The Hairy Ape* (both 1922), *Desire under the Elms* (1924), *The Emperor Jones* (1925), and *Strange Interlude* (1928) as anything other than spectacular, but there were other amazements during the decade. John Barrymore created a Broadway sensation in *Hamlet* (1923), and Konstantin Stanislavsky and the Moscow Art Theatre presented Russian plays in repertory. In short, it was a dream decade for any college drama major.

On the musical side, *Variety* noted in March 1920 that Irving Berlin would write "numbers and scenes" for the second act for *Ziegfeld Follies*. Berlin also contributed songs to several editions of the annual *Music Box Revue*, which included such hits as "Always," "What'll I Do," and "Blue Skies." Jerome Kern had a big success with the 1920 *Sally* (with lyrics by Otto Harbach). But the most enduring musical of the decade was *Show Boat*, adapted from Edna Ferber's novel by Oscar Hammerstein II, who also wrote the lyrics to Kern's music. In an era of tuners with featherweight plots, this one featured serious themes and songs including "Ol' Man River," "Bill," and "Can't Help Lovin' Dat Man." It was a change of pace for Florenz Ziegfeld—or Zieggy, as *Variety* called him February 9, 1927—but the January 4, 1928, review read: "It has everything, and tops everything ever done before by Ziegfeld." Reviewer Abel (Abel Green) wrote, "It's a corking production and the best in its class" and noted that there was already a backlash to the positive reviews and word of mouth "and the second night commenced opining that while it's a great show there's nothing phenomenal about it."

So theater, novels, and movies were thriving. And on September 21, 1927, E. F. Albee insisted vaudeville was thriving too, making a statement to the press that the form was never so stable and firmly entrenched as it is today in America.

This is what is now known as "positive spin."

There were early warning signs. On September 23, 1921, a report from Charleston, West Virginia, stated, "For the first time in its history this city is without anything but picture theatres. The spoken drama has passed indefinitely...." Chicago was described as the traditional source of road-show attractions since it usually originated between 175 and 200 per year. The city, however, was expecting the year's total to be only thirteen.

What killed vaudeville? Most concede it was the combo of radio and "talkers," but here's something to consider:

A November 9, 1927, story said big vaudeville circuits, such as Keith-Albee, and independent bookers were clamoring for "sideshow freaks." A group of nine had recently appeared in New Brunswick and nearly broke the house record, so Loew Circuit exec Fred LaReine snapped them up: "In LaReine's layout are Albert and Alberta, half man and half woman; armless wonder, snake charmer, spider boy, fat woman, living skeleton, midget, giant and sword swallower." Accompanying the "freaks" were a barker and "hooch dancer."

The story added that the "activity in freak hunting" has proven a great opportunity for them. On Coney Island, "they have to sit for a 12-hour trick and get far less money than handed for their vaude work. Vaude contract mean only four shows a day."

And vaudeville was getting competition from other innovations of the decade, such as air shows.

The September 21, 1927, issue carried several tales of terror, including a "daredevil aerialist and parachute jumper" who dropped 1,500 feet to his death, and another, Ben Seger of Detroit, who was in a Jacksonville, Illinois, hospital, "probably fatally injured" when his parachute didn't open.

World War I had been the first major war to use aerial combat, and it exposed people to airplanes, which were a thing of thrills and awe. But, as always, some performers take the awe too far.

In the same issue:

> "Ben Kahl, a farmer residing near the landing field of Davenport [Iowa] Airport, became as frightened as the chickens and cows on his farm last week when planes operated from the airport flew low over his property. . . . He met Alfred Sporrer, one of the aviators, and smacked him down. Sporrer has filed information charging assault and battery against the farmer. . . . Kohl has consulted his lawyers about getting an injunction to protect rights to the air over his farm fields."

But the real key was carried in the same issue. As usual, there was a vaudeville section, but this one was different, since the main headline was "Passing of Vaudeville." The unnamed writer quotes from an article by W. A. S. Douglas in the October issue of *American Mercury*, a magazine founded in 1924 by acerbic journalist H. L. Mencken and drama critic George Jean Nathan (it ceased publishing in 1981). Douglas asserted that the two-performances-a-day, all-star bill of vaudeville—which carried the now-ironic nickname of the Big Time—was gone.

Douglas had written: "Big Time slumbered while the picture show-men were racing forward" and added, "*Variety* warned the vaudeville magnates of what was coming. At the same time it shouted in its columns to every two-a-day actor or actress to get on to this picture racket before it's too late."

Douglas said *Variety* lost vaude advertising due to this, "but not one whit deterred, *Variety* moved its picture news to a preferred position in the paper and continued to play John The Baptist to the vaudevillians. Finally *Variety* predicted the complete disappearance of Big Time."

That changed the lives of some people, but the death of vaudeville was hardly the biggest tragedy of the 1920s. That dubious honor goes to the stock market crash. *Variety*'s memorable headline "Wall St. Lays an Egg" was a lighthearted touch to a glum story that labeled it "The most dramatic event in the financial history of America . . ." The story estimated that 22 million individuals had money in the stock market. But this wasn't just an American tragedy; the ripples were quickly felt worldwide. And, as *Variety* predicted in its October 30, 1929, story, some people never recovered.

Right: It is paramount to use the word "Paramount."

the PARAMOUNT way!

¶ There's a vast difference in the way PARAMOUNT makes pictures from the methods of other producers. That's why PARAMOUNT leads the picture business. That's why PARAMOUNT hits like "INTERFERENCE", "THE WOLF OF WALL STREET", "ABIE'S IRISH ROSE", "THE DOCTOR'S SECRET" and others are rolling up the biggest box-office grosses in history. ¶ The PARAMOUNT way is illustrated afresh in "THE CANARY MURDER CASE". This company set out to make the greatest mystery-detective-melodrama in history. We bought the rights to the biggest selling book of this type ever known —"THE CANARY MURDER CASE"— with over a million readers. Featuring "Philo Vance", the most popular fictional "master mind" since Sherlock Holmes. ¶ We picked William Powell, with a gorgeous talking voice, to play "Vance", supported by an all-star cast of James Hall, Louise Brooks and Jean Arthur. We assigned a splendid money director, Malcolm St. Clair, to the job. We lavished time, money and care. ¶ The result is a KNOCKOUT! ¶ Only the vast resources that are PARAMOUNT'S made such a clean-up picture possible. And PARAMOUNT exhibitors again reap the profits.

THE BIG THRILL!

"THE CANARY MURDER CASE"

another PARAMOUNT all-talking hit!

1930s

In the summer of 1933, the *Inverness Chronicle* reported that a London man saw a huge, hideous beast slither into the water. The international press was riveted and the world read about the Loch Ness Monster for the first time. The *Daily Variety* of September 25, 1934, stated,

> "If that Loch Ness monster really does exist as attested to by sober Scots, it will be shown on the screens of the world. J. E. Williamson is lugging his deep sea photographic equipment to the Scotch pond and will go down as deep as 1,000 feet."

That's the entire story. It barely suggested that the creature could be a hoax or mirage and didn't ask how a large, prehistoric beastie could have kept such a low profile for so long. That's because in those days, people needed magic.

Variety fretted, back in 1932, about Adolf Hitler and the Nazi party, "whose influence is growing daily." Benito Mussolini and Spain's Francisco Franco were steadily gaining power by tapping into the public's poverty and fears, and the Second Sino-Japanese War was brewing. Meanwhile at home, America was hit by severe drought and dust storms, and gangsters such as John Dillinger, Baby Face Nelson, and Pretty Boy Floyd alternately horrified and enchanted the population.

Al Capone himself gave a June 30, 1931, interview to *Variety*. He said he'd been approached "many times" to appear in movies and received up to two thousand fan letters a week. Reporter Lou Greenspan noted that Capone's friends called him "Snorky," his home included seventy bodyguards, and a picture of him on the wall was flanked by portraits of George Washington and Abraham Lincoln.

Snorky snorted at most gangster films, but he loved watching "moving pictures and has private showings with professional projectionists to run the show."

He wasn't alone. With radio keeping people up to date on crime and poverty at home, they escaped to movie theaters to see screwball comedies, swashbuckling adventures with Errol Flynn, and musicals starring Shirley Temple or Fred Astaire and Ginger Rogers.

Talking pictures—or "talkers," as *Variety* called them—were a novelty

Right: September 16, 1935.

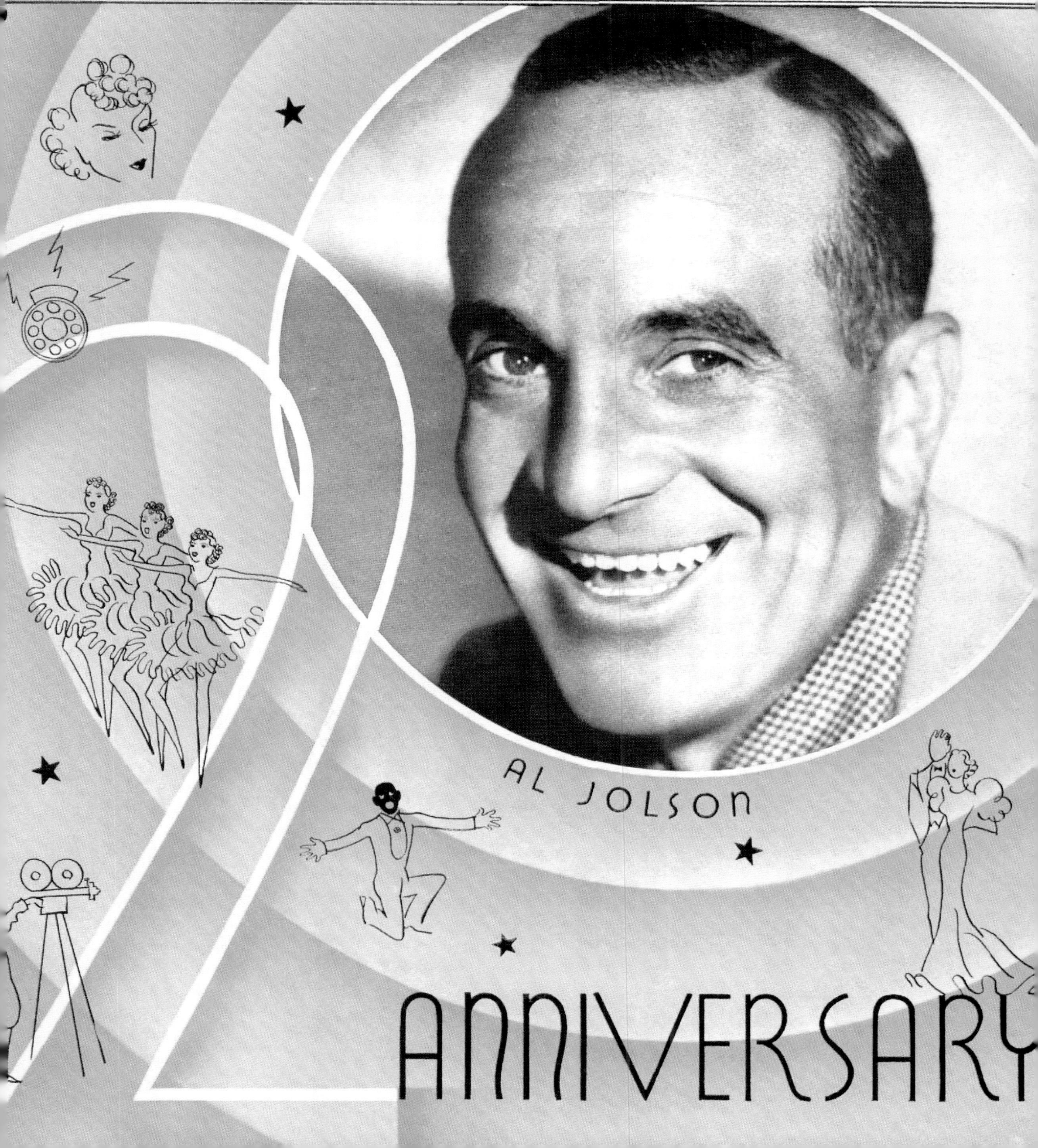

DAILY VARIETY DAILY

FIRST ANNIVERSARY EDITION

OUT MONDAY

OCTOBER 1
IN TWO SECTIONS

ORDER YOUR COPY TODAY

NO TILT IN PRICE — IT'S STILL

5¢

Left: September 29, 1934.

Above: Al Capone; James Cagney and the cast of *The Public Enemy*.

that helped box office boom at the start of the decade.

Variety reported on December 3, 1930, "Despite general depression, the film industry's leaders will pass the fiscal period of 1930 to their biggest net profit in history, amounting in all to nearly $55,000,000."

But it didn't last. Though the persistent myth says that moviegoing thrived throughout the Depression, a *Variety* study from June 21, 1932, showed that talkers had boosted box office but the craze was short-lived: "Theatre operators and distributors, who complain that grosses are off 39% to 40% . . . in the same breath charge that Hollywood is doing nothing through its studios to balance the situation."

But Hollywood's bottom line was hardly the world's biggest concern. The harsh times were reflected in many ways in every issue of *Variety*. For example, the December 8, 1931, issue reported on "hunger marchers" who arrived in Washington, a bankruptcy filing by an unnamed theater producer identified only as "one of the Broadway boys who blames it on the Depression," Disney's laying off three animators, and the opening of five-cent restaurants in Hollywood. These "grease pastures" offered "the answer to the problems of picture extras; . . . [each of them] works one day and looks for work the other six."

But as bad as it was on the home front, things were worse overseas. The June 21, 1932, issue contained a small item on page fifty-two from Berlin: Nazis, identified as a radical political party, "caused considerable disturbance at the Kleines Theatre in Kassel," which led to the closing of Robert Sherwood's *Waterloo Bridge*, a play about the romance between a soldier and a prostitute in World War I–era London. The local Nazi paper denounced the production, and the director closed it after "he'd received a number of threatening letters. . . . It's only one of many headaches caused to show business in Germany recently by the National Socialistic party whose influence is growing daily."

This wasn't particularly surprising. Back on November 12, 1930, a story from Berlin reported,

> "Adolf Hitler's party has opened a theatre here which is called the Nationalsozialistische Volksbuhne (National-Socialistic People's Theatre). It is being financed partly by German industrialists, as for instance Director-General Vogler, Kirdorf, etc., and partly by funds from the party itself."

The story then listed seven plays lined up for the theater.

So, even from the beginning, popular culture and the arts were a key building block for the Nazi agenda.

On September 5, 1933, Wolfe Kaufman summed up the actions that had occurred since Hitler's rise to chancellor only eight months before.

> "The world's stage was dominated during the past year, and for the first time in history, by an individual. Germany's brown-shirted Mr. Hitler and his activities stand out like thorns in a perusal of the year's activities. And thorns is a good word because the activities tell only of troubles and headaches and heartaches."

Under the February 27, 1934, *Weekly Variety* headline "Nazis Must Control Pix," the story read, "Dr. Goebbels, the Reich's minister for Public Enlightenment and Propaganda, told various reps of the Federal Film Corp. filling the Kroll Opera house in Berlin,

> "We are convinced that the film is one of the most modern and far-reaching means for influencing the masses . . . a government can therefore not possibly leave the film world to itself."

Left: Adele Astaire points at Fred Astaire.

Right: Fred Astaire points away from Ginger Rogers.

A Berlin story from May 2, 1933:

"Coupled with the new regime's very outspoken anti-jazz attitude is the new German ruling that no more works of Jewish composers or lyric writers are to be played in cafés, music halls, etc. Besides, radio is boycotting any work created by or credited to Jews."

The report added that the ban applied to records as well.

Two years later, a story quoted *Der Stürmer*, called the "most vitriolic anti-Semitic periodical" by *Variety*, as saying, "It is quite wrong when people say that Jazz hails from the Negroes. The Negro race has nothing to do with Jazz, since Africans don't know any Jazz music. It's the Jewish race that invented jazz, made to fit the Jewish idea of life with its disharmony and distortion."

By 1935, it was clear that the Nazis were targeting more than Jews. *Der Stürmer* was railing against Catholics, and the Nazi party was shutting down existing theater unions representing actors, managers, and chorus members due to their "Marxistic" tendencies, according to general manager Hinkel of the Reichskulturkammer (Chamber of Culture) and divisional organizer Frauenfeld, according to a September 25 story. The story added that three other showbiz unions had recently been disbanded; the International Artists' Lodge, International Variety Managers' Union, and Professional Performers' Association.

Hitler enlisted Leni Riefenstahl, a former dancer and actress, to film documentaries. The results were the 1935 *Triumph of the Will* and the 1938 two-part *Olympia*, which recorded the 1936 Olympics in Berlin. To this day, scholars and movie fans wonder whether they can morally admire her filmmaking skill, considering the content.

Riefenstahl traveled to the United States to explore movie-making deals but *Variety*, on November 29, 1938, issued a full-page ad on page five, urging Hollywood not to hire her. The

following day, *Daily Variety* front-paged this:

"Leni Riefenstahl, hailed as head of the Nazi film industry and Hitler's close friend, who came to Hollywood to survey American picture-making methods, yesterday found studio gates locked against her entry. Attaché of German consulate who sought to pave way for actress-director to enter lots was met with word that 'American films are barred from Germany, so we have nothing to show Miss Riefenstahl that would interest her.' Prominent nitery on Sunset Strip declined reservations for a party of 16 planned in her honor."

Meanwhile, film studios were doing everything possible to stay in business, convinced that they could outlast the Depression. In most cases, they were right.

The final player of the major-studio era was born in 1935 when the two-year-old 20th Century, created by Joseph Schenck and Darryl F. Zanuck, merged with William Fox's veteran company. The result, 20th Century-Fox, would be the last major studio created until DreamWorks was born fifty-nine years later.

This was the era of the movie mogul—execs so colorful and powerful that even the public recognized their names and faces.

Schenck (who'd been head of production at United Artists [UA] since it began in 1919) became chairman of 20th Century-Fox after the merger. His brother Nicholas Schenck was based on the East Coast and had been second-in-command to Marcus Loew, who died in 1927.

Loew's studio, Metro-Goldwyn-Mayer (MGM), boasted Louis B. Mayer and head of production "boy wonder" Irving Thalberg. Jack and Harry Cohn and Joseph Brandt were at Columbia Pictures; Adolph Zukor and Jesse Lasky at Paramount Pictures; Jack Warner became the best known of the brothers Warner at Warner Brothers; and the Laemmles (founder Carl and his son Carl Jr.) ran Universal Pictures.

The other major, RKO, was the one exception, and always in trouble. William LeBaron became head of production when it was formed in 1928 by linking RCA's Keith-Albee-Orpheum theater chain, the fledgling Pathé Studios, and the company of successful businessman (and founder of a political dynasty) Joseph Kennedy. But LeBaron was quickly replaced by David O. Selznick in 1931, who was in turn replaced by Merian C. Cooper. It went into receivership in 1933, with Samuel Briskin becoming head of production in 1935.

During this tumultuous time, though many of RKO's films are long forgotten, several have stood the test

Above: Louis B. Mayer allows Norma Shearer and Irving Thalberg off a train.

Right: September 15, 1936.

DAILY VARIETY
NEWS OF THE SHOW WORLD

Vol. 13 No. 7   Hollywood, California, Tuesday, September 15, 1936   5 Cents

SCREEN DARKENED

Irving Grant Thalberg
May 30, 1899   Sept. 14, 1936

TOP man of the picture industry — Irving Grant Thalberg was called home by his Maker. It's the Maker's gain and the loss of the entire amusement world.

Thalberg was the miracle man of the pic industry.

HE came into it in a quiet, humble, and unassuming way. That demeanor did not change as he mounted the rungs of the ladder to fame and success. To everyone he was 'Irving.' There was no false pride or vanity in his makeup. He was a modest but dominant human being who profited by experience. Nothing was impossible with him. Whether it was in forward step in the industry, strife in the industry, or the

Continued on page 4

H'wood Hushed In Homage to Thalberg

Irving G. Thalberg, 37, executive vice-president of Metro, died yesterday at his home in Santa Monica from an illness contracted while at Del Monte over Labor Day which resulted in lobular pneumonia. Thalberg had been ill at his home for a week previous to his death. From the outset, his illness had not been believed critical. It was stated it was 'just a cold.' However, on Saturday the lobar condition set in and an oxygen tent had to be utilized.

At his bedside at his passing were his wife, Norma Shearer, his father and mother, Mr. and Mrs. William Thalberg, his sister, Mrs. Lawrence Weingarten and her husband, Mrs. Edith Shearer, mother of Norma, and Mr. and Mrs. Bernie Hyman.

In attendance on Thalberg was Dr. Phillip Newmark and Dr. F. Groedel of New York, who was called into consultation. The ill-
Continued on page 4

Arthur, Boyer as Leads In Wanger 'History'—

Walter Wanger has signed Jean Arthur to co-star with Charles Boyer in 'History is Made at Night,' Gene Towne and Graham Baker story which Frank Borzage will direct.
Set to start Oct. 26.

Whiting, Mercer Join Warners for Year—

Song writing team of Richard A. Whiting and Johnny Mercer has joined Warners on a year's ticket.
First assignment is tunes for 'Ready, Willing and Able.'

Mono Dickers O. Henry Topic by Jennings—

Monogram Pictures, through W. Ray Johnston, president, is negotiating for the screen rights to the book 'Through the Shadows With O. Henry,' by Al Jennings.

Stantons in GN 'Hats'

Val and Ernie Stanton have been set for comedy roles in 'Hats Off,' which Boris Petroff is producing for Grand National. Flo Browne set deal.

Previewed
MISSING GIRLS (Ches.)
Preview on page 3

Services Wed. A.M.

Funeral services for Irving Thalberg will be held Wednesday morning in B'nai Brith Temple on Wilshire boulevard. Rabbi E. J. Magnin will officiate. Provisions for 1,200 invited friends will be made in the temple. There will be no honorary pall bearers.

Levers Launch Jolson's Airings In Mid-Nov.—

New York, Sept. 14. — Al Jolson, Sid Silvers, Martha Raye and Victor Young's orchestra will start a new commercial for Lever Bros., which controls several products, in mid-November. Levers will, in the meantime, signify which product will be actually plug-
♣ Continued on page 8 ♣

Hersholt Joins Henie By Zanuck Decree—

Jean Hersholt, who returns today from Callandar, Ont., after appearing in scenes with the Dionne quintuplets for 'Reunion' (20th-Fox), has been assigned by Darryl F. Zanuck to take a featured role in 'One in a Million,' the first Sonja Henie skating musical.

Buzzell Edits 'Luckiest'

Eddie Buzzell is cutting Universal's 'The Luckiest Girl in the World.' Morrie Ryskind produced. Director also working on story preparation of his next U pic.

Irene Dunne Stricken

With Irene Dunne at home with a cold, Director Richard Boleslawski is shooting around player in 'Theodora Goes Wild' at Columbia.

60 Speak for DeMille

Speaking cast in C. B. DeMille's 'The Plainsman' reaches 60 with addition of Frank Albertson and Francis Ford.

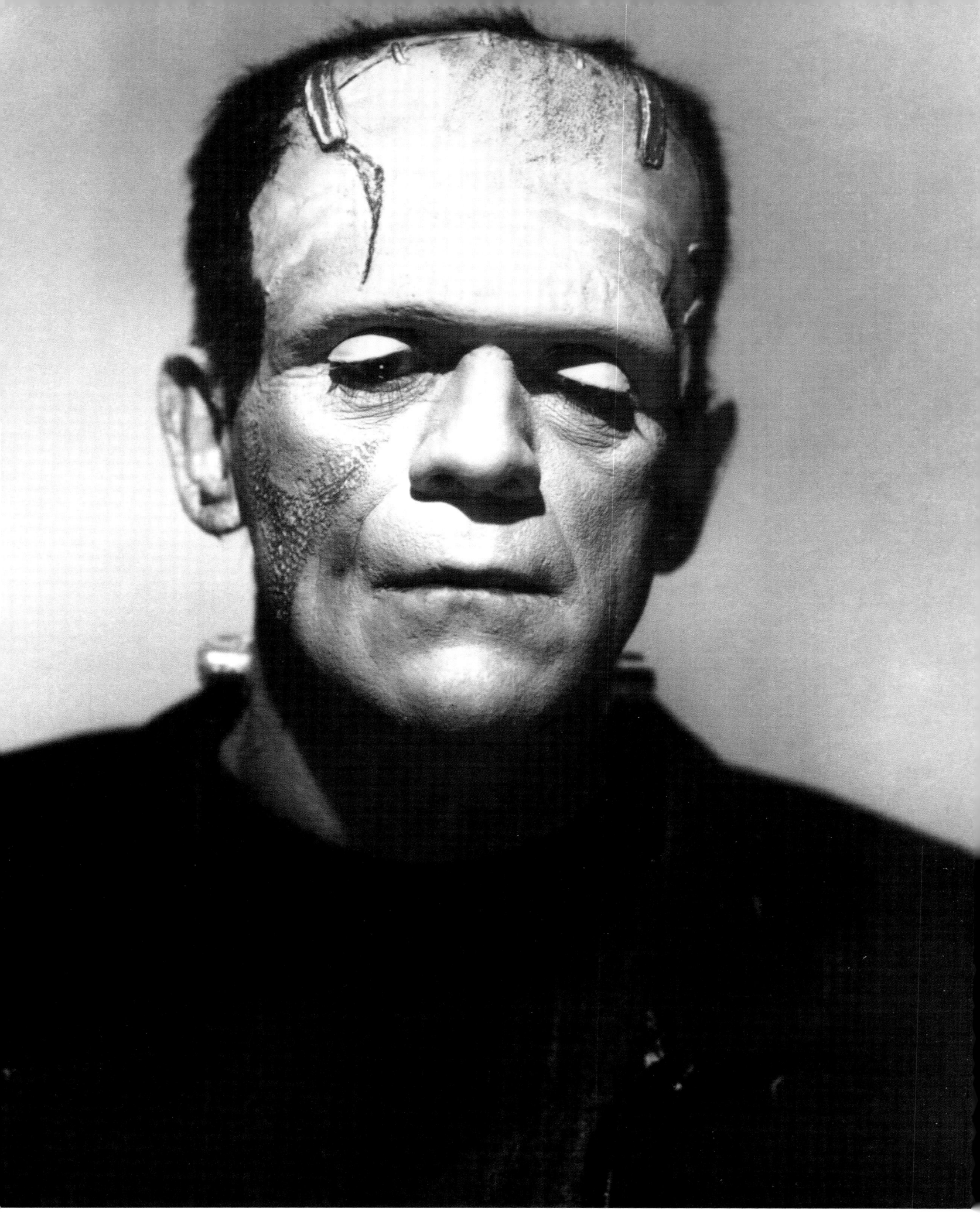

Left: Boris Karloff as The Monster in *Frankenstein*.

of time as outstanding examples of cinema, including the 1933 *King Kong*; most of the Fred Astaire–Ginger Rogers musicals; Katharine Hepburn's *Little Women* (1933), *Alice Adams* (1935), and *Bringing Up Baby* (1938), directed respectively by George Cukor, George Stevens, and Howard Hawks; *The Informer* (1935), 1939's *Gunga Din* and *The Hunchback of Notre Dame*, with Charles Laughton; and, in the 1940s, *Citizen Kane*, *Notorious*, and *It's a Wonderful Life*.

RKO, or "Radio" as it was sometimes called in *Variety*, also distributed Walt Disney's animated features. Though RKO didn't make these films, it got to bask in the reflected glory of *Snow White and the Seven Dwarfs*, *Dumbo*, *Fantasia*, and *Bambi* in the late 1930s and 1940s.

In 1928, Universal founder Carl Laemmle named Carl Jr. as head of production as a twenty-first birthday present. Cynics rolled their eyes at the blatant nepotism, but Carl Jr. was progressive, smart, and an advocate of color and sound. All that spending on production and new technology in the Depression took a toll, though, and the Standard Capital Corporation seized control of the studio, and the Laemmles were removed.

Carl Jr. was also the force behind Universal's greatest legacy during this period: its monster movies.

Universal kicked off the decade with *Dracula*, starring Bela Lugosi, and *Frankenstein* (both 1931) and *The Mummy* (1932), the latter two making a star of Boris Karloff. John L. Balderston, who as a reporter had covered the opening of King Tut's tomb in 1922, contributed to all three scripts. When Lord Carnarvon, who had funded the search for the tomb, died a year after the expedition opened it, rumors of "the curse of the Pharaohs," who allegedly took revenge on those who disturbed their tombs, began to circulate. People liked magic.

Studios capitalized on audiences' fear of the supernatural, and films such as *Dracula* and *Werewolf of London* (1935) hit theaters, as did films exploring the dangers of tampering with the natural order. Aside from Victor Frankenstein's attempts to play God, mad scientists were central in *The Invisible Man* (1933), directed by Universal stalwart James Whale, Paramount's 1931 *Dr. Jekyll and Mr. Hyde* (with Fredric March winning an Oscar), and 1932's *Chandu the Magician*, *Dr. X*, *The Island of Lost Souls*, and many others.

After a few decades of major technological upheavals (electricity, radio, automobiles) and frightening changes (aerial warfare, bombs, World War I mustard gas), the public seemed to be unsettled by the concepts of "progress" and science.

Many of the decade's classic fright films take place in Europe and not just because of their source material; after the war, there was something about Transylvania and foggy London that inspired a sense of dread that small-town America didn't.

In his December 8, 1931, review of *Frankenstein*, Rush (the sig line of Alfred Rushford Greason) wondered if the public would be interested in this relatively new genre:

> "The audience for this type of film is probably the detective story readers and the mystery yarn radio listeners. Sufficient to ensure financial success if these pictures are well made."

Horror was newish. There had been a few isolated precedents, including the eye-popping German Expressionism of *The Cabinet of Dr. Caligari* (1920; directed by Robert Wiene), *Nosferatu* (F. W. Murnau's 1922 unauthorized version of Bram Stoker's *Dracula*), and some influential Lon Chaney vehicles including *The Phantom of the Opera* (1925) and *London after Midnight* (1927).

Unlike the villains of chiller films from the 1970s to the 1990s, many of the 1930s "monsters" were more sympathetic than the protagonists. Karloff's

Frankenstein creature and mummy, the sideshow performers in the 1932 *Freaks* (directed by Tod Browning), and the 1933 *King Kong* were outcasts, trying in vain to understand a heartless world they'd been thrust into. Of course, that was also true of many victims of the Depression.

Big cities were perfectly frightening as well; victims of the 1929 Wall Street collapse must have had a special thrill at watching King Kong wreak havoc on New York City, and there was a real magic—that word again!—in watching Kong battle airplanes atop the Empire State Building.

On September 5, 1933, in the same year that *King Kong* was released, *Variety* opined, "Film is still the topmost branch of show business. Radio in the United States has made great strides. Abroad it has not gotten very far. Legit, through the world, is probably second to pictures, despite that in the U.S. it's lost a good deal more prestige than that. . . ."

The story was written by Wolfe Kaufman, the same reporter who'd been reporting on Nazi actions from *Variety* since their earliest days. His assessment of film was correct, but his legit theory was only partly true. Thanks to film and radio, stage performance had ceased to be the number one entertainment for the masses, resulting, in 1931, in the powerful Shuberts entering into receivership. Lee Shubert and Irving Trust Company were named as receivers, determined to keep Shubert, Broadway, and theater alive during the economic crisis. (Don't worry, they succeeded.)

But even during the hardest times, theater was thriving creatively.

The decade boasted plays such as *The Children's Hour*, by Lillian Hellman (1934), which dealt with lesbianism; Noël Coward's 1932 *Design for Living*, which dealt with a ménage à trois; *Private Lives* (1931); and *Tonight at 8:30* (1936), ten one-acts that were rotated in performances, with three being performed each evening. In 1935, the Group Theatre mounted Clifford Odets's *Awake and Sing!* and *Waiting for Lefty*, addressing unions and the Depression itself. Group Theatre members Elia Kazan, Luther and Stella Adler, Sanford Meisner, and Harold Clurman, as directors and acting coaches, influenced a generation of actors with their emphasis on naturalism and bringing personal experiences into the performance.

Other highlights in the late 1930s included *The Petrified Forest*, by Robert Sherwood; Thornton Wilder's *Our Town*; *You Can't Take It with You*, by George S. Kaufman and Moss Hart; *The Millionairess*, by George Bernard Shaw; and Ben Hecht and Charles MacArthur's *Twentieth Century*.

Musically, there was the 1935 *Porgy and Bess*, by the Gershwins and DuBose Heyward; Rodgers & Hart debuted *On Your Toes*, *Babes in Arms*, and *The Boys from Syracuse* between 1936 and 1938; and Cole Porter turned out a musical each year for the decade, including *Gay Divorce* (yielding the song "Night and Day"), the Ethel Merman–starrer *Anything Goes* (with the title song as well as "You're the Top" and "I Get a Kick Out of You"), *Red Hot and Blue* ("It's De-Lovely"), and *Leave It to Me* (starring Sophie Tucker and marking the Broadway debuts of Gene Kelly and Mary Martin, who stole the show singing "My Heart Belongs to Daddy").

Not bad for an art form that had lost prestige.

Marc Blitzstein's 1938 *The Cradle Will Rock* was a musical that tackled corporate greed. Directed by Orson Welles and produced by John Houseman, its tunes were recorded for 78 rpm discs, a novelty for the day.

One of the biggest hit plays of the era was *Life with Father*, a family comedy by Howard Lindsay and Russell Crouse, adapted from the turn-of-the-century memoirs of Clarence Day Jr. It opened in 1939 and ran for more than seven years—3,224 performances—and is still the longest-running non-musical ever on Broadway. It broke the also-impressive record of the scandalously

Above: Fay Wray and friend in *King Kong*.

Maybe • It's • You!

Stars and Exhibs Mingle at Great Banquet Given For MPTOA by Southern California Colleagues

Josef Von Sternberg squired the exotic Marlene Dietrich, who seemed to enjoy the party as much as anyone present.

Dick Dickson and Al Hanson, Fox-West Coast division managers, took an evening off from their convention and host labors to escort their wives to the industry's biggest blowout of the week.

Lowell Sherman, who rarely goes for 'those banquet things,' turned up for this one at the Ambassador and liked it.

West and East Meet in the banquet hall, the twain being Mrs. Harold Lloyd and Odd McIntyre, Hearst columnist.

Vivacious Daughter of Secretary Fred Meyer was captured by John Boles for several dances and they looked oke.

You may be looking at the next president of the Southern California Indie Assn., for it's Harry Hicks and his party. Harry is regarded as successor to Ben Berinstein, now a MPTOA v.p.

One of those that way couples, Lee Tracy and Isabel Jewell, had a perfectly swell time and won many friends among the showmen.

Another Rare Banquet bird who showed up for this one was Harold Lloyd, left, who sat with Mr. and Mrs. Jas. J. McGuinness of Boston. All seem to get a real kick.

Three guesses allowed you on what Leo Carrillo is saying to Jean Harlow, or vice versa. Whatever it is, they're enjoying the gag—and it certainly was a good night for it.

Left: April 14, 1934.

Above: George and Ira Gershwin.

Right: Cole Porter.

At the beginning of the decade, *Variety* glumly reported that studio scouts were finding an "acute" lack of potential talent for pictures. Theater proved to be a great hunting ground for executives searching for new stars. With talkers the norm, Broadway and the West End offered actors who could speak as well as emote with their faces. Several of film's biggest stars, all with a distinctive way of speaking, came from the theater, including Bette Davis, Mae West, Humphrey Bogart, James Cagney, Katharine Hepburn, Claudette Colbert, Irene Dunne, Henry Fonda, and Cary Grant, whose "natural grace" in his performance in *A Wonderful Night* was

hailed in the November 6, 1929, issue of *Variety*.

Hollywood imported Ronald Colman, Charles Laughton, Basil Rathbone, Claude Rains, Leslie Howard, Laurence Olivier, Michael Redgrave, and Sydney Greenstreet from Britain.

On March 4, 1931, *Variety* reported that "selling of the forthcoming year's feature product will be almost wholly on a star basis." Studios were signing actors to contracts. Gary Cooper,

funny *Tobacco Road*, by Jack Kirkland, adapted from the novel about dirt farmers by Erskine Caldwell, which debuted in 1933 and eventually ran 3,182 performances.

Aside from its booming creativity, theater had another value: it served as source material for film (which, as Kaufman reported, was the "topmost branch of show business").

By the end of the twentieth century, film adaptations of hit plays were rare; but in the first half of the century, theater was a key source of content. Two best-picture Academy Award winners of the 1930s, *Cavalcade* and *You Can't Take It with You*, originated on stage, as did plenty of nominees, including *The Front Page*, *Shanghai Express*, *Stage Door*, and *Pygmalion*.

The film biz grabbed many of its most "classy" writers from theater.

Imports included George Bernard Shaw (who won an Oscar for his 1937 adaptation of *Pygmalion*), Frances Goodrich and Albert Hackett, Ben Hecht and Charles MacArthur, George S. Kaufman, Sidney Howard, Robert Riskin, Morrie Ryskind, R. C. Sherriff, Sidney Buchman, Dudley Nichols, and Dorothy Parker; and many of Broadway's biggest songwriters who became key to Hollywood musicals, including Irving Berlin, the Gershwins, Jerome Kern, and Cole Porter.

Left: Ingrid Bergman.

Right: Greta Garbo.

Marlene Dietrich, and Mae West at Paramount; Cagney, Davis, Bogart at Warner Brothers; Jean Arthur, Columbia; Irene Dunne, RKO; Henry Fonda, Shirley Temple, Alice Faye, Tyrone Power, Fox; Deanna Durbin, Margaret Sullavan at Universal. MGM boasted "more stars than there are in heaven": Clark Gable, Greta Garbo, Norma Shearer, William Powell, Myrna Loy, Joan Crawford, and all of the Barrymores (John, Ethel, and Lionel). But it wasn't all heaven for the stars. Actors were often suspended by studio executives. In the 1930s, *Variety* reported on battles between Fox and Spencer Tracy, MGM and Jean Harlow, Paramount and George Raft, Warner Brothers and James Cagney, Warner Brothers and Pat O'Brien, Warner Brothers and Ann Dvorak, etc.

A few actors, including Cary Grant and Katharine Hepburn, managed to avoid long-term pacts, while others switched from one studio to another. Spencer Tracy moved from Fox to MGM, and W. C. Fields and the Marx Brothers worked at Paramount then moved to Universal and MGM, respectively.

Meanwhile, Hollywood imported stars and directors from Europe. In the silent era, foreign accents (or even a limited knowledge of English) were no hindrance. And as the movies learned to talk, English-language audiences proved surprisingly open to accents. Exhibit A: Garbo, whose beauty made her a silent star while moviegoers loved her from her first sound-synched words—"Gif me a viskey with ginger ale on the side and don't be stingy, baby"— in MGM's 1930 *Anna Christie*, based on Eugene O'Neill's play. ("Garbo talks!" was the tagline for the posters, and a German-language version, also

NEWS OF THE SHOW WORLD

Vol. 4 No. 59   Hollywood, California, Tuesday, August 14, 1934   5 Cents

Garbo Deal at 300 G's

FWC SETS B.O. TILT POLICY—

Fox West Coast figures on getting the jump on other Los Angeles exhibs by putting into effect a general box office tilt in all of its local houses, starting next week. Boost will range from 5c to 10c, depending on calibre of houses, with a 20c minimum in any case.

Circuit execs were mulling the admission price boost throughout
(Continued on page 3) ●

Wanger Figures Technicolor 'Beau Geste'—

New York, Aug. 13.—Paramount and Walter Wanger are huddling on deal that would provide for three Wanger productions made during the coming year to be released through Paramount.

Wanger has on tap plans for remake of 'Beau Geste,' and is selling Paramount execs here on the idea of producing the picture in the new three color process of Technicolor.

According to reports here, Erpi is in line to participate in partial financing of the Wanger group of pictures.

Finger
Grand Jury investigators tabbing the speaks and clubs around Hollywood and listing the names of patrons for future reference.

Sneak Previews Due For Early Embalming—

Sneak preview nuisance is expected to be automatically legislated from the industry locally with the start of the new product season, through the recent action of the L. A. zoning-clearance board in fixing a minimum box office price of 50c for these advance screenings.

Under the new ruling, price tilt to 50c, plus tax, becomes mandatory on exhibs showing previews, and unless such an increase in the
(Continued on page 3) ●

Rosenbloom Parks Mitts, Beautifies Ears For Films—

Maxie Rosenbloom, light heavyweight champ, seems to have forsaken the prize ring for the screen.

Maxie will not don the gloves any more, for yesterday he had a plastic gent chisel away the cauliflower which blooms on his left ear.

Par and Col Knocking Head Off Coin Barrel In N. Y. Ads

New York, Aug. 13.—Paramount and Columbia are skeded for big campaigns on 'Cleopatra' and 'One Night of Love.' Columbia will eclipse the $31,000 all-time high expenditure hung up for Goldwyn's 'Nana,' by spending $32,000 in advance of its picture's entry into Radio City's Music Hall, probably Sept. 6.

Paramount is going for $30,000 on 'Cleopatra,' opening next Thursday (16), of which $20,000 is going into newspapers.

'Treasure Island' Set
'Treasure Island' (Metro) goes into Loew's State next Thursday for a two weeks' run. Will be followed by studio's 'Chained.'

Jobs for a Day
Central Casting has called 491 extras for picture jobs today. Roy William Neal will use 140 at Columbia. Recalls number 175.

WILLIAM SEITER
Now Directing
"The Richest Girl in the World"
For RKO

EDINGTON AGAIN METRO STAR'S REP

Greta Garbo again has Harry Edington handling her business affairs and the first result of the reunion is a readjustment of her contract raising the ante from $250,000 to $270,000 on 'Painted Veil.' He also is negotiating a new deal for two next year at $300,000 each.

Gaumont-Fox Distrib Deal On Fire—

New York, Aug. 13.—Aggressive invasion of the American market is under way by Gaumont-British, with the company negotiating deal with Fox Film whereby Fox exchanges in this country would handle physical distribution of the G-B features for the coming year. Jeffrey Bernerd, Gaumont general manager, admitted the nego-
(Continued on page 3) ●

Polly Walters In U's 'Princess'—

First picture for Polly Walters under her contract with Universal will be 'Princess O'Hara.' Actress is currently in the legit 'She Loves Me Not' in New York.

Doris Malloy and Harry Clork have completed the script.

Bergner Will Do One For 20th—

London, Aug. 13. — Elizabeth Bergner will make one picture for Twentieth Century next summer. She starts work on 'Escape Me Never' for British Dominion, Oct. 1, and then stars in the same show in New York in January for Harold Franklin and Arch Selwyn.

Edington was called in by Miss Garbo about two months ago to be her personal representative in studio matters, in place of her New York attorney, Joseph S. Buhler, who took over the job in May, 1933.

Edington was called in when Miss Garbo was getting ready to make 'Painted Veil,' the second and final deal, and requested to
(Continued on page 3) ●

Clarence Brown In Parley On 2 Yrs. More—

Metro is talking over a new directorial contract with Clarence Brown to run two more years. Brown came to the lot eight years ago from United Artists and has been considered the 'ace prestige' director on the lot.

He has been getting $75,000 a picture and the new deal is said to call for a minimum of two-a-year at that figure.

Col Shows Moore Opera Today—

Columbia will preview its 'One Night of Love,' with Grace Moore, for the trade and invited guests at the Ambassador hotel theatre at 1:30 p.m. today. Screening will be preceeded by a luncheon.

More than 200 exhibs and guests expected to attend.

Register Keith Loss of 59G—

New York, Aug. 13.—Net loss of $59,000 is shown by the B. F. Keith corporation for the 26 weeks ending June 30.

For same period, Keith-Albee-Orpheum reported a net profit of $485.

Luke Barnett Flits
Luke Barnett, daddy of ribbing and Vince, has departed by motor for his home in Pittsburgh.

80   VARIETY

Film Row Calls It a Good Time

The gals always give 'Bud' Lollier plenty of attention. Tiny Copeland, one of the F-WC financial wizards, feeding him while Lucille Hill and Marie Harris wait their turn.

Paul Neuerberg who helps operate Arlington and Gem with Harry Hicks casting a sharp eye in the direction of a group of F-WC execs, figuring if latter are trying to work out new clearance schedule.

Earle Johnson of the Knoll theatre and Mike Gore learning about UA product from Guy Gunderson, office manager of the UA exchange.

Indie Theatre Owner Association big moguls. Left to right: Harry H. Vinnicof, Bob Poole, Irving Carlin, N. C. Son and Max Sinker.

A bunch of those F-WC secretaries who are known as the 'sunshine' gals of the home office. Left to right: Ruth Sussman, Gertrude Cassel, Margaret McPhee, Estelle Ryan, Florence Sigmond, Elsie Rothschild.

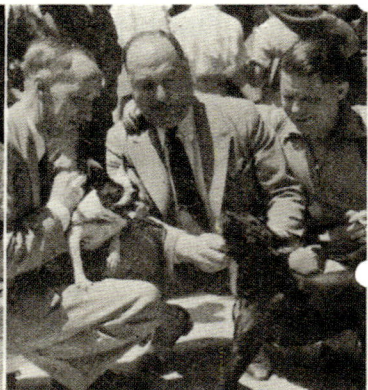

Trio of Indie exhibs getting their canine guards pepped to ward off any sales onslaught from Jake Milstein and the other film hawkers. Left to right: Bill Wall, Manny Hoffman, Louie Berkowitz.

Bill Quinn, in charge of the picnic arrangements, warning Jack Goldberg to deliver his films on time while he is away on his Honolulu vacation, while Paul de Outo the Gaumont-British exchange manager is looking over the gals.

Adolph Ramish and his missus having a grand time watching the baseball game and getting a big laugh out of the F-WC team taking a four to one beating from the indie group.

Three of the really prosperous Indie exhibs who have no worries, J. E. Schwartzbein, W. E. Weinman and George Bromley.

Photos by Bill Phillips, Daily Variety Staff Photographer

starring Garbo, was also made.) Stars of the decade included Ingrid Bergman, Maurice Chevalier, Charles Boyer, Luise Rainer, and Peter Lorre; directors Fritz Lang, Ernst Lubitsch, Eric von Stroheim, Josef von Sternberg, William Wyler, Otto Preminger; composers Wolfgang Korngold, Miklos Rosza, and Franz Waxman. Many other artists, including Igor Stravinsky, Arnold Schoenberg, Otto Klemperer, Thomas Mann, Bertolt Brecht, and Kurt Weill, whose 1928 *Die Dreigroschenoper* (*The Threepenny Opera*) made its Broadway debut in 1933, fled Nazi Germany and eastern Europe to the creative and personal safety of London, New York, or Hollywood.

Despite Al Capone's dismissal of gangster films, early 1930s audiences ate up James Cagney's *Public Enemy*, Edward G. Robinson's *Little Caesar*, and Paul Muni's *Scarface*. Evil is always seductive, and in the Depression, the Robin Hood/antiestablishment aggression was fascinating and cathartic.

Back when moviegoing was a major meal, cinemas showed double-bills, trailers, a short subject, a newsreel, and a cartoon. In contrast with most cartoons, Betty Boop served as a surprising reflection of life in the 1930s. Betty lived in a poor neighborhood and encountered unsavory and/or sexual people. She was a "jazz baby," and Fleischer Studios, under brothers Max and Dave, who also brought Popeye to the screen, used such musicians as Cab Calloway for Betty's soundtrack. Disney's and Warner Brothers' cartoons were wildly popular, especially with the advent of color. Mickey Mouse had been a favorite from his 1928 debut in *Steamboat Willie*, with Donald Duck debuting in 1934's *Silly Symphonies*, a series of music-related shorts that Walt Disney used to build his business. This series also served as practice for his full-length 1937 *Snow White and the Seven Dwarfs*, which stunned everyone with its level of success.

Warner Brothers also created music-centric shorts with *Looney Tunes* and *Merrie Melodies*, introducing Porky Pig in 1935, Daffy Duck in 1937, and Bugs Bunny in 1940.

These animated shorts endured well into the twenty-first century, as do some live-action shorts, including those starring the Three Stooges, Laurel & Hardy, and the *Our Gang* comedies (known as *The Little Rascals* on TV).

But, naturally, the main course of the evening was the movies. Studios began to crank out "programmers," lower-budget films with shorter running times to accommodate double bills (*Frankenstein* and the 1935 *Bride of Frankenstein* run seventy and seventy-five minutes, respectively.)

When reviewing *Frankenstein*, Rush talked about "the essential touch of monstrous human evil." To audiences of 1931, that may have conjured up the evil of the Great War. But at that point they had only a glimmer of the evil that was growing around the world. Horror movies may have been cathartic, but radio and newsreels gave them a glimpse—a brief, understated glimpse—of real-life horrors and evil.

The December 8, 1931, *Weekly Variety* bannered a story by Tom Waller, "21 Big Newsreel Stars," tallying the most frequently featured individuals in the past year. The easy winner was President Herbert Hoover, with forty-six clips. Distant runners-up included New York's Mayor Jimmy Walker, thirteen; and, with eleven apiece, Italy's Benito Mussolini and Britain's prime minister Ramsay MacDonald.

They were followed by the Prince of Wales, with ten; Governor Franklin Delano Roosevelt, seven; "Mayor Cormack" (presumably Chicago mayor Anton Cermak, who was engaged in a heated election that year), six; German president von Hindenburg and the Lindberghs, with five apiece; Gandhi, four; and Hitler, three.

During the decade, *Variety* regularly offered reviews of newsreels and on July 14, 1937, Char. (the pen name of Richard Gersh) felt the strongest piece was on the "search of many forces for the missing Amelia Earhart and her flying companion."

In 1937, American newsreel companies moved camera teams from Shanghai and Tokyo to near the troops in Tientsin, due to the "probability of hostilities between Japan and China." An August 11, 1937, story pointed out a key clue to "the danger of an armed conflict in Europe": Lloyds of London upped its rates on cameramen by seven times. Newsreels also gauged public

---

Previous Spread: August 14, 1934; June 28, 1935.

Above Left: Not just my gang, *Our Gang*.

Below Left: Shirley Temple.

Below: Bugs Bunny.

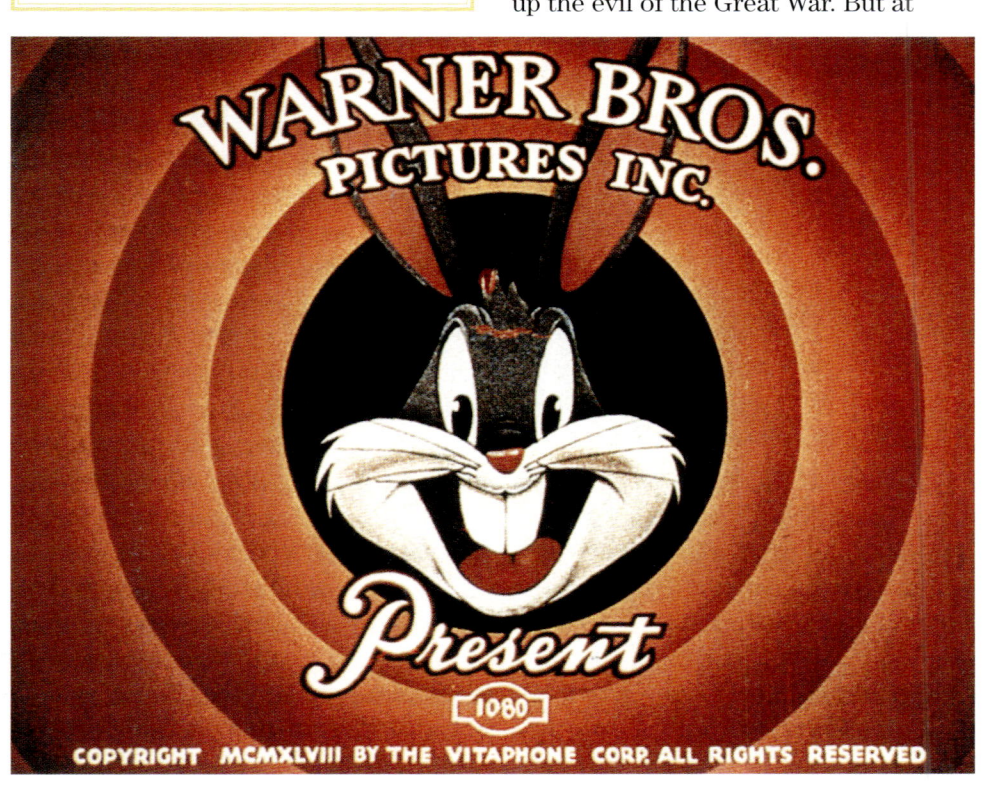

reaction. A December 12, 1936, story reported on the audience watching the newsreel at London's New Gallery cinema the evening of King Edward's abdication:

> "Edward VIII, the retiring king, was greeted with applause and hissing in equal proportions and the salute to Mrs. Wallis Simpson was three-fourths hissing and no applause. Greeting for Prime Minister Stanley Baldwin was 100% applause."

It's easy to forget the news pace of the 1930s. On May 24, 1939, *Variety* noted that newsreels had begun to ship via commercial transatlantic flights: "newsreel officials believe this commercial plane service opens up vast potentialities. Stories photographed in Europe may be shown in U.S. in three days, it is hoped."

Meanwhile, radio was providing updates that were even more immediate. On the day of Edward VIII's abdication, *Daily Variety* reported that the film *Parnell*, starring Clark Gable, was filming a scene set in the House of Commons on the MGM lot: "Most of the players in the scene are British. A radio was hooked up in the 'House' to listen to Prince Edward's farewell to the throne. The silence was complete."

The growth in number of radios that households owned was reflected frequently in both the *Daily* and *Weekly Variety*. In the latter's October 9, 1934, issue, the two national networks posted booms in ad income, or "time money," as *Variety* called it. NBC saw September jumping 20 percent over that same month in 1933; CBS was 26 percent above the year-ago numbers.

February 2, 1938, *Weekly Variety* quoted Philco vice president Sayre M. Ramsdell as saying more than 55 percent of the nation's farms were without radios, but set manufacturers were about to start an "ad campaign directed at the stix." Ramsdell declared that seventy-seven out of one hundred American families had radio, but the farm average was far below that. "Stix population, he said, is highest it has ever been," at 34 million, living on 6.8 million farms. Of those, only 800,000 had electricity, according to a survey done by the radio company Philco, and 3.8 million did not have radios.

It's doubtful Ramsdell himself ever used the word "stix." That was *Variety*'s contribution to the report. On July 17, 1935, *Variety* ran its most famous headline:

"Sticks Nix Hick Pix."

The story said that Joe Kinsky, of the Davenport, Iowa–based movie chain Tri-State Amusement Corporation, offered insights into tastes in the Midwest (i.e., the sticks):

> "Farmers are not interested in farming pictures" (i.e., "hick pics"). He also urged the studios "to educate fans to see pictures from the beginning, instead of hopping into a theatre at any time."

Meanwhile, the decade's expansion of radio was an international affair. An October 16, 1934, *Weekly Variety* bannered the fact that an "impressive" number of U.S. companies were setting up overseas sales-distribution offices to penetrate the foreign radio markets. Kotex Corporation, which also manufactured Kleenex, was targeting Cuba, Puerto Rico, the Philippines, South Africa, and Shanghai, while gum company Wrigley was looking at Japan and China. England was "displaying marked interest in American internal political affairs," so NBC and CBS were setting up speaking engagements in Britain for political commentators. The interest was inspired by President Franklin Delano Roosevelt, who introduced the New Deal and his radiobroadcasted *Fireside Chats*, designed to update and reassure listeners.

A 1939 roundup of the year in radio noted that there weren't many new stars, but long-popular shows went on to "higher planes of popularity,"

Above: Laurel and Hardy.

Right: July 9, 1935.

Camera Does Nip-up on UA'ites

Pittsburgh salesmen have a chance to duck B. M. Stearn, their branch manager, and get together for an informal how-de-do. Left to right: Charles L. Dortic, Leonard Cantor, William Scott, Harry Rees.

Sam Glazer, who is branch manager at Toronto, remembers a few things to discuss with Mike Wilkes, his publicity chief. The boys were hot at it when the camera man caught up with them.

On the prowl for baked beans, the Boston boys were among the early risers, but finally compromised on orange juice. Here they are, left to right: George Hager, Sam Stern, A. I. Weiner, Lou Wechsler.

Ed MacLean, who pilots Los Angeles sales gang, takes time out to congratulate B. M. Stearn, Pittsburgh branch manager, who's combining business of the convention with honeymoon trip.

Before going into yesterday's business session, Al Lichtman got his two sales managers, Paul Lazarus and Harry Gold together, and told them what he expected in way of sales and profits from the Charlie Chaplin and Mickey Mouse product. Boys were told that alibis wouldn't count.

Al Hoffman, branch manager at Denver, took advantage yesterday to renew his long time friendship with A. H. Kloepper, who hails from Seattle, and what a gabfest they had.

Three of the sales boys stage a lovefest when they meet Hank Mann, who's acting in Charlie Chaplin's current picture, that they'll be selling pretty soon. Left to right: B. J. Robins, Detroit; Mayer Lieberman, New York; S. J. Bowman, Detroit; Hank Mann.

Part of the foreign delegation got together with a pow-wow. Left to right they're Lester Sussman, in charge at Porto Rico; Walter Gould, South American representative, and Emanuel Silverstone, who's here for London Films.

Quartet of those Chicago sales pushers who can't forget shop, even at a convention. From left to right they're Charles Kamp, Harry Goldberg, Joe Hartman, Ernest Pickler.

Photos by Bill Phillips, Daily Variety Staff Photographer.

including "Fibber McGee and Molly" and shows starring Bob Hope, George Burns and Gracie Allen, Jack Benny, Kate Smith, Bing Crosby, and the "dance orchestras" of Guy Lombardo and Paul Whiteman.

Even as radio was booming, showbiz was looking ahead. A short item on July 17, 1935, said that Sam Goldwyn was trying to buy film rights to Edna Ferber's *Come and Get It*, but the author was holding off because she wanted to retain television rights. Calling it the "see-hear angle," *Variety* noted, "It's the first instance of television figuring in a story sale controversy."

In a brief front-page story on November 30, 1938, *Daily Variety* dubbed the new medium "Telvish," reassuring readers (quite accurately, as it turns out) that

> "Television, as the public has come to expect it, won't be available for at least 10 years, according to Dr. Leon Levy, president of WCAU, [Philadelphia's] local Columbia outlet. Therefore, he adds, claims by industry leaders that visio is imminent will cause public disappointment as well as decrease sales of radio sets."

("Visio" was an alternate moniker, in the way that "wireless" was first used to describe radio.)

OK, so visio-phobia was temporarily quelled. But there were plenty of other things for Hollywood to worry about.

Starting in 1934, the industry cracked down on what was allowed on-screen.

To quiet those demanding censorship, the Motion Picture Producers and Distributors (MPPDA) of America was created in 1922. Will H. Hays was named president.

But it wasn't until 1930, eight years after Hays's hiring, that the MPPDA unveiled the Motion Picture Production Code, which came to be known as the Hays Code. The new Production Code Administration would require all films released after July 1, 1934, to have a certificate of approval.

To get that certificate, the film had to observe a list of no-no's, as outlined on page nine in the February 19, 1930, issue of *Variety*. For example, films could not show extramarital sex that was "presented attractively," mock the clergy or the flag, or depict miscegenation or dances with "indecent movements," and no portrayal of criminals could be sympathetic.

The August 29, 1934, *Daily Variety* reported audiences hissing when the seal appeared on-screen. But moral crackdowns weren't limited to movies. On April 11, 1933, NBC radio execs asked the publisher of the song "I Lay Me Down to Sleep," to find a substitute for the word "impunity," on the theory some might mistake it for "impurity." *Variety* added, "NBC execs issuing the order doubted whether the average radio fan would know the meaning of 'impunity' anyway."

On October 31, 1938, *Daily Variety* reported that the previous evening's

Left: Mae West.

Above: In case you were wondering what Mr. Leroy was up to.

Harry Hunter, manager of Par Washington branch, snapped alongside his salesman, J. J. Oulahan, only film seller to win the 100% club button four years in a row.

Following their lunch the Paramount theatre associates grabbed a bit of sunshine to show off their summer togs.

Mel Schauer demonstrating the Hays cleanser to his cousin, Eugene Zukor, during the bathing hour at the party Mel tossed for the visiting Conventioneers.

airing of Orson Welles's adaptation of H. G. Wells's *The War of the Worlds* had tied up Columbia Broadcasting's phones for ninety minutes.

A week later, *Daily* reported NBC radio comics who'd planned to joke about the Welles broadcast "are finding their scripts badly mutilated and even the slightest mention of the hair-curler is deleted." Though the show aired on rival CBS,

> "NBC, having had its inning with the Federal Communications Commission on the Mae West episode, has no desire to be hauled before the powers again when CBS is to be chastised for spreading terror through the land."

The Mae West episode was a reference to her appearance on *The Chase and Sanborn Hour*, hosted by Edgar Bergen. West's trademark deadpan delivery made every line sound like a slight groan of pleasure. She flirted with dummy Charlie McCarthy, who was "all wood and a yard long," and as Eve to Don Ameche's Adam asked him to "get me a big one. . . . I feel like doing a big apple."

A month later, the FCC sent the twelve NBC stations carrying the show "a precedent-setting letter which declared all licensees are obligated to censor the output of their transmitters."

"Dangerous" material was not limited to the United States. In 1939, the British censor decided that children could only see *Snow White* if accompanied by parents. (The ruling was eventually overturned.) The film had the same problem in other territories.

> "After being reviewed by the censors four times, 'Snow White' has been admitted for universal exhibition in Holland. First three verdicts sanctioned it only for those above 14 years of age but the final one approved it after the picture took several more cuts."

There was another code for Hollywood to deal with. In 1933, as part of his economic recovery plans, President Roosevelt introduced the National Industrial Recovery Act, a many-faceted law working to ensure that businesses tone down greed and cutthroat tactics for the good of the nation. It was to be enforced

Above: Conventioneers try to act casual.

Right: June 27, 1934.

U.S. MAY CUT IN ON SMUT BRAWL

Daily VARIETY Daily
NEWS OF THE SHOW WORLD

Vol. 4 No. 19 — Hollywood, California, Wednesday, June 27, 1934 — 5 Cents

MAE WEST FIGURES 'SIN' GOING OUT NAMELESS

Mae West may decide to challenge the censors to outlaw her from the screen by having the interdicted picture, 'It Ain't No Sin,' go forth nameless and letting exhibs bill her instead. Expecting censorial action on any handle that might be affixed to a revamped 'It Ain't No Sin,' following the thumbing by the New York regents, the actress is known to be seriously considering the daring novelty of merely hoisting her own name on the marquee and relying on her personality and previous exploitation to bring 'em in.

'Mae West's Picture,' the legend would probably read, if Paramount accedes to a suggestion relayed by Miss West from one of her advisers. Without a title, there would be no focal point for any ban except the name of West herself, or on material in the sapolioed picture.

The actress is going to comply with eliminations which are expected to get 'It Ain't No Sin' past the censorial portcullis, for within
(Continued on page 6)

Romberg at MG For Music Stint On 'Tip Toes' Pic

Sigmund Romberg arrived yesterday from New York, joining the Metro writing staff. He will work with Oscar Hammerstein, 2nd, on preparation of the filmusical 'Tip Toes' from story by Vicki Baum, with Romberg writing the music and Hammerstein the libretto.

Picture, slated for fall production, will co-star Ramon Novarro and Evelyn Laye under direction of Dudley Murphy.

Ida Lupino Wins Clear of Scourge

Ida Lupino's doctor, T. Perceval Gerson, has given the Paramount actress good news with the assurance that she will have no after effects from her siege of infantile paralysis.

Dr. Gerson says she is making rapid recovery and probably can return to work by July 15. She is convalescing at home.

Irving Trust Set As RKO Trustee

New York, June 26.—Irving Trust company has been named permanent trustee of RKO by Federal Judge Coxe, acting on a petition filed by attorneys for Radio under the new corporate bankruptcy act.

Objections by parties seeking to intervene in the action were overruled.

Minor Watson at Par

Minor Watson, New York actor, will play in 'Pursuit of Happiness' for Paramount. Watson, who came here last week, was set through the William Morris office.

Clayton Sheehan Bringing Inside On Foreign Setup

Clayton Sheehan, foreign head for Fox gets here July 5 for a ten day stay. During that period he will confer with his brother Winnie on the matter of American films for the foreign market as well as foreign product.

Likely that Winnie Sheehan will return east with his brother the middle of July to start on his European trip which will last about six weeks.

HELEN MENCKEN REFUSES TEST IN 'GOOD EARTH'

Helen Mencken has arrived in Hollywood on a vacation to visit relatives. Actress has no picture deals on.

Miss Mencken refused Metro's offer in New York of a test for 'The Good Earth,' believing that too much counted on the success or failure of the few feet of film.

Eugene Forde on New 'Charlie Chan'

Eugene Forde draws assignment at Fox to direct 'Charlie Chan in London,' next in the series of Chan features, which will star Warner Oland.

Others set for parts in the picture include Drue Leyton, Hugh Williams, Mona Barrie and Walter Johnson. All the latter are Fox contract players. Picture starts next month with John Stone producing.

Jane Wyatt in 'One More River'

Jane Wyatt, Universal's newest legit importation, is in 'One More River,' garners the name part in 'Fanny.'

Latter goes in Monday with William Wyler directing.

Ex-Fawcett Editor In U Flack Dept.

Arthur C. Janisch, who has been editor of several Fawcett fan mags, is on his way here to join the Universal publicity staff. He will be fan mag contact.

Strike May Send Col to Honolulu

Columbia is slated to decide today on plan to send Lewis Milestone and entire company working on 'Captain Hates the Sea' on a round trip to Honolulu to make needed ship scenes for the picture.

Company has been endeavoring to charter a liner at San Pedro, but excessive rental plus difficulties likely to be encountered by the longshoremen's strike, has swung studio execs over to the idea of the Honolulu trip, which is an unbudgeted extra expense.

'World Moves On' At $2 in New York

New York, June 26.—Fox opens 'World Moves On' at the Criterion Theatre Thursday night for a run at two a day and $2 top.

Company figures the picture to do at least four months in the house.

Frank Joyce on Way

Frank Joyce is en route to Hollywood by train. He left New York yesterday.

Back-to-Raw-Nature Routs Sex in MG Policy

Schulberg Mystery

Taking a special plane, B. P. Schulberg flew to New York on a mysterious mission Saturday (23), saying only that it was a hurried business trip.

RALPH SPENCE
DIALOGUE
"STUDENT TOUR"
For M-G-M

HAYS CODE WHIP UP TO NRA

Washington, June 26.—The Federal government is prepared, through its Recovery Administration, to step into the film decency scrap when and if the occasion arises, it was learned today.

It is believed possible that in the end the NRA will ask the CA to call on producers to observe the Hays pledge without providing any guide by which decency could be determined, and that if criticism then persists more drastic steps may
(Continued on page 2)

Pan Going Dual After 2-Wk. Single

After two weeks under single feature policy, Pantages winds up engagement of 'Little Man, What Now' tonight (Wed.) and tomorrow goes back to duals.

Feature program will comprise 'Sisters Under the Skin' and 'Hollywood Party.'

'Repeal' Carded As Harlow's Next

Jean Harlow's next for Metro will be top spot in 'Repeal,' from story by Charles Francis Coe.

Following that assignment, player is slated for lead in 'China Seas,' which Tay Garnett directs with Irving Thalberg producing.

Metro will go heavy during the next few months of production on outdoor adventure material and play down the parlor, bedroom and bath sexy stuff as its answer to the current anti-dirt campaign.

Leading off with 'Treasure Island' that it is expected will hit kids of all ages on the adventure angle the studio will put into production several yarns which have been on and offers for months and in some cases years. The outdoor action element of these stories is
(Continued on page 6)

Jobs for a Day

Central Casting placed 561 extras today with 80 held over from yesterday. Ernst Lubitsch is using 238 at Metro.

by the NRA, or National Recovery Administration.

As part of this, *Daily Variety* on November 6, 1933, reported Roosevelt's imminent signing of the NRA Code of Fair Competition for the Motion Picture Industry. That meant "the whole film industry, from executive to extra and from studio to theatre will be under control of the NRA-sponsored trade authority," which forbade company unions.

After Roosevelt was inaugurated in March 1933, his first act was to declare a "bank holiday," closing banks for three days to stop the runaway closures. An ad on page twenty-two bragged that even with "no money" available last week, *King Kong* played to 189,402 paid admissions at Radio City Music Hall. Now with "confidence restored!" the RKO movie was assured of even more business.

But the financial landscape was creating much bigger repercussions for showbiz.

The *Weekly Variety* of March 14, 1933, reported that the Hays organization of producers had ordered a 25 to 50 percent pay cut for workers, to last at least eight weeks. Though admitting the size of the cut was unprecedented, it seemed appropriate to "film leaders who contend that the picture business is run on a scale different from that of any [other] industry."

Production was shut down amid the wrangling, but Metro, Warner Brothers, RKO, and Paramount sent out word that staff must report for work the following day. The producers sent for the emergency committee of the Academy of Motion Picture Arts and Sciences (AMPAS) "and the heated words that were reported . . . hinted at a possible collapse of the Academy."

AMPAS had five branches—actors, writers, directors, technicians, and producers—and served as a "common parliamentary seat for all Hollywood problems," also including unions and talent agents.

A separate story put the cutbacks into perspective: in the past two years, 90,000 showbiz people had lost their jobs, and the annual payroll of the "major picture business" in the United States was estimated at $50 million compared to $156 million two years ago.

The push for unions grew stronger. In 1933, both the Screen Actors Guild (SAG) and the Screen Writers Guild were formed, and the Directors Guild of America was born in January 1936.

They joined veteran industry unions, including the American Federation of Musicians (founded in 1896), International Alliance of Theatrical Stage Employees IATSE Local 33 (also 1896, at first representing Los Angeles legit then adding films in 1918), and the Teamsters (1903).

The October 9, 1933, issue of *Daily Variety* contained multiple stories on the growth of SAG, including a report on a formative meeting. Eddie Cantor said, "He was surprised at the heavy attendance, especially in view of the reports he had heard earlier in the night of threats being made against players if they attended. . . .

> 'Some Academy members say we are all going screwy forming such an organization as the Guild,' Cantor continued, 'but we are not screwy. We just want to be 100 percent represented in an organization not subsidized by any one. We just want to be 100 percent Americans.'"

The situation heated up on May 27, 1935, when the Supreme Court justices unanimously invalidated the NRA, including the Code of Fair Competition for the Motion Picture Industry, saying Congress had overstepped its bounds.

Though the NRA was short-lived, some of the government's other economic programs were more long lasting.

On January 22, 1935, *Weekly Variety* alerted readers about a series of new taxes that would affect "every employer in the amusement field within the next two years under President Roosevelt's four-point social security

Left: Bert Lahr, Jack Haley, Ray Bolger, Judy Garland, Toto, a Flying Monkey, and Margaret Hamilton in *The Wizard of Oz*.

Left: Bessie Smith.

Above: Billie Holiday.

program outlined last week." Aside from Social Security, there was a proposed unemployment tax for states, to "relieve the Federal government of the burden of providing relief in future depressions. . . . "

On June 11, 1935, *Daily* reported on California's

> "state income tax at a quarter of the federal rates . . . If bill goes through here are the approximate amounts that Californians would be compelled to pay to the state and federal government under this arrangement . . ."

That was followed by a chart, showing that anyone with an annual income of $3,000 would pay $8 per year. However, the tax showed a big jump to incomes over $500,000 while an income of $1 million would pay $571,396.

Meanwhile, back at the ranch, *Variety* observed its own milestones during the decade. *Daily* was started in Los Angeles, with its first issue on September 6, 1933, publishing six days a week. Arthur Ungar was editor. In the same year *Variety* founder Sime Silverman died on September 22 of a heart attack. *Daily* ran a front-page obit. For the first time in its twenty-eight-year history, the reins were handed over to somebody new.

Artistically, the decade ended on a high note. *Life with Father* opened on Broadway; *The Grapes of Wrath* and the first *Batman* comic book were published; and Billie Holiday recorded "Strange Fruit," a haunting song about lynchings.

1939 was also the year some film historians consider Hollywood's greatest single year. The Oscar roster of Best Pic nominations listed *Dark Victory*, *Goodbye, Mr. Chips*, *Love Affair*, *Mr. Smith Goes to Washington*, *Ninotchka*, *Of Mice and Men*, *Stagecoach*, *The Wizard of Oz*, *Wuthering Heights*, and the eventual winner, *Gone with the Wind*.

Margaret Mitchell's novel had become an immediate sensation when it was published in 1936, and anticipation was high for the David O. Selznick–produced film. In its unsigned review, *Variety* hailed it as "one of the screen's major achievements, meriting

DAILY Variety DAILY
NEWS OF THE SHOW WORLD

Vol. 4 No. 32   Hollywood, California, Friday, July 13, 1934   5 Cents

FAIR IS FAIR

Reprinted with permission of Variety from its current issue.

There is every indication that the church campaign against the picture business is getting out of hand. The extremes to which some churchmen and newspapers are going to emphasize the 'menace of the screen' seem out of all proportion to the case at hand.

It's getting to be a race to break into print, with pictures the springboard behind which the boys and girls are lining up in single file and down which they run to take off to see who can make the biggest splash. There are two institutions which can put a quietus on this free-for-all which has reached such exaggerated dimensions—the Catholic Church, which instituted the campaign, and the press. It's a long leap, a deplorable leap, from the well considered Cincinnati conference on the subject, held by a committee of bishops, to the matter which is now breaking into print despite that the bishopric round table only took place last month.

There can be no doubt that the picture producers have been guilty of errors but they are taking definite steps to correct those errors and have so pledged themselves. If those closest to the situation from outside the business, the committee of bishops, are satisfied with the producing companies' sincerity as to making correction, and realize that proof will be invested or lacking in those pictures scheduled for fall release, it casts a doubt upon the true purpose of those who continue to broadcast anti-film statements almost promiscuously. The committee of bishops said their say direct to picture men and have said no more. Those who are trying, with no little success, to bathe in the reflection of that meeting must remain in poor light with anyone giving the subject a modicum of reflection.

It is unfair for Cardinal Dougherty, of Philadelphia, to have commanded an outright boycott of all pictures by his diocese just before taking a boat; it is unfair for Archbishop Curley to have made his statement just before taking a boat, and it is unfair for Dr. S. Parkes Cadman to deplore the screen also just before taking a boat. They hit and run.

There is no condoning Cardinal Dougherty's action in Philadelphia. It was and is an unjust and extreme measure. Such an edict is as much an affront and overt act as if some studio were to deliberately rush into production and release an indecent picture. It is a gesture which is unnecessarily harsh. Stay away from all pictures. Why?

The attitude of the press in this campaign against pictures is difficult to fathom. Have the newspapers of the country a grudge against pictures? The way the press has hooked to the campaign, the space it is giving to practically everyone and anyone with some kind of an organization title who cares to berate the screen, makes it seem as if editors are paying off a grouch of years' standing. Yet the best explanation would seem to be that the dailies deem the campaign a hot story and figure it for circulation.

But in playing up the film agitation the papers have also been opening their columns to the professional reformer, other offshoots of the original Catholic intent and publicity grabbers. It's amazing what the desk men are letting get by. Anyone familiar with the picture business can spot the blundering stories immediately. Some of the yarns which delve into block-booking flagrantly reveal that neither the spokesman, the writer, or desk men know what they're talking, writing, or reading about.

Maybe the papers believe they are giving the picture business an even break. But that must remain their own conception so long as they hang it on the line for the professional reformer and the publicity hound. It's not difficult to discriminate and normally the press bunch can smell a phoney a block away. Nevertheless they seem to look upon the present situation as a set-up and are hungry for anything which pertains to the matter.

Both the Catholic Church dignitaries who are closest to the picture exigency and film men realize the danger of the professional reformers and the limit to which they may go. Neither side wants this aspect to creep in but the newspapers are making it easy for a third angle where there are only two. There is a certain element which has joined in the current movement whose presence may be inspired only by what it sees to be gained from the effort, and that doesn't necessarily mean clean pictures.

This all makes it the more difficult to understand the position the press has taken for practically all newspapers are wary of the professional reformer and do not like anything for which he stands. Meanwhile, the picture business rates an even break before the public—but there has been no beacon to date.

It cannot be denied that the film producers have been wrong many times and in many ways. But their mistakes have not been malicious. Rather have they been on the side of bad judgment or poor taste and a bad error has been in ignoring for so long a warning which was sounded as far back as 1932. And beyond that the most grievous mistake has been their failure to realize their responsibility to the public.

Whether they choose to think so or not those who make pictures have a responsibility to the public. It amounts to their unwritten license to make pictures. The obligation is to the community and if going back over the record it will be found that the producers have also done much to uphold that trust, although this aspect has become buried in the barrage of violation citations.

People forget very easily but there is no reason to overlook that the picture business gave to the screens of

(Continued on Page 4)

FAIR IS FAIR

(Continued from Page 1)

the world 'Ben Hur,' one of the finest presentations of a religious story ever conceived and worthy, as to sincerity and delicacy of handling, of ranking with the Passion Play of the Oberammergau Players, and, incidentally, witnessed by hundreds of thousands of more people. That was a long time ago, but before and since 'Ben Hur' there have been films of national import which, for instance, have helped the east understand the west, made the north realize the situation in the south; historical and educational films of inestimable value in bringing home to a public such subjects more vividly than books and particularly to a people not given to concern themselves with such matters after leaving the schoolroom. Nor has there been anything finer on stage or screen than 'Cavalcade,' probably the highest tribute ever paid a foreign nation by the amusement business anywhere and a picture of international significance in aiding the world to understand England. Is there any question that the picture business is basically a national asset and, from the commercial angle, can it not be said that the American business man owes a debt to American pictures? For the screen has been his silent salesman in many things.

In view of these things it is going too far to figuratively brand the picture men as wolves in celluloid clothing and publicly make them the targets of irresponsible accusations. In not taking cognizance of their responsibility the film men have often gone off the track, too often, but they have said that correction will be made and there is plentiful evidence that measures to this end have been inaugurated. Anyone is entitled to a hearing but there is no let-up in the din of condemnation. Granted that severe measures were necessary to make the producers see their mistakes, nevertheless this has now been achieved. What more is to be gained by the hounding until Hollywood has had an opportunity to demonstrate what it is going to do?

Neither has a belligerent attitude by film men a place in the present situation. That is only asking for more trouble and plenty of it. Any business can ill afford a fight with the church of any denomination. With the professional reformer, yes, but not the church when the latter's purpose is well founded. The closing of theatres in Philadelphia, and then blaming it on the boycott by that Catholic diocese, would be equally as wrong as Cardinal Dougherty's action in telling his people to abstain from all pictures. Corrective measure to the Cardinal's action must come from the other side of the fence for the film industry will but further jeopardize its position in trying to force the issue. It goes back to the old adage that two wrongs don't make a right.

It is also deplorable that even producers from the legitimate theatre are rushing into print with denunciations of the picture people. One such producer and manager got himself some easy publicity by terming a leading film executive the country's 'highest priced nit-wit.' Which is bad enough without knowing that this picture official rejected one of the same producer's plays as unfit for the screen. It's no time to be washing dirty linen.

There can be no questioning the right of the Catholic, Jewish or Protestant churches to tell their people to stay away from pictures which they deem objectionable. That is their right. There can also be no doubting the sincerity of the Catholic Church in the present campaign as judged on the meeting of bishops in Cincinnati. That meeting brought forth rational and constructive suggestions to which picture men agreed and have paid heed. Those bishops stated that they do not desire that the studios only make pictures for the church, that they remain vehemently opposed to censorship, do not want to tell the picture business how to run that business and are only concerned with obscenity on the screen. They further agreed to give Hollywood time in which to keep its promise during which period they would go ahead with the formation of the Legion of Decency. They also seemed well satisfied with the results of that meeting.

It is regrettable that the campaign has gotten out of the hands of these four men and that they, as bishops, have no authority over some of the other bishops in the matter. There are 103 bishops in this country all ruling their individual diocese. It is, of course, not known whether the Cincinnati committee can or would care to step into the breach but it is to be lamented that other church dignitaries have not seen fit to allow this committee to handle the campaign.

As one priest put it, and was so quoted in a New York newspaper, 'Each bishop is running his own show.' And that now appears the keynote of the entire campaign and the situation the picture business is up against. It's become too much of a show.

The picture business in making correction, has devised the best system for self censorship it has ever had and is entitled to a truce until results can be judged on the screen. An answer to those who think and say block-booking forces 'objectionable' films into the theatres wi probably be generally released this week.

The anti-film campaign is being allowed to go to extremes for which there is no excuse and the press can do much to sift the chaff from the wheat.

Fair is fair.

Milestone Ends Sea Shooting—

Lewis Milestone finished maritime scenes aboard the Ruth Alexander yesterday, bringing 'Captain Hates The Sea' company back to the studio for interiors.

Director ran into foggy weather while shooting the boat sequences, and was delayed four days.

Lennon Laugher July 20

'The Laughing Journey,' novel by Tom Lennon, news editor of Radio publicity staff, has been set for publication release on July 20.

Moratorium on Theatre Building Urged by Bard

A moratorium on theatre construction in this territory, particularly in Altadena where erection of a picture house is reported under consideration, has been suggested by Lou Bard, operator of the independent Colorado, in Pasadena, in a complaint against zoning-clearances for that community, filed yesterday with the local z-c board here.

Bard points out that Altadena, suburb of Pasadena, is already heavily overseated for pictures.

Zoning-clearance protest filed by Bard objects to a seven day clearance for Pasadena first runs after the Los Angeles first run closing, and he also wants a 77-day clearance for South Pasadena instead of the 21 days provided in the new schedule.

Z-c board will begin wading through a batch of protests today.

Wanger Starts Here Sept. 15—

New York, July 12.—Walter Wanger, flying coastward Friday, says he is set to produce four films, two in Hollywood and two in London, but distribution arrangements not yet set. He expects to start his first Hollywood production about Sept. 15.

Lyda Due Sunday

Lyda Roberti due in at Paramount from her New York engagement Sunday

highest respect and plaudits," concluding "a great picture, by every measure."

In 1958, MGM's head of publicity Howard Dietz estimated that the film's Atlanta premiere "drew 1,000,000 persons to a town with a population of 300,000." Dietz credited Selznick with doing the pioneer work on the *Wind* promotion.

The film has endured as the type of work that Hollywood excelled at: epic yet intimate, and filled with memorable performances, scenes, and lines of dialogue. However, the depiction of slaves was not as universally beloved. Though Best Supporting Actress winner Hattie McDaniel's Mammy and Everett Brown's Big Sam were among the most multidimensional and sympathetic portrayals of African Americans ever in a mainstream Hollywood film, some thought the slaves shown were depicted merely as the extended family of their owners and not as slaves truly had been treated at the time.

Also in 1939, after the Daughters of the American Revolution refused to let contralto Marian Anderson perform in Constitution Hall, Franklin and Eleanor Roosevelt invited her to perform at the White House and helped arrange an open-air concert in front of the Lincoln Memorial.

On December 27, 1939, *Variety* reported on the second annual Theatre Arts Committee's "Spirituals to Swing" concert at Carnegie Hall in New York City: "Sterling Brown, of the faculty of Howard University, Washington, D.C., Negro school, did the introes, he being introduced at the outset by John Hammond, of Columbia Records and lil white father of the boogie-woogie hotcha cult."

Well, that's a job description for you.

But Hammond certainly deserves some kind of special label. He was credited with discovering Billie Holiday, Count Basie, Bessie Smith, and Benny Goodman, and, later, Bob Dylan, Aretha Franklin, and Bruce Springsteen, among many others. He also worked hard for decades to integrate the music industry and shone a spotlight on black music by lining up performers in traditionally Caucasian venues, such as Carnegie Hall.

Racial tension was only part of the troubles on the domestic front.

In an interview with *Variety*, published December 27, 1939, J. Edgar Hoover said he and his G-men were going to keep an eye on gambling in Miami. "Hoover said that all kinds of rackets are attracted to the Miami area, much in the same manner as pickpockets used to follow the circuses. 'It's not a very wholesome picture down here,' the head G-man said in an interview at the Flamingo Hotel, Miami Beach." He said Capone associates had come to Miami for the winter.

War seemed imminent in Europe, but in America, there was still a strong sense of jittery isolationism. As *Weekly Variety* reported in 1939, NBC's St. Louis affiliate, KWK, cut off the broadcast of Dorothy Thompson: "The station took her off the air just after she had charged Hitler with thinking only of his own prestige and not the horror that might be caused his people by a general European conflict."

Robert Convey, head of KWK, denied that this was censorship. He said Thompson "was expressing some personal opinions" and that it "does not seem, in view of the present tension in international affairs, that anything but reportorial matter would be in the public interest."

In the same issue (September 6, 1939), a separate story stated that network executives were internally debating their goal of news objectivity after Nazis sank British steamship *Athenia* as it left Glasgow. Given the U.S. public's mood, "the imposition of strict neutrality" would be going against the public grain and could lead to backlash. "The networks on the other hand feel that it is their duty to stem the spread of mob hatred and prevent being used to cement public opinion toward America's entry into the European conflict."

Americans continued to debate their potential role in the conflict for another two years.

On September 6, a *Weekly Variety* report from London stated, "With theatres and every other form of amusement enterprise dark, the British Broadcasting Corp. has assumed the gigantic job of providing the United Kingdom's only diversion."

Even before hostilities were actually declared on Sunday morning, the BBC began its task. It scrapped its existing program plans on Friday and went into emergency mode, with news broadcasts every hour, alternating with "programs of light music and talks."

Once again, radio was a unifying force for people, and it would build on that role in the following decade.

As the decade ended, it was the best of times, it was the worst of times—but the worst was devastating.

Everyone was still looking for magic, but the chances seemed ever slimmer that it would arrive.

Previous Spread: July 13, 1934.

Right: November 8, 1935.

Following Spreads: Mr. Hearst doesn't like it here anymore; Mrs. Roosevelt likes movies; On sound stages or on location?

30 YEARS

Make no mistake about it — show business has decentralized.

The departments used to be distinct — vaudeville, legitimate, pictures, circuses.

Then came radio. And radio erased the boundaries. Talent expanded its former restricted fields. Scores of outstanding personalities excel in several divisions. Others strive for recognition. It is the era of versatility.

For 30 years VARIETY has held the mirror up to show business. Its columns tell the story of transition. Not limited to one form of professional entertainment, it covers all branches and divisions. Not confined to one country, it is recognized throughout the world as the only authentic and universally accepted news and advertising medium of the artist, manager, theatre and broadcaster. The vitality of its editorial policy has served show business in public relations outside of entertainment for a generation.

In December VARIETY publishes its 30th anniversary number, a text book and guide for the ensuing 12 months.

Reservations for space are now being made.

NEW YORK	CHICAGO	HOLLYWOOD	LONDON
154 W. 46th STREET	WOODS THEATRE BLDG.	1708 NO. VINE ST.	8 ST. MARTIN'S PLACE TRAFALGAR SQUARE

Why I Am Leaving California, by W.R. Hearst

PAR POISES GUILLOTINE FOR TYPE PLAYER NECKS

Feeling that number of its stock players who are typed as to performance and characters, are so familiar to audiences that their appearance on screen telegraphs story was in advance of its enfoldment, Paramount is surveying its contract players with eye towards weeding them out.

Studio will go over their work, try to determine how familiar audiences are with particular players and their typing and drop those it feels are detrimental to story development.

New faces cry has been an old one in major studios but this is the first time story tip-off angle has come up. Studio will rebuild stock company with eye towards obtaining more versatile players with personalities which may possibly deceive fans as far as story development is concerned.

N.Y. Lists Legit 'Substitute' As Likely for Pic—

New York, Oct. 22.—'Substitute for Murder,' comedy by William Jordan Rapp and Leonardo Bercovici, which opened tonight at the Ethel Barrymore theatre, has chance for a moderate run, providing the critics don't slate it too hard. Play has some good laughs and fine situations, but also some dull spots in dead center.

Mob should like it, once they start coming. Cast includes Francis ster, Jessie Royce Landis and Myron McCormick. William Harris, Jr., produced and staged. Comedy could be filmed nicely.

Previewed

MAN WHO BROKE THE BANK AT MONTE CARLO
(20th-Fox)
Great for Colman fans. Turnstiles should whizz. Well paced.

FRISCO KID (WB)
Smash for b. o. Sure everywhere. Top-notch Cagney.

LOVE FEVER (Invincible)
Mediocre. Leads sparkle, story limps.

RENDEZVOUS (MG)
Happy. Headed for big grosses if edited. Comedy first rate.

Previews on page 3

Wall Street Sights Loews in RKO—

New York, Oct. 22.—Wall Street has new angle on purchase of RKO control by Atlas Corp. and Lehman Bros., bankers, from RCA. That is that David and Arthur Loew are in the deal as financial participants on Lehman end of the transaction.

Not known how extensive such participation is. Loew boys resigned from Loew directorate some time ago, and David recently became associated with Hal Roach in film production.

Rockefeller Bidding Chaplin at 50-50—

New York, Oct. 22.—Rockefeller interests have offered United Artists 50% of gross and eight week run guarantee at Music Center theatre for Charlie Chaplin's 'Modern Times.'

Fred Allen Air Ghost Ticketed at 20th-Fox—

New York, Oct. 22.—Harry Tugand, radio script collaborator for Fred Allen, has been signatured as writer by 20th-Fox.

Los Angeles Examiner
OFFICE OF THE PUBLISHER
BROADWAY AT ELEVENTH ST., LOS ANGELES

October 16, 1935.

Editor of VARIETY DAILY,
Hollywood, Calif.

Dear Sir:

I read your article of September thirtieth stating that I am leaving California.

I hope still to be able to spend some time in California, but I am compelled to close my places and live almost entirely in New York.

Heaven knows I do not want to leave California. No one does, least of

[Concluded on Page 4]

Metro Rolls Own!

Metro is putting dozen masseuses on payroll to slap and rub 40 dancers in 'Great Ziegfeld.' Seymour Felix, dance director, sold studio idea girls should be kept in condition.

Solow Gusting 'Simoom'

Gene Solow signed by Walter Wanger to write screen treatment of 'Simoom,' original story by Humphrey Cobb. Set by Feldman office.

AT&T Shedding Erpi If Price Entices—

New York, Oct. 22.—American Telephone & Telegraph is desirous of disposing of its subsidiary, Electrical Research Products, Inc., to private interests if possible, and if able to get a price. In wanting to let go of Erpi, phone company is following definite policy reported handed down by President Walter Gifford, that AT&T has no desire of engaging in any business actively out of field of the telephone and public service domain.

WHY I AM LEAVING CALIFORNIA, by W. R. Hearst

[Continued from Page 1]

all a native son whose father was a pioneer; but it is utterly impossible for me to remain here and to occupy a place like San Simeon, on account of the federal and state tax laws.

The California income tax law goes to fifteen percent. Add this to the federal income taxes, and the New York taxes, plus many other taxes, and I find that over eighty percent of my income will go in taxes—in fact, it may be nearer ninety percent.

Under these circumstances, it is absolutely necessary for me to eliminate the high income tax of California.

What I do, however, is of little consequence; but I fear that a great number of people with considerable incomes are planning to reside elsewhere, and that a great many who had in mind to come to California, and to remain here for at least half of their time, are realizing the utter impossibility of doing so.

The California law contains the peculiar provision that if anyone, even though a citizen of another state, remains in California six months of any year, he thereby becomes for that year a citizen of California, and is subject to California income taxes in addition to the taxes he has to pay in the state where he has actual and legal residence.

This, of course, will prevent many well-to-do people from being even part-time residents of the state.

It would seem also that a number of moving picture people who earn considerable salaries are unwilling to pay the high income taxation of California, and are accepting engagements in the East or abroad.

I am inclined to think that if some alert moving picture company should establish studios in Florida or Delaware or New York City, or some suitable Eastern place, they could get many of the most valuable stars from California.

This would be better for the nation than allowing them and many leading directors to go abroad, to build up English pictures and foreign pictures generally.

The California income tax was an unhappy move—very unhappy for us who are compelled to leave the state, but also somewhat unfortunate for the state, which may lose some useful people and enterprises.

However, the state is so great and so rich that it will easily sustain the loss. The great misfortune falls upon those who have to leave it.

Sincerely,

W R Hearst

On Sept. 30 Daily Variety printed a story under the caption 'Hearst Quitting California' to effect that William Randolph Hearst is reported ready to pull stakes from California, abandon use of his San Simeon Ranch, near San Luis Obispo and confine his motion picture production activities of Cosmopolitan productions to his Cosmopolitan studios in New York as well as make his residence there.

Eleanor Roosevelt Sees Films As Force for Culture

By ELEANOR ROOSEVELT

WASHINGTON. — I have been asked to write these few words on the motion picture industry, and anyone less gifted to write on this subject could hardly be found.

I see movies occasionally, but I realize that I am not a really good critic. However, I have one great interest in the movies, namely, how can the movies become a force in education.

☆ ☆ ☆

THE great majority of our people see motion pictures as part of their regular recreation. They like something which will make them forget themselves and their daily round. They want to be thrilled, to live in another world for a time; so it is easy to see why great spectacles have been put on the screen, thrilling detective stories, stories which have the element of horror and suspense.

☆ ☆ ☆

YET here is a medium by which we can develop taste and artistic appreciation. Here stories can be told in such a way as to develop an interest in literature, and in the arts and history. It is a great field, this field of visual education and propaganda, if you use the word propaganda as the South Americans do, meaning education.

☆ ☆ ☆

YOU can teach ideals and standards and values through the medium where all the school precepts and readings of books will fail. I look for a time when the culture—the culture of our country will be immeasureably improved by the quality of our movies.

First Lady of the Land, from a photograph taken during a visit to her son, James, at the Samuel Goldwyn Studios.

HOLLYWOOD PAYS LAST HONORS TO LAEMMLE

'He was a little man who was a big man,' was the tribute paid at the funeral services of Carl Laemmle, Sr., by Rabbi Edgar F. Magnin at the Wilshire Boulevard Temple yesterday, as Hollywood leaders gathered to pay their last respects to the man who had done so much to develop the motion picture industry.

Commenting on the producer's many and little-known charities, Rabbi Magnin said 'he used his office for the welfare and improvement of his fellow men.

'Famous stars and producers, people of all creeds and classes, the simple workingmen, bankers and industrial potentates all mourn his loss.'

Adding that although Laemmle had never forgotten his German birthplace, he was always an American, Magnin continued. 'He had one allegiance and one loyalty to the country of his adoption and if there were more like him in America today, there would be less of alienisms and distorted European propaganda.'

Active pallbearers included Jack Ross, Dr. Leland Hawkins, Sam Behrendt, Fred S. Meyer, Ben Strauss, Sam Von Ronkle, Herman Einstein and David Tannenbaum.

Among those paying their last respects were Louis B. Mayer, Adolph Zukor, Mr. and Mrs. William Thalberg, Edward Small, Rabbi Jacob Sonderling, Walter Wanger, Clarence Brown, Wesley Ruggles, Kurt Newman, Leon Schlessinger, Harry Sherman, Walter Woolf King, E. J. Mannix, Sid Grauman, Hugh Herbert, Guy Kibbee, Bryant Washburn, Gibson Gowland, Charlie Murray and George Sidney.

Morris, Mercer Join In Publishing Firm—

New York, Sept. 26. — Buddy Morris, former operating head of Warners music firms, and Johnny Mercer, songwriter, will have their own publishing firm in operation within a week. Morris and Mercer already are primed for entry into the legit field as Mercer is to work with Hoagy Carmichael on scores for Shubert's 'Three Blind Mice' and 'Ziegfeld Follies.'

Breen Film Halted

Production on 'Escape to Paradise,' Sol Lesser's Bob Breen feature, was called off yesterday due to continued illness of Kent Taylor with severe cold. Picture, which shot around Taylor Monday, hopes to be able to resume today.

James, Spence Spotted

Rian James and Ralph Spence set at 20th-Fox to write the screen play on 'Down Rio Way,' South American yarn slated for the Sol Wurtzel unit.

Trio Spotted at 20th

Roland Young, Mary Healy and Lyle Talbot drew featured assignments yesterday in 'He Married His Wife' at 20th-Fox.

Friends Say Goodbye To 'Uncle Carl' Over Radio—

Friends to whom he was 'Uncle Carl' paid a final tribute to Carl Laemmle last night in a special broadcast over KFWB, presented jointly by Daily Variety and the Warners station. Eulogies delivered by all the speakers spoke of Laemmle, the great humanitarian, friend to the humble and great alike.

Arthur Ungar, editor of Daily Variety, sketched the film pioneer's early struggles, the opportunities he gave others, his altruism and kindness that endeared him to all who knew him. Others who spoke their reverence and admiration of the Universal founder were Robert Z. Leonard, who was an actor at the studio in 1911; D. W. Griffith, Henry MacRae, general manager of the studio under Laemmle's regime; Herbert Rawlinson, Universal star of the silents; William Wyler, director who was brought here from Europe by Laemmle, and David Broekman, onetime general musical director of the studio.

Memorial program opened with a tribute by Rabbi Maxwell Dubin against background of a Yiddish chant by Sons of Liberty choir, composed of Saul Silverman, Molio Sheron, Howard Ross, David Solovieff and Paltiel Buchner. With Leon Leonardi at the piano and conducting the studio orchestra, Clarence Muse sang 'Old Man River' from 'Showboat,' one of the biggest pictures turned out by Laemmle.

Program was produced by Bill Ray, assisted by Manny Ostroff. Lou Marcelle handled the introductions.

Blair In Today

Aubrey Blair checks in tonight from San Francisco to confer with tops in Associated Actors & Artistes of America on organizational work for American Guild Variety Artists. Blair is supervising organization work between Salt Lake City and Portland.

Pat Casey at Desk

Pat Casey, producer-labor contact, returned to his office yesterday after several weeks in east for conferences with labor tops and film executives. Did not reach city until 4 a.m., train being marooned by flood waters east of Needles.

Stothart Ork Records

Herbert Stothart and orchestra of 50 balalaikas have started recording of Russian background music for Metro's 'Balalaika.'

MICHAEL KANIN left the Cedars of Lebanon yesterday.
IVY WILSON home from the Cedars of Lebanon.

Jean Harlow Dies; Private Services Wed. at 11 a.m.—

Jean Harlow died yesterday morning in Good Samaritan hospital, to which she had been taken from her home on Sunday after a week's illness. She was 26.

Services, which will be said tomorrow at 11 a.m. at the Wee Kirk o' the Heather, Forest Lawn,
Continued on page 6

Jean Harlow, 26, Dies; Private Services Wed.

Continued from page 1

will be strictly private. Pierce Bros. mortuary is in charge of arrangements.

The actress was transferred to Good Samaritan when she became so ill that oxygen had to be resorted to in an attempt to save her life. Drs. E. C. Fishbaugh and Leland S. Chapman were in attendance.

Death Came in Morning

Early yesterday morning Miss Harlow lost consciousness. An inhalator crew of the Los Angeles fire department worked for two hours in an unsuccessful effort to prolong her life. She died at 11:37. Uraemic poisoning was given as the cause of death.

At Miss Harlow's bedside were her mother and step-father, Marino and Mrs. Bello; an aunt, Mrs. Jetty Chadsey; her maid, Blanche Williams, and William Powell.

Mrs. Bello was escorted to her home, 512 North Palm drive, Beverly Hills, and placed under care of a physician.

Miss Harlow was born March 3, 1911, in Kansas City. Her father was Dr. Monte Carpentier, a dentist, and she was christened Harlean Carpentier.

When she was 16, the girl eloped with Charles F. McGrew, 22, and they came to California. While she was visiting a studio, an executive noted her striking beauty and suggested a screen tryout. A few days later she was registered at Central Casting Bureau and received many extra calls.

However, when she appeared in a picture her grandparents called a temporary halt. After a divorce from Mc Grew Miss Harlow decided on another attempt at films.

Howard Hughes placed her under contract and she drew the feminine lead in 'Hell's Angels.' That was in 1929. Her salary was low and Hughes had many requests to lend his discovery. A Hughes publicity man then tagged her the 'platinum blonde.'

Miss Harlow secured a release from Hughes and signed with Metro in 1931. 'The Secret Six' was her first under the Metro banner and she became big boxoffice. Since that time, she has had top billing in 16 Metro pix, exclusive of 'Saratoga,' on which she was working when she became fatally ill.

Married Bern in 1932

During her early days at Metro, Miss Harlow met Paul Bern, associate producer. Their marriage on June 2, 1932, followed. Two months later, Bern shot himself. A year later, Miss Harlow eloped to Yuma with Cameraman Hal Rosson. In December, 1934, this marriage ended in divorce.

Friends estimated Miss Harlow's estate as a large one with a great share of it represented in insurance policies. One policy was recently taken out through Lloyds of London.

1940s

In the 1940s, news could be divided into two categories: World War II and everything else. And the "everything else" was distinctly the lesser of the two. That's because the effects of World War II endured even into the second half of the decade—the rise of the middle class, reconstruction in Europe, and atomic energy were all direct results of the war. And for decades to come, the economy, public attitudes, and the arts reflected the war and its effects.

On January 3, 1940, the first issue of the new decade, *Variety* carried a front-page report from London by the managing director of MGM, Samuel Eckman Jr. He said that only three months into the war, the mood had changed from chaos to confidence.

> "Confidence in the future. And confidence that Great Britain in wartime is not too bad a place to be in . . . When war was declared, we all heard on the radio that every place of amusement was to be shut until further notice. . . . Some assurance might perhaps have been given that the amusement houses would be reopened at the earliest possible moment—as in fact they were. . . ."

Ah, those Brits. Stiff upper lip and all.

Americans were plucky too, but practical. On December 10, 1941, three days after the bombing of Pearl Harbor, *Weekly Variety* ran the headline "Hollywood Takes Stock of Itself; Sure to Lose Much Manpower to War." General conversation at the studios "centers on war and what will be expected." Actors and workers were "jittery on what is in store for them. That considerable of the youthful manpower in the studios would be utilized by the armed services is a foregone conclusion." Considering the age limit of thirty-five years under the draft law, "it is understood that up to 35% of studio manpower would come under the call to service. In extra ranks the toll would run as high as 50% of those registered with Central Casting and indie offices."

That issue also ran a story about the government's plan to support the war effort by selling bonds, under the now-appalling headline "Slap-the-Japs Bond Drive." Other stories revealed that the Metropolitan Opera had

Right: Ingrid Bergman burned up the screen as *Joan of Arc*.

Wed., Dec. 4, 1940

MOTION PICTURE DAY AT BILTMORE BOWL

Members of the motion picture division of the Los Angeles Community Chest drive, as well as the studios' 17,911 pledgees, were extolled as 'real inspiration' for all other divisions making up the Los Angeles area yesterday, when Motion Picture day was celebrated at a meeting of campaign leaders in the Biltmore Bowl. Filmites have already contributed $465,718.52, which is a 47% increase over the Chest collections last year. Final Hollywood reports may raise the figure by another $5,000 to $10,000. Paul K. Yost was enthusiastic in his commendation of picture industry folks for their generosity, pointing out that the record sum was rolled up under the stress and strain of war that has greatly affected the talker business and the people in it. Louis B. Mayer, who led the film division; Will Hays, Edward Arnold and Jane Withers also added words of praise for the filmites money-raising accomplishments. Scores of execs and stars, directors and writers, were seated at the tables.

Frank Capra and Tyrone Power talking over the Chest setup.

Louis B. Mayer, with Will H. Hays and Archbishop J. J. Cantwell, who opened the meeting with an eloquent invocation.

Jane Withers and Hugh Herbert applaud efforts of the Industry.

Other studio captains shown here, L. to R. are: Fred S. Meyer, 20th-Fox, Eddie Seltzer, Warner Bros., William Koenig, 20th-Fox, and W. K. Craig, Metro-Goldwyn-Mayer.

George J. Schaefer, president of RKO Radio pictures, and Harry Warner, of Warner Bros.

Some of the studio captains in the drive are—L. to R.—Gunther Lessing, of Walt Disney's, Fred W. Beetson, of the Producers Association, Abe Lastfogel, Danny Winkler, of RKO Radio, and B. B. Kahane, of Columbia Studios.

Paul K. Yost, campaign chairman, Edward Arnold and Mary Pickford.

Ellen Drew, Wendy Barrie, J. J. Nolan, studio chief at RKO Radio, and Anne Shirley.

Nate Blumberg, president of Universal, and Cliff Work, the company's studio head.

"BACK THE ATTACK—BUY WAR BONDS"
THIRD WAR LOAN

DAILY Variety DAILY
NEWS OF THE SHOW WORLD

Vol. 41 No. 19   Hollywood (28), California, Friday, October 1, 1943   5 Cents

World Film War Looming

Left: Happy Motion Picture Day!

Above: Uh-oh.

Following Spread: January 10, 1940.

canceled all perfs of *Madame Butterfly*, while Greenwich Village Savoyards yanked *The Mikado* from its schedule.

A month after the United States joined the war, *Weekly Variety* headlines of January 14, 1942, showed that showbiz was being mobilized: "Army May Soon Take Over Par's L.I. Studios for Production of Training Pix"; "N.E. Theatres Prepared for Air Raids; Each House Has 2 to 10 Wardens"; "FDR Talks to Be Piped into Coast Theatres"; and "Glamour in Overalls: Defense Worker as Screen Hero—That's Type of Propaganda Gov't Wants From Hollywood . . ."

To translate: L.I. is Long Island; N.E. was the Northeast; the Theatre Defense Bureau proclaimed that presidential broadcasts will be heard between movie shows; and "in case of emergency news from the Government, the pictures will be interrupted if necessary. After any such broadcast, the National Anthem must be played before resuming the performance."

Daily Variety's December 8, 1942, Hollywood Insider column showed the studios grappling with gas rationing. One unnamed exec said his studio's gas consumption was 20 percent below normal for December, aiming for 35 percent in February. Theater owners were trying to get extra gas rationing for "taggers," who carry film prints between theater circuits. Meanwhile, RKO filled its need for messengers by using local high school students, working half days.

Food scarcity was an issue for the film *Meet John Bonniwell*, which was filming in Kernville, California. According to a story (December 8, 1942), 160 Hollywoodites were in the area (costing the production $5 per day per person). The manager of the local Mountain Inn traveled to Bakersfield for supplies and became irate when told she couldn't have any of the food in front of her: "Her burn did not subside when she was informed that the large consignment of butter and eggs was destined for consumption by Jap internees at Manzanar."

The item did not explain Manzanar, because it didn't need to. On February 19, 1942, President Roosevelt authorized internment of Japanese Americans. Under the measure, the military designated some locations as "military areas" or "exclusion zones," where certain people were not allowed. And that meant Japanese Americans were excluded everywhere—except internment camps, mostly on the West Coast of the United States. Otherwise, headlines over the next few years give an overview of the times:

May 13, 1942:

"Still Complain That H'wood Makes Too Few Hard-Hitting War Films"

May 13, 1942:

"Despite tire 'n' gas shortage, resort band bookings still OK"

| RADIO | SCREEN | STAGE |

Variety

PRICE 25¢

Published Weekly at 154 West 46th Street, New York, N. Y., by Variety, Inc. Annual subscription, $10. Single copies 25 cents
Entered as Second-class matter December 22, 1905, at the Post Office at New York, N. Y., under the act of March 3, 1879.
COPYRIGHT, 1940, BY VARIETY, INC. ALL RIGHTS RESERVED

VOL. 137. NO. 5   NEW YORK, WEDNESDAY, JANUARY 10, 1940   56 PAGES

BOOM IN POP MUSIC BIZ

Phono. Discs—Not Radio—Develop Singers; NBC Flopped on Ink Spots

Ad agency impresarios generally agree that the phonograph industry has taken over from radio the function of developing singers. It's been four or five years since a single vocalist has been made by radio but phonograph records can lay claim to the clicking of such singers as the Andrew Sisters, Bonnie Baker and the Ink Spots. The latter (colored) combination was on NBC for years but they made no headway in popularity until they started making records for Decca. Their 'If I Didn't Care' started them. As a result of this shift in material developing sources agency men have begun to make themselves more conversant with the latest output of the disc mills.

Not so long ago it was radio that produced candidates for popular attention in other media such as films, stage and discs. Now the course is reversed, with radio waiting to see what the other media succeed in grooming to headliner brackets.

Refugee Lawyer Writes Play, Starring Himself, To Hurdle U. S. Barrier

Ingenious attempt to get into the United States via a play which has written to star himself is being made by a former top-ranking Berlin attorney. Drama, now going the rounds of New York agents, is by Dr. Erich M. Frey, who is exiled in Chile and unable to obtain a permit to enter this country under the quota law.

With plenty of time on his hands, Dr. Frey set out to hurdle the immigration technicalities. So he wrote the play and tailor-made the major role to fit himself. Now he hopes to find a producer to stage it and thus obtain a visiting actor's permit, which would allow him to enter the country without awaiting the quota allowance.

Play deals with various aspects of criminality, with the leading player an attorney—the part Dr. Frey would essay. It is titled 'Das Dritte Ohr' ('The Third Ear') and has just been translated from the German by the Hans Bartsch agency, international play brokers. Dr. Frey, who is Jewish, appeared as defense counsel in many famous Berlin political trials.

Having Fun for $1.50

Des Moines, Jan. 9.
Mary Little, radio columnist for KSO-KRNT in the Des Moines Register and Tribune, is organizing a contest for Alka-Seltzer on 'How to Have Fun on $1.50.'
The two winners will have an all-expense paid trip to Chicago.

Brain Operation Filmed

Tokyo, Dec. 15.
The first medical picture in sound to be produced in this country will soon be released for educational purposes.
Pic is the work of Dr. Kagoto Saito, head of a section of the Nagoya Medical University, and will show a delicate piece of surgery upon the brain of an epileptic. Operation will be accompanied by music.

BOWLING NEW MENACE TO B.O.

Minneapolis, Jan. 9.
Bowling is the latest concern of exhibitors in the territory. With the public going strong for the game in ever increasing numbers, alleys are springing up like mushrooms everywhere. What's more, they're playing to capacity business, diverting much trade away from the showhouses.

The alarming part of the development is that women are becoming as good customers of the bowling allies as the men, it's pointed out by exhibitors. Leagues are being formed right and left. Here in Minneapolis they've even formed a film league, with all of the exchanges and many exhibitors represented.

Bowling is being exploited as a weight reducer for the fair sex, but its adds up as an additional headache for exhibitors.

WHAT TO CALL BABY A 15G RADIO CONTEST

Pepsodent will give away $15,000 as prizes in a name picking contest, slated to start on the Bob Hope program Jan. 30. The object of the name will be the infant daughter of Bill Goodwin, announcer and stooge on the show. She was born two weeks ago. Winner of the name that's pinned on the youngster will get $5,000.

The last time that Pepsodent had a similar name picking contest it involved Madame Queen's baby in the Amos 'n' Andy script. The contest drew 2,500,000 boxtops.

3d Starrer At 2

Hollywood, Jan. 9.
Baby Sandy starts her third Universal starrer, 'Sandy Is a Lady,' this month, shortly after she reaches the age of two.
Moppet celebrates her second birthday Jan. 14.

BREAKS TERRIBLE THIRTIES' GLOOM

Song Sheet and Phonograph Disc Sales Figures for 1939, with Promise of Even Better 1940, Marks Recovery From Headache Decade — And One of Few Industries in America to Really Turn the Tide

LEADERS NAMED

So far as the popular music industry of the United States is concerned the Terrible Thirties decade has ended with a complete restoration of vigor and public affection. Tentative estimates for both song sheet and phonograph record sales for 1939 are sensational when contrasted with the snails-pace of only a few years ago. Taken together with the present number and popularity of name dance orchestras the figures are eloquent of one of the most amazing comebacks ever scored within amusements and, in a wider sense, makes the music industry one of the few American businesses to really climb out of the 1930-40 vale. Through a check on jobber sources it is estimated that the turnover of
(Continued on page 55)

AUTOGRAPH SECRETARY SAVES WEAR AND TEAR

Detroit, Jan. 9.
Here's a tip to all autograph-hounded actors, actresses, politicians, prizefighters, authors and other celebrities who wear out their good right—or left—arms in signatures or handclasps. Gov. Luren Dickinson, no mean shakes at copping publicity, has just appointed a Secretary of Autographs. He picked out Velma Jean Spotts, 19 and attractive, as his glad-handing secretary.

Wherever the Governor goes there will go Velma. She will hand out pretty little autographed cards, signed by the Governor at leisure, embellished, what's more, by the State seal of Michigan. She also will help to greet visitors, doubling for the Governor on the hand-pumping business.

The aged Dickinson has been called upon to address what he calls 'mob meetings' at least 25 times since his eastern junket, when he returned from the conference of Governors in New York to criticize 'high life in high places.'

To avoid handshakes and autograph hounds he has been ducking out of the backdoors, but the crowds and his political chums don't like that. He figures that he still is good for about 10 minutes of finger crushing, but after that the secretary cuts in.

Laughton Meets Memphis Femmes And They Express Their Sorrow

What About Stripes?

Ft. Worth, Jan. 9.
Convicts at the Huntsville state penitentiary have a weekly radio program, '30 Minutes Behind Prison Walls.' Over the recent holidays the cons got 6,000 pieces of fan mail.
One fan wrote: 'I love your voice. Meet me in the lobby of the hotel. Wear a white carnation.'

PARIS NITE LIFE GIVEN A HYPO

Paris, Jan. 1.
A few more shades of gay are being put back into 'gay paree' following several new decisions taken by local military authorities towards normalizing the capital's night life.
The ban on public dancing, on since the start of the war, has been lifted and 40 dancehalls have received permission to reopen. This was decided upon after the one-day trial of resuming dancing, on St. Catherine's Day (Nov. 26), was considered a huge success.
The 11 p.m. curfew was set aside to permit merrymaking over the Christmas holidays, according to another official announcement. Prefect of Police Langeron was authorized to permit cafes, restaurants, dancehalls,
(Continued on page 55)

S. A. LYNCH, PIC EXHIB, BUYS FLORIDA RAILROAD

Miami, Jan. 9.
S. A. Lynch, veteran showman and partner of Paramount in the operation of a circuit of theatres in Miami and vicinity, has acquired control of the Florida East Coast Railway. Bonds on the line have been in default for some time.
Negotiations were carried on through J. P. Morgan & Co. of New York.
Lynch, owner of numerous hotels in Miami as well as other real estate, has sold Venetian Islands, development near Miami.

Film Radio's History

Twentieth-Fox is readying a story concerning the rise of radio from the crystal sets to television and plans using Alice Faye and Don Ameche in the leading roles. It may be one of the ace productions on the company's 1940-41 schedule. Radio stars of the past decade would be included in the cast.

Memphis, Jan. 9.
Charles Laughton's one-day excursion here for Dixie premiere of 'Hunchback of Notre Dame' won general favor from all save the ladies of the Memphis Better Films Council.

Academy award winner generally made favorable impression at cocktail party, two brief personals on Malco Palace stage, where picture is showing, and with the press. But Better Filmers are still snorting their displeasure.

Femmes squawked that Laughton was untidy, wore no vest, had twisted string for necktie and dirty shirt. Hair wasn't combed, they said. Nor were they pleased with the frankness of the passage about women from 'Rembrandt' which he read to them, topped by awkward remark that he hoped all the ladies' little boys would feel that way about them. About 400 females were there; at least a dozen telephoned the newspaper later to complain about its guest.

Funny twist to incident was that this was the only chore arranged by Terry Turner and Don Prince, handling visit, to which Britisher had objected. He said he was no lecturer and couldn't bear to face so many women at once.

Cheese Was Too Much, So Philly's City Hall No Longer OK's Free Ads

Philadelphia, Jan. 9.
Theatrical and film press agents who were able to promote free ads in lights on the sides of City Hall ballyhooing their productions in the past will get the thumbs-down treatment on this gag in the future. Mayor Robert E. Lamberton, who went into office New Year's Day, put the kibosh on it with the ukase that the municipal lights would only be used for civic and charitable events.

Advertising men said the mazda signs, right in the heart of the city, were worth a couple of hundred dollars a day. These were given gratis in the past to any p.a. who had an in with the Mayor or his secretary.

A couple of months ago an exploitation artist was successful in getting a sign: 'Welcome Hour of Charm' on the side of the Municipal Building ballyhooing the engagement of Phil Spitalny femme orch at the Earle. The 'Leave It To Me' troupe at the Forrest also got the same break.

Even nitery artists were able to nail the choice spot with a 'Welcome Joe Doakes' in big, blazing lights. The low spot was reached when 'Eat More Cheese' was shown above Broad and Market streets, heralding a convention of cheese manufacturers.

HAYS MAY SURVEY PUBLIC

Goldwyn's $975,000 'Westerner' May Find Berth on Shelf; WB Deal Off

Unless Samuel Goldwyn has something very unique up his cuff, general trade opinion is that the United Artists legal battery has jockeyed him into the unhappy position of possessing almost $1,000,000 worth of film for which he has no release. 'The Westerner' will shortly cross the finish tape at a cost of approximately $975,000 and, unless Goldwyn is willing to gulp a heavy dose of his pride and give it to United Artists for release, he apparently will have to put it on the shelf.

Although there is no official statement from Warner Bros. that the deal announced last week for distribution of the film is off, there is likewise no denial of reports to that effect. Paramount and RKO have declined becoming legal guinea pigs for the Goldwyn strategy of UA contract 'terminating' and it appears unlikely that other companies will offer themselves.

Goldwyn, who arrived in New York Friday (5) night, in accordance with instructions from his attorney, Max D. Steuer, kept his lips tightly zippered on the entire matter. Steuer was little more voluble except to express indignation at the trade press reports of the 'Westerner' deal being off.

Goldwyn trained from the Coast to Chicago with James Mulvey, his eastern rep, and planed the remainder of the distance. He ostensibly came in to accept the New York film critics' award Sunday (7) for 'Wuthering Heights' as the best picture of the year, but has held a series of huddles in his Waldorf suite with Steuer. He returns to the Coast today (Wednesday) or tomorrow.

Warner break resulted from a letter by Charles Schwartz, co-counsel for UA with O'Brien, Driscoll & Raftery, to WB's legal department. This so upset the Warner counsel they immediately advised breaking off the Goldwyn deal, which had been negotiated on the Coast by Harry Warner; Gradwell Sears, sales chief; Abe Schneider, company treasurer, and Joe Bernhard, Warner circuit head.

Threatens Injunction Suit

Schwartz letter threatened an injunction suit against WB to prevent distribution and an action for dam-

(Continued on page 53)

M-G, PAR, 20TH CUT TO 40 PIX

Hollywood, Jan. 9.

Only 40 pictures each will be released by Metro, Paramount and 20th-Fox for 1940-41, according to advance indications.

Many will be made in England, hopped up with Hollywood names. The three studios have each announced up to six English pictures for next season, but it's understood their quota for new season won't exceed 40 pictures, which constitutes heavy trim numerically over past seasons.

Par Narrows Down Cartoon Feature Field

Several votes by Paramount execs during the past few weeks have reduced from about 20 to four the possible subjects for a feature-length cartoon by Max Fleischer to succeed 'Gulliver's Travels'. Final selection will be made within the next few weeks.

Getting the right subject, it is said by Par's story department, is made difficult by demand of the company's heads that it not be scarey, yet have suspense.

'Pinocchio' In After 2 Years of Cartooning

Hollywood, Jan. 9.

Walt Disney wound up camera work on his animated cartoon, 'Pinocchio,' after two years of shooting and turned it over to crew for the working-in of sound track on the master print.

Tentative release is set for Feb. 23. Original plan was to send it out this month.

UA-PRODUCER DEAL NEAR CLOSING

Addition of another producer to the United Artists fold is expected this week, with deal having been virtually worked out and only signaturing of the papers needed to make it official. Name of the newcomer is being kept secret, even the UA staff not being let in on it. Murray Silverstone, company's chief, is known to have been negotiating recently with the Frank Capra-Robert Riskin unit. It is not believed, however, that the Capra-Riskin deal is up to the announcement stage yet.

Another change in the UA producer setup being arranged, it is said, is for Alexander Korda to transfer his activities from London to Hollywood when he finishes his present propaganda film for the British Admiralty, 'Chasing the U-Boat.' Korda, Silverstone and other UA execs confabbed on the switch when the English producer-owner was in the U. S. about a month ago.

James Roosevelt's unit, product of which will be distributed by UA, will get underway on its first picture, 'The Bat,' in April. Roosevelt has also purchased 'Storm in Paradise,' by David Boehm and Henri Verstappen, and 'Love Song,' which will be published in novelette form in McCall's mag in February. Latter is for fall production.

Silverstone was careful to point out that Samuel Goldwyn, with whom Roosevelt was associated and who is now in a battle with UA, will not be the financial or directing angel behind the new producer. 'Mr. Roosevelt has not only financed and organized his own company,' Silverstone said, 'but will be, in every way, the guiding spirit behind his pictures.'

LEVY GOES WEST TO MAKE 'SYRACUSE'

Set with Universal for the production of one picture, to be followed in all probability by others, Jules Levy left for the Coast last night (Tues.) to prepare for the filming of 'The Boys From Syracuse,' his initialer as a producer. Setting up his own producing company, known as Mayfair Productions, Levy's deal is one for release only.

Until recently Levy was general sales manager of RKO, his entire career having been spent in distribution and theatre operation. He resigned from RKO about two months ago, his deal with U following.

Einfeld Heading East

Charles S. Einfeld, WB v.p. in charge of publicity-advertising, is due in New York Friday (12) for homeoffice huddles. Grad Sears probably will return from the Coast shortly afterwards.

Einfeld probably will devote part of his time to personally supervising the premiere of 'Fighting 69th.'

TO QUERY LACK OF ATTENDANCE

Film Companies Particulary Anxious to Know What Is Keeping Public Away From Theatres — Though Basic Industries and Agriculture Showed Definite Upturn in '39, Admish Scales Dropped Slightly

ALONG RADIO LINES

Strong possibility looms that the motion picture industry in the spring will employ a professional agency to send interviewers into thousands of homes of every type in every part of the country to determine why people are not attending films. It'll be a takeoff on a radio survey.

While business statistics indicate a decided upturn in basic industries and agriculture—which it is figured should be reflected in increased theatre attendance—there is no proportionate gain at the boxoffices. Fact is, confidential Hays office figures show that film admissions during 1939, with the average admission price lowered, have been considerably below expectations.

Problem of what is keeping the public away from theatres is one for which production, distribution and circuit execs have been unable to find a satisfactory answer. They have not only pondered it for the past year, but worried over it plenty. They feel it is one of the toughest nuts the industry has ever been called upon to crack and one that is vital to its future existence.

Several quiet confabs have been held by circuit and distribution officials with members of the Hays office staff on a plan, or method for

(Continued on page 55)

RKO PAYS 160G TO FORGET PIC BY WELLES

Hollywood, Jan. 9.

RKO is shelving 'Heart of Darkness,' which was to have been the first film by Orson Welles, due to the estimated budget of $1,100,000.

Studio figured the film was overboard on coin, so it discharged its obligations to Welles and cast he assembled by paying off $160,000 to forget about 'Darkness.'

Welles and John Houseman have dissolved their partnership, Houseman going back to Broadway and Welles remaining in Hollywood.

They had been partners since birth of the Mercury Theatre. Houseman insists that Welles belongs on Broadway, in spite of his ambition to make pictures.

Freeman Will Huddle With Par Heads in N.Y.

Y. Frank Freeman, vice-president of Paramount in charge of the studio at Hollywood, is due in New York early next week for home office conferences with Barney Balaban, Stanton L. Griffis, Neil F. Agnew, Austin C. Keough and others. Matters on the agenda are of a general character, including production plans of the immediate future as well as for 1940-41.

Since going out to the studio two years ago, Freeman has been east only on one occasion since then.

La Guardia Claims $25,000,000 Will Be Spent and 125 Pix Made in N. Y. In Next 2 Yrs.; Vague on Tee-Off

New York's Mayor Fiorello La Guardia Monday (8) told reporters that the next two years would see $25,000,000 spent on product and more than 125 pictures made in the metropolis. The mayor declared that N. Y. was contributing 27% of the total income of Hollywood and it was only fair that an equal proportion of work should come to this city.

'We have made pretty good progress, not as much as I would like, but a great deal more than some of the stand-patters can possibly absorb.'

The mayor also disclosed that 'several major film companies have approved our plans for eastern production.' A cinema city is under consideration with developments far past the talking stage.

It was disclosed in this regard that all producers would work together on this lot, which will be large enough to handle all production. In the meanwhile, production will be carried on at the Eastern Service and Biograph studios. The Mayor refused to divulge the location of the new studio, pointing out that should it become known the real estate values would jump considerably.

La Guardia stated that he had spoken to many executives of the film industry, some of whom had vision and were willing to cooperate. He admitted failure to get together with others.

Wants 'Harmony'

'New York does not want to take anything away from Hollywood,' La Guardia declared, 'We expect to work in complete harmony and with the cooperation of Hollywood. We realize there is a great deal of capital invested in Hollywood, but we feel we should be able to make our share of films the same as London does.'

As to when actual production would start La Guardia was somewhat vague. He declared that various producers would gradually start to work in the east. Pinned down for a date, he said that some films would be shot before summer. He hastened to add that they would not all be grade A productions, but

(Continued on page 18)

Stahl, Starr Combo To Produce Col Pair

Hollywood, Jan. 9.

John M. Stahl closed a deal to produce two pictures this year on the Columbia lot in association with Irving Starr.

Financing will be equally split between Stahl and the studio.

HORNER HEARS BIOFF MATTER TODAY (WED.)

Chicago, Jan. 9.

Matter of ordering William Bioff's extradition from California, which has become a local political issue and the cause celebre of a $250,000 libel suit filed by Gov. Horner against the Chicago Daily News, will come up again tomorrow (Wed.) in Springfield when the Governor resumes hearings on the application. Motion for the return to Illinois of Bioff, coast labor leader and representative of George E. Browne, president of the IATSE, is being made by Thomas Courtney, Chicago prosecutor, who is in possession of records that Bioff in 1922 slipped from under a six-months sentence in the Bridewell.

Bioff was detained by Los Angeles police on telegraph request by Courtney and subsequently released pending issuance of an extradition order by Gov. Horner. Latter is reported to have asked the state's Attorney General, John Cassidy, for an opinion and investigation, and it is believed generally in political and labor circles here that the state's top legal officer will advise that the necessary papers be issued immediately by the governor.

Bioff's attorneys have contended that the records of the one-time conviction of the labor negotiator were dug up at this time because of animosities created by labor disputes in the film studios.

BERMAN TO METRO ON 3-YR. PRODUCER DEAL

Hollywood, Jan. 9.

Pandro Berman signed a three-year pact as producer at Metro, moving in about Feb. 1.

Deal calls for straight salary, without the percentages he formerly collected as executive producer at RKO.

Ross Quits As Exec, But Will Produce For Roach

Hollywood, Jan. 9.

Frank Ross, executive vice-president of Hal Roach studio since last spring, resigned that job to produce two pictures on the same lot.

Ross joined the Roach outfit two years ago as a reader, later becoming story editor and stepping up to the vice-presidency after the resignation of Milton Bren.

Look's Shorts Via Par

Paramount is discussing a deal with Look magazine to distribute a series of shorts the mag proposes making.

The first, already completed, has been viewed by Par but so far a deal has not been closed.

VARIETY
Trade Mark Registered
FOUNDED BY SIME SILVERMAN
Published Weekly by VARIETY, Inc.
Sid Silverman, President
154 West 46th Street, New York City

SUBSCRIPTION
Annual..... $10 Foreign..... $11
Single Copies..............25 Cents

Vol. 137 No. 5

INDEX

Bills 46-47
Chatter 53
Dance Bands..................38-40
15 Years Ago................... 42
Film Booking Chart............ 18
Film Reviews................... 14
Film Showmanship.............. 8
Forum 55
House Reviews...............44-45
International News............ 12
Inside—Legit 50
Inside—Music 40
Inside—Pictures 22
Inside—Radio 34
Literati 52
Legitimate 48-51
Music 38-40
New Acts....................... 47
Night Clubs.................41-43
Night Club Reviews............ 42
Obituary 54
Pictures 2-22
Radio 23-37
Radio—International 27
Radio Reviews...............36-37
Unit Reviews................... 47
Vaudeville 41-43

Above: Humphrey Bogart and Dooley Wilson in *Casablanca*.

Right: An uncensored letter from William Hays.

June 8, 1943:

"Biz Fears U.S. Driving Ban"

September 13, 1944:

"N.Y. Radio Station Pushes Jobs for GIs"

September 13, 1944:

"London Theatres Gradually Returning to Normal as Robot Menace Passes"

While that last one sounds like a sci-fi headline, "robots" were actually robot bombs. The 1940 *Foreign Correspondent*, directed by the British-born Alfred Hitchcock, was one of several Hollywood films of the period that were genre entertainments that carried subliminal messages about the serious threat of the Axis and the dangers of isolationism.

Once the United States entered the war, flag-waving became popular. Though movies about World War I are rare, Hollywood cranked out endless films dealing with the second one. It's no coincidence that the Oscar-winning films for 1942 and 1943, *Mrs. Miniver* and *Casablanca*, were war themed.

At the 15th Academy Awards, for the year 1942, honorary awards went to Noël Coward "for his outstanding production achievement 'In Which We Serve,'" and to MGM "for its achievement in representing the American Way of Life" in the Andy Hardy film series. The first was a patriotic look at the British military in wartime, and the latter kind of explains itself.

Many of Hollywood's A-list filmmakers worked on pieces depicting war heroism and nobility. Which is not to say that all the films of the time were pieces of art. Many were low-budget programmers designed to fill out double bills and to make audiences feel better about the sacrifices they were making.

Except Preston Sturges. He was a screenwriter who made history by transitioning to the role of director, which he did to protect his scripts from what

MOTION PICTURE PRODUCERS & DISTRIBUTORS OF AMERICA, INC.
28 WEST 44TH STREET
NEW YORK CITY

WILL H. HAYS
PRESIDENT
CARL E. MILLIKEN
SECRETARY

December 15, 1941

OFFICE OF THE PRESIDENT

The Editor,
VARIETY,
154 West 46th Street,
New York, N. Y.

Dear Sir:

VARIETY deserves the warmest commendation of all who would preserve unimpaired, untrammeled, unsullied what you so brilliantly term "The Fifth Freedom - the freedom of self-expression in artistic terms".

This is a never-ending fight. It does not permit of complacency or indifference or neglect. Those who would destroy freedom of expression sometimes move forward in frontal assault; more often they attack by flank, subtly, deviously, stealthily, raising, when the occasion suits them, false banners and slogans to entrap the unwary and the unsuspecting.

Freedom of expression is not a particular virtue of the screen, the press, the stage, the radio, literature and the arts. It is a basic tenet of our way of living. An attack on one is an attack on all. If one freedom falls, all freedom is threatened.

Our industry has always stood with those who have fought and won the many notable battles in behalf of freedom of expression. No challenge to that freedom will find us unprepared to do our share.

With kind regards, I am

Sincerely yours,

Will H. Hays

Below: Betty Grable. And her legs.

Right: Rita Hayworth shows how to show off a leg on a red carpet.

he considered idiotic directors. After working as a writer on the 1935 *The Good Fairy*, the 1937 screwball classic *Easy Living*, and doing uncredited rewrites on numerous films, Paramount let him direct the 1940 *The Great McGinty*. Over the next two years, the writer-director had three hits, *The Lady Eve*, *Sullivan's Travels*, and *Palm Beach Story*.

Arguably his biggest landmarks were his 1944 pair *The Miracle of Morgan's Creek* and *Hail the Conquering Hero*. The former is a comedy about a young woman (Betty Hutton) who goes out dancing with some GIs, hits her head, and wakes up pregnant, with no idea who the father might be. The latter concerns a small-town nice guy who is rejected by the army but passes himself off as a military hero. With overlapping rat-a-tat dialogue, wacky character names (Trudy Kockenlocker, Sergeant Heppelfinger, Woodrow Truesmith), and an ensemble of actors who shone in small roles, Sturges had an amazing string of hits. Their success was especially surprising considering his outrageous themes, including the mockery of small-town values, honesty, and motherhood, in the midst of World War II patriotism.

Interestingly, Sturges had five major hits in four years, then, like a comet, trailed off. His 1948 *Unfaithfully Yours* concerns a conductor (Rex Harrison) who fantasizes three times about murdering his wife, each fantasy to the accompaniment of classical music (Rossini, Tchaikovsky, and Wagner). During the war years, his perverse black humor was unique. Later, when the world caught up with his outrageous POV, his films fizzled.

Though movie audiences kept up with current events via newsreels, their real lifeline was radio. With news programs, commentaries, and President Roosevelt's reassuring addresses to the nation, perhaps the most calming was the music.

In 1942, there were three hit versions of "Don't Sit Under the Apple Tree (With Anyone Else But Me)," one by the Glenn Miller Orchestra (with vocals by Tex Beneke, Marion Hutton, and the Modernaires), another by the Andrews Sisters (with the Harry James Orchestra), and still another by Kay Kyser. The up-tempo song concluded with ". . . till I come marching home!" A wholesome image of romance to be sure, but by the twenty-first century, most people wouldn't know where to find an apple tree, much less dream of sitting under one with a sweetie. But in wartime, this simplicity of emotion trumped the Cole Porter–style sophistication of the previous years.

113

Songs in the 1940s reflected the tearful optimism of folks back home separated from their loved ones. Songs like "Sentimental Journey" and "I'll Be Seeing You" by Glenn Miller, Tommy and Jimmy Dorsey, Benny Goodman, and Bob Crosby & His Orchestra soothed a worried population and, of course, bobby-soxers screamed and swooned over Frank Sinatra.

Every country had its own musical heroes. Britain had Vera Lynn, who immortalized "We'll Meet Again" and the plucky-English optimistic idea that soon there'll be bluebirds over "The White Cliffs of Dover."

France had Edith Piaf, Tino Rossi, and Charles Trenet, whose French "La Mer" became a huge hit for singer Bobby Darin in the 1950s when lyricist Jack Lawrence translated it into English as "Beyond the Sea."

Like every other industry, show business was preoccupied with war, which *Variety* reflected as it talked about deals and about the comings and goings of such stars as Rita Hayworth and Betty Grable, both favorite pinups of the soldiers.

Sometimes it felt like a small-town newspaper, showing the effect of a war as seen through one individual's eyes. For example, the November 15, 1944, *Daily Variety* ran a small story about a 20th Century-Fox executive: "Spyros Skouras, president of Greek War Relief, may visit Greece shortly, either on behalf of the relief organization or the United Nations Relief and Rehabilitation Administration. UNRRA is now working to feed peoples of countries decimated by the Nazis. It is reported that both Spyros and brother, Charles Skouras, own various commercial enterprises in Greece. Nephew of the two film execs, son of a fourth brother now living in Greece, was executed by the Germans shortly after Greece was overrun."

Meanwhile, that Puccini opera was again causing problems, but from a different perspective, as reported in *Daily Variety* on March 15, 1944: "Gestapo has banned the operas 'Lakme' and 'Madame Butterfly' in France. Former, by Leo Delibes, had been recently sung in Marseilles and, after the way the audience applauded the British officer who is one of the characters, the Nazis decided that they wanted no more of that. 'Madame Butterfly' has an American Naval officer in one of the leads, and the Gestapo is taking no chances on future demonstrations favorable to the Allies by the French."

Virtually every page of *Variety* reflected the global war.

A September 13, 1944, story said film and legit theaters in London were seeing a return to normal business, partly due to resumption of public transportation, while the partial lifting of the blackout "is seen as improving evening attendances as much as the lack of bombings, but the government is chary at predicting that the robot menace has passed for good."

After years of the fighting, the world had another reason to mourn: the death of President Franklin D. Roosevelt. An April 13, 1945, a *Daily Variety* story observed,

> "Never before in the history of a President's passing were the millions of Americans so speedily told of the nation's tragedy. Within minutes after the network flash came through, the word was passed along from mouth to mouth, long before the extras [i.e., newspaper special editions] appeared on street corners."

Daily featured a regular column by the single-named Flannery, identified as "CBS News analyst," who wrote about the hard news of the war, with no concessions to finding a showbiz angle. His As It Looks to Flannery column on May 2, 1945, stated,

> "The story of Hitler's death is being discredited by some persons because we have it only from German sources. We cannot, of course, have it from any other until the Russians complete the liberation of Berlin and are able to view the body. It's suggested that the death story may have been faked to enable Hitler to escape, that perhaps one of his doubles is dead instead. Hitler, since he looks like a million other Germans, could easily lose himself in any German crowd."

Flannery snorted that the Nazi announcement described Hitler as "a hero fighting the Bolsheviks" when he died.

His May 24, 1945, entry began,

> "This will be my last column for awhile. . . . I'm off on a trip that will enable me to know a little more, I hope. As I leave, the German picture is shaping up well. We hear from the Russian intelligence service that Hitler is dead, and we can be certain that when the Russian intelligence service comes to a conclusion like that, it's true. We need no longer worry about a Hitler popping up somewhere."

It's a sign of the times that, even a month later, no one was certain about Hitler's death.

Nearly three months later, the war reached its end when Japan surrendered. August 15, 1945, *Daily* ran stories about the outpouring of celebrations on both coasts.

DAILY VARIETY DAILY
NEWS OF THE SHOW WORLD
Vol. 47 No. 29 Hollywood (28), California, Friday, April 13, 1945 5 Cents

H'D MOURNS ROOSEVELT

A Martyr to Freedom

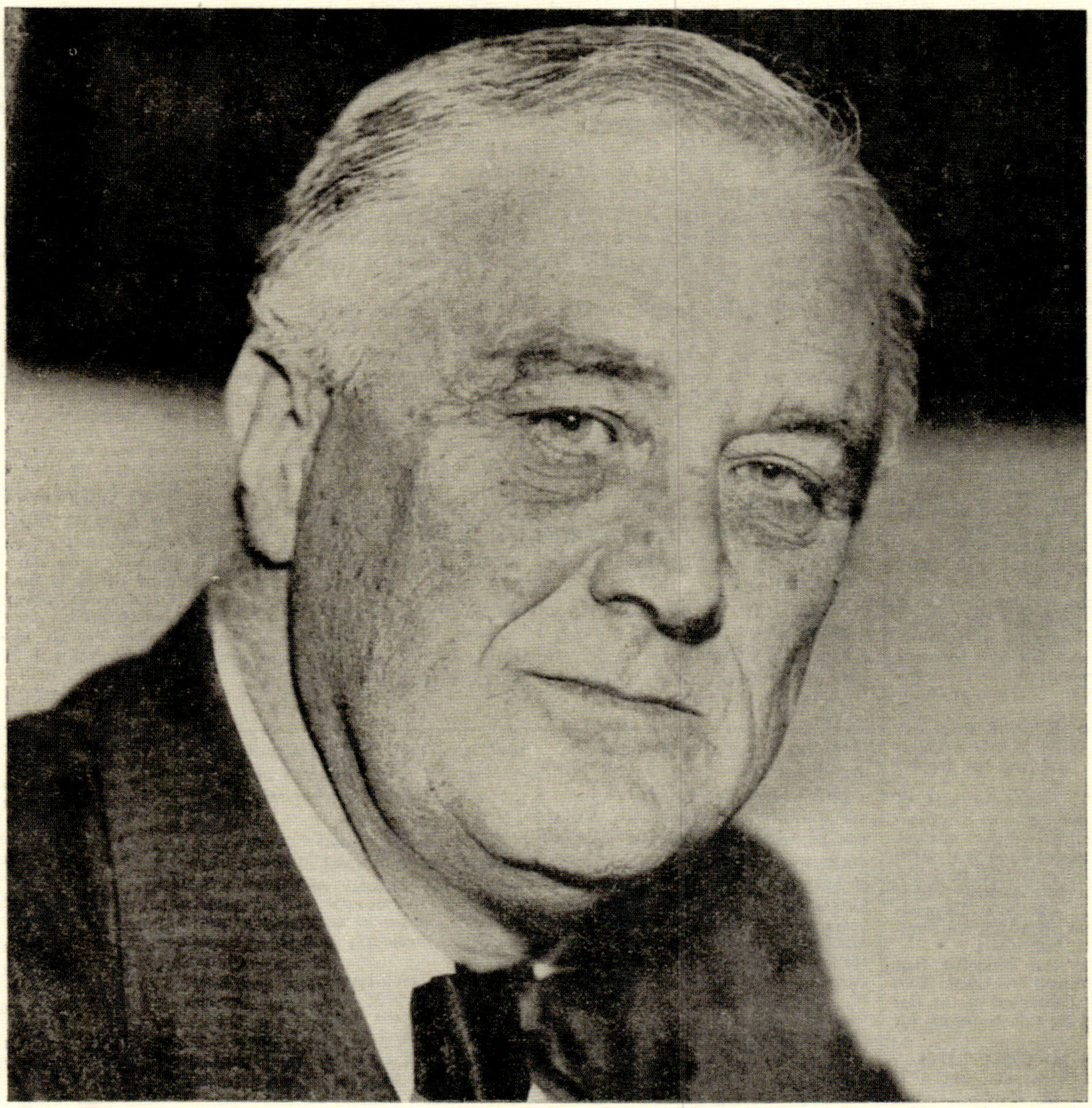

Franklin D. Roosevelt—His Favorite Photo

DAILY *Variety* DAILY
NEWS OF THE SHOW WORLD

Vol. 48 No. 48  Hollywood (28), California, Monday, August 13, 1945 5 Cents

Official Peace Message Due

EXTRA MERGER LOOMS; MIGHT END WALKOUT

New peace move to unite the Screen Extras Guild and Screen Players Union into "on strong American Federation of Labor union" and which might pave the way for settlement of the studio strike, has been launched by the Strike Strategy Committee, it was learned last night. Several secret conferences between various leaders already have been
◆ Continued on page 6 ♥

Morris, Here, Maps Peace Era Plans

William Morris, head of the William Morris agency, who conferred here all of last week with his agency partners Abe Lasfogel and Johnny Hyde on post-war plans returned to New York Saturday. Morris probably will go to London and Paris to check office operations some time next month.

MacDonald Starts His Next 40 Years In Pix

J. Farrell MacDonald, starting his 40th year in motion pictures, left for Kanab, Utah, over the weekend to take a role in 20th-Fox "Smoky," filming on location there.

Variety Raises Fund

Minneapolis, Aug. 12. — Northwest Variety Club has launched a campaign to raise $325,000 to build and equip heart hospital on University of Minnesota campus as its principal and most pretentious charity project. Club also has pledged itself to contribute $25,000 a year for hospital maintenance and research.

Yoohoo, Yehudi!

Violinist Yehudi Menuhin has been ordered by his draft board to report Thursday for induction into the armed forces. He recently completed a G. I. concert tour in Europe.

Mexican Romance

Mexico City, Aug. 12. — Janet Riesenfeld (Raquel Rojas), daughter of late Hugo Riesenfeld who has been acting in and writing for Mexican films, was married here Thursday to Luis Alcoriza, Spanish actor.

REVIEW
THE GAY SENORITA
(Col) (Page 3)

POWERS QUITS ASCAP FOR MGM MUSIC POST

Richard Joseph "Dick" Powers is leaving American Society of Composers, Authors and Publishers after 12 years to join Metro as music coordinator, a new post created for him. He moves over to the Culver City studio late this month on a straight three-year deal. In his new duties he will act as liaison between the studio and music publishers and songwriters on its pictures and music properties and the record com-
◆ Continued on page 7 ●

Par Has 20 Going Through Various Mills

With the completion of "Calcutta" over the weekend, Paramount now has six recently-finished features and three tinter musical shorts in the cutting rooms. Three pix currently are before cameras at the studio: "To Each His Own," "Blue Skies" and "The Bride Wore Boots."
Studio producers and writers are readying eight additional productions scheduled to get the starting gun during the next two months.

McIntyre Retires From Goldwyn Casting Post

Robert B. McIntyre will retire Wednesday from post of casting director for Samuel Goldwyn. McIntyre has been a casting director for the past 26 years and previously was production manager for Samuel Goldwyn. He will be succeeded by Edward A. Blatt, who directed several films for Warners.

Sturges Starts Sept. 15

"The Sin of Harold Diddlebock," which Preston Sturges will produce and direct for United Artists release, goes before cameras at Samuel Goldwyn studios on Sept. 15.

Theatres Remain Open On VJ Day

Los Angeles film houses will remain open on V-J Day, according to showcase tops, representing major and independent operators in this area.
Houses will be fully staffed, with emphasis on male employes for the next few days and individual managers have been given jurisdiction to close houses if celebrants prove overly exhuberant.

FORD LEAVES NAVY; JOINS REPUBLIC

Capt. John Ford, USNR, who has been on the continent making films for Office of Strategic Services of scenes to be used in the trials of the European war criminals, has completed his mission and is on his way home from London.
Ford, who has been in the Navy since Pearl Harbor, plans to retire from the Navy on his return. He has a deal at Republic where he will be a producer-director.

Savitt Improves

Jan Savitt is recovering from throat ailment at his North Hollywood home.

ARMY DECIDES ITS OWN RADIO A POST-WAR NEED

Washington, Aug. 12. — Armed Forces Radio Service will be maintained after the war as a new section of the Army, according to reports. It would mark the first time that a definite place in the Army's setup was made for a morale or entertainment unit. This is interpreted as high tribute to the work done by the AFRS radio group in Hollywood under command of Col. Tom Lewis, onetime radio production chief of Young & Rubicam agency. The unit previously had been decorated for its important contribution to morale of GI's around the world. Most of the officers and enlisted men in the AFRS unit were recruited from Coast radio and include some of the top writers and directors of big-time network shows.

STUDIOS READY TO SHUT SHOP FOR 1 DAY

Hollywood and the film industry are awaiting official word of peace before completing celebration plans. If the Japanese surrender is announced by President Truman this morning or any other week-day morning, the remainder of that day will be a holiday in studios. If the word comes during an afternoon, studios will close for the remainder of that day
♠ Continued on page 7 ♠

Houseman Quits OWI; Will Return To Par

New York, Aug. 12. — John Houseman, Paramount producer who took leave of absence last May to join OWI on temporary assignment as chief of film, theatre and music control division for U. S. occupied Germany, has resigned his government post. He will remain in New York indefinitely until reporting back to Paramount in few months for one-picture commitment.

Mozart Next In Cycle Of Great Artists' Pix

Both Republic and Metro are planning stories centering around Mozart, the Austrian composer, in line with present vogue for pictures based on lives of famous musicians. Herman Millakowsky has been working on story, "Mozart's Trip To Prague," for Republic. Joe Pasternak is starting preparations on untitled story of celebrated composer, at Metro.

Hopes For More Film Hits Postponement Snag

Washington, Aug. 12. — Crimp was put into hopes that current regulations on raw film would be immediately lifted, with the announcement of postponement of industry advisory meetings which had been slated for tomorrow by the WPB. The WPB has set the meetings ahead for August 27-29.

Parsons Off Air

After less than two minutes of broadcasting last night, Louella Parsons' air show suddenly blacked out, due to power failure at KECA Playhouse. Records were cut in from main studio to fill out her five-minute program.

One of the stories began:

"New York went stark mad with the arrival of peace news this evening. Times Square never saw such jam-packed humanity and from all parts of Manhattan came similar reports. It was without doubt the wildest outpouring of humanity in New York history, exceeding the celebration of Armistice Day 1918 by ten times and making the May hipdedee on German surrender pale into pastel shades."

There was also a big hipdedee in Los Angeles at Hollywood and Vine:

"At approximately two minutes after four p.m., air raid sirens, car horns and whatever other noise-making devices were at hand, exploded into the usual afternoon traffic noises. . . . Here and there small American flags popped up, waved by all ages and types of people. And here and there, there wasn't a smile on someone's face . . . someone perhaps who had lost a dear one in the almost four–year-old conflict. . . . Aside from that it was just a noisy, happy, frolicking group of people, who might have been at any given corner in any given city anywhere in the U.S. instead of Hollywood and Vine."

An accompanying story (*Daily Variety*, August 15, 1945, page eleven) talked about the role that "radar motion pictures" played in the bombings of Japan:

"It was disclosed yesterday for the first time that the uncanny accuracy with which the American airmen bombed Nipponese strategic points was made possible by the work of motion picture technicians at the Culver City unit. The B29's are equipped with special radar to bomb through clouds or overcast, but the radar operators have to have a preview of the target area to know exactly when to release their bombs."

So the motion picture unit created models of the targets.

"They succeeded so thoroughly that before radar operators took off from Saipan to bomb Japan for the first time the motion pictures showed them exactly what the target would look like in the radar scope."

The August 15, 1945, *Daily Variety* also said Los Angeles film box office was down 90 to 100 percent for V-J Day.

"The potential box office was all out in the street celebrating V-J Day. . . . From about 4:05 p.m. on, the houses began to empty and no one came in to drop their ticket stubs in the box. . . . Coming hard on the heels of a none-too-good weekend, the grosses for the coming week look to be slimmer than a Dachau breakfast."

Previous Spread: April 13, 1945.

Left: August 13, 1945.

Right: Shirley Temple all grown up.

Yes, *Variety* has had many proud moments over the years, but this wasn't one of them.

In its multistory coverage of V-J Day on August 15, 1945, *Daily Variety* addressed the business opportunities going forward for American film distribution in Asia. The story predicted only a 4 percent jump in box office from local audiences, but a "much greater market for U.S. picture distributors while some 1,000,000 American troops are patrolling land of the Fallen Sun."

However, a story a few months later had a different angle. The November 8, 1945, story quotes a letter that the Screen Actors Guild (SAG) was sending to all its members: "There's work to be done in Japan, not only for General MacArthur's men, but for the men of Hollywood. The United States Government plans strict control over Japan's film industry, and wants Hollywood executives and production personnel to go to Japan and take charge."

The report continued, "They'll find about 20 studios, located mainly in Tokyo, with an aggregate of 68 sound stages." In one year, the SAG missive revealed, Japan's studios turned out 554 feature films and 456 documentaries: "Japan also had before the atomic bomb, 1,885 theatres, many of them large and modern. . . .

"Judging from stills reproduced in the Japanese Cinema Yearbook, the artistic quality of Japanese films, their composition and camera work are excellent. The actors are attractive, too, in a strange sort of way. . . ."

Variety concluded that the SAG memo "pointed out that Hollywood execs and technicians taking over Japanese studios will find many peculiar customs, but expresses the belief that the job of reconstruction will prove fascinating."

The optimist would see this as postwar assistance; the pessimist would see this as plundering and carpetbagging.

Almost immediately, the postwar cleanup began—physically for ravaged areas, and emotionally for every country that had participated.

On November 21, 1945, Flannery looked at the war trials that had just begun in Nuremberg, where the "biggest Nazis were caught" and being tried. As a contrast, he pointed to 1918, when the Allies had compiled a list of nine hundred Germans who should be tried for their actions, but the list had eventually been cut to forty-five.

"Most of these had disappeared, were living abroad or could not be located. Even the witnesses could not be rounded up, or refused to testify. The result was but a few sentences and even these were farces, since none served his sentence. . . ."

A story from Cleveland on January 14, 1946, reported on the first public showing of the Army's official film, *The Atomic Bomb Strikes*, held at the city's opening of the National Air Show:

"Picture, running 40 minutes, shows first experimental blast in New Mexico and aerial views of Hiroshima and Nagasaki bombing. Previously, film was accessible only to high military officials and members of Congress."

Co-Starring in "THE STORY OF SEABISCUIT" Warner Bros.

SHIRLEY TEMPLE
A SELZNICK STAR

Co-Starring in "A KISS FOR CORLISS" A Colin Miller Production

The public sensed that the use of an atomic bomb on Hiroshima was a turning point in the war. The initial elation and excitement among the Allies transitioned into fear and unease as details emerged about the effects of neutron bombs—concerns that manifested in early-1950s horror films.

Scary films are always a good gauge of public mood, so it's notable that the 1940s seemed to have fewer iconic horror movies than any other decade. There were *Cat People* in 1942 and 1943's voodoo version of *Jane Eyre* and *I Walked with a Zombie*, and the Robert Wise–directed 1945 *The Body Snatcher*. In these films, the scares were from the unseen and unknown (a woman fears she will turn into a killer cat, and maybe she does; grave robbers terrorize Britain).

But on the whole, audiences had their fill of real-life horrors. They wanted escapism from the movies, so they embraced comedies, or musicals starring Bing Crosby or Judy Garland or Mickey Rooney. In the 1940s, horror often came with a big dose of comedy, such as the 1940 *The Ghost Breakers* with Bob Hope, or the 1948 *Abbott and Costello Meet Frankenstein*. (Universal's series of A&C comedies were running out of steam and so were the horror staples, so the studio combined them.)

But a different type of material emerged to unsettle audiences: film noir. Crime dramas filled with sexual manipulation and greedy motives, film noir showed that life was cruel and few people could be trusted. Helping to set the tone was John Huston's 1941 *The Maltese Falcon* (the third film version of Dashiell Hammett's novel in ten years). But the genre really kicked into high gear with Billy Wilder's 1944 *Double Indemnity*. *Falcon* may have had a sympathetic protagonist in Sam Spade, but in the darkest noir films, nobody was guilt free. See *Gun Crazy* (1950), *Out of the Past* (1947), *Detour* (1945), *Gilda* (1946; featuring Rita Hayworth singing "Put the Blame on Mame," possibly the sexiest musical performance ever on film), the 1946 Robert Siodmak–directed *The Killers*, with Burt Lancaster and Ava Gardner, and Otto Preminger's 1944 *Laura*, with its haunting music by David Raksin as prime examples.

Often visually stylish, with dark streets, shadows of Venetian blinds, and garish blinking neon lights, and filled with hard-boiled dames, manipulated saps, liars, swindlers, and murderers, these films featured tough-talking narrators. Take this line from Raymond Chandler's *The High Window*: "From thirty feet away she looked like a lot of class. From ten feet away she looked

Above: Judy Garland and Mickey Rooney.

Right: Betcha can't wait till tomorrow!

Following Spread: January 24 and May 16, 1945.

like something made up to be seen from thirty feet away."

There were also two films that, like *Indemnity*, were adaptations of James M. Cain novels: the 1945 *Mildred Pierce* and the 1946 *The Postman Always Rings Twice*. And Chandler, who has a co-script credit on *Indemnity*, also wrote the 1946 *The Blue Dahlia* and saw adaptations of two of his novels: *The Big Sleep* (also 1946) and a 1944 adaptation of *Farewell, My Lovely*, starring Dick Powell. The studio feared audiences would think it was a musical so they renamed it *Murder, My Sweet.*

Directors began to mix non-actors with professionals, shooting on war-ravaged locations and featuring themes of rebuilding amid impossible odds. Roberto Rossellini led the way with *Rome, Open City*, while other directors, including Luchino Visconti, Vittorio De Sica, and Federico Fellini emerged as well.

Rome, Open City (1945) was one of the winners at the first Cannes Film Festival, created by French minister for education and fine arts Jean Zay, who had wanted an international event for France to rival the Venice Film Festival. Cannes had been targeted for a 1939 launch under festival president Louis Lumière, but the war delayed it until September 20, 1946. Aside from *Open City*, the winners included Billy Wilder's *The Lost Weekend*, Britain's *Brief Encounter*, and Mexico's *Maria Candelaria*, which was voted by French film critics as "most interesting film of the festival."

By 1947, Flannery was back with his *Daily Variety* column.

In his June 13, 1947 entry, he wrote about one example of Europe's postwar turmoil. He praised Dersoe Sulyok, "who dared to stand up in the Hungarian Parliament, and say what he thought of the Communist government." Flannery concluded that a Hungarian revolution would not get far and the supportive U.S. government wouldn't do much more than take the case to the new United Nations:

THE SURPRISE OF 1941

IS IN

VARIETY

OUT TOMORROW
(SATURDAY, SEPT. 6)

Containing—

A COMPREHENSIVE SUMMARY
of the
1940-1941 SEASON'S

TOP BOX-OFFICE STARS
TOP BOX-OFFICE DIRECTORS
TOP GROSSING PICTURES
(Tabulated by Studios)

ON SALE AT ALL
PACIFIC COAST NEWSSTANDS **25¢**

"We're talking about financial aid, but that's to states outside the Iron Curtain, which has now clamped down on Hungary. The sums mentioned by counselor Ben Cohen of the State Department as needed for rehabilitation in the next three to four years are a staggering $5 to $6 billion a year compared with the $400 million to Greece and Turkey and the $350 million for general relief, but not so great as what we've been spending $350 million to the Netherlands since July 1945; $1,958,794,000 to France in the same period; $850 million to Italy, $356 million to Germany, etc. It's still a huge sum, of course, one that we cannot afford not to afford."

On February 2, 1948, he mourned,

"Mahatma Gandhi was one of the two or three great men of all time. . . . His great cause was the freedom of India, but it was more than that. It was to help his people to be able to live better, in working conditions, in their efforts, and in their consciences. . . . That Gandhi, who preached and practiced non-violence, was finally killed by one of his own people; that he who tried to make men love one another died because of the flame of hate, is a supreme tragedy. . . ."

On Oct. 24, 1949, Flannery observed:

"We may have decided to delay recognition of the Communists as the government of China, but with Russia recognizing the Reds, and we continuing to recognizing the nationalists, a test is certain in the United Nations. . . . Is Red China the de facto government? Is it in actual control of the territory that it purports to govern?"

While some news events were addressed directly, other news events

"PLEASE, MISTER, DO YOUR BEST"
1945 March of Dimes • January 25-31, 1945
THE NATIONAL FOUNDATION FOR INFANTILE PARALYSIS

Published Weekly at 154 West 46th Street, New York 19, N. Y., by Variety, Inc. Annual subscription, $10. Single copies, 25 cents.
Entered as second-class matter December 22, 1905, at the Post Office at New York, N. Y., under the act of March 3, 1879.
COPYRIGHT, 1945, BY VARIETY, INC. ALL RIGHTS RESERVED

VOL. 157 No. 7   NEW YORK, WEDNESDAY, JANUARY 24, 1945   PRICE 25 CENTS

SHOW BIZ EDUCATES EX-GI'S

Name Talent Clicks as Columnists; Orson Welles Latest Word Juggler

Newspaper columns by top show biz personalities are clicking on an unprecedented scale, with the result that several new byline features are being offered for syndication. Current emphasis on such features is traced to the success scored by Gracie Allen's daily report, with Bob Hope, who started scrivening later, similarly delivering readers.

Newest name to undertake a column is Orson Welles, with Eddie Cantor and Frances Langford also reported in line for a whack at it. Welles, who gained considerable political stature during the recent Presidential campaign, started his "Almanac" in the N. Y. Post, Monday (22). First piece dealt mainly with political questions in connection with Welles' attendance at FDR's fourth inauguration Saturday (20). Post's syndicate is handling, starting with 11 outlets.

Columning by the show folk is in keeping with the growing social awareness evidenced by performers since the outbreak of the war. It's been manifested by their campaigning, GI entertainment, war bond endeavors, etc. In the past, the most
(Continued on page 44)

Disc Jockey Rides 'Frivolous' Tunes, Causing Radio Stew

Contending there's insufficient awareness on the home front of music's potency as a propaganda weapon, and that there's a need for distinguishing between honest war songs and "frivolous tunes that are hurting the war effort," Alan Courtney, WOV (N. Y.) disc jockey, aroused a storm of controversy last week when he announced over the air he was "burning" a Louis Prima recording of the tune, "I Want to Go to Tokyo."

Courtney's editorial expression, unusual for disc jockeys, in which he declared he would refuse to play the tune, and his subsequent recital of songs that he considered good or bad for the war effort, resulted in a deluge of
(Continued on page 47)

CLARE BOOTHE LUCE AIR SHOW DEAL ON

Rep. Clare Boothe Luce, Republican representative from Conn. and playwright ("The Women") before she turned to politics, may shortly become a radio commentator. Deal is being negotiated between Mrs. Luce and Textron, textile outfit now engaged principally in war work, producing parachutes. Proposed air deal is being handled by J. Walter Thompson.

Should Mrs. Luce turn commentator, her program is headed for Mutual as a Sunday night airer.

Fatal Repeat
Muskegon, Mich., Jan. 23.
The fates—or whatever it may have been — caught up with Mrs. Amelia Schwab, former opera singer.
In 1903 she was so seriously burned in the Iriquois theatre fire in Chicago that she had to give up her career. About a week ago she was burned to death in a local hotel fire.

Million Income In '44 for T. Dorsey

Tommy Dorsey's orchestra piled up a gross income last year of approximately $1,000,000. This figure is the highest take ever amassed by a popular dance band. Kay Kyser might have equalled it several years ago, but his income was based mostly on his then Lucky Strike radio commercial.

Back in August, it was estimated that Dorsey's gross would be closer to $1,200,000, which unquestionably would have been an all-time high. However, his enforced layoff on the Coast, from August to early November, put a crimp in the expectations even though he did work weekends at the Dorsey Brothers-owned Colonnades Ballroom.

Figured in that $1,000,000 take is a sizeable income from the sale of 6,000,000 RCA-Victor recordings in 1944. Such a record sale was as unusual as the band's total gross since Dorsey had not made a new record during the previous 18 months, due to the record ban.

WB Plea to Arnold Gets MD's Planed to Jolson

Hollywood, Jan. 23.
Al Jolson, whose "Jazz Singer" and "Singing Fool" were particularly significant milestones not only for Warner Bros., but also for the entire film industry, may owe his life to Jack and Harry Warner, in addition to General Arnold. The brothers were granted a request to General Arnold, head of the Army Air Forces, for a special plane to fly two New York specialists here to attend the seriously ailing Jolson.

The actor contracted malaria while entertaining servicemen overseas, and a lung condition developed, resulting in the hurried call for medicos Mayer and Hertz. An operation has been successful, and while his condition is still serious, doctors are now convinced that Jolson will recover. No visitors are allowed to see him at the Cedars of Lebanon hospital, where he was rushed recently.

PAVES WAY FOR PEACETIME JOBS

Show business once again is harnessing its forces to cope with the next job facing the country in reestablishing the peace—the rehabilitation and reorientation of the returning GI to civilian life. Just as show business fully assumed its responsibility in keeping up the morale of the fighting men via its all-out mobilization of entertainers, so, too, is the entertainment industry on the march in taking up the job which presents itself as Phase No. 2 in the broad canvas of Show Biz at War.

Recognizing the need to lay a firm foundation to cope with the biggest task that will confront the nation, when demobilization comes, the various show biz media are already at work. It's not only a case of an
(Continued on page 21)

Look to Day When 'Aida' Is Done Under Water, With Midgets
St. Paul, Jan. 23.
St. Paul Civic Opera Assn. has come through with something new in the way of entertainment. It's grand opera on ice. "Hansel and Gretel" was skated successfully, the ballets and frequently the singers doing their stuff on the ice, at the St. Paul Auditorium before large audiences.

All of which prompted John K. Sherman, Minneapolis Star Journal music editor, to inquire "if 'Hansel and Gretel' can be skated, is there any reason why 'Carmen' can't be swum, 'Tristan and Isolde' put on roller skates and 'Aida' made a fireworks spectacle?"

"It's my prediction," commented Sherman, "that the old operatic staples, from now on, will not be let alone or untampered with. A straw in the wind is 'Carmen Jones,' played by a Negro cast in a modern hi-de-ho setting. Another is the Nine O'Clock Co.'s clever modernizing of Mozart operas and 'The Merry Wives of Windsor,' done with good taste, but opening the door, nevertheless, to what may be a weird succession of adaptations of old operas to modern conditions and audience demands. Harry James may yet enact 'Rigoletto' on the trumpet."

FINKLEHOFFE PIC BASED ON LIFE OF ELLA LOGAN

Author Fred Finklehoffe, under contract to Metro, has completed a film script based on the life of his wife, singer Ella Logan, which will be the first of two films to mark his debut as a pic producer for Metro. "Peg o' My Heart" will be the second production, after which he'll do a comedy of his own authorship, with music, on Broadway next fall.

OWI Kayoes 'Tomorrow World'; Seen As 'Too Sympathetic' to the Nazis

—And Cigarets, Too
Hollywood, Jan. 23.
When George Topper, Fox-West Coast treasurer, was held up and robbed of his $15 bankroll, repercussions were heard all over the F-WC circuit.

Charles P. Skouras, prexy, issued orders that all F-WC execs must carry at least $150 on their persons at all times from now on.

Nazi Radio in U.S. 'Atrocity' Attacks

With the attacks on Germany growing more critical for that country each day, the Nazi radio has just introduced the most ominous propaganda note yet recorded, according to veteran American students of the German air technique. Introduced almost at the same time the Russian attacks on the eastern front started, the new Nazi technique has been to accuse American soldiers of atrocities, against troops and civilians alike. Knowing the psychological purposes to which the Berlin radio has been devoted, the opinion is now offered that the cur-
(Continued on page 46)

Muni As 'Jazz Singer' In Warners' Remake
Hollywood, Jan. 23.
Warners is planning a remake of "The Jazz Singer," which originally was done with Al Jolson by the same company in 1927.

This time it's for Paul Muni and straight, meaning that the Frank Sinatra musicalized version is cold.

Office of War Information has refused to approve "Tomorrow the World" (Cowan - UA), reportedly owing to feeling in both official and semi-official circles that the treatment of the German problem in the film (based on the play) is entirely too sympathetic to the Teutons. The OWI nix means that the film will not be given an export license unless some important changes are made in the picture.

Belief is that "Tomorrow," which stars Fredric March, Betty Field and Skippy Homeier, is the wrong kind of a picture for European and other areas because it raises question that if an American family is unable to cope with a single Nazi-indoctrinated youngster, then what will be the approach in handling the millions of little mobsters in Germany after the war?

Thematic criticism has also been heard on grounds that such a film pre-supposes U. S. inclination towards a "soft peace" for Germany.

Foreign market for "A" product represents 40 to 50% of the domestic rentals, in some cases higher, and 70 to 80% of the net profits to a producer.

Anti-Nazi Airer Yanked By Agency When Army Disclaims Responsibility

"The Only Good Nazi," by Eve Merriam, did not go on the air last Thursday night (18) as a substitute for ailing Major Bowes' half-hour on CBS. The Chrysler company, via its agency, Ruthrauff & Ryan, decided that if the War Department shied away from taking the responsibility for the program, then the program would not be heard.

Situation caused some puzzlement in radio circles as Miss Merriam's
(Continued on page 44)

FIVE CONCERTS at $4.80 Top!
ALL S.R.O.
CONSTITUTION HALL, Washington, D. C.
ACADEMY OF MUSIC, Philadelphia, Pa.
ZEMBRO MOSQUE, Harrisburg
BUSHNELL MEMORIAL, Hartford
LYRIC, Baltimore, Md.

Booked by HARRY SQUIRES

THE HOUR OF CHARM
ALL GIRL ORCHESTRA AND CHOIR
Under the direction of
PHIL SPITALNY

2 DOWN AND 1 TO GO -- ON TO TOKYO!

'Showmen's 7th' Will Speed the Deed!

VARIETY

Published Weekly at 154 West 46th Street, New York 19, N. Y., by Variety, Inc. Annual subscription, $10. Single copies, 25 cents.
Entered as second-class matter December 22, 1905, at the Post Office at New York, N. Y., under the act of March 3, 1879.
COPYRIGHT, 1945, BY VARIETY, INC. ALL RIGHTS RESERVED

VOL. 158 No. 10 — NEW YORK, WEDNESDAY, MAY 16, 1945 — PRICE 25 CENTS

RADIO, PRESS BLITZ WAR CENSORS

Envision Public Ready for Gang Pix As Mob Stories Clean Up at the B.O.

Based upon the way certain gangster pictures are going, opinion in show business is that perhaps the public is ready for a cycle of this type of film fodder as relief from war stuff. It is also pointed out that murder mystery product, much of which has a gangster angle, has been selling heavily of late.

What may be an index to a change in public tastes in favor of gangster stuff is the way "Dillinger" (Monogram) opened on Broadway at the Victoria. It set a new house record of $35,800 the first week and last week (its 2d) did $27,800 in the 720-capacity house. "Dillinger" cost $200,000 to make and is likely to cue Mono to making additional films of this type, though Steve Broidy, v.p. in charge of sales, states nothing is set at the moment. According to Broidy, "Dillinger" has opened strongly in about 25 spots.

In the reissue field many gangster pictures are claimed to be cleaning
(Continued on page 8)

Palisades Park's New Gimmick — Happiness Of People Who Earned It

By SAUL CARSON

Palisades Amusement Park opened for the season last Saturday (12). The day was perfect, the evening gorgeous—and so was the take. It was a 100% Jersey Bounce.

Seventy-five thousand customers paid two-bits apiece to get in at the preem of this people's playground. For it was really a debut, since 90% of it was destroyed by fire just before last season closed. Only the stage, restaurant and those close to him among the major attractions. The rest of the place is new.

In the eating places and at the rides, in the penny arcade and casino, at all the concessions, the moola rolled faster than a shill's tongue. If the tills didn't add up to 250G, they didn't total a dime. And
(Continued on page 22)

CHI KIDS NOW FRISKED FOR CAP PISTOLS AT PIX

Chicago, May 15.

Kids who ride the range on Chi's northside have to check their gats before entering Essaness' Argmore Saturday afternoons from now on, juve enthusiasm for Republic's "Zorro's Whip," wild west serial that teed off three weeks ago, having reached such a pitch by last Saturday (12) that they began bringing their own cap pistols to augment the screen sound effects.

Harvey Cahn, manager, now frisks 'em, making them leave their weapons at the b.o., and will keep it up, he says, till S-E day, meaning the day the S-erial E-nds, nine weeks hence.

George Sidney's Epitaph

Los Angeles, May 15.

George Sidney's will, filed for probate here, left an estate of more than $100,000 to two brothers and three sisters, to be shared equally. His own epitaph was written as a codicil: "No fuss—no feathers—chuck me in a hole and forget it. I lived, I had fun and the world owes me nothing—love to all."

Louis K. Sidney, the Metro exec, is one of the brothers; and L. K.'s son, George, a Metro director, was named for his late uncle.

Crosby Off 'KMH' Reported—Again

Reports are current in the trade that Bing Crosby, who heads up the "Kraft Music Hall" Thursday night show on NBC, will step out of the radio picture for good at the end of the current season, and there's a feeling in the trade that this time Der Bingle means it.

It's become a fairly perennial affair, those late-spring and early-summer rumors that Crosby wants to scram out of radio, do some recordings, a picture or two a year, with perhaps some guest air shots and otherwise relax, but in the past he's always showed up for Kraft when the new broadcasting season rolled around. However, it's known that the Groaner would like to take things easier and those close to him say that come Sept. or Oct. it's likely that Kraft might find itself shopping around for a new star.

Just how Crosby's exit from the radio show will rest with his Decca associates is something else again, for it's generally acknowledged that his Thursday night air show is one of the strong factors in the continued booming of Crosby disc sales. On the other hand it would give him more extra time to record.

LaG. Nixes Radio Career

Mayor LaGuardia, who has eliminated himself as a candidate for another N. Y. mayoralty term, has also closed the door to any potential sponsored radio commentary program when he steps out of office.

"Frankly," the mayor bluntly told "Variety," when it was suggested that, on the basis of the reaction to his Sunday afternoon WNYC broadcasts he might fit into the network commentary picture, "it just wouldn't work out. For one thing I wouldn't let them censor any of my copy and I know they wouldn't hold still for that."

SEEK TO NIP E.T.O. NIPUPS VS. NIPS

By GEORGE ROSEN

Washington, May 15.

With the war in the Pacific still to be won, American radio and press correspondents are taking steps to avoid duplication of "too-severe" censorial treatment accorded them by military press relations officers in Europe. Right now the radio-press boys are in a state of apoplectic rage. The irritations and criticisms of the news-gatherers have been partially reported in the United States for some time, but the explosion last week, following the reportorial "fiasco" of the V-E Day developments, has brought the issue squarely into the open.

The radio trade, both here in Washington and around New York, is buzzing with speculation about the probable aftermaths. It is an unprecedented situation wherein the men who feed a nation its news are bitterly hostile to the military
(Continued on page 18)

H. M. Warner Points Up Value of Films for Int'l Education to D.C. Solons

Washington, May 15.

Value of American films as a medium of educating Axis nations was impressively brought home to a group of Senators last week by Harry M. Warner, who was a guest of Sen. Millard E. Tydings (D.-Md.) at a private luncheon at the Capitol attended by 15 other Senators, Joseph E. Davies and Leslie Biffle, secretary of the Senate.

Warner suggested to the Senators an educational program which would pull no punches. "It would bring the atrocities and war damage be-
(Continued on page 55)

Abbott & Costello Agree to Break Up, Go Single When U Pic Pact Ends in '47

Abbott and Costello, who have been together for 14 years, will split when their contract with Universal Pictures expires in two years. Lou Costello will go along for five years beyond 1947 under management of their current pilot, Eddie Sherman. His partner, Bud Abbott, is said to have favored Sam Steifel as a handler.

Costello is going out next month on three weeks of vaude appearances with singer Connie Haines, who is vocalist on the comedy team's airshow for Camels. They will make one-week p.a.s at Izzy Rappaport's Hippodrome, Baltimore; the Steel
(Continued on page 18)

Pix and Radio Execs May View Nazi Murder Camps

U. S. radio and film executives have been invited by Secretary of War Stimson to go to Germany, as did newspaper editors, and see for themselves the brutal evidence of German atrocities.

War Department, it is said, is anxious to make sure that no one, after this war, will brush off atrocity stories by swallowing the subtle Nazi line which alleges that these accusations are "propaganda."

Goebbels' American Stooges Being Tracked Down for Treason Trials

Await Mufti for Pixites

Hollywood, May 15.

Film industry is looking for the return of numerous producers and directors as a result of the collapse of the war in Europe and the reduction of the Army's program of training shorts.

Understood Col. Frank Capra will soon shift from his uniform into indie production. Others in line for discharge include Lieut. Col. Robert Lord, Major Robert Carson and Major John Huston.

Probe Drama Schools in Chi

Chicago, May 15.

"Variety" stirred up a hornet's nest here with its story, April 25, about the $5,000,000 a year you-too-can-be-a-star racket in Chi, as witness investigation started last week by State's Attorney William J. Tuohy following filing of complaints by four pupils against Metro College of Drama, Voice and Radio Arts; Talent Scouts and Broadcast Productions School; and others. Appointed to head investigation is Ota P. Lightfoot, assistant State's Attorney.

Also joining in the hubbub were Chi Herald-American, spearheading dailies' blasts, and Better Business Bureau, with Station WCFL cancelling a 13-week contract for half-hour Sunday afternoon airers "dramatizing" sudden rises to "fame" of such performers as the Dinning Sisters, Yvonne de Carlo, etc., latter's biography having been skedded
(Continued on page 20)

A rat hunt of special interest to radio is under way in Europe now. Rodents are Americans who acted as radio propagandists over Nazi and fascist DX transmitters. A few Englishmen are also involved, most notorious of these being 'Lord Haw-Haw.'

So far, the arrest of only one of the spielers of hate has been announced. He is the poet Ezra Pound, under indictment for treason. He was trapped when Mussolini folded, and is now in the hands of the Fifth Army in Italy. But he's coming back "home"—to stand trial on the treason charge.

Those really in the know can't do any talking, since the inside info is under security wraps. But it is believed that at least some of the other Americans who spewed Hitler's line over the shortwave have already been tabbed. Others are being sought among prisoners of war and suspect civilians in Europe who are being
(Continued on page 8)

Nothing Harvey-ish About Pulitzer Prize, Author Chase Finds

By JACK PULASKI

Most surprised over the "Harvey" (48th Street, N. Y.) Pulitzer prize award was Mary Chase, who wrote the comedy. Show's producer, Brock Pemberton, who had just returned from San Francisco, where he was present at the second anniversary of the Stage Door Canteen there, learned of the author's amazement when he reached Mrs. Chase on long-distance telephone. She had been visiting in New York but returned to her home in Denver three days before the Pulitzer announcement. She felt "Harvey" didn't have a chance at the honor citation.

Mrs. Chase's husband, Bob Chase, managing editor of the Rocky Mountain News, published in Denver, got the Pulitzer flash and hustled to a picture theatre where his wife was looking at newsreels. When he told her, Mrs. Chase screamed and nearly started a riot in the house. Author admitted she had one day-dreamed of winning a Pulitzer cita-
(Continued on page 8)

R.R. TRAVEL POST-VE EVEN TOUGHER NOW

Picture of rail-travel as a consequence of V-E has already started to change for the worse. Railroad accommodations westward which were fairly easy to obtain, have become extremely difficult and acts needing passage only to Chicago have to go through all sorts of grief to get space.

Situation in east to west travel is expected to become increasingly difficult as more men and supplies are
(Continued on page 20)

often were covered more peripherally. On December 16 1948, *Daily Variety* enthused,

> "Hottest race of the year has teed off among studios. The heat is to see who'll be first to make a picture on the Berlin Airlift, a story that has copped more page one space than any other this year and is expected to maintain its news value for more than a year to come."

On May 21, 1948, columnist Radie Harris gushed,

> "Raymond Massey's speech on behalf of the Actors' Fund at the Habima performance of 'The Golem' the night the state of Israel was born was spine tingling. . . ."

Daily Variety's page-one story five months later stated that eight thousand British exhibitors belonging to the Cinematograph Exhibitors Association had imposed a "tacit ban" on the work of Ben Hecht, a long-successful American writer and producer:

> "Action against Hecht was expected, since he is one of the most vociferous critics of Britain's attitude in the Palestine situation and a champion for the new state of Israel."

Hollywood was involved with Israel from the earliest days. On page seven of the June 16, 1948, *Daily Variety*:

> "Mrs. Golda Myerson, first official representative of the new Jewish state of Israel, will be welcomed here at a special invitation dinner headed by Dore Schary and Samuel Goldwyn next Sunday. She'll make a report to local Jewish leaders on the Palestine situation. Mrs. Myerson is administrator of Jewish areas in Jerusalem and only woman member of the Israel provisional government. Dinner will be held at the Biltmore."

Mrs. Myerson was born Golda Mabovitch in 1898 and became prime minister of Israel in 1969 under the name Golda Meir.

The Samuel Goldwyn who co-hosted her visit was a producer known for films like *Dodsworth*, *The Little Foxes*, *Ball of Fire*, and the 1939 *Wuthering Heights* with Laurence Olivier. When the war ended, Goldwyn was determined to film a story about GIs returning home. Skeptics thought it was too soon, and not what the public wanted. But he persisted. The result was the 1946 *The Best Years of Our Lives*, written by Robert E. Sherwood (from MacKinlay Kantor's story) and directed by William Wyler, and which is still one of the most wrenching depictions of post-military life ever shown.

The film captured the new world that GIs were adjusting to. The GI Bill of Rights gave returning GIs the right to go to college, buy homes, and apply for loans, giving rise to the American Dream of owning a little home with a white picket fence—and a radio and telephone.

Jack Helman wrote a regular *Daily Variety* column about radio, and his April 11, 1946, entry offered stats from Gallup's audience research: The study figured that 40 million families in the U.S. had radios, meaning an estimated 100 million listeners (Gallup figured 2.5 persons per set). The study also said that in Los Angeles and Minneapolis, the majority of homes had telephones, though home phones were in the minority elsewhere.

> "Rural areas, which have more phones per capita than urban, are rarely if ever checked by the radio raters. In the matter of car radios it is presumed that sets in use are greater numerically than in homes during the summer months."

But home telephones were growing, beyond L.A. and Minneapolis (and why Minneapolis, rather than Chicago or New York?).

On February 18, 1947, it was clear the phone company was branching out:

> "Telephone company is working on another assist to local transmission of television and FM programs with crews constructing a three-story building on Mt. Wilson to serve as a clearing house for sound synchronization with pictures and relaying to individual transmitters..."

And in *Daily Variety* on July 11, 1947:

> "Largest television screen yet devised, measuring 19x25 inches and projecting an image on an area more than six times greater than standard 10-inch screen, has been offered for sale here by United Television Corp. . . . New home receiver is projection type and not direct vision screen, comparable to but larger than Philco, Radio Corp. of America and DuMont sets."

The seeds were planted for the TV world, but radio was making its own tech strides, and by Eleanor Roosevelt no less. On November 9, 1948, *Variety* reviewed a radio show hosted by Anna and Eleanor Roosevelt, airing three days a week at 11:15 a.m. on KECA-ABC. The reviewer said the show

> "made for relaxed listening and on yesterday's tee-upper [Anna's] pear-shaped tones came through with greater clarity than her mother's, who was shortwaved in from Paris. . . . As a sample of what's to come, both devoted considerable wordage to the Truman victory and Mrs. Roosevelt was all for ousting the Dixiecrats from the Democratic party. . . . ABC is carrying the series sustaining but its commercial possibilities are very promising, especially in view of the sweeping Demo victory. Mrs. Roosevelt will continue to be shortwaved from Paris while she is attending the United Nations meetings as an accredited delegate."

And then *Variety* recognized a milestone in a fledgling business. The June 9, 1948, front page trumpeted "Texaco TV Show Hits Milestone." It elaborated that the sixty-minute first episode of *Texaco Star Theater* on NBC, costing $10,000 to produce, earned an audience of several million. The article from New York gushed that the new "vaudeo baby"—vaudeville-video, get it?—was the greatest single boost yet given to the new medium of TV.

Performers on the show included ventriloquist Señor Wences, singer Pearl Bailey, and, of course, comic and host Milton Berle.

As showbiz was exploring technology, it was also changing some fundamental working relationships. The Taft-Hartley Act (formal name Labor-Management Relations Act) of June 23, 1947, was designed to monitor activities of labor unions. Among other items, it limited the ability to call a strike and forbade radicals from leading unions. States were allowed to pass "right-to-work" laws that outlawed union shops. The following day, *Daily Variety*'s front page carried the banner "New Law Hits Film Unions," adding "17 Closed Shops on Way Out." (A closed shop said the employer could only hire labor union members.) In all, the Taft-Hartley law affected forty-two showbiz unions and guilds and forced the studios to divest their stakes in theaters. The November 3, 1948, *Daily Variety* banner read "Par Speeds Divorcement." Paramount was "following fast on the heels of Howard Hughes' plan for the breakup of RKO joint theatre holdings, and presently is in negotiations with theatre partners to dispose of a number of its joint interests." Paramount had submitted proposals to the Department of Justice,

Those Lilies For Radio May Be a Few Yrs Too Soon

By JACK HELLMAN

RADIO—that obselescent thing! You've doubtless heard it a hundred times since Milton Berle hit an 80 in Manhattan, and not always tongue-in-cheek. If memory serves, we believe it was Hans Kaltenborn who coined what is now a cliche, and it caught on in a big way with the alarmists. They were looking for some such phrase to ease their own suspicions about the dark days that lie ahead.

The cry was even taken up in the big agencies and they in turn passed it along to the men who pay the way less 15%. It was beginning to take hold and radio shows were dropped like hot potatoes at a clambake. "Let's look into this thing called televisoin," they counselled, and the hucksters started compiling voluminous reports. "By all means, television," they recommended, and radio's defenders slunk away into dark corners to await the day of reckoning, which they were sure would come.

Nothing succeeding like success, all sponsors ordered the same kind of show—like Berle's—so "we can get high rating quick." it sounded like a good idea but there was only one thing wrong with it—when they made the Berles there was only one Milty. Others tried to ape Berle's mad antics (and a big assist to Producer Ed Cashman) but it just didn't come off. Already the clients were getting frantic and here theyve were only getting their feet wet in the new medium. "What about the others who are so powerful in radio, pictures and night clubs? Is television out of bounds to them?"

"Oh, them," meekly replied the commission men, "they're out in Hollywood."

"I haven't heard about any quarantine out there," flipped one of the big ulcer breeders. "Get them."

What the shiny brass didn't know was there's a barrier higher than a quarantine in Hollywood to keep those big picture names out of television. And those free to make their own TV deals just didn't relish the idea of either moving to or running back and forth to New York.

Studio heads must be fumbling for new excuses to keep their stars off video now that it's fairly certain the big swing will be to the west before another season rolls around. It used to be fairly stock, and it stuck, that tele wasn't ready for the big names. "Come around when you grow up," was the withering retort to those seeking a few sparklers from the cinema plants. What few free lancers that dared the cameras of the TV stations set a bad example for a frightened industry. They were poorly photographed due to lack of know-how in lighting and much of the equipment was either obsolete or manned by amateurs. That proved their point, up to a point, and the studios held fast against any of their contractees going over to the opposition. But that was many months ago and the excuse is pretty threadbare by now. No longer can they say the medium hasn't grown up and their bread winners have nothing to gain by going tele-wards. Of course it's something else again when they run a trailer on a station with their stars in action. Just now television producers are trying to work out some compromise with the picture studios—somewhere in between a trailer and a short feature. Once arrived at, the vignette will serve both as a trailer for the picture and a short feature for the station. It may also be a foot in the door for TV, long seeking a common ground for the affinity of their interests.

THE admen knew it was coming so they immediately briefed their clients on the high cost of the coaxial when the transcontinental strand is completed, the present inadequacy of the kinescope and the high fees for filming. Both the sponsor and the admen frowned on these offshoots of live tele because it would move the seat of TV 3,000 miles away and they were determined to nail it down in New York. How, then, could the sponsor or his wife, take a party of friends over to see MY television show without hopping an airliner. But it looks like a losing fight. When Ed Wynn went east on kine and "Life of Riley" on film the ice was broken and it looked again like the old cry all over again—"California, here we come."

In their low dudgeon the sponsors, looked for a graceful out, found one. "What about circulation after w pass Chicago on the coaxial?" they wanted to know. "After all, y'know, we're still buying circulation or are we?" They were told that roughly there are two million-odd television sets around the country and better than 60,000,000 radio receivers. They began scratching their heads. Wasn't someone being too hasty about obsoleting such a far reaching medium of reaching so many millions of people? So back came the admen to grudgingly concede that radio is still a going thing and a long way from gone.

MANY of the seven-figure spenders in radio were beginning to revise their thinking—and their budgets. They took particular head when such industrial leaders as Gen. David Sarnoff and Leve Charles Luckman openly remarked that radio had a good many profitable years ahead and would be with us for as long as they would be around. Netwrok prexies shared their optimism and a new note of cheer ran through radio's ranks.

The end results began to show up before the curtain was raised on the new season. The two majors—NBC and CBS—had only a few open time slots, and the others would show billings this year comparable to last. That this is radio's most critical year is freely admitted by even the die-hards. The ratings will tell the story. Should Hooper's First 15 fall short of last year's or previous markers it can only mean that television is making deep inroads. Radio has survived all other competition so the heavy must be video if the AM audiences drop off alarmingly. Sure, as one sour puss put it, "they're the same old tired shows," but no one seems to be able to do anything about it. This season the quality is bound to suffer because of lower budgets and tighter spending. Television will more than double last season's billing and most of the coin is being siphoned off from radio, regardless of what you hear. If not, howcum shows that brought $10,0000 a week have been bought and sold for seven?

IN the transitory process of changing mediums, Hollywood won't come off the loser—for long. In show biz there's always the c for names and right here you'll find them anchored. The advantages of pictures and climate is not so easily overcome so in the final analysis television will become big time only when this lost horizon (to easterners) is at the originating end of th big shows as it has been in radio. Far-sighted leaders in TV see film as the only salvation and when you can knock off a half hour show in less than a day's shooting time and keep down the cost to the level of a live telecast, who's to quarrel with that conclusion? Not only is price a factor but quality must be a reckoning virtue. What tape is to radio film will be to tele and you just ask any producer or director about the qualitati margin.

Radio may be on its last legs and its days numbered but in the money temples they'll tell you that the old man will have to support the poor relative for a few more years at least. Color will come in tele and giveaways will be scuttled, too, but don't make any bets that it will happen this year or next. They'll be doing business at the old stand until the new one is ready. They can mark a "hold for release" on radio's obit but don't put it too far up front. Time will dim its pages before it goes down to the composing room.

Left: Poor, poor radio!

which would pave the way "for agreement on a separate consent decree peace pact."

Under that inside-baseball gobbledygook was a story with huge implications. Moviegoers in 1948 might not have noticed, but the Paramount Consent Decrees changed the studio system.

As the story reported, Paramount owned a 25 percent stake in 90 of the 112 houses in the Butterfield circuit, and a 33 percent stake in the other 22. RKO owned 10 percent of the 90 houses, and 33 percent in 22 venues. The Federal Trade Commission had been looking at the studios since the silent era. Many of the major studios were created in the 1920s, as theater chains needed product to fill their pipeline. And by 1945, the majors owned 17 percent of theaters, which accounted for 45 percent of rentals (i.e., the amount of money returned to the studio after the theater owner had deducted his operational costs, aka the "house nut," and his share of the income).

The studios had been settling for a lower share of the box office income from houses they owned. So the Department of Justice sued for unfair labor practices in 1938, which was settled by a consent decree two years later. Under that agreement, studios had to comply within three years, or the government would reinstate the lawsuit.

Among the requirements were the elimination of block booking (i.e., a theater owner agreeing to a package of films rather than individual consideration) and blind bidding (forcing exhibitors to agree to book a film sight unseen). It finally went to trial in 1945, with the "Big Eight"—Columbia Pictures, 20th Century-Fox Film Corporation, Loew's, Paramount Pictures, RKO Radio Pictures, United Artists, Universal-International, and Warner Brothers—as well as the American Theatres Association and W. C. Allred as defendants.

The Supreme Court forced the studios to divest themselves of theaters. The *Daily Variety* story stated that Paramount had submitted proposals to the Department of Justice, which would pave the way "for agreement on a separate consent decree peace pact."

Without block booking, studios became more selective in the movies they made. This fact, along with the boom in television, meant that the old studio system was fading fast. Another nail in the coffin came from sweet-faced actress Olivia de Havilland, who sweetly portrayed the endlessly sweet Melanie in *Gone with the Wind*.

For decades, the studios often signed actors to seven-year contracts, maintaining that this legally meant seven years of actual work. When de Havilland's contract expired, Warner Brothers claimed she still owed the studio six months, due to time she'd been suspended. On March 15, 1944, *Daily Variety* ran the headline "De Havilland Free Agent." The article stated,

> "Warners contended that they were entitled to 'seven years' actual working time' and that because she had been suspended seven or eight times, they could add the suspension time to the seven-year period."

The court, under Superior Court judge Charles S. Burnell, said this would make the contract one of "peonage."

The actress's legal victory marked the end of an era when stars were essentially indentured servants—but pampered and protected ones. Studios groomed stars by giving them classes in acting, voice, and movement, and sometimes changing their looks (Rita Hayworth underwent painful electrolysis to change her hairline). Execs controlled their image by putting out press releases and hushing up scandals (Loretta Young's "adopted" daughter was really her illegitimate child by Clark Gable). In exchange, stars went where they were told, dated whom they were told, and performed in whatever movie they were told.

Above: Vivien Leigh and Hattie McDaniel in *Gone with the Wind*.

With Hollywood in turmoil, things on the East Coast were cooking. On Broadway, Arthur Miller and Tennessee Williams wowed critics and audiences with back-to-back hits in the late 1940s—*All My Sons / Death of a Salesman* and *The Glass Menagerie / A Streetcar Named Desire*, respectively.

And the 1943 *Oklahoma!* was hailed as a revolution in musicals by seamlessly blending book, songs, and dances. In truth, the 1927 *Show Boat* did the same thing, but *Oklahoma!* was the right show at the right time, mixing homespun values and creative sophistication. It also marked the start of the long and successful team of Richard Rodgers and Oscar Hammerstein II.

The 1947 *Finian's Rainbow* broke new ground as well. With a score by E. Y. Harburg and Burton Lane, the show contained pleasant tunes, but it was the book that made headlines as Harburg and Fred Saidy addressed Southern racism in a fanciful tale of love and leprechauns.

Showbiz was not always sensitive to racial issues—look no further than the long tradition of minstrel shows, the treatment of non-Caucasian races in plays and films, and Caucasians being cast as Native Americans, Latins, or Asians.

But the 1940s saw a few stirrings of the racial changes that were about to come to the forefront in the 1950s and 1960s.

At the February 29, 1940, Academy Awards at the Ambassador Hotel's Cocoanut Grove, Hattie McDaniel became the first black to win an Oscar, for her supporting role in *Gone with the Wind*. Newsreel footage captures her moving acceptance speech. But the cameras don't show that McDaniel was seated in a section of the room reserved for blacks.

That ceremony also led to another bit of Oscar history: the secret envelope. Usually, newspapers were leaked the winners and told to hold them until the ceremony concluded, but the

ALL-DAY DEBATE ON CURB FOR COMMIES

New York, Nov. 24.—After meeting all day and well into the evening, film leaders huddling with Eric Johnston on the Red menace in Hollywood adjourned tonight without working out any conclusions. A sub-committee went into immediate session, in effort to come out with a report for presentation when full body convenes again tomorrow morning.

Today's stanza teed off with a small executive board meeting in the morning, after which whole group, numbering 48 industry leaders, assembled at Waldorf-Astoria for main confab of the day. Open discussion of the problem at hand, including plans for combatting subversive elements in studios, was held here, with Johnston acting as presiding officer.

It was agreed that a most serious public relations situation is facing motion picture industry, as a result of the "unfriendly 10" and their refusal to answer
♥ Continued on page 11 ♥

Above: The hearts at the end are a nice touch.

Herald Examiner hit the newsstand before the rites started. After that, the Academy of Motion Picture Arts and Sciences instructed its accounting firm to keep the secret, which has been upheld since then.

Jackie Robinson broke the color barrier in 1947 by signing with the Brooklyn Dodgers. In October 7 of that year, *Variety* announced,

> "Jackie Robinson, Brooklyn first baseman, will topline stage show at Million Dollar week of Nov. 18. The Negro major leaguer will head three standard vaude acts and Gerald Wilson's ork, with show getting 50-50 split of gross after first $2,500 at wicket. General Artists agency will group show around Robinson who, after stand, will start role in 'Courage,' PRC film. Prior to coming Coastward ballplayer will personal at Apollo, New York; Howard, Washington, and Regal, Chicago."

OK, what's the most confusing part of that story: the fact that it took so long to integrate sports; the fact that celebs made personal appearances at movie shows; or the fact that *Variety* used the word "ork" for "orchestra"?

Even though multiple races served in the armed forces, racism persisted. Between June 5 and 8, 1943, were the Zoot Suit Riots in Los Angeles, which were set off when sailors in L.A. attacked Mexican Americans. Five years later, *Daily Variety* ran a review of the play *City of Angels*, on June 16, 1948. The review began, "Problem play dealing with treatment of Mexicans in Los Angeles, 'City of Angels' is too local a topic for general acceptance and stands small chance of survival." And it concluded with "Action is fairly realistic but subject matter not conducive to good theatre." John Bright's play at the Musart Theatre may not have survived long, but the director, Anthony Quinn, did, as did the problems of Mexicans and other minorities.

So, too, did Hollywood's obsession with World War II. Aside from the three Best Picture Oscar winners of the decade (*Mrs. Miniver* (1942), *Casablanca* (1942), and *Best Years* (1946)), other winners in the years to come went on to include *From Here to Eternity*, *The Bridge on the River Kwai*, *Patton*, *Schindler's List*, and *The English Patient*. The war also figures prominently in later winners *The Sound of Music* and *The King's Speech*. And, as a signal of the film biz's continued fascination, three of the five Best Pic nominees for 1998 were set during World War II: *Saving Private Ryan*, *The Thin Red Line*, and *Life Is Beautiful*.

War is hell, except in Hollywood.

But the next decade would provide its own style of wars—and its own style of hell.

George M. Cohan Dies at 64; Show Biz 'Yankee Doodle Boy'

■ Continued from page 1 ■

est inspiration show business has given to this nation in all its history.

Death came to the 'song and dance man' at 5 o'clock in the morning three hours after he had passed into a merciful coma. For many months he had been suffering from a dread malady. As some men cling to life from fear of death, Cohan characteristically clung to life with a tenacity that amazed his physicians as the direct result of his life's consuming emotion, love of country. With the United States at war, the 'Yankee Doodle Boy' had to know what was going on.

Another factor that helped to prolong his life was his keen interest in the Warner Bros. filming of his life story in the James Cagney picture 'Yankee Doodle Dandy.' Though long at outs with Hollywood, the breach was largely healed by the intense satisfaction he derived from this motion picture.

Cohan's wife, long ill, his three daughters and one son, and his closest friend, Gene Buck, were at the bedside when death came.

The body remains at home until funeral at St. Patricks Saturday and will be placed in the mausoleum, Woodlawn cemetery next to that of Sam H. Harris.

BORN IN PROVIDENCE

Cohan was born July 4, 1878, in a cheap theatrical hotel at Providence, R.I. His father was Jeremiah Cohan and his mother was Helen Costigan Cohan, both in legit and vaudeville. His sister was Josie Cohan, also an actress.

By the time he was eight years old he was playing second fiddle in an orchestra for 'Daniel Boone on the Trail' and shortly thereafter appeared in velveteen pants as 'Master Georgie — Violin Tricks and Tinkling Tunes.' At 11 he was in vaudeville as a buck and wing dancer. Two years later he was the star of 'Peck's Bad Boy' and at 15 he made his Broadway debut at Keith's as a 'song and dance artist.'

There is only one epitaph Cohan would wish—that he would be remembered as America's greatest song and dance man. Early in his youth he was cocky; but he was able, too, and he never fooled himself into believing that he was a great artist or anything else save a topnotch theatrical craftsman.

Within a few years after his first Broadway appearance with his sister in 'The Lively Bootblack,' he was playing with 'The Four Cohans' and had created his novel curtain speech, 'My mother thanks you, my father thanks you, my sister thanks you, and I thank you.'

QUARRELED WITH MANAGERS

During these days he always wore a derby hat or a straw topper pulled down over his right eye. He delivered his wisecracks out of the right side of his mouth and carried a cane.

Sometimes when the Four Cohans were given the first spot in vaudeville, he would quarrel savagly with theatre managers and frequently announced that he was quitting the stage. Once or twice he did quit, but he couldn't stay away longer than six months. Sometimes he told managers he would be famous some day and come back and buy the house 'just so I can throw you out.'

Once he sent a song to Witmark's, which the music firm accepted and published. It came out with entirely new lyrics, however, and Cohan was furious. In 1919, 25 years later, Witmark's asked him to revise an operetta then called 'Cherry Blossoms.' He might have remembered then the rewriting of his own cherished lyrics, for he practically rewrote 'Cherry Blossoms' and it emerged as 'The Royal Vagabond,' to become a smash hit.

At 26 Cohan really began stepping out in the theatre. He joined forces with Sam H. Harris (they were both broke at the time) and put on 'Little Johnny Jones,' which turned out to be a hit despite the lukewarm attitude of the critics. Cohan and Harris remained together for 15 years. After being apart 18 years they joined hands again in 1937 to produce 'Fulton of Oak Falls.'

During his 50 years in the theatre Cohan acted in more than 5,000 performances. He wrote or produced or collaborated on 100 plays and composed 300 songs. Critics are divided on his greatest performance, but he did score effectively in his 'Seven Keys to Baldpate,' in 1913, and 'Song and Dance Man,' which he wrote in memory of his father, in 1923. Other plays which won him acclaim were 'Ah, Wilderness,' by Eugene O'Neill, and 'I'd Rather Be Right,' in 1937.

WAS TWICE MARRIED

He was married twice, first to Ethel Levey, vaudeville actress, by whom he had a daughter, Georgiana. He married Agnes Nolan, of Boston, in 1907 and there were three children from that marriage, George, Jr., Helen and Mary.

He was making big money as far back as the time of his second marriage, when he was reputed to have an income of $500,000 a year.

His most famous song was 'Over There,' which he wrote in 1917. Congress voted him a medal later, which was presented to him by President Franklin D. Roosevelt on May 1, 1940. Cohan was modest about the honor, insisting that if he 'hadn't written it on Thursday, somebody else would have written it on Friday. It just had to come.' He also admitted then that he was 'pretty handy at song-writing.' As he accepted the medal he said, 'I hope America will never need another war song. But if we do need one, it will

---

OPPORTUNITY FOR ACTORS WISHING TO BE SEEN
Important Broadway Play
READINGS STARTING MONDAY, NOV. 9
Courtesy to Agents
THE MARY STEWART PLAYHOUSE
1737 N. HIGHLAND AVE.　　　HOllywood 0681

1882　John Barrymore　1942

◆ Continued from page 1 ◆

pleted until he had to be taken almost forcibly to the hospital for his last fight. On May 19, suffering wracking pain, Barrymore went through the entire preview of the Rudy Vallee ether show for the next day. When he finished, those on the show knew he would not be back to play it. But John seemed to sense that he owed a duty to his public. He said to Dick Mack, 'When do I go through this again?' Smilingly, and knowing he was tampering with the truth, Mack said, 'Jack, you were perfect. We won't have to do it again. Next week we'll have another show.' But Barrymore, swollen with pain, said, 'Stop kiddin', Dick, I've another show to do.'

That was John Barrymore—a trouper to the end. He had a colorful career in the theatre and on the screen. He always made good newspaper copy, as well as never intentionally doing anything to hurt show biz.

John Barrymore is gone, but the other two members of the Royal Family will carry on the tradition of the clan, one of the most outstanding in show biz.

—A. U.

Obituary

JOHN BARRYMORE

John Barrymore makes his final exit at 11 a.m. tomorrow, when funeral services for the great actor will be held at Calvary cemetery.

Starting at 7 o'clock last night and continuing through today, Barrymore's body lies in state at Pierce Brothers chapel, 720 West Washington blvd., but only relatives and close friends are being permitted to view the body.

Funeral arrangements call for a simple and private ceremony, with requiem mass being celebrated by Father John O'Donnell, pastor of Immaculate Heart church, in Calvary Mausoleum chapel.

Active pallbearers will be John Decker, Gene Fowler, E. J. Mannix, W. C. Fields, C. J. Brider and Stanley Campbell. Honorary pallbearers are Edward Sheldon, Charles MacArthur, Roland Young, Thomas Mitchell, Alan Mowbray, Ben Hecht, Arthur Hopkins, George M. Cohan, Herbert Bayard Swope and Bramwell Fletcher.

The chapel where final services over Barrymore will be read accommodates only about 75 persons. Among those to whom invitations have been sent and who are expected to be present are: Fredric March, Clark Gable, Herbert Marshall, George Cukor, Errol Flynn, Katharine Hepburn, L. B. Mayer, Greta Garbo, David O. Selznick, Spencer Tracy, Rudy Vallee, Nunnally Johnson and A. Edward Sutherland.

Death came to the great actor at 10:20 p.m. Friday at Hollywood hospital, which he had entered May 19 following a sudden collapse brought on by an attack of the kidney and liver ailment from which he had suffered for years.

Almost from the moment of his collapse, hope for his survival had been abandoned. Although he rallied sharply for a few days early last week, physicians told Barrymore at 7 a.m. on May 21 that he could not live.

'Send for Diana and let me say goodbye to her,' Barrymore ordered, when told that he was facing death. 'When she's gone I'll stage for you the greatest death scene you ever saw, greater than that in Henry VIII.'

But John never played that scene. He failed so rapidly after his brief rally that he made his exit with but one line, albeit a line that summed up in just four words the whole philosophy behind an amazing life: 'It's a wonderful place.'

Death followed but a few hours after the actor received the last sacrament of his church from the hands of an old friend, Father O'Donnell. At the deathbed were only his older brother, Lionel, and his physician, Dr. Hugo M. Kersten. His daughter, Diana Barrymore, was in the hospital, as were three of his closest friends, Gene Fowler, novelist; John Decker, artist, and Alan Mowbray, actor. His sister, Ethel, in Boston, closed her play there Saturday night.

Born Feb. 15, 1882, in Philadelphia, John Barrymore was a son of America's first and greatest theatrical family. His father was Maurice Barrymore, his mother Georgianna Drew. Death of his mother while he was still a small boy left his early training in the hands of his maternal grandmother, Louisa Lane Drew, also a famous actress.

Art, in which he remained interested all his life, claimed Barrymore's first interest, although he took part in backyard theatricals with Lionel and his sister, Ethel, both older than he. John studied art in Europe, was recalled by his father when his bills assumed unwarranted proportions. He started his career as a cartoonist on the New York Journal under Arthur Brisbane, who fired him, urging Barrymore to follow in the theatrical footsteps of the rest of the family.

Barrymore was 21 when his stage career began. And he had but indifferent success until a role in 'The Dictator' allowed him scope for his comedy talents. In this play he toured America and Australia, returning to appear in 'Stubborn Cinderella' and 'The Fortune Hunter', the latter vehicle definitely launching him as a star.

'Kick In', 'Justice', 'Peter Ibbet-

Fri., Dec. 15, 1944 — DAILY VARIETY

AMERICAN MAJORS DOING $5,000,000 BIZ IN BRAZIL

New York, Dec. 14. — Business being done by American majors in Brazil is now running between $5,000,000 and $6,000,000 annually, a 40% increase over pre-war rental receipts, Sigwart Kusiel, general manager for Columbia in Brazil, stated here yesterday at a press interview.

He predicts that there will be a substantial further increase after victory when there will be additional theatres in that country. During the past five years 50 new houses have been built and plans are in work for 20 more. Total now is 1,500.

Kusiel, who is here for three weeks of home office conferences, does not vision any governmental control for the picture industry in Brazil.

'Spirit' Cast Complete

Universal completed casting for "That's the Spirit" yesterday with setting of June Vincent, Gene Lockhart, Edith Barret and Andy Devine. Film rolls Dec. 18 with Charles Lamont directing.

"THE PICTURE BOOK HOME"
EARLY AMERICAN, created by famed Architect and Decorator, 27 ft. living room, chummy den with fireplace, 2 bedrooms with large closets and adjacent sundecks. Harmonizing colors throughout. Wide lot. Pecan trees, etc. Near markets, transportation. Price $21,000 including rugs, curtains and drapes.
SU 22015   ED B. WELCOME   SU 16828
12240 Ventura Blvd.

CORONER ORDERS AUTOPSY IN DEATH OF LUPE VELEZ

An autopsy was ordered yesterday on the body of Lupe Velez, 36, found dead in her Beverly Hills home yesterday. Two phials of sleeping tablets, bearing labels showing they had originated in Mexico, were found in the star's home, Chief C. H. Anderson of Beverly Hills Police Department said. One of the phials was empty and the other contained three of the pills. It is believed the tablets were taken by the actress and were the cause of her death.

Mexican star was discovered by her housekeeper about 10 a.m. when she went to awaken her. Getting no response from the actress, the housekeeper called the Beverly Hills police station, and coroner estimated death had occurred approximately two hours before the body was discovered.

FAREWELL LETTERS

Beside the bed on which the body lay were two notes. One was addressed to Harold (Harold Ramond, the star's latest heart interest) and the other to Mrs. Kinder, long-time friend and confidante of Miss Velez. First note read:

"Harold:
"May God forgive you and forgive me but I prefer to take my life away and our baby's before I bring him with shame or killing him. How could you, Harold, fake such great love for me and our baby when all the time you didn't want us? I see no other way out for me, so goodbye and good luck to you. Love.
"Lupe."

The second note, which was addressed to Mrs. Kinder, read:

"My dear friend, Mrs. Kinder:
"My faithful friend, you and only you know the facts for the reason I am taking my life. May God forgive me and don't think bad of me. I love you many. Take care of my mother. Say goodbye and try to forgive me. Say goodbye to all my friends and the American press that were always so nice to me.
"Lupe."

"P.S.: Take care of Chips and Chops."

Chips and Chops were the actress's two dogs.

HER LAST PHONE CALLS

Mrs. Kinder, it is understood, received a call from Miss Velez four hours before her death. She had called to say good night. At that time the actress gave no hint of her impending action, according to Hallam Cooley, agent for the actress.

Born Lupe Velez de Villalobos in San Luis Potosi, Mexico, Miss Velez started her entertainment career in Mexico City in the musical comedy "Rataplan." Coming to Hollywood, she appeared in "The Music Box Revue," staged by Fanchon & Marco, and then was chosen by Douglas Fairbanks to star as the fiery mountain girl in his film, "The Gaucho," in 1927, after she had appeared in several Hal Roach comedies.

Following her screen bow she appeared in "Stand and Deliver," "Masquerade" and "The Wolf Song."

"SPITFIRE" LAST PIX

Her career in films took her to every major studio, and she had last worked in "Mexican Spitfire" series at RKO. She was married to Johnny Weissmuller for several years, but the marriage ended finally after three divorce suits had been instituted.

She is survived by her mother, Josefina, who lives in San Luis Potosi, and her two sisters, Josefina and Queenie, who lived with her, and one brother.

CLEAN HOUSE WINDOWS, CEILINGS, WALLS AND FLOOR WAXING. ALSO WEEKLY SERVICE
CEntury 24692

Film Review

Dancing In Manhattan
(Comedy Drama)

COLUMBIA RELEASE. Producer, Wallace MacDonald. Director, Henry Levin. Original screenplay, Erna Lazarus. Photography, L. W. O'Connell. Film editor, Richard Fantl. Art director, George Brooks. Set decorations, George Montgomery. Assistant director, Ivan Volkman. Sound engineer, Lodge Cunningham.
CAST—Features Fred Brady, Jeff Donnell, William Wright, Ann Savage, Cy Kendall, with Howard Freeman, Eddie Kane, Sally Bliss, Adelle Roberts, Jean Stevens, George McKay, Dorothy Vaughan.
REVIEWED at Grauman's Chinese, Hollywood, Dec. 14, 1944. Running time: 60 MINS.

"Dancing In Manhattan" is first-rate supporting fare, containing many chuckles and a fast pace that makes for advantageous spotting on twin bills. Wallace MacDonald's production guidance gives full value for the budget allotment, and Henry Levin's direction gets the best from the excellent original script by Erna Lazarus. Making a strong bid for not too far distant screen prominence is Fred Brady, a personable young man who does a deft job in the lead role.

When a young garbage collector (Brady) finds a nice roll of lettuce worth $5,000 in refuse from a night club he promptly quits his job, drags his girl away from her package-wrapping job and they step out for an evening of high living. Roll of money found its way into garbage when blackmailers William Wright and Ann Savage discovered police were wise to payoff by victim Howard Freeman at the night club. Crooks and the detective, Cy Kendall, soon trace Brady, and efforts of Wright and Miss Savage to recover money, not knowing it's marked, add laugh suspense. Finale comes when crooks grab what's left of the bankroll and the cops move in for the arrest.

Brady milks the easy chuckles as the brash garbage expert trying to turn society for a night. Jeff Donnell gets in her moments of fun as his slightly bewildered best girl. Wright and Miss Savage do smooth chores as the heavies. Kendall's detective job is excellent. Freeman, the victim; Eddie Kane, Sally Bliss, Adelle Roberts, Jean Stevens, George McKay and Dorothy Vaughan add capable support to principals.

Photography by L. W. O'Connell, Richard Fantl's film editing, art direction and sets, etc., count in giving expert quality touch to this programmer.

Tinturin In Civvies

Peter Tinturin, composer with 60 picture scores to his credit, was discharged from Army yesterday, following two years with Signal Corps. He will continue his career here.

Photography
by
RUSSELL METTY

THE MASTER RACE

JAMES B. CASSIDY
Presents
FRANCIS LEDERER   PHILIP MERIVALE
DALE MELBOURNE
LYLE TALBOT   JANE DARWELL
in
— Ibsens Immortal Stage Play —
"A DOLL'S HOUSE"
BILTMORE THEATRE ONE WEEK ONLY — DEC. 17 TO 23

1950s

Today, the souvenir shops on Hollywood Boulevard are filled with watches, key chains, lighters, commemorative plates, and T-shirts bearing the images of stars. And none are more popular than James Dean, Marilyn Monroe, and Elvis Presley. That showbiz holy trinity has endured long past other celebs, including those who rose to fame many years after them. All three were talented, all were sexy, all died at relatively young ages—and all three were products of the 1950s. What is it about that decade that still intrigues and confuses us so much?

Though suburbia was springing up in the postwar prosperity and families tried to keep an upbeat and calm aura, there was turmoil beneath the tranquility. While such 1970s works as *Grease* and *Happy Days* portrayed the 1950s as a carefree time of hot rods, malt shops, and rock and roll, it was the era of the Cold War, Nikita Krushchev, Fidel Castro, and the Joseph McCarthy anti-Communist witch-hunts—in other words, sociopolitical fear and repression. It was the decade of Rosa Parks, Jack Kerouac, Disneyland, Hugh Hefner, *Lolita*, Sidney Poitier, quiz-show scandals, Samuel Beckett, Hula-Hoops, *The Lord of the Rings*, *Lord of the Flies*, Cinerama, Technicolor, Jerry Lewis, Audrey Hepburn, beatniks, LEGO, Grace Kelly and Prince Rainier of Monaco, Alfred E. Newman, "the Golden Age of Television," and the Ricardos and the Mertzes.

Does this seem confusing and contradictory? Yessiree-bop, it was both squaresville and crazytown, and that's how it felt to those who lived through it.

The decade got off to an ominous start in 1950 when Senator Joseph McCarthy (R-Wisconsin) claimed to have a list of members of the Communist party who were working in the State Department.

The rumblings had started a few years earlier. On June 22, 1948, *Daily Variety* ran an ad taken out by the so-called Hollywood Ten, bemoaning the "first mass victims" of the House Committee on Un-American Activities. That's it's real name, though it's been abbreviated as HUAC. I guess HCUA was too hard to pronounce....

> "History may record it as ironic, but perhaps it is only fitting that the first mass victims of the House Committee on Un-American

Right: James Dean.

OPEN LETTER

JUNE 22, 1948

TO ELEVEN HONORABLE AND DISTINGUISHED AMERICANS WHO ARE ABOUT TO SERVE THEIR COUNTRY BY ENTERING FEDERAL PRISON

Greetings:

To Dr. Edward K. Barsky, Chairman of the Joint Anti-Fascist Refugee Committee and Board members:

Howard Fast	Dr. Jacob Auslander	Ruth Leider
James Lustig	Marjorie Chodorov	Harry Justiz
Dr. Louis Miller	Charlotte Stern	Manuel Magana
	Dr. Lyman Bradley	

HISTORY MAY RECORD it as ironic, but perhaps it is only fitting that the first mass victims of the House Committee on un-American Activities should consist of the following:

Three noted physicians
A world-renowned author who has chosen to celebrate American democracy in his novels
A housewife
Two trade union organizers, A.F. of L. and C.I.O.
A business man
Two attorneys
A professor of Languages at New York University

LET US RECORD THE CRIMES FOR WHICH YOU ARE NOW TO BE IMPRISONED:
FOR TEN YEARS YOU ADMINISTERED RELIEF to the Republican refugees from Franco Spain. You supplied them with hospital beds, physicians, bandages, clothes, medicine . . . <u>CRIME!</u>

YOUR CHARITABLE WORK has been executed abroad by the UNITARIAN SERVICE COMMITTEE and the QUAKERS. Your records have been regularly inspected by the U. S. GOVERNMENT AGENCY that licensed your work . . . <u>CRIME!</u>

BUT THE THOMAS COMMITTEE announced that opposition to the Franco government is un-American and subversive. The Thomas Committee demanded your books and records.

AS HONORABLE MEN AND WOMEN you refused to hand over to this committee the names of decent, humane Americans who had contributed funds for this medical aid . . . in order to protect your donors from persecution, investigation and black-listing . . . <u>CRIME!</u>

AS ANTI-FASCIST AMERICANS you refused to hand over to the announced friends of Franco those names of Spaniards who had received your aid . . . lest their families inside Spain be reached in reprisal by Franco's executioners . . . <u>CRIME!</u>

AND NOW, convicted of Contempt of Congress, your court appeals denied, you are to go to prison. Six months for Dr. Barsky. Three months for the Executive Board.

WE HONOR YOUR "CRIMES." We honor Americans who have not forgotten the tradition of liberty, the tradition of Jefferson and Paine, Emerson and John Brown, Garrison and Thoreau.

WE PROTEST the shame of our nation that sends you to prison while fifteen American Fascists who spoke treason over the Italian, German and Japanese radios during the war are at Liberty.

WE ASK ALL CITIZENS OF GOOD-WILL to telegraph the President and urge that he extend pardons for the honor of the country.

WE ASK CITIZENS OF LOS ANGELES to come to the Embassy Auditorium, 847 Grand Ave., at 8:00 P.M. on Monday, June 28, to honor you and to ask the President for a redress of grievances.

WE SALUTE you with respect and pride.

Alvah Bessie	Edward Dmytryk	Samuel Ornitz
Herbert Biberman	Ring Lardner, Jr.	Adrian Scott
Lester Cole	John Howard Lawson	Dalton Trumbo
	Albert Maltz	

IN ASSOCIATION WITH THE ARTS, SCIENCES AND PROFESSIONS COUNCIL
1515 CROSSROADS OF THE WORLD—HOLLYWOOD 28, CALIF.

"Activities should consist of the following: Three noted physicians, a world-renowned author who has chosen to celebrate American democracy in his novels, a housewife, two trade union organizers, A.F. of L. and CIO; a business man; two attorneys; a professor of languages at New York University . . ."

Left: June 22, 1948.

Above: Will the real Charlie Chaplin please stand up?

Below: Everyone likes colorful profits.

The ad extolled their accomplishments and urged protests of their impending imprisonment.

The anti-Commie hunt shifted into high gear in the early 1950s. On April 11, 1950, *Daily Variety* ran the headline "Supreme Court Nixes Lawson-Trumbo Appeal; Ten Scribes Face Jail Time." The front-page story reminded readers that, in October 1947, the House had issued contempt citations for the ten, who refused to answer the question whether or not they were Communists. John Howard Lawson and Dalton Trumbo were tried and convicted in October 1948 while the other eight never went to trial, agreeing to let their fate be tied in with the decision of the duo, who had appealed. The Supreme Court refused to hear the case so the paper concluded on April 10: "It means they will all probably go to jail for a year and pay a $1,000 fine for contempt of Congress."

No one in Hollywood felt safe. Even future icons such as Katharine Hepburn and Lucille Ball were under suspicion. But the highest-profile target of HUAC was Charlie Chaplin.

Chaplin's morals had been under scrutiny for a long time. Actress Joan Barry filed a 1943 paternity suit against him. Though blood tests proved he wasn't the father, the results weren't admissible in court and he was ordered to pay child support. That same year, Chaplin, aged fifty-four, married Eugene O'Neill's eighteen-year-old daughter. It was his third (or fourth) marriage. (Chaplin and Paulette Goddard had been together for nine years, claiming to be married, though some contemporaries were dubious.) And as if that wasn't enough, he never publicly supported the U.S. war effort during World War II, but he did support Russia. Russia had been fighting off Nazis at the time he offered his support, but after the war, Russia was still Russia.

After Chaplin traveled to Europe in 1952, he was told he couldn't return to the United States. On October 3, *Daily Variety* on page two reported a D.C. press conference during which Attorney General James P. McGranery said it was a question of "morals," referring to Chaplin as "a menace to womanhood," and said that the Department of Justice planned to deport one hundred "unsavory characters"—mostly gangsters—who were foreign born. Chaplin fit into that category.

On the same issue, Assistant Secretary of State Howland H. Sargeant seemed to contradict McGranery, saying Chaplin "has every State Dept.

COLOR . . . For Extra Profits *Color by* **Cinecolor** for the lowest color cost in the industry

paper he needs to get back into the country," and that it was actually the Department of Defense that deemed him a security risk.

The same issue carried two other reports: a pair of "friendly" witnesses volunteered the names of twenty-five members of screen and radio "cells" of the Communist party, while a new pact among the four major networks and National TV Committee included a clause that the networks "will not use political criteria as a basis for employment."

In 1953, Arthur Miller's *The Crucible* debuted, a play theoretically about the Salem witch trials but actually a thinly veiled indictment of HUAC hysteria and finger-pointing.

In April of that year, Chaplin got his first defender in Hollywood: Samuel Goldwyn said Chaplin's U.S. exit was a great loss because he is "the greatest artist we have ever had." At a press conference, Goldwyn added Chaplin was a sometimes "misguided liberal, but no Communist."

Weekly Variety, November 21, 1951, reported that CBS had, a year earlier, asked staffers to sign a loyalty oath, but there were unconfirmed reports whether there was a policy on performers working for just one-shot work. The actors' guilds are "increasingly fearful of the dangers inherent in the 'clearance' policies" and were figuring out a strategy. Meanwhile, some directors and casting supervisors were thwarted in attempts to cast actors who were not listed in the can't-hire roster *Red Channels*, giving rise to a fear that agencies and sponsors may have their own private blacklists, apart from the *Red Channels* listings, to prevent actors they suspect of Red leanings from appearing on TV.

The hysteria eventually died down in 1954, due in large part to TV and its live broadcast coverage of the Army-McCarthy hearings. Senator Stuart Symington told McCarthy, "The American public have had a look at you for six weeks. You are not fooling anyone." And, under questioning, Joseph N. Welch asked, "Have you no sense of decency, sir, at long last?" Respected journalist Edward R. Murrow aired specials that took a hard look at McCarthy and his tactics. Like all bullies, McCarthy and his cohorts eventually crumpled, but the damning blacklists stayed in place for years afterward.

TV grew increasingly important to the American public. Though it took off in the late 1940s, fueled by Milton Berle's *Texaco Star Theater*, nobody in the industry was quite sure what to do with the medium. Some thought it should become an educational tool; others thought it could become basically radio with visuals. Naturally, the latter argument won out because there was more money to be made that way.

On April 5, 1950, *Weekly Variety* ran a story that proved "radio and television outlets, operated side by side, can both do good business." The story said NBC's AM station, WNBC, and its TV outlet, WNBT, had both signed a number of advertisers "in a flurry of spring billings." Among the TV station's renewals: Bulova, generally credited with creating the first TV ad to air on a commercially licensed TV station. Bulova is said to have paid nine dollars to run the ad on WNBT during a 1941 Brooklyn Dodgers-Philadelphia Phillies baseball game, which showed a U.S. map and the slogan "America runs on Bulova time."

The startup TV networks wanted to transfer radio successes like George Burns and Gracie Allen, Jack Benny, *Our Miss Brooks*, and *The Lone*

Below: Remember "film?"

Right: July 12, 1950.

| FILMS | RADIO | VIDEO | MUSIC | STAGE |

VARIETY

Published Weekly at 154 West 46th Street, New York 19, N. Y., by Variety, Inc. Annual subscription, $10. Single copies, 25 cents.
Entered as second class matter December 22, 1905, at the Post Office at New York, N. Y., under the act of March 3, 1879.
COPYRIGHT, 1950, BY VARIETY, INC. ALL RIGHTS RESERVED

VOL. 179 No. 5 — NEW YORK, WEDNESDAY, JULY 12, 1950 — PRICE 25 CENTS

VIDEO NOW VAUDE'S VILLAIN

NBC Planning Star Suds Sagas In Drive for Housewife Audience

Hollywood, July 11.
Stars in the suds is the new soap opera formula. Top Hollywood names—including Mary Pickford, Rosalind Russell, Charles Boyer, Burt Lancaster and Gloria Swanson—may soon be bending over the washboard weepers as part of a new NBC daytime programming offensive.

The plan follows completion by the web of a special survey, which covered rating histories for the past four years and reveals that the sentimental sagas continue tops in before-dark audience preferences. To the proven appeal of the serials, NBC's AM program veepee Bud Barry now wants to add the lure of established picture personalities.

Miss Pickford is being mulled as narrator of "The Bough Breaks," an airer dealing with the problems of divorce. Miss Russell would star in "Boss Lady," dramatizing a career woman's life. And Miss Swanson would play in a strip on which romantic and family problems would be enacted, with the screen actress then giving her solution.

Lancaster is being considered for "The Doctor," expansion of a half-hour once-weekly show NBC has
(Continued on page 47)

Oiler's Dramatic Series From H'wood First War Casualty

Hollywood, July 11.
First TV casualty attributable to the shooting war in Korea is "Writers Theatre," half-hour dramatic series, which was, to all intents and purposes, sold, sealed and delivered. A major oil company "firmed" the deal but at 11th hour abandoned it temporarily after a hastily-called board meeting in New York.

If conditions improve in the Pacific between now and September, the contracts may be called up for signing. Time had been reserved on one of the networks and series was to be filmed in Hollywood but oilmen decreed this is no time for an entry into television.

Paul and Jack Warwick came out from N. Y. to negotiate the deal with Don Sharpe, agenting for "Writers Theatre," and returned with everything they needed except what they needed most—the sponsor's John Henry.

DECCA'S '45' DECISION LAID TO WAR SITUATION

War situation in Korea and its threatening implications are regarded in industry circles as a key factor in Decca's decision to convert to 45 rpm. (Details in Music section).

War threat means shortage of shellac which comes largely from the Far East. The new platters represent at least a 25% material saving.

Bea Lillie's U. S. Nitery Bow at Persian Rm., N.Y.

Beatrice Lillie looks set to reopen the Henry Dreyfus-redecorated Persian Room of the Hotel Plaza, N. Y., this fall. It is a matters of terms now. This would set back Celeste Holm, who can only do the supper show because of her legit commitment, "Affairs of State," a straight play.

Marlene Dietrich nixed the Plaza's bid, stating she is not a saloon artist. This marks Miss Lillie's debut in U. S. cafes, although she has worked in London niteries.

Miami 'Summer Resort' Bally Now Paying Off

By LARY SOLLOWAY
Miami Beach, July 10.
The greater Miami area seems to have come into its own as a summer (as well as winter) resort, with the twin cities and other South Florida sun-fun spots jammed with tourists from the majority of the 48 states. Influx can be credited to all-out ad campaigns by the airlines and heavy expenditures on space by agencies handling the resort cities, as well as all Florida.

With the jamup, which began in mid-June, reports by the leading hostelries indicate this sector of the country can look to heavy biz until end of August. It is the first time in the area's history that families are content to stay in and watch video rather than go out even for an inexpensive evening.
(Continued on page 53)

Conrads Quit Show Biz For Volunteers of America

Detroit, July 11.
William Conrad, former trumpeter with name bands, and his wife, Marianne Dunn, former torch singer, have renounced the dance band world for the Volunteers of America. They're now stationed at Detroit.

The pair were "converted" by a minister of the Evangelical United Brethren Church. Conrad now works with truck collectors. His wife, a blonde looker, serves in the group's public school clothing center.

Miss Dunn's parents, Major and Mrs. John H. Dunn, were former vaudevillians. They're in the Volunteers in Akron.

Conrad played with Gene Krupa, Ted Weems, Joe Venuti, Frankie Masters and others. Miss Dunn sang with Jack Teagarden, Ted Weems and others. She appeared in "Birth of the Blues" (Par), with Bing Crosby in 1942.

ACTS AND AGENTS FEAR TV INROADS

Talent agency men are beginning to worry about the effects of television variety shows on the vaude industry. Tele's free shows are proving too much competition to theatres. While many are still saying that video is trailerizing live talent and effects won't be fully noted for some time, a pessimistic note is currently clouding the thinking on that subject.

Reason for an increasing doubt as to the efficacy of tele as an aid to stage shows has come with the realization that the current summer is one of the worst that vaudeville has experienced since the depth of the depression. Bookings, except for New York and Chicago, and a handful of theatres in scattered cities, have been steadily dwindling. The fall is expected to see an upswing, but whether the increase will hold up in view of the expensive vaudeo shows set for the fall, remains to be seen.

Agency men feel that there's no remedy in sight for tele's boxoffice inroads. It may be possible to overcome the slim b.o. by top film names, but most aren't taking to theatre dates and those that might turn the tide are demanding prohibitive guarantees.

Percenters are looking for some idea, such as the swing band vogue, which when introduced in 1936 brought hefty grosses into vauders and helped open up a multitude of time throughout the country. Today, only a handful of bands can draw heavy grosses.

Some agency men feel that while tele is cutting into theatre grosses, basic reason for decline in vauders is tied in with the general economy. Costs of necessities are still high and amount of money available for entertainment is believed to be at a low ebb. It's declared that because of high prices, many families are content to stay in and watch video rather than go out even for an inexpensive evening.

Lower prices for television sets and lineup of top talent to be preemed in the fall indicate to the percenters that the worst is still to come.

Foy's Feel for Felons

Chicago, July 11.
Let Bryan Foy smell a new angle on a prison yarn and it would take an Alcatraz to hold him back. That's how come the Warner Bros. producer arrived here this week, less than 48 hours after four inmates at the Marquette prison in Marquette, Mich., attempted to take Gov. G. Mennen Williams as a hostage while he was on an inspection tour.

Foy, whose production activities have taken him in and out of more jails than a four-time offender, is here to get more dope on the Marquette incident and will head to Michigan this week for a first-hand look.

20th-Fox Brass Huddling on Pix-TV; Films for Video Seen Possibility

Margaret Truman's Commercial TV Bow

Washington, July 11.
Margaret Truman is set to make her debut on a commercial video variety show on Ed Sullivan's "Toast of the Town" over CBS, Oct. 29.

Daughter of Pres. Truman has made an occasional tele appearance, but this will be her first on a program without a public-service aspect. Miss Truman appeared several years ago on a telecast of a Boy Scout conclave at Madison Square Garden, N. Y.

NBC $2,000,000 Bid for Schnoz? Vamps M-G Pact

New wave of bidding between NBC and CBS for services of Jimmy Durante on TV broke out anew this week following reports from the Coast that the comedian had bought up his contract from Metro at $75,000, making him a free agent in the video programming sweepstakes. M-G contract still had a year to go.

Durante recently broke off with his Camel radio sponsor because of his refusal to turn over TV rights to the tobacco company upon expiration of his Metro contract.

NBC reportedly has the inside track on Durante's services, with a figure of $2,000,000 for an exclusive AM-TV contract prominently mentioned. If Joe McConnell & Co. grab him off, it's expected that he'll join the round-robin of comics (Fred Allen, Eddie Cantor, etc.) in the Sunday night 8 to 9 Colgate series.

Goldwyn, Jr's Foreign Pic Snafued By War Crisis

First projected pic to feel the axe as a result of increasingly international tension in recent months is "No Time Like the Present," which was to be Sam Goldwyn, Jr.'s, initialer under his father's banner. Young Goldwyn had planned to make the postwar yarn in Italy, Germany and Hollywood, but has found recent international pressure too great to enable him to draw all the ends of his project together.

Goldwyn, Jr., returned to New York last week from several months spent abroad working on the story and trying to set up his production. Army and occupation authorities have discouraged him from going ahead. He's planning to return to Hollywood shortly to set up a new project under his deal with his father.

Hollywood, July 11.
Entire relationship between films and television will get a onceover by 20th-Fox's top executives here this week, with a possibility that out of the huddles may come a decision to produce films specifically for video. Prez Spyros Skouras and veepee Al Lichtman flew in yesterday (Mon.) from the homeoffice to join studio exec Joseph M. Schenck and production veepee Darryl F. Zanuck in the discussions.

Twentieth toppers will also review production plans in line with impending divorcement, as well as blueprints for expanded studio facilities. Provision of more space for production was ordered some months ago by Zanuck and Skouras at a cost of $6,000,000 to enable 20th to boost its production and releasing rate. Series of huddles here follows Schenck's decision last week to remain with the studio instead of ankling 20th to devote full time to his theatre interests.

Twentieth's entry into the making of films specifically for TV is believed to have been greenlighted two weeks ago with announcement of production plans for a series of religious films. Pix, to be made at 20th's Beverly Hills studios under
(Continued on page 53)

Berle Unit Into Roxy At $27,500 Plus %; New Try to Make Tele Pay

Milton Berle has been set to play the Roxy theatre, N. Y., starting Aug. 18.

It's his first date at that house in nearly three years and first New York vaudate since he started on video for Texaco. He'll get $27,500 plus percentages and will pay for several supporting acts. Latter haven't been set as yet. It's a straight two-week stand, without options. Film slated for the Berle run is "Stella."

Berle's booking represents a further attempt by Roxy booker, Sammy Rauch, to cash in on television headliners. Previous attempts by the Roxy to lure biz with TV names have met with varying success. House didn't click with its presentation of the Ken Murray show, but succeeding program headed by Sid Caesar, Imogene Coca and Faye Emerson fared better. House hit nicely with the CBS "Lucky Pup" display (Bunin Puppets) coupled with Robert Merrill, whose Met rep has been enhanced by video appearances.

Berle's previous stand at the Roxy grossed $463,000 in four weeks with the film "Foxes of Harrow" (20th). It's problematic whether the same kind of tally can be racked up these days because of downbeat in theatre attendance.

Comedian left for a short vacation on the Coast yesterday (Tues.).

DAILY Variety

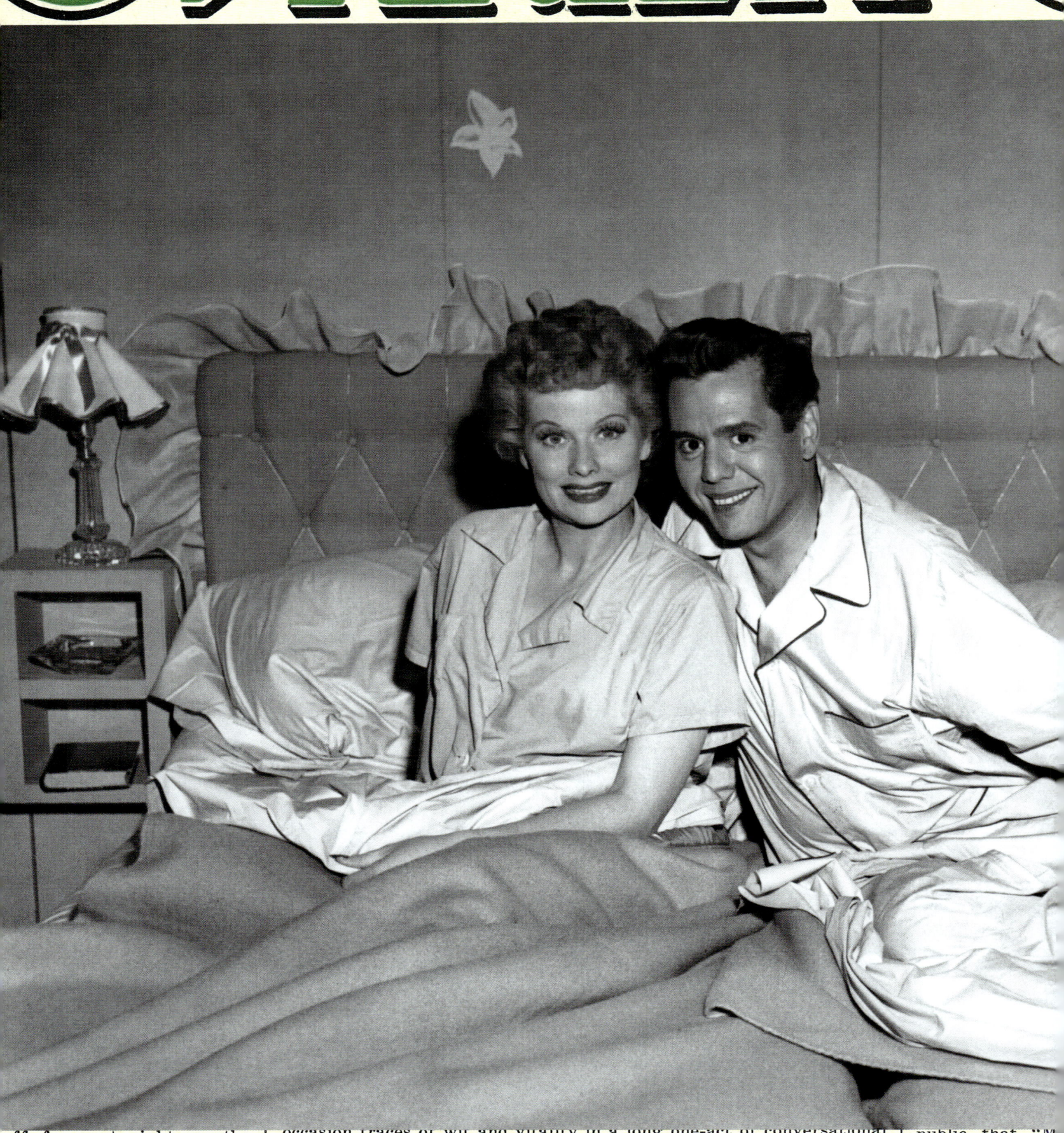

off for past eight months, osed just as contracts were e inked, according to Roy all, IB head locally. Tindall CBS had agreed to all de- ls of the new contract but at ast minute refused to recog- the NLRB's certification of IB's jurisdiction over web's o's B and C—used almost ely for television.

occasion traces of wit and vitality in a long one-act of conversational fluff. If play is comparable to Fry's recent London smash, "The Lady's Not for Burning," Broadway is in for a major letdown when John Gielgud brings "Lady" here next Fall.

"Phoenix," satirical treatment of Petronius story, is blank-verse spoof of how a young Greek widow, preparing to sacrifice herself on husband's grave, decides she prefers life after having a drink with a handsome young soldier. Nina Foch, Vicki Cummings and Richard Derr are ingratiating in overlong piece that probably not even Lunt, Fontanne and Gertie Lawrence could quite put across. Kenneth

(Continued on Back Page)

public that "M given "art-hous fore general e The Charles Fe starring Orson Rep two years from release a lease engagem year ago. Firs will be in the area.

Above: We love Lucy and Desi.

Ranger to the television. CBS pursued Lucille Ball, a film actress who was in the hit radio show *My Favorite Husband*. Rather than adapt that series, Ball insisted that husband Desi Arnaz star with her in a live broadcast, every two weeks. Cigarette company Philip Morris, sponsoring the show, demanded a weekly series; Ball and Arnaz also wanted to work in Los Angeles, at a time when live broadcasts generally emanated from New York, since the East Coast accounted for the vast majority of the TV audience.

Everyone finally compromised to filming weekly episodes out of Los Angeles, but costs ballooned, and Ball and Arnaz were asked to take a salary cut. The couple and their business advisors came up with a plan: they would take the lower salary but would own the negative. CBS and Philip Morris agreed—because at that point, there were no such things as reruns. Who would watch a TV episode after it's already aired?

And so, once again, an entire industry was changed not by CEOs, not by money barons, but by artists trying to make a living.

On May 7, 1952, *Variety* reported that *I Love Lucy* was being watched in ten million U.S. homes, with 2.9 people viewing the comedy in each of those homes.

By any standard, the show was a phenomenon, but it also indicates the medium's growing popularity. In June 1951, there were an estimated thirteen million TV sets; by June 1953, there were twenty-five million homes (or 50 percent of U.S. homes) with sets.

On October 12, 1955, a story said that the Radio-Electronics-TV Manufacturers Association predicted eight million sets would be sold that year, with the first nine months of the year running 25 percent higher than the same period in 1954.

The December 5, 1955, *Daily Variety* front-page story confirmed that advertising tallies were just in for 1954 (yes, that's a year prior!) and, for the first time, TV overtook radio.

The early days of TV created some templates that would last seven decades: daytime talk shows and soap operas, the late-night comedy-interview shows like *Tonight* with Steve Allen then Jack Paar, the airing of old movies and, thanks to Arnaz and Ball, the invention of reruns.

Some hail this as the Golden Age of Television, giving the world talents including Neil Simon, Mel Brooks, Carl Reiner, and Woody Allen, who wrote for Sid Caesar's *Your Show of Shows*; Mary Martin's performance in *Peter Pan*; Julie Andrews's star-making turn in Rodgers and Hammerstein's *Cinderella*; original teleplays by Paddy Chayefsky, Rod Serling, Horton Foote, and Gore Vidal; work from directors including Sidney Lumet, John Frankenheimer, and Robert Mulligan; popular series like *Gunsmoke*; and high-class fare like *The Bell Telephone Hour* and concerts by Leonard Bernstein and Van Cliburn.

The popularity of *Gunsmoke* helped inspire TV westerns so much that the late 1950s and early 1960s saw a glut of primetime westerns. *Variety* used various "slanguage" terms like "oater" and "horse opera" to avoid constant repetition of "western." But within a few years, the audience had OD'd on the genre and terms like "oater" bit the dust.

Technically, TV ambitions were growing. In 1958, Robert A. Seidel, RCA executive vice president in charge of consumer products, met with five hundred distributors to show off the "RCA tv-radio-hi-fi line." He said hi-fi and transistor radio sales were booming and that record sales were at an all-time high. Though black-and-white TV set sales were down, color set purchases were growing. The meeting unveiled RCA's new seven-function remote control tuning unit, developed exclusively for the RCA color sets.

Viewers began to see the news of the world primarily through a TV lens. In February 13, 1952, *Weekly Variety* exclaimed,

> "First trans-oceanic tele transmission is expected to take place when Queen Elizabeth's coronation will be microwaved to the U.S. NBC is currently blueprinting the pickup of one of the most colorful ceremonies in the catalog of British pomp."

The network planned to use six DC-6 planes cruising at a height of 35,000 to 45,000 feet equipped with microwave equipment, with engineers to monitor the relays.

The following year, NBC scored another coup immediately after the death of Josef Stalin when its *Today* show offered excerpts from a 1944 interview he'd done with Eric Johnston, who had become president of the Motion Picture Association of America. Referring to the taped show as a "taper," *Variety* reported it "also was heard on the Mutual radio network the same day and Telenews Productions serviced TV stations across the country with an interview session with Johnston re Stalin."

An August 2, 1956, *Daily Variety* front-page item related,

> "The Egyptian seizure of the Suez Canal has led to a sudden demand for bookings on Louis de Rochemont's 26-minute documentary, 'Suez Canal,' according to producer, who is releasing film through his Louis de Rochemont Associates. . . . Film recently played five-month engagement with 'The Ladykillers' at Sutton Theatre. Color film, produced on location last year, depicts story of Ferdinand DeLesseps building the canal."

Songs on the hit parade reflected U.S. audiences' curiosity about other parts of the world: there were popular revivals of European oldies like "Isle of Capri," "La Vie en Rose," and "Fascination," plus new tunes like "Volare," "Chanson d'Amour," "Melodie d'Amour," "Non Dimenticar," "That's Amore," "I Love Paris," "Istanbul Not Constantinople," "Mambo Italiano," and "You Belong to Me," which opened with the line "Fly the ocean in a silver plane," a funny phrase signaling a time when a "silver plane" was still a novelty concept.

In truth, flying in a silver plane was a bit of a novelty. And as it became more affordable, travel increased, and this wanderlust, coupled with the threat to film biz from those dang TV sets, meant studios had to give audiences something spectacular, such as films with a big travelogue component (*Love Is a Many-Splendored Thing* (1955), *Three Coins in the Fountain* (1954), *King Solomon's Mines* (1950)).

Though film executives saw TV as competition, that didn't stop them from using the new technology. Exhibit A: On March 20, 1953, *Daily* marveled that

> "Oscar turned 26 last night and an estimated 91,000,000 people via TV and radio helped him celebrate. . . . And the film industry's cousin-by-marriage, and currently its chief competitor for the entertainment time of American audiences, made much of the excitement possible with a dazzling display of electronic ingenuity."

In the story, reporters Mike Kaplan and Bill Brogdon congratulated the Pantages audience for "remarkable self-control" in not waving at the cameras. "Bob Hope then took over as emcee to kid television, old movies and the crop of former screen greats now enjoying new careers via TV. He quoted Jack L. Warner's description of TV as 'the piece of furniture that stares back at you.'"

Hollywood was trying to define its relationship with the new medium.

Above: Grace Kelly.

Right: Rin Tin Tin.

Following Spread: There was a time when people didn't know who Audrey Hepburn or Rosemary Clooney were.

An August 9, 1950, article explained one reason for a jump in movie attendance, while also hinting that it might not last.

The story made a connection that might seem farfetched: the United States' invasion of South Korea was improving box office. But the story explained that improved attendance "is particularly noticeable in the west. That's in line with experience in World War II, when giant aircraft factories and other war industries hyped Coast biz. These plants again are starting up."

In other words, more jobs, more moviegoing.

But there was the TV question, called "video" at the time: "How severe a drain on the b.o. is being made by video continues subject to debate. Most theatre execs feel, however, that competition of other forms of summer amusement are having a considerably more serious effect than TV. They point out that in some medium-sized towns there are as many as 15 other forms of entertainment and sport for the public to choose from. These include roller derbies, harness racing, dog racing, night baseball, etc. While each may draw only a few thousand customers, the aggregate is a considerable drain on the film potential."

So the movie biz decided to lure audiences with razzle-dazzle.

On March 26, 1953, *Daily Variety* reported,

> "First major first-run theatre to swing into an exclusive 3-D policy will be Fanchon & Marco's Hollywood Paramount. House, a 1,430-seater on Hollywood Boulevard, already has two stereopix booked which will carry it through June 17 and intends to continue screening the new dimensional films thereafter."

The story stated that the venue had found success with its November 1952 booking of *Bwana Devil* and would open *House of Wax* in April and Columbia Pictures' *Fort Ti* in May. *Variety* had often coined terms for industry trends, like "sitcom" and "soap opera." For 3-D pics, *Variety* came up with "stereopix" and "depthies." Neither term lasted, but then neither did that style of 3-D.

The story continued, "With the Hollywood Paramount swing to 3-D, the Boulevard will have two theatres exclusively devoted to dimensional pictures. The Warner Hollywood is now converting to Cinerama and will open 'This Is Cinerama' on a hard ticket basis the end of April."

Paramount called its wide-screen process Vistavision, while 20th Century-Fox called theirs CinemaScope.

> "Because European manufacturers can retool quickly for production of CinemaScope screens, lenses and stereophonic sound equipment, theatres on the Continent after next January will be fitted with widescreen systems faster than their U. S. counterparts, 20th-Fox prexy Spyros P. Skouras declared on his return from Paris here Sunday . . . The 20th topper reported the company was sinking 'millions' in financing and commitments to get manufacturers in Germany, Italy, France and Spain to push the production of magnetic sound reproduction gear, tailored to the 20th system of four sound tracks on the same film as the image. Sound units have been a CinemaScope bottleneck. German firm, Siemon-Halske, is now turning out 250 pieces of sound equipment a month, but expects to raise the total to 500 by October. An Italian outfit promises 400 a month by October."

March 3, 1954, *Variety* reported that the new Mar del Plata film Festival in Mar del Plata, Argentina, would feature a CinemaScope screen, ensuring that 20th Century-Fox's *The Robe* could screen there.

"The cost of conversion is estimated at over $20,000. [WB had proposed 3-D projection for its 'House of Wax.'] To cover this expenditure the circuit has been authorized to increase admission scales of CinemaScope pix to around $4 in Mar del Plata, and $2 at the Broadway here."

On March 3, 1954, *Weekly Variety* crowed that Cinerama was raking in two hundred grand every week. "All companies involved in Cinerama—Stanley Warner, Cinerama Productions, and Cinerama, Inc., the equipment and installation firm—are extremely upbeat about the medium. Receipts took a slight dive during November and December when 20th-Fox unveiled Cinemascope, but the grosses are on the upbeat again. Cinerama's main problem currently is to find a subject suitable for another picture. The Louis de Rochemont 'Cinerama Holiday'"—yes, the same Louis de Rochemont of Suez Canal fame—"will be ready for release about May, but it's considered a 'transition' film, being mainly another scenic film with a slight story line. . . . Anything put on the Cinerama screen, it's felt, must be capable of running at least a year."

In September 1952, *This Is Cinerama* opened and established the format, with three projections on a curved screen giving viewers the illusion of being there, with documentary-style footage of a roller coaster, Niagara Falls, Florida water-skiing, etc.

In every way, the film biz was thinking big. Previously, "prestige" productions were targeted for months-long engagements at one theater in any given city. But two decades before *Jaws* "pioneered" the idea of a wide release, Warner Brothers was doing it to capitalize on (what else?) television. As reported in *Daily Variety*, June 16, 1953,

"Warners will make use of TV and radio on an unprecedented scale to campaign for the record 1,422 saturation territorial bookings of its science-fiction release, 'The Beast from 20,000 Fathoms,' pub-ad veepee Mort Blumenstock reported yesterday. Simultaneous air programs in 11 areas nationally will be tied in with the usual newspaper campaigns, and will be used to effect the quickest playoff in key and secondary runs in WB history, according to Blumenstock."

Within a week of its New York-L.A. bows, *The Beast from 20,000 Fathoms* spread to 1,500 theaters. In June 1954, Warner Brothers released *Them!*, another nuclear monster film. As always, horror films are an excellent gauge of the public's concerns, and Hiroshima had unleashed a fear of long-term effects of nuclear power, resulting in films about giant ants, tarantulas, and even *Attack of the 50 Foot Woman*.

In keeping with the 1950s mantra of thinking big, studios embraced spectacles. The 1951 *Quo Vadis* was a big-enough hit to set off a chain of toga epics, including *The Robe* (1953), *The Egyptian* (1954), and Cecil B. DeMille's 1956 *The Ten Commandments*. The trend continued into the 1960s, but it really reached its climax with William Wyler's costly ($12 million!) *Ben-Hur*, which scored big box office and held the record of eleven Oscar wins, which was unmatched for decades until the 1997 *Titanic* and the 2003 *The Lord of the Rings: The Return of the King* tied its record.

Things were expanding on-screen. Offscreen changes were less noticeable, but maybe more profound. After the de Havilland decision of 1945, everyone was trying to figure out new formulas for actor-studio relationships. In 1950, Lew Wasserman of MCA negotiated a deal for James Stewart to defer most of his salary on three Universal films in exchange for a share of income. The first, 1950's *Winchester '73*, was a big hit; as Mike Connolly reported in

Right: Note the asterisk.

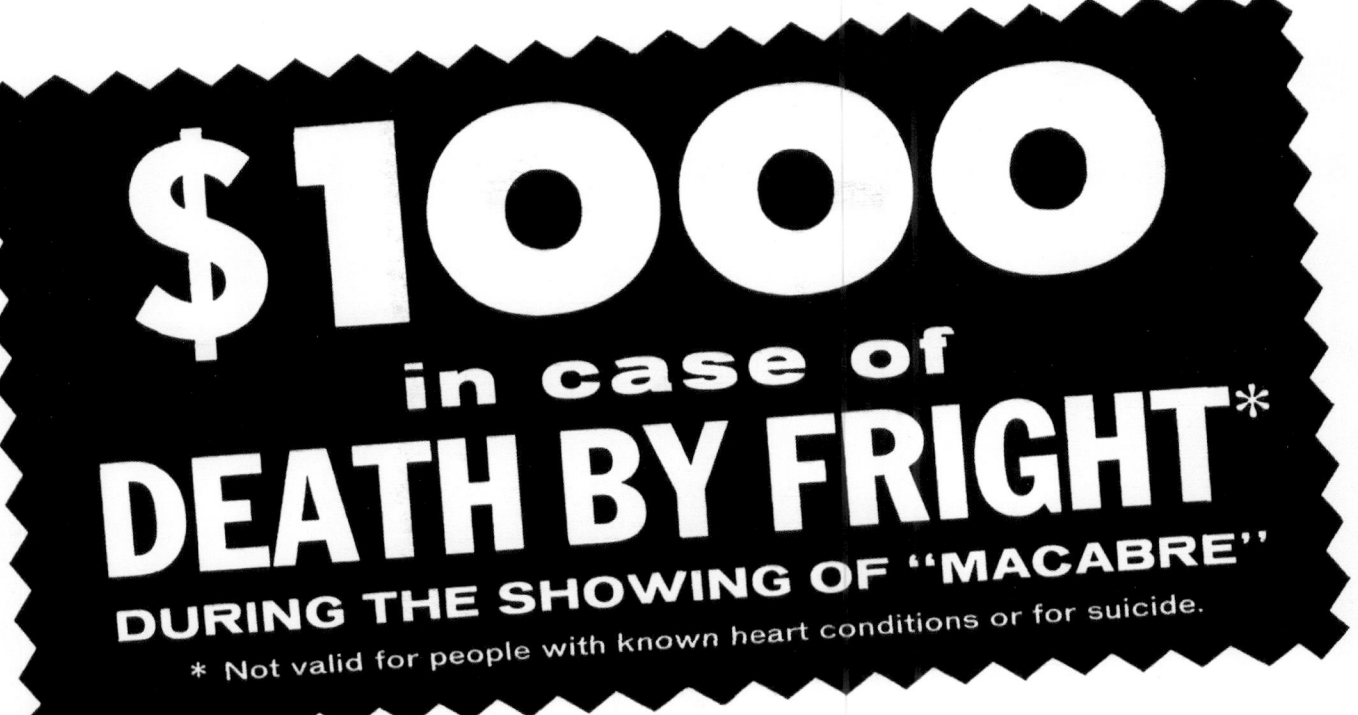

EVERY PATRON GETS A BONA FIDE POLICY ISSUED BY THE WORLD'S FOREMOST INSURANCE COMPANY!

THIS IS THE AMAZING OFFER YOU CAN MAKE WHEN YOU PLAY ALLIED ARTISTS' SENSATIONAL SHOCKER!

YOU GET POLICIES FOR DISTRIBUTION IN ADVANCE!

HERE'S SHOWMANSHIP FOR TODAY'S TICKET BUYERS!

Phone or wire ALLIED ARTISTS today! Play it HOT!

Thurs., Feb. 27, 1958

1944 – "NATIONAL VELVET"

FILM CHATTER

Joanna Barnes, Warners contractee, christened six new helicopters yesterday at the Marine Corps Air Force Base in Santa Ana . . . Craig Stevens winds his role as heavy in Col's "The Name's Buchanan" and leaves for Palm Beach, Fla., with wife Alexis Smith to rehearse play, "The King of Hearts," opening March 10 at the Poinciana Playhouse . . . UA district manager Ralph Clark heads for Frisco today to set up area dates for "Witness For the Prosecution."

Former Metro flack Carolyn Pfeiffer has joined the Hollywood office of Brenon & Morgan praisery . . . Actor Corey Allen, currently appearing in Warner Bros.' "Darby's Rangers," returns to his alma mater, Verdugo Hills High School, March 8 to direct a Community Theatre production of "The Fifth Season" . . . Don Porter guests next week at Ron Carver's UCLA professional comedy class and at Columbia College of Los Angeles' public relations class.

Benjamin Zemach, dance and drama director of the University of Judaism, will direct an Israeli folk program Saturday and Sunday at the University . . . Filmercial's Jack Rabin planes to Chicago and NY today . . . C. Alvin Bell tonight replaces Sidney Blackmer in the Pasadena Playhouse's production of "Inherit the Wind" as Blackmer wings to Phoenix to star in the same show at the Sombrero Theatre.

Bert Gordon Acquires Wechsler's 'Affair'

Producer-director Bert I. Gordon has bought Simon Z. Wechsler's novel, "Internal Affair," and plans to put it into production as soon as he completes the currently shooting "Revenge of the Colossal Man," both for American International.

Gordon is now negotiating for Wechsler to come here to do the screenplay on his book, which is concerned with a struggle for power in a large corporation.

'Connie' Leads Set

Dorothy Provine and Jack Hogan have been signed to co-star in "Tommy Gun Connie," theatrical film which Stanley Shpetner will produce and William Witney will direct for American International Pictures at Ziv studios. It rolls March 10 and will be released with AIP's "Machine Gun Kelly."

North Tunes 'Seas'

Alex North has been signed to score the fifth Cinerama production, "South Seas," and the Norman Luboff Choir will provide the vocal background. Pic produced by Carl Dudley is scheduled to open late this year.

Out Of The Horn's Mouth

Jay Livingston, Ray Evans and Larry Shayne have formed their own pubbery which will operate under the Livingston & Evans, Inc., tag. First publication will be "Oh Captain" which L&E penned for the Broadway staging.

Anna Maria Alberghetti set to sing with the Boston Philharmonic June 11. Prior to this she will guest on NBC-TV's "Dinah Shore Show."

Dick Contino, backed by the John Williams orchestra, pre-recorded four tunes for Elmer C. Rhoden, Jr.'s production, "Daddy-O", in which he co-stars with Sandra Giles. Songs are "Angel Act," "Rock Candy Baby," "She Just Wants To Rock" and "Wait'll I Get You Home, Baby."

Frankie Laine opens at the Americana Hotel in Miami, Fla., March 5 for one week.

Actress Erin O'Brien has been signed to a disk pact by Coral Records.

Frank Sinatra has been booked into the Sands in Las Vegas for a three-week engagement starting April 9.

Ray Bolger will open for four weeks at the Flamingo in Las Vegas the early part of June. Opening date will be either June 5 or June 12.

Songstress Jane Froman has been set by the William Morris Agency to open May 2 for four weeks at San Francisco's Fairmont Hotel.

Movie chanteuse Jane Powell will open for a two-week engagement March 18 at the Havana Riviera Hotel in Havana, Cuba.

Comedian Dick Shawn will play London for the first time when he opens April 7 for a two-weeker at the London Palladium.

Tiny Lockheed Riveter Making Acting Debut

John E. Carter, a former Lockheed riveter, makes his acting debut in "Rip Van Winkle," filmed episode of NBC's "Shirley Temple's Storybook."

Carter, who measures only 3 feet, 6 inches, was signed by director Harry Horner to portray the role of a claustrophobic dwarf.

French Envoy Honored

Washington, Feb. 26. — Herve Alphand, French Ambassador to the United States, will be guest of honor tomorrow at the benefit premiere of Warners' "Lafayette Escadrille" here. Proceeds go to a local youth center named after James Henry Baugham, hero of the early air unit.

Big Extra Call in Africa

Director Fred Zinnemann used 50 Belgian colonials and 750 Congolese extras this week for chapel scene in Warner Bros.' "The Nun's Story," shooting in the Belgian Congo. It was the largest call to date.

1957 – "RAINTREE COUNTY"

"ESTABLISHES ELIZABETH TAYLOR AS A FAVORITE FOR THE OSCAR."
—EDWIN SCHALLERT, L. A. TIMES

his Just for Variety column, on June 22, 1951: "Jimmy Stewart has stashed close to 150G's so far as a result of his percentage deal on 'Winchester '73.'"

It was more than a clever one-time deal. It changed the DNA of Hollywood deals. Within a few years, agents were in the driver's seat. In 1957, producer Joe Pasternak complained that "Hollywood is now bossed not by the studios but by the deal-makers representing stars." Strangely, MCA ended up owning Universal, and Wasserman was put in charge. The man who had helped drain the studios' once autocratic power, was himself now a studio head—and, ironically, he became more powerful than most of the moguls of the studio heyday. In addition to overseeing the studio for the next forty years, he also became Hollywood's chief negotiator, strategist, and peacemaker.

A piece from December 11, 1957, fretted over a source of income that might lead to long-term danger—selling recent films to TV:

> "Picture industry is coming face to face with the prospect of releasing relatively new (post-1948) pictures to television interests and the prospect, to many, is alarming though there is no specific evidence of a major-scale selloff to TV at present. But such a move is 'sensed.' Above all it is 'dreaded' as a case of the film industry mixing its own suicide potion. A prominently-placed eastern film industry official said he anticipates such unloading within nine months."

Film companies will do this because "they are financially under strain and need the money."

Communists, 3-D, and TV. What else did the 1950s offer? Why, wholesome fun, of course!

Calling it a $17 million gamble, *Variety* heralded the launch of Disneyland. Admission was one dollar for eighteen ticketed attractions. In the first six months, it attracted one million visitors.

A July 13, 1955, piece in *Weekly Variety* previewing Disneyland describes it as a

> "moppet-sized 'World's Fair,' which will run year round . . . All showmen agree that the project is of staggering imaginative concept, a sure winner, one of the true wonders of modern entertainment. As a family thrill there is only one flaw in the outlook—will it cost too much for the average parents and their brood? Disneyland management says it wants the average family outlay to be held to around $2 but others see $10 or $12 nearer the mark . . ."

On that same day, *Daily Variety* headlined "Disneyland Aims at $10 Million Yearly B.O.; 160-Acre 'Dream' Park Opening July 18." And while Disneyland embodied a childlike wonder and innocence, the 1950s also found its symbols of sex. In 1955, *The Seven Year Itch* scene with Monroe's skirt billowing became one of the most iconic images in the history of Hollywood. Elvis Presley appeared on *The Ed Sullivan Show*, during which Elvis the Pelvis created a sensation with his gyrations.

Yes, sex was rearing its head. And perhaps it is no coincidence that this was the dawn of the teenager. With their parents' prosperity, teens had disposable incomes, and pop culture catered to them. Transistor radios and record players, with some able to play 45s *and* LPs (i.e., long-play albums, which could contain a then-impressive thirty minutes of music), played Bill Haley & The Comets' "Rock around the Clock." The rock and roll movement was crystallized, and James Dean became the patron saint of teenagers in *Rebel without a Cause* and *East of Eden*.

Dean died on September 30, 1955, shortly after finishing his third and final starring role, in *Giant*. A year later,

Left: February 27, 1958.

Above: Marilyn Monroe.

Right: March 26, 1953.

Vol. 79 No. 15   Hollywood (28) California, Thursday, March 26, 1953   Ten Cents

H'W'D PARAMOUNT GOING ALL 3-D

CBS SCRAPS ITS TV TINT; RACE OPEN

Washington, March 25. — Disagreement between RCA and CBS as to the readiness of a compatible color TV system appeared today when CBS prexy Frank Stanton indicated to the House Interstate Commerce Committee that development of such a system at a price within reach of the public is still some time off.

Stanton told the Committee CBS has no plans, "so long as the present circumstances exist," to go ahead with its FCC-authorized system. Whether or not the Government ban on production of color sets is revoked, he said, "I think we would be tilting at windmills
(Continued on Page 3)

Pam Robinson Making Film Bow In 'Robe'

Pamela Robinson, daughter of 20th-Fox producer Casey Robinson, has been set to make her screen debut in company's "The Robe."

Miss Robinson, who has had no previous professional acting experience, will play the role of Richard Burton's sister, Lucia, in the film.

Cast Jaeckel in 'Sea'

Richard Jaeckel yesterday was signed by Republic for second male lead in "Sea of Lost Ships." He'll topline with John Derek and Wanda Hendrix in the Joseph Kane production, which rolls April 1 with Kane also directing.

Actor's last pic, on loanout from Paramount, was Metro's "The Big Leaguer."

20th Reoptions Crain

Option on services of Jeanne Crain has been picked up by 20th-Fox for another year.

Actress next goes into "Three Coins In the Fountain," which rolls in Rome Aug. 3. Sol C. Siegel will produce; Jean Negulesco direct.

2-Way 'Canyon'

Columbia, to beat the high cost of conversion for the exhib not yet ready for 3-D, will shoot "Renegade Canyon" with two cameras strapped together, from exactly the same angle.

Thus, theatres without 3-D projection equipment can project "Canyon" as a flat film, for which a number of additional closeups will have to be made during shooting, in 2-D.

Both the 3-D and the flat will be otherwise identical.

Lovelace Quits Disney Bd.; Youngman Succeeds

Resignation of Jonathan B. Lovelace as a member of the board and the election of Gordon E. Youngman to succeed him was announced yesterday by Walt Disney Productions. Lovelace, a director of the Disney organization for more than 10 years, bowed out due to pressure of his own business affairs.

Youngman formerly was veepee and chief legal counsel of RKO in NY for many years, as well as an RKO board member. He currently is a partner of the law firm of Bautzer, Grant, Youngman and Silbert.

Gladys George In 'Law'

Gladys George yesterday roped a featured lead in a "I Am the Law" telepic which rolls Saturday. Deal was set by Jack Donaldson.

First Major 1st-Run House To Swing Into Exclusive 3-D Policy; 'Wax', 'Fort Ti' Set

First major first-run theatre to swing into an exclusive 3-D policy will be Fanchon & Marco's Hollywood Paramount. House, a 1,430-seater on Hollywood Boulevard, already has two stereopix booked which will carry it through June 17 and intends to continue screening the new dimensional films thereafter. F&M pioneered in Hollywood with "Bwana Devil," the first feature-length 3-D film, last November. Boulevard showcase starts its exclusively 3-D policy when it opens Warners' "House of Wax" April 17 for a run and follows it on May 20 with Columbia's "Fort Ti," which is in for a minimum of four weeks. By the time these two stereopix have finished runs, similar 3-D product, now in various stages of production, will be on the market to sus-
(Continued on Page 3)

Rank Exec Sees H'wood Need For Standardization

New York, March 25. — Enthusiasm over the development of widescreen and concern over the apparent lack of standardization was voiced here by John Davis, managing director of the Rank Organization. Davis, who visited the Coast and viewed CinemaScope and the new Paramount widescreen system, planed to London yesterday.

"I like the idea of the large screen very much, but I can't see
(Continued on Page 3)

Cy Howard Spurns CBS' $1,000,000 Bid; Objects To Exclusivity Aspect

Cy Howard broke off negotiations with CBS for a new producer contract and is leaving the network after nine years. Although the new pact would involve more than $1,000,000, Howard refused to sign a deal that would make his services exclusive to the net. This would have prevented him from writing or producing pictures. Last week Howard conferred
(Continued on Page 8)

Ike Proposes Sarnoff's Star Be Permanent

Washington, March 25. — RCA head David Sarnoff was nominated by President Eisenhower today for permanent rank of brigadier general.

Sarnoff, who headed a commission under President Truman to seek economies in the Defense Department, is now a member of a similar committee under Eisenhower.

Sholem Leaving UI

Lee Sholem, UI contract director now piloting the retakes for "The Golden Blade," checks off the Valley lot upon completion of his present chores to free-lance. Sholem is subbing at present time for Nathan Juran, who's tied up on "Three Were Renegades."

During the association, Sholem directed "Ma and Pa Kettle At Waikiki," "Redhead From Wyoming" and "The Stand At Apache River" for UI.

COMMUNIST 'BLACKLIST' OF ANTI-RED WRITERS GETS HOUSE PROBE AIRING

By Mike Kaplan

Existance of a Communist "blacklist" operating against writers unfriendly to the party was brought out again before the House Un-American Activities Committee yesterday. However, before the witness, Bart Lytton, one-time writer, could document his testimony completely, the Committee excused him until today's session and went on to delve into an alleged top secret Communist Party meeting in Crestline last December and garner a few names from an attractive radio writer.

It was a session marked by the stormiest colloquies to date as the Committee blacked out television on two of the day's four witnesses,
(Continued on Page 10)

CONSOLIDATED FILM INDUSTRIES

PROCESSING PERFECTION
From PRODUCTION to PROJECTION

HO 9-1441

16 M/M • 35 M/M • COLOR • BLACK & WHITE

Daily Variety ran a front-page headline "WB consults psychologists on handling 'Giant' problem of James Dean cultism." The story detailed how the studio was trying to deal with Dean's fans as it prepared the release of *Giant*. The problem was how

> "to channel the adoration of Dean . . . into affirmative directions rather than let the macabre aspects get out of control. The amazing popularity of Dean goes beyond ordinary dimensions. He is some sort of a symbol—though exactly what sort is not yet fully evaluated."

Some skeptics wondered if Warner Brothers was creating this hoopla in advance of the film's release, but most thought it was genuine.

> "Old-timers groping for a comparison go back to Rudolph Valentino and wonder if the fabulous success of another 'modern' youth—'Elvis the Pelvis' Presley—doesn't have an affinity."

Hm. Prescient.

In his October 3, 1955, column, Army Archerd wrote, "It's still hard to believe James Dean's quick, tragic passing. . . . Dennis Hopper, one of Dean's close friends, is in a complete daze . . . Kathy Case fainted when told the news; Lori Nelson collapsed in tears . . . Steve Rowland, who had been invited to accompany Dean on the ride North, is curbing his reckless side. He sold his motorcycle . . ."

With his brooding charisma, Dean was sometimes compared to Marlon Brando, who introduced the world to Method acting. Brando created a sexy sensation in a torn T-shirt and his animal behavior in the 1951 Elia Kazan–directed film adaptation of Tennessee Williams's *A Streetcar Named Desire*.

That film was adapted from a play, and these legit-to-screen transfers threatened to break screen taboos, because theater was generally more daring than films. Also in that category was *The Moon Is Blue*. The 1951 play had been a saucy sensation, and the 1953 film adaptation created a scandal by using the word "virgin"; United Artists defied the Motion Picture Production Code by releasing the film without code approval. Robert Anderson's play *Tea and Sympathy* dealt with homosexuality. It, too, was later filmed in 1956.

William Inge featured "adult themes," as they were called, in *Picnic* (1953) and *Bus Stop* (1953), while Eugene O'Neill's autobiographical *Long Day's Journey into Night* (1956) debuted after his death, according to his wishes.

In Britain, John Osborne's 1950 play *Look Back in Anger* depicted an

Below: Kim Hunter and Marlon Brando in *A Streetcar Named Desire*.

Right: Elvis Presley. Did you really need this caption?

angry young man, a startling contrast to the well-made plays by Noël Coward and Terrence Rattigan. Osborne's 1958 *The Entertainer* offered a glum look at post-Imperial Britain, a sharp contrast to the admiring stiff-upper-lip studies from the previous decade.

But not all theater was boundary breaking . . . and not all of it was good. But when it *was* good, it was phenomenal. Due to some harmonic convergence, the 1950s offered some of the greatest musicals of all time: *My*

Vol. 97   No. 47   Hollywood (28), California, Monday, November 11, 1957   13   Ten Cents

RKO ENTERS FEEVEE SWEEPSTAKES

SCALE OF JUSTICE

The small print in an acting contract prompted a dietetic discourse by L.A. Superior Court Judge Harold Schweizer.

Judge Schweizer approved a seven-year contract between 18-year-old Diana Francis and ABPT Pictures, the pact calling for $120 per week to start and rising to $1,250 per week at the end of the term if all options are picked up.

But he noted a clause that permits the company to cancel the contract on the grounds of "disfigurement," if Miss Francis' weight goes below 105 or over 130. Judge Schweizer ascertained that the young actress now weighs 117.

He pondered the problem judiciously then gave his opinion. "Don't," he said, "eat potatoes."

Solons Fear TV's Own SP(utnik) Form Of Blurb

Washington, Nov. 10.—As a result of a report from the FCC, a member of Congress has proposed that "subliminal perception" commercials be prohibited on television pending completion of an investigation by the agency of the new advertising technique.

SP, which the process is called, sends messages across the screen which are too fast for the eye to catch but which make an impres-
(Continued on Page 4)

Rexall Takes Dim TView of Tint Kines

Because of "the poor quality of color kinescoped programs seen on the Coast," Rexall Drug, which is sponsoring "Hansel & Gretel" on NBC April 27, has ordered the show to be telecast in black-and-white, not tint.

Justin Dart, Rexall prexy, who lives here, does not like the quality of color programs seen here via kine. That's why Rexall-sponsored "Pinocchio," also on NBC, was telecast in b-and-w.

Even shows televised live in color here are repeated later via kines.

Meanwhile, Yasha Frank, producer-stager of Rexall series, has arrived from NY for casting confabs on "Hansel."

Nathanson Exits Globe

Sam Nathanson has resigned as general sales manager of Globe International Releasing Corp., with prexy Theodore J. Ticktin taking over active supervision of sales policies.

U of 'Ghoulifornia' Students Demand 'Blood', Get Cops

San Francisco, Nov. 10.—Chance remark on Russ Coglin's weekly "Nightmare" film show on KRON turned out more than 1,000 University of California students on the Berkeley campus Thursday midnight.

Said Coglin, at 10:30 p.m.: "Greetings to my followers at the University of Ghoulifornia. Berkeley believers will meet at the Big C at midnight."

Then he unspooled 1933's "Dracula."

When it was over, students started assembling, many wearing sheets or hooded sweatshirts. They
(Continued on Page 6)

Poitier Balks At 'Porgy' As Goldwyn Balks At Giving Him Script Approval

Sidney Poitier, announced last Tuesday as signed for the star role of Porgy in Samuel Goldwyn's production of "Porgy And Bess," vacated spot over the weekend.

According to Goldwyn, Poitier requested script approval which he (Goldwyn) would not grant, resulting in producer releasing the actor from his commitment.

Meantime, director Rouben Mamoulian and screenwriter N. Richard Nash begin confabs in NY this week with Oliver Smith and Irene Sharaff, who have been signed by Goldwyn as production designer and costume designer, respectively. Both Smith and Miss Sharaff were associated on Goldwyn's "Guys and Dolls."

Bill Harpell Buys Into KXLE, Ellensburg

Bill Harpell, CBS newscaster-announcer, has bought a majority interest in radio station KXLE, Ellensburg, Wash.,

He'll continue his newscasting, rotating between L.A. and Seattle.

Asking FCC For OK To Test Aerial System That Offers 'Choice Of Free And Pay Shows'

New York, Nov. 10. — Thomas F. O'Neil, prexy of RKO Teleradio, disclosed today company is filing for FCC okay to participate in feevee tests, and already is negotiating with manufacturers of toll-tv systems for employing one or more in invading what O'Neil terms "the tide of the inevitable." i.e., feevee.

O'Neil envisions using a through-the-air toll system, welcoming "a real opportunity for the viewer to choose among free and pay programs."

As operator of five television stations, O'Neil holds "it would be economically and socially wasteful for broadcasters not to take their rightful place (among those) who seek to broaden the base of tv entertainment."

Two months ago the FCC stated it would start licensing applicants in March for a test of toll-tv, us-
(Continued on Back Page)

Dicker Widmark, Newman for 'Fury'

Deals are pending for Richard Widmark and Paul Newman to essay star roles in "The Sound and the Fury," a Jerry Wald production for 20th-Fox which rolls next month under Martin Ritt's direction.

Negotiations were previously started for Kirk Douglas to essay a star role in film.

Par's Balaban Sees Feevee Upping Pix Prod'n 50% By '62

New York, Nov. 10.—Hollywood production will have increased 50% by 1962, Paramount president Barney Balaban asserted at a "Ten Commandments" first anniversary buffet-luncheon at the Criterion Theatre here Friday. This will come with the "audience extension" that is to be brought about with home toll-tv, he predicted.

Film rentals derived from both
(Continued on Back Page)

Col Amends Astor's Pact, Ups Zeeman

New York, Nov. 10. — Louis Astor, member of Columbia's top homeoffice sales staff since 1933, will switch to a consultative basis Dec. 31 under terms of an amended employment contract.

In another personnel change, Bernard E. Zeeman, treasurer of Col Pictures International since 1951, has been named a v.p. of the foreign operation. Zeeman joined Col in 1935 as a traveling auditor, having switched from Universal where he served in the same capacity. He subsequently became assistant manager of branch operations and, in 1944, head of foreign branch operations.

Sol Siegel to NY

Metro producer Sol C. Siegel leaves for NY this morning to huddle on exploitation plans for "Merry Andrew," Danny Kaye starrer which was sneaked Friday in Santa Barbara.

HAYWARD SIGNS TO DO PAR FILM

Paramount has inked Leland Hayward to a producer's contract. Pact calls for Hayward to indie-produce a film in NY for release through Paramount. In confirming the deal yesterday, studio tomorrow after looking over the British production of "Annie Get Your Gun." His wife and daughter got in yesterday.

Reisman on Tour

New York, Jan. 4.—Phil Reisman, RKO foreign chief, leaves for South America this weekend for a tour of company's south-of-

Johnston Leaving for Hawaii Vacation

Eric Johnston is leaving for a Honolulu vacation this weekend. Motion Picture Association of America prexy planed in Tuesday for huddles with studio chieftains on preliminary details of U.S. demands at the upcoming huddles Janet Blair and Blackburn Twins' engagement.

Van Heflin Package

New York, Jan. 4.—Van Heflin leaves for the Coast Sunday, following a video guest shot on Ken Murray's CBS-TV show Saturday night. MCA is now packaging Heflin deals under capital gains

---

Mel Brooks:
"*VARIETY*: News and reviews to amuse Jews."

Left: November 11, 1957.

Fair Lady, Gypsy, Guys and Dolls, The King and I, West Side Story, The Music Man, and *The Most Happy Fella.*

Theater offered another breakthrough: Lorraine Hansbury's *Raisin in the Sun* (1958), with its depiction of a lower-middle-class black family. The play and its film adaptation also offered a meaty role for Sidney Poitier. The early deaths of the 1950s holy trinity turned them into romanticized icons, but in fact Poitier may have had a bigger effect than any of them.

Rarely has a single performer changed perceptions so radically and so firmly. The 1949 *Home of the Brave* starred James Edwards as a textured, sympathetic black man; Edwards continued to work but didn't achieve stardom. The following year, Poitier starred in *No Way Out*, directed and co-written by Joseph L. Mankiewicz, as a doctor treating a racist white patient. *Raisin in the Sun* (1961), *Blackboard Jungle* (1955), and *The Defiant Ones* (1958), in which he was a fugitive chained to a racist (Tony Curtis), helped redefine blacks in cinema.

Previously, Hollywood majors created all-black films for black audiences, like *Stormy Weather* and *Cabin in the Sky* (both 1943). Lena Horne kinda-sorta helped integrate films. MGM would film her singing in "Till the Clouds Roll By" (1946) and "Words and Music" (1948), but her segments were often cut from prints sent to the South, where many exhibitors were uncomfortable booking films that showed blacks in anything other than servant roles.

The 1950s offered *Carmen Jones*, *Porgy and Bess*, and a few interracial dramas like *Island in the Sun*, but aside from Dorothy Dandridge and Harry Belafonte, few other leading black actors worked as regularly as Poitier. Whatever "star quality" is, he had it. He brought intelligence, integrity, and heart to roles, and audiences of all races seemed to like him. Soon Hollywood began to tailor films to match his talents.

On January 27, 1954, *Weekly Variety* ran a story stating the apparently surprising premise that black audiences should be wooed by the industry. Under the headline

"Sensational 10-Year Upsurge of Negro Market; Worth 15-Billion-$," the story by Robert J. Landry began: "Despite segregation, which is weakened but still general, the American Negro has become the most important, financially potent, and sales-and-advertising serenaded 'minority' in the land. During the past 10 years while foreign-language publications and broadcasting have declined notably, the Negro market, which during the depression was despised as marginal and underprivileged, has became a 15-billion-dollar market. In numbers it exceeds the total population of Canada."

Landry continued,

"Those most expert in the problems of selling branded merchandise to Negro retailers have issued practical warnings. 'Don'ts' include avoidance of racial slurs such as the double-g form of the word 'Negro,' or a patronizing, or talking down, or overselling approach. Not the least arresting angle about the new status of the Negro is this: few or no Negro film theatres have closed in recent years, in sharp contrast with the high rate of closings (several thousand houses) in the white exhibitor ranks. C.J. Mabry has observed: "They aren't losing patronage—they are gaining patronage."

On November 21, 1956, *Weekly Variety* ran a letter from Thurgood Marshall, who at the time was special counsel to the National Association for the Advancement of Colored People. He wrote that he was interested in

"the recent series of letters commenting upon the spotty use of Negro actors and actresses on the legitimate stage as well as in television and films save in 'token' jobs or in stereotyped roles . . . The plight of Negroes in the theatre may be considered typical of Negro labor in the north generally . . . the purpose of this note is to commend Variety for providing—in the true tradition of our press—a forum for public discussion of this problem. I sincerely hope that this discussion will not only broaden the views of your readers but also will lead to the wider use of Negro theatrical personnel—not merely because they are Negroes, but rather because they represent a significant segment of the fabric which is the American scene."

A few black singers crossed the music boundaries, such as Nat King Cole, Louis Armstrong, and the mellow

Johnny Mathis. But frequently "colored music" was segregated on radio stations. White audiences heard Pat Boone's 1956 "Tutti Frutti" and Ricky Nelson's 1957 "I'm Walking," which were "whitened" versions of records made respectively by Little Richard and Fats Domino.

Pearl Bailey had appeared on the first telecast of *Texaco Star Theater* in 1948 and Ed Sullivan, a New York columnist who began hosting a variety show in the early days of television, stood up to sponsors who balked at some of his proposed bookings. As *Variety* recalled in a 1964 article,

> "He is the man who went to the mat with a sponsor in the beginning 15 years ago, declaring that a variety show could not be run without Negro talent, and goodbye to the bankroller who thought otherwise. Sullivan has again and again guested Ella Fitzgerald, Lena Horne, Louis Armstrong, Pearl Bailey, Harry Belafonte, Nat King Cole and other major Negro stars . . ."

But integration was slow. *Daily Variety*, on November 24, 1953, reported,

> "The first time in many years in Memphis a Negro performer has worked on the same stage with white performers. Moreover, he wowed the all-white audience. In one-niting here with his troupe, Fred Waring presented in his show Negro baritone Frank Davis, who got a salvo of applause—probably heaviest accorded any of the troupe—for his rendition of 'Ol' Man River.' Heretofore, Lloyd T. Binford, Memphis' headline-getting censor czar, has always refused to permit white and Negro performers to appear in the same show. He invariably rules that all-Negro troupes must work together and all-whites together."

Left: Louis Armstrong.

And if it wasn't civil rights, the decade was hosting censorship battles. On December 17, 1957, *Variety* reported,

> "Memphis' topsy-turvy censor board has come up with another baffling 'reason' for putting its proverbial kibosh on pix—this time the board saying it was banning two juvenile delinquency films because of 'general principles.' Chairwoman of the four-woman board said that the board passed 'Peyton Place.' Mrs. Edwards said 'Peyton' was 'all right,' but nixed 'Street of Sinners' and 'The Careless Years,' which were to open today."

Daily Variety reported that Jerry Wald, the producer of the 1957 *Peyton Place*, changed one word to please the Legion of Decency, the powerful Catholic organization that rated films for their levels of acceptability: "It was when the girl comes to the doctor, asking for an abortion. He says: 'I can't do anything for you now.' Legion asked that the 'now' be removed since it implied he might have performed an operation earlier."

The sex-sational film was based on Grace Metalious's book, which remained on *The New York Times*' best-seller list for fifty-nine weeks and was said to have sold more copies than any other book in its time, except the Bible. It centered on a New Hampshire town where people have ugly (and usually sexy) secrets under the demeanor of New England niceties: illegitimate children, sexual abuse, marital infidelities, and abortion.

The late 1950s also saw the beginning of a series of trials on another front. Book publishers and sellers were on trial for obscenity, for D. H. Lawrence's 1928 *Lady Chatterley's Lover*, Henry Miller's 1934 *Tropic of Cancer*, John Cleland's 1748—yes, 1748!—*Fanny Hill* (aka *Memoirs of a Woman of Pleasure*). Most of them had been published long ago in Europe but were printed for the first

Radio—Television

Tele Review
THE DICK CLARK SHOW
(Sat., 8 p.m., KABC-TV)

"The Dick Clark Show" is sort of television's little window on today's young people. That the glass is stained with the shattering hysteria of their musical tastes is no fault of the show's, for it is designed to please that vast audience alone, and to sell them on Beech-Nut chewing gum, which Clark alternately describes as "the only flavorific chewing gum in the whole wide world" or, somewhat more to the point, "a swinging gum." The program is as commercial as the birth rate, and figures to linger on the network until teenage idols go out of style.

Clark has brought his show to Hollywood for three weeks while he makes a feature motion picture. The switch of locale is notable in that his young Hollywood audience seems more subdued than its New York counterpart. There is less screeching hereabouts. Only guest star Fabian inspired the shriek brigade into action.

Sharing the bill with Fabian were Bobby Darin, Dodie Stevens and Mitchell Torok. Darin by far was the most poised and most effective. He is the only one of the four likely to survive when rock 'n' roll goes the way of all fads. His work on "Mack the Knife" and "Dream Lover" was youthful and refreshing, particularly on the former selection. Miss Stevens offered one pleasingly innocuous vocal on "Miss Lonelyhearts." Torok brought a country-style presentation to his rendition of "Caribbean." Fabian's piercingly self-conscious stares, graceless movements and totally undistinguished voice nevertheless elicited the major response of the evening from the studio crowd, as he battled through vocals of "Come On and Get Me" (a few of the assembled young ladies seemed on the verge of such an urge) and "Got the Feeling."

Clark ties all this mayhem together with a note of relative sanity and casual respectability (shirt, tie and jacket, and disposition to match). This, along with his clean-cut, boyish good looks, is his principal charm.

Some lavish sets whipped up by ABC-TV's Coast crew served as a replica of a Hollywood motion picture star's home as an appropriate gesture in honor of Clark's visit. They were tasteful and useful. Producer Deke Hayward's show got another lift from Garth Dietrick's smooth direction, particularly since all vocals were lipsynced on this show. *Tube.*

TV STORY EDITOR—WRITER
Woman desires position with Producer or Story Department. Experience with contract procedure top network live and film shows —research, editing, analysis, rewrites and originals.
Box 960, Daily Variety

Dick Clark:

❝ When I first started reading *Variety*, I was working in Philadelphia doing *American Bandstand*. Because I wasn't in New York or Los Angeles, *Variety* gave me the feeling of being a little closer to the "Main Street" of entertainment. ❞

Leslie Caron:

❝ First, when I arrived from France to do *An American in Paris* with MGM I couldn't decipher the slanguage. I waited for colleagues to tell me when and what my next film was going to be. That's the way I learned that MGM had cast me for *Lili*. I was thrilled. Then when I lived in London, there was, once a year, a fancy gala, a premiere, one of my films or someone else's, when we stood in line and curtseyed to royalty who shook our hand. That's how I learned that *Variety* gave money to charities. I have five or six precious photographs of these glamorous events. ❞

Below: Airline food used to be free.

time in the United States. The books contained sexual descriptions and language. In 1960, U.K. publisher Penguin was put on trial for *Lady Chatterley's Lover*, tried under the recent Obscene Publications Act, but found not guilty. Similarly, U.S. courts decided the books had enough redeeming social value to offset their shocking content.

And Americans discovered foreign-language films were much sexier than local fare. Sophia Loren, Brigitte Bardot, Marcello Mastroianni, Jean-Paul Belmondo, Anna Magnani, Claudia Cardinale, Jeanne Moreau, Raf Vallone, Simone Signoret, and Yves Montand offered a sensuality that was exotic and attractive.

Foreign-language films were so good that they got their own Oscar category, with Federico Fellini's 1956 *La Strada* winning the first one. The film was a breakthrough for Fellini. While his striking (and sometimes surreal) images led to the term "Fellini-esque," the accent on his visuals shortchanges his deep insights about self-doubt, religion, sex, and identity. The *La Strada* trophy was assigned to producers Dino De Laurentiis and Carlo Ponti. De Laurentiis's credits at that point included the 1949 Italian *Bitter Rice*, famous for its sexual energy. De Laurentiis went on to a long and unique career, moving from low-budget Italian art films to epics like the 1956 *War and Peace* (directed by King Vidor and starring Audrey Hepburn and Henry Fonda) through such Hollywood movies as *Serpico*, *Mandingo*, and *King Kong* in the 1970s through a 2001–2 pair of *Silence of the Lambs* sequels, *Hannibal* and *Red Dragon*. But after *La Strada* won, the Academy decided the director, not the producer, should be handed the foreign-language trophy, and Fellini won three more for *The Nights of Cabiria*, *8½*, and *Amarcord*.

Sex was always a selling point in foreign-language films during the decade, but worldwide audiences also found other joys: Akira Kurosawa's 1950 *Rashomon*, his *Seven Samurai* (1954), and *The Hidden Fortress* (1958), which was one of George Lucas's inspirations for *Star Wars*. Japan also offered the trend-setting 1956 *Godzilla*.

And as films from the East were gaining popularity, Miyoshi Umecki

won the supporting actress Oscar for the 1957 *Sayonara*, the first Asian thespian to nab an Academy Award. But it wasn't exactly a breakthrough—more of an anomaly, since it would be another twenty-seven years before another Asian actor won, Haing Ngor for the 1984 *The Killing Fields*. Since then, nada. So sayonara to progress.

The civil rights and sexual-liberation battles of the 1960s clearly had strong precedents in the 1950s.

The decade also witnessed two key changes at *Variety*. The March 22, 1950, *Weekly Variety* reported the death of Sid Silverman, who had inherited the reins of the paper when his father, Sime, died in 1933. Sid Silverman's obit said,

> "Variety ownership has passed on to his son, Syd, just past 18. It remains a wholly owned Silverman property, with no change in management, policy, or direction, following the precepts and standards set down by Sime Silverman when he founded the paper in 1905 . . . (Syd Silverman's) virtual 100% stock control and ownership of Variety and Daily Variety, the latter published in Hollywood, is held in trust for him until he comes of age. Meantime, the same editorial and business direction of both publications remain as before."

And in Hollywood, Thomas M. Pryor became editor of *Daily Variety*, a post that he would hold for nearly thirty years.

Carl Reiner:

"A morning without *Variety* is like a morning without coffee...!"

Right: January 11, 1957.

Following Spread: January 28, 1957; February 1, 1957.

158 VARIETY

Radio—Television

TV ACAD CUTS EMMY AWARDS FROM 41 TO 29; SCANT LIVE, PIX DISTINCTION

(Continued from Page 1)

most drastic cutback, from 11 in 1956, to six. Gone are best children's, daytime, documentary, audience participation, action or adventure, variety, music and dramatic series classifications.

Performer groupings lost four classes in the reshuffling — specialty acts, male singer, femme singer and emcee-host. However, creation of overall best male and best femme personality class brought total awards to 11, from 13 last year.

In writing, best tv adaptation was dropped, but best original teleplay grouping was divided between half-hour and hour-or-more categories, bringing total to three, against four last year.

Production and technical awards were narrowed to nine, from 13 last year. Gone are choreography,

Burning Questions

Among pointed questions to be decided by a new committee on ethics, currently being named by Southern California Radio-TV News Club prexy John Holbrook, will be:

How long can a newsman continue to promote himself as "award-winning," after the award is made?

Definition of the word, "exclusive."

How many new shows can advertise as "highest rated" in the L.A. area?

Already named, and accepting, appointment to the committee are Sam Zelman, CBS-TV Coast news topper, and George Putnam, of KTTV.

producer (both film and live), commercial campaign. Directors and art directors divisions were also changed, from separation between live and film to between half-hour and hour-or-more.

In looking over new structure, prexy of the Hollywood ATAS branch, and Ed Sullivan, NY prexy, both paid tribute to respective award and structure committees; in Hollywood, headed by Al Scalpone and John Guedel, and with Frank Cleaver, Fenton Coe, J. English Smith and James T. Aubrey as principal members; and in NY, headed by Robert Lewine, Marlo Lewis and Mark Goodson.

The full list of awards, as revised, follows:

(1) Best Single Program of the Year; (2) Best New Program series; (3) Best series (half-hour); (4) Best Series (hour); (5) Best Public Service Series; (6) Best Coverage of a Newsworthy Event; (7) Best Continuing Performance In A Dramatic Series (actor); (8) Best Continuing Performance In A Dramatic Series (actress); (9) Best Continuing Performance By A Comedian In A Series; (10) Best Continuing Performance By A Comedienne In A Series; (11) Best Single Performance (actor); (12) Best Single Performance (actress); (13) Best Supporting Performance (actor); (14) Best Supporting Performance (actress); (15) Best Male Personality (continuing performance); (16) Best Female Personality (continuing performance); (17) Best Commentator.

Writing Awards

(18) Best Teleplay (half-hour); (19) Best Teleplay (hour); (20) Best Comedy Writing.

Production, Technical Awards

(21) Best Direction (half-hour); (22) Best Direction (hour or more); (23) Best Art Direction (half-hour); (24) Best Art Direction (hour or more); (25) Best Cinematography; (26) Best Live Camera Work; (27) Best Editing Of A TV Film; (28) Best Musical Contribution To TV; (29) Best Engineering or Technical Achievement (if merited).

Emmy nominations will be telecast over NBC Feb. 16, the Awards March 16, sponsored by Oldsmobile and RCA.

'Today' to 'Tonight'

New York, Jan. 10. — Jack Lescoulie is withdrawing from NBC-TV's "Today" to become anchor man in NY for the new three-way format for "Tonight" teeing up Jan. 28.

Obituaries

MRS. FANNY GANG

Services for Mrs. Fanny Gang, 80, mother of Martin Gang, showbiz attorney, who died suddenly of a heart attack Wednesday night in her home here, will be held at 11 a.m. today at Malinow & Simons Mortuary, 818 Venice Boulevard, with cremation to follow. Rabbi Max Nussbaum of Hollywood Temple will conduct the rites.

Mrs. Gang also leaves Mrs. Violet Kopp of the law firm of Gang, Kopp & Tyre, and four other daughters.

ISOBEL McREYNOLDS GRAY

Services will be held tomorrow, 11 a.m., St. Paul's Episcopal Cathedral, 6th & Figueroa, for Mrs. Isobel McReynolds Gray, 75, dramatic coach who died Monday.

On The Air Waves

Betty White, who shortly starts toplining the vidpix series, "Date With Angel," last night was kudosed by Hollywood Women's Professional and Business Club as "most glamorous" gal of the town.

Disk jockey Bob Kennedy has role in Alfred Hitchcock vidpic.

Guesting on KTLA "Mike Stokey Presents" tomorrow night are Gail Robbins, George O'Hanlon, Hans Conried and Jackie Coogan.

Berne Giler has just been signed to do his sixth telefilm in Warner Bros.' "Cheyenne" series, starring Clint Walker.

Clint Eastwood, who recently completed role in Warners' "Lafayette Escadrille," planes to NY over weekend for location shooting on "West Point" series vidpic segment, "White Fury."

Joe Corey flies to NY tomorrow via American Airlines for tv commitments.

Telecastings: Robert Easton, "The Brothers;" Joan Vohs, femme lead in Rod Cameron "State Trooper" series.

Pat O'Brien will film a tv clip Monday for the national Easter Seal campaign.

Additional TV Film Production Chart

(Continued from Page 15)

"77TH BENGAL LANCERS"
Cast: Phil Carey, Warren Stevens.
Prod., Herbert B. Leonard; Dir., Frank MacDonald; Cam., Fred Jackman, Jr.

"CIRCUS BOY"
Cast: Mickey Braddock, Noah Beery, Robert Lowery, Guinn "Big Boy" Williams.
Prods., Herbert B. Leonard, Norman Blackburn; Dir., George Archainbaud.

DON W. SHARPE & WARREN LEWIS PRODS.
(Filmed by Desilu)
(Motion Picture Center —HO. 9-5981)
29 "WIRE SERVICE" (1-hr.).
Cast: Dane Clark, Mercedes McCambridge, George Brent.
Prod., Warren Lewis; Dirs., Alvin Ganzer, Tom Gries; Cam., Joe Novak; Film Ed., Les Orlebeck.
39 "DuPONT THEATRE" (½-hr.).
Prod., Warren Lewis; Dir., Laslo Benedek; Cam., J. Novak; Film Ed., Marsh Hendry.

STAGE FIVE PRODS., INC.
(General Service—HO. 7-3111)
39 "ADVENTURES OF OZZIE & HARRIET."
Cast: Ozzie, Harriet, David and Ricky Nelson.
Prod.-Dir., Ozzie Nelson; Cam., Neal Beckner; Film Ed., William Murphy; Sound, Max Hutchinson.

STUDIO CITY TV PRODS.
(Republic—PO. 3-8411)
Casting: Harold Rossmor
39 "FRONTIER DOCTOR" (½-hr.).
Cast: Rex Allen.
Prod., Edward J. White; Dir., William Witney; Cam., Bud Thackery.

TCF TELEVISION PRODUCTION
(Fox-Western Ave.—HO. 2-6231)
Casting: Marvin Schnall
20TH-FOX HOUR
Prods., Peter Packer, Ben Feiner, Jr.; Dir., Various; Cam., Lloyd Ahern; Film Ed., Art Seid.
39 "BROKEN ARROW" (½-hr.).
Cast: John Lupton, Michael Ansara.
Prods., Mel Epstein, Alan Armer; Dir., Various; Cam., Charles V. Enger.

WARNER BROS. TV DIVISION
(Burbank, Calif.—HO. 9-1251)
"CONFLICT"
Cast: Will Hutchins, Rex Reason, Edward Binns, Ray Teal.
Prod., Roy Huggins; Dir., Walter Doniger; Cam., Edwin DuPar; Film Ed., George Nicholson.
"CHEYENNE"
Cast: Clint Walker, Bob Hover, Buddy Baer, Merry Anders.
Prod., Art Silver; Dir., Joe Kane; Cam., Hal Stine; Film Ed., Harold Minter.

WESMOR, INC.
(California Studios—HO. 2-7141)
Casting: Lynn Stalmaster
39 "DR. HUDSON'S SECRET JOURNAL" (½-hr.).
Starring: John Howard.
Prods., Eugene Solow, Brewster Morgan; Dir., Peter Godfrey; Cam., Hal McAlpin, Film Ed., Jerome Young.

ZIV-TV
(American-National—OL. 4-2800)
Casting: Bub Miley
"DOCTOR CHRISTIAN"
Cast: Macdonald Carey.
"HIGHWAY PATROL"
Cast: Broderick Crawford.
"MEN OF ANNAPOLIS"

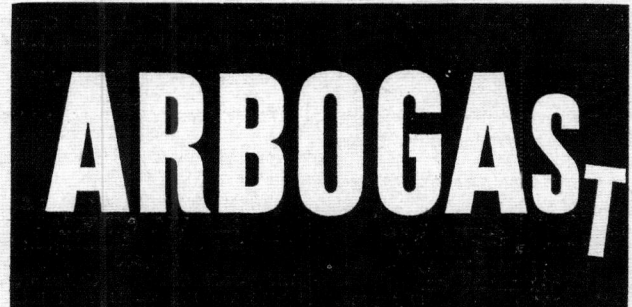

FOR SALE BY OWNER
Newly Decorated Longridge Estates Home. 3 Bdrms. two and ¾ baths—Carpets & Drapes. Over ½ Acre of flat ground. Beautiful hillside view. Heated and filtered swimming pool, badminton court. Beautifully landscaped. Large parking area. $46,500. Courtesy to Brokers. 3613 Longridge, Sherman Oaks.
PO. 1-2865   ST. 7-0703

"Love Me Tender" In A . . . **KINGSIZE**
Innerspring Mattresses ● Box Springs
Hollywood Beds Custom Built
ANY Length ★ Any Width ★ Any Shape
HOLLYWOOD BEDDING MFG. CO.
8418 Santa Monica Blvd. OL. 4-1294 — OL. 4-2957

Vol. 94 No. 36 Hollywood (28), California, Monday, Jan. 28, 1957 Ten Cents

WRITERS VOTE H-H-L, TODD STRIKE

$3,000,000 BUDGET ON 6 AM-PAR PIX

New York, Jan. 27.—A budget of $3,000,000 has been allocated for six Am-Par productions, to be made during the next six months, Irving H. Levin, prexy of Am-Par, AB-PT production subsid, reported yesterday.

Decision was reached at two-day meet of Am-Par's exhibitor advisory committee last week in New Orleans, according to Levin, who disclosed that three of the six will

(Continued on Page 4)

Presley 'Pornographic', Mexico Decrees; Can't Play in Any Gov't Bldg.

Mexico City, Jan. 27. — Elvis Presley is banned from appearing in any government-owned establishments in Mexico because his style of singing "lacks esthetic values and is markedly pornographic," Education Minister Jose Angel Ceniceros said here today.

'Decision' Pends at UI For Abner Biberman

Negotiations are on for Abner Biberman to return to UI, where he formerly was under contract, to direct "Decision at Durango," Gordon Kay production starring Fred MacMurray.

Biberman's UI pact expired three months ago. Release of his last pic on lot, "The Night Runner," starring Ray Danton and Coleen Miller, is upcoming.

Heap Legit 'Praise' On Louise Beavers

Louise Beavers has been set to star in Huntington Hartford production of Charles O'Neal's "Praise House," which will preem in Frisco's Alcazar Feb. 24, followed by Mar. 4 fortnight here, and Cleveland and Washington bookings prior to late April Broadway bow.

Where Angels Fear

Chicago, Jan. 27. — Janet Kern, Chicago American's television editor whose freewheeling comments are well known in the trade, tomorrow starts as a twice weekly regular on WBBM-TV's "Chicago Story" talk show. Miss Kern's doubling into tv evoked this comment from her mother:

"What's the matter, can't you make enough enemies with your column that you have to open a branch office?"

Mary Martin Will Star In 2 Civic Light Opera Shows in One Season

Mary Martin has been signed by Civic Light Opera's Edwin Lester to topline both "South Pacific" and "Annie Get Your Gun" this coming season, on a 20-week guarantee deal.

Thus, Miss Martin becomes the first star ever to appear in two CLO shows in a single season. She opens five-week San Francisco stand in "Pacific" June 3, then plays five weeks here. "Annie" opens in Frisco Aug. 20 and after five weeks comes to the Philharmonic here to close the CLO season. Only other CLO show set for season is road company of "My Fair Lady."

WGAW Takes Action Despite Hecht's Offers To Negotiate; Production Co. Threatens Suit

Strike action was authorized against Hecht-Hill-Lancaster and Mike Todd by the Screen Writers Branch of Writers Guild of America West at a special membership meeting Thursday night. Also at the meeting, WGAW execs reported that the Guild membership had approved, by mail vote, establishment of a "strike list" in addition to present "unfair list." Under new rules, Guild members shall not only be prevented from working for struck producers, but also may not sell or license any literary or dramatic work to them.

Action against H-H-L is outgrowth of hassle in which WGAW charges that the production company refuses to negotiate a pact, a charge which prexy Harold

(Continued on Page 4)

B-52s' Record Hop Cues 20th to Rev Up 'SAC'

Record global flight of three B-52s two weeks ago has cued 20th-Fox to speed up start of its "SAC Saboteur," originally slated to roll next fall.

Anthony Muto, who will produce, has been instructed to rush scripting and get film before the cameras as soon as possible, probably within 60 days.

Muto also was given the speed-

(Continued on Page 2)

Chi News Hastily Replates After Printing Nudes Next To 'Violent' Rap At TV Fare

Chicago, Jan. 27. — The Chicago Daily News got caught in one of those "which page of the News did you read?" embarrassments that occasioned considerable comment in Windy City television circles last week.

For five years the John S. Knight newspaper has been sniping at tv and its advertisers, charging "crime and violence" on children's programs. Impact of the crusade was blunted to some extent by the general recognition that it was one way by which the paper could cash in on the public's interest in a competing medium.

News' tv writer Ethel Daccardo last week detailed rough stuff she

(Continued on Page 22)

Offer TV 'Princess' Role to Teresa Wright

Teresa Wright is being paged to star in "The Princess Back Home," on Goodyear Playhouse, NBC-TV, Feb. 14.

John Van Druten scripted the romantic comedy for producer Phillip Barry, Jr.

Nab Frisco Chinatown Exhib; U.S. Eyes Theatre As Pro-Red Pix Distrib

San Francisco, Jan. 27. — Security officials of the U.S. Immigration and State Departments have had a Frisco film theatre's co-owner arrested on grounds he made a false statement in connection with a 1951 passport application.

He's Fong Ying, 42, who runs

(Continued on Page 17)

AA to Release NY Indie's Pix; 'Frankenstein' Kick

In continuing its search for outside product to release, Allied Artists is finalizing a deal with Motion Picture Releasing, NY outfit.

First of the films probably will be "The Curse of Frankenstein," title of which has been filed with the MPAA Title Registration Bureau. AA also has registered "Dr. Frankenstein's Monster" and "The Frankenstein Monster."

Disney Offers 'Old' Role to Peter Graves

Walt Disney has opened negotiations for Peter Graves to essay a top role in "Old Yeller," which also toplines Dorothy McGuire, Fess Parker, Jeff York, Tommy Kirk and Kevin Corcoran.

Jelling of deal depends on whether Graves can free himself temporarily from his starring role in TPA's "Fury" vidpix series. Meanwhile, "Yeller" goes before the cameras today under Robert Stevenson's direction.

Vol. 94 No. 40   Hollywood (28), California, Friday, Feb. 1, 1957   13   Ten Cents

$85,000,000 IN 35 WB FILMS

TOA SAYS 7 MAJORS WILL EASE TERMS

New York, Jan. 31. — Theatre Owners of America prexy Ernest G. Stellings today said he has obtained assurances from seven majors that they will "do everything in their power" to assist smalltown theatres and adopt a national sales policy based on theatres' ability to pay rather than percentage terms.

While the seven assured cooperation, not all promised to drop the 50% policy for small houses, Stellings reported, adding, "we hope to get the rest around to our view soon." He refused to identify the seven at the companies' re-
(Continued on Page 2)

MGM to Bankroll Indie Vidpix, Split Profits; Also Make Own Series

Metro's telefilmery is prepared to make outside deals with actors, producers or packagers with program ideas acceptable to the operating heads of the studio's video division. Adrian Samish, director of programming, said yesterday such independent arrangements have been integrated into the
(Continued on Page 3)

1st Disney Common Div

Walt Disney Productions yesterday declared its first cash dividend on common stock. Board voted to pay 10¢ a share April 1 to holders of record March 8 as a quarterly melon.

Board also has the intention of supplementing cash dividends with an annual stock dividend, according to prexy Roy O. Disney. Latter
(Continued on Page 4)

Marshall 'Sad' Megger

George Marshall has checked on the Paramount lot to prep direction of the Hal Wallis production, "Sad Sack," Jerry Lewis starrer.

New Chanteuse

Tillie Balaban, wife of Paramount prexy Barney Balaban and mother of three, turned disk artist this week, cutting four sides as a vocalist backed by a five-piece combo. It was an independent effort for which she is picking up the tab. The tunes, conducted by Bernie Richards, included a pair of French songs, "Two Different Worlds," and "My Reckless Heart."

Parenthetically, Paramount Pictures is in the process of acquiring Dot Records. Mrs. Balaban's disk efforts, however, are not presently tied to that label's activities.

KTTV Covers Air Crash So Fast Rival Stations Don't Send Remoters

KTTV again scored a beat on the tv local opposition in covering yesterday's Pacoima air crash, dispatching a live remote crew to the scene and getting a picture on the air approximately 45 minutes after the Air Force plane hit the school. Station got the beat on the recent Malibu fire disaster, too.

KTTV also scored a news beat when Nancy McFayden, wife of a
(Continued on Page 14)

Here We Go Again! Ann Sothern Lashes Emmy Awards; Wants 'Investigation'

Ann Sothern yesterday demanded an investigation of the manner in which the Academy of Television Arts and Sciences sets up its lists of "reminders" or Emmy pre-nomination ballots, terming them "unfair" and "a great injustice."

Outburst by the star of the "Private Secretary" telefilm series is the first such blast this season at the Acad, subjected to a continual barrage of criticism on its awards structure last year by Groucho Marx, Dick Powell, Jerry Lewis, Jack Webb, Frank Ferrin, Ben Fox and others. Webb was so critical he withdrew two nominations.

Miss Sothern minces no words in
(Continued on Page 6)

Sothern Vidpix Re-Runs $1,500,000 in Year

Importance of residuals in vidpix was again emphasized yesterday with the disclosure Ann Sothern's "Private Secretary" reruns, shown under the tag "Susie,"
(Continued on Page 6)

Jack Warner Says Company Has Faith In Pix Biz Future; Names 3 New Properties

New York, Jan. 31. — Warner Bros. will spend $85,000,000 on 35 pictures skedded for future release, prexy Jack L. Warner disclosed today, following windup of firm's national conclave of district execs at home office here. Warner, however, did not indicate over what length of period films would be released. Last year, company put out a total of 22.

Twelve of the 35 releases already are completed, six are now shooting and 16 are slated for future production. Warner, who listed "The FBI Story," one of the 35, as still in the negotiation stage, also announced three new properties. These include "The Whip," to star Gary Cooper; "Young Strangers," a stage comedy now in rehearsal; and "Tears of Hollywood," from an original by William A. Wellman. Warner today likewise revealed purchase of "Home Before Dark," a new novel by Eileen Bassing, not included in the 35 releases.

"This large investment," Warner said, "reflects our faith in the bright outlook for our company and offers concrete evidence of our confidence in the future of theatrical motion picture exhibition."

Heading list of completed films
(Continued on Page 3)

RKO Studio Shrouds 2 More Departments

Two more studio departments at RKO, including the still and transportation, will be closed tonight, in a continued exodus of personnel and shutdown of operations at Gower St. lot.

Margaret Stevenson, head of the still department, checks out after a 24-year association, and Red Ken-
(Continued on Page 6)

Balaban Here; To Shuffle Top Personnel at KTLA?

Barney Balaban, Paramount prexy, aired in yesterday from NY for a week's stay.

Reports he will reshuffle the top personnel at Paramount-owned KTLA are questioned by Henry Flynn, assistant general manager of the local tv indie.

Head of the station, Lew Arnold, assumed post shortly after the death last summer of Klaus Landsberg.

Only change, according to Flynn,
(Continued on Page 4)

Borzage Will Direct Batjac's 'China Doll'

Frank Borzage has been signed by Batjac Productions to direct "China Doll," scheduled to roll shortly.

To be tested by director for a featured role in film is Columbia contractee Sheridan Comerate, with whom Borzage appeared before the cameras in scenes for "Jeanne Eagels" at Columbia.

hotel SAHARA — Now Appearing ★ XAVIER CUGAT and ABBE LANE ★ las vegas
for reservations, phone CR. 6-0231, BR. 2-7995

100G-PER-PIC PACT IN WORKS AT WB AT TIME OF JAS. DEAN'S FATAL CRASH

Services for James Dean, 24-year-old actor who was killed Friday night in a head-on auto collision, will be held Saturday, 2 p.m., at Hunt Funeral Parlor in Fairmont, Ind. Burial will be in Marion, Ind., Dean's birthplace.

At time of his death, a new contract was being negotiated for James Dean by Famous Artists and Warner Bros., whereby the young actor would have received $100,000 per picture for WB. His pact at Warners had three years to go, but nonetheless the new deal was being negotiated to give the actor a considerable hike in coin.

Accident occurred about 19 miles East of Paso Robles, as Dean was driving to Salinas to participate in weekend road races.

Dean, after majoring in dramatics at UCLA, started his thespic career in NY legit, in "See the Jaguar." He subsequently appeared in "The Immoralist," a performance which won him the David Blum Award as "the most promising newcomer of the year." During that time he also appeared in numerous tv roles.

After run of "Immoralist," Dean was signed by Warner Bros. to a long-term contract and went directly into the starring role in "East of Eden." He subsequently starred in "Rebel Without a Cause," as yet unreleased, and then went into a top role in "Giant," which he completed only last week. George Stevens, producer-director of the latter film, termed Dean's death a "great tragedy . . . he had extraordinary talent."

Dean is survived by father, Winton Dean.

Obituary

BILLIE HOLIDAY

Billie Holiday, 44, widely recognized as one of the great modern jazz singers, died Friday in New York of lung and heart complications following a lengthy illness. Miss Holiday, also called "Lady Day" in jazz circles, had perhaps a greater influence in molding female singing styles than any other jazz singer of her day.

She came to prominence in about 1935 through a series of recordings with Toddy Wilson, later singing with Lester Young, Artie Shaw and others, then branching out as a nightclub soloist on her own. She is survived by her husband, Louis McKay.

LOUIS B. MAYER

Another pioneer is gone. The ranks of the giants of the picture business, the colorful, adventuresome trailblazers of a then infant industry, succumb to the actuarial statistics. In the perspective of time the film industry they forged created an impact never equalled—and that includes television.

You can be the king of the Nielsens but you're a secret in a Savoy Grill or the Ritz Bar compared to some yesteryear Laurel & Hardy or Leo Carrillo. Such is the magic of celluloid. Such has been the import of America's best known export—Hollywood films.

And it was the L. B. Mayers with their stable of stars which created the global boxoffice impact. No cracks about L. B.'s "arrogance" detracts from his pioneering. His role was unique.

It was in his era, with his "three or four Notre Dame teams of stars, producers and directors" that money was no object because money always brought back bigger dividends. Louis B. Mayer once said to a VARIETY man, "Don't you know that I call Culver City 'the Valley of Metro Retakes' and, if it's not right, I shoot it and re-shoot it, until it's right for the boxoffice?" (This was after a criticism of a Marion Davies picture which had greatly upset W. R. Hearst).

It was Louis B. Mayer whose name was part of the name of the most potent film production and distribution powerhouse in the history of the motion picture business. All of which dwarfs his latterday hurt pride and anger against successor managements. The glory that was Metro-Goldwyn-Mayer under Louis B. Mayer can never be erased from the record.

Mayer Dies 'In Exile' From Films

Once 'King of Hollywood' and a Power In National Politics Succumbs To Leukemia

Louis B. (for Burt) Mayer, symbol of Hollywood in its heyday and one of the founders of Metro-Goldwyn-Mayer, died in Hollywood yesterday (Tues.) of leukemia. He was 72. He had been ill for several months. Death came at the UCLA Medical Center.

Mayer, immigrant boy whose keen business sense, imagination and eye for talent, helped develop the world's biggest motion picture studio, was perhaps the most important single figure in the industry's growing pains days. He invented and developed the star system, bringing to Metro (and occasionally to personal contract to himself) a roster of boxoffice luminaries whose names still figure importantly in film annals.

He also brought to Metro Irving Thalberg, still regarded as the industry's most creative producer. It was in this skill at developing personalities and executives that Mayer excelled; that and his shrewd talent for negotiation and dealing with people.

Anecdotes of his business dealings are many; they're as famous as tales of how he was able to turn on the charm and tears alternately in order to get what he wanted in a deal.

Born in Minsk, Russia, he was brought to St. John, New Brunswick, at the age of three, and was in business at eight, lugging a little red wagon loaded with junk behind him. The junk business led him into ship salvage, which forced expansion of his activities to Boston where he saw and became enthralled with flickering images at nickelodeons.

A newspaper ad in 1907 offering a small Haverhill, Mass., theatre for sale launched him on his motion picture career. He bought the rundown house, refurnished it, installed an organ, one of the first in theatres. It was a move typical of the subsequent Mayer incentive to try something new in an effort to keep abreast, or even ahead, of changing public tastes in entertainment.

Against all precedent, Mayer launched his new activity with the hand-tinted "Passion Play," opening the film on Christmas Day. Success of the show, with Mayer concentrating on clean, salable entertainment, gradually forced a revolution in the motion picture industry, pushing it out of ranks of a freak attraction into its eventual position as one of major industries of the world.

Gradually Mayer added to his theatre holdings, eventually developing a chain of theatres, a move which subsequently forced him into his greatest career as a production executive. Dissatisfied with the product he was getting, he began booking leading stage attractions and other adjuncts. He created his own repertory company and finally decided he needed to be in better position to acquire product. So he formed the American Feature Film Co., located in Boston, which served houses in six New England states besides his own. With this affected, he became the biggest film booker in country. Simultaneously, his judgment on films began to be recognized. His audacious buying of pix was always justified. It became automatic that Mayer could measure to within the small percentage point the final gross of films. Thus, his bid on "Birth of a Nation," which his competition considered would be ruinous for him, actually sharply appraised the true worth of the picture and made him a fortune before he was 30.

"Nation" also convinced him the public was ready for feature films. With a group of showmen he organized Metro Films in 1915. At first, he remained east, keeping only a long distance eye on production. But after two years, dissatisfied both with the quantity and quality of productions, he trekked west, set up Louis B. Mayer Productions, and began a production career that continued actively for almost a quarter of a century until, after a series of disagreements, he walked out of his offices at Metro-Goldwyn-Mayer never to return.

Short and stocky, a man who never for a minute forgot the power of his position and acted accordingly, Mayer was a bundle of emotion. His temper was invariably uncertain and he rarely bothered controlling it. He was not noted for consideration or concern re the impact of his behavior. Once, in an argument in his office, he ran around his desk and punched a producer in the nose. His relations with the press weren't improved by the episode of his marriage in 1948, when he "ducked" the reporters. Some extremely unflattering stories were written about him in consequence.

He was positive in his opinions, brooking no arguments from his aides. He was not always an accurate prophet since he predicted that television would never make trouble.

During Herbert Hoover's time the influence of the Metro chief in national politics, especially as concerns California, was determining. A VARIETY man once sat in Mayer's presence and overheard

(Continued on page 21)

1960s

The front page of *Weekly Variety* on December 27, 1961, carried twelve stories. One reported on a Christian film distributor pressuring a North Carolina theater owner to integrate his movie house. (The theater man argued, "This could set a tremendously dangerous precedent.") Another article told about merchandise based on "The Twist." A third story mentioned Riverside Records putting out a disc with the newfangled title *Isometric Exercises*, tied to President John F. Kennedy's fitness program. A report from Europe referenced the Berlin Wall.

Almost a decade later, on July 16, 1969, the nine front-page stories included a preview on the thirty-one hours of network coverage planned for the moon landing, headlined "Greatest Show Off Earth." A month before Woodstock, a reporter addressed the headaches of mega-music festivals. President Nixon was contemplating a woman appointee to the Federal Communications Commission. Paramount's *Medium Cool* was about to make history as the first studio release to use the f-word (or, as the headline exclaimed, "gutter sexual lingo"), while final numbers were tallied to find that 1967's fall re-release of *Gone with the Wind* had helped the 1939 classic surpass *The Sound of Music* as America's biggest-grossing film of all time.

On just two pages, which bookend the decade, you have JFK, Nixon, dance crazes, civil rights, the Berlin Wall, rock music, women's lib, the moon landing, dirty words, and Julie Andrews. Ladies and gentlemen, that was the 1960s!

However, one key element was missing from this two-page time capsule: Vietnam. Though it wasn't on the radar of most showbiz folk in 1961, by 1969, it was a wearying fact of daily life, perhaps too mundane a fact to be carried on the front page every week.

It was a decade filled with trauma, and one of the biggest turning points was the assassination of the president. On November 25, 1963, the Monday after President John F. Kennedy's Friday shooting in Dallas, *Daily Variety* canceled its usual stories and ads to publish a special four-page edition under the banner "All Showbiz Mourns Kennedy."

Right: Julie Andrews takes a break from spinning and singing in *The Sound of Music*.

Following Spread: July 16, 1969; November 25, 1963.

| FILMS | VIDEO | TV FILMS | RADIO | MUSIC | STAGE |

VARIETY

PRICE 50¢

Published Weekly at 154 West 46th Street, New York, N.Y. 10036, by Variety, Inc. Annual subscription, $20. Single copies, 50 cents. Second Class Postage Paid at New York, N.Y., and at Additional Mailing Offices. © COPYRIGHT, 1969, BY VARIETY, INC., ALL RIGHTS RESERVED

Vol. 255 No. 9   NEW YORK, WEDNESDAY, JULY 16, 1969   80 PAGES

GREATEST SHOW OFF EARTH

Miami Beach Yens Casino Loot & Glam To Keep Stars in Those 50G-a-Wk. Fees

By JOE COHEN

Whether Miami Beach niteries can continue in their present state without the aid of gambling is becoming increasingly doubtful among both operators and talent agencies. By now, salaries in the Beach hotels have risen to $50,000 weekly, and very few performers getting that kind of money have turned in a profit for the bonifaces.

The current mood for reappraisal comes from the Hilton Plaza, which goes off the nitery standard and into the legit format, starting Dec. 5 with "Can Can" with Tony Martin & Cyd Charisse in the leads. John Kenley of the Kenley chain of playhouses in Warren, Columbus and Dayton, is producing, and it's believed that he can bring in the shows at a far lower rate than it would cost to bring in a headliner. Besides, the nitery room with armchairs
(Continued on page 75)

TV-AM WEBS BET $13-MIL ON MOON

By STEVE KNOLL

That 31-hour tv super-special scheduled for next Sunday (20), and lasting through midday Monday (21), will be "the world's greatest single broadcast," in the view of Robert Wussler, exec producer of CBS' coverage. Wussler says that not only will the moon landing be "a most historic event, but our own coverage will be up to matching it." That same sense of pride and anticipation, of course,
(Continued on page 54)

Nixon May Name a Femme To a Berth on the FCC

Washington, July 15.
President Nixon last week told concerned Republican Congresswomen that he hopes to appoint a woman to the FCC this year.

Reps. Florence Dwyer (R-N.J.), Catherine May (R-Wash.), Charlotte Reid (R-Ill.), and Margaret Heckler (R-Mass.) asked the President to make greater efforts to
(Continued on page 75)

Pop Festivals 'Fistful of Dollars'; Do $1-Mil Gates Generate Violence?

By MARTY BENNETT

In the wake of the outbreak of recent en masse break-ins at pop fests, the music biz is turning its eye to the storm clouds which now hover as fixtures over all similar rock packages coming up.

Promoters' intricate security strategies for repelling or avoiding the uninvited gatecrashers are making the huge pop music festivals resemble diplomatic showdowns between selling and consuming factions of the youth market, as much as they are more simply structured orgiastic celebrations of some of pop culture's louder product.

The next blowouts include the Seattle Pop Fest in Woodenville, Wash., July 25-27; the Midwest Rock Festival the same weekend in Milwaukee; the Atlantic City (N.J.) Pop Fest, Aug. 1-3; and the Woodstock Music & Art Fair —
(Continued on page 78)

See Saudi Arabia $12-Mil Financing 'Ibn Saud' Epic

Paris, July 15.
Kingdom of Saudi Arabia, out of its oil royalties, is reportedly putting up $12,000,000 for an epic on the life of its demised king. This would bear the title for world release of "Ibn Saud, Leopard Of The Desert." French producer Henri Gebrier states that the deal is
(Continued on page 78)

'Wind' Tops Anew; 'Sound of Music' Revised as No. 2

MGM's "Gone With the Wind" has regained its position as the biggest domestic film grosser of all time.

It has already passed $74,000,000 in U.S.-Canada net rentals, and by Labor Day (says Metro), the figure will equal $76,000,000 as result of the sixth reissue of the 1939 David O. Selznick production. In contrast, when 20th-Fox sales chief Peter S. Myers disclosed a few weeks ago that "The Sound of Music" would be taken out of release on Labor Day for a period of four years, he added that by that time it would have taken in $68,000,000 in rentals.

This raised a delicate point. Fox
(Continued on page 78)

'Laugh-In' So Big a Lure To Teacher, He Rules Out Monday Night Classroom

Neil Compton, the Canadian literature prof who's been regular video critic for Commentary mag for the past few years, this month briefly departs from his usual brand of academic carping to sum up those things he likes about commercial video.

"I was a little irritated with one of my English department colleagues the other day," he writes. "This very strict and uncompromising scolar peremptorily reject-
(Continued on page 78)

Why WMAR-TV, CBS-TV Affiliate in Baltimore, Selected 459 "Films of the 50's and 60's" (246 in Color) including

VOLUMES 12 & 13

"WMAR-TV has been pre-eminent in the presentation of feature films in the Baltimore market for 21 years. To perpetuate our leadership, we have included Warner Bros.-Seven Arts' features in our million dollar library since they first became available. Our excellent vertical and horizontal scheduling flexibility is based upon Warner Bros.-Seven Arts' features in Volumes 1, 2, 3, 4, 5, 7, 8, 11 and Starlite 1. Volumes 12 and 13, our latest purchase, presented an opportunity to acquire only first-class features without dilution in our movie schedule which includes:

14 WEEKLY LOCAL MOVIES

Channel Two Theatre (Sun.-Thurs.) .... 11:25 PM
Twilight Movie (Mon.-Fri.) .... 4:30 PM
Friday's Big Movie .... 11:30 PM
Big Movie of the Week (Sat.) .... 11:00 PM
Saturday's Top Movie .... 5:30 PM
Picture for a Sunday Afternoon .... 12:00 PM

Represented by Katz Television

Donald P. Campbell, Vice President and General Manager, WMAR-TV

Friday's Big Movie Coming Attraction
SPENCER'S MOUNTAIN
Henry Fonda, Maureen O'Hara, James MacArthur

WARNER BROS.-SEVEN ARTS
NEW YORK · CHICAGO · DALLAS · LOS ANGELES · TORONTO · LONDON
PARIS · ROME · BARCELONA · SYDNEY · TOKYO · MEXICO CITY

NATO Asking If MPAA's Code Is 'Really' Working

Kansas City, July 15.
National Assn of Theatre Owners is currently conducting a check throughout the country to determine how well the Motion Picture Assn. of America's voluntary code and rating system is doing.

Sponsored by young NATOites supervised by Richard M. Durwood of Kansas City, the check involves the sending of a three-page questionnaire to theatre throughout the nation and to regional NATO units.

In the accompanying letter, the exhibitor is told to be honest. He is further told his answers and
(Continued on page 78)

Gutter Sexual Lingo In Film Breakthrough Via Par's 'Medium Cool'

"The vernacular terms for fornication, and the related tools, are expected to be just around the corner, according to reports," wrote VARIETY in a frontpage lead story "No End to Gutter Film-Talk," in the Oct. 30, 1968 issue. Now, nine months later, they're here.

Previewers of Paramount's "Medium Cool," the film which takes place against the background of last summer's Democratic National Convention in Chicago, say that it contains liberal use of the most common
(Continued on page 75)

DAILY VARIETY DAILY

Vol. 121 No. 58   Hollywood (28), California, Monday, November 25, 1963   13   Ten Cents

ALL SHOWBIZ MOURNS KENNEDY

REACTION OF PIX B. O. SPLIT

Biz Here Good, But N.Y. Is Dented By Tragedy

It was virtually biz as usual at Los Angeles firstruns over the weekend, but not so in New York where death of President Kennedy made a shambles of Broadway box-office.

There was this difference, too, between situation on two coasts: Broadway cinemas closed Friday night, with trade very thin Saturday and yesterday; all L.A. film theatres remained open Friday, and virtually all did normal or even better biz Saturday, yesterday being only slightly off.

Locally theatres with new pix
(Continued on Page 4)

Assassination Cues TV Shows Revamp Coming Programs

A number of future program changes were made by networks in view of the sombre weekend events.

Ed Sullivan's CBS-TV show next Sunday was to have featured the Obratsov Russian Puppet Theatre, but this taped performance, devoted to comedy and satire, has been postponed.

Comedy will be omitted from the Sullivan show now being prepared.

Garry Moore cancelled taping of the CBS-TV show he would have aired tomorrow, so a rerun of an old Moore show probably will be seen.

"Route 66," also CBS-TV, had scheduled a drama, "I'm Here To Kill A King," about the assassination of a foreign monarch, for next Friday. This will be replaced by another "66" drama.

Tomorrow's CBS-TV Red Skelton show is changing its script in view of the tragedy.

Unprecedented Broadcasting Coverage Costing $30 Mil

Unprecedented, all-out four-day news "crash coverage" by the three television networks, sans all entertainment programming and commercials, began Friday immediately word was flashed that President Kennedy had been murdered. It's estimated, on basis of annual gross of approximately $2,000,000,000, that when the final bill is toted up the four-day tab will exceed $22,000,000. Figure includes losses on tv network day and nighttime programming as well as national spot business that would have accrued to the tv stations throughout the country.

The seven Los Angeles tv stations, in cancelling all forms of commercial programming over the four-day span, will lose approximately $150,000 in revenue.

The 31 radio stations in the L.A. area, also foregoing commercialism over four days, will lose around $250,000 in revenue.

Nationally, radio stations are giving up around $7,000,000.

Final total might go higher than $30,000,000 for tv, making this the
(Continued on Page 2)

Showbiz Stox Hit By Death Of JFK

Before stock exchanges could close at 2:30 p.m. Friday — scant half hour before regular shutdown — the death of President Kennedy reflected a major setback in entertainment stocks as 14 shot downward.

Biggest skid was by MCA, down 6¾ to 52½. Paramount fell 5⅝ to 48¼, RCA 5½, to 85.

Other losses included Ampex, down 3⅜ to 16; ABPT, down 2⅝ to 28; United Artists, down 1⅝ to 19½. Eastman Kodak and Tech-
(Continued on Page 3)

B'way Blacks Out Signs; Legit Shows, Opera And Niteries Shroud Tonight

New York, Nov. 24. — Broadway put on its most sombre dress in mourning President Kennedy. Shortly after it was made known the President was dead, nightclubs, restaurants, legit theatres, Met Opera, N.Y. Philharmonic, as well as some of the major restaurants announced that they would not open that evening. There were some exceptions, but niteries that elected to remain open would do so without music or entertainment.

Adding the most austere touch was the absence of most of the Mazda spectaculars. Douglas Leigh Inc., which operates some of the largest signs in the world obtained permission from 90 percent of its clients to shut off signs' power. They were trying to make it 100 percent.

All Broadway legit theatres have cancelled Monday programs. Tick-
(Continued on Page 4)

Pioneers' Dinner Postponed In N.Y.

New York, Nov. 24. — William J. Heineman, prexy of the Motion Picture Pioneers, issued a terse statement late in the afternoon announcing "postponement" of the annual Pioneers Dinner tomorrow (Monday), at which 20th-Fox prexy Darryl F. Zanuck was to have been feted as Pioneer of the Year.

Dinner will be rescheduled at a later date. Zanuck, in Rome all week, was due back here this weekend.

STUDIOS, CLUBS, FILM THEATRES CLOSED TODAY

The assassination of John Fitzgerald Kennedy Friday had far-reaching, almost unparalleled impact on the entertainment industry.

Certainly not since the death of Franklin D. Roosevelt in April, 1945, has showbiz generally been so "moved" — and moved to cut back operations today, the national day of mourning, on all levels and sundry facets.

If the decisions seemed to come slowly, and amid confusion, it was because the entertainment industry, along with the whole world, simply could not believe the dire news. Then, as the hours passed and all attention was galvanized on the shocking events and aftermaths, as
(Continued on Page 3)

Rod Serling, Froug Speed USIA Film On New President

Writer Rod Serling and producer William Froug jetted to Washington last night at the request of the USIA to prepare a half-hour documentary on President Lyndon Johnson, for showing abroad. Serling will write and narrate the documentary.

Kenneth Boles, project producer with USIA, called Serling from Washington and asked him and
(Continued on Page 4)

Col Now 'Worrying' About Releasing 'Bomb'

New York, Nov. 24. — Columbia, which had skedded a sneak preview of "Dr. Strangelove, Or How I Learned To Stop Worrying And Love The Bomb" at the RKO 86th St. Friday night, called off showing.

There also was some question expressed at Col as to whether the company would go ahead with
(Continued on Page 2)

ON STAGE! 5TH ALL NEW! Greatest of the Spectaculars! **Le Lido de Paris** "Bravo" Revue!   **STARDUST HOTEL** LAS VEGAS   1295 DELUXE ROOMS CALL 274-5801 272-8301

International Sound Track

London

Yolande Donlann is doing a guest star stint in "Jigsaw," written, produced and directed by her husband, **Val Guest** for Brittania Films. It's her first screen role since "Expresso Bongo". . . **Walt Disney's** latest British production, "The Horse Without a Head," starts rolling on location in Paris on April 30 and moves into Pinewood Studios on May 7. Scripted by **T. E. B. Clarke** from a novel by **Paul Berna,** pic will be directed by **Don Chaffey. Michael Stringer's** set, a replica of a French village, will occupy the whole Pinewood lot and is said to be twice the size of the "Cleopatra" set in Rome . . . Wessex Films' "Mix Me a Person" has now moved into Shepperton Studios after locations in and around London. **Anne Baxter, Adam Faith** and **Donald Sinden** are playing the leads under **Leslie Norman's** direction. **Victor Saville** is exec producer . . . **Carl Foreman** has signed two British and two Swedish actors for "The Victors," which he's now filming in Stockholm, and which will star **Sophia Loren** and **Simone Signoret.** They are **Peter Arne, Charles Conabere, Alf Kjellin** and **Veid Bethke.** Film, which marks Foreman's debut as a director, is for Columiba release.

Paris

Yank director **Robert Aldrich** in lookseeing a possible pic directorial stint here via a U.S.-French coproduction. Project is yet to be disclosed . . . Pic star **Jeanne Moreau** says she chooses her directors rather than her roles. Her last three pix were with the noted Italian **Michaelangelo Antonioni** "The Night," the Yank filmmaker living in England **Joseph Losey,** who has become the favorite of the avant garde film set here, in an Italo-French coproduction "Eva," and with leading French young director **Francois Truffaut** in "Jules et Jim." She is now doing a small part in **Orson Welles'** currently shooting "The Trial." She then goes into a French-Italo coproduction "Mata Hari," doing the spy role that Garbo once did, with American **Edgar Ulmer** helming, and then turns producer for "Banana Skin," with new director **Marcel Ophuls,** son of the late **Max Ophuls,** doing his first feature.

Michel Subor to New York to huddle with **Elia Kazan** on a possible lead role in Kazan's next pic . . . An offbeat film club, The Cine Club Nickel Odeon, specializes in showing its members little known U.S. films that may have been second features or only fillers in the U.S. but are held up as examples of fine dynamic and true cinema by buffs here. Group is also trying to unearth many pix that Yank majors usually do not distribute here. Among pix showing the next weeks at the bimonthly screenings are **George Sidney's** "Jeanne Eagels," **Douglas Sirk's** "Mystery Submarine," "Summer Smoke." **Zoltan Korda's** "Sahara," **Don McGuire's** "Johnny Concho," **Charles Walter's** "Torch Song," **Lewis Milestone's** "Of Mice and Men," **Hugo Fregonese's** "Untamed Frontier," **Karl Malden's** "Time Limit," and **Ray Enright's** "Trial Street."

Anthony Perkins will do his first French pic in which he speaks French after his English speaking role in Orson Welles' presently shooting "The Trial." He is also hoping to do a legiter here sometime in '63 when he thinks his improving French will allow it . . . A recent poll shows France still one of the lowest per annual capita countries in re attendance at an average of eight times a year for filmgoers . . . In an article on the growing trend of multimillion dollar film spec giants being made by Yank majors both at home and abroad, in the big selling local news weekly L'Express, **Darryl Zanuck,** who just wound his $10,000,000 "The Longest Day" (20th) here.

Rome

Joseph Fryd set release rights to "Invincible Gladiator" with Seven Arts during recent stateside jaunt . . . also purchased pic rights to bestselling "Gold for the Caesars," which he plans for upcoming Italo production . . . Arco Film has started work on **Anna Magnani's** new pic, "Mamma Roma," which **Pier Paolo Pasolini** directs from his own script . . . Cineriz will release . . . "Eclipse" (**Hakim**) opens in Rome prior to its Cannes debut . . . pic, directed by **Michaelangelo Antonioni,** got raves in its Milan opener . . .
. . "Mondo Cane" (Cineriz), **Gualtiero Jacopetti's** feature documentary, breaking records throughout Italian run . . . Rome first two days pic raced up $10,000 new high for Adriano Theatre . . . **Christopher Fry** spent two days conferring with **Dino DeLaurentiis** on "The Bible" project . . . **Stewart Granger** may do **Franz Wisbar's** "Marcia . . . o Crepa" (March . . . or die) next for FICIT-Tempo-Midega . . . foreign legio yarn would be shot in Spain . . . "Smog" (Titanus-Metro) shot in L.A., has been invited by Spoleto Festival . . . Spoleto also plans series of screenings of great films of yesterday and today now being set up by **Denis Horne** . . . **Marlon Brando** being paged as **Gina Lollobrigida's** partner in "The Thaw," which **Franco Rossi** directs this year . . .

"Marco Polo" sale by Jolly Films to American-International now official . . . deal was announced some time ago, but some hitches apparently developed . . . "Polo" gets mass U.S. release in early July . . . **Ermanno Donati** and **Luigi Carpentieri** made pic for Jolly release . . . it stars **Rory Calhoun** and **Yoko Tani,** with **Hugo Fregonese** directing . . . Italian government has extended usual aid money to Venice Festival (reported $170,000) for another year . . .

Joseph E. Levine's Embassy Pictures trying to enlarge the corner it already has on Cannes Fest entries . . . Yank distrib already has three pix to be screened at event, "Boccaccio 70," which opens fest out of competition, "Divorce, Italian Style," the official Italo entry, and a Yank production, "The Strangers," which will be screened at Canneson special invite by French Film Critics group. Levine also has bought "Seven Capital Sins," an Italo-French coproduction, which may be entered by France, and is currently mulling purchase of one, two, or three more features, all in the Italo French orbit, some or all of which may likewise show up at the Riviera do. One is currently being mulled as the wind-up entry at the fest, which would unusually give the purchaser both opening and closing spots at same event.

Edinburgh Fest Bosses Plan Revamping of Own Setup to Curb Losses

Edinburgh, April 17.

The Edinburgh Festival bosses, faced with continued losses, will streamline their own setup and exercise a stricter control over finances. The 1961 Edinburgh Fest incurred a record loss of $350,020 compared with $272,274 in 1960. First steps will be to make a drastic pruning in council membership from 45 to 21.

According to Lord Cameron, leading Scot judge, who stays on the council, the time has come for plain speaking. "This Festival Society requires a drastic reorganization," he said. "Quite bluntly, I think it is time some of us went out. Many of us have been in the Society since its inception. No man can go on giving of his best all the time."

Sir John Greig Dunbar, chairman of the Festival Society Council, said: "The effect of this reorganization will be to speed up the administration of the Festival and allow earlier decisions to be made."

The Festival's biggest loss last year was in productions by Covent Garden Opera, amounting to $115,500. This was despite the fact that they played to audiences of 94% capacity. At the Empire Theatre, the cost of producing "Luther" and "Triple Bill" was $90,000, with a deficit of about $27,000. Smaller losses were made by orch concerts.

French Crix Select 'Viridiana,' 'Sat. Night'

Paris, April 17.

The Academie Du Cinema, composed of French film critics and others from most art and show biz categories, handed out its Crystal Stars, with the best foreign film nod going to the Spanish pic, "Viridiana," naming as the best local pic, "Jules Et Jim."

Best foreign thesps were Lena Winnicka for the Polski film, "Mother Jeanne and the Angels" and Albert Finney for the British pic, "Saturday Night, Sunday Morning." Best French actors were Jeanne Moreau for "Jules Et Jim" and Alain Delon in Rene Clement's Italo-French pic "What Joy of Living."

Debut in Spain Of Film Finance For World Marts

Madrid, April 17.

Financiera Europea S. A. will make its debut as a Spanish film finance company this month to underscore an accelerated trend here toward world market coproductions. The new Madrid company, in which a half dozen Spanish producers have invested, will boast sufficient capital to provide coproducers with below-the-line Spanish costs as well as to guarantee Spanish coproducer commitments against counterpart commitments of future foreign copartners.

Going beyond mere financing, FESA plans to package as well by supplying a Spanish producer, key production personnel and film guidance as related to the local scene. Another aspect of the ambitious FESA structure is the organization of finance links in France and Italy to spur three-way Continental coventures. Film circles in Madrid expect fuller light soon on the individual participation of prominent industry nabobs and announcement of sending first co-project under the FESA aegis.

Japan Exhibs Agree To Lower Admissions

Tokyo, April 17.

Japan's film industry told the government it would agree to lower admission rates equal to amount of expected reduction in ticket taxes. This is a change from earlier proposal that half of tax slashes be added to basic ticket costs in considering the fading film biz.

Taxes will probably be sliced from high of 30% to 10% this spring. Industry did turnabout in anticipation of government aid in form of subsidies at a later date.

British Film Prods., Exhibs Agree On 30% Quota for '63, Not on Relief

London, April 17.

British film producers and exhibitors are agreed that the 30% quota should stay for 1963 but they are split on the question of relief. The filmmakers contend that the quota should be met without qualification in three-way competitive situations. Exhibs fear that there may not be enough product to maintain a triple release, and want provisions for a lower quota rate in such circumstances.

Producers estimate that around 100 first feature films will be available in 1963 which, in their view, is adequate supply for three releases. But the exhibs want the National Circuit, or third release, to be given the "greatest possible freedom" in order that it can have the best chance of survival.

Failure of twoway meetings between the Cinematopraph Exhibitors Assn. and the two producer organizations, British Film Producers Assn. and Federation of British Film Makers, to hit on common ground on the question of relief means that separate recommendations have now to be made to the Board of Trade which sets the level of quota.

Further meetings with the filmmakers are being sought by the CEA on the subject of a ceiling on levy coin. Exhibitors feel the present no-limit formula possibly has a depressive effect on the general level of feature pix production. Subject already has been debated and rejected by the producers.

16 YEARS ENOUGH

Marchent Bows, Cebollada Heads Film Writers Assn.

Madrid, April 17.

Spanish Film Writers Assn. (Circulo de Escritores Cinematograficos — CEC) elected a new slate of officers at its annual elections last week and gracefully retired group's founder and former president for the past 16 years, Joaquin Momero Marchent, by naming him honorary president.

CEC prexy is Pascual Cebollada (editor of La Revista Internacional de Cine); Fernando Mendez-Leite was elected secretary; Alberto Cambronero, vice-secretary; Antonio de Santiago, treasurer. Rafael Capilla, Victor Andresco and Santiago de la Cruz were named executive members.

New roster of officers, in one of their first public acts, called on the director general of cinema, Jesus Suevos, who expressed his intention to consult with the CEC in reorganizing Spanish film industry. The CEC incorporates screen writers, film critics and film commentators.

Tax Chile Cinema To Pay Teachers

Santiago, April 17.

After a two-month hassle between the cinema trade organizations and the Ministry of Economy, a new tax on cinema admissions is finally being implemented, with a partial compensation for distribs and exhibs via a ticket price hike. Object of this new tax is to finance a raise in teacher salaries. It puts Chile in the position of being one of the few countries where films are most heavily taxed. The previous 61% on net has now been raised to 69%.

When Congress first approved this additional levy, it was described as "confiscatory" by Guillermo Carter, president of the Film Distributors Assn. Trade opinion still agrees with this description.

The price of ducats has been raised from 585 pesos to 650 (65c). Even though this means an increase of 65 pesos on gross (95 was initially asked) most of this is absorbed by taxes leaving a net raise of around 21 pesos per ticket.

Films running over 135 minutes, as before, are allowed special scales. For example the current "Guns of Navarone" (Col) gets 1,000 pesos ($1).

Prods. Saltzman, Broccoli Face Big Decision on 2d James Bond Thriller

London, April 24.

Prospect of challenging the security of Fort Knox faces producers Harry Saltzman and Albert R. (Cubby) Broccoli if they finally decide on "Goldfinger" as the second of their James Bond subjects under the deal with United Artists. It is, at the moment, a tossup between that and "The Spy Who Loved Me." Both yarns are now in the scripting stage. The choice will be made when the screenplays are complete.

First of the famed Ian Fleming adventures, filmed by Saltzman and Broccoli under their Eon Productions banner, is "Dr. No," which was lensed on location in Jamaica, with interiors at Pinewood Studios. It is a Technicolor production, and was budgeted at around $1,000,000. It is expected to preem in London next September, and will open next year in the United States.

Sean Connery, a little known actor, who was chosen to essay the secret service agent role of James Bond, opens out of-town next week in the new Christopher Fry play, "Judith." If it turns out a hit, he'll probably repeat the role later in the year when Harold Clurman presents the play on Broadway. It is claimed to be the first time that the Foreign Office has permitted the work of its secret service branch MI 6 (the British equivalent of the CIA) to be depicted on the search.

James Bond's code number in MI 6,007, has been adopted by Eon as the peg for their publicity, and is now being used on the cover of all new books in the series. Book tieups, in fact, are forming a major part of the campaign for launching "Mr. No." Pam Books is publishing a special edition with an initial print order of 1,000,000, reputedly the largest ever for a paperback. In the U.S., it is to be published in the Signet series, with a print order of 5,000,000 copies.

Apart from Connery, principal rales are filled by Joseph Wiseman, as the title character; Jack Lord and Swiss born Ursula Andress. Terence Young directed.

In addition to their commitment to make a minimum of three James Bond films for UA at the rate of one a year, Saltzman and Broccoli are readying another subject for filming in the fall. Under their deal with the distrib, UA has first refusal on all their other projects.

Although actively involved with Saltzman on the Eon Company's production sked, Broccoli retains his 50% interest in Warwick Films, in which he's partnered with Irving Allen.

Veit Harlan Pic Provokes Riots

Zurich, April 17.

Lifting of the Zurich banning, pronounced in 1959 "in the interest of public peace and security," against Nazi director Veit Harlan's film, "The Third Sex," has caused new protest demonstrations in front of the local Stauffacher Theatre, a 460-seater. The exhibitor as well as the film's distributor, Favre-Films of Geneva, had made continuous efforts with the Zurich authorities to have the 1959 ban revoked, reasoning that the film had been released in a number of Swiss cities since then (censorship in Switzerland is in the hands of individual cantons) without major disturbances.

Zurich city council finally gave in, allowing the film's release, but the local police expressly authorized protest demonstrations provided they are carried out in a dignified manner.

On the first day of the re-showing (in 1959, picture had to be ankled after two days due to "disturbances"), over 1,000 reps of primarily Jewish and Socialist youth organizations gathered in front of the Staffacher, carrying transparents with inscriptions such as: "Harlan Picture — a Disgrace for Zurich," "Morals Before Business," "Go Home to the Reich" etc. They tried to prevent patrons from entering the theatre, resulting in riots and physical action.

Protest action against the notorious "Jew Suess" director's film, which has been released sans newspaper ads, was initiated by an action committee against Veit Harlan pictures via large ads in local dailies. This committee includes members of Jewish, Protestant and Catholic associations, political groups, the Zurich Teachers' Association, the Swiss Actors' Assn. and several youth and students' groups.

In view of repeated demonstrations on subsequent days, the exhibitor decided to restrict showings of the film to matinees on weekdays, to refrain from any Saturday and Sunday shows and to remove the picture altogether after a six days' run, including the unplayed weekend.

Later: In consequence of the uproar over "Third Sex," or more accurately its creator, the film has again been banned outright. Reason: "unworthy of Zurich."

Left: *Variety* covers the international beat.

Right: Debbie Reynolds, Carrie Fisher, and Todd Fisher.

The lead story on page one began, "The assassination of John Fitzgerald Kennedy Friday had far-reaching, almost unparalleled impact on the entertainment industry. Certainly not since the death of Franklin D. Roosevelt in April 1946 has showbiz generally been so 'moved'—and moved to cut back operations today, the national day of mourning, on all levels and sundry facets. If the decisions seemed to come slowly, and amid confusion, it was because the entertainment industry, along with the whole world, simply could not believe the dire news."

Some of the reporting was anecdotal: On the MGM lot on Friday, "the focal point on each soundstage suddenly became the familiar transistor radio," reported Army Archerd. Debbie Reynolds told Archerd, "That's why I work for mental health—one out of 10 people today is potentially as sick as the president's murderer. But what can you expect?" Reynolds became emotional:

"With so many slutty books, dirty movies and material going thru the mail. Teenage pregnancies are at all-time high and parental discipline at an all-time low. The country's morals are at a new low."

The small edition carried only nineteen stories. Almost all dealt with biz repercussions, such as stock market reaction, canceled performances of plays, and postponed "blurb talks" (i.e., contract negotiations over advertisements) between the Screen Actors Guild and the American Federation of Television and Radio Artists. There was a twenty-four-hour blackout of all entertainment in Las Vegas.

Another front-page story began, "Unprecedented, all-out four-day news 'crash coverage' by the three television networks, sans all entertainment programming and commercials, began Friday immediately word was flashed that President Kennedy had been murdered. It's estimated, on basis of annual gross of approximately $2,000,000,000, that when the final bill is toted up the four-day tab will exceed $22,000,000. Figure includes losses on TV network day and nighttime programming as well as national spot business that would have accrued to the TV stations throughout the country."

169

Left: Ruth Gordon, John Cassavetes, Sidney Blackmer, and Mia Farrow in *Rosemary's Baby*. It doesn't end well.

Right: January 2, 1962.

The story estimated the seven Los Angeles TV stations, in canceling all forms of commercial programming over the four-day span, would lose approximately $160,000 in revenue. The area's thirty-one radio stations, also foregoing commercialism over four days, would lose around $260,000 in revenue. "Nationally, radio stations are giving up around $7,000,000. Final total might go higher than $30,000,000 for TV."

There were three additional obits, including one for *Brave New World* author Aldous Huxley, whose death on November 22 received scant attention anywhere throughout the world.

Just five years later came another national nightmare: the assassination of Martin Luther King Jr. in Memphis. The April 10, 1968, *Weekly Variety* read, "Not since the assassination of President John F. Kennedy Nov. 22, 1963, has America blacked out economic and social pursuits in memory of an individual American." A report from Washington, D.C., read,

"As might be expected, this city's massive rioting and looting, followed by curfews and liquor sale suspensions, brought all facets of the entertainment industry to a shuddering stop. There were virtually no exceptions to the weekend shutdowns. Although some suburban film houses stayed open, there will be very little activity until the curfew is lifted, probably tomorrow (Wed.)."

Two months after that, in the June 12 *Weekly Variety*:

"Massive TV coverage of Sen. Robert F. Kennedy's assassination over four days totaled roughly 100 hours of network time, worth about $7,000,000 in gross billings. The national debate set off by the depiction of violence in 'Bonnie and Clyde' is almost certain to be paled by the concern over violence in the mass media, particularly television and motion pictures, that has been generated by the assassination of Sen. Robert Kennedy. Sure to be at the center of the discussion is the new commission on violence in America appointed by President Lyndon Johnson after the Kennedy shooting."

These assassinations capped a decade in which the Republic of the Congo's first legally elected prime minister, Patrice Lumumba, was deposed, imprisoned, and executed by a firing squad; four black girls were killed in a

Vol. 114 No. 18 — Hollywood (28), California, Tuesday, January 2, 1962 13 — Ten Cents

JOHNSTON BULLISH ON FILMS IN '62

Too Many 'Second' Helpings May Give 20th 20G Bellyache

By Martin Kivel

Almost everyone agrees that "The Second Time Around" is usually the result of somebody's goof. But for those who doubt it, 20th-Fox has found a rather expensive way to prove it. And therein lies the tale of too many "Second" helpings.

Film company's boo-boo, which may cost it at least $20,000, was using, without permission, a disk by Gogi Grant to plug via paid radio blurbs its Debbie Reynolds
(Continued on Page 11)

Legion Of Decency Blasts 'Liaisons'

New York, Jan. 1.—The Roman Catholic Legion of Decency has given a condemned (C) rating to Astor Pictures' French import, "Les Liaisons Dangereuses." Announcement of the rating is accompanied by an especially sharp denunciation which states that "the film's theme of seduction is more nearly a diabolical mockery of virtue," and adds that there "are numerous sequences which are pornographic in their intent."

Pointing out that the film does
(Continued on Page 4)

Violence Down, Sex Up In '61, Says NAB

Washington, Jan. 1. — "Violence for the sake of violence" declined on television during 1961, but sex reared its head a little more than before.

This was the New Year's word from National Assn. of Broadcasters in reporting results of its TV Code monitoring for the past 12 months. The NAB release summed it up this way:

"A continuing decline in violence for the sake of violence but
(Continued on Page 11)

PIX DIVVY MELON SLICED IN '61

Washington, Jan. 1. — Dividends of film companies lagged slightly behind the 1960 pace during the first 11 months of 1961, according to the Commerce Dept. Through November, stockholders received a $21,649,000 melon as against $22,049,000 for the same 1960 span. Dept. pegged the November total at $1,539,000 compared with $1,074,000 for November, 1960.

Film dividends departed from the national uptrend for dividend-paying corporations. Publicly reported cash dividend payments through last November totaled $11,400,000,000 — a 2.5% gain over 1960.

L. A. Racks Up $10,431,221 At B.O. In '61; Down 5% From '60

Los Angeles firstruns, with considerably fewer openers than in recent years, ran up a sock $10,431,221 during calendar 1961. Total repped a 5% dip from 1960's $10,980,744, but still 4.04% over '59's $10,070,212.

Statistically, the '59 tally was 9.8% under 1958's $11,164,455, which in turn was 3.2% below 1957's $11,534,700. The 1956 great of $11,918,400 repped the highest take since 1949's colossal $13,596,400, down from 1948's record $14,686,800.

Strong entries were responsible for first quarter of 1961 topping all others by a substantial margin — $3,122,774, against third period's $2,673,948, nearest contender, and the fourth's $2,303,500. Latter was the weakest of the year through the absence of any outstanding product strength. Second quarter for '61 was $2,330,999. Comparative figures for '60 showed third quarter the highest, $2,924,-
(Continued on Page 4)

20th's 20th Salute To Prexy Skouras

All 20th-Fox divisions, including the record arm, are behind a three-month business booster campaign, starting this week, as a tribute to mark the 20th anniversary of Spyros P. Skouras as company president.

William C. Michel, exec veepee, is serving as worldwide chairman, according to general sales manager C. Glenn Norris. Murray Silverstone, prexy of 20th's International Corporation, already is in Europe to get the tribute going there. Michel is skedded to tour in
(Continued on Page 10)

TOP PIX-TV STORIES IN 1961

The majority of the big 10 film-tv stories of 1961 were far from one day headline sensations. In fact, some will continue to make important news this year as their full effect upon the destinies of individuals, corporations and the industry generally remains to be played out.

1. THE CODE, CENSORSHIP AND CLASSIFICATION

Criticism of the current state of film morals continued to mount and the propaganda for a system of self-classification by the industry grew hotter, capped in November with a warning by the Catholic Bishop's Committee on films, radio-tv that segregation of pix not suitable for children was the only bulwark against censorship. The Motion Picture Association of America continued adamant against classification, however, even liberated the Production Code more than
(Continued on Page 11)

Predicts Big Rise In Gross Biz And H'w'd Filming, Too

Eric Johnston, after consulting his shiny new crystal ball, predicts that 1962 will be a year of big progress for the film business at home and abroad. The prexy of the Motion Picture Assn. of America forecasts:

(1) A two million weekly increase in average weekly theatre attendance from the 44 million mark reached in 1961;

(2) At least a $100 million rise in total U.S. boxoffice gross, which was estimated at $1.5 billion last year;

(3) A hike of from $10 to $15 million in the more than $200 million annual income the industry takes back to this country from the world market.

Johnston predicted the foreign
(Continued on Page 4)

Labor & Industry Sked Parleys On 'Runaway' Prod'n

At behest of the Hollywood AFL Film Council, labor and industry have agreed to go into conclave early this month in an effort to at least partially solve some of the problems surrounding "runaway" film production. Meeting, which will be held before Jan. 10, will be chaired by Association of Motion Picture Producers veepee
(Continued on Page 4)

Revue Elects Four As New Officers

Four execs at Revue studio have been elected officers of the Revue division of MCA. Production company personnel upped at the Universal City lot are Jere Henshaw, assistant to Pat Kelly, in charge of talent; James Nicholson, in the production department; Gordon Forbes, in studio operations; Gerald Adler, who is in charge of co-ordinators. New titles will be announced later this week.

Las Vegas RIVIERA HOTEL LAS VEGAS, NEVADA — HARRY BELAFONTE (Dec. 21 - Jan. 21) — FINEST ACCOMMODATIONS IN Las Vegas — RESERVATIONS BRadshaw 2-0421 MAdison 3-3102

Left: The Supremes.

Above: The Beatles.

Birmingham, Alabama, church bombing; Medgar Evers was assassinated in Mississippi; three civil rights workers were also lynched there; and Malcolm X was shot by three gunmen in New York City.

While all of these carried their own horrors, the shooting of Lee Harvey Oswald, coming just two days after the Kennedy shooting, was troubling in a different way. His death meant one thing: there would never be answers. Horror films always reflect the collective anxiety. In the May 29, 1968, review of the Roman Polanski–directed *Rosemary's Baby*, the reviewer talks about Rosemary (Mia Farrow) being "the lone victim of a conspiracy . . . audience interest focuses on rooting for the heroine, and finding out what the conspiracy is all about." The key word in the review and in the decade was "conspiracy." Everyone around you is a potential source of danger. You are alone. Nobody will help you.

That fear was validated with the 1969 Tate-LaBianca murders by the Manson family. The most famous of the victims, Sharon Tate, was the actress wife of Polanski.

Kitty Genovese's 1964 murder in Queens illustrated that you could get killed in public and nobody would help you. The Tate-LaBianca murders took it one step further, showing you could be killed by a stranger in your own home. You were not safe from anyone. You were not safe anywhere.

But the mood of the 1960s wasn't always somber. Because we had The

Beatles. The Beatles influenced music for decades to come (virtually every artist post-Beatles has been expected to come out with something different and remarkable with each album), as well as fashion (long hair was unthinkable before them) and lifestyle (Transcendental Meditation and drug experimentation came into vogue). The Beatles' effect is especially remarkable considering their short span: they began to hit it big in the early 1960s and officially disbanded in 1970.

The Fab Four spawned the British Invasion, a group of U.K. musicians set to conquer the world, including the Rolling Stones, The Who, The Kinks, Petula Clark, Tom Jones, Manfred Mann, and Dusty Springfield.

Americans had their homegrown stars in the decade as well, including the "surf sounds" of the Beach Boys and Jan & Dean, plus The Four Seasons, Sonny & Cher, and the more folky-influenced The Byrds, The Lovin' Spoonful, Simon & Garfunkel, The Mamas & the Papas, Judy Collins, Jefferson Airplane, The Doors, Buffalo Springfield, and Creedence Clearwater Revival.

There was also the empire of Motown, founded by Berry Gordy Jr. in 1959 with The Miracles' "Bad Girl," though the Detroit label had its first hit the next year with the group's "Shop Around." Motown (from the Detroit nickname "Motor City") launched the careers of Stevie Wonder, The Jackson 5, Marvin Gaye, the Four Tops, the Temptations, Martha and the Vandellas, Gladys Knight and the Pips, and The Supremes (which in 1967 became Diana Ross & the Supremes), while

Above and Right: Gene Hackman, Warren Beatty, Faye Dunaway, Michael J. Pollard, and Estelle Parsons in advertisements for *Bonnie and Clyde*.

NOMINATED FOR . . .
Best Picture
Best Actor: WARREN BEATTY
Best Actress: FAYE DUNAWAY
Best Supporting Actor: GENE HACKMAN
Best Supporting Actor: MICHAEL J. POLLARD
Best Supporting Actress: ESTELLE PARSONS
Best Direction: ARTHUR PENN
Best Story & Screenplay (Original): DAVID NEWMAN & ROBERT BENTON
Best Cinematography: BURNETT GUFFEY
Best Costume Design: THEADORA VAN RUNKLE

the Miracles were renamed Smokey Robinson & the Miracles. Like the Brill Building, which cranked out numerous hits in the 1950s and 1960s, Motown used a stable of songwriters to keep creating the hits, with Gordy's company indebted to the team of Holland, Dozier, and Holland (respectively Brian, Lamont, and Edward Jr.). Other black artists were also breaking down the barriers, including Ray Charles, James Brown, Dionne Warwick (with a string of hits written by Burt Bacharach and Hal David), the Marvelettes, The Drifters, The Shirelles, and Little Eva. And, of course, there were also the musicians who died too early, including Otis Redding and the "three J's," all of whom died at age twenty-seven: Jim Morrison, Jimi Hendrix, and Janis Joplin.

Years before the U.S. government passed civil rights legislation, artists were paving the way toward equality. The *Weekly Variety* headline on October 11, 1961, announced

"Segregation in Professional Legit Theatres in the U.S. Is in Its Last Season." The story read, "Actors Equity and the League of N.Y. Theatres have agreed that beginning next June 1, productions will not play houses practicing segregation. Each booking contract will contain clauses providing that no discrimination or segregation will be practiced against any performer or patron at the theatre by reason of race, color or creed."

Two months later, *Variety* carried a story about a Greensboro, North Carolina, movie-theater owner who was protesting pressure to integrate. On the same page was a headline "Gathering the Facts on Negro Casting." It told of various showbiz factions meeting to formulate a plan for "presenting a true picture of the Negro in films and video [television]." And here's the complete story from *Weekly Variety*, January 31, 1962, headlined

"Negro Heads Art Dept.": "Harold Van Riel, a staff advertising designer at 20th-Fox for the last 20 years, has been named the company's advertising art director, a post which has been vacant since 1956 when Victor Sedlow resigned. Van Riel is believed to be the first Negro to hold a comparable post."

The August 28, 1963, March in Washington for Jobs and Freedom was the setting for Martin Luther King Jr.'s historic "I Have a Dream" speech. The following day, *Daily Variety* reported that over 200,000 demonstrators heard a show business pledge "to do everything possible" to bring the "evils of discrimination to an end." Among those who spoke or performed, according to the report, were Harry Belafonte, Ossie Davis, Joan Baez, and the singing group Peter, Paul, and Mary, as well as Odetta, Ruby Dee, Josh White, Bob Dylan, Leon Bibbs, Lena Horne, Bobby Darin, Marian Anderson, Mahalia Jackson, Dick Gregory, and Burt Lancaster.

James Earl Jones:

"On September 16, 1963, an article appeared in *The Washington Post* (as, I must assume, in national papers across the nation—perhaps including *Variety*), "Six Dead After Church Bombing." In that same season, Off Broadway, at the Saint Marks Theater in the East Village in New York, a play by the Frenchman Jean Genet titled *Les Negres* (or "The Blacks") was playing to sellout audiences. The play, a highly symbolic ritual play, had two groups of negro performers. The upper tier, wearing white masks, represented white people. The lower tier, with no masks, represented The Blacks. The ritual enactment was of rape, trial, and murder. Each group was led by a queen, and each queen would launch into an incantation of ethnic iconic symbols. At one performance, the queen of The Blacks shouts out, "Dahomey Dahomey!" which unleashes a torrent of incantations and dance accompanied by drum, and in the din of all this excitement, a voice says, "And six little girls in Birmingham." The leader of the troupe halts the proceedings to suppress this bit of unscripted dialog too late—it was out. The connection was made. That outburst never happened again; it was left to be interpreted as, "some actor got carried away.""

Right: Americans looked forward toward civil rights.

Following Spread: Katharine Hepburn, Spencer Tracy, Sidney Poitier, and Katharine Houghton in advertisements for *Guess Who's Coming to Dinner*.

THE TV SCENE

Tragic Touch Is a Minor Miracle

BY CECIL SMITH

Television achieved a minor miracle Monday night—a sociological play that touched the universal heart.

The play was "Who Do You Kill?" by Arnold Perl, which occupied "East Side, West Side." In the usual manner of this series, it brimmed with social indignation. But it also told in glowing terms a tragic tale that belonged to no time or place. It was a tragedy set in Harlem; it could have been set in Elsinore.

Quite simply, the story was of a young Negro couple, superbly played by Diana Sands and James Earl Jones, whose baby is killed by a rat bite in the infested tenement that is their Harlem home. There was a great deal of sociological noise about the conditions under which Negroes live in New York, the lack of job opportunities and the like, but this was of lesser value than the drama itself.

The play showed the coming to manhood of a youth through tragedy—a major theme in the minor world of television. In the beginning, Joe Goodwin (Jones) is a surly, bitter lad, whose wife (Miss Sands) supports him, working as a bar waitress, while he minds the baby and studies for a job he's certain he won't get.

When the child dies, the wife disintegrates. She is the bitter one, brooding over her bourbon. But the boy she married finds phoenix-strength in the tragedy, the maturity to rise from the ashes of his baby's death and flex his muscles, spread his wings.

Magic Moments—Beautifully Made

The play was beautifully made under the direction of Tom Gries, shot almost wholly on the cluttered, drab and dirty streets in New York's Harlem. There were magic moments—Jones dashing in to the onrushing traffic of the street with his stricken baby; Diana's soundless grief at the news her child was dead.

There was one passionate scene wherein a preacher told the bereaved parents the story of the great Civil War Negress Harriet Tubman. Gries kept his cameras on the couple, caught their agony while the banal tale of ancient heroism washed over them.

This was a tale of Negroes but not a Negro story. Despite its racial arguments, it was a story of all humankind caught in remorseless fate and transformed by tragedy. It was not a story of color but of the eternal struggle of man in an imperfect world.

L.A. Times, Wed., Nov. 6, 1963

TV: A Drama of Protest
Predominantly Negro Cast Enacts Story of Frustration Set in Harlem
By JACK GOULD

Drama of protest, a theme rarely found on television, made an impressive and moving appearance last night on "East Side / West Side," a series built loosely around the life of a social worker played by George C. Scott.

The play, "Who Do You Kill?" from the pen of Arnold Perl, was the story of frustration experienced by a young couple living in the slums of Harlem. The motivating incident was the tragedy of wretched housing—the couple's child was fatally bitten by a rat.

But the larger narrative, told by Mr. Perl with lean and perceptive understanding, dealt with the erosion of the human spirit that accompanies exploitation of a minority. The damage to dignity that attends unequal employment and unequal education finds release in bitterness. But in the sequel to the accident that befell the couple's daughter Mr. Perl made his telling point: disaster, suffering and finally the healing balm of love know no color line.

"Who Do You Kill?" for all practical purposes was the first television drama to employ a predominantly Negro cast since the revival of "Green Pastures." As the young mother, Diana Sands was extremely touching and heartrending. James Earl Jones, playing the father, was first rebellious and then filled with humility; it was a portrayal of dimension. Tom Gries did the superb direction, and the camerawork of Jack Priestley was an editorial in itself on Harlem living conditions.

New York Times, Tuesday, Nov. 5, 1963 (Review)

Telepix Review

EAST SIDE, WEST SIDE
(Who Do You Kill?)
Mon., 10-11 p.m., KNXT-CBS-TV

"East Side, West Side" presented a powerful, scathing indictment, a searing social wallop, in "Who Do You Kill?" In the intensely hard-hitting script of Arnold Perl was a savage yet accurate picture of the plight of the second-class American—the Negro who lives in ugly, rat-infested slums.

It's a gripping, morbid drama, a tale of despair and futility, and there undoubtedly are many who uneasily will wish this had never been made. Yet ugly and unpleasant as the situation is, it's better to have it exposed honestly, than to sweep it under the rug.

Perl's tale has to do with a young Negro couple living in the dregs of Harlem. A rat bites their young child, who eventually dies. The father's angry frustrated rage at the world echoed in his anguished cry, "Who do I kill?" is one to rub all consciences. There is no resolution of the twofold, yet single problem of segregation plus poverty and slums, and it would have been presumptuous to attempt one in a 60-min. drama. It is a generally depressing story because it is etched in realism.

Diana Sands is excellent as the young Negro mother trapped in squalor and heartbreak. James Earl Jones contributes a powerful performance as her husband, and the scene wherein he frantically seeks help while carrying his rat-bitten child is a study in despair. Godfrey Cambridge, George Gaynes, Maxwell Glanville and John McCurry also give good portrayals, and there is the usual fine acting by George C. Scott, as the social worker, plus competent help from Elizabeth Wilson and Cicely Tyson, who are regulars.

Tom Gries' direction is sensitive and perceptive, an excellent contribution to the overall impact of the drama. *Daku.*

Daily Variety, Wed., Nov. 6, 1963

TV DRAMA CLEARS TENEMENT YARDS
Businessman Sends Truck for Garbage in Harlem
By EDITH EVANS ASBURY

A businessman sent a truck and crew of men to Harlem yesterday to clear away, at his expense, rat-infested rubbish and garbage in the yards behind tenements on Lenox Avenue between 117th and 118th Streets.

The dozen men began removing the debris at 1 P.M. under the direction of Sidney Rosenblatt, who estimated that the job would take a week and cost $10,000.

Mr. Rosenblatt, general manager of City Service Cleaning Contractors, a subsidiary of the Kinney Service Corporation, had been sent to Harlem by Steven J. Ross, Kinney's president.

Mr. Ross, tall and impeccably dressed, visited the site during the afternoon. He explained that he had decided to "do something to help Harlem" after viewing a television drama depicting the tragic plight of Negro families trapped in the slum there.

The drama, "Who Do You Kill?" was presented on "East Side/West Side," a series shown on Monday nights on WCBS-TV, starring George C. Scott as a social worker.

Daniel Melnick who, with David Susskind, produces the series, also visited the site, and expressed pleasure at Mr. Ross's reaction.

"I just hope other people will become aroused enough to do something about it, too," Mr. Melnick said.

Exterminators Are Next

Mr. Ross, whose company has five subsidiaries and includes a real estate department, said he had encountered so much difficulty in ascertaining the true ownership of the tenements that he had decided to go ahead with his plan without the permission of the landlords. He had been advised by his legal department to get permission . . .

N.Y. Times, Friday, Nov. 22, 1963 (Article)

AGAIN TONIGHT · CHANNEL 2 · 10PM

NOMINATED FOR 10 ACADEMY AWARDS

BEST PICTURE

BEST ACTRESS
Katharine Hepburn

BEST ACTOR
Spencer Tracy

BEST SUPPORTING ACTRESS
Beah Richards

BEST SUPPORTING ACTOR
Cecil Kellaway

BEST DIRECTOR
Stanley Kramer

BEST SCREENPLAY
William Rose

BEST FILM EDITING
Robert C. Jones

BEST ART DIRECTION
Robert Clatworthy

BEST SET DECORATION
Frank Tuttle

BEST MUSIC AND SCORE
DeVol

COLUMBIA PICTURES presents a
STANLEY KRAMER
production
SPENCER TRACY | SIDNEY POITIER | KATHARINE HEPBURN

guess who's coming to dinner

and introducing
KATHARINE HOUGHTON
with CECIL KELLAWAY, BEAH RICHARDS
Written by WILLIAM ROSE, Produced and Directed by STANLEY KRAMER
Music by DeVOL TECHNICOLOR®

More "dinner" talk

```
              Christina
The most obvious mistake you're making is in under-
estimating your own daughter.  She'll fight you...and
when she fights you, and for what it may be worth,
I'm going to be on her side.
```

NOMINATED FOR 10 ACADEMY AWARDS

BEST PICTURE / BEST ACTRESS Katharine Hepburn, **BEST ACTOR** Spencer Tracy
BEST SUPPORTING ACTRESS Beah Richards, **BEST SUPPORTING ACTOR** Cecil Kellaway
BEST DIRECTOR Stanley Kramer, **BEST SCREENPLAY** William Rose, **BEST FILM EDITING**
Robert C. Jones, **BEST ART DIRECTION** Robert Clatworthy, **BEST SET DECORATION** Frank Tuttle
BEST MUSIC AND SCORE DeVol

Columbia Pictures presents A STANLEY KRAMER PRODUCTION

guess who's coming to dinner

Right: Robert Culp and Bill Cosby in *I Spy*.

"Also in from Hollywood were Steve Cochran, Gregory Peck, Anthony Quinn, Robert Ryan, Marlon Brando, Tony Franciosa, James Garner, Rita Moreno, Peter Brown, Nate Monaster, Sam Peckinpah, Eugene Frenke, Ben Rinaldo, Antoinette Bower and Frank Silvera. In from Gotham were Susan Strasberg, committee chairman Charlton Heston, Sidney Poitier, Diahann Carroll, Paul Newman and Joanne Woodward, Joseph Mankiewicz, Tony Curtis, Lorraine Hansberry, Arthur Canton, Marvin Levy, Mike Merrick, John Killens, Ina Balin, Jan Sterling and Dolores Grey. Sammy Davis Jr. came in from Detroit."

But, never forgetting its industry readership, the front page also carried a story from Washington, D.C., that began "The civil rights 'march on Washington' killed showbiz in the capital today. The matinee performance of 'Cleopatra,' at the 1,250-seat Warner Theatre, sold 68 tickets. . . ."

Historic moments can inspire millions—or they can inspire people to cash in. As reported in the December 18, 1963, issue of *Variety*:

"The 'I Have a Dream' speech made by Rev. Dr. Martin Luther King in Washington, Aug. 22 was ruled to be the property of the speaker and not in public domain by Judge Inzer B. Wyatt in N.Y. Federal Court last week. Decision puts an injunction on albums issued by 20th Century-Fox Records and the Mr. Maestro label which used the speech. Rev. King's suit against 20th and Mr. Maestro was based on his feeling that their exploitation of the 'March On Washington' and his 'I Have A Dream' speech diverted funds from the civil rights movement."

Slow progress was reported in July 1964 in New Orleans:

"Negroes testing the new Federal Civil Rights law Monday . . . found doors opened at previously all-white downtown and nabe theatres, drive-ins, restaurants and hotels. In some instances, Negroes made reservations for the Roosevelt Blueroom but failed to show up after they were accepted. There were no major incidents reported since the legislation barring discrimination in public accommodations went into effect Thursday night."

On that November 18, 1964, *Weekly Variety* front page stated:

"Sheldon Leonard's projected one-hour series, 'I Spy' for NBC-TV next season has a unique distinction in casting. Negro comedian Bill Cosby has been cast. . . . There have been a few occasions in which Negroes have had running supporting roles in dramatic series, notably, 'East Side, West Side' and 'Nurses.' Unlike the projected 'I Spy' series, no series has had a Negro costar in a running role."

Four months later, *Variety* reporter Bill Greeley talked about the booming popularity of primetime TV series showcasing popular music acts, which "has created what is probably the most important breakthrough yet for Negro performers in the medium. It all started early this year when the Liverpool Beatles, in a sense, introduced Americans to American music on Ed Sullivan's CBS-TV vaudeville hour. The Beatles hit a 45.3 rating and 60.5 share (an estimated 73,000,000 homes), and the numbers held up very well through two more appearances and two repeats. Then came ABC-TV's 'Shindig,' the youthful musical half-hour show that will boom into an hour at midseason, and it is this slick and lively boomchucker that has been important to the young Negro troupers whose fame was previously preserved in perishable disk wax and one-nighter and split weeks of the r&r vaude circuit."

Among the "mostly young Sepia performers" who were performing for TV audiences of all colors were Jackie Wilson, The Miracles, The Supremes, and Sam Cooke, who sang "the Bobby Dylan integration folk number 'Blowing In the Wind.'"

Bobby Dylan?

Robert Zimmerman had changed his name to Bob Dylan in honor of Dylan Thomas. While the nickname "Bobby" didn't stick (thankfully), the press and public did feel a connection to him. Dylan and The Beatles ushered in the era of the singer-songwriter, who went beyond the usual love songs to write about personal doubts, hopes, and social concerns. Close on their heels were the Rolling Stones, The Who, Simon & Garfunkel, Leonard Cohen, Laura Nyro, and Harry Nilsson.

During the first half of the twentieth century, there had been songwriters and there had been singers. Andy Williams and practically everyone else recorded the Henry Mancini–Johnny Mercer "Moon River," but the songwriters didn't sing it themselves. The same was true of other hit songs like "More," from the 1962 hit shockumentary *Mondo Cane*, and "The Girl from Ipanema," by Antonio Carlos Jobim. If one singer had a hit song, other singers were expected to create their own version.

There were manufactured singing groups (The Chiffons, The Shangri-Las, etc.), who had stables of writers creating material for them.

The music scene certainly had its ups and downs—the eight-track tape phenomenon is clearly in the latter category—but the musical diversity offered further proof that creativity blossoms in tough political climates.

Aside from America, other countries were dealing with their own racial unrest. Apartheid had been an official policy in South Africa since 1948, but it wasn't until the 1960s when people noticed. A January 5, 1966, *Variety* report stated,

> "Despite South Africa policy on 'Apartheid,' Brit artists are boycotting, but top stars and companies from other countries are signing up and find arrangements satisfactory. . . . Ster Films, financed by Volksbeleggings, an investment company, is buying up as many cinemas as possible. . . . The

Left: Charlton Heston.

Above: Robert Zimmerman/Bobby Dylan/Bob Dylan.

Above: The Jackson 5.

Right: October 29, 1963.

DAILY VARIETY

News of the Show World
(Trade Mark Registered)
FOUNDED BY SIME SILVERMAN
Published Daily, Except Saturdays,
Sundays and Holidays, with a
Special Edition the Last Week
in October
By Daily Variety, Ltd.
Syd Silverman, President
6404 Sunset Boulevard
Hollywood (28), California
Phone HOllywood 9-1141

Vol. 121   Oct. 29, 1963   No. 38

Copyright 1963, by Daily Variety, Ltd.
Single Copies, 10 Cents
Annual $20 .. Foreign, $25
Second class postage paid at Los Angeles, California.

THOMAS M. PRYOR, Editor

Who's Where

David A. Lipton, Universal pub-ad veepee, to N.Y. h.o. confabs and TOA convention.

Mark Robson, in last night from global tour, checks into Columbia today for script confabs with Nelson Gidding on "The Centurions."

Charles Boasberg, Paramount general sales mgr., back to N.Y. after studio confabs.

Julie Andrews due today from London to start role in "Americanization Of Emily" at Metro.

Vincent Edwards and Michael Callan plane to Frisco today for preem of "The Victors" at the film fest.

Selig J. Seligman, "Alexander The Great" teleseries exec producer, returns today from St. George, Utah, location. Leon I. Mirell, Selmur Prods. veepee, and series femme lead Ziva Rodann plane to St. George today.

Arch Hall Sr. to Gotham screening of new Fairway-International product and to attend TOA convention.

Ruth McDevitt jets in today from N.Y. to start role in "The Out-Of-Towners" at Warners.

Frankie Laine due today from stand at Palmer House, Chicago.

Tom Harmon planes in tomorrow from Chi convention of General Motors personnel.

Connie Stevens and husband James Stacy jetted back from Mexican honeymoon to report for tv stints.

Bobby Vinton due back from Maine today.

Habimah To Play L.A.

America-Israel Cultural Foundation, which holds third annual $100-a-plate dinner-concert at the BevHilton Nov. 24, will sponsor a spring tour of Habimah Theatre, to wind in Los Angeles in April. Trek begins at New York's Little Theatre.

JUST FOR VARIETY
By ARMY ARCHERD

GOOD MORNING: When Carl Foreman bows his "Victors" at the Frisco film fest tomorrow it will be minus Romy Schneider's nekkid footage . . . Miss S., currently displaying her charms and talents in "Good Neighbor Sam" at Col's Gower St. lot, was asked by director David Swift if she could drive an American car. "I can drive — but I don't know how to stop," Schneider said . . . Swift follows the sexy "Sam," "Yum Yum Tree" and "Grindl" tv'er with an all-femme series, sezze . . . Deborah Kerr is Ross Hunter's choice to play the nympho in "The Easy Way" — Jane Fonda to play her dotter . . . A German film company is picking up shots in L.A. and Palm Springs for a Deutsche feature, "The Corpse Of Beverly Hills" . . . After 1,600 miles of location-hunting in the southwest, John Sturges decided to lense "Satan Bug" outside Palm Springs, the principal set to be built near Palm Desert for a Dec. 5 start . . . Producer Bernard Smith back from the Monument Valley location of John Ford's "Cheyenne Autumn," met with Spencer Tracy who works in scenes to be Burbank-lensed. "Autumn" has winter scenes awaiting snows in Colorado — Moab locations as well . . . Lawrence Welk queried on a possible biopic by Universal — his early life bubbling with more than champagne music. Decision on the deal isn't dough, assures Sam Lutz, but the script . . . Roger Edens, associate producer to Lawrence Weingarten on "Molly Brown," and ditto on "Sound Of Music" (formerly with William Wyler), sez "Music" now vamps until September '64. Or later? . . . The "Oliver" film pact with the Mirii now looks set result of Harold M.'s N.Y. trek . . . Hy Averback looms as producer-director of Gene Barry's indie feature "Girl In The White Mercedes" . . . J. Lee Thompson tossed one big celebration at 20th to commemorate the "What A Way To Go" finale . . . Barbara Eden sez it's okay with her if the "NEW Interns" cast is listed alphabetically, she'll use her married name — Mrs. Michael Ansara.

* * *

Film version of "The Best Man" will include integration, the Cuban situation and a zealot character — not named as a Bircher — but . . . Hank Fonda and Cliff Robertson, the pic's Presidential hopefuls are both Demos. while Lee Tracy, the ex-Prexy whose endorsement they both seek is a GOP'er . . . Doubleday soon publishes "Two Worlds Of Charlie Gordon," which Robertson will indie feature. He played the vidversion, bought it for pix after losing the bigscreen'd "Hustler" and "Days Of Wine And Roses," which he originally tv'd . . . Tommy Farrell now in "Kissin' Cousins" at Metro, prepping a vidseries, "Woodrow Perkins," with Jerry Hopper. They tackle a new profession: insurance salesmen. "There's no one with endurance like the man, etc. etc." . . . Glenda Farrell in "Cousins" with her sprig playing a "Ma Kettle"-like role, claims the moth-eaten sweater she wears was once owned by Marie Dressler . . . Elvis Presley didn't attend the sneak of his "Viva Las Vegas" but got the final tabulation: 10 Presley songs to Ann-Margret's two. (The La Mirada mob A-OK'd the Jack Cummings-George Sidney pic) . . . Walter Seltzer showed "Man In The Middle" to 20th in N.Y., they dug it, gave a Jan. release date for the Bob Mitchum starrer. Seltzer now preps "The War Lord" for Charlton Heston — no release deal set yet . . . Four Star's Tom McDermott in N.Y. talking distrib pacts for "Man And Boy," which Charles Boyer will feature for 'em . . . Vic Damone back from his Vegas wedding, starts rehearsals for this week's Judy Garland taping . . . Bobby Darin sez he discovered how to beat the "Vegas throat" — a vaporizer puffs away all night in his room.

* * *

The mad (4) whirl: Stanley Kramer started testing "World" at midnight last night on the countdown sked for Sunday's preem of his pic and the Cinerama theatre. The theatre checkoff list is now down to stopwatch timing . . . June Allyson took her two kids outta BevHills school, is selling the house, will live at Newport Beach where hubby Glenn Maxwell works . . . Lucy Ball and Gary Morton in the audience at the Joey Bishop show where pals Paula and Jack Carter guested. After the seg, Lucy checked her Cahuenga stages, noted, "I may paint it" . . . Janice Rule talking "Outrage" with Marty Ritt . . . Bob Newhart joins Marty Ransohoff's "Muscle Beach" boys — Jim Garner will probably star . . . They love Mike Connors south-of-the-border where his "Tightrope" series is mucho big. His nitery dates in Mexico, Venezuela, expand south to Buenos Aires where he's offered $7,500 per frame plus fringe benefits . . . The "Beverly Hillbillies" and "Petticoat Junction" bunch will be on hand Friday for Rufe Davis' bow at the BevWilshire . . . Diahann Carroll inked to be personally managed by Norman Rosemont whose stable includes Roberts Goulet and Horton . . . Don Rickles inked for a CBS series about a coupla N.Y. firemen, "Kibbee Hates Finch," heads to Gotham to test for a firehose partner.

POLL PRODUCING PAR'S 'SYLVIA'

Martin Poll and Paramount have concluded a deal under which Poll will produce "Sylvia," novel by E. V. Cunningham, for Par release through Poll's Marpol Productions Inc.

Cunningham is a pseudonym for Howard Fast, who originally had been slated to script. Picture had been announced in June, 1961, as a coproduction with Poll, Martin Ritt and Paul Newman, with Richard Carr signed to screenplay, then was dropped. Poll now has complete ownership and will begin filming late next spring in Hollywood. He will assign new scripter and director.

Producer has four pix remaining on his deal with United Artists. Among films he is now prepping are "Twist Of Sand," "Abby A The Girls," and "Love And Taxes." Latter is the film version of the Carolyn Green legit comedy, "Janus," which Abe Burrows is scripting.

3 Pix Univ. Pact For Carl Reiner

Carl Reiner has been signed to a three-pix producer-writer deal by Universal, under which performer will establish his indie production company, Acre Enterprises, on the lot early next year.

Reiner scripted "The Thrill Of It All" and the upcoming "The Art Of Love" for Universal.

Bourguignon On 20th Lot To Direct 'Wedding'

Director Serge Bourguignon checked onto the 20th-Fox lot yesterday to prep "Cassandra At The Wedding," Natalie Wood starrer, to be produced by Martin Manulis.

Manulis also opened an office on the 20th lot and will be bicycling between it and Warners, where he is producing "The Out-Of-Towners."

Levy 'Love' Director

Ralph Levy has been signed to direct "Some Other Love," projected Doris Day starrer for the Melcher Co. Martin Melcher will be exec producer. Levy and Milt Rosen also will script.

Bal Denver 'Doll'

Jeanne Bal, regular in MGM-TV's "Mr. Novak," during Christmas hiatus will do a Denver revival of "Guys And Dolls."

Name-Dropping

Bernie Hamilton reports getting a role in a new entry in tv's title-stretching derby, the "Dick Van Dyke Show" segment tagged: "The Sound Of The Trumpets Of Conscience Falls Deafly On A Brain That Holds Its Ears . . . Or Something Like That."

Says Hamilton, ". . . It's a good thing I only have to memorize the part . . . and not the title."

Left: Sidney Poitier.

Right: Audrey Hepburn in an advertisement for *Wait Until Dark*.

20th Century-Fox Organization of S. Africa concluded arrangements to open Cinerama theatres here [in Capetown], Johannesburg and Durban. . . . 'Mary Poppins' and 'Sound of Music' have broken all records in Capetown. . . ."

Adding to the global anxiety was Southeast Asia. A May 1, 1963, review of a one-hour TV documentary began,

"'The War That Creeps' was an interesting report on the war in Vietnam which became particularly timely last week in light of the outbreak of new conflict in the Laotian corner of Southeast Asia. This documentary about Vietnam successfully conveyed the idea that the struggle against the Communist forces in this area of the world will be a long, difficult and expensive commitment for the American government."

As the military was beefing up, so were news teams. A front-page August 10, 1964, *Daily Variety* story was headlined

"CBS Rushing News Reinforcements to Cover South Vietnam, 7th Fleet" and continued with "CBS is rushing a task force of correspondents and camera crews to Saigon to report on the growing crisis in South Vietnam. Charles Collingwood, European staffer, flew to the trouble spot from Istanbul, where he covered the Cyprus dispute. Murray Fromson of the West Coast bureau has departed with a camera crew. . . ."

The newsies' rapid disillusionment was chronicled on August 31, 1965, in a story from Hong Kong:

"ABC network commentator Peter Jennings stopped over here after a three-week assignment in Vietnam and observes, 'Before I left the States, I was not too sure, along

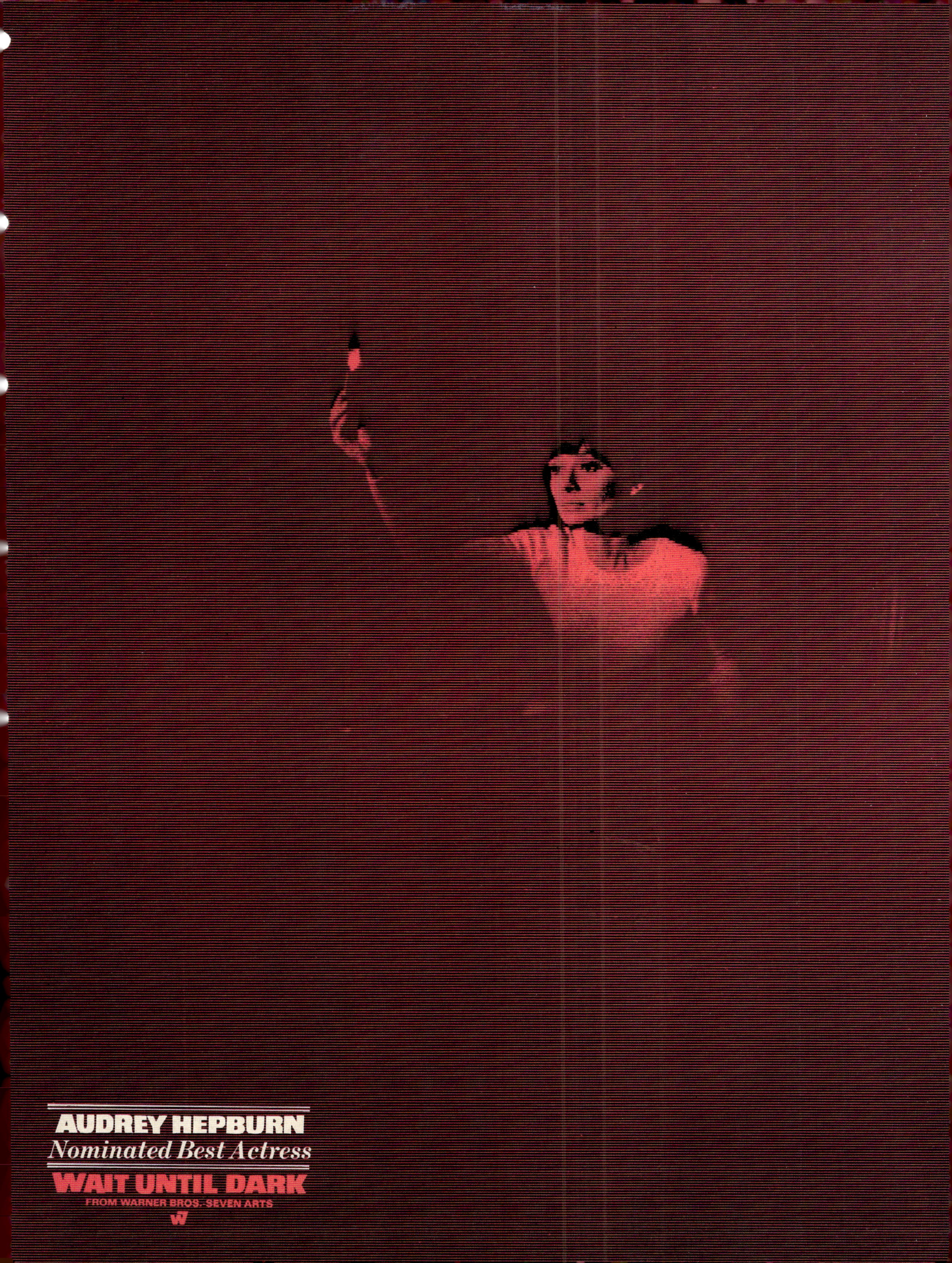

Right: Janis Joplin.

with a lot other people, just how much of a war was going on there in Vietnam or even if there was a real war. Now I'm dead sure.'"

After serving several missions there, Jennings concluded,

"This is a dirty, muddy and lonely war, and one that the Vietnamese have to win themselves."

That creeping doubt, in sharp contrast to American support in World War II, was taking its toll. January 5, 1966:

"Hugh O'Brian, back from troop visiting in South Vietnam, reports the need for more solo tours by showbiz people in order to reach servicemen on remote outpost duty. . . . O'Brian toured the battlefront via helicopter, and reports morale as high despite domestic picketing and draft-card burning incidents."

The 1960s popularized the term "generation gap," but the tension was political as well as generational, as demonstrated by the clash between a flag-waving vaudeville veteran and a protest singer, as reported on January 5, 1966:

"George Jessel, whose plane was shot at while personaling for the GIs in Vietnam, took pacifistic Joan Baez to task for the folk-singer's anti-Viet pronunciamentos and financing of a school which teaches methods in non-violent resistance in civil rights causes."

This could also be read as:

George Jessel, whose plane was shot at while he was in Vietnam entertaining the troops, berated folk singer Joan Baez for her anti-war statements and for financing "a school which teaches methods in non-violent resistance in civil rights causes."

A story from Washington, D.C., in the January 19, 1968, *Daily Variety* was headlined "Eartha Kitt's Tirade Stuns Lady Bird at D.C. Luncheon." The story said the singer-actress

"shouted angrily at the First Lady that the war in Vietnam is responsible for the widespread youth rebellion, crime in the streets and rioting." The story added that "White House historians knew of no incident in modern times equaling such a show of bad manners by an invited guest in the mansion."

Some felt that it wasn't bad manners, but rather just telling the White House what it needed to hear. Years later, Kitt said she'd been blacklisted as a result, and clubs and theaters, fearing CIA or FBI reprisal, refused to book her.

The *Daily Variety* story didn't carry a byline, but the writer concluded Kitt was "a rebel without a cause," because earlier in the day she had visited Representative Roman Pucinski (D-Illinois) to explore a Vietnam trip to entertain the troops. The reporter thought this contradicted her antiwar sentiments. That was a sign of the times: many Americans thought U.S.

soldiers were dupes or blind patriots for going to Vietnam, and had little compassion for them (despite the fact that many of them had been drafted). It was only in subsequent wars that Americans realized they could be against a war and yet "support our troops," as the bumper stickers read during the Gulf and Iraq wars.

Kitt was far from the only high-profile war protester. In 1968, "the increasing candor of broadcast commentary on Vietnam reached a high point last Thursday . . . as NBC's David Brinkley declared his opposition to the war on his nightly radio report."

A week later, America's participation in the war received a fatal blow from CBS's Walter Cronkite. A February 29, 1968, *Daily Variety* review of the half-hour CBS special *Report from Vietnam: Who, What, When, Where, Why?* concluded, "As Cronkite factually and graphically demonstrated, it's a dirty war."

Cronkite, aka Uncle Walter, delivered an editorial stating that it seemed certain the war would end in a stalemate. His statement was devastating. Americans were not accustomed to losing anything. According to an anecdote at the time, President Lyndon B. Johnson concluded, "If I've lost Cronkite, I've lost Middle America." The day before that review appeared, a story headlined "LBJ-B'Casters' Gap Widening: New Nadir Cued by Vietnam-Plus." The story talked of "the alienation gap" between newsies and President Johnson: "The White House of late has come under mounting criticism from segments of the industry on a number of counts, not least of them being Johnson's credibility standing."

If the decade ended on a note of alienation, it began with energy as the country and the world tried to make a transition between the pent-up 1950s and the changes that were being reflected in the entertainment industry.

On May 25, 1960, a Cannes Film Festival critic praised *Never on Sunday*. It seems like just another review of a saucy comedy but the film's backstory hints at the times. The writer-director was Jules Dassin, who had been blacklisted and was working overseas (in this case, an English-language comedy in Greece). The tale of a professor trying to educate a prostitute—or "joy girl," as she's called in the review—seems like a Pygmalion retread but was actually radical for a film released by an American distributor. Since the Motion Picture Production Code was still in force, United Artists was treading where few Hollywood studio would. Under the code, sex-for-hire women had to either atone or be punished for their sins, often by dying (*Camille* [1936], *Waterloo Bridge* [1940]), but *Sunday*'s prostitute (Melina Mercouri) ends up happier than anyone else in the film. It was dangerous turf but, as the reviewer hints, "the tactful treatment should probably avoid any possible censorship troubles."

On the same page was a story about Lenny Bruce's arrest when a police officer attending his show called

Above: "Uncle" Walter Cronkite has news.

Right: October 6, 1961.

Fri., Oct. 6, 1961 — DAILY VARIETY — 3

Film Review

Breakfast At Tiffany's
(Romantic Comedy-Drama; Technicolor)

Paramount release of Martin Jurow-Richard Shepherd production. Stars Audrey Hepburn, George Peppard; features Patricia Neal, Buddy Ebsen, Martin Balsam, Mickey Rooney; with Vilallonga, John McGiver, Dorothy Whitney, Stanley Adams, Elvia Allman, Alan Reed, Beverly Hills, Claude Stroud. Directed by Blake Edwards. Screenplay, George Axelrod, based on the novel by Truman Capote; camera, Franz F. Planer; editor, Howard Smith; art directors, Hal Pereira, Roland Anderson; music, Henry Mancini; sound, Hugo Grenzbach, John Wilkinson; assistant director, William McGarry. Reviewed at the studio, Oct. 5, 1961. Running time: 115 mins.

Whitewashed and solidified for the screen, Truman Capote's "Breakfast At Tiffany's" emerges an unconventional, but dynamic, entertainment that will be talked about and, resultantly, commercially successful. Out of the elusive, but curiously intoxicating negative of Capote's fiction, scenarist George Axelrod has developed a surprisingly moving positive, touched up into a stunningly visual motion picture experience by the screen artisans assembled under the aegis of producers Martin Jurow and Richard Shepherd and surveillance of director Blake Edwards.

Capote buffs may find some of Axelrod's fanciful alterations a bit too precious, pat and glossy for comfort, but enough of the original's charm and vigor have been retained to make up for the liberties taken with character to erect a marketable plot.

What makes "Tiffany's" an appealing tale is its heroine, Holly Golightly, a charming, wild and amoral "free spirit" with a latent romantic streak. Axelrod's once-over-Golightly erases the amorality and bloats the romanticism, but retains the essential spirit ("a phony, but a *real* phony") of the character. And, in the exciting person of Audrey Hepburn, she comes vividly to life on the screen. Miss Hepburn's expressive "top banana in the shock department" portrayal is complemented by the reserved, capable work of George Peppard as the young writer whose love ultimately enables (in the film, not the book) the heroine to come to realistic terms with herself.

Especially excellent featured characterizations are contributed by Martin Balsam as a Hollywood agent, Buddy Ebsen as Miss Hepburn's deserted husband, and Patricia Neal as Peppard's wealthy "sponsor." Mickey Rooney's participation as a much-harassed upstairs Japanese photographer adds an unnecessarily incongruous note to the proceedings. Others prominent and valuable in support are John McGiver, Vilallonga, Dorothy Whitney, Stanley Adams, Elvia Allman and Alan Reed. Putney, as Miss Hepburn's symbolic no-name feline pet, is definitely PATSY bait.

Cinematically, the film is a sleek, artistic piece of craftsmanship, particularly notable for Franz F. Planer's haunting Technicolor photography and Henry Mancini's memorably moody score. The latter's "Moon River," with lyrics by Johnny Mercer, is an enchanting tune with great commercial prospects. Other ace contributions are those of art directors Hal Pereira and Roland Anderson, set decorators Sam Comer and Ray Moyer, editor Howard Smith and wardrobe designer (for Miss Hepburn) Hubert de Givenchy. *Tube.*

'Breakfast' Hearty 25G On 1st B'way Day; 'Hustler' Still Hot On 2d Lap

New York, Oct. 5. — Strong new fare, plus continued cool weather, is giving Broadway first-run biz nice fall hypo despite first two World Series games here. Diamond tilts naturally hurt most matinee trade but this was generally made up by night upswing. Hot newcomer is "Breakfast At Tiffany's" which, with stageshow, looks like smash $25,000 or near opening day, today, the Music Hall.

After wow initial week, "The Hustler" is holding up, eyeing, for three days of second round daydating at the Paramount and arty 72d Street Playhouse, socko $22,000 or close. Pic also is doing remarkably big $7,000 or close first two days of initial week at the Brooklyn Paramount.

"Thunder of Drums" wound first Capitol stanza with mild $21,000; reissue combo of "Earth Is Mine," "Sapphire" looks for good $15,000 initial Palace week. Another oldie dualer, "God's Little Acre," "La Parisienne," is heading for okay $10,000 at the Victoria. "Guns Of Navarone" shapes to solid $25,000 in 15th Criterion week. "Young Doctors" finished sixth Astor frame with mild $13,000. "Francis Of Assisi" looks like okay $10,000 in 10th Rivoli round, "Spartacus" lusty $18,000 in 52d DeMille session.

Meanwhile, starting Wednesday "Spartacus" will switch from the DeMille to Palace and play 16 other RKO houses simultaneously in the greater N.Y. area.

"La Dolce Vita" held to great $21,000 in 24th stanza at Henry Miller. "Exodus" is fair $14,000 in 41st week at the Warner. Oldie combo, "Picnic" and "Twinkle And Shine" slipped to good $9,000 second Forum round.

State closes after today to prep for preem of "King Of Kings" next Wednesday. "Honeymoon Machine" dipped to $8,500 in sixth week there.

Lenny Bruce Runs Afoul Frisco Laws On 'Obscene' Lingo

San Francisco, Oct. 5. — Comic Lenny Bruce, arrested Wednesday night after his first show for using "obscene language in a public performance," yesterday was booted out of his room at the Clift Hotel.

Bruce was told by the management that "his reservation had expired." Episode followed a day-long hassle which began when Bruce appeared at the Hall of Justice on the obscene language charge and got a continuance until Oct. 16. He is currently scheduled to appear in Philadelphia Oct. 9 on a charge of illegal possession of drugs which police claim they found in his room.

Bruce opened at the Jazz Workshop here Tuesday and did two SRO shows at $2.50 a head in the 150-seat club without episode. Wednesday night uniformed Frisco police officer James Ryan was present for the first show and when he heard Bruce utter a vulgate term for homosexual called Sergeant James Solden. Bruce was arrested after the show as he walked out to the street and greeted the cop with, "Cold tonight, eh?"

The police said they were acting on an anonymous complaint despite fact no customers walked out or objected at Bruce's shows. Booked and charged for violation of Section 205 of the Police Code. Bruce made bail and was back at the Jazz Workshop in time for a second show at 1 a.m. in which he related the entire experience to his audience. Bruce claims artistic privilege and cites the dismissal of charges on poet Allen Ginsberg's use of the same word in "Howl" several years ago. Sgt. Solden said, "We're trying to elevate this street. Our society is not geared to this word. How can you break it down?" To which Bruce replied, "By talking about it."

'Lust' For Saunders

Mary Jayne Saunders has been set to star in "Lust For Innocence," indie to be produced next year in New York by Ralph S. Hirshorn, former executive assistant to Arthur Kramer at Columbia. Film is based on a novel by Dianne Doubtfire, with author also to adapt for the screen.

Alex Gordon Fights Woolner Pic Plans

Producer Alex Gordon yesterday charged independent producers who are not members of Motion Picture Assn.'s Title Registration Bureau take advantage of properties registered by actual members.

There is no protection, Gordon adds, and says he plans to fight Woolner Brothers Productions announcement regarding plans to film Edgar Allan Poe's "Mask Of The Red Death" (listed by Woolner as "Masque Of The Red Death"), which, Gordon says, he has been prepping 18 months.

He asserts he already has a script by Mildred and Gordon Gordon from an adaptation by Ruth Alexander of the Poe story. Vincent Price is to star and has a percentage of the pic, to be budgeted at $750,000. All Poe works, it might be noted, are in public domain.

Gordon stresses producers who are members of the Bureau pay an annual fee of $65 for membership plus $70 for every 10 titles registered. Non-members, of course, pay nothing.

Lewis In 'Hathaway'

Robert Q. Lewis has been cast in "TV Or Not TV," seg of "The Hathaways" vidfilm series.

BROADWAY OPENING

BLOOD, SWEAT & STANLEY POOLE
(Continued from Page 1)

for a moderate run on Broadway, besides having the makings of a hilarious pic.

Idea is that a not-too-bright lieutenant, having won his commission in combat, is required under a new Army regulation to pass a test in order to retain his rank. As the company supply officer, he is in a jam because he has been taking supplies to pay off the captain in return for passing him. If the stock shortage is discovered he'll not only be dishonorably discharged but probably sent to prison. With the help of an intellectual wizard private, however, he passes the test legitimately and even gets revenge on the captain.

Perhaps because the basic situation isn't preposterous in itself, "Blood, Sweat And Stanley Poole" tends to be funny rather than sidesplitting. As with most farces, essential premise doesn't stand close examination, but it's plausible enough for practical purposes and the co-authors have cooked up a pretty good assortment of comic twists. The key sequence, in which the elaborate scheme to defeat the villain is pulled off, is ingeniously staged, although it has to take the form of description of the off-stage event, with sound effects.

As adroitly and economically staged by Jerome Chodorov, the performance is generally proficient. Darren McGavin is skillful and properly virile as the beset lieutenant. Peter Fonda, Henry Fonda's son making his Broadway debut as the high i.q. private, makes a lean, blond appearance and has an attractive manner. With considerably more experience, he may also be a good actor some day.

As for the others, John McMartin is excellent as the contemptible captain, and there are helpful supporting portrayals by Gene Roche, Hy Anzel, J. Talbot Holland, Pat Polen, Robert Weil, Reed Brown Jr. and Elisabeth Fraser. Donald Oenslager has designed an authentic looking supply office setting and J. Michael Travis has provided the various uniforms.

At risk of dooming with faint enthusiasm, call "Stanley Poole" a passably funny show. *Hobe.*

London's K.C. Date

Julie London has been signed to headline at Riviera Club, Kansas City, Mo., for two-week engagement starting Nov. 2. Date follows singer's stand at the Club Russo, Middleton, Conn., where she opens next week.

'Young' Sound Dept.

Jerry Young has been set by executive producer David L. Wolper to head new sound department at Wolper Productions. His assistant will be James Young.

JALEM PRODUCTIONS

Gratefully acknowledges the contributions of all of the actors, artists and technicians whose efforts contributed so meaningfully to the critical and boxoffice success of "COOL HAND LUKE." Jalem also points with pride and gratitude to the Academy Award nominations voted for:

PAUL NEWMAN — *Best Actor*
GEORGE KENNEDY — *Best Supporting Actor*
DONN PEARCE & FRANK R. PIERSON — *Best Screenplay (Adaptation)*
LALO SCHIFRIN — *Best Original Music Score*

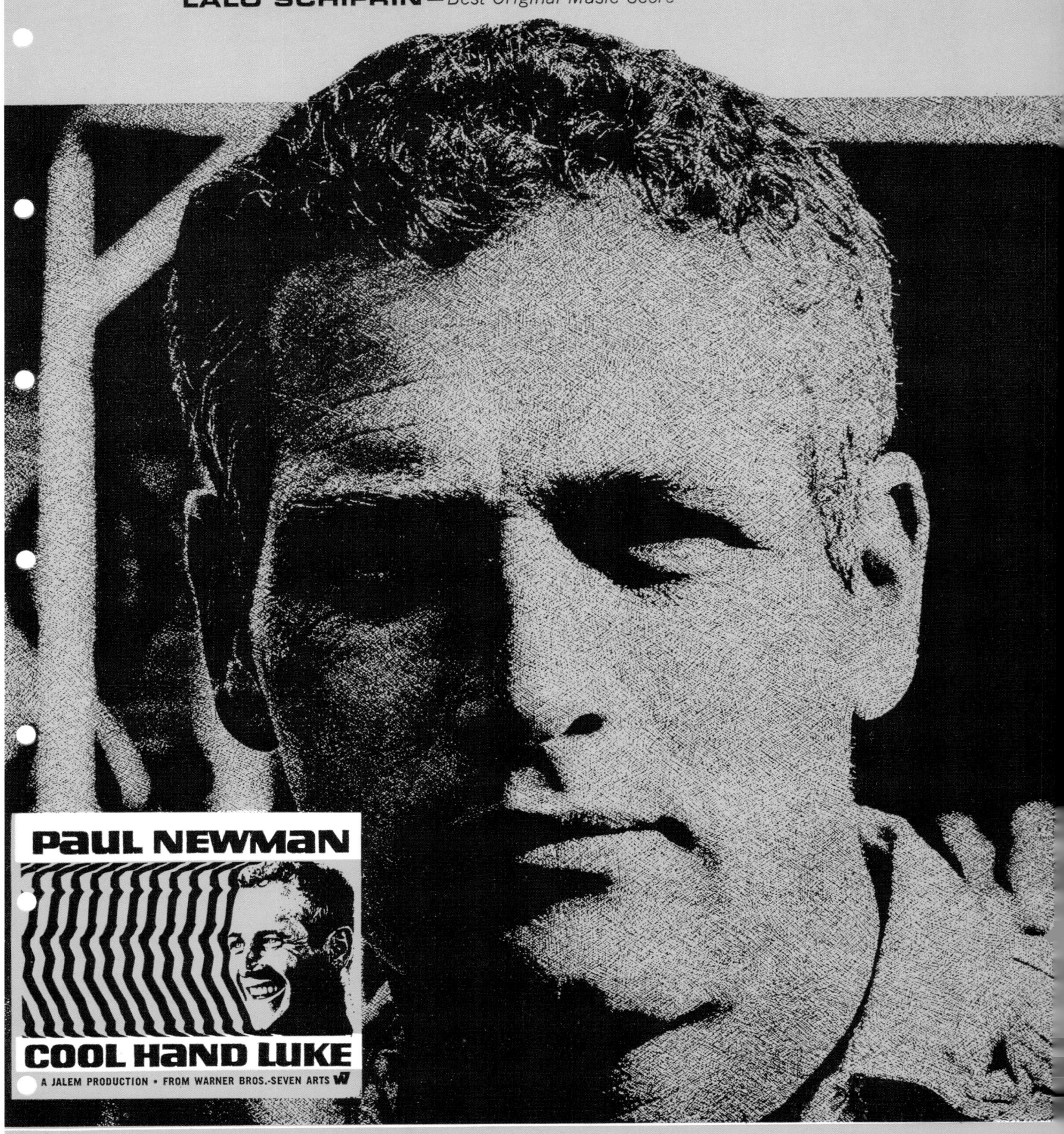

"A film as beautifully executed as any made this year" — HOLLIS ALPERT, *Saturday Review*

FIRST 4 DAYS 3RD WEEK "PLANET" BREAKS RECORD SET BOTH 1ST AND 2ND WEEKS!

Loew's Capitol

First 4 Days of 1st week $70,533
First 4 Days of 2nd Week $60,844

First 4 Days of 3rd Week $72,097

72nd Street Playhouse

First 4 Days of 1st Week $14,547
First 4 Days of 2nd Week $13,566

First 4 Days of 3rd Week $16,688

BOOK IT NOW FOR EASTER!

Co-starring RODDY McDOWALL · MAURICE EVANS · KIM HUNTER · JAMES WHITMORE · JAMES DALY · Introducing LINDA HARRISON as Nova
Produced by APJAC PRODUCTIONS · Associate Producer MORT ABRAHAMS · Directed by FRANKLIN J. SCHAFFNER · Screenplay by MICHAEL WILSON and ROD SERLING · Music by JERRY GOLDSMITH · Based on a Novel by PIERRE BOULLE · PANAVISION® · COLOR BY DELUXE

Previous Spread: Paul Newman and George Kennedy in advertisements for *Cool Hand Luke*.

Left: Advertisement for *Planet of the Apes*.

his captain "when he heard Bruce utter a vulgate term for homosexual."

In the March 2, 1960, *Weekly Variety*, the Cartier Cinema in Hull, near Quebec, bleeped out two words from the film *Look Back in Anger*. In John Osborne's play and the film, angry-young-man Jimmy sings, "I'm in love with you" to a woman who's not his wife—so the theater cut the last two words.

In the same issue, the Independent Film Importers and Distributors of America griped that they couldn't afford two simultaneous censorship battles. In Fort Worth, Kingsley International's *And God Created Woman* had been judged obscene. Atlanta had banned a number of films, including two that had received Production Code approval. *Variety's* article asked:

> "Are the censorship battles worth it? Not financially, according to one interested film attorney, but every victory, no matter how limited, serves to whittle down general censorship powers and, in addition, serves to instill a little more caution into censor board members."

Meanwhile, American TV was seeing its own battles on this front.

The June 17, 1960, banner read, "Sex-Violence under TV Code Fire." The story out of Washington was an interview with National Association of Broadcasters Television Code review board chairman E. K. Hartenbower. He said that Frank Morris, director of the Code's Hollywood office, "has reviewed and edited 209 TV scripts and 74 syndicated films other than those handled by the networks. According to Hartenbower, none of these would have been checked for Code compliance if the Hollywood office had not been set up."

The tallies had been in the months since August 1959.

> "Overall, Hartenbower said the code staff analyzed some 90,000 monitoring hours last year, breaking down to a total of 740 reports on individual stations. Of the 740 reports, more than 258 showed no Code violations whatsoever, Hartenbower said."

Doing the math, this means that 482 *did* have Code violations, which raises the question: was the Code that strict or was Hollywood being naughty?

Possibly both.

The moral climate was shifting, as the review pages indicate. Look at the October 6, 1961, review of *Breakfast at Tiffany's*, in which the critic thought scripter George Axelrod's

> "once-over-Golightly erases the amorality and bloats the romanticism, but retains the essential spirit ('a phony, but a real phony') of the character. And, in the exciting person of Audrey Hepburn, she comes vividly to life on the screen."

Hepburn and the film are so charming that audiences then, as now, could overlook the fact that this was a romance between a call girl and a paid gigolo. Two months later, Hepburn starred in *The Children's Hour*, a chaste film that addressed lesbianism (like prostitutes, lesbians and homosexuals had to end up unhappy or dead, and frequently both).

Hepburn's costar in *The Children's Hour* was Shirley MacLaine, who also starred in Billy Wilder's 1963 *Irma La Douce*, as a Paris prostitute who also finds a happy ending. Meanwhile, thirty-eight-year-old Doris Day was still trying to hold on to her virginity in films like *That Touch of Mink* (1962).

Though the Motion Picture Production Code was still in place, the rules began to loosen.

The stage had traditionally been more open to adult themes than the movies, which, in turn, were more permissive than TV. The public acceptance of changing standards was put to the test in 1966, with Warner Brothers' release of *Who's Afraid of Virginia Woolf?* Edward Albee's play was a

195

Above: Richard Burton and Elizabeth Taylor in *Cleopatra*.

Right: Bette Davis looks for work.

sensation on Broadway in 1962, with its then-shocking language like "screw you," "bugger," "up yours," and "hump the hostess."

Shortly before the film's debut, a *Weekly Variety* story read, "Although he didn't explain how he expects to enforce it, Warner Bros. president Jack L. Warner said last week that an 'adults only' policy for

'Who's Afraid of Virginia Woolf?' would include a clause in all contracts with exhibitors, prohibiting theatres from admitting anyone 'under the age of 18 unless accompanied by his parent.'"

The report said this was

"admittedly the first time such a clause has been included in a Warner Bros. contract covering motion picture rentals (and probably any other company) . . ."

An accompanying story speculated that the over-eighteen move came from a recommendation by the National Catholic Office for Motion Pictures, which gave the film an A-IV rating, which meant "morally unobjectionable for adults, with reservations." (A "condemned" rating from the group was considered box-office poison.)

The report explained,

"A-IV rating by the Catholics is one that has been used of late for 'class' offerings which might in the past have been condemned on subject matter alone. Titles in this category have included 'Tom Jones,' 'The Servant,' 'La Dolce Vita,' '8-1/2,' 'The Knack' and 'Darling,' which won an award from the Catholic group as best film for adults of 1965."

With the A-IV rating "some people have been saying that the Church is more aware of 'artistic' considerations

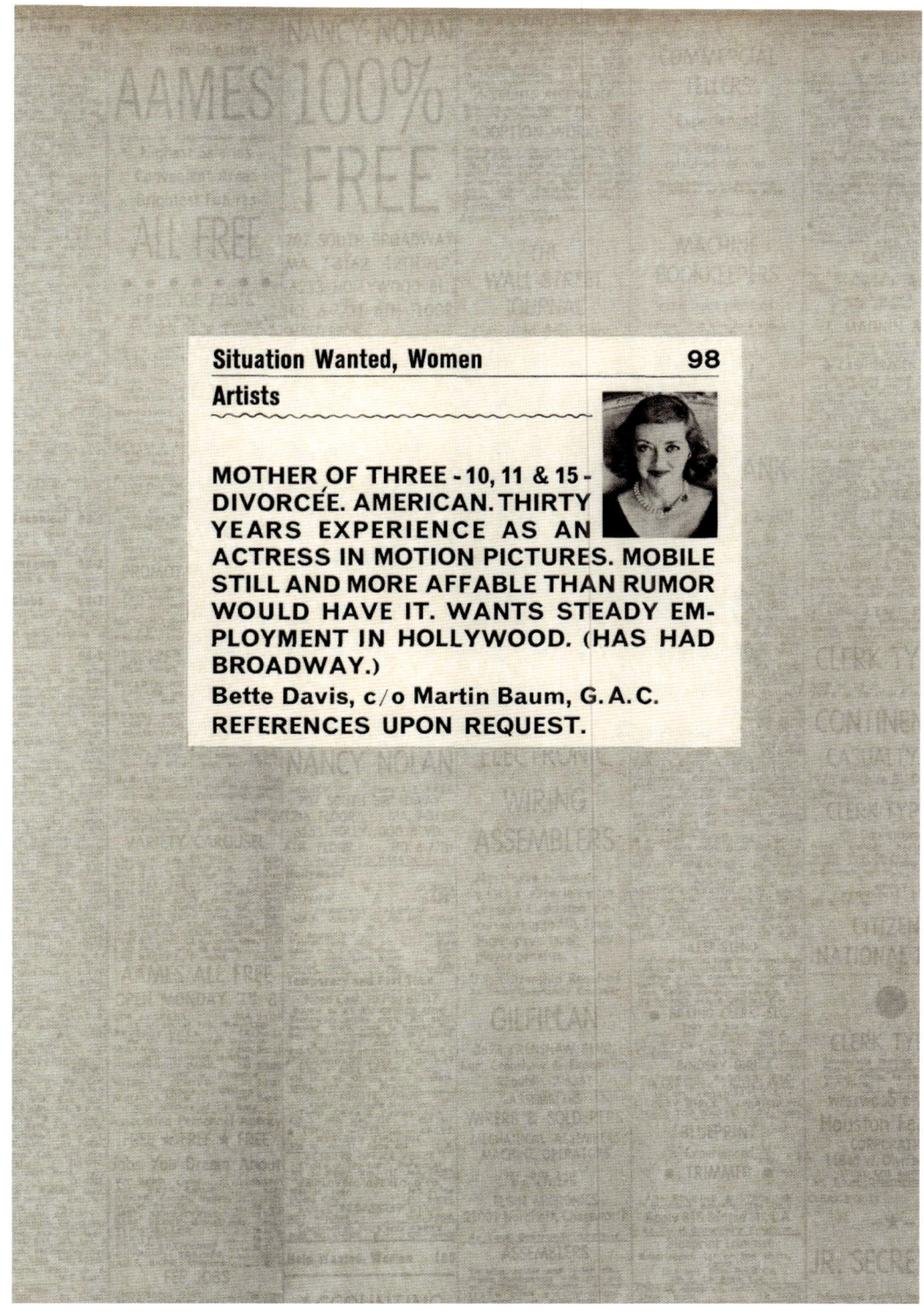

than the Code, and is consequently more 'liberal' in some areas."

Those previously mentioned daring films, it should be noted, were from the U.K. and Italy. Clearly, other countries were pushing the envelope more than the United States because they weren't forced to adhere to the Code. The story concluded, accurately, "Nevertheless, the 'Virginia Woolf' fracas may serve to hasten the public debut of a revised code, still 'under discussion' by the MPAA."

Elizabeth Taylor and Richard Burton found themselves at the center of the decade's morality self-exam. Again.

Taylor made a name for herself with *National Velvet* in 1944 but became a leading lady with the 1950 *A Place in the Sun*. As she was gaining more respect as an actress, she became a young widow when her husband producer Mike Todd died in a plane crash. So the world embraced her. As did singer Eddie Fisher, who left his America's Sweetheart wife Debbie Reynolds for her. Those three became tabloid fodder for ages, which heightened further still when Taylor in turn left Fisher for Richard Burton, whom she had met on the set of *Cleopatra*.

Burton and Taylor earned as much tabloid attention as Brangelina and William & Kate combined, but in a different way. Their sexy good looks were mingled with drinking, diamonds, and a lavish lifestyle that were all breathlessly reported.

Cleopatra had been envisioned as a $5 million film, and Taylor had been signed for the unprecedented salary of $1 million. It began filming on September 15, 1960. A series of setbacks delayed the film: sets destroyed by weather, changes in co-stars, the exit of director Rouben Mamoulian and entrance of director Joseph Mankiewicz, numerous rewrites, Taylor's near-fatal illness, and other calamities. Filming was completed in 1962, two years after the start of production. On January 9, 1963, *Variety* editor Abel Green pronounced that the film's final production cost was $35 million, or seven times the original budget. Others have estimated it cost even more.

The media and the fickle public blamed Taylor and Burton for the costs. And when the Century City complex in Los Angeles opened in the 1960s on acreage that was once the 20th Century-Fox back lot, Hollywood lore said *Cleopatra* had forced Fox to sell the land. Actually, on November 24, 1958, long before *Cleo*, *Daily Variety* reported that Fox was near a deal to sell 176 acres for $40 million. The following May, *Daily Variety* covered the dedication of the land, which was purchased by William Zeckendorf, who would help turn it into the current Century City. *Cleo* was not the culprit: TV was to blame, as dwindling film audiences forced all studios to rethink their cost structure. This is not to say that *Cleopatra* was benign. The movie forced massive layoffs and killed many of the studio's planned films.

A similar myth says *Who's Afraid of Virginia Woolf?* put the final nail in the coffin of the long-running Motion Picture Code. The film certainly helped, but actually changing morals had meant that the old Code was an anachronism.

Audiences were getting more sophisticated. Stars like Sean Connery, Steve McQueen, and Clint Eastwood were too cool and too sexy to be constrained by any code. British films from directors Tony Richardson, John Schlesinger, and Lewis Gilbert dealt with adult themes and starred sensations like Julie Christie, Vanessa Redgrave, Michael Caine, Albert Finney, Peter O'Toole, Alan Bates, and other inhabitants of swinging London.

International directors Federico Fellini, François Truffaut, Ingmar Bergman, Akira Kurosawa, Sergio Leone, Luis Buñuel, Michelangelo Antonioni, Mario Bava, and Jean-Luc Godard were offering works considered radical at the time. So were Americans John Cassavetes, Stanley Kubrick, Richard Lester, and Andy Warhol. Warhol's 1964 *Empire* docu is a

Right: Clint Eastwood.

Following Spread: Katharine Ross, Dustin Hoffman, Anne Bancroft, and Mike Nichols in advertisements for *The Graduate*.

single shot of the Empire State Building that runs eight hours; his 1966 *Chelsea Girls* and 1968 *Lonesome Cowboys* were more accessible, but still genre breaking.

The Code was beginning to erode, but in 1968, it bit the dust as the Motion Picture Association of America, and its new topper Jack Valenti, unveiled its four-tier ratings code. It was to be a voluntary system—no censorship!—and intended as a guide for parents, according to an August 7 *Daily Variety* story. It was also intended to put an end to all the local groups that were censoring or banning films.

And just a few years after the "shocking" debut of *Virginia Woolf*, the coarse language seemed tame. On October 30, 1968, *Variety* predicted, "The vernacular terms for fornication, and the related tools, are expected to be just around the corner." A front-page story on July 16, 1969, confirmed, "Now, nine months later, they're here."

Under the headline "Gutter Sexual Lingo in Film Breakthrough via Par's 'Medium Cool,'" the story announced that the Haskell Wexler–directed film featured verboten language too frequent to be bleeped out. The film merged a fictional story with documentary footage of police-protester clashes at the Democratic National Convention in 1968: "A lot of the obscenities, according to reports, are heard during scenes of hippie-yippie confrontation with Chicago cops."

The story continued,

> "The words utilized in 'Medium Cool' represent the last language barrier for major-company pix. The common euphemisms for urine and defecation are now commonplace, albeit a small sensation occurred only 18 months ago when 'In Cold Blood' broke the ice."

A few days later, *Daily Variety* carried a statement:

> "Hollywood AFL Film Council, composed of unions and guilds representing more than 25,000 employees in the motion picture industry of Southern California, has become deeply concerned over the marked increase in the excessive and offensive portrayal of sexual acts, nudity, perversion, sadism and brutality in films being made and shown today. . . . Many members of our unions and guilds are reluctantly forced to accept employment on

Katharine Ross

"Possibly the most beautiful and talented new young female on the screen ...surely this year's Julie Christie!"
— Liz Smith, Cosmopolitan

"Beautiful, real, warm, a rising young star!"
— Charles Champlin, Los Angeles Times

"Excellent!"
— Jack Heisel, Philadelphia Daily News

"A delight!"
— Peggy Doyle, Boston Record American

Dustin Hoffman

"superb!"
— Bosley Crowther, New York Times

"perfect!"
— John Hartl, Seattle Times

"tremendous!"
— Clifford Terry, Chicago Tribune

"remarkable!"
— Sam Lesner, Chicago Daily News

"extraordinary!"
— Alta Maloney, Boston Herald Traveler

"one of the best actors of his generation. Certainly he is the best American film comedian since Jack Lemmon."
— Stanley Kauffmann

Anne Bancroft

"Miraculous!"
— Hollis Alpert, Saturday Review

"Superior!"
— Bosley Crowther, New York Times

"Magnificent!"
— Sam Lesner, Chicago Daily News

"Excellent!"
— Jack Heisel, Philadelphia Daily News

"Perfect!"
— Pat Colonna, Trenton Sunday Times Advertiser

"A gem!"
— Hap O'Daniel, Cincinnati Post & Times Star

"A magnificent performance!"
— Bernard L. Drew, The Hartford Times

drama, something "they are beginning to permit in their news and documentaries. If this is their view, and not an illusion, this is what I want to write."

He said topicality of the subject is what prompted him to go into the venture, not the coin. While Silliphant will draw the "Playhouse" top of $25,000, it's far below his price of $150,000 for screenplays. Silliphant is an Oscar nominee for his "In The Heat Of The Night" screenplay.

the airways must be regulated.

A stinging attack on Wasilewski's statement was made by fellow panelist Frank Orme, exec director of the National Assn. for Better Broadcasting. He said it is "propaganda designed to serve the special economic interest of the commercial broadcasting industry."

After all the panel presentations, subcommittee chairman Harley Staggers (D.-W. Va.) invited panelists to submit recommendations for changing the law.

Tetragrammaton Post For Dave Briggs

David Briggs has been signed as the first of five a&r men to be pacted by the new Tetragrammaton Records.

Prexy Arthur Mogull said the waxery is releasing its first vinyl Murray Roman's "You Can't Beat People Up And Have Them Say I Love You" album. Firm is a subsid of the Campbell-Silver-Cosby Corp.

LOIS ADAMS — DISCUSSES NUDITY
STARS CINEMA THEATRE

REP. HO 4-5161   TODAY 2 P.M. - CH. 9

FOR BEST RESULTS ADVERTISE IN

DAILY **Variety** DAILY

25' COMMODORE CRUISER

225 H.P. Graymarine, only 550 hrs. Deluxe ship/shore. Spacious dinette & galley. Dual outriggers. Bait tank & pump. Insured $4800. Owner moving East.

$3700.
(714) 673-9579

Left: Read that page just for the articles.

such objectionable motion pictures because other work opportunities have been reduced due to 'runaway' foreign film production. . . ."

A trio of films perfectly captured the zeitgeist: *Bonnie & Clyde*, *The Graduate* (both 1967), and 1969's *Easy Rider*. All three films centered on restless characters butting heads with the establishment as they pursue their ever-more-elusive goals. While these rebellious films helped define the decade, the 1960s were also marked by fare that was more traditional and reassuring to mainstream audiences.

The best-picture Oscar winners of the 1960s include *West Side Story* (1961), *My Fair Lady* (1964), *The Sound of Music* (1965), and *Oliver!* (1968). If you look at that list, you might think this was the golden age of movie musicals. But you would be wrong. *The Sound of Music* was hugely profitable for 20th Century-Fox after the money drain of *Cleopatra*. But the Rodgers and Hammerstein film also inspired a raft of money-losing imitators, including Paramount's *Paint Your Wagon* (1969) and Fox's own trio of *Doctor Dolittle* (1967), *Star!* (1968), and *Hello, Dolly!* (1969), as well as such A-for-effort tuners from other studios like *Camelot* (1967), *Finian's Rainbow* (1968), and *Sweet Charity* and *Goodbye, Mr. Chips* (both 1969).

Old rules were falling in other countries, too. When the Broadway hit *Hair* opened in the West End, it was the first play to be publicly performed in London since the start of the sixteenth century without a license from Lord Chamberlain. Parliament had revoked the Chamberlain's licensing power in July 1967. The Chamberlain's strictures were firm, but *Hair* featured lyrics about sodomy and fellatio and an Act I closer in which members of the cast appeared nude.

All of these changes might indicate that the 1960s were years of progress and forward movement. In truth, for every story about change, there was evidence showing that the population was rooted in the past.

For examples of the contrasts, *Variety* stories in June 1960 told about the "Bamboo Curtain" of Red China, while Israel was addressing "various aspects of the Adolf Eichmann case." The same issue featured ads for the Steve Reeves gladiator movie *The Last Days of Pompeii* ("See! The Shameless Orgy as Drunken Pompeii Abandons Itself to the Goddess Isis! See! The Yawning Jaws of the Flesh-Ripping Alligator Death Pit!"); a 1961 story concerned a documentary produced by the Canadian Broadcasting Corporation, *¡Cuba Sí!*, which was yanked from viewing in the United States due to its alleged "pro-Fidel Castro slant."

In that same issue, a front-page banner trumpeted "New 'Twist' in Cafe Society," with the subhead, "Adults now dig juves' new beat." It told of the Twist—which, in *Variety* lingo, was termed a "terp craze" ("terp" referring to Terpsichore, the Greek muse of dance). The Twist inspired scarves, dolls, and lapel buttons with such slogans as "Do the Twist." In the same issue was a story about "society bandleader Ben Cutler."

What exactly were café society and society bandleaders?

The mixed messages were abundant. Under the headline "East-West Paar Berlin Crisis," *Variety* wrote of congressional outrage over Jack Paar doing an NBC show from the newly built Berlin Wall, but Paar said he had full military cooperation.

In 1965, the August 4 *Weekly Variety* carried front-page stories about troops pouring into Vietnam, apartheid in South Africa, and Broadway newsstands removing "flesh magazines" as tourists arrived for the World's Fair. That same year, the top-rated TV shows were a family-friendly group reflecting no turmoil: *Bonanza*, *Gomer Pyle U.S.M.C.*, *The Lucy Show*, *The Red Skelton Hour*, and *Batman*, and the Best Pic Oscar winner was *The Sound of Music*.

The January 5, 1966, *Weekly Variety* recounted the tale of Daniel Burros, Ku Klux Klansman and American Nazi Party activist who killed himself after the *New York Times* wrote about his Jewish origins. Burros also had connections with Hatenanny Records, described as "a right-wing 'message' diskery whose prime artists were a singing trio aptly called The Three Bigots." The issue, offering a roundup of the previous year, added, "What else marked 1965? Burning of draft cards, Teach-ins. President Johnson's kidneystones."

Standards were changing, but not everywhere. The very Catholic Italy did not recognize divorce. A *Variety* item read,

> "Roman laws which looked askance at Sophia Loren and Carlo Ponti's marriage—the director had been previously married, hence under state-church statutes this was a 'bigamous' marriage—got headlines. They're still seeking a Vatican annulment and meantime have also taken a penthouse apartment in Paris and he's gotten a French divorce from his first wife so as to remarry Miss Loren."

The issue also contains an ad that seemed lifted from the vaudeville pages fifty years earlier: "the deceptive artistry of the amazing George Val George," presenting his magic act "Dovetail Rhapsody" at the Town Casino in Buffalo, New York. (The ad asks the provocative question, "Where do the doves come from? Where do they go?")

The paper also mentioned the death of Dr. Albert Schweitzer in his African hospital at age ninety, adding that there was "much showbiz interest and support" for him and his work. The Aussies nixed the nitery tour of London playgirl Mandy Rice-Davis, and later in the year the number one "London playgirl" Christine Keeler, who figured in the 1964 John Profumo sex scandal, got headlines when she married and announced her endeavor to "settle down as a housewife."

Meanwhile,

> "on the heels of Walt Disney World, a $100,000,000 tourism project near Orlando, Fla., Roy Rogers' Western World amusement development in the same area—a $10,000,000 undertaking aimed to 'complement' the Disney layout—augurs much for Florida tourism."

A story said there were five thousand discotheques in the United States, with twenty-one in Manhattan alone. The Beatles

> "set an all-time, one-night showbiz record in August at Shea Stadium, Flushing, when 55,000 screaming-meemies paid $304,000 at $6.65 top. Score was Beatles, 55,000, Music, 0, because as a point of fact none out front heard any Beatle, singular or plural. It was the most spectacular display of teenage frenzy this side of a Holly Roller meeting."

The January 1966 anniversary issue weighed in on the changing moods in various overseas locales. Paris was expensive, but the discotheques were filled with youngsters and oldsters "ready to twist, watusi, frug etc. till the wee hours." Men and women in communist countries like Yugoslavia and Poland "are notably prudish," but there were plenty of spots catering to tourists, charging expensive prices while fresh fruit and green vegetables were nowhere to be found.

The most insightful story was headlined "Seoul a Sinful Swinging City." The piece by Jim Knight begins on the premise that, only thirteen years after its invasion from North Korea and being razed twice, there was no evidence of that: "cinemas and sinful night clubs and tearooms all seem to be filled to capacity" and the fifty thousand U.S. soldiers "mingle quite freely" with locals.

However, he painted a portrait of an economy and an attitude that still bore battle scars. Though the city had

Right: Connery. Sean Connery.

a population of three million, "most Koreans cannot afford a car and most rely on public transportation." Most taxis were from Japan, he added.

"One of the most popular GI spots is the Happy Room atop the Continental Hotel. Here hostesses are available and the room generally employs a Caucasian stripper. Strip act is usually done to the limit." (Though he never specified what the limit was.) "Hostesses will sit with customers, charging 500 won ($1.75) an hour. Some hostesses will make after-hour arrangements with the customer and this is where the hotel comes in handy. In fact, a certain amount of rooms are set aside for this purpose." One wonders what Mr. Knight's expense report looked like. "Hotel also boasts one of the better restaurants catering to foreigners. However, waitresses work 24-hour shifts and are then off for 24 hours so if you come in at the end of their shift the service is not so good."

There was also a nightclub act featuring "an ersatz 'Egyptian slave trader' who cracked the whip while his 'slave girl' writhed and moaned on the floor.

"As mentioned, tea rooms abound, majority of them employing jockeys who spin records in glass booths. Most places put the accent on American rock 'n' roll."

"The city only has six or seven first-rate downtown film houses. These are always crowded. Generally three of the theatres show foreign flicks, mainly American. Subtitles are used for the foreign films—very little dubbing is done." There were three TV stations, two of them Korean owned (one commercial, one by the government): "City has a plethora of radio stations."

Everywhere in the world, people were experiencing fast changes. Sometimes the changes were welcome because it helped them forget a painful past.

Twenty years after World War II ended, a 1966 *Weekly Variety* page one story reported *The Sound of Music* had opened at Munich's City Palast "with about one-third its running time eliminated, ending with the wedding of Baron von Trapp and Maria." All references to Nazis were cut. According to the story by John Kafka (interestingly, the same surname as the twentieth century writer who mastered in existential absurdity), "'Sound of Music' slashing came only a short time after a banner headline in local Deutsche paper, "*National und Soldatenzeitung*, reading, 'Will Hollywood's Hate of German (CQ) Never End?' There was an implied threat of German boycott of films guilty of rubbing it in about the Nazis."

While some wanted to forget the past, others were feeling a nostalgia for times that were outmoded.

A 1961 story began, "The chorus girl, one of the last remaining glamour symbols of the nitery biz, is following the stage-door Johns into limbo. . . . The supply of the prancing babes has dwindled to the vanishing point a victim of café economies and the lure of other showbiz media."

In the first *Weekly Variety* edition of 1966, editor Abel Green marvels, "The mixture of politico, social, economic and diplomatic events highlights again that 'showbiz' adjunct, television. It is today's constant catalyst of public understanding." He continued,

"Television yields a new immediacy to Watts (Los Angeles' 'black hell') race riots or Berkeley (Calif.) students' protestations, brings

Below: A little understated.

Max von Sydow:

"Dear Jean,

Regarding Mr Gray's request:

I had a music teacher in highschool, who often dared to encourage our youthful tastes. He used to tell us not to listen to the politicians but to the poets, the musicians and the comics. "They will tell you the truth" he used to say. I very often follow his advice.

Much love from us.

Max."

home problems of the Dominican Republic, Vietnam and Castro's approval for Cubans (stripped of all personal belongings) to emigrate in the U.S. to join their relatives."

There is something admirable about his recognition of world events and television's role in enlightening viewers—but something quaint about his still marveling at the power of this newfangled entertainment "adjunct."

That same 1966 issue featured a guest column by actor Robert Taylor from Madrid recalling the studio heyday of the 1930s and 1940s, which seemed to him "200 years ago." He recalled, "There was a 'style' in living and making motion pictures which no longer exists, which has been coldly modernized into something very factual, very efficient—and, I'm afraid, not very much fun." That style ended, he concluded, in the late 1940s, "with the unexplained but seemingly premeditated murder of glamour. Television, taxes, actors pricing themselves to the skies are all part-causes, but not the definitive one. I don't know really. I can't explain the demise. Perhaps if someone could correctly explain the phenomenon of rock 'n' roll, Beatle haircuts and beatnik wardrobes we will start to understand. In any case, it was 200 years ago."

To anyone from the 1940s, the 1960s must have come as a shock. But the decade set the stage for even more upheavals in the 1970s, when political and social changes must have made the previous years—a time of the Twist, chorus girls, screaming-meemies, and "gutter language"—seem like innocent, simple times.

Judy Garland Dies In London At 47; Autopsy Likely

London, June 22—The ill-starred career of Judy Garland, 47, ended here last night when her fifth husband Mickey Deans found her dead. Scotland Yard investigation continues and probably an autopsy will be performed.

Born Frances Gumm in Grand Rapids, where her father Frank managed a theatre, she made her stage bow at three, during an amateur night when her sisters Virginia and Mary Jane were performing. Judy made an impromptu dash onstage and sang a chorus of "Jingle Bells."

By time Judy was nine she was in a professional act with her sis-

(Continued on Page 11)

Mon., June 23, 1969

JUDY GARLAND
(Continued from Page 1)

ters. When playing a Chicago vaude theatre with George Jessel, marquee misspelled billing, it reading "Glum Sisters." Jessel had it corrected and suggested act rebill itself Garland Sisters — after his friend, Robert Garland, drama critic on N.Y. World-Telegram. VARIETY's review of act at that time noted, "The youngest . . . handles ballads like a veteran and gets every word and note over with a rsonality that hits audiences. Her sisters merely form a backdrop."

In 1932 Frances became Judy, despite her mother's objection, and when playing L.A. four-a-day house, Judy was signed in 1936 for her first film, "Pigskin Parade."

Thereafter for more than a decade she was under MGM contract, doing mostly musicals, along with a skein of Andy Hardy pix. A lateau was reached in the 1939 "\ zard of Oz" with her singing of "Over the Rainbow."

Suspended By MGM

Among her better-known films were "Broadway Melody of 1938," "Babes in Arms," "Strike Up the Band," "Little Nelly Kelly," "Ziegfeld Girl," "Babes on Broadway," "For Me and My Gal," "Thousands Cheer," "Meet Me in St. Louis," "Harvey Girls," "The Pirate," "Easter Parade," "Words and Musi

In that era Miss Garland did dramas (such as "The Clock") as well as tuners and had a big two-dimensional career going until she came a cropper, failing to report for filming of "Annie Get Your Gun" in 1950. MGM, after enduring a number of no-shows by her, suspended Miss Garland and borrowed Betty Hutton from Paramount to essay Annie Oakley.

That sent her back to the stage.

1955 Warners signed her for remake of "A Star Is Born" and production was greatly impeded by her tardiness and no-shows.

Her stage and nitery appearances became more infrequent and no-shows (at this period many one-niters) more frequent. Her career had toboggoned downhill.

Miss Garland was married five times, to David Rose, Vincente Minnelli, Sid Luft, Mark Harron. She was wed to Deans in January, bi it was determined divorce from Harron was not final, so subsequent March 15 ceremony was held in London, where Miss Garland largely had based last few years. Daughter, Liza Minnelli, survives, with the Luft children, Joey and Lorna.

DISNEY'S DEATH STUNS H'WOOD, TOTS, WALL ST. -- THE WORLD

By A. D. Murphy

The sudden death yesterday of Walt Disney — like that of any prince of government or industry — precipitated worldwide reverberations among saddened film-tv audiences, shocked industry associates, some temporarily panicked stockholders, and more than 4,000 stunned Disney employes. The Disney tradition and in-depth organization, however, indicate clearly that, while the ship has lost its captain, there is a well-trained crew to maintain course, artistically and commercially.

Services will be private, restricted to his family, and no dates or me will be disclosed. He is survived by widow Lillian, and two married daughters, Diane (Mrs. Ron Miller) and Sharon (Mrs. Robert Brown); two brothers Roy

(Continued on Page 24)

DISNEY'S DEATH STUNS H'WOOD, TOTS, WALL ST. --- THE WORLD

Walt Disney, Hollywood's Most Luminous 'Star'

(Continued from Page 1)

and Raymond A. and a sister Mrs. Ruth Beecher.

In lieu of flowers, family requests that contributions may be made to the California Institute of Fine Arts, c/o Walt Disney Prods., Burbank. Disney was instrumental in the founding of this college-level professional school for the creative and performing arts.

Death came to the 65-year-old showman at 9:35 a.m. in St. Joseph's Hospital in Burbank, and was ascribed by his physicians to an acute circulatory collapse. Disney on Nov. 6 entered the hospital for removal of his left lung, and

NBC Airing Tribute

A tribute to Walt Disney by an industry personality will be integrated in Sunday's "Wonderful World Of Color" on NBC. Scheduled show will be "Disneyland Around The Seasons."

re-entered on Nov. 30 because of complications. An attending cardiologist was at his bedside when he died.

The astute, showmanly manner in which the Disney name was exploited — above-title billing as befits a true star, and one of the few non-performing names ever to mean a thing to the man in the street — inevitably created the impression of a one-man company, contrary to shrewd, far-sighted planning on the part of Disney and his brother Roy, board chairman and prexy of the company.

Thus, when news of his passing flashed across the world, an immediate void was created. The Disney Studio closed at noon, and as many of the Buena Vista distrib offices as could be reached. Today, however, in the show-must-go-on tradition, the company resumes full-scale operations.

Disneyland and other corporate arms continue to provide temporary diversions into a world of tension-relieving fantasy, just as Disney intended that they should. After all, unhappiness and gloom have no place in a make-believe world. Two Disney-sponsored children's parties, set for this week, will be held, while many an adult in charge may be fighting back tears.

In the real world of hard-headed finance, however, news of Disney's passing provoked fiscal tremors. It was early afternoon on the floor of the N.Y. Stock Exchange when the word was flashed. Brokers immediately received calls from jittery stockholders — "Shall I sell?" The responses were varied, but sell orders began to pile up, and after 9,000 Disney shares were sold, depressing the price from its opening 67 to 64½, trading was suspended for a couple of hours.

This is not uncommon procedure, when the big board determines that a panic of sorts may be setting in. Later, just before the market closed, a buy order totalling 22,500 shares was executed at 69, thus closing out the day with Disney stock one point above previous day's closing.

On the Pacific Coast Exchange, open for three hours after N.Y. shuts down, Disney stock was off to 67⅝, on a volume of 2,400 shares.

In a statement by Roy Disney, he expressed the sentiments of all — "There is no way to replace Walt Disney." At the same time, he noted that Walt Disney "gathered the kind of creative people who understood his way of communicating with the public," and that "we will continue to operate" the company "in the way that he has established and guided it."

Roy Disney's assurances of on-course operation make explicit the implementation of long-range plans, already set for the company in the fields of pix, tv programs, amusement parks and recreation centers. For example, $25,000,000 is earmarked for Disneyland in the 1966-70 period, a spectacularly successful pioneering concept already endowed with a $55,000,000 investment which has grossed over $200,000,000.

Also, the Mineral King Valley project in the Sierra Nevada range is allocated already some $15,000,000 in the 1969-71 period, total investment to reach $35,000,000. Then, too, the Florida Disneyland-type park will involve capital expenditures of over $60,000,000.

(Continued from Page 22)

Services, pix on health still used around the world by the U.S. State Dept., and propaganda films.

With the return of personnel from the war in 1945, Disney resumed full cartoon production. While continuing his animation he expanded to live-action and embarked upon his "True-Life Adventure" series, at first two-reelers, which gradually gave way to full-length features. Disney, as he had with his cartoons, became the leader in such nature study films, some of which required as much as 18 months to complete.

Videbuted In 1954

Following the success of Disneyland, which since its $17,000,000 investment in 1955 has grown into an almost unheard-of project of more than $50,000,000, and which more than 50,000,000 persons have attended, Disney focused his fuller attention upon television, which he originally entered in 1954.

He entered the field of color tv in 1961 with his "Wonderful World Of Color" over NBC, which today still stands as a hallmark. This followed seven years of "Walt Disney Presents" and "Disneyland" programs, and the "Mickey Mouse Club" and "Zorro" series. He acted as his own host, adopting a folksy approach which created the image the whole world has come to know.

Enthused over the popularity of Disneyland, Disney decided to open a second amusement park near Orlando, Fla., where in addition to such recreational facilities plans called for the building of two new cities, to act as a buffer area around the whole complex. This was done through buying up 500 parcels in the area over an 18-month period at a cost of around $5,000,000, and because Disney didn't want what he thought of as a honky-tonk neighborhood which surrounds Disneyland.

Still another recreational project planned by Disney is Mineral King near Sequoia National Park, which is skedded to be a ski resort during a 120-day season within the next 10 years. Both the Florida and Sequoia projects will be continued, according to studio plans revealed yesterday.

'Mr. Clean', Esquire

Disney's passion for "clean" entainment, a mark of all his undertakings regardless of what field, was further extended during the N.Y. World's Fair. He had four exhibits, which included homespun America and the fabulous Abraham Lincoln replica with its secret lifelike animation, as well as a Fantasia-like view of Creation and pre-historic life. These were attended by an average 135,000 daily through the first season, entertainment hit of the entire fair.

An interviewer once quoted Disney's veepee in charge of studio operation, William H. Anderson, as saying: "I guess Walt is the only man in Hollywood to whom you don't tell a dirty joke. When you do, somehow it doesn't come out funny."

While willing to spend untold sums on technical and all sorts of electronic development for use in his various enterprises, Disney among all the studio heads of Hollywood was probably the lowest pay. He paid a minimum for stories, stars' salaries frequently were less than at other studios and he lost some of his best men through refusing to meet pay demands.

Stopped 'Signing Papers'

In 1960, Disney gave up his titles of prexy and board chairman because he "spent too much time signing papers," and functioned merely as "executive producer in charge of all production." His relations with his company were unique; he had the right to make one picture annually outside the company, an option he never exercised.

His agreement with com ny called for a basic salary of $182,000 yearly, plus a deferred salary that accrued at $2,500 a week. One of the interesting features of his agreement was that it gave him options to purchase interests of up to 25% in firm's feature-length live-action films, but had to make his selection prior to start of production. He paid his share of the cost and then took a proportionate share of any profit or loss.

This sharing right started in 1953 but Disney didn't exercise such options until 1961. He took however, only 10%, not 25% rights. Roy Disney, who succeeded his brother as prexy-board chairman, explained the reason for Walt not exercising his full 25%. "It's money," he said. "Ten percent costs Walt around $1,250,000 a year."

Disney had assigned all his profits to a family company he set up called Retlaw (Walter spelled backward), formed originally in 1953. In fiscal 1965, Retlaw received $292,349 from merchandising royalties alone.

Peak 'Poppins' Profit

One of Disney's most profitable undertakings was "Mary Poppins," which introduced Julie Andrews to screen audiences. On film's first time out through the international market, plus domestic, the estimate is that it will gross perhaps as high as $47,000,000, top money-maker in Disney history.

Disney, who once played polo extensively, than abandoned the sport when it became too time-consuming, was perhaps Hollywood's hardest worker. His entire time and energy was devoted to his work. Even in the pleasant atmosphere of his Holmby Hills home, he spent most of his time reading scripts. He always checked in at his office by 8:30 each morning.

But always he was a family n. He enjoyed them, confided in them, asked their advice. That is one reason why he was able to strike such a popular chord, he once remarked.

Assign 4 'Veni' Roles

Eddy Ryder, Gil Lamb, Wil Jordan and Don Newman have been set by Five Oaks Productions toppers Ric Marlow and Fletcher Fist to round out the male featured roles in "Veni, Vidi, Vici," fea re which rolls Jan. 15. John Ireland toplines.

THE SCREEN
PRODUCERS GUILD

*mourns the loss of its
fellow member*

Walt Disney

Dec. 5, 1901   Dec. 15, 1966

In Fond Memory

John Hyde

December 18, 1950

From Associates and Friends

XXX

1970s

In the 1970s, American TV viewers were shocked at and rocked by Archie Bunker's bigotry in *All in the Family*. CBS's Korean War–era comedy-drama *M*A*S*H* began a run that lasted eleven years (eight years longer than the actual war). ABC estimated that 130 million people saw all or parts of its miniseries *Roots*. But the biggest TV star of the decade was Richard Nixon. From his "I am not a crook" speech to the Watergate hearings to his on-air resignation, viewers around the world witnessed a drama that no fictional work could match: a presidential administration writhing and collapsing under TV's harsh spotlight.

The intersection of TV and world events also provided moments of inspiration. On September 18, 1978, *Daily Variety*'s lead story noted that the 30th Annual Emmy Awards had been preempted for twenty-nine minutes as President Jimmy Carter, Prime Minister Menachem Begin of Israel, and President Anwar Sadat of Egypt announced a Middle East peace breakthrough following a summit conference at Camp David. *Variety* reporter Dave Kaufman noted that the announcement, which aired on all three U.S. networks simultaneously, "was far more dramatic than what was offered in the awards ceremony."

The Middle East had enjoyed a thriving and sophisticated culture for centuries, but many Americans had no understanding of the Arab-speaking world—or, if they did, it was gleaned from images of Ali Baba, the Great Pyramids, *Lawrence of Arabia*, and maybe the Israel-Palestine conflict. "The Mideast situation" had been a familiar topic on primetime news, but America really came to grips with the Middle East in the 1970s.

Between the oil crisis drawing attention to the region, Nixon's visit to China, and the prolonged Vietnam trauma, Americans were forced to rethink their country's role in the global community.

Inspired by the civil rights battles of the previous decades, minds were expanding in other directions with the rise of women's lib and gay lib.

And there was another subtle yet far-reaching change afoot. As Frank Segers reported on October 6, 1971, a committee of Broadway honchos had "been working out a uniform credit card system for Broadway box offices. Only cash and checks are currently

Right: During the filming of *Jaws*.

Following Spread: August 9, 1974.

DAILY VARIETY DAILY

VOL. 164 No. 46   Hollywood, California-90028, Friday, August 9, 1974   20 Pages   25 Cents

NIXON'S PRIMETIME FADEOUT

FCC's Benjamin Hooks Goes After Nets Over Coverage Of Blacks; Calls For A Change

By STEVE TOY

Federal Communications Commissioner Benjamin Hooks yesterday blasted the networks for alleged distorted news coverage of blacks, saying, "It's time to change the standards."

Hooks, in a vigorous speech before National Association of TV & Radio Artists convention at the Century Plaza that had members standing and cheering, and in a subsequent press conference, said, "We've got to let these stations know their definition of news is not good enough if it doesn't let us in."

Hooks, admitting his FCC position doesn't give him overall power to correct the situation, nonetheless said he will use his position as a podium to bring about change.

Blames The Nets

He said, while local media do a good job, networks are the ones at fault, citing news standards which "systematically exclude blacks."

"Black folk cannot continue to be invisible," Hooks said. "I'm not an overregulator. But I'm trying to convey a sense of urgency to the networks. They need a new standard of journalistic interpretation that includes blacks.

"News is what the news director says it is. We've got to educate the people."

He said the situation is either "a
(Continued on Page 18, Column 3)

Wolper Reveals Volleyball, Net Coverage Plans

Film and tv exec David L. Wolper revealed plans yesterday for a professional volleyball league with franchises in 10 major cities and regular network telecasts of the games.

Wolper will serve as founding prexy. Others who shared the platform during a press conference in the BevWilshire Hotel included Barry Diller, v.p., ABC; exec prez David Gerber, Columbia Pictures TV; Berry Gordy, Motown Industry prexy; Gerald J. Leider, prez of Warner Bros. TV, and Martin Starger, prez of ABC Entertainment. Basketball star Wilt Chamberlain also was there.

League administrator will be Chuck Nelson, a former Olympic volleyball player. Nelson said the teams will have a three-month season, starting in June, 1975, and
(Continued on Page 19, Column 1)

A. C. Lyles Returns To Par Lot As Vidpic And Series Producer

A. C. Lyles, vet theatrical film producer, has joined Paramount TV to develop and produce telefilms and series, production chief Bud Austin revealed yesterday. For Lyles, who is making his debut in tv, this represents a return to the studio where he spent 30 years, beginning as a mailroom boy and working up to producer status.

Lyles said yesterday that he is currently discussing several projects with the studio, but was not yet ready to release details.

Lyles left Par three years ago to produce a picture at Metro. At Par he had formed his own A. C. Lyles Prods. Inc. 10 years ago and produced many features under a contract whereby he turned out a minimum of 10 theatrical films each year.

Lyles' move to Par TV brings to 15 the number of production developers now with the telefilmery. Others are Harry Ackerman, Gerald Di Pego, Ivan Goff and Ben Roberts, David Karp, Emmet G. Lavery Jr., George LeMaire,
(Continued on Page 10, Column 3)

Surgery Not Necessary For Dr. Jules Stein

Following a spinal myelogram test on Dr. Jules Stein, founder of MCA Inc., his doctors, Paul Crandall of UCLA and William Scoville of Hartford, Conn., have concluded that his planned laminectomy (spinal surgery), is unnecessary.

Stein entered UCLA Medical Center Wednesday in anticipation of corrective surgery. He will return to his home this afternoon or tomorrow.

JOHN EGER SEEN IN OTP'S TOP POST AS WHITEHEAD QUITS

By PAUL HARRIS

Washington, Aug. 8 — Jealously eyeing the exit sign for the last eight months, Clay T. Whitehead, chief of the Office of Telecommunications Policy, submitted his resignation this week effective Sept. 15. Deputy director John Eger will be named acting director of the office, and is said to have the inside track for the job full time.

Whitehead submitted his letter to President Nixon shortly after testifying before the Senate Communications Subcommittee on a bill to provide long-term funding for public broadcasting. The resignation was announced today. The measure was the last major project before Whitehead, who was tapped to head OTP when the department was formed four years ago.

Whitehead's letter to President Nixon, which was accepted during Nixon's waning moments of the Presidency, made no mention of the Watergate scandal, nor was the resignation prompted by it. Rather, Whitehead has for months longed to return to private life, and work on a book about his OTP tenure. He is also expected to take a consulting position with either MIT or Harvard.

The controversial director, a former Rand Corp. official, began
(Continued on Page 15, Column 3)

AFI EXEC COMMITTEE SESH CALLED AUG. 22; DANIEL ISSUE GROWING

By A. D. MURPHY

An executive committee meeting of the American Film Institute has been called for Aug. 22 in N.Y., it has been learned, and mounting pressure for a reconsideration of the Frank Daniel matter is thought likely to be an agenda item. Daniel's resignation as dean of the Center for Advanced Film Studies was accepted Aug. 1, provoking strong reaction from many AFI trustees and CAFS fellows, present and past.

At issue was Daniel's insistence that CAFS be strengthened in its financial and administrative autonomy in order that various centre projects, including film production, be carried out in an orderly and stable manner. He came up against AFI director George Stevens Jr., and the exec committee decided to accept Daniel's resignation, effective Sept. 1, thus backing Stevens.

Meanwhile, further expressions
(Continued on Page 18, Column 1)

John Wayne Takes On 'Maude' Next Season

John Wayne, no comedian he, will guestar on the opening segment of CBS-TV's "Maude" series this coming season — thanks to some ingenuity on the part of Max Bercutt, an old friend of Wayne's from the days when Bercutt was p.r.-ad chief at Warner Bros.

Bercutt, who also conceived the idea of Wayne's being paraded in a tank to the Harvard Lampoon club last January, came up with the
(Continued on Page 15, Column 3)

Had More Hours On Tube Than Any President In History; Last Official Act Is High Drama

By DAVE KAUFMAN

Six years to the day after he was nominated by the Republican Party to be President, Richard Nixon last night resigned as Chief Executive — an historic, unprecedented event which was viewed by millions of Americans over the electronic miracle known as television.

Nixon's Resignation Allows Senate Time For B'casting Bill

Washington, Aug. 8 — President Nixon's reluctant decision to succumb to the voices demanding his resignation means more to the broadcast industry than just an escape from devoting mass amounts of free air time to an impeachment and Senate trial. It now virtually assures it that license renewal legislation will be given ample time for Senate passage.

Nixon for the last time today asked the networks to yield primetime for an address to the nation. The request followed a 70-minute talk between Nixon and Vice-President Gerald Ford, when the two discussed the precedent-setting transference of power.

Networks were being given last-minute information about tomor-
(Continued on Page 19, Column 1)

CBS, NBC and ABC all aired the farewell address of President Nixon, as he confirmed earlier reports that he was resigning — all the backlash of Watergate and what had been a pending impeachment hearing in the House and possible trial and conviction in the Senate.

Nixon, who for almost all of his political career was at odds with the news media, did not take any parting shots at tv news in his resignation, a fact duly noted by CBS' Eric Sevareid, himself often the target of Administration criticism when it had zeroed in on tv's "instant analyses." So sharp was CBS reaction to such criticism that it dropped those for a time.

Sevareid also observed that
(Continued on Page 10, Column 1)

Wm. J. Heineman, Veteran Industry Exec, Dies At 74

New York, Aug. 8 — William J. Heineman, 74, motion picture theatre owner, producer and former UA vice president and member of its board, died today in N.Y.C. following a long illness. A resident of Yonkers, N.Y., Heineman had been associated with the film industry for more than half a century.

He was a member of the original management group that took over operation and ownership of United Artists Corp. from Charles Chaplin and Mary Pickford in 1951. Two other members of the group, lawyers Arthur B. Krim and Robert S. Benjamin, still hold top posts at UA, as chairman and co-chairman of the board, respectively.

Born in Athens, Wis., Heineman entered the film business in 1918 as a booker for the old Pathe Co. in Seattle. He subsequently served as a sales manager for First National in Seattle; owned and operated a subfranchise for WB Classics of
(Continued on Page 15, Column 4)

CREST NATIONAL FILM LABORATORIES
1141 N SEWARD, HOLLYWOOD, CA. 90038   (213) 462-6696

NOW PROCESSING THE NEW ECN II 7247 & 5247
DAYLIGHT DEVELOPING AVAILABLE

Nixon's Primetime Fadeout

(Continued from Page 1, Column 5)

Nixon's farewell was unlike that of former Vice President Agnew, who when he resigned last year assailed the tv news media and press.

President Nixon appeared a bit grim in his final appearance as the nation's leader, but he was in control of his emotions. It was one of the shortest Nixon speeches in memory, just 16 minutes long.

The President's resignation, due to the fact he had lost almost all support in Congress and thus faced the alternative of conviction in the Senate, undoubtedly drew a record number of viewers for an address by a politician.

Net Skeds Wrecked

Nixon's history-making move played havoc with network schedules, as they junked regular primetime programming for special news reports, reaction from here and abroad, devoting the entire night and then some to the ramifications of the Presidential decision.

ABC-TV was on until the wee hours of this ayem, with the focus on reaction, as correspondents were brought in from all over the world via satellite to bring the American public global response to Nixon's action. Domestic reaction was not overlooked.

CBS-TV also junked its regular sked, and was on until 4 a.m. Coast time, with reaction from around the world via satellite, as well as on the home front.

NBC-TV, too, turned the night over to coverage of the fast-breaking Washington events, with its final coverage at 11 p.m. Johnny Carson's "Tonight" show was bumped by the news special, as were the primetime programs.

All three networks were on before Nixon's address, covering all aspects of the President's situation, Watergate, the events leading to the unprecedented resignation. Walter Cronkite anchored it all for CBS; John Chancellor, for NBC; Howard K. Smith and Harry Reasoner for ABC.

Irony

There was irony in Nixon's fateful move being proclaimed on television, a medium he has bitterly assailed many times during his political career, charging tv news with "liberal bias," with slanting news, with unfairness in its coverage of him. As a matter of fact, no

Music Frat's Awards For Radio-Tv To ABC

ABC-TV will receive both 1974 national radio and tv awards given by Sigma Alpha Iota, the international music fraternity which is honoring the web for "The Strauss Family" series and for pianist Artur Rubinstein's appearance on "The Dick Cavett Show."

Awards, to be given Sunday (11) at the fraternity's convention in Kansas City, Mo., are for outstanding music programming in a series and in an individual program.

"The Strauss Family," a seven-week dramatic series, included music arranged and conducted by Cyril Ornadel and played by members of the London Symphony Orchestra. The Cavett show aired May 17, 1973, and included 13-year-old violin prodigy Lilit Gampel as a guest.

Chief Executive in the 26-year history of the electronic medium has ever waged such an all-out assault on tv as had Nixon, the barrage reaching its peak with tongue-lashings aimed at tv news by former Vice President Agnew.

It is probable no President has used tv as extensively as has Nixon during the years he functioned as Chief Executive. He had been on CBS on 164 occasions since his inauguration Jan. 20, 1969. That network had no figures to compare this with previous Presidential tv appearances.

Nixon appeared on NBC 75 times, with major addresses or press conferences, those appearances totalling 48 hours, 38 minutes. This was over the 5½-year period since he became President. By comparison, the late President Johnson was on NBC 97 times, but the total for those appearances amounted to 47 hours, and it was over a longer period of time, from Nov. 22, 1963, to Jan. 20, 1969.

ABC reported he was on that network 78 times since his first inauguration, that this added up to a total of 38 hours and 37 minutes.

No Friend Of Tv

Nixon was no friend of the tube, and it was while he was President that the Federal Communications Commission hit tv hard in many ways, including slapping network primetime with the access rule; the Dept. of Justice-pressed antitrust action against the nets; he

A. C. Lyles Returns To Paramount Lot

(Continued from Page 1, Column 2)

Garry Marshall and Sheldon Keller, Thomas L. Miller and Edward K. Milkis, E. Jack Neuman, Norman Steinberg and Tony Wilson.

Par also has Carson / Paramount Prods. company, formed a year ago by Johnny Carson and Paramount Pictures.

appointed a director of telecommunications, Clay T. Whitehead, whose main job initially seemed to be lashing out at tv with special attention to tv news.

It was the Nixon Administration which took great umbrage over the CBS spec, "The Selling Of The Pentagon," a show critical of Pentagon p.r. methods. That hassle resulted in the government taking CBS to court, with the network eventually the winner, a victory which scarcely eased the Administration ire against tv news.

Nixon's antagonism to tv undoubtedly began in the 1960 campaign in which his opponent was John F. Kennedy. Turning point there were those Kennedy-Nixon debates, and Nixon always blaming tv for this, claiming the tv cameras made him look less than good.

Moody-Threshold Exex Reshuffled

Major reshuffling of top echelon of Moody Blues, Threshold Records, Threshold Music and all tour activities has been announced by Jerry Weintraub, Management III topper who recently was appointed to manage biz affairs of the music group.

New assignments are Gerry Hoff as Threshold Records European manager; Peter Jackson as liaison between Weintraub and Moody Blues, London, and Steven H. Weiss, U.S. attorney for Moody, Threshold Management III.

Continuing in their present posts are Cyril Simons, Leeds Music head who handles Threshold catalog and individual publishing companies for all territories except U.K. and Canada; United Kingdom legal advisor Michael Balin; Ivor Casson, chartered accountant; Colin Berlin and Barry Clayman as agents, and Nick Massey, publicity head.

Par Currently Has Eight Pix Playing Locally

Paramount currently has a total of eight films playing the L.A. market, largest spread of pix here for any one company in several years. All are in first release except "Harold And Maude," which opened a reissue stand Wednesday at UA Cinema Center 1.

"Apprenticeship Of Duddy Kravitz" teed exclusive engagement Wednesday at Bruin and "Parallax View" entered first general release in 17 situations on same date. "Death Wish" is in second round at Avco 3, Pantages and Pickwick Drive-in; "Chinatown" in eighth at Chinese and National, and "White Dawn" in Village third. "Malizia" continues in sixth lap at the Plaza.

"The Great Gatsby," which went into first general release a week ago, currently is showing in 12 spots in second.

109 Stations Lined Up For 'National Velvet'

MGM Family Network has signed 109 American tv stations for a Sept. 8 broadcast of "Natio.. Velvet," among them Los Angeles' KABC-TV and the four other ABC-owned outlets. Elizabeth Taylor and Mickey Rooney star in the film.

Edward A. Montanus, MGM-TV senior v.p., said he expects station clearances for this pic to far exceed the 146 signed last March for the company's "Knights Of T Roundtable."

PANAVISION
16mm & 35mm
KEM & STEENBECK
DAILY, WEEKLY, MONTHLY
2-plate 4-plate 6-plate 8-plate
Call Gary (213) 826-6565
DENNY HARRIS, INC.

Fast-paced Theatrical Agency
NEEDS
Bright, "Together" Secretary
Preferably with knowledge of Music Industry. Typing & light steno required.
Salary commensurate with skills
Regency Artists, Ltd.
273-7103

WANTED
EXP. SCRIPT TYPISTS
Must be fast, accurate & excellent at spelling. Full time days or nights.
Barbara's Place
273-1015

LEARN ITALIAN CONVERSATION
650-0978

CUSTOM BUILT
TV OR FILM SET
Excellent condition . . . Living room, kitchen, and patio including Blue CYC and Chromakey Flat.
MAKE OFFER
PHONE (213) 980-2030

COMPLETE REHEARSAL HALL FACILITIES...
at
PAUL DE ROLF STUDIOS
12117 Moorpark St., Studio City
just west of Laurel Canyon Blvd.
Call now for information: 769-2233

JUNERO JENNINGS

Appearing
as
House
in
"THREE THE HARD WAY"
soon to be seen
in
"BLACK SAMSON"
Just completed
Starring
IN
"SOUTH OF SULO"
soon to be released
Representation — Murry Weintraub Agency — 652-3892

LAST PERFORMANCES FRIDAY & SATURDAY AT 8:30

The National Theatre of Great Britain
WORLD FAMOUS PRODUCTION OF SHAKESPEARE'S
AS YOU LIKE IT

"..WILL PROVE TO BE THE HIT OF THE SEASON .. THE PRODUCTION IS ONLY HERE UNTIL SATURDAY .. IF YOU MISS IT, YOU HAVE ONLY YOURSELF TO BLAME." — Sylvie Drake, L.A. Times

— GOOD SEATS AVAILABLE —
TICKETS AT BOX OFFICE, AGENCIES & WALLICHS • FREE PARKING

GREEK THEATRE GRIFFITH PARK
2700 NORTH VERMONT AVENUE
LOS ANGELES 90027 • PHONE 666-6000

OPEN AUDITIONS
Male and Female Rock Singers or Musicians with acting experience. Production company forming rock group for committed Network TV project. Be prepared to play or sing. Provide own music. Pix & Resume. Friday, August 9. Rehearsal Room 4.
1313 North Vine Street
(use Homewood Entrance)
9:00 A.M. and 1:00 P.M.

RENT A USED CAR
daily — weekly — monthly
low, low rates
BUNDY RENT-A-CAR
478-0676

INTERNATIONAL DISTRIBUTOR
is interested in purchasing completed pictures or those where principal photography is completed. Must be good commercial pictures and no X-rated product. Have cash available. Will be in Calif. within 10 days to look at pictures. Write: TRANS-INTERNATIONAL FILMS, 104 Crandon Blvd., Key Biscayne, FLA 33149
(305) 361-3341

OPPORTUNITY FOR MODELS
Who can do eye makeup and have pleasant speaking voice.
Professional Schools International
657-3750

honored. . . . " Yes, the 1970s saw the glorious rise of the credit card, which had profound effects on everyday transactions and fundamentally changed people's relationship with money and personal finance.

The 1970s were also the time of Pong, roller disco, the Eagles, Captain & Tennille, *Deep Throat*, *The Godfather*, "blaxploitation," "chopsocky" movies starring Bruce Lee, and two films that changed the business of showbiz: *Jaws* and *Star Wars*.

These entertainments were an antidote to the unrest carried over from the prior decade. And when people's worst suspicions about their leaders, fueled by Watergate, were added to the unease from the 1960s, the new decade was ripe for years of existential despair and alienation.

On May 13, 1970, Bill Greeley wrote a piece for *Variety* pointing out that ABC, CBS, and NBC had avoided live coverage of such protests as the November 1969 Peace Moratorium, which he cited as the "largest political demonstration in the history of the country. . . . But this time around, with the expansion of the war into Cambodia and Laos, and four Kent State Univ. students killed by National Guardsmen, and the nation's educational system in a state of unprecedented chaos, the networks opened up. That would seem natural under such pressure of events, but from all reports the moves to coverage came at the 11th hour after internal struggles and indecision in high places."

There were battles in the streets and, apparently, in TV network offices, too. Was no place sacred? Clearly not. On August 6, Anaheim city police entered Disneyland for the first time in its fifteen-year history to quell a "Yippie riot." *Daily Variety* reported that 260 "longhaired Yips" had entered the park and there were eighteen arrests: sixteen on misdemeanor charges and two on felonies for possession of narcotics. Disneyland management would reassess their admissions policy:

"Not only will the park bear down on long hair, which up to this season has virtually been banned, but the general attitude of the individual also will be considered. Should he show a belligerent attitude he'll be refused admittance."

But belligerent attitudes were becoming the norm. In the July 15, 1971, in a review of CBS's *The Pentagon Papers: What They Mean*, *Variety* concluded, "There was agreement [among the subjects being interviewed] that the 'papers' have undermined public confidence in its leaders; and there will be a slide to isolationism and an antimilitary attitude to 'Let others fight their own wars.'"

The *Pentagon Papers* were the result of Defense Secretary Robert McNamara commissioning a classified "top secret—sensitive" (not a military security risk) study of U.S. strategies in Vietnam from 1945 through 1967. The study, leaked to the *New York Times* by Daniel Ellsberg and Anthony Russo, concluded that administrations of four presidents—Harry S. Truman, Dwight Eisenhower, John F. Kennedy, and Lyndon B. Johnson—had lied to the public about America's intentions in Vietnam, including planned coups, the extent of troop involvement, and false promises of cutting down troop involvement.

Though Nixon was not directly targeted, the *Pentagon Papers* added to the public's ongoing tensions with his administration.

> **Norman Lear:**
> "When he died, I arranged with others to start a scholarship at UCLA in the name of Army Archerd. No one loved the entertainment business more than Army, and in thirty years he never had a bad word to say about anyone and made every column interesting without the trashing. It was blessed *Variety* that kept Army Archerd writing daily and I'll always be grateful for that."

Right: Advertisement for *The Osterman Weekend*.

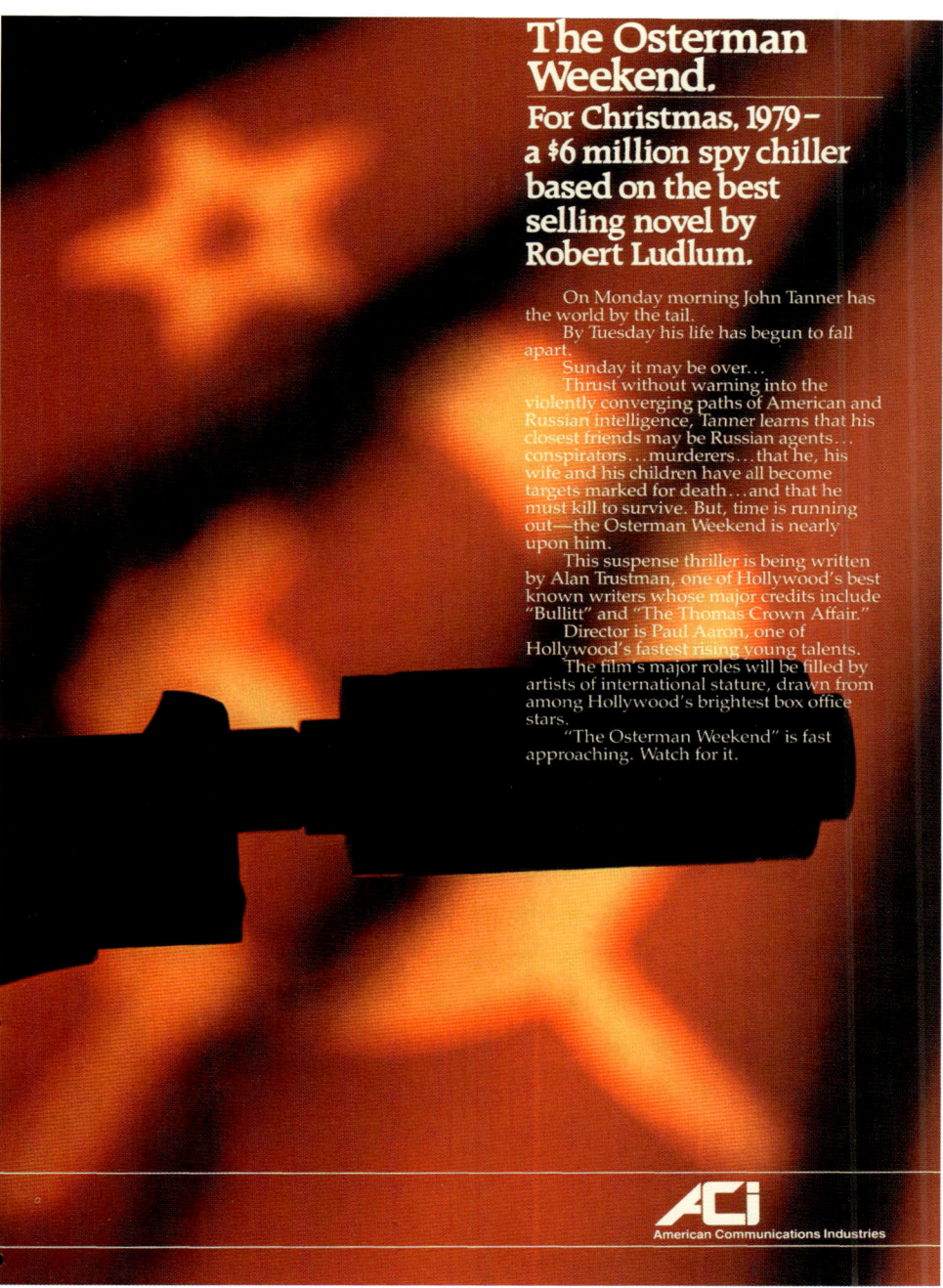

In a July 1, 1974, *Daily Variety* column, Dave Kaufman wrote that TV news had

> "survived the most powerful assault ever waged on the medium from men in the highest places in the government. What is referred to here, of course, is the all-out attack initiated by the Nixon Administration against TV news about three years ago. Never before had an incumbent administration spent so much time waging war against the media, both TV news and print, although the sharpest attacks were directed at TV because of its impact."

He cited John Ehrlichman's demand that CBS fire news anchor Dan Rather, but "that powerful assault failed principally because of the events put under the umbrella of Watergate. . . ."

Ah, yes, Watergate. The August 9, 1974, *Daily Variety* headline: "Nixon's Primetime Fadeout." Kaufman labeled Nixon's on-camera resignation "an historic, unprecedented event which was viewed by millions of Americans over the electronic miracle known as television."

On September 11, *Weekly Variety* ran the headline "You Can Lead ter-Horst to Watergate but You Can't Make Him Sink." The story revealed that new White House press secretary Jerald terHorst exited only nine hours after President Ford pardoned Richard Nixon, because, as he said in an interview,

> "I felt in good conscience I could not support his decision. Because I didn't know how I could credibly defend it in the absence of pardons for those who avoided the war in Vietnam in good conscience and former Nixon aides who suffered under the same Watergate troubles (as Nixon)."

TV was arguably the public's primary source of news during the 1970s, but a July 20, 1977, *Weekly Variety* post mortem of the July 13–14 New York City electricity blackout noted that national TV offered occasional bulletins but generally kept to regular programming. It was another, older medium that offered the most help: "radio stations did a sterling job of keeping the populace informed."

In sharp contrast to the 1930s, when newsreel footage was flown from Europe to the United States, radio and TV in the 1970s were immediate indicators of the political health (or disease) everywhere in the world.

In 1972, TV networks around the world covered the story as Arab gunmen invaded the Olympic Village in

| FILMS | VIDEO | TV FILMS | RADIO | MUSIC | STAGE |

Variety

PRICE
60¢

NEWSPAPER
Second Class P.O. Entry

Published Weekly at 154 West 46th Street, New York, N. Y. 10036, by Variety, Inc. Annual subscription, $25. Single copies, 60 cents.
Second Class Postage Paid at New York, N. Y., and at Additional Mailing Offices.
© COPYRIGHT, 1973, BY VARIETY, INC., ALL RIGHTS RESERVED

Vol. 273 No. 3   New York, Wednesday, November 28, 1973   34205   64 PAGES

FUEL SHORTAGE 'SCARES' SHOW BIZ

ECONOMIC FEARS WORSE THAN RESTRICTIONS

B'way 'Niger' Out; Nixed Cut-Rates; Tourer In Wash.

"The River Niger," which closed Sunday night (25) at the Brooks Atkinson Theatre, N.Y., was an exception to the general Broadway rule — it never used twofers or other cut-rates and did not allot any tickets for sale at the Times Square Theatre Center, the cooperative boxoffice where seats are sold at half-price.

The theory among most Broadway managers and boxoffice personnel is that the Joseph A. Walker drama might have run several more months if it had distributed tickets through the TSTC, which sells seats the day-of-performance only and thus presumably does not discourage advance buying. It's also figured that twofers would have helped prolong the life of the Negro Ensemble production.

Douglas Turner Ward, a cofounder of the Ensemble and one of its directors, as well as the stager-star of "Niger" was reportedly responsible for the decision not to use twofers or allot tickets to the TSTC. His reason is understood to have been that he wants to build up a Broadway theatregoing habit among the black public.

(Continued on page 54)

Royal Variety Show's 25th Anni Sparks LP Set Of Bygone Talent

London, Nov. 27.
While the event itself dates back to 1910, yesterday's (Mon.) Royal Variety Show marked the 25th consecutive year of its presentation at the London Palladium, which anni has cued a double-album of tracks by past RVS talent such as Petula Clark, Tony Bennett, Max Bygraves, Herb Alpert, Jack Jones, Buddy Rich and Andy Williams.

Due out as a pre-holiday release on the Pye label, the LP set will retail for L5 a throw (about $12) with proceeds destined for the Variety Artistes Benevolent Fund. A 24-page booklet recapping the history of the royal shows goes with it.

Pye, like the Palladium, is a subsid of Sir Lew Grade's Associated Television operation. Louis Benjamin, the label's chieftain, doubles as Palladium ditto.

By SYD SILVERMAN

The real impact of the energy crisis on show business has yet to be determined. But even at this early stage in the saga of basic power shortages, the huffing and puffing politicians in Washington seem to be doing their best to scare the hell out of the American public and seem to be succeeding at the unhappy task.

Show business has lived through all the presently proposed restrictions, gas rationing, brownouts, dimouts and even blackouts and somehow managed to survive.

The most obvious danger of the present situation is the worldwide crisis in confidence. Recession in 1974 is now almost taken for granted in the U.S. and if the European and Japanese economies suffer similar traumas, the U.S. can look forward to a domestic recession and a collapse of foreign markets at the same time. That spells trouble for all business.

Europe and Japan have already come to grips with the problem and six countries now have bans on Sunday driving. Detailed below

Arab Oil Flows Again But Crisis Not Solved

Reports yesterday (Tues.) that the Arab nations had decided to lift the oil embargo gave some relief to the American economy, but the longrange U.S. strategy of self-sufficiency may still lead to energy shortages. Even before the Arab embargo, America was facing an energy squeeze!

It's expected that Arab decision to let the oil flow once again will ease the crash program suggested by Pres. Nixon, but for this winter at least, shortages are slated to be widespread around the country.

FCC HITS CBS, ABC ON NEWS 'STAGING'

Washington, Nov. 27.
The FCC today (Tues.) admonished CBS and ABC for alleged "staging" or distortion of news reports, and failure to make complete investigations into certain incidents.

CBS, cited for six "staging" incidents, was told it failed to make adequate initial investigations into two of them. ABC, told that only one of three investigations was adequate, is expected to complete its probes in the near future, the commission said.

and in other departments of this issue are stories spelling out some of the specific actions implemented or planned in the U.S. or overseas to meet the present crisis.

The ban on Sunday gasoline sales in the U.S. is most likely to effect resorts more than 100 miles from their primary population centers. Las Vegas and Reno could both feel the impact of lessened weekend auto traffic and that, coupled with a cutback in regular and charter flight service to these resort areas, could add up to serious problems.

Films would seem to be in fairly good shape since downtown theatres are accessible via mass

A Gasser

CBS commentator Dan Rather is credited with one of the sharpest comments on the current energy crisis:
"You can fuel some of the people all of the time and all of the people some of the time, but you can't fuel all of the people all of the time."

transit and even suburban and shopping centre sites don't require that much travel. Dimmed marquees may be a drawback, but elimination of weekday matinees and perhaps Monday night shows can be effected without unduly unbalancing anyone's balance sheet so long as the customers continue to come in the evenings and on weekends.

Broadway legit should be largely okay since the suburban theatregoers on whom live theatre relies so heavily, can make it via train what with the early curtain. Regional theatres and other concert arenas should also be all right since they are generally close to population centers, and they might even benefit from lessened weekend travel with more people seeking entertainment locally. Same would also be true for local cinemas.

If more people stay around home over weekends, record and tape sales should also benefit and, of course, broadcasters figure to

(Continued on page 61)

Advertisers Wary Of Buying Time On 'Dirty' TV Shows

Stop Immorality on TV, the crusade to "clean up" the medium, appears to have some advocates along Madison Ave.

SIT queried several tv sponsors on their moral stance in programming and found them men of high purpose. They are quoted in the SIT newsletter.

Says Miles Lab's media director Mitchell B. Streicker, "Miles has never sponsored the 'Maude' show, nor do we intend to, until we are clearly convinced that the network intends to make suitable program format changes."

Gillette's advertising veepee Thomas R. Ryan says, "We also share many of your concerns about the nature of television programming today. As a matter of policy, we try to see that our advertising runs in programs which are suitable for general family viewing. Under this policy, we have declined to participate as sponsors in programs such as 'The Smothers Brothers' and 'Laugh-In.'"

Says Carnation Milk veepee P.H. Wills, "We are critical and selective as to the program con-

text in which our product commercials appear. We do not condone programming which may be objectionable or offensive to the public ... we register objections with the networks in an effort to maintain a high level of program quality ... and have on occasion cancelled commercial participation when, in our judgment, the programs were substandard."

Eastman Kodak's Bruce R. Wilson says, "In programs we sponsor on a regular basis, we do preview all scripts before the airing of the program. If we find a script is offensive, we will withdraw our commercials from that program."

Says Woolworth's advertising program director E.H. Hunt, "It is the policy of the Woolworth Co. to maintain good taste in all of its dealings with the public including our advertising and its content. We pursue this policy in all media and guard it carefully."

Needham, Harper & Steers' Peter A. Nelson (the McDonald's account) says, "In those cases where there may be some doubt

(Continued on page 54)

CBS-TV In Deep Think Vs. NBC On Late Late Fridays

CBS-TV programming brass is close to a decision on a scheme to compete with NBC in the post-1 a.m. timeslot Friday night (Saturday morning).

Plan would see the CBS movie, which begins at 11:30, followed by a second film for a latenight double feature. The show, if it goes, would offer an alternative to network audiences who may not appreciate rock format of NBC's "Midnight Special." It might also grab off some of the younger audiences caught up in current nostalgia fashion for old films.

CBS' director of latenight programming, Ed Warren, said the idea had been kicking around CBS for several months, and that no firm decision has been made. But, he indicated, decision time is near.

NBC recently started a Monday-Thursday 1 a.m. talk strip with some success. A success in the post-1 a.m. slot on Fridays might cue CBS into thinking about a longer schedule of films in that spot. The web's selection of 11:30 p.m. films has not been notable for quality — being composed largely of recent potboilers and

(Continued on page 61)

Britain's ACTT Shifts $1,200,000 Assets Into A Swiss Bank Account

London, Nov. 27.
Guess who's got a numbered Swiss bank account? The big British show biz craft union, Assn. of Cine, Television & Allied Technicians (ACTT), with a membership of around 18,000.

Per recent revelation, it has switched the bulk of union assets, close to $1,200,000 including stocks and bonds, to Geneva, reportedly with approval of the Bank of England.

The move is designed to foil possible future seizure of union assets in lieu of cash penalties that might be imposed under the nation's new industrial relations act. Union is a militant opponent of the new law.

At the moment, the union is clear with the government, but in hot water with its own membership over attempts to force all feature production here into the major studio plants.

proof that some people thought Berry benefited from a double standard, coupled with "the proof of irrelevant inaccuracies, together fall short of establishing the 'malice' needed to sustain a ver-

THEATRE FOR RENT
183 Seats
Available Immediately
HOLLYWOOD CENTER THEATRE
1451 N. Las Palmas off Sunset
463-1845

For The Best In CANTONESE FOOD
Luncheon • Dinner • Cocktails
Food to Take Out
ANAHEIM • (714) 635-7072
BEVERLY HILLS • CR. 6-1034
HOLLYWOOD • OL. 6-2226
ENCINO • 783-8533

AH FONG says:
Try Our
New Location!
424 N. BEVERLY DR

FANTASTIC FEMALES
are averaging $4 per hour selling sandwiches. Must have car and insurance. Working area — L.A. and Valley. Call
THE MOVEABLE FEAST
836-8616

YOUR CHOICE
Of Industry Jobs
We have a variety of temporary secretarial & typing positions waiting for you.
EMPLOYERS OVERLOAD
1737 North Ivar   462-7394

TELEPHONE SALESMEN
Make $300. wk. commission or more!
559-5588

✓ **SCRIPTS TYPED**
We do professional accurate script typing with complete set up, including copying at a reasonable fee.
AMERICAN SECRETARY
(213) 477-9829

GIRL FRIDAY
Sharp intelligent girl.
Experience required for production office. Lite shorthand—typing.
Call for appt. 464-7313

Typing/Secretarial Services
— *Scripts a Specialty* —
Conveniently located for Valley residents in the Union Bank Building
Marcom Office Service
15233 Ventura Blvd.
Sherman Oaks, Suite 602
(213) 990-1324

Left: November 28, 1973.

Above: Want ads? *Variety* had ads.

Munich and killed two Israelis and took nine others as hostage; all nine were eventually killed.

Weekly Variety on July 3, 1974, reviewed a one-hour primetime special of Walter Cronkite with "the first-in-depth interview with Alexander Solzhenitsyn, exiled in February from the Soviet Union." Solzhenitsyn "suggested that the press place greater restraint upon itself in dealing with people, suggesting that in the demand for news, it seemed to overstep the bounds of decent conduct."

CBS landed the first interviews with Fidel Castro in six years, airing a one-hour special in October 1974 that was a compilation of two separate interviews (by Frank Mankiewicz and Kirby Jones, and by Dan Rather).

The reviewer Tone (Tony Scott) found Castro "a master of the medium," articulate, and "as ardent about his politics as ever, but less strident." Castro presented himself as "an affable dictator." At the end of the broadcast, Rather reminded viewers that, make no mistake, Castro is a Marxist.

Amid the eighteen-month civil war in Lebanon, the October 20, 1976, *Weekly Variety* declared Ziad Rahbani a star for his political program *We're Still Alive* on Radio Lebanon.

A November 22, 1977, *Daily Variety* page one story reported that two thousand print and electronic journalists were arriving in Israel to cover Sadat's meetings with Begin, "one of the most important news events since the end of World War II."

In a July 23, 1973, column, Army Archerd mentioned a state dinner at Nixon's White House, where the guest of honor was the Shah of Iran. By 1979, the Shah had left Iran, and the United States was wondering about the fate of Iran as a site for festivals, international production, or even as a showplace for U.S. films. (A January 24, 1979, story noted there were 430 film theaters in Iran and "it had been part of the Shah's ambitions to prod Iran into the modern world.")

But, starting November 4, 1979, TV was once again center stage when Iranians took over the U.S. Embassy in Tehran and held fifty-two Americans hostage. On December 12, 1979, *Weekly Variety* reported that House Democratic whip John Brademas (D-Indiana) had blasted NBC for airing an interview with one of the hostages,

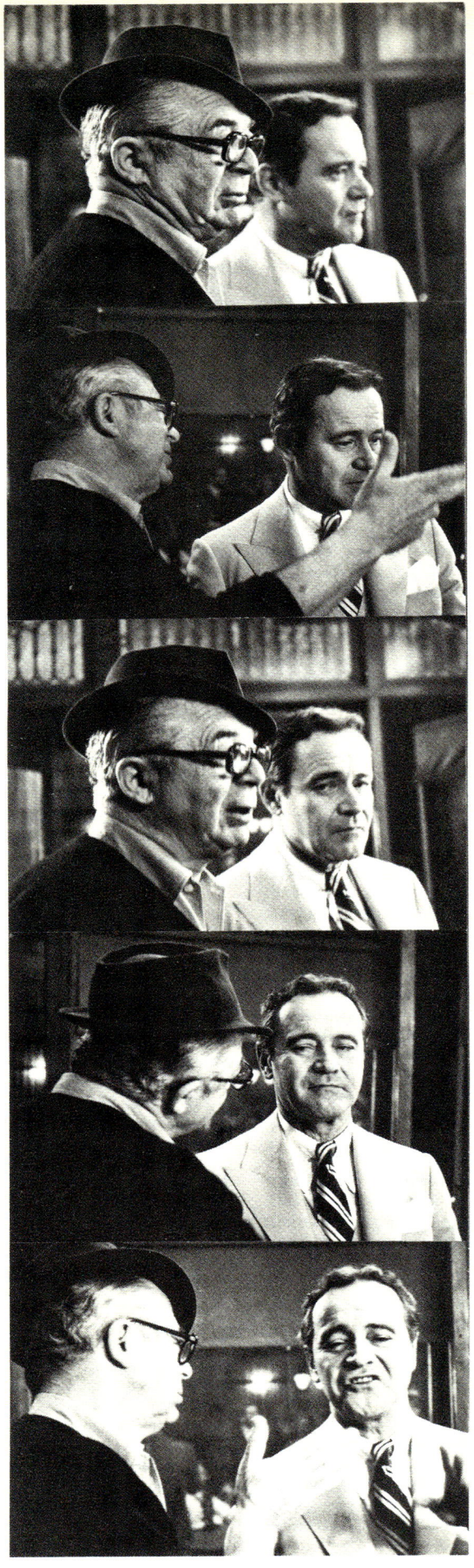

Daily Variety 41st Anniversary Issue

which he labeled as Iranian propaganda: "Brademas said 'no respectable network' would have agreed to air the session, and praised ABC and CBS for not accepting the conditions for the first such interview with a captive." A *Daily Variety* headline on December 17 says it all: "Webs become whipping boy for some in Iranian crisis."

"The fierceness of the competition among the networks for news ratings was on display last week as ABC, CBS and NBC dispatched key correspondents to Iran—at risk of life and limb—to get interviews with the Ayatollah Khomeini," according to the November 21, 1979, *Weekly Variety*. The big "get" went to Mike Wallace because *60 Minutes* executive producer Don Hewitt had started negotiations on November 13 with the Iranian radio and television authority for the interview.

But showbiz in that decade was expanding its global view beyond the Middle East. President Nixon's groundbreaking plans to visit China—yes, Red China! Communist China!—got Hollywood thinking. *Weekly Variety* reported on October 13, 1971, that agent Frank Cooper was heading for Hong Kong and Japan, since the presidential visit (or, as *Variety* called it, the "Nixon peek-in") was a hint of East-West cooperation.

Three years later, a *Weekly* story on January 30, 1974, indicated Hollywood was still trying to get in on the ground floor. More than thirty years after that, Hollywood was still trying to make headway in China.

Showbiz was also trying to figure out its role in the U.K. On May 7, 1979, *Daily Variety* predicted, "Thatcher's win may be mixed showbiz blessing." Margaret Thatcher, running on the Conservative Party, had pledged to cut income tax. Many in showbiz hoped this could mean a return to the U.K. of many British "tax exiles," particularly in the music and film industries: "Upper-bracket earners in Britain are currently clipped at a tax rate of 83%, whereas the Tory axe would seek to chop it down to around 60%."

Left: Billy Wilder and Jack Lemmon.

To the delight of supporters and the dismay of detractors, at the end of the 1970s, both Thatcher and Ronald Reagan won office and used TV to effectively promote their agendas.

TV's expanding international coverage was dangerous, and not just for those risking their lives in war zones. As *Weekly Variety* reported, Don Harris, forty-two, and cameraman Robert Brown, thirty-six, were

> "part of an 18-member mission trying to find out whether a religious cult called the People's Temple was keeping Americans against their will at Temple headquarters in the Guyana village of Jonestown. Leading the investigative mission was Representative Leo J. Ryan (D-California), who was also killed in the Saturday attack. . . ." In all, five were murdered when cult members attacked the group at an airstrip in Port Kaituma, Guyana. "Following the five murders . . . [915] members of the cult committed suicide. Their bodies were found in Jonestown by Guyana authorities. . . ."

Groups and individual fought for their rights, in both peaceful and violent ways, throughout the 1970s. Britain was hit by a "wave of Irish terrorist bombings in the London area," according to a September 10, 1975, report. The new round of violence

> "reactivates the jitters around the show trade. This foresees a resultantly softer box office for films, legit, etc., as happened last year—assuming of course that the terrorism continues apace. . . . Same dimmer B.O. prospect also applies to department stores, pubs. . . ."

And the women's lib movement finally gained momentum, long after Simone de Beauvoir's 1949 feminist manifesto *The Second Sex* and Betty Friedan's 1963 *The Feminine Mystique*.

Betty White, who shortly starts toplining the vidpix series, "Date With Angel," last night was kudosed by Hollywood Women's Professional and Business Club as "most glamorous" gal of the town.

Disk jockey **Bob Kennedy** has role in **Alfred Hitchcock** vidpic.

Guesting on KTLA "Mike Stokey Presents" tomorrow night are **Gail Robbins, George O'Hanlon, Hans Conried** and **Jackie Coogan.**

Berne Giler has just been signed to do his sixth telefilm in Warner Bros.' "Cheyenne" series, starring **Clint Walker.**

> **Betty White:**
> "WHY I FIRST STARTED READING *VARIETY*: Since I am in the business, I wanted to be updated and aware of everything going on.... and I love reading the project reviews."

Germaine Greer's 1970 *The Female Eunuch* was followed by the 1972 debut of *Ms.* magazine under Gloria Steinem, while the "new" movement gained such spokeswomen as Shirley Chisholm, Bella Abzug, Jane Fonda, and Vanessa Redgrave (the latter two starred together in the 1977 *Julia*).

And just as nature hates a vacuum, whenever there's a sociology-political movement, Madison Avenue steps in. Altria Group (formerly Phillip Morris Companies) in 1968 introduced Virginia Slims, cigarettes targeted at women with the tagline "You've come a long way, baby."

An August 26, 1970, *Weekly Variety* story began,

> "CBS has come a long way, baby. In an internal memo issued this week, CBS exec veepee Jack Schneider extended formal recognition to the Women's Liberation Movement. He declared, 'Television must show a new image of a woman as a doer, as an educated serious-minded individual person. Not just a kitchen slave or a single swinger. Acceptance of advertising hostile to women's dignity denigrates and causes the existent ridicule. It has been suggested that the television industry become as sensitive about women in program content and advertising, as they are concerning blacks.... One thing is certain: the movement is definite and it is not going to go away."

Sexual liberation gained momentum with the Food and Drug Administration's 1965 approval of the sale of oral contraception pills. At first, some states mandated that only married women could get a prescription. It wasn't until 1972 that all states allowed all women to get the pill.

Of course, showbiz tried to make money off women's lib, which some male chauvinist pigs simplified as just a battle between men and women. ABC on September 20, 1973, aired a tennis game between Billie Jean King (the eventual winner) and Bobby Riggs, which *Daily Variety* called the "hustle of the century" match. ABC sold ads during the game for $80,000 per minute.

To some, women's lib meant bra burnings and hairy legs, while others believed it to be synonymous with the debate on abortion.

On August 15, 1973, *Daily Variety* ran a front-page story about thirty-nine CBS affiliates refusing to air the episode of Norman Lear's *Maude* that dealt with her abortion:

> "A network source confirmed the dropouts, and attributed it mainly to what he called a 'highly organized campaign by many Catholic organizations who feel the show advocates abortion.'"

Because TV producers and networks worry about offending ad buyers, TV is often less willing to take risks than film. But great strides were made during the 1970s. In fact, 1970's *The Mary Tyler Moore Show*, about a single woman finding fulfillment without a man, debuted years before movies like *An Unmarried Woman* (1978) and *Norma Rae* (1979).

Similarly, 1975's *Hot L Baltimore* sitcom (produced by Norman Lear and based on Lanford Wilson's play) and 1977's *Soap* (created by Susan Harris)

Right: April 15, 1970.

featured lead characters who were gay, likable, and funny—a much more evolved attitude than the gay-themed films like 1976's *Norman . . . Is That You?* and 1980's *Cruising*.

Those series were also far ahead of the sniggering "straight guy pretending to be gay" gags of 1976's *Three's Company*. But, of course, the giggly approach is always more popular than the more enlightened ones.

As women were fighting to change their image, gays were fighting to have an image—any image—after being virtually invisible. For centuries, some plays would feature a butch, domineering woman or a fussy, fluttery male, but none ever directly addressed their sexuality. Such similarly circumspect stereotypes were carried over into radio shows, films, and TV series (was *Bewitched*'s Uncle Arthur gay?). It was literally the love that dared not speak its name.

There was the occasional work that addressed homosexuality, such as the 1931 German film *Mädchen in Uniform*, Robert Anderson's *Tea and Sympathy* (1956), Lillian Hellman's *The Children's Hour* (1961), and Mart Crowley's *The Boys in the Band* (1970). They were so somber you'd never know that a gay person could be fun or funny. And most had sad endings. But Brits led the way with 1961's *Victim* and *A Taste of Honey*, in which gay characters were not only likable, but they didn't kill themselves!

Gay lib may have started with civil rights legislation in the 1960s, but it got a boost with the Stonewall riots. On June 27, 1969, crowds of gay people in Manhattan felt a sense of unity as they gathered to mourn Judy Garland's death. That feeling carried over into the early morning hours of June 28, as police raided The Stonewall Inn in Greenwich Village. Gay people, lead by drag queens, had finally had enough of constant harassment and fought back.

Even at the start of the 1970s, it was clear that the fight for gay lib would not be easy. A headline on page one on August 26, 1970, read "Vatican Ban on Homo Marriages Cues Filming."

"Italian screenwriters are already at work on a socio-religious conflict arising out of a request from two homosexuals for a church-sanctified marriage. Last week, L'Osservatore Romano flailed the local gay liberation effort as 'unnatural.'"

The story said that Father Gino Concetti affirmed "that marriage can only take place between male and female humans. . . ."

Daily Variety offered insights into the public's attitude toward gays on August 3, 1971, as Norman Lear explained the growing success of *All in the Family*.

Dave Kaufman's column began,

"Not in a long, long time has a series scored with the impact of 'All in the Family,' sneaked in by CBS-TV last midseason. 'Sneaked in' is a phrase used advisedly, since there was no advance publicity, no promo, as a nervous network didn't quite know what to do with a show in which the hero is a bigot. The web expected an avalanche of protests, and hired extra operators to handle them. There was an avalanche, but 99% of the callers liked the show, recalls producer Norman Lear."

Lear continued,

"Archie is a fool. . . . The world is changing so fast around him, attitudes on everything are changing, that's why he is lashing out at everything. . . . We did one [episode] on homosexuality, and the network had said the public finds that repulsive and repugnant, and wouldn't laugh at it. But the audience liked it. We even got mail from homosexuals saying they loved it."

So the early 1970s were enlightened enough to deal with it, but *Variety* was unenlightened enough to spotlight that idea with the boldface subhead, "Even homos loved it." Which was, obviously, not an exact quote.

You've come a long way, baby.

The October 20, 1976, *Weekly Variety* covered a five-part news series from WAGA-TV Atlanta that focused on such topics as swine flu, Legionnaires' disease—and homosexuality. That episode looked at

"the 100,000-plus metro Atlantans considered and/or admitted homosexuals. . . . A gay doctor tells [*News Scene* correspondent Barbara] Nevins that there is simply no answer why men and women turn to the homosexual life as they reach adulthood."

One step forward, one step back. Note the phrase "turn to the homosexual life as they reach adulthood"

| FILMS | VIDEO | TV FILMS | RADIO | MUSIC | STAGE |

VARIETY

PRICE 50¢

Published Weekly at 154 West 46th Street, New York, N. Y. 10036, by Variety, Inc. Annual subscription, $20. Single copies, 50 cents.
Second Class Postage Paid at New York, N.Y., and at Additional Mailing Offices.
© COPYRIGHT, 1970, BY VARIETY, INC. ALL RIGHTS RESERVED

Vol. 258 No. 9 — NEW YORK, WEDNESDAY, APRIL 15, 1970 — 64 PAGES

TV HAVEN FOR FILM STARS

Spelling Sees FCC's Primetime Trim As a $60,000,000 Blow to Hollywood

By DAVE KAUFMAN

Hollywood, April 14.
Industry circles in Hollywood and N.Y. are shaken by a proposed FCC ruling that would in effect shear a half-hour a night from network primetime programming beginning in 1971.

Production execs and producers in Hollywood are worried because of the impact on production if such an edict is approved. It would severely dent tv production in Hollywood, since webs would be restricted to three hours primetime each night for entertainment. Knowledgeable sources estimate loss of 11½ hours weekly in program time would mean loss in production coin of about $2,500,000 weekly, and some figure over sea-
(Continued on page 62)

San Antone Strippery Op 'Switches to The Lord'

San Antonio, April 14.
The Green Gate, a local stripper haven, closed last week when Guy Linton, the spot's operator, said he was switching to "the Lord's side." The closing came on the heels of a preaching session held at the club by the Rev. Bob Harrington, who calls himself in
(Continued on page 62)

BRYNNER, FORD EYE VIDSERIES

By LES BROWN

The convulsive changes within the motion picture industry, and its new order of "now generation" stars, increasingly are driving screen names into television. With picture deals hard to come by today for the quondam boxoffice names, the security of a regular tv base, with latitude for one theatrical film a year, has become attractive.

They can get between $600-$750,000 a year for a tv series, usu-
(Continued on page 61)

Bacall Fave for Tuner Star 'Tony'; Figure 'Applause' as Best Musical

Oscar Triggers Cafe And Fair Bids for Goldie Hawn

Hollywood, April 14.
Following her Academy victory as best supporting actress, Goldie Hawn has received a flock of offers for p.a.'s at fairs and niteries throughout the country, including moveup of a date at Vegas' Caesars Palace, according to APA agency v.p. Marty Klein.

However, the only booking this year will be at the Palace, accord-
(Continued on page 61)

Tight voting is expected this year in the Antoinette Perry Award sweepstakes. Unlike recent years, the competition in most of the 16 Tony categories appears to be neck-and-neck.

The race commanding the most interest, both in and out of the trade, is that for best actress in a musical, with Lauren Bacall (of "Applause") vying with Katharine Hepburn (of "Coco"). Both are major stars making hit legituner debuts, and neither has won a Tony in the past.

Their only competition, Dilys Watling, the British actress who starred in the short-lived "Georgy," is not figured a serious threat. Trade speculation has Miss Bacall as the favorite to win.

Her show, "Applause," is also deemed the favorite to cop the
(Continued on page 60)

Vegas Casinos Won $338-Mil In '69, a 24% Rise

Las Vegas, April 17.
Las Vegas casinos won $338,-000,000 during 1969, according to the Gaming Commission.

Tally was $338,399,052—24.4% or $66,000,000 more than the $272,-372,772 won during 1968.

Figure is the gross taxable revenue earned by the 475 licenses who operate 83 table games (pan and poker), 797 games such as Keno, craps, 21 and roulette and 16,391 slot machines.

Operating expenses such as salaries and promotions are not included in the total win, which was
(Continued on page 50)

UK Gambling Faces Rigid Controls With New July 1 Statutes

London, April 14.
Gaming club operators are in for a tough time under the new laws which will come into force on July 1. Sir Stanley Raymond, chief of the new Gaming Board, has made it clear that there will be no kid-glove treatment for those clubs that flout, or try to wriggle around the new laws.

In a White Paper and at a news conference Raymond vigorously denied that he and his part-time team were trying to dictate the way people can "have a little flutter."

Said Raymond: "We are going to allow gaming—a highly dangerous and volatile business—on
(Continued on page 62)

He'll be stealing audiences locally this fall.

Especially 18 to 49ers.
Even the biggest prime-time strongholds on CBS and NBC were penetrated by the "Thief." We've got the record to prove it.
When he starts stealing in your market, make sure it's for you.

It Takes A Thief.

Robert Wagner as Alexander Mundy
International jewel thief turned U.S. counterspy.
65 ALL COLOR HOURS from mca tv

Winchell Memoir Fusing Into Biog By Bob Thomas

By ABEL GREEN

Bob Thomas, the Associated Press Hollywood columnist and author of "King Cohn" (Harry Cohn) and (Irving) "Thalberg" and other show biz books, will next do a biography on columnist Walter Winchell. Doubleday is Thomas' publisher and was to have published "The Uncensored Letters of Walter Winchell," which was a working title of the autobiog he, Winchell, signed to do first for McCall's (serialization) and coincidental publication by Doubleday.

It may be coincidence or a practical way to salvage WW's notes (and a reported $75,000 advance) when the now retired columnist
(Continued on page 61)

Turin Cops Round Up 2 'Rodeo Far West' Injuns On Firewater, Knife Raps

Turin, April 14.
More trouble for "Rodeo Far West," some of whose other difficulties have been previously reported. This time, two of the show's Sioux Indians were arrested for drunkenness and illegal possession of knives. The incident took place the night of April 2 in Turin, where the company of 80 cowboys and 16 Indians is now putting in a last stand on Italian soil before crossing the Alps to Zurich.

The two Sioux, Paul Randel-
(Continued on page 54)

DAILY Variety DAILY

Vol. 149 No. 5 Hollywood, California - 90028, Monday, September 14, 1970   13 15 Cents

ROCK DOC FILMS NEW TREND

Spurt In Showbiz Stocks Greater Than General Market

By A. D. Murphy

Showbiz stocks last week outperformed a generally consolidating market, with major gains posted in the long-lagging film production-distribution group. MCA on Friday leaped 2¾ points to 20¾, climaxing a 4¾-point gain over a six-trading-day period. Unconfirmed reports are circulating that MCA is contemplating a bond issue, through Lehman Bros., in part to retire $50,000,000 in bank debt (half to Bank of America, rest to a Chi bank) due next March 31.

MGM on Friday jumped 1½ points to 18½, for a 3½-point gain on the four-day trading week. And 20th-Fox added another ¼ on Friday to climax a two-point gain on the week. Queried in N.Y., 20th said it has no idea why the stock is rising, but denied any new takeover/merger events. However, there remains speculation that the rising price, plus strengthening of its Eurodollar bonds, presages new corporate developments.

Walt Disney Prods. jumped 2⅝
(Continued on Page 4)

Paramount Today Will Unveil Its New Look For '70s

Paramount will take a look at its product line-up for release through next summer during a three-day national sales convention which starts today at the Bev-Wilshire Hotel.

Theme for the series of meetings is "A New Look for the '70s." Participating in the convention will be exhibitors, producers, directors, screenwriters, performers and sales and advertising personnel.

Distribution v.p. Frank Yablans will conduct the sessions which run through Wednesday, during which he will outline the sales approach on all of Par's releases through next summer.

Attending will be 150 leading exhibs from the U.S. and Canada, producers Dino De Laurentiis, John Foreman, Stuart Rosenberg, Howard G. Minsky, Albert S. Ruddy and stars Ali MacGraw, Ryan O'Neal, Ray Milland, John Marley, bert Redford, Walter Matthau and Lee Grant.

Par prexy Stanley Jaffe will
(Continued on Page 5)

From Horse's Mouth

London, Sept. 13 — Letter from a Beatle, photo-printed in a British pop sheet:

"In order to put out of its misery the limping dog of a ews story which has been dragging itself across your pages for the past year, my answer to the question, 'Will the Beatles get together again?' ... is no."

(signed) Paul McCartney

Warners Sues Western Union

Warner Bros. on Friday filed a suit in Superior Court seeking $122,000 in damages from Western Union, charging WU failed to deliver 224 of 300 telegrams.

Wires were press invitations sent last Jan. 12-13 to meet Helmut Berger, star of "The Damned." WB alleges only a few showed up at the receptions and thus WB failed to get the publicity sought.

Huntley In Group Paying $4,325,000 For 5 Stations

Washington, Sept. 13 — Horizon Communications Corp. has won Federal Communications Commission approval of its purchase of KPAT-AM-FM in Berkeley, Calif., and Wisconsin stations WKOW-TV in Madison, WXOW-TV in La Crosse and WAOW in Wausau.

Total price is about $4,325,000, with $3,000,000 of that sum going for the Wisconsin outlets. The
(Continued on Page 15)

Mgmt. And Labor Meet This Morning On Concessions

Top labor and management execs of Hollywood are due to meet at 10 a.m. today to reexamine the industrywide concessions agreement on pix budgeted at $1,000,000 and under, amid indications labor will agree to its continuance if there are guarantees against further alleged violations.

At a meeting of all Hollywood local business agents of International Alliance of Theatrical Stage Employees with IA International prexy Richard F. Walsh which lasted almost five hours last Thursday, decision was reached that Walsh would arrange the labor-management confrontation with Assn. of Motion Picture & TV Producers, and on Friday the sesh was set.

Business agents said Friday that in their face-to-face meeting with
(Continued on Page 4)

A&M, WARNERS, UA PREPPING SUCH PICTURES

By Rick Setlowe

Don't write off Warner Bros.' "Woodstock" as an isolated phenomenon. Its boxoffice success could mark the breakout of an entirely new genre of film, the rock doc—the unstructured cinema verite that captures the mystique and myths of the subculture of pop music.

At least three other projects with major studios or record companies involved are currently in the works. Although the medium technically is film, the appeal is to the rock freaks—the record buyers and rock concertgoers — although, as with "Woodstock," there is always the possibility of large general audiences. However, at the planning stage the market of a project is best evaluated by those in the music business.

A current example is a film totally financed and produced by A&M Records, "Joe Cocker—Mad Dogs and Englishmen." At a total cost of about $500,000, including the soundtrack for the album, A&M
(Continued on Page 11)

Burch Says It Is FCC's Responsibility To 'Keep B'casting An Open Medium'

By Bill Edwards

Federal Communications Commission's function is "to keep broadcasting an open medium of expression, to supply the framework within which the industry can—and must—present a diverse fare of information and views on significant public issues."

FCChairman Dean Burch told American Political Science Assn., "Beyond this, we can encourage the development of structural diversity through new and competing modes of expression. This is the primary challenge of the '70s. It is also a primary mandate given to the commission by Congress."

In a paper presented to the 66th annual meeting of the APSA at the Biltmore Hotel Friday, Burch
(Continued on Page 15)

Jerry Lewis To Do Broadway Musical

Jerry Lewis has signed with legit producer David Black to star in a Broadway show next year. Property has not been determined, but it's likely that it will be a musical.

Black, whose last Broadway production was "George M," is currently prepping musical "W. C.," in which Mickey Rooney will star as W. C. Fields.

FRANK WEBB...
one actor in search of a
good, **clean**, movie role...

DON SCHWARTZ
and Associates

---

224 VARIETY

Left: September 14, 1970.

and compare it to the 2011 Lady Gaga anthem "Born This Way." Also note use of the word "admitted" to describe what later became known as "openly gay." Better, but is anyone ever described as being "openly straight" or "openly vegetarian"? Still, it was an improvement over the dismissive "homo."

Just as the defeat of the Equal Rights Amendment had fueled women's lib, gay solidarity gained strength from its setbacks, such as the campaign fronted by singer Anita Bryant, former Miss America and 1970s pitchwoman for the Florida Citrus Commission. Bryant was the leader of Save Our Children, a coalition of local religious groups who successfully worked to repeal a law giving equal rights to gays and lesbians in Dade County, Florida.

LGBT groups, as they came to be known (i.e., lesbian, gay, bisexual, and transgender), began to push back and to move forward. On August 24, 1977, *Weekly Variety* ran a story about *Gay USA*, a documentary shot "during the Gay Pride marches held on June 26 in New York, Los Angeles, San Francisco, Chicago, Houston and San Diego. The non-profit venture was the brainchild of director Arthur J. Bressan Jr., conceived on 'Orange Tuesday,' the day singer Anita Bryant won the anti-homosexual referendum in Dade County, Florida. The gay pride rallies which followed had a large turnout in various U.S. cities and Bressan wanted to lense them to show the positive side of the gay lifestyle. . . . Pic, lensed in 16mm, came in under $10,000, according to producer David Pasko."

Harvey Milk was the center of another trauma that spurred activism. On November 27, 1978, Dan White shot and killed Milk, the first openly gay man elected to public office, and pro-gay Mayor George Moscone in San Francisco. The defense argued that White was so depressed that he had "diminished capacity," so could not have committed premeditated first-degree murder. The jury bought the argument and convicted White only of voluntary manslaughter. But many considered it a hate crime since White had appeared uncomfortable with Milk's gayness. Various actors and directors planned a film version, but that didn't happen until 1984, when Rob Epstein's documentary *The Times of Harvey Milk* was released, and 2008, when the scripted film *Milk* was made—and won two Academy Awards.

On September 6, 1979, reporter Dale Pollock declared that the upcoming film *Cruising*, directed by William Friedkin and starring Al Pacino, marked the first time groups had protested a film "during production, and not at the time of release. In this case, it was New York's homosexual community that was up in arms over charges that 'Cruising' not only exploited gays, but would cause a rash of antigay violence across the United States."

Producer Jerry Weintraub insisted he did not make an exploitation picture, but admitted, "There's no way you could buy this kind of publicity."

Protesters had the same concerns that blacks had expressed over D. W. Griffith's 1915 silent *Birth of a Nation* or even the 1950s TV series *Amos 'n' Andy*—namely, it's OK to portray a minority in a negative light, but where are the positive portrayals to balance that?

"Homos" weren't the only minority to receive insensitive treatment in the pages of *Variety*. An April 15, 1970, issue said that a Wild West show, Rodeo Far West, featuring a company of eighty cowboys and sixteen Indians, had been performing in Turin. However, two Sioux performers had been arrested for drunken behavior and possession of knives. *Variety* ran with the headline "Turin Cops Round Up 2 'Rodeo Far West' Injuns on Firewater, Knife Raps."

Like gays, Native Americans raised their profile in the 1970s after a late-'60s kick start. They were also tired of Hollywood's frequent depiction of them as monosyllabic savages, bloodthirsty lunatics, or comic drunks.

Their unhappiness got a global forum on the March 27, 1973, Oscar telecast, when Marlon Brando won the Best Actor prize for *The Godfather*. Brando was a no-show and sent Sacheen Littlefeather, in full Indian regalia, to accept the statuette and convey his message.

Two days after the ceremony, *Daily Variety* ran a column from editor Thomas M. Pryor:

> "The Academy of Motion Picture Arts & Sciences should vote a 1973 Oscar to Marlon Brando—for bad manners. Brando didn't use the Awards platform to protest social injustice to the American Indian; he abused the privilege of the occasion. . . . The question is not whether Brando had the right to criticize the government's treatment of Indians and/or their portrayal on the screen. No doubt many in the audience and among the general

Right: August 23, 1972.

Following Spread: Enter the theater for a preview of *Enter the Dragon*.

public did sincerely applaud his remarks. The point is that Brando should have had the courtesy and the courage to come on the stage before TV cameras and speak his piece himself instead of sending an emissary to represent him . . . . The Academy and its producer, Howard W. Koch, did the wisest thing under the circumstances by permitting Brando's representative, a personable Apache lady, Sacheen Littlefeather, to come on stage and deliver his refusal to accept the award, explaining that she would make a four-page letter by the actor available to the press."

A few months later (August 20, 1973), Tony Scott (aka Tone) in *Daily Variety* reviewed an episode of the KNBC public-affairs program *Impacto*. The show looked at "the tragic confrontation at Wounded Knee, S.D., and its implications," with contributions from American Indian Movement national field director Dennis Banks and chief counsel Ramon Roubideaux.

"'They have offered us a life span of 44.5 years,' comments one brave at Custer, S.D., about the way the white man has treated the Indian. The indictment suggests the desperate straits, with Banks stating he is sorry Wounded Knee was ended, since the treaty was broken by the whites less than two hours after it was signed."

While many racial and sexual minorities gained momentum in the 1970s, other groups continued their long struggle toward equality. The Oscars for 1972 gave a hopeful note as Diana Ross, Cicely Tyson, and Paul Winfield earned nominations in the lead acting categories. Remarkable, considering only nine other black actors had been nominated in the history of the Academy Awards (with wins only for Hattie McDaniel and Sidney Poitier).

And, lo, the birth of the low-budget "blaxploitation" film. Actors like Richard Roundtree, Tamara Dobson, Pam Grier, Jim Brown, and Fred Williamson were the heroes of these movies. Not the drug-dealers, not the scary lowlifes, not the jive-talking sassy sidekicks, but the heroes. And Caucasians were the villains. Audiences ate up pics like 1971's *Sweet Sweetback's Baadasssss Song* and *Shaft*, 1972's *Super Fly* and *Blacula*, 1973's *Cleopatra Jones* and *Coffy*, and 1974's *Foxy Brown*, from such directors as Melvin Van Peebles and Gordon Parks.

"The black-slanted film market, whose fiscal importance dates back about four years, has so far yielded only a few films which have achieved what the trade calls 'crossover' status; that is, films which, despite black story and casting elements, has appeal to white audiences as well,"

according to a July 17, 1974, story about the Warner Bros. Poitier–Bill Cosby–Harry Belafonte comedy actioner *Uptown Saturday Night*, which was hoping to change that.

However, that film ran into its own controversy.

According to a story on July 17, 1974, studios would book black-oriented films in downtown theaters but refused to book those same films in black neighborhoods until later in the film's run.

According to Walter Brecher, whose Brecher Theatre chain includes Harlem's Apollo Theater, Warners "refused to open 'Uptown' in a Harlem day and date [engagement] because it didn't want pic to be tagged as merely a black attraction.'"

Asian actors, meanwhile, got a global boost that can be summed up in one name: Bruce Lee. The good-looking, charismatic actor had moves like no one else. He became, briefly, America's first Asian superstar. Until this time, many Asian protagonists had been portrayed by Europeans (Mr. Moto and Charlie Chan were played, respectively, by Germany's Peter Lorre and Sweden's Warner Oland, among others).

On July 23, 1973, *Variety* ran Lee's obit.

His films were few but influential. *Variety* editor David Fox coined the word "chopsocky" to describe *Fists of Fury* and the flurry of the martial-arts films that ensued, making a global star of Jackie Chan and others.

When speaking of films, it's always fun to check that old, reliable gauge of public mood: scary films. The 1970s created some doozies, including *The Exorcist* (1973), *The Texas Chainsaw Massacre* (1974), Mario Bava's cult fave *Suspiria* (1977), and John Carpenter's *Carrie* (1976) and *Halloween* (1978)—both of which borrowed the "big scream" first seen in the 1967 *Wait*

FILMS | VIDEO | TV FILMS | RADIO | MUSIC | STAGE

VARIETY

PRICE 50¢

Published Weekly at 154 West 46th Street, New York, N.Y. 10036, by Variety, Inc. Annual subscription, $20. Single copies, 50 cents.
Second Class Postage Paid at New York, N.Y., and at Additional Mailing Offices.
© COPYRIGHT, 1972, BY VARIETY, INC., ALL RIGHTS RESERVED

Vol. 268 No. 2 — NEW YORK, WEDNESDAY, AUGUST 23, 1972 — 64 PAGES

GOP'S GREAT VIDEO FREEBEE

Crime Ties To Show Biz Stirs Nerves But Skeptical On P.R. Porno 'Raids'

Probably nothing will come of the present "tall talk" in New York, perhaps akin to Mayor John V. Lindsay's recent porno shop raids (a day or two later, they were back doing business at the same addresses) but show biz, bars, grills, jukebox and music biz could come under an unwelcome spotlight if the City Hall palaver about organized crime syndicates' financial stakes in "legitimate" business ever becomes public property. It is no secret that any number of liquor licenses are held in the individual names of trusted employees, often of blood relationship, fronting for pubs, clubs, bars and grills owned by "the boys."

Risk capital in "services" companies from syndicate sources has run the gamut from laundry and diaper services to garbage carting, coal, oil and garment trucking, and the like.

The Prohibition era spawned (or accelerated) mob control of niteries
(Continued on page 62)

Davis As Black 'Hyde'; Muhammad Ali's Project; Spangler Repeats 'Nigger'

Hollywood, Aug. 22.
Sammy Davis Jr. viewed American International's "Blacula," and called producer Joe Naar to express an interest in a black "Dr. Jekyll and Mr. Hyde." Naar says he also is talking a black remake of a white classic with boxer Muhammad Ali's lawyers. Ali's condition: no sex in the pic.

"Legend of Nigger Charley" producer Larry Spangler reports he'll start a sequel Sept. 26 and the title will definitely include the words "Nigger Charley" once more.

Spangler has remained indifferent to the criticism that he has revived the double-g of racial derogation after 40 years of objection got it pretty well buried. Spangler's angle: "Nigger is boxoffice."

BERNSTEIN-LERNER MUSICAL FOR SUBBER

Leonard Bernstein and Alan Jay Lerner may collaborate on a Broadway musical for production next season by Saint Subber. The project is tentatively titled "Opus 1," and the official word is that the composer and librettist-lyricist "are exploring the possibility" of such a work.

Bernstein, besides being a concert composer and the retired musical director of the N.Y. Philharmonic Symphony, has written the scores for such Broadway
(Continued on page 61)

Adult Radio

Minneapolis, Aug. 22.
A sign of the updated morality in the broadcast media are the themes listed for this month on WLOL-AM's "Girl Topic," a sex-oriented telephone-talk show. Among them:
"What do you do that turns your man on?"
"Did you ever have sex with a man for sex's sake, without feeling?"
"Do you ever fake your response during a romantic encounter?"

UN & Show Types Dig 'Deep Throat'

Sources close to the operation of the World Theatre in Manhattan, where "Deep Throat" was the target of a well-publicized seizure last week, report that upwards of 5% of the weekly audience for that porno hit is made up of off-duty policemen, Broadway stage personalities, judges and United Nation officials, many of them "repeaters."

The World, like other sexpo houses, generally gives cuffo admission to police who flash their badges for entry and to celebrities who call for passes as they would to one of the major distribs. One prominent Broadway legit actress is known as a World "repeater" in the company of her famous husband. Lately there's been a rash of calls from the U.N. for passes for foreign dignitaries. The porno crowd in Manhattan has always been composed of a number of foreign tourists and officials who
(Continued on page 62)

Jerry Lucas Heads ABC's 3-Hour Kidspec For Nov.

ABC-TV will air a three-hour kiddie variety show featuring New York Knicks basketball player Jerry Lucas Friday, Nov. 25, from 10 a.m. to 1 p.m.

The spread will be produced by Kirshner Entertainment Corp. and sponsored in full by Ideal Toy Corp.

Titled, "The Jerry Lucas Super Kids Day Music and Magic Jamboree," the show will cast Lucas as a magician and mentalist. Don Kirshner is exec producer with David Yarnell as producer. Scoring will be by Ron Dante with the 50-piece children's symphony from Allen Stevenson School in New York featured.

PARLEY STYLED FOR THE MEDIA

By LARRY MICHIE

Miami Beach, Aug. 22.
There are two major producers of television spectaculars here, each equally avid for air exposure. At the opening of the Republican National Convention, it appears that the antiwar demonstrators will have to outdo themselves to cut significantly into the tv show being mounted by the GOP.

With two networks committed to gavel-to-gavel coverage, and very little party business to transact, it was a setup for the Grand Old Party to lay in the old controlled "sell"—whether in the form of industrial films (euphemistically called documentaries) or parading the first family, or evangelizing for the discontented Democrats. In all, the biggest commercial freebee since television began.

Republican planners frankly made this a "media convention."
The absence of news is breathtaking. So the GOP set dull business for afternoon sessions, leaving major speeches, films extolling the Nixon Administration, and other entertainment tidbits for primetime.

The news media generally have
(Continued on page 30)

Munich's Hotels, Eateries, Cafes All Revved Up

By JOHN KAFKA

Munich, Aug. 22.
In addition to the two new Yank-modeled, German-bankrolled hotel towers, the Holiday Inn and the Sheraton, the Munich Hilton finally opened and got ready for the Olympiad. It's a 15-decker on the fringe of this city's Central Park, Englischer Garten, and offers, to a guest potential of 900, apartments, four restaurants (Marco Polo Roofgarden, Tivoli Grill, Isar View, Atrium Cafe), two night clubs as well as ballrooms, convention halls, swimming pools, gyms, saunas and an indoor shopping street.

Hilton, Sheraton, Holiday Inn as well as Munich's older tourist palaces (Continental, Bayerischer Hof, Vier Jahreszeiten, Regina, Koenigshof, Ambassador, Residence, Arabella) are sold out for the duration of the Games, each getting its share of royalty (England, Holland, Sweden, Denmark, Iran), reigning princes (Monaco, Luxembourg, Liechtenstein), presi-
(Continued on page 61)

FCC Plus U.S Agencies Co-Op To Stem Drug-&-Sex Payola Tide

The March Of Color

Color tv is now in 56.1% of American homes with sets, according to research conducted by NBC-TV. As of July 1, there were 35,400,000 color sets in the country, per NBC intelligence.

That's twice the number of color homes in 1968. NBC research anticipates that 60% of American tv households will have color by next Jan. 1.

Racial Minorities And Film Casting

Hollywood, Aug. 22.
Black Artists Alliance has been formed to protest the "gross and deliberate distortion of black life in motion pictures, television, radio and commercials."

Organization, according to a spokesman, includes 400 actors, directors, writers, producers, announcers and technicians.

"We will no longer tolerate the cheap movies about us" the spokesman said. "We will no longer tolerate the visual images of black people that are paraded across the screen as little more than reincarnations of racist stereotypes which demean our women and make ludicrous caricatures of our men."

Minorities want to appear in roles which do not reflect ethnic background, Association of Motion Picture & Television Producers has been told by a Screen Actors Guild committee.

SAG's ethnic minorities committee listed minority actors' grievances at a meeting with AMPTP. Cited were lack of opportunity to vie for roles which have nothing to do with ethnic background; requirements that stereotypical
(Continued on page 62)

BBC Reviving 'Death,' Source Of U.S.' 'Family'

London, Aug. 22.
After a lapse of four years BBC-TV this fall revives the hit sitcom "Till Death Us Do Part," inspiration for CBS-TV's "All in the Family."

Johnny Speight repeats as writer, and the show's set for a seven-week run (not uncommon for the British medium) with the same cast as before, including Warren Mitchell as hard-hat bigot Alf Garnett (Carroll O'Connor is his counterpart in the Yank edition).

Washington, Aug. 22.
The FCC has "reinforced" and "strengthened" its liaisons with the Justice Dept. and has begun to "deal directly" with the Bureau of Narcotics & Dangerous Drugs in a renewed attempt to cure the continuing payola and plugola problem nationwide.

A top FCC official has urged that the Commission, for the first time, conduct public hearings into the matter, revealing four closed-door hearings that have been held, the last as recent as two months ago.

William B. Ray, chief of the FCC Complaints' & Compliance Division, detailed latest schemes that see marijuana and other drugs being used as bribes for disk jockeys, as well as the furnishing of girls, paying doctor bills and rent, and sending "huge quantities" of records to deejays who can
(Continued on page 62)

Caesar Donating His Children's Song Rights To Scandia Kids Funds

When "No, No Nanette" debuts its Scandinavian tour on Sept. 21 in Skilstuna, Denmark, under auspices of the Swedish Risteatern, lyricist Irving Caesar will code the copyrights to his "Sing A Song of Safety" and "Sing A Song Of Friendship" series to the children of Sweden, Denmark and Norway. All rights to the children's song series, which have been widely translated and performed, but never in any of the Scandinavian countries, will go to local children's welfare or other usages.

The coincidence of Caesar attending the Norsk preem of "Nanette" sparked a longtime
(Continued on page 61)

DANNY KAYE'S GLOBAL PITCH FOR DC-10 PLANE

London, Aug. 22.
Danny Kaye, who often globetrots as a UNICEF goodwill ambassador, is back on the Coast after a 21-day global sales sojourn with the McConnell-Douglas DC-10 airbus. Latter is the competition for the new Lockheed Tristar in the big passenger payload (350-400) sweeps.

Kaye, a certificated jet pilot, was invited along by Douglas topper Jack McGowan, and spent the aloft portions of the tour on the plane's flight deck. Fellow passenger during a run over Greece was Aristotle Onassis, the shipping tycoon who also owns the Greek-flag Olympic Airlines.

227

Warner Bros. is Proud to Announce Trade Screening Sneak Previews of One of its Major Productions — the Ultimate in Martial Arts Excitement and Adventure.

BRUCE LEE · JOHN SAXON · AHNA CAPRI in "ENTER THE DRAGON"
Co-Starring **BOB WALL · SHIH KIEN** and Introducing **JIM KELLY**
Music: Lalo Schifrin · Written by Michael Allin · Produced by Fred Weintraub and Paul Heller in association with Raymond Chow · Directed by Robert Clouse · PANAVISION® · TECHNICOLOR®

TRADE SCREENING SNEAK PREVIEWS – SAT. AUG. 4*

ATLANTA Fox	8:00 PM
BOSTON Savoy	8:30 PM
CHARLOTTE Tryon Mall	10:00 PM
CHICAGO United Artists	8:00 PM
CINCINNATI Grand	8:30 PM
CLEVELAND Center Mayfield	9:00 PM
DALLAS Medallion	8:00 PM
DENVER Centre	8:00 PM
DES MOINES Galaxy	8:00 PM
DETROIT Madison	8:05 PM
JACKSONVILLE Florida	8:00 PM
KANSAS CITY Metro #4	9:00 PM
* LOS ANGELES Pantages Hollywood* Jul. 27	8:30 PM
MEMPHIS Malco	8:00 PM
MILWAUKEE Palace	8:00 PM
MINNEAPOLIS Cina #4, St. Paul	8:00 PM
NEW ORLEANS Saenger	8:00 PM
* NEW YORK Loews State 2 Fri. Aug. 3	8:30 PM
OKLAHOMA Sheppard #1	8:00 PM
PHILADELPHIA Milgram	8:30 PM
PORTLAND Broadway #2	8:30 PM
SALT LAKE Utah	8:00 PM
SAN FRANCISCO Warfield	8:30 PM
SEATTLE U.A. 70	8:45 PM
ST. LOUIS Loews State	8:00 PM
WASHINGTON Town #2	8:00 PM

until Dark when the audience thought the villain was dead... but he wasn't! Big scream! *Carrie* also made Stephen King a household name, as the prolific author wrote numerous books over the next decades, many of them adapted for film and TV including *Salem's Lot* (1979), *The Shining* (1980), 1983's *Christine* and *Cujo*, *The Stand* (1994), and *Misery* (1990).

The Wes Craven 1972 *The Last House on the Left* was probably the only fright movie ever based on an Ingmar Bergman film (in this case, the 1960 *The Virgin Spring*). It was released with the memorable ad line "To avoid fainting, keep repeating—it's only a movie..."

The decade also gave rise to a different kind of scary pic. On September 5, 1973, *Weekly Variety* led page one with a story about the film biz's "Fascination with Assassination"; it listed 20th Century-Fox's *The Chairman* (1969), Costa-Gavras's *Z* (1969) and *State of Siege* (1972), National General's *Executive Action* (1973), Universal's *Day of the Jackal* (1973), Claude Chabrol's *Nada* (1974), and many others. In the next few years, the topic would also be covered in more U.S. pics such as *Parallax View* (1974), *Nashville* (1975), and *Winter Kills* (1979). In 1976, director Martin Scorsese tapped into the decade's unrest in *Taxi Driver*. Working with Paul Schrader's script, Scorsese presented a portrait of Vietnam vet Travis Bickle, played by Robert DeNiro, whose mind slowly unhinges and who becomes a political assassin.

The topic was also movies about corruption and cover-ups, like Roman Polanski's *Chinatown* (1974), and paranoia, like Polanski's *The Tenant* (1976). And, of course, there was *All the President's Men*, the 1976 white-knuckle suspense film based on Bob Woodward and Carl Bernstein's account of their exposure of the Watergate crimes.

When you're talking about scary 1970s movies, special attention must be paid to *Jaws*.

OBITUARIES

Bruce Lee

Bruce Lee, 32, a Chinese-American actor who parlayed his kung-fu expertise into a screen career, died July 20 in a Hong Kong hospital of undetermined causes. He had been in L.A. only a month ago, at which time he underwent a complete physical examination.

Born in San Francisco, where his father was appearing with the Cantonese Opera Co., Lee Jung-fan returned with his parents to Hong Kong and began appearing in films there at the age of four. As a teenager he changed his name to Bruce Lee and began studying kung fu. He returned to the U.S. at 18 to attend the University of Washington, where he eventually wrote a master's thesis since expanded into a 1963 paperback called "Chinese Kung Fu, The Philosophical Art Of Self-Defense."

After graduation Lee opened a kung-fu school in Seattle, then moved to L.A. and appeared in a number of small tv roles. In 1967 he was cast as Kato on "The Green Hornet" video series, and in 1971 he was a guest performer in the initial segment of the "Longstreet" show. That led to several starring offers in Hong Kong, where Lee returned with his American wife Linda and two children. He and producer Raymond Chow formed Golden Harvest and made two substantial b.o. successes: "Fist Of Fury" (released this year in the U.S. by National General as "The Chinese Connection") and "The Big Boss" (another 1973 NGP release under the title of "Fists Of Fury"). Both pix also proved successful in this country.

Prior to his death, Lee had completed his first U.S.-financed kung-fu film, "Enter The Dragon," for Warner Bros. and producer Fred Weintraub. Film is skedded for release here next month.

As a tribute to his popularization of kung fu (or jeet kune do, as he called his technique), Black Belt Magazine recently named him its man of the year.

Elsie Illingworth

New York, July 22—Elsie Illingworth, 87, concert soprano who became a longtime biz exec with S. Hurok Attractions, died last week in a Huntington, L.I., nursing home. She retired last year.

Mrs. Alice Goorwitz

Lebanon, N.J., July 22—Funeral services were held at the weekend for Mrs. Alice Goorwitz, 59, mother of actor Allen Garfield, who died Thursday of heart failure in Beth Israel Hospital, Newark. Burial was in Mt. Lebanon Cemetery.

In addition to son Allen, she is survived by a daughter, Lois, and two sisters, Mrs. Marion Agress and Mrs. Charlotte Amster.

Right: The Bicentennial was a pretty big deal.

IT WAS THE BIGGEST BIRTHDAY BASH OF ALL TIME.

ON JULY 4TH, WE SET ASIDE OUR REGULAR PROGRAMMING TO THROW A MAMMOTH 16-HOUR BICENTENNIAL CELEBRATION.

AND WHAT A CELEBRATION IT WAS! AN AUDIENCE EQUAL TO EVERY FAMILY IN THE UNITED STATES CAME TO OUR PARTY—MORE THAN ATTENDED FESTIVITIES ON EITHER OF THE OTHER TWO NETWORKS. BY FAR.

THE PARTY WAS SUCH A SUCCESS, IN FACT, THAT THE FOLLOWING SUNDAY, BY OVERWHELMING DEMAND, WE BROADCAST A SPECIAL HOUR OF HIGHLIGHTS.

AS YOU CAN SEE FROM JUST A FEW OF THE RETURNS, JULY 4, 1976 WAS A DAY WE'LL CHERISH THE REST OF OUR LIVES.

Impressive! Inspiring! Magnificent! T.V. at its finest!
SAN FRANCISCO, CALIFORNIA

To me there never has been a television day and night that gave us the enjoyment and entertainment that came with your July 4 accomplishment.
BUFFALO, NEW YORK

It was a once-in-a-life-time experience.
NILES, MICHIGAN

It was the finest thing my husband and I have ever seen on television. It reminded me of the many wonderful things about America that we are apt to forget when the bad things happen.
EUREKA, CALIFORNIA

A *Beautiful* Birthday Party! It was by far the most wonderful thing we've ever seen on television.
ST. PETERSBURG, FLORIDA

Thank you for the most fantastic program I've seen, "In Celebration of U.S.," which made this holiday far more than I had expected. You've captured the diversity of the American spirit.
SILVER SPRING, MARYLAND

Sincere congratulations and heartfelt thanks for your wonderful coverage of the July 4th Bicentennial Celebration. In such coverage T.V. seems to have realized its potential as a constructive and cohesive force in our society.
TARRYTOWN, NEW YORK

T.V. has certainly come of age. Congratulations and many many thanks.
BETHESDA, MARYLAND

We consider this the all-time landmark of television.
YAKIMA, WASHINGTON

You made history live and I felt I was a living part of that history.
HEMPSTEAD, NEW YORK

Tears and goose bumps had to be in every home watching.
FLORIDA

What a wonderful, joyous celebration it was, which, thanks to T.V. we all could share.
SEATTLE, WASHINGTON

I hope you taped the whole day's events and will present them to the National Archives.
OMAHA, NEBRASKA

I am astonished at my reaction to it all. It prompted an outpouring of reflection about my feelings about being an American.
YPSILANTI, MICHIGAN

Beautiful! Fantastic! The July 4th show covered by you and the CBS crew made me and, I'm sure, millions of Americans proud of our heritage.
FT. WORTH, TEXAS

Never have I personally felt such a deep love for my country and my fellow man.
KINGSPORT, TENNESSEE

It made us proud to be Americans.
PRESCOTT, ARIZONA

You made us proud to be Americans.
INDIANAPOLIS, INDIANA

Made me feel proud to be a part of this nation.
SAN DIEGO, CALIFORNIA

I am proud to be an American and what a marvelous opportunity you have given us to renew our belief and faith in ourselves.
SCHENECTADY, NEW YORK

As we watched we thought, this is really a country united, when so many can come together from one ocean to another. May this day linger long with all of us.
CORNING, IOWA

It was very patriotic, very beautiful, very emotional and very American.
TOPEKA, KANSAS

Watching CBS coverage made me proud to be an American.
CUMBERLAND, RHODE ISLAND

I'm truly proud to be an American; you made me feel even more proud. What a great job you did.
N. SUBURBAN, ILLINOIS

| FILMS | VIDEO | TV FILMS | RADIO | MUSIC | STAGE |

VARIETY

PRICE 75¢

NEWSPAPER
Second Class P.O. Entry

Published Weekly at 154 West 46th Street, New York, N.Y. 10036, by Variety, Inc. Annual subscription, $30. Single copies, 75 cents.
Second Class Postage Paid at New York, N.Y. and at Additional Mailing Offices
© COPYRIGHT, 1977, BY VARIETY, INC. ALL RIGHTS RESERVED

Vol. 287 No. 12   New York, Wednesday, July 27, 1977   34205   80 PAGES

FILM EFFECTS MEN TURN TRICK AT B.O.

Interpol Told To Track Down Film Pirates

Rome, July 26.
Minister of the Interior Francesco Cossiga has ordered the Italian head of Interpol, Romeo Iola, to help coordinate the international campaign against film piracy in close association with the Italian motion picture industry, according to ANICA prexy Carmine Cianfarani who headed a trade delegation at a recent meeting with the minister. Also present at the meeting were Francisco Rodriguez (20th-Fox manager), Franco Cristaldi of Vides, Paolo Ferrara for the exhibs and Gino De Dominicis, all members of the industry's anti-piracy committee.
At a meeting last week, Interpol
(Continued on page 77)

Bare-Foot Talent Swings On Streets Of World Capitals

Frankfurt, July 26.
A sign in the London subway states that "no loiterers and no musicians are allowed" in the area. Less than a meter away, a young American rock trio is jazzing it up as a pretty blond songstress, barefoot and in a ground-scraping Indian wraparound, shrills along with the music.
Along the Zeil, Frankfurt's walking street between rows of towering department stores, Bach is being
(Continued on page 67)

BRITISH MUSICIANS REPUDIATE CURB ON WAGE RAISES

London, July 26.
The Musicians' Union is the first showbiz trade union to join in the general unionite call for an end to the "Social Contract," which limited pay increases over the past two years but never kept the lid on prices.
In common with others within the Trades Union, Congress the tooters want an immediate return to unrestrained bargaining.
As to that aspect, with inflation apparently at 17%, a Common Market survey sponsored by the European Commission, noted an adverse British reaction to their declining lifestyle.

'STAR WARS' SPOTLIGHTS NEW BREED OF WIZARDS

By JAMES HARWOOD

Hollywood, July 26.
Hollywood's renewed interest in special effects wizardry, made even more acute by the current smash of 20th's "Star Wars," is attracting a new breed of technicians to the film industry, people whose original training is far afield from the traditional motion picture arts and crafts.
Producers eager for more realistic special effects and mechanical gadgetry are concluding the best results can be achieved by hiring those familiar with the latest scientific advancement in building materials and high-technology, especially electronics and micro-circuitry.
Significantly, the immigration has been eased by a period of high-employment in Hollywood, when union resistance to newcomers is low. Also, the new talent is rapidly filling the vacuum discovered a few years back when special effects pix like "Earthquake" had a hard time rounding up enough trained people. Instead of having to teach old methods to a new generation, Hollywood is adapting what the youngsters already know — and finding the results are often much better.
Typical of the new arrivals is 37-year-old Curt Brubaker, who works with his wife Lee and a small staff designing transportation of the future. Formerly with General Motors in Detroit, Brubaker has had his own shop since 1969 where he's developed a steam taxi for the Department of Transportation and the state of California, an aerial ambulance for the Marine Corp., hydrofoils and helicopters and is currently designing three prototype electric cars for the Federal Energy, Research and Development Administration.
Accustomed to working on pro-
(Continued on page 76)

Aud-Arena Biz In Transition To New Format

By JOE COHEN

San Francisco, July 26.
The largest convention held by the International Assn. of Auditorium Managers is current at the Fairmont Hotel with nearly 400 members in attendance. The 52d annual confab also drew the largest number of exhibitors with more than 80 companies housed in two rooms of the hotel. The hotel's main ballroom was insufficient and an adjacent floor had to be put into service.
The large number of operators and managers meeting here reflects the growing concern of the
(Continued on page 76)

Argues Vid Tape Not Copyrightable Until Jan. 1, 1978

Hollywood, July 26.
Arthur Stanley Katz, a prominent BevHills copyright expert and former studio lawyer, has published a rather novel — and extreme — opinion that no programs created on videotape are now protected by copyright and won't be until the new copyright law goes into effect Jan. 1.
His argument, appearing in the current issue of the legal Daily Journal Report, seems certain to cause some discomfort. Asked to boil the complex cases study down to laymen terms, Katz commented: "It means if I'm right, the whole industry goes down the tube."
Seemingly, Katz has enough
(Continued on page 77)

L.V. SHERIFF CAST AS THE BAD GUY IN FEDERAL TAX SUIT

Las Vegas, July 26.
Sheriff Ralph Lamb, one of the most powerful political figures in southern Nevada who wields heavy control over gambling and liquor, began facing charges today in Federal court of failing to pay income taxes of about $34,000 from 1970-72. Lamb, 51, was indicted April 13 on three charges of tax evasion.
Maximum penalty, if guilty, would find Lamb
(Continued

A PERSONAL STORY OF EPIC PROPORTIONS ABOUT FIVE YOUNG MEN IN THE VIETNAM WAR — AS IT REALLY WAS!

CPL. TYRONE WASHINGTON, USMC – AGE: 21 – OCCUPATION: GHETTO SURVIVOR – CHARACTERISTICS: HARD-NOSED, RUGGED, DESTINED TO LEAD.

HE IS ONE OF...

THE BOYS IN COMPANY C

DIRECTED BY SIDNEY J. FURIE

PROUDLY PRESENTED BY
RAYMOND CHOW'S GOLDEN HARVEST GROUP
CONSULTANT: MAX E. YOUNGSTEIN (213) 274-0371

Left: July 27, 1977.

Above: Mark Hamill and Carrie Fisher in *Star Wars*. [And my world changed. -ed.]

Following Spread: June 25, 1975; December 16, 1975.

The June 25, 1975, *Daily Variety* was agog over the opening weekend for the Steven Spielberg–directed movie. The report from A. D. Murphy began, "Universal Pictures reports a smash three-day [weekend] opening domestic box office tally of $7,061,513 for Jaws in 409 situations."

Murphy and fellow reporter Steven Ginsberg virtually invented modern-day box office reporting. After *Jaws* and the 1977 *Star Wars*, studios began to release films in more theaters simultaneously. The old model had been to book a big film in one or two theaters in key cities, hope that it ran for a year there, then it would roll out to more theaters and eventually make it to small towns or to "dollar houses" in major cities. With the money being paid for ads in newspapers' entertainment listings and on TV, studios finally realized it made more sense to open a film wide.

But studios were reluctant to give out box office figures. So *Variety* rounded up estimates from key cities that would offer a representative sampling. As a film's opening became a national phenomenon in the late 1970s and early 1980s, Murphy and Ginsberg would call exhibitors and come up with an estimate. Studios were not happy, but they eventually began to cooperate. For years, these figures were part of *Variety*, and then they began to appear in mainstream newspapers and on TV and radio news. The reluctant dragons at the studios began to see box office reporting as a marketing tool and bragged if their film "won the weekend box office."

The *Jaws–Star Wars* one-two punch also helped reshape the way films were made and the studios' emphasis on visual effects.

And to make the deft oral segue from *Jaws* to *Deep Throat*, the business of adult films was a regular feature in *Variety* during the 1970s. The sexual revolution of the 1960s, along with plenty of savvy marketing, helped middle-class people feel less guilty about attending porn theaters. Some of *Variety*'s attention was due to the legal implications for mainstream Hollywood films. Some of it was a reflection of the times when it was cool, or at least acceptable, for young couples to go to the Pussycat Theatre. And some of it may have been due to the personal interests of a few *Variety* staffers. Who can say, really?

On June 14, 1974, *Daily Variety* announced that the X-rated *Deep Throat* made L.A. movie history by earning $3.2 million at the Hollywood Pussycat Theatre, a record gross in a single theater in L.A. The story saucily punned, "'Throat' got its big thrust when a N.Y. judge in last week of February, 1971, threw the book at Gotham exhib of pic, and film instantly zoomed to national attention."

Variety even ran reviews of adult films and carried stories about adult films loosely based on the 1974 kidnapping and "radicalization" of newspaper heiress Patty Hearst.

But in January 30, 1974, *Weekly Variety* ran the headline "Porno Chic Fades; N.Y. Post Muting its Editorial

Just for Variety

By ARMY ARCHERD

GOOD MORNING: Burt Lancaster will costar with Paul Newman in Bob Altman's "Buffalo Bill And The Indians, Or Sitting Bull's History Lesson" for UA. Lancaster plays Ned Buntline, the man who "invented" Buffalo Bill. Altman, in town briefly, says he set Indian Chief Frank Kaquits to play Sitting Bull. Asked whether this is Kaquits' acting debut, Altman smiled, "He's either never acted before — or he's acted all his life." Besides Geraldine Chaplin, femmes added to the cast are opera stars Mary Cross Leuders and Noel Rogers. Altman's also here talking with Dino De Laurentiis for whom he'll do "North Dallas 40," scripted by John Binder and hopefully with Jimmy Caan, Elliott Gould and a host of pro football players, also, "Ragtime" — an epic set at the turn of the century being scripted by Joan Tewkesbury. The latter two pix are probably for Par. In answer to those who seek special "meaning" to his "Nashville," Altman replies, "I just show what I see." Is the pic related to the JFK or George Wallace shootings? "Neither — and both," Altman answered . . . Rod Serling is due to undergo open heart surgery tomorrow at Strong Memorial Hospital in Rochester, N.Y. . . . Jack Haley Sr. at St. John's Hospital, happily says he's waiting an OK from medics to go home. "I'm feeling fine," he says, "but — I had a close call." When George Burns visited Haley, latter gave Burns the title for his new book — "How To Become Old Without Aging" . . . Tony Bill, who once told us his "Shampoo" role was his thesping swansong, did a cameo in "Las Vegas Lady" for pal, producer-director Noel Nosseck. The scene was lensed at the blackjack table in Las Vegas' Circus Circus and Bill admits, "I lost more than I made." Tony's prepping two properties apart from his WB pact: Rob Thompson's ("Hearts Of The West") "Killers Don't Kiss" and Bronte Woodard's "My Blue Heaven." Latter's a love story.

* * *

Among those offering congrats to Jimmy Caan at Arthur Krim's Chasen's party post-"Rollerball" screening at the Directors Guild was Darryl Ponicsan, who scripted the Caan starrer, "Cinderella Liberty" — and who has just completed the book and screenplay of "Tom Mix Died For Your Sins" for producer Jerry Zeitman, also there. Caan, a bona fide rodeo star, looms as the latest contender to play Mix. (Burt Reynolds and Steve McQueen had previously been mentioned). Caan, by the way, is still suffering from an injury to his right hand, crushed while steer-roping prior to "Killer Elite's" start. Jimmy admitted he had been asked to help coach President Ford's son Steve in the not-so-gentle rodeo arts — when Caan was at the White House with "Funny Lady." But — his injury and the just-wound "Elite" sked preempted working with young Ford . . . Producer Zeitman and scripter Ponicsan are also in confabs with "Rollerball" boss Norman Jewison to direct the Tom Mix biopic . . . Among the 400 guests at the UA president's party was Jim Stacy, who house-guested with the Jewisons in England while being fitted for appliances. Stacy, who scores in "Posse," is completing his autobiodoc for a tv spec. . . . Other "Rollerball" cast members taking a bow at the bash included John Houseman, Maud Adams, and Pamela Hensley (with Jim Aubrey) . . . Showbiz and politics make sweet music: WB Records president Joe Smith and wife Donnie welcomed Demo Presidential candidate Jimmy Carter, ex-Governor of Georgia, with a lavish party in their Beverly Hills home (formerly owned by the Delbert Manns and previously, Eddie Cantor). Carter had gotten word earlier in the day from the Smiths' neighbors, Lucy Ball and Gary Morton, that they were joining his campaign. The very affable, yet outspoken-for-morality-in-government Carter is no stranger to showbiz — both in music and films. He'll be back here for a Lew Wasserman-hosted party pre-Demo telethon, July 26-27 ABC. Carter told the showbiz guests, "Wallace must be stopped."

* * *

Conn.'s Gov. Ella Grasso is an active cochairman with Greg Morris for the Children's Charity celeb golf tourney the thesp heads July 27 in Hartford, Conn., bringing a planeload of names east for the event . . . Art Fisher will not return to direct the Cher shows this fall. He's busy readying the "Night Dreams" for late night NBC viewing launching Aug. 1 and 8. He promises a "totally different visual approach for tv." George Schlatter set Emmy-winning director Bill Davis for Cher. That's some switch for Davis — from Julie Andrews to Cher . . . Fisher also makes his film directing bow with "Happy Days" and "Petrocelli" assignments.

DAILY VARIETY DAILY

(Trade Mark Registered)
Copyright ©1975 by Daily Variety, Ltd.
Founded 1933 by Sime Silverman
Syd Silverman, President

Published Daily Except Saturdays, Sundays and Holidays with a Special Edition the last week in October by Daily Variety Ltd., 1400 N. Cahuenga Boulevard, Hollywood, California — 90028. Telephone (213) 469-1141, Telex #674-281.

Vol. 168 June 25, 1975 No. 14

Second class postage paid at Los Angeles, California
Thomas M. Pryor, Editor

Principal Offices
New York, Variety, 154 West 46th Street, N.Y., 10036 (212) Judson 2-2700, Telex #1-26335.
Washington, D.C., 1050 Potomac St., N.W. 20005; (202) 965-4301. Telex 89568
Chicago, 400 North Michigan Ave., (312) Delaware 7-4984, Telex #2-53268.
London, 49 St. James's Street, Piccadilly, SW1A1JX. Tel. 493-4561, Telex #24547.
Rome, Via Marche 23, Tel. 463-290.
Paris, 80 Ave. Charles de Gaulle, Tel. 722-07-12.

West End B.O. Up Moderately; 'Locust' 24G

London, June 24 — West End business recovered some lost ground in this frame, but aggregate trade remained on the lethargic side despite a nice influx of new contenders. Pacesetting premiere stanza was the cheering $24,318 pulled by Par's **"Day Of The Locust"** for the Empire theatre.

UA's **"Brannigan"** initialed with nice $22,191 for the big Odeon Leicester Sq., while **"Yakuza"** (WB) copped a good $12,819 for Warner West End-2.

Among others bowing, **"Klansman"** (via Hemdale) nailed a sock $19,505 grinding a recut and shorter version, and EMI's **"Barry McKenzie Holds His Own"** sequel comedy picked up hep $10,659 at three small-seaters.

"Godfather II," no patch in b.o. terms here on its forerunner, registered only fair fifth lap $29,795 at four sites. **"Passenger"** rang up sock $16,896 in second turn at two houses, and **"Shampoo"** sustained with a terrific $21,369 eighth at Odeon Haymarket.

"Uptown Saturday Night" did oke $10,246 in second at two, with **"Alice Doesn't Live Here Anymore"** rated busy $11,682 in ditto session at Curzon. Combo of **"Projectionist"** plus **"Cars That Ate Paris"** was mild $3206 in second at Rialto.

New in town are Metro's "Man Who Loved Cat Dancing" (via CIC) at the Plaza-2, with "Julia" (Sylvia Kristel) at the Columbia theatre via indie Focus distrib.

14 TV Acad Prexies Meet In San Diego

The fairness doctrine, confidentiality of news sources, and station license challenges are among broadcast issues slated for discussion at the second annual national presidents meeting of the National Academy of Television Arts & Sciences beginning tomorrow in San Diego.

Prexies of local chapters from 14 cities across the country will join the Acad's national officers and board of trustees for the three-day conference at the Westgate Hotel. Positions on critical broadcast issues will be decided by the group.

Weitman Chairs Aug. Israel Bonds Dinner

Robert M. Weitman has been named chairman of the Beth Jacob Congregation's second annual Israel Dinner of State on behalf of Israel Bonds.

The affair, which also will honor Rabbi Solomon I. Mizrahi, will be held Aug. 24 at the Beverly Hilton Hotel. Rabbi Mizrahi, former spiritual leader of the Sephardic Hebrew Center, will receive the "Freedom Award" for his devotion to the country, the faith, the language and the people of Israel.

Charlton Heston Resigns SAG Bd. Seat

(Continued from Page 1, Column 1)

were also appointed — Monte Markham, Barbara Barron and Bella Bruck, to sit in for board members Jay Silverheels, Jack Kruschen and Robert Vaughn, who, according to a guild spokesman, have "indicated that their work schedules make them temporarily unavailable for full participation in Guild activities."

'Jaws' Grabbing Bay Area B.O. With Whopping 75G First 5 Days; 'Race' 18G

San Francisco, June 24 — A mighty newcomer is attracting all the attention this week.

"Jaws" is grabbing stupendous $75,000 in first five days at Coliseum, Serra and Spruce Drive-in.

"Death Race 2000" doing speedy $18,000 in preem at Empire 3, Golden Gate and Geneva Drive-in.

"Lepke" faring okay $10,000 in debut at Golden Gate 2, Royal and El Rancho 2 Drive-in.

"Adam And Eve" and **"Kama Sutra"** teeing off to frail $2200 at Crest.

"Monty Python And The Holy Grail" going wacky $20,000 at Stage Door for second romp.

"The 7th Voyage Of Sinbad" slowing to fair $16,000 in second try at Empire, Mission, Warfield and Spruce 2 ozoner.

"Benji" acting cute $16,000 at Stonestown 2 and El Rancho Drive-in for second lap.

"Rosebud" wilting to drab $3000 in second at Regency 2.

"The Middle Of The World" clocking fast $6000 at Clay for second race.

"The Day Of The Locust" bagging fine $13,000 in fifth sweep at Ghirardelli.

"French Connection II" showing bright $14,000 at Alexandria for fifth act.

"Mandingo" looks frisky $8500 in fifth about at Baronet and Mission Drive-in.

"The Eiger Sanction" holding firm $4000 in fifth at Cinema 21.

"Cornbread, Earl And Me" swinging light $3000 in fifth quarter at El Rey.

"The Lion In Winter" feels slack $4500 in fifth reissue week at Alhambra 2 and Stonestown.

"The Passenger" going for swell $7000 in eighth ride at Regency.

"Tommy" eyes rich $10,000 for ninth Northpoint round.

"Chinatown" in 11th subrun week at Balboa seems pallid $2400.

"Shampoo" reaching for zippy $6500 after 14 weeks at Metro.

"Funny Lady" stays sweet $9000 in 15th stanza at Coronet.

"Emmanuelle" remains shapely $5000 in 20th viewing at Cannery.

"Alice Doesn't Live Here Anymore" orbs steady $3500 in Alhambra 19th.

"Murder On The Orient Express" holds firm $3200 in Larkin 22d.

"The Godfather, Part II" offering rich $5000 at Bridge after 27 weeks.

Phoenix Increases Efforts To Lure Location Lensing

Phoenix has beefed up its drive to woo filmmakers to that city by publishing a brochure extolling Arizona virtues and establishing a motion picture coordinating office as arm of city manager's staff.

Although Arizona's present share of motion picture filming market is already $10,000,000 annually, 70-80% of this business goes to Tucson and southeastern part of the state. Phoenix mayor, Timothy A. Barrow, wants more of it.

The coordinating office is a one-stop source which fields inquiries from industry people and aids them in location searches. That office also insures cooperation from city departments in such matters as street closures, use of fire equipment and police cars, and traffic management.

Brochure, titled "Phoenix — A Single Source For Your Creative Film Needs," is available at that office and describes facilities available, typical locations, architecture and scenery offered.

In addition to numerous tv commercials, several episodes of "Movin' On" and a British industrial, an Italian film production company currently has its h.q. there while making a $5,000,000 feature film in northern part of the state.

'Jaws' Chomping 370G In Five Chicago Sites

Chicago, June 24 — It's all **"Jaws"** in the Windy City this round, with the great white blockbuster teeing off to a wow house-record $110,000 at the United Artists and a monstrous $260,000 at four outlyers.

"The Wilby Conspiracy" is preeming to a crisp $24,000 at the Woods.

"The Return Of The Pink Panther" is grabbing a fine $120,000 in second sesh at eight nabes.

"Monty Python And The Holy Grail" is pulling a boffo $22,000 in third glide at the Carnegie.

"Young Frankenstein" is notching a nice $104,000 in seventh trip at nine spots.

"Bug" bows to $20,000 at the State-Lake.

"A Brief Vacation," in first moveover stanza at the Cinema, is grabbing an okay $7500.

"Dolemite," in first moveover trip at the Loop, pulling a sunny $9500.

"Mandingo," in first moveover canto at the Roosevelt, is drawing a handsome $32,000.

"Cornbread, Earl And Me" has slowed down in fifth try at the Oriental to a still tasty $24,000.

"Day Of The Locust," in last week at the Playboy, is tallying a dull $4000.

NEW SUBSCRIBER! MOVING!

DAILY VARIETY DAILY
1400 N. Cahuenga Boulevard, Hollywood, Ca. 90028
$40 Annually $25 Semi-annually • Foreign $50 Annually

SUBSCRIBE NOW! Attach your check For fast service.
MOVING? ATTACH LABEL Showing current address Print new address below

NAME
STREET
CITY STATE ZIP

Subscription Payable In Advance

Tues., Dec. 16, 1975 — 15

FBI Jane Fonda Lie Fizzles

(Continued from Page 1, Column 5)
that the Nixon Administration put together an organized campaign to discredit her political activities.

"Those of us who opposed the Nixon Administration were being made to appear irresponsible, dangerous and foulmouthed," Fonda told reporters outside the court of Judge Malcolm Lucas. She denied making any threats against Nixon's life.

Inside, attorneys for the American Civil Liberties Union representing the actress, successfully persuaded Lucas to order the government to turn over all FBI data on Fonda to the defense.

In Grapp's original memo to Hoover, the apparent inspiration for the fraud was a two-line item in Archerd's column of June 11, 1970, noting that Fonda would appear at a fund-raiser for the Black Panther Party. Grapp suggested the following be faked:

"Dear Army,
"I saw your article about Jane Fonda in 'Daily Variety' last Thursday and happened to be present for Vadim's 'Joan of Arc's' performance for the Black Panthers Saturday night. I hadn't been confronted with this Panther phenomena before but we were searched upon entering Embassy Auditorium, encouraged in revival-like fashion to contribute to defend jailed Panther leaders and buy guns for 'the coming revolution', and led by Jane and one of the Panther chaps in 'we will kill Richard Nixon, and any other M----- F----- who stand in our way' refrain (which was shocking to say the least!). I think Jane has gotten in over her head as the whole atmosphere had the 1930s Munich beer-hall aura.

"I also think my curiosity about the Panthers has been satisfied.
"Regards,
/s/ "Morris."

"If approved," Grapp wrote Hoover, "appropriate precautions will be taken to preclude the identity of the Bureau as the source of this operation."

FBI director's reply amounted to one-paragraph preceding a summfary of Grapp's proposal. "You are authorized to prepare a letter as set forth in relet and mail to Army Archerd, the Hollywood 'gossip' columnist. Insure that mailing cannot be traced to the Bureau."

Both memos are topped by capital letters apparently indicating the subject matter: "COUNTERINTELLIGENCE PROGRAM. BLACK NATIONALIST-HATE GROUPS. RACIAL INTELLIGENCE. BLACK PANTHER PARTY."

Yesterday, Archerd said the FBI plan was "news to me," adding, "the information doesn't show if the so-called letter was ever sent. If it were, I don't recall getting it. And I wouldn't use any information without checking it."

'W.O.G.' Spec Airing Jan. 10

"W.O.G." ("Way Out Games") will be presented as a Saturday afternoon special, Jan. 10 on CBS-TV.

Soupy Sales will host the special, which is a pilot for a possible series.

DESIRE
PRINCIPAL NUDE DANCER
Minimum height 5'10" for
FOLIES BERGERE
TROPICANA, Las Vegas, Nev.
CONTACT MITCH DeWOOD
TROPICANA PRODS. (702) 739-2222
P.O. Box 14460, Las Vegas, Nev. 89114

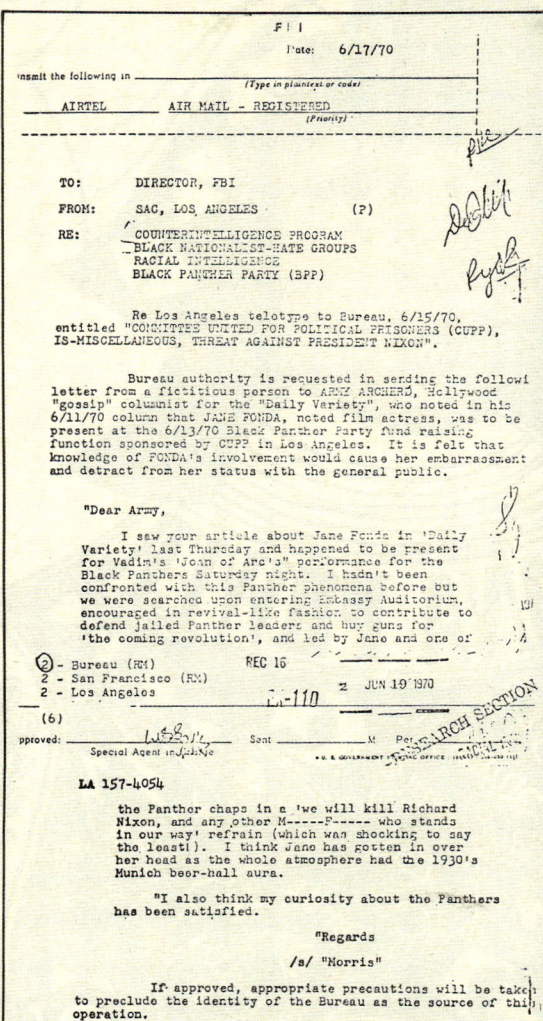

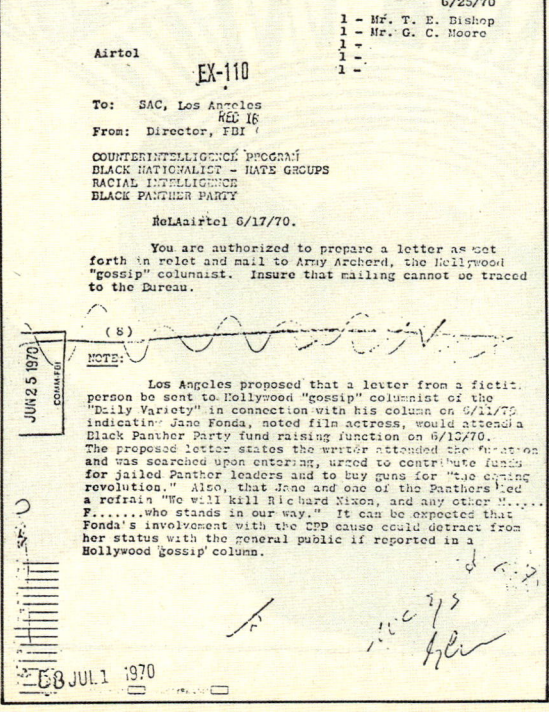

Peak $40 Mil Budgeted This Season By QM Prods. For Tv Series, Telepix, Features

(Continued from Page 1, Column 2)
sic tales. Martin would be exec producer, also may be the narrator. As to whether he would host it, the exec commented "NBC is doing research to see if a host is still viable in tv."

'Firecreek'
Calvin Clements is writing "Firecreek," described as a "western Waltons" and produced by Saltzman. It's a "family hour" potential. The d.a. show would be located in Santa Barbara. William Yates is producer-writer of series which also could be for family time. "The Cop And The Professor" deals with a street-tough cop who becomes involved with a professor emeritus. It concerns the world of academia and police. Mayo Simon scripted, and Saltzman is producer. Show has a contemporary Holmes-Watson relationship.

"Most Wanted" is being readied by Larry Heath, deals with a team of four specialists with different backgrounds who find the most wanted criminal each week. One is an electronics expert, another a homicide lieutenant, another a female psychiatrist, the other an undercover operator.

"Easy Street" producer-writer is John Wilder. It's about a three-generation family of con artists who now are out to help people recover losses when they have been bilked by con men.

Peter Nelson scripted "Bodyguard," a variation of the private-eye format. No producer has been assigned yet.

Other Action
Other QM action includes the currently shooting tv film, "Crime Of The Century," for CBS, with Saltzman as producer, Bob Lenski the writer, Marvin Chomsky director.

Upcoming is "Laurette," which Irving Pincus is producing for QM and CBS-TV. Phil Epstein is writing the Laurette Taylor bio, and Martin is talking to George Cukor, a friend of Taylor's, about directing it, and to Anne Bancroft for the starring role.

ABC-TV has asked Martin to develop new two-hour films for tv, and he is currently seeking classic yarns for this particular group of films.

Martin's newest series, "Superstar," stars Paul Sorvino, debuts on ABC-TV in midseason. It will be shot in San Francisco.

PRESS SECRETARY RON NESSEN'S MEDIA PROBLEMS SURFACE AGAIN

Washington, Dec. 15 — White House press secretary Ron Nessen's problems with the media have flared up again, the upshot of harsh criticism from regulars over the recent trip to Peking.

A lengthy story in the Washington Post detailed many of the problems of the press during the trip, and highlighted a longstanding feud between the former NBC correspondent and secretary of state Henry Kissinger. The Post claimed Nessen's Peking conduct "was distinguished chiefly by long absences from the press room and by the presentation of inadequate information when he appeared."

By way of example it noted that Nessen had assured one scribe that President Ford would not be visiting with Chinese party chairman Mao Tse-tung on the same day the two met. Nessen, who was not invited along on the visit, said later that he was not informed it was taking place.

Adding to the problem, it appears, is the imminent departure of two highly regarded Nessen assistants, William I. Greener to the Defense Dept., and Carl Rosenberger to private industry. The Post speculated that two other assistants, John Hushen and Arnold Noel, would also be ankling soon.

Meanwhile, wagers are again being made by press corps regulars that Nessen would be shown the door before Ford gears up for his campaign.

But if that's the case, it doesn't come from official sources. Ford today, Monday, reaffirmed his "full confidence" in his press chief "because he feels he is fully professionally qualified to do the job," said Greener in an announcement during the daily briefing. Nessen is on vacation until year-end. As for the departure of Hushen and Rosenberger, Greener said they "had no definite plans."

Columbia College Salute To Director Mark Rydell

Columbia College will honor Mark Rydell on Jan. 23 with a seminar in which the entire enrollment of the college will participate.

Symposium will cover all of his pictures and television product over the past 10 years.

Woody Kling Named Co-Exec Producer Of Tandem's 'Family'

Woody Kling has been named coexec producer of Tandem Prods.' "All In The Family" series on CBS-TV, sharing that stint with Norman Lear.

Kling formerly was producer of Lear's "Hot l Baltimore" series on ABC-TV.

RENTA YENTA Will Shop And
Schlepp For Christmas
881-0844

ENTERTAINMENT LEGAL SECRETARY
Motion Picture Company. Excellent typing and shorthand skills.
Call 278-8118, Ext. 256
An Equal Opportunity Employer

A GOOD PHOTO IS YOUR BEST AGENT
8 x 10 Black & White Glossies
LOW AS 12¢
Duplicate Photo Lab
1522 No. Highland
Phone 456-7544

50 BEST-SELLING POP SINGLES

The Variety singles chart is a current reflection of records active on the national retail level. The tabulation is derived from a broad sampling of sales data obtained from the top 25 markets. It is based wholly on retail sales. Album titles appear in lower case beneath the single record title due to a percentage of the public buying the album to get the single. Relative Sales Index measures the difference in sales power between any two disks. (It thus shows the relative lead of the No. 1 disk over the rest of the field.)

● Indicates an increase in sales for two consecutive weeks.

RELATIVE SALES INDEX	WKS. ON CHART	TWO WKS. AGO	ONE WK. AGO	THIS WEEK	ARTIST	NUMBER
96.49	8	2	1	● 1. AFTERNOON DELIGHT / starland vocal band	Starland Vocal Band	Windsong 10588
81.51	12	3	2	2. KISS & SAY GOODBYE / manhattans	Manhattans	Columbia 10310
79.52	15	1	3	3. SILLY LOVE SONGS / at the speed of sound	Paul McCartney & Wings	Capitol 4256
77.77	12	5	4	4. LOVE IS ALIVE / dream weaver	Gary Wright	WB 8143
77.39	17	4	5	5. MORE MORE MORE / more more more	Andrea True Connection	Buddah 515
73.86	8	9	8	● 6. MOONLIGHT FEELS RIGHT / moonlight feels right	Starbuck	Pvt. Stock 039
72.25	3	46	18	7. LET 'EM IN / at the speed of sound	Paul McCartney & Wings	Capitol 4293
71.13	6	14	11	● 8. YOU'LL NEVER FIND ANOTHER LOVE LIKE MINE / all things in time	Lou Rawls	Phila. Int'l 3592
70.97	6	19	14	● 9. GOT TO GET YOU INTO MY LIFE / HELTER SKELTER / rock n' roll music	Beatles	Capitol 4274
70.78	4	22	9	10. TEDDY BEAR / teddy bear	Red Sovine	Starday/Gusto 142
70.36	12	8	6	11. SHOP AROUND / song of joy	Captain & Tennille	A&M 1817
70.04	10	18	15	●12. GET CLOSER / get closer	Seals & Crofts	WB 8190
68.62	17	11	12	13. SARA SMILE / darly hall & john oates	Hall & Oates	RCA 10530
68.47	2	-	33	●14. DON'T GO BREAKING MY HEART / no album	Elton John & Kiki Dee	Rocket 40585
67.03	18	6	7	15. GET UP & BOOGIE / silver convention	Silver Convention	Midland Int'l 10571
65.82	16	7	10	16. MISTY BLUE / misty blue	Dorothy Moore	Malaco 1029
65.49	12	13	13	17. I'LL BE GOOD TO YOU / look out for no. 1	Brothers Johnson	A&M 1806
64.95	12	24	21	●18. I'M EASY / i'm easy (asylum)	Keith Carradine	ABC 12117
63.88	7	20	17	19. THIS MASQUERADE / breezin'	George Benson	WB 8209
63.45	23	10	16	20. BOOGIE FEVER / showcase	Sylvers	Capitol 4179
62.89	2	-	40	●21. YOU SHOULD BE DANCING / no album	Bee Gees	RSO 853
62.67	9	34	26	●22. LET HER IN / john travolta	John Travolta	Midland Int'l 10623
61.89	6	37	22	23. ROCK & ROLL MUSIC / fifteen big ones	Beach Boys	Brother/Reprise 1354
61.70	10	17	20	24. TEAR THE ROOF OFF THE SUCKER / mothership connection	Parliament	Casablanca 856
61.16	9	21	23	25. TAKE THE MONEY & RUN / fly like an eagle	Steve Miller	Capitol 4260
61.06	7	23	27	26. THE BOYS ARE BACK IN TOWN / jailbreak	Thin Lizzy	Mercury 73786
60.56	7	29	28	●27. YOU'RE MY BEST FRIEND / a night at the opera	Queen	Elektra 318
60.07	6	41	35	●28. HEAVEN MUST BE MISSING AN ANGEL / sky high	Tavares	Capitol 4270
59.14	11	16	24	29. NEVER GONNA FALL IN LOVE AGAIN / eric carmen	Eric Carmen	Arista 0184
58.72	16	12	19	30. LOVE HANGOVER / diana ross	Diana Ross	Motown 1392
58.62	11	32	30	●31. TURN THE BEAT AROUND / never gonna let you go	Vicki Sue Robinson	RCA 10562
57.01	10	26	31	32. YOUNG HEARTS RUN FREE / young hearts run free	Candi Staton	WB 8181
56.37	10	27	34	33. SOPHISTICATED LADY / natalie	Natalie Cole	Capitol 4259
55.78	4	45	38	●34. BABY I LOVE YOUR WAY / frampton comes alive	Peter Frampton	A&M 1832
54.31	16	15	25	35. SHANNON / release	Henry Gross	Lifesong 002
54.09	9	28	29	36. TODAY'S THE DAY / hideaway	America	WB 8212
53.56	3	48	44	●37. A FIFTH OF BEETHOVEN / no album	Walter Murphy & Big Apple Band	Pvt. Stock 073
53.55	11	25	32	38. TAKIN' IT TO THE STREETS / takin' it to the streets	Doobie Brothers	WB 8196
53.27	7	31	37	39. SOMETHING HE CAN FEEL / "sparkle" soundtrack	Aretha Franklin	Atlantic 3326
52.98	4	43	42	●40. IF YOU KNOW WHAT I MEAN / beautiful noise	Neil Diamond	Columbia 10366
51.84	8	30	36	41. MAKING OUR DREAMS COME TRUE / no album	Cyndi Grecco	Pvt. Stock 086
50.00	1	-	-	●42. SHAKE YOUR BODY / part 3 (album to be released)	K.C. & Sunshine Band	TK 1019
48.19	2	-	50	●43. LOWDOWN / silk degrees	Boz Scaggs	Columbia 10367
48.08	1	-	-	●44. GETAWAY / no album	Earth, Wind & Fire	Columbia 10373
45.80	1	-	-	●45. PLAY THAT FUNKY MUSIC / wild cherry	Wild Cherry	Sweet City/Epic 50225
45.61	2	-	47	●46. ANOTHER RAINY DAY IN NEW YORK CITY / chicago x	Chicago	Columbia 10360
43.82	1	-	-	●47. SAY YOU LOVE ME / fleetwood mac	Fleetwood Mac	Reprise 1356
42.51	1	-	-	●48. I'D REALLY LOVE TO SEE YOU TONIGHT / no album	England Dan & John Ford Coley	Big Tree 16069
41.16	1	-	-	●49. TRY ME I KNOW WE CAN MAKE IT / a love trilogy	Donna Summer	Oasis 406
36.37	1	-	-	●50. A LITTLE BIT MORE / a little bit more	Dr. Hook	Capitol 4280

Left: July 21, 1976.

Above: Gloria Gaynor survives.

Above Right: People from The Village People.

Play." Reporter Addison Verrell said that newspapers had recently considered it fashionable to write stories, reviews, and columns about the X-rated industry, but that "the chic is thoroughly tarnished now." That craze would breathe its last gasp in the 1980s, when videocassettes signaled the end of adult-movie theaters.

No discussion of the 1970s would be complete without another craze that made a lot of people happy and then quickly faded: disco!

Herm Schoenfeld in the *Weekly Variety* of September 10, 1975, trumpeted,

> "The disco beat is getting stronger in the music biz. Well over 100 discos are now operating in the New York metropolitan area and they still are proving to be solid launching pads for disk talent. . . . The basic beat of the disco described as chugga-chugga-chum, runs through all of the disks. It's typical of the biggest disco hit of them all, Van McCoy's 'The Hustle'. . . ."

Schoenfeld observed that New York discos have a wide variety of formats: "Some are private clubs and others have open admission, albeit for fancy prices of up to $10 per head. There are discos for the singles, couples. Latins, blacks and gays. . ."

And that equal-opportunity approach may explain the eventual disco backlash. Disco provided a musical forum for black women such as Donna Summer and Gloria Gaynor (whose 1978 "I Will Survive" turned into a gay anthem). There were the Village People with their gay-in-joke costumes and songs like "Y.M.C.A." and "Macho Man" (both 1978); and there was Sylvester of 1978's "Dance (Disco Heat)" and "You Make Me Feel (Mighty Real)," who was a gay drag performer. KC and The Sunshine Band were racially integrated.

The Bee Gees were in some ways anomalies: straight, male, and Caucasian. Yet the Brothers Gibb became closely identified with disco due to their multiple hits on the soundtrack to 1977's *Saturday Night Fever*, which captured the zeitgeist of disco. Disco quickly fell out of fashion and was reviled. But then it changed its identity to "dance music" and nobody seemed to mind.

Otherwise, the decade was musically bookended by a very specific ending and a new beginning. In 1970, Paul McCartney confirmed the breakup of The Beatles. Though many blamed (and still blame) John Lennon's wife Yoko Ono for the split, the official cause was given as artistic and financial reasons.

The year 1977 marked the end of an era with the death of Elvis Presley—though, like The Beatles, his songs continued to entertain people (and rake in bazillions of dollars) for generations to come. And 1979 saw the unofficial birth of hip-hop, or rap music, as Sugarhill Gang's hit "Rapper's Delight" set the stage for decades of songs that incorporated a strong beat with samplings of other songs and lyrics about politics, pride, and sex.

The singer-songwriter trend of the 1960s continued well into the 1970s with now-former Beatles John Lennon, Paul McCartney, and George Harrison, as well as Carole King, James Taylor, David Bowie, Neil Diamond, Elton John, Randy Newman, Lou Reed, Van Morrison, Barry Manilow, Joni Mitchell, Al Green, Marvin Gaye, Stevie Wonder, and the musically radical reggae sounds of Bob Marley.

While television was chronicling the world changes, the medium itself was undergoing its own transformations by the end of the decade.

Aside from Norman Lear revolutionizing primetime TV, daytime TV got its own groundbreaker, thanks to the Public Broadcasting System: *Sesame Street*.

On December 24, 1969, Les Brown in *Weekly Variety* made an accurate prediction:

"It may be just the show to put public television on the rating map," and he gushed, "The show moves, seduces, diverts, dazzles, amuses and infects, and in the captivating course of things it teaches the very young basic human values, the meaning of numbers, the alphabet and solutions to simple problems."

The publicly-funded group of stations known as PBS also offered mini-series that set a high standard for quality TV: *Masterpiece Theatre*, with such offerings as *Upstairs Downstairs*; the 1973 documentary series *An American Family*, which took cameras inside the home of the Loud family and eventually led to the twenty-first century's glut of so-called reality TV; and British comedies including the wildly popular and influential *Monty Python's Flying Circus* and *Fawlty Towers*.

Another groundbreaker in daytime was *The Phil Donahue Show*, which went from a local show and into

Above: The cast of *Sesame Street*.

Right: December 24, 1969.

'SESAME STREET': WUNDERKIND

CBS Echoes NBC Plan on AT&T Hike; Affils Seek 'Compromise'

CBS-TV last Friday (19) revealed to its affiliate board its new proposal for sharing the increase in AT&T line charges which has been in effect since Oct. 2. CBS' plan was in most respects similar to that which has been adopted by NBC. It involves a proposed 6.5% reduction in station compensation which would allow CBS to recoup the majority of the additional AT&T expense, which totals about $6,800,000 for that network. In return, CBS proposed to expand all station breaks that follow one-hour programs from 42 to 62 seconds. Programs ending at 11 p.m. would not be included in this proposal, since station time follows at that hour.

In addition, CBS proposed adding two new 32-second station breaks in its Thursday and Friday feature showcases.

The affiliates advisory board in turn responded with a suggested compromise idea. Board noted that CBS had originally proposed a different method of sharing AT&T costs under which the affils would have paid the $3,000,000 increased tab for local loops, and the network would itself have absorbed the $3,800,000 increase in intercity charges. This initial CBS proposal had been rejected by the affils board. Responding to the latest CBS offer, the board suggested a compromise under which CBS itself would still have to pay the $3,800,000 it would have absorbed under terms of its original proposal. The board proposed an alternative to the 6.5% reduction in compensation advanced by CBS. Under this alternative, CBS would have to reduce station comp only by the percentage that would recoup the $3,000,000 in local loop charges.

However, the affiliates board also proposed that CBS still give its stations the expanded station breaks "in order to allow us to be competitive with NBC affiliates," as one source put it. The next move is up to CBS, though no formal date has been set for its response.

Affiliate sources stress that the affils advisory board is not empowered to negotiate on behalf of the affiliates, but can only act in an advisory capacity.

Effective Jan. 5, NBC-TV adds three minutes of blurbs to the "Tonight Show" and shortens 10 primetime programs by 20 seconds as part of its quid-pro-quo

(Continued on page 34)

Indians B'casting From Alcatraz

Pacifica Foundation's KPFA-FM (Berkeley, Calif.), which is bankrolled by listeners and operating on a very tight budget, has installed $2,000 worth of equipment on Alcatraz Island where 200 American Indians are living and staking a claim to the abandoned U.S. Government penal isle.

Since the Indians made their claim under a Federal act of 1868 stipulating Sioux braves can claim unused Federal territory, all Alcatraz phone and electric service has been cut off. The station's remote operation is powered by a gasoline generator, and the Indians will broadcast a live Indian Affairs report every Tuesday, Wednesday and Thursday night. The 15-minute shows covering Indian culture and history as well as running comment on the island claim, will be carried by all three Pacifica stations, KPFA, KPFA-FM Los Angeles, and WBAI-FM New York.

First show was last night (Tues.) during the Indians' first national powwow from the island. Pacifica estimates there are about 100,000 Indians within the listening areas of the three stations.

NAB Cig Correction

Washington, Dec. 23.

The Jan. 1, 1971 date given for the effective date of the National Assn. of Broadcasters rejection of cigaret advertising for radio-tv is incorrect. Correct date is Sept. 1, 1971.

Inaccuracy resulted from a typo in an NAB press release.

Eight Ky. Burley Growers Sue Nets On Anti-Cig Spots

Louisville, Dec. 23.

Airings of anti-cigarets spots on the three tv networks, CBS, NBC and ABC, have roused the ire of Kentucky burley tobacco growers. Eight growers in this state filed suit last week in U.S. District Court asking for an injunction against the nets.

Plaintiffs said the suit was brought "in behalf of all tobacco growers who are citizens and residents of the Commonwealth of Kentucky." Following up, another suit will probably be filed in a state court this week asking for damages for the anti-cig spots already aired by the networks.

Suit charges that the nets have aired "at large and within the Commonwealth of Kentucky on numerous occasions in words or substance that 'cigarets will kill persons who smoke them'," that "each of said statements (aired) by each of the corporate defendants was false, or made with reckless disregard of whether said statement was false or not because there is no scientific evidence of any causal connection between cigaret smoking and lung cancer, heart disease, tuberculosis

(Continued on page 34)

ST. JOAN'S CLICK FOR PTV & UHF

By LES BROWN

Not until the closing weeks of 1969 did television offer a program series that really answered the long-standing criticism of the medium—namely that it takes of a viewer's time without giving anything in return—and held out hope for a more substantive future. Significantly, the program has come from outside the commercial tv realm, and its brief rating history already suggests that it may be just the show to put public television on he rating map, and UHF in the bargain.

The show, of course, is "Sesame Street"—a daytime strip for underprivileged pre-schoolers which seems to owe a certain debt to "Laugh-In" and to the sell techniques of Madison Avenue's commercials. One of the few shows in memory that has lived up to its advance ballyhoo, it is the apotheosis of education through show business, and anyone who thinks it is only for the smallfry ought to give it an hour. The show moves, seduces, diverts, dazzles, amuses and infects, and in the captivating course of things it teaches the very young basic human values, the meaning of numbers, the alphabet and solutions to simple problems.

It is a sweet show, and a forceful one, and if racial peace and harmony should visit this country 15 or 20 years from now when the tots grow up, "Sesame Street," as the most naturally integrated show in television, may be one of the reasons why.

It could be wishful thinking, but "Sesame" may well be the opening volley in an entirely new kind of television that exploits the medium's faults and turns them into virtues. Repetition, slapstick, running gags, fast cuts, short takes, monsters, catchy ditties and even commercial interruptions (letters of the alphabet are the "sponsors") are the stuff of the program. And if in five or six weeks a certain suburban two-year-old learned

(Continued on page 33)

FCC's Fairness Doctrine Cited in Bid By S.F. Crusader to Match Recruiting Pitches With Anti-Military Message

By MORRY ROTH

Chicago, Dec. 23.

If Chicago's eccentric politico Lar Daly can be considered the keystone of the broadening of Section 315 and John F. Banzhaf 3d is credited with putting a new light on the FCC's doctrine, then San Francisco's Don Jelinek may someday be remembered as bringing fairness into the broad area of social dissent, more specifically dissent with government policy.

Jelinek has written the 31 radio and television stations in the San Francisco area asking "fair time" for spots in response to Army, Navy, Air Force and Marine recruiting pubservice announcements. In a move first given national attention in the New Republic two weeks ago, Jelinek has prepared a series of spots rebutting the recruiting announcements and suggesting "alternatives" to both the draft and enlistment.

In a telephone interview, Jelinek said he was not too sure that the recruiting spots are much of a "public service" to young viewers and listeners. "Ninety percent of the public service announcements are innocuous," Jelinek said, "and 99% of the public would go along with them. But when you treat military service in an unpopular war as a fait accompli, you are taking an editorial position and the least a station can do is afford time for information on alternative action."

No, Politely

So far, the Bay area stations have not shown any great enthusiasm for the principle. As of today, eight stations said no in various polite ways, one station said that it was turning the matter over to its lawyers and 23 have not answered in the three weeks since Jelinek wrote to them.

Jelinek is not too surprised at the response. On Jan. 20 he will file a formal complaint with the FCC, an action in which he is somewhat pessimistic. He will give the Commission 60 days to respond, and if they don't or respond unfavorably, he will begin his court attack in the Circuit Court, he says.

"We're going to win," Jelinek said. "Hopefully in the Circuit Court, but if not there then in the Appellate or Supreme Court. The

(Continued on page 35)

Movies Stand Tall

Network tv's hottest sell, movies, continue this season to average very substantial overall rating shares as well attract the Nielsen demographics Madison Ave. loves.

Rating boxoffice score for films so far this season shows NBC's three nights a week of pix averaging a 20.1 rating and 35 share, CBS an 18.3 rating and 32 share for two nights and ABC a 19 rating and 32 share for its two nights a week.

B'cast Newsmen's 'Notes' Sought In Chi Rain of Writs

Chicago, Dec. 23.

The blizzard of subpoenas that have descended on Chi radio and tv stations and newspapers in the wake of court cases since the Dem convention, continued unabated last week—but with one significant twist. For the first time, an attorney for one of the Black Panther defendants has received court permission to subpoena print and broadcast reporters' handwritten notes. It's an area long considered too fraught with pitfalls to warrant the legal demand.

The subpoena to all the media asks for "all photographs, film, videotape and sound recordings, whether or not broadcast, and all documents, notes, drafts, manuscripts, memoranda and other written matter, whether or not published. . . ."

The Chicago Sun-Times and

(Continued on page 32)

CBS May Move Merv to Coast

There is a strong probability that CBS-TV's latenite "Merv Griffin Show" may soon be shifted from New York to Hollywood origination. Griffin is on his second trip to the Coast, and if his H'wood ratings show any discernible improvement, his show is likely to be moved there permanently.

Since debuting on CBS last August, Griffin has failed to make any inroads into the "Tonight Show's" dominance of post-primetime ratings. Despite the fact that such low-budget shows can be profitable even if way behind the leader, there has been a certain restiveness at CBS over Griffin's below-expectations performance to date. This has recently led to speculation anent changes afoot; principal change, it's now learned, is the projected move to the Coast.

Switching to Hollywood also solves the guest problem that would have arisen with three latenight shows originating from Gotham (Dick Cavett debuts next Monday). It had been envisioned that the same old faces would be turning up ever more frequently on Manhattan's desks and sofas, but the switching of Griffin to Hollywood would diminish the prospect of a guest scarcity.

DECLARE A YEAR-END DIVIDEND ON YOUR STANDING IN THE TRADE . . .

You can imply you as a person or you as a company, an organization, a group. Whichever it is, nothing is more primary than your standing in, your impact upon the trade. Everything you are or hope to be starts with the trade. Hence the force of your advertisement in

The 64th Anniversary Edition of

VARIETY

Here is the Image of your Issue, the Prospectus of your Anticipation, the Biography of Your Performance. You need only authorize publication. Don't Delay. Act Forthwith.

NEW YORK 10036
154 W. 46th St.

HOLLYWOOD 90028
6404 Sunset Blvd.

CHICAGO 60611
400 N. Michigan Ave.

LONDON, S.W.1
49 St. James's Street
Piccadilly

PARIS
80 Ave. de Neuilly
Via Marche 84

ROME
Neuilly-Sur-Seine

FILMS | VIDEO | TV FILMS | RADIO | MUSIC | STAGE

VARIETY

PRICE **85¢**

NEWSPAPER
Second Class P.O. Entry

Published Weekly at 154 West 46th Street, New York, N.Y. 10036, by Variety, Inc. Annual subscription, $35. Single copies, 85 cents. Second Class Postage Paid at New York, N.Y. and at Additional Mailing Offices
© COPYRIGHT, 1979, BY VARIETY, INC., ALL RIGHTS RESERVED

Vol. 294 No. 4 — New York, Wednesday, February 28, 1979 — 34205 — 128 PAGES

PAYCABLE SHOWS HIT BY LABOR PAINS

DIRECTORS GUILD ORDERS NO WORK WITHOUT PACT

By LARRY MICHIE

Paycable is trying to give birth to a new and distinctive body of original programming, but it's suffering labor pains. The Directors Guild of America still doesn't have an agreement with the paycablers, and it is cracking down on at least some DGA members who have done shows for Home Box Office and Showtime, the two major paycable suppliers who do original entertainment programs.

One of the directors being disciplined, Chuck Braverman, who turned out "Willie Nelson At Lake Tahoe" for Showtime, fears that "the DGA's efforts have backfired in that English, Canadian, and non-union directors will be directing all future paycable tv shows."

Braverman said he has been assessed a stiff fine, but he didn't want to discuss specifics because of the possibility of an appeal.

Another director whose wrist may be slapped is Joshua White, who did "Disco Beaver From Outer Space" for HBO. That show is of particular interest because paycable entrepreneurs are gradually easing into regular series in addition to their theatrical features and sports. "Disco Beaver" is one of a pair of series ideas that HBO is trying out this month, the other being potentially more significant as a breakthrough — "The Great Consumer Rip-Off" from Gateway Productions is another series pilot, and it's a documentary. Independent docu-makers have few outlets; perhaps paycable will expand the market.

"Disco Beaver" is from National Lampoon — the theatrical "Animal House" and ABC spinoff series "Delta House" are among its credits — and if HBO goes to series the irreverent production house would have a natural outlet for its brand of
(Continued on page 94)

Italo Radio Play Written By Pole Who Became Pope

By MARGO HAMMOND
Rome, Feb. 27.

Karol Woytyla, a former Polish actor, playwright and now leader of the Catholic world as Pope John Paul II, still has show biz in his blood. On March 1 a drama written by the Pontiff, under the pseudonym of Andrzej Jawien, will be broadcast — with the Pope's blessing — by the Italian Radio Two (second state channel) at 4 p.m. All author's rights have been granted by the Pope to Third World countries.

John Paul II wrote the drama, "The Goldsmith Shop," nearly 20 years ago when he was Bishop of Cracow and published it in 1960 in the magazine Znak. His interest in the theatre, however, dates well before that time. As a boy he took part in school plays and in the years before World War II, he partici-
(Continued on page 90)

Arabs To Film How Oil Money Is Spent

Manama, Bahrain, Feb. 27.

Seven Arab Gulf States have joined forces to invite foreign filmmakers and authors to help explain, to the Western countries, how oil money is spent at home. The seven Information Ministers, meeting here, dropped original plans for an oil information center to counter "Western allegations that Arabs waste their oil wealth."

They said, instead, that filmmakers and writers could better show, in their own way, how the cash flow from the oil wells was properly utilized. They'd be paid, of course.

Participating were Bahrain, Saudi Arabia, Kuwait, United Arab Emirates, Qatar, Sultanate of Oman and Iraq.

Foreign Embassies In Jerusalem Chip In With Talent For Spring Fest

Jerusalem, Feb. 27.

The fifth edition of the Jerusalem Spring Festival is going to be the biggest and the most expensive one yet. The Festival, scheduled for April 12 to May 17, will take place in a half a dozen theatres and in the streets.

Budgeted at '8,000,000 pounds
(Continued on page 126)

Vidtape-Of-Month Club Taps New Biz Via Rental Route

Opening a new route to tap the home videotape market, a vidtape-of-the-month club is due for a major launching in early May. Video Corp. of America will be renting out, rather than selling cassettes of feature films, sports, etc. at from $9 to $14 per week, contrasting to the $40 to $75 prices now prevailing for outright purchases of similar material.

Video Corp. of America, which operates a production studio set in New York, has wrapped up deals with Avco Embassy for its feature film catalog and with Major League Baseball Productions for sports material. Pitch to vidtape machine owners for the rental operation will
(Continued on page 90)

Northern Freeze Heats Fla. Tourism

Fort Lauderdale, Feb. 27.

The cold weather which recently walloped the northeast and midwest has given South Florida's tourist economy a big boost.

Traffic patterns for January showed increases in virtually every section. Miami International Airport reported a 15% increase in arrivals compared to the same period last year. Fort Lauderdale-Hollywood International advanced 12%. Palm Beach International could not offer figures for the month, but estimated total traffic had increased 30% (including departures).

Some individual carriers, geared
(Continued on page 125)

Showfolk On Both Sides On Eve Of Election Day For Scot Independence

Edinburgh, Feb. 27.

The pattern already established in U.S. political campaigns, where presidential candidates often reveal a bandwagon of celebrity supporters, is being followed here in the drive leading up to voting for Scotland's independence.

Devolution vote day — Yes or No for a separate governmental system for Scotland — is March 1. More than 20 noted Scots, many in show business, will urge their fellow Scots to say "No." Among them is the singer Lulu, actor Iain Cuth-
(Continued on page 115)

THE DEAN'S LIST:
Woody Allen, Tim Conway, Peter Falk, Goldie Hawn, Carroll O'Connor, Frank Sinatra (continued on pages 72 and 73)

The Dean averaged a 37% share for his entire nine network seasons. The Best of Dean Martin. 100 very funny half-hours. Ready to strip starting Fall 1979. **MCATV**

Source: NTI, subject to survey limitations. — NATPE Hospitality Suite, Penthouse, 26th Floor.

syndication in January 1970. It was an issue-oriented program, with guests discussing topics—then Donahue would go into the audience to get questions or comments. It wasn't a radical concept, but it was so successful that many others, including Oprah Winfrey, copied it.

In late night, NBC debuted the Lorne Michaels–produced *Saturday Night Live* in 1975, mixing topical humor with goofy comedy and launching numerous careers. It also spawned numerous imitators, with only the syndicated *Second City Television* (SCTV) achieving real writing-performing brilliance.

More radical were formats on the horizon beginning to challenge the dominance of broadcast television: cable TV and home video.

A March 1977 *Weekly Variety* report said the courts were reshaping TV structure. The U.S. Court of Appeals in Washington, D.C., threw out the Federal Communications Commission's 1975 pay-cable rules. That meant pay-cable television was given the green light, paving the way for HBO.

The ad side was changing as well. On February 9, 1971, *Daily Variety* carried a story about six radio stations telling the U.S. District Court in D.C. that the new law forbidding cigarette advertising on radio and TV "reflects a legally schizophrenic policy on the part of Congress." A week later, the February 17 *Weekly Variety* indicated that this was a global concern.

Germany's Federal Ministry of Health set out guidelines for tobacco companies, which spent

> "about $55,000,000 for advertising last year. . . . Models who look as if they are under 25 will no longer be featured on German TV cigaret commercials, there will be no backgrounds of beat hangouts and discotheques in such ads and popular sports figures cannot be portrayed as smokers on the homescreen. . . ."

Content was also in question. In June 2, 1971, *Daily Variety* carried a story that read, "Because of the rash of airplane hijackings, ABC-TV is chilling any dramatic stories involving hijacks on ground 'it would not be in the public interest.'"

But TV's changes in the decade weren't always about restrictions; they were also about expansion. The February 2, 1977, *Weekly Variety* declared in a headline "Roots Remakes TV World in 8 Nights," describing how the show scored record ratings and set a new standard for network quality.

The *Variety* article points out that the show lifted other ABC series that aired just before *Roots* in those eight nights, including *Captain & Tennille*, *Baretta*, the *Barney Miller/The Tony Randall Show* hour, *Donny & Marie*, *Starsky & Hutch*, and *The Six Million Dollar Man*, as well as a repeat of the ninety-minute special "Fonzie Loves Pinky."

Roots was a pinnacle in "appointment television," when viewers would arrange their schedules to catch a TV "event." But the era was to be short-lived: in less than a decade, the home-video boom meant that viewers could watch a show the minute it aired. Or later, if they wanted.

The undisputed primacy of the three broadcast networks, ABC, CBS, and NBC, was coming to an end.

Seeds were planted for a twenty-first-century plethora of entertainment

Previous Spread: February 28, 1979; Neil Diamond rocks a 'fro.

Above: Phil Donahue probes.

Right: February 2, 1977.

Vol. 285 No. 13   New York, Wednesday, February 2, 1977   34205   96 PAGES

BEIRUT CINEMAS: RUBBLE TO RICHES

BUY BACK GEAR FROM UNDERWORLD

By MOUNIR ABBOUD

Beirut, Feb. 1.
There's a film-going boom on in Lebanon these days, so soon after the deadly Christian-Moslem civil war, and it's comforting to some distributors that most of the action is taking place outside of Beirut. Decentralization is under way, with business improving in such spots as Bybles, Reyfoun, and other towns.

The director of the regional office of one major U.S. company said that deals with proprietors outside Beirut will, henceforth, prove more lucrative. "They're paying more for the product, but they're also doing much more business so it is still profitable for exhibitors." (In nearby areas as Amman, Cyprus and the Gulf, business during 1976 more than doubled.)

Beirut is beginning to come out of the havoc that partially or completely demolished many of its theatres. The Saroulla and Piccadilly are the most active, followed by the Strand, Pavillion, Orly, Versailles and Etoile, all of which have acquired generators to overcome the power cuts. The films doing the biggest business are Egyptian, U.S. and some European product.

One theatre owner even believes the audiences have changed — "we've acquired a new clientele, particularly among the young." But another believes this is because audiences have become displaced, forced to frequent situations in, to them, strange parts of town, because their own theatres are still out of operation. One sidebar curiosity is that an astonishing number of banned films or product, which would ordinarily never be considered, have found their way to Beirut's screens.

(Continued on page 86)

Wolper Tied To Haley Comet Via A 'Roots' Sequel

Los Angeles, Feb. 1.
While ABC-TV's Nielsen foliage from "Roots" was still blotting out the ratings sun of its rivals, producer David Wolper said in Hollywood last week that a sequel may be in the works.

He said that there is enough material unused from the Alex Haley book that he may go ahead with another miniseries (he ruled out a continuing series, a la "Rich Man Poor Man"). The tv series ended after the Civil War, but the

(Continued on page 92)

Sinatra-Martin In B.O.-Busting Date At Westchester Th.

The highest grossing take ever for a hardtop theatre is expected during the two weeks starting May 16 when Frank Sinatra and Dean Martin combine for a double header at the Westchester Premiere Theatre, in Greenburgh, N.Y. The 3,500 seat house has been scaled at $30, $23 and $16. The two-week gross could go over $1,000,000.

This is the first time that Sinatra and Martin have joined on a single bill. Sinatra has played several dates at Harrah's and Lake Tahoe with John Denver, although each did shows singly.

Although terms were not revealed, trade believes that this is a three-way partnership arrange-

(Continued on page 86)

Try Infrared For Better Film Sound

London, Feb. 1.
Infrared sound transmission, designed to give additional soundtrack clarity, is to be used for the preems in London and New York of Joseph Strick's version of James Joyce's "A Portrait Of The Artist As A Young Man."

Snag is that earphones must be worn to achieve full effect and this clearly won't suit everyone. It will still be possible, however, to listen to the soundtrack in the conventional way.

Extra cost of the system, which is

(Continued on page 92)

Feds Eye Disks Not For Payola But Anti-Trust

Los Angeles, Feb. 1.
Speculation that a network record subsidiary may be a prime target broke the otherwise tight-lipped industry reaction to the sweeping Federal grand jury investigation shaping up on alleged anti-trust violations in the manufacture, promotion and merchandising of records.

While the east coast was digging itself out of snowstorms, Los Angeles-based record companies and rackjobbers found themselves in-

(Continued on page 93)

BBC Bids $1-Mil For Henry The K. As News Jockey

London, Feb. 1.
Henry Kissinger, former U.S. Secretary of State who has reportedly been talking to the American networks, is meantime also being paged by the British Broadcasting Corp. as pundit on a series on global trouble spots.

BBC is reported to have offered him around $1,000,000 for the stint. Program chieftain Alasdair Milne confirms an approach was made "about two or three months ago," but exec declined further comment. Apparently, the proposition is still cooking, or at least not yet vetoed by Kissinger, who's probably weighing a whole flock of proposals from book publishers, foundations, universities, big business, etc.

Niteries Suffering From B.O. Frostbite

Baby — it's cold inside — at the boxoffice, that is. B.o is in the cold belt, which now includes most of the U.S., has dwindled considerably during the advent of the new ice age which is figured to have started in October for many parts of the country.

The nitery business hasn't yet officially been declared a disaster area, but many operators are conceding that it is so.

It takes either a hardy spirit or a blockbuster attraction to overcome the chief headliner of the tv and radio news shows, the cold wave. On

(Continued on page 86)

platforms. Movies were initially just for theaters, then expanded to TV, then airplanes, then hotel rooms.

However, the real revolution was in "the home videotape market," as Herm Schoenfeld analyzed in the August 24, 1977, *Weekly Variety*.

Also in 1977, Andre Blay asked the studios permission to transfer films to videotape, with the intention to sell. Only 20th Century-Fox agreed. An August 8, 1977, *Daily Variety* headline announced "Fox Pix into Home Tape Market." In 1979, Fox bought out Blay for $7.5 million.

As with everything, the early days of home video involved experimentation. People knew there was a business here but weren't sure how to reach viewers. One idea was similar to a book-of-the-month club, with consumers having the option of buying a new title each month. On February 28, 1979, *Weekly Variety* offered an alternative plan:

> "Video Corp. of America will be renting out, rather than selling cassettes of feature films, sports, etc. at from $9 to $14 per week, contrasting to the $40 to $75 prices now prevailing for outright purchases of similar material."

Meanwhile, another business plan was moving quickly: electronic games that were light-years beyond Pong.

On February 1, 1979, *Daily Variety* reported

> "Warner Communications said its Atari subsid will enter the handheld computer toy and game industry as part of its expansion into the consumer electronics field. Warner said Atari's first computer hand-held game, called 'Touch Me,' will be introduced at New York's February Toy Fair and will be Atari's first non-video consumer electronics product. The company recently announced its entry into the personal home computer field with the Atari-400 and Atari-800."

As the decade ended, the lingering 1960s paranoia had leveled off into everyday wariness, which was arguably an improvement. And two decades after the boom of television, the medium hit its stride, exposing people to new worlds, new thoughts, and new forms of entertainment. But the blossoming of TV was like a good news/bad news joke. The good news was that the average citizen had a heightened awareness of world politics and of social issues. The bad news is, these were often distressing— and there was much more to come in the following decades.

Above: Were you an *SNL* or *SCTV* person?

Right: Yes, this is the third time Carrie Fisher appears in this book.

"CHEERS! IT'S SMASH-HIT DEBBIE"
— London Evening News

"The Debbie Reynolds Show" at The London Palladium

PHOTO BY TERRY O'NEILL

"TRIUMPHANT"
"Triumphant was the European debut of Debbie Reynolds. As the curtain fell, the audience stood to cheer. The London Palladium prays for that kind of happening. Carrie Fisher stopped the show herself with two songs. She is obviously heading high in show business."

James Green — London Evening News

"ANOTHER GARLAND-MINNELLI"
"We were in for a surprise when we saw a delightful talent which Debbie's film roles never allowed her to indicate. Carrie Fisher turns out to be a handsome girl who sings in a strong contralto voice of great dramatic power. This will be another Garland-Minnelli situation."

Judith Simons — London Daily Express

"A CHEERING OVATION"
"Debbie was given a cheering ovation. The undoubted hit of the evening was her young daughter Carrie Fisher, who sang two songs in a strong deep voice which delighted the audience."

London Evening Standard

"A RITZY NIGHT"
"The scene was set for a ritzy night. It was all that and a little bit more. Carrie Fisher sings a couple of powerful songs and proves in the process that her famous mother does not exactly have a monopoly of all the family talent."

Keith Nurse — The Daily Telegraph

"A DREAM"
"Debbie Reynolds' show has been transplanted into the London Palladium like a dream. The opening night crowd stood, clapped, yelled and clamoured rapturously after a show which offered talent, style, laughs and production values on a scale seldom seen hereabouts. It was a big click, too, for Carrie Fisher. The dramatic power and depth of her young pipes mark her as a strong bet in the immediate future. All-pro at 17 years of age, she appears to have all the ingredients for a powerhouse career."

Watt — Variety

"A TRIUMPH FOR DEBBIE"
"Debbie Reynolds came, saw and conquered. At the end of her 90-minute opening show she had the London Palladium eating out of her hand. It was a triumph for Debbie."

Peter Noble — Hollywood Reporter

"Carrie Fisher sang with the skill and verve of a Judy Garland."

Sidney Williams — London Daily Mirror

Debbie Reynolds stars in "Irene," opening at the Shubert Theatre in Los Angeles October 24 with a Benefit Preview for The Hollywood Motion Picture and Television Museum.

Elvis Presley, 42, Discovered Dead In His Memphis Manse, Possibly Of A Heart Attack

By TODD EVERETT

Elvis Presley, often credited as the single performer to introduce the mass white audience to the black boogie and blues rhythms of his native south, died yesterday at age 42, possibly of a heart attack.

Presley's apparently lifeless body was found in his elegant Memphis mansion, Graceland, at 2:30 p.m. by his road manager, Joe Esposito, who went to wake him. Performer's father, Vernon Presley, and other relatives were present in the house and summoned an ambulance, but the singer never regained consciousness. An hour later, his personal physician, Dr. George Nichopoulos, abandoned efforts to revive him at Baptist Memorial Hospital.

Nichopoulos said heart attack was a possible cause of death, but an autopsy was in progress late in the day.

Elvin Presley as he appeared in NBC-TV's 1973 special, "Elvis: Aloha From Hawaii."

Presley was to appear today in Portland, Maine, and his long-time manager, Tom Parker, was there when the singer died. He also had a sold-out concert set for Aug. 27 in Memphis.

Elvis Aron Presley was born in Tupelo, Miss., on Jan. 8, 1935, the son of farmworker Vernon Elvis Presley and the former Gladys Smith. A twin brother, Jesse Garon, died at birth.

His family was strongly religious, and Presley was a regular churchgoer; singing along at Assembly of God camp meetings, revival tents, and church conventions. When he was still a boy, he asked his parents for a bicycle; so poor that they couldn't afford one, they volunteered to buy him a $12.95 guitar, instead. That investment was to change the course of popular music.

When Presley was 13, his family moved to Memphis. He

(Continued on Page 17, Column 1)

Wed., Aug. 17, 1977 — DAILY *VARIETY* DAILY — 17

Elvis Presley, 42, Found Dead In Memphis Mansion

(Continued from Page 1, Column 2)

attended L. C. Humes High School, working as an usher at Loews State Theatre evenings for $15 a week. When he was offered a job with the Crown Electric Company, driving a truck for $35 a week, he took it immediately.

1st Recording

Presley was sufficiently talented as a singer that he was able to work occasional engagements with bands, at church and social functions. His first recording session, however, was a strictly private affair — a song for his mother as a birthday present. For $4, he cut two songs — "My Happiness" and "That's When Your Heartaches Begin," at the Memphis Recording Services studios.

A secretary liked what she heard and saw, and recommended Presley to studio owner Sam Phillips. He listened to the crudely cut disk, and passed. A few months later, on Jan. 4, 1954, Presley cut two more sides at the studio. This time, Phillips was present, and somewhat more impressed.

Two months after that, Phillips tracked down Presley, to try his voice on a song the studio owner had liked. Presley was unable to record an acceptable take of that song or any of several others.

Phillips arranged for Presley to meet a local guitarist, Scotty Moore, who brought in a neighbor, bassist Bill Black. On July 6, 1954, the three returned to the recording studios. The first song taped was a country ballad standard, "I Love You Because."

During a break in the session, Presley began to sing a country blues tune by black singer Arthur (Big Boy) Crudup, "That's All Right."

Phillips knew that what he heard had tremendous potential. For years, Phillips had been telling friends, "If I could find a white man who had the Negro sound and the Negro feel, I could make a billion dollars." Presley met those requirements like nobody who had been heard before.

The second song recorded at that session was an uptempo version of a bluegrass tune, Bill Monroe's "Blue Moon Of Kentucky." That disk would set Presley's style for years; a fast, rhythmic tune backed by a slow, country number. Presley's most recent single, currently on the charts, was a turn on that formula: a fast, gospel-flavored tune, "Way Down," backed by the rhythm and blues classic, "Pledging My Love."

At first, local disk jockey reaction was slow to come. And when it did, the reaction was often one of confusion and dislike for what was, by all current standards, a most unusual record. Fans, however, took to Presley immediately. The first single, on Phillips' soon-to-be-historic Sun label, became a regional hit on both country and rhythm and blues stations.

Presley's success as a live performer came quickly. Billed as "The Hillbilly Cat," he toured the south incessantly with Moore and Black, driving crowds to hysteria with his vocalizing and hip-swinging theatrics.

His first single to reach the national country charts was another Crudup tune, "Baby, Let's Play House." It reached No. 10 nationally.

Presley released five singles on Sun; for the last sessions, Moore and Black were joined by drummer D. J. Fontana, who became a regular member of Presley's backup band until the unit broke up in 1960 (Black went on to become a successful bandleader until his death in the mid-'60s; Moore and Fontana are currently recording engineers in Tennessee).

Enter Parker

It was at about that time that Presley's management was picked up by Col. Tom Parker, a former carnival owner and medicine show huckster, who had been involved with country music performers like Eddy Arnold.

In 1955, RCA Victor Records purchased Presley's recording contract, plus all existing master tapes, from Phillips for $35,000. Presley himself received a $5000 bonus from the company.

With a major label behind him, Presley was in short order booked on national television programs hosted by Tommy and Jimmy Dorsey, Milton Berle, Steve Allen and Ed Sullivan. Offended by Presley's hip-swinging, tv directors ordered his image cut off at the waist. It didn't matter. Presley became a national superstar overnight.

In the ensuing years, Presley released more than 80 singles for RCA, and nearly that number of albums — including two boxed sets of 50 "golden hits" and various recouplings. In 1965, *Daily Variety* estimated that Presley's recordings had grossed $150,000,000 for RCA. Presley's most recent album, "Moody Blue," was pressed in a blue-vinyl "limited edition" of some 250,000 copies; after those are sold, says the label, disk will be pressed on regular black compound.

Army Hitch

Presley was inducted into the Army in 1958. Fears that his recording career would slow down proved false. Serving in an armor unit in Germany, passing up an opportunity to sing in Special Services at Army pay, he had stockpiled enough tapes to see him safely through. His first postservice single, "Stuck On You," reached No. 1 within weeks of release.

Presley's film debut, "Love Me Tender," was released by 20th-Fox in 1956. A Richard Egan-starrer originally titled "The Reno Brothers," the pic was quickly retitled to capitalize on the fame of the singer, whose role was relatively minor.

He went on to make 33 films, of which the last two were documentaries of the singer on tour. Ensuing Presley vehicles were generally released by Paramount and MGM. Presley maintained a long-standing relation-

(Continued on Page 18, Column 1)

OBITUARIES

DUKE ELLINGTON

Edward Kennedy (Duke) Ellington, 75, American Negro jazz conductor and composer, and a dominant theatrical figure for 45 years, died May 24 at Columbia-Presbyterian Medical Center, New York. He had been hospitalized since early April with a respiratory infection that developed into pneumonia.

For career details, see Music section, this issue.

DONALD CRISP

Donald Crisp, 93, outstanding screen character actor and Academy Award winner, and onetime west coast banker, died May 25 in a Van Nuys (Calif.) hospital. His Oscar was for best supporting actor in 20th's "How Green Was My Valley."

For career details see Pictures.

In Memoriam

HENRY W. HERRMAN

1890 - 1974

Beatrice Coe
Ann and Bill Countrymen
Sandra Drew
Alice Knick
John and Jean Lehti
Jack Vaughan
Romaine Weil

STEWART ALSOP

Stewart Alsop, 60, nationally-syndicated columnist, died May 26 at the National Institute of Health, Bethesda, Md., where he had been undergoing treatment for leukemia.

Alsop's book about his impending death, "Stay of Execution: A Sort of Memoir," was published last year, after he had been diagnosed as afflicted with acute myeloblastic leukemia. He started as a reporter in 1945 when his brother, Joseph, asked him to be his partner in writing the Washington column for the New York Herald Tribune, "Matter of Fact," which they wrote for 12 years for as many as 137 national papers.

He is survived by his wife, Patrica, five sons and a daughter, as well as brothers and a sister.

KITTY GORDON

Kitty Gordon (Mrs. Ralph) Ranlet, 96, stage and vaudeville actress, retired for many years, died May 26 at a Brentwood, N.Y., nursing home. Born in England, she started her theatrical career there. Between 1901-02 she was seen in "Kitty Grey" and "The Girl From Keys," as well as in a Gus Edwards company.

In New York she was seen in the 1904 "Veronique," as well as "Three Kisses" and "Nelly Neil" plus roles in "Dollar Princess," "Girl and the Wizard," "The Enchantress" and "La Belle Paree." She toured in "Lady Kitty" and was seen in vaudeville in "A Pink Nightgown" and "Alma's Return."

Her last appearance was in 1952 on television in "Life Begins At 80." There are no known survivors.

Variety's "New Acts" file has entries on Miss Gorodn going back to 1906, as "Kitty Gordon and Her Broadway Comediennes," plus later reviews of her vaude turns in 1906, 1911 and 1913. In a 1919 review of her turn by the late Joshua Lowe (*Jolo*), afterwards chief of the London bureau, cited her gowns. "She is as beautiful as ever and knows how to wear clothes" but her voice appeared to have grown tired. One song number was "Nowadays It's All The Craze To Have A Jazz Band."

DORA WEISSMAN

Dora Weissman, age unreported, an actress of the Yiddish theatre and American film, stage and television, died May 21 in Flower Fifth Avenue Hospital, New York. She lived at the Beacon Hotel, Manhattan.

The widow of Yiddish playwright and theatre manager Anshel

In Memoriam

DAVE APOLLON

May 30, 1972

Schorr and the daughter of Rubin Weissman, a Yiddish playwright and founder of the Hebrew Actors Union, she started playing children's roles and later appeared in the Yiddish Art Theatre, N.Y., and director and actress of the Arch Street Theatre, Philadelphia. She also toured extensively.

Her English-speaking stage debut was "Hitch Your Wagon" in 1937 and she was later seen on Broadway in "Two On An Island," "The Man With Blond Hair," "A New Life" and "Down to Miami." She toured with Luise Rainer in "Biography."

Her films included "The Gorilla Girl," her radio-tv stints, "The Goldbergs" and the Milton Berle show. She formerly conducted the Dora Weissman School of Performing Arts in Manhattan.

KARL J. LAMBERTZ

Karl J. Lambertz, 78, retired executive of WFAA and WFAA-TV, died May 15 in Dallas. He retired in 1962 as assistant to the managing director of WFAA and became director of public relations for Business Music Inc., distributors of Music by Muzak. He retired from Business Music in 1971.

Lambertz conducted various theatre orchestras in Missouri, Illinois and Arkansas before moving to Dallas in 1923. He joined WFAA in 1930 as a staff musician and became musical director in 1933, a position he held until 1946 when he moved to Albuquerque, N.M. He returned to WFAA in 1952 as assistant manager and program director and was promoted assistant to the managing director in 1957.

He is survived by his wife, daughter and two grandchildren.

MILT DEUTSCH

Milt Deutsch, 56, longtime personal manager and agent, died May 25 in Hollywood following a lengthy illness. He managed Jim Bailey, Tony Martin & Cyd Charisse, Billy Eckstine and Barbara McNair.

Deutsch started as an agent in the Frederick Bros. Agency in New York and later went to Associated Booking Corp before going to the Coast to head the ABC office there. He later operated his own agency before going into personal management. Active until recently, he was in New York last for the opening of Martin & Charisse at the Waldorf-Astoria.

Survived by wife, Marion a former dancer, son, daughter, and sister.

JACK DOYLE

Jack Doyle, 64, Desert Inn exec prior to Howard Hughes ownership, died May 18 at Methodist Hospital, Houston, Texas. He was admitted to Sunrise Hospital, Las Vegas, last January after suffering a stroke, but when his condition deteriorated he was transferred to the coronary ward in Houston under care of heart specialist Dr. Michael Debakey.

A 25-year Vegas resident, Doyle was active in civic endeavors, was past chief barker of Variety Club, Tent 39. He was former secy of Nevada Athletic Commission, honored by former Gov. Paul Laxalt with the Silver State Plenipotentiary. He was a charter member of Nevada Kentucky Colonels.

He is survived by his wife, son, two daughters, three grandchildren and one great-grandchild.

JAMES JOYCE

James Joyce, 53, singer-arranger for films and television programs and choral arranger-director for The King Sisters and the King family for many years, died May 17 in Los Angeles.

Joyce had also worked with Frank and Nancy Sinatra, Nelson Riddle, Ray Coniff, Kay Starr and had arranged for such films as "The Great Gatsby" and "Tom Sawyer." His tv credits included "The Smothers Brothers," "The Bobby Darin Show" and "The Red

In Loving Memory
of
MARY WELCH

BRYAN O'BYRNE

Skelton Hour." He served on the local and national boards of the American Federation of Radio and Television Artists and the American Federation of Musicians.

He is survived by his wife, five sons and mother.

SILVIO D'ALEXANDER

Silvio D'Alexander, 87, clarinet player who toured in the old-time orchestras of Phil Spitalny, Maurice Spitalny, Angelo Vitale and Al Russo, died May 20 in Cleveland. He was an active member of Musicians Union, Local 4, for 61 years, playing in various Italian groups, although he worked 54 years steadily in a day-time job for Central Brass Manufacturing Co. He retired from it seven years ago.

D'Alexander migrated from Italy in 1904, at age 17, as a clarinetist with a concert band making a tour of the United States. He became a citizen, married an American-Italian girl in Cleveland and performed in pit orchestras at silent film theaters for many years. (The Spitalnys originated in Cleveland and were prominent pop names in presentation house era-Ed.)

Survived by a daughter, son, five grandchildren and two great-grandchildren.

SHERLOCK FELDMAN

Sherlock Feldman, 73, whose gambling stories were used by many comedians, died May 17 at Sunrise Hospital, Las Vegas, following a lengthy illness.

Feldman passed along many stories to entertainers playing Las Vegas and they gave him full credit, making him a well-known gambling character for years.

Born in St. Louis, in 1901, he moved to Las Vegas in 1949 and was employed in casinos of El Rancho Vegas, Royal Nevada, Sands, Silver Slipper and Riviera Hotels prior to joining the Dunes Hotel in 1960. He was an honorary life member of Al Malaikah Temple, Peace Officers Shrine Club and Las Vegas Shrine Club.

He is survived by his wife, daughter, son, five grandchildren.

ALAN DUNN

Alan Dunn, 73, New Yorker cartoonist and author, died May 20 at his home in Manhattan. The most prolific of the mag's artists, he had 1,906 drawings and nine covers published therein between 1926 and 1974. He left work that will still be published.

Dunn, an architecture student, also contributed articles on the subject to the Architectural Record. He introduced the work of his fiancee, later wife, Mary Petty to the New Yorker. His collected works include "Rejections," "Who's Paying For The Cab?," "The Last Lath," "East of Fifth," "Should It Gurgle?," "Is There Intelligent Life On Earth?" and "A Portfolio of Social Cartoons — 1957-1968."

He is survived by his wife.

MICHAEL J. CUNEEN

Michael J. Cuneen, 52, a longtime broadcaster, died May 23 in an automobile accident in Deposit, N.Y.

Vice president and general manager of radio WDLA, Walton, N.Y., Cuneen was a member of the radio board of the National Assn. of Broadcasters and a charter member of the New York Broadcasters Assn.

Cuneen began his broadcasting career after World War II at WESB in Bradford, Pa., and in 1950 he and two associates bought WNLK Norwalk, Conn. He sold that station in 1953 and moved to WKLA.

Survivors include his wife and two children.

MARK A. BUSHNER

Mark A. Bushner, 67, administrator of Motion Picture Industry Pension Plan since its formation, died May 18 of cancer in Los Angeles, following a three-month illness.

Native of Boston, Bushner came to L.A. as a young man and received his education here, receiving an LLB degree from Southwestern University School of Law in 1928.

He joined the film industry in 1935 as timekeeper at Paramount, then moved to Selznick International in 1937. In 1940 he joined RKO-Radio Pictures as industrial relations director and remained in that post until 1953, when he became administrator of the pension plan.

Surviving are his wife, daughter and son.

CASEY ZIGA

Casey Ziga, 56, Hungarian gypsy violinist in orchestras that played in many of Northern Ohio's niteries, restaurants and at wedding receptions since he was a youngster, died May 15 in Cleveland. He was part of the George Jurvic Melody Orchestra for the past 18 years.

A group of 30 Hungarian gypsy violin players who were his friends paraded through the streets, playing "Gypsy Farewell March," as they followed the hearse carrying his body to the church and the cemetery as a tribute to him. Ziga, one of the leading musical members of Cleveland's Hungarian Cultural Club, was also honored by it in several receptions held for survivors in his family.

STEWART CHASE

Salvatore Capilli, 48, who under the name of Stewart Chase was associated with several Philadelphia and Trenton, N.J., radio stations as newscaster, announcer and disc jockey, died May 22 at West Park Hospital, Philadelphia.

News and sports director of WHAT and WWDB-FM, which he joined as a d.j. in 1964, he also did weekend newscasts on KYW and, for the past two years, WCAU-FM.

A member of AFTRA and a World War II veteran, he is survived by his wife, two sons and three daughters.

CHARLES SQUIRES

Charles Squires, 46, one of Britain's top telefilm documentarians, died May 22 at a London hospital while undergong treatment for a heart condition.

He came up through feature-film production at various London studios, starting as a "tea boy" and graduating to film editor. He switched to video with the inception of a commercial channel in the U.K. in the mid-1950s, and in recent years had made films for London Weekend Television. His best known pic was "Derby Day," shot at Epsom Downs.

Survived by wife and two children.

BILLY WELU

Billy Welu, 41, former bowling great who had served as expert commentator for ABC Sports' "Professional Bowlers Tour" telecasts for the past 10 years, died May 16 at his Houston, Tex. home.

A former president of the Professional Bowlers Assn., he had won PBA titles in 1962 and 1964 and the American Bowling Congress Masters in 1964 and 1965. He was to have returned to the bowling telecasts for the 1974-75 season along with longtime colleague, sportscaster Chris Schenkel.

A bachelor, he was survived by his father and sister.

GUY BOSWELL

Guy Boswell, 66, a trombonist who formerly played in Cleveland Symphony Orchestra, died May 13 in Cleveland, Ohio. A graduate of Curtis Institute of Music, he worked for the Euclid (Ohio) Music House after World War II and also performed in the Cleveland Orchestra's summer concerts when Rudolph Ringwall was its conductor. Boswell retired in 1972.

Survived by wife.

JOE QUINN

Joe Quinn, 75, veteran stage,

1980s

There were many great social, political, and artistic achievements made during the 1980s. So why does the decade now seem so depressing?

Maybe it's because the 1980s gave us Milli Vanilli, Wrestlemania, *Howard the Duck*, *Heaven's Gate*, the Luciano Pavarotti romantic comedy *Yes, Giorgio, Manimal*, infomercials, *The Brady Brides*, Luke and Laura's wedding, big hair, heavy-metal headbangers, one-hit wonders, *Breakin' 2: Electric Boogaloo*, and a lot of *Star Wars* wannabes, Madonna wannabes, *Dallas/Dynasty* wannabes, and the term "wannabe."

It was also the decade of Chernobyl, Tiananmen Square, *Exxon Valdez*, the space shuttle *Challenger* disaster, Nicaraguan Contras, and AIDS. The 1980s had no shortage of words that can immediately evoke distress, misery, and despair.

Despite this, however, there were some profound improvements that, though receiving little media coverage at the time, went on to change the world. The Apple Macintosh computer was launched. The U.S. Supreme Court made its so-called Betamax decision, ruling that individuals could videotape programs for their own use. Ted Turner's "superstation" TBS expanded and, along with the launch of his CNN, changed the landscape of TV.

Apple, founded by Steve Jobs and Steve Wozniak, gave the average person extensive information at their fingertips. The two built an empire of ever smaller, ever more portable, and ever more powerful forms of communication. While Apple may have not been the first on the IT scene, since Paul Allen and Bill Gates officially launched Microsoft in April 1975, and though there were others, the Mac offered hardware and software that were aesthetically pleasing and backed by efficient tech support. In other words, they made new technology accessible, even desirable, which fueled a revolution as far-reaching as any political uprising.

Just as important was the Betamax decision. The new Betamax and VHS systems allowed private citizens to videotape programs from the TV—in other words, to own copyrighted material. Before then, audiences could only watch a film or TV show when it was scheduled by someone else. If you wanted to go to the movies, you had to wait for the starting time. If a movie disappeared from theaters, you had to

Above: Steven Spielberg and Henry Thomas on the set of *E.T.: The Extra-Terrestrial*.

VOL. 202 No. 30　　44 Pages　　Hollywood, California-90028, Wednesday, January 18, 1984　　Newspaper Second Class P.O. Entry　　50 cents

HOLLYWOOD LOSES TO BETAMAX

L.A. Supervisors Order Development Of Program To Curb Runaway Prod'n

By WILL TUSHER

The Los Angeles County Board of Supervisors yesterday voted unanimously to instruct the nonprofit L.A. County Economic Development Corp. to develop an antirunaway program "providing for advertising and other incentives in support of the motion picture industry."

Howard Mull, named to coordinate the 30-day study, said the objective will be to match other states incentive for incentive.

Others on the study unit are Ted Howard, president of the County Economic Development Corp., and D.E. Slusser, chairman of the newly formed industry-multifilm commission coordinating committee.

The motion to help the industry was moved by Supervisor Mike Antonovich, and met with no opposition. Mull is an Antonovich deputy. Mull said he plans to hold a series of meetings before reporting back to the Board of Supervisors in a month.

He interpreted his mission as
(Continued on Page 42, Column 1)

'Zone' Defense Attacks Charge Of Cover-Up

By DAVID ROBB

Attorneys for the "Twilight Zone" defendants yesterday presented new physical evidence and a "surprise" witness that they claim proves their clients had not, as the prosecution claims, engaged in a "cover-up" of the use of children around helicopters and explosives the night of the fatal "Twilight Zone" crash.

Physical evidence came in the form of a script sent to Ed Morey, a Warner Bros. v.p. who was the studio's liaison with the Landis production team. That script, received in Morey's office on July 8, 1982 — nearly two weeks before the fatal crash — indicates the production team's intention of using children at night around helicopters and explosives.

Morey, however, testified yesterday that he was on vacation when that script came across his desk and he'd not had a chance to read it until the afternoon before the fatal crash on July 23, 1982.

The final scene in the script, clearly labeled a "night" shoot, reads in part: "Bill (Vic Morrow's character) finds children. Helicop-
(Continued on Page 38, Column 1)

Seligman Associate Producer Of Oscars

Michael Seligman will be associate producer of the 56th annual Academy Awards show, according to Jack Haley Jr., producer of the show for the Academy of Motion Picture Arts & Sciences.

Seligman's assignment marks the sixth time he has been associate producer of the Oscar show.

Oscars will be handed out April 9.

'JACKET' 1ST OF 3 KUBRICK FILMS FOR WB

As part of a new three-picture accord with Warner Bros., Stanley Kubrick, unrepresented on the world's screens since "The Shining" was released in 1980, will write, produce and direct "Full Metal Jacket," an account of a young Marine's training and his experience in Vietnam.

Production is scheduled to start this fall, according to a joint announcement by Kubrick and WB's prexy and chief operating officer, Terry Semel.

Based On Novel

The pic will be based on the novel, "The Short-Timers," by Gustav Hasford, who served as a Marine in Vietnam during 1967-68. The novel, hailed by some book critics as one of the best works of fiction dealing with the Vietnam war, "follows 18-year-old Marine recruit, Private Joker, from his carnarge-and machismo initiation rites" at training camp "to his climactic involvement in the heavy fighting in Hue during the 1968 Tet offensive."

According to WB, Kubrick will launch a nationwide search for new faces to play the young Marines whose average age was 18. "Kubrick plans to stick very closely to that age in casting the film," says WB.

Kubrick's last three films, "A Clockwork Orange," "Barry Lyndon" and "The Shining," were made for Warner Bros.

Sky Channel Makes Its Bow On U.K. Cable

By JACK PITMAN

London, Jan. 17 — Satellite-to-cable television bowed in Britain last night with the start of a five-hour Sky Channel feed to some 10,000 basic cable subscribers in western England.

Sky Channel, which carries American and Scandinavian spot advertising, is operated by London-based Satellite Television Ltd., whose majority holder is Rupert Murdoch.

Outfit also has around 500,000 cable subs in Norway, Finland, Switzerland, France (limited to hotel cable systems) and West Ger-
(Continued on Page 42, Column 3)

High Court Rules Homevid Taping Does Not Violate Current Copyright Laws

By PAUL HARRIS

Washington, Jan. 17 — The U.S. Supreme Court ruled today that the widespread practice of homevideo taping is not a violation of copyright laws. In a 5-4 decision that amounts to a crushing defeat for Hollywood, the court ruled in the Sony Betamax case that "time shifting," the practice of taping shows for later viewing, is a fair use of vid product protected by law. Similarly, it ruled that manufacturers of VCRs are not "contributory infringers," as program suppliers alleged.

The long-awaited decision, written by Justice John Paul Stevens, overturns an appeals court verdict that home use of a VCR is not legal under current copyright laws.

"One may search the Copyright Act in vain for any sign that the elected representatives of the millions of people who watch television every day have made it unlawful to copy a program for later viewing at home, or have enacted a flat prohibition against the sale of machines that make such copying possible," Stevens wrote.

"It may well be that Congress will take a fresh look at this new technology, just as it so often has examined other innovations in the past. But it is not our job to apply laws that have not yet been written."
(Continued on Page 38, Column 3)

Sony Warns Against Home Taping Limits

Obviously delighted over the Supreme Court's hometaping ruling in its behalf, Sony Corp. yesterday urged the public to guard against any Congressional push to undo the ruling.

"There may be efforts by some to undermine this decision in Congress and through further litigation," Sony said. "We hope that this decision focuses attention of consumers on the importance of being actively involved in efforts to protect their rights to continue to utilize new homevideo technology."

Sony said the ruling was an "important victory for consumers."

EIA Rejoices While MPAA Asks Congress For Royalty System

By DENNIS WHARTON

Washington, Jan. 17 — While champagne flowed freely in the corridors of the Electronic Industries Association following today's U.S. Supreme Court Betamax decision, the mood was decidedly less jubilant a few blocks away at Motion Picture Association of America headquarters.

"It's great, isn't it?" shouted EIA veepee of government and legal affairs Gary Shapiro. "After two years of fighting, it's a fantastic feeling. There's a lot of celebrating going on here."

Meanwhile, MPAA chieftain Jack Valenti spent most of the day poring over the decision with staff attorneys. At a press conference
(Continued on Page 38, Column 3)

Producers Quiet On VCR Ruling

By JIM HARWOOD

While the electronics industry led by Sony Corp. was crowing over the Supreme Court decision upholding homevideo taping, Hollywood producers were generally quiet yesterday, privately hoping they will stand to gain more than they'll lose from the rapid spread of vidtape.

Only 20th Century-Fox issued a formal statement, urging Congress to amend the copyright laws to provide film companies a royalty of blank tape of vidrecording equipment, the solution championed all along by the Motion Picture Association of America.

Other studios essentially echoed the same sentiment by referring queries to the MPAA, which will now carry that fight into Congress, thus maintaining a united front in
(Continued on Page 42, Column 4)

Pano Alafouzo To Step Down As President Of UIP

London, Jan. 17 — Pano Alafouzo has turned in his badge a prexy of United International Pictures and is expected to be replaced in that role by UIP's senior sales v.p., Michael Williams-Jones.

Alafouzo, who presided over the formation of UIP in 1981, told a meeting of UIP partners — Universal, Paramount and MGM/UA — that he would step down at the end of his contract, June 30. He was 65 last month.

Williams-Jones' appointment has
(Continued on Page 42, Column 4)

Roy Evans Gets V.P. Stripes At UA Circuit

Roy Evans has been elevated from southern division manager to veep of United Artists Theaters, effective immediately. His new duties will include overseeing all advertising and p.r. for the circuit.

UA Theaters also has made the following additional appointments: Larry Levin has been tabbed western division theater operations v.p.; Terry McIntire becomes v.p.-film buyer for the Dallas division, and Milt Daly is now v.p. in charge of theater operations for the eastern division.

NEW YEAR . . . NEW MEXICO!!!

THE NEW MEXICO FILM COMMISSION is a full-service team dedicated to serving you on all your film and video projects. Call us on our TOLL-FREE number: 1-800-545-9871 or write for our Production Manual: SJON UECKERT, Director, New Mexico Film Commission, 1050 Old Pecos Trail, Santa Fe, New Mexico 87501.

Left: January 16, 1984.

Right: The cast of *Dallas*.

wait for its re-release. If you couldn't watch a TV episode, the only option was to await the rerun. But Betamax and VHS put the power into the hands of the consumers. Audiences could see a show any time, any day they wanted. For the first time, audiences were in control.

Studios sued the system manufacturers, and showbiz execs were horrified when the court approved such home use. Until, of course, those same executives figured out how they could make money from it. That decision, and the studios' eventual marketing of videocassettes, was a revolution in entertainment, and a much more profound moment than most people in Hollywood realized at the time.

On September 24, 1980, a prescient *Variety* article talked about how broadcasters, cable operators, and ad agencies were all speculating on "an approximate date when the whole mix of cable, pay-cable, videocassette recorders and videodisk players effect a change in TV ad spending and viewing patterns that is no longer a matter of percent or degree but a matter of kind." The story quotes a report from Ron Kaatz, J. Walter Thompson's vice president and director of broadcast operations, who predicted, "People will no longer watch simply what is on—they will watch what they want to view when they want to view it, sometimes free of any commercial messages whatsoever." On June 17, 1981, *Daily Variety* carried a Reuters story from Tokyo reporting a huge boom in earnings for Sony Corporation, mostly due to the demand for videotape recorders (or VTRs, as they were called then), color TV sets, and Walkman sets.

On November 1, 1984, *Daily* carried a story elaborating on 20th Century-Fox leading the studios' move into home video:

> "From the day in August 1977 when Fox stepped forward as the first studio to license its films into the vidcassette market, to last Oct. 17 when CBS/Fox collected the largest initial-order total ever for a $79.95 vidcassette, Fox has been deeply involved in the industry,

often before and/or more profitably than any other major."

And when the U.S. Supreme Court ruled on January 17, 1984—with *Daily* bannering the headline "Hollywood Loses to Betamax"—folks in the industry quickly realized that if you can't beat 'em, join 'em, so they threw themselves fully into the new medium.

A day after the Supreme Court ruling, the paper carried four stories on the topic, with Sony crowing that this was an "important victory for consumers," and an executive at the Electronic Industries Association saying, "There's a lot of celebrating going on here." One story read, "Hollywood producers were generally quiet yesterday, privately hoping they will stand to gain more than they'll lose from the rapid spread of vidtape."

In the short term, many in Hollywood concluded that this *was* a victory, since the income from videocassettes, and later DVDs, gave a healthy boost to the bottom line.

However, an April 24, 1985, story from Sydney pointed up that there were problems whenever new technology is introduced.

Reporter Don Groves wrote that the

"Long-awaited recovery of the Australian theatrical market which began late last year with 'Ghostbusters' and which got a terrific charge this month from 'Beverly Hills Cop's' massive opening numbers is now under threat due to a fast-growing bottleneck at the Federal Film Censor's office which is resulting in a three-to-four-month delay in clearing cinema titles."

Groves said no one was blaming censor Janet Strickland. "For months she has been pleading for extra staff to enable her office to cope with the added responsibility of classifying videotapes." As filmmakers around the world, and particularly Hollywood, rushed to release films on videocassettes, they created a logjam for the censors.

Groves added ominously,

"Last year some 152 screens shuttered, equivalent to about one-sixth of the national screen-spread; 742 remain, and distribs are confident that no more will be lost. Of the 152 casualties, 108 were in rural areas, and 74 were ozoners"

("ozoners" being *Variety*-speak for drive-ins).

But the points were clear: vidcassettes were a goldmine, but they carried hidden hazards—and this boom coincided with a decline in movie going.

Another hazard: the March 31, 1981, *Daily Variety* carried a story about police in Willoughby Hills, Ohio, confiscating more than $2 million worth of equipment used to manufacture pirated tapes. Piracy still existed when films were shown on reels of celluloid, but digital technology enabled piracy on a much bigger scale.

By the end of the twentieth century, the income from videotape and later DVDs and Blu-Rays easily accounted for the bulk of a film's revenue.

Above: We were going to colorize this picture of Ted Turner.

> **Steven Bochco:**
> " I have three framed *Variety* front pages, the first one of which headlines 'Hill Street Cops Most Emmys,' the second one of which headlines 'NBC, "Law," Top Emmy Nominations,' and the third headlining '"Blue" Collars 26 Emmy Noms.' "

Ted Turner, a colorful and charismatic businessman who'd expanded his father's billboards company into radio and TV was key in changing the TV scene. In the first few decades of television, viewers had only a few stations to choose from, usually ABC, CBS, NBC, some local independent stations, and, eventually, PBS.

In January 1970, Turner bought the low-rated UHF channel WJRJ in Atlanta, changed its call letters to WTCG, and built the audience by showing reruns of old movies, TV series, and sports.

WTCG became one of a handful of "superstations," independent TV stations that broadcast outside their local regions. In 1977, the November 16 *Weekly Variety* hailed it as "the first satellite-distributed indie TV station for cable," calling it a superstation and predicting more would come. By 1978, the station was in all fifty states. By 1979 it was officially called Superstation WTBS.

This was the birth of basic cable. The 1980s gave viewers numerous options. And despite Bruce Springsteen's faux lament "57 Channels and Nothin' On," Turner and his Turner Broadcasting System had bought MGM Entertainment then sold most of the assets seventy-four days later, as reported in the June 9, 1986, *Daily Variety*. Former MGM owner Kirk Kerkorian got the production and distribution businesses and the home entertainment group; Lorimar-Telepictures bought the studio lot and MGM laboratory.

Turner kept the one MGM element that he'd wanted in the first place: The studio's library of films. As *Daily Variety* reported,

> "Turner has always maintained his main reason for buying MGM was for its extensive library of classic MGM, Warner Bros, and RKO films, which he wanted and needed for programming on TBS-run superstation WTBS."

New channels sprang up, targeting specific audiences. Advertisers jumped on board. As the undisputed dominance of broadcast television was ending, basic cable became the norm, and new powerhouses emerged, including MTV (Music Television) and "premium" pay-cable channels like HBO (Home Box Office).

Turner was branching out. On January 9, 1981, *Daily Variety* ran a story than began,

> Less than a year after CNN began, "Ted Turner's Cable News Network, which came into existence seven

253

VOL. 186 No. 22   44 Pages   Hollywood, California-90028, Tuesday, January 8, 1980   Newspaper Second Class P.O. Entry   35 Cents

SHARPENED EXHIB CONCERN ABOUT FEEVEE

Lorimar To Acquire Allied's Pic Library, Vidcassette And Tv Operations For $7 Mil

Lorimar Prods. said yesterday it pacted to acquire Allied Artists' entire pic library, its vidcassette and tv operations, plus a few other properties for more than $7,000,000.

Included in the deal is AAIndustries' half-interest in "The Betsy," plus AAPictures inventory, which notably includes "Cabaret" and "Papillon."

Allied said it expects to use the proceeds from the sale to repay debts of its three Chapter XI entities — AAIndustries, AAPictures and AA-TV — as part of the arrangement these operations will submit to the bankruptcy court on Feb. 20.

Allied has apparently worked out an arrangement with the creditors committees to allocate the Lorimar proceeds among Allied's divisions, which are debtors in chapter XI proceedings.

Initial beneficiary of the negotiated sale will be lead secured creditor Walter E. Heller & Co., who will receive about $2,400,000 against its claims, some of which will be cash and the rest in various assets.

According to an attorney close to the deal, Lorimar will put $2,600,000 down, plus another $2,100,000 a year later on top of the Heller settlement. The attorney estimated that the remaining creditors should recoup between 25¢ to 55¢ on the dollar.

Lorimar also picks up the leasehold on Allied's Gotham base at 15 Columbus Circle with about 10 years to run on the lease.

(Continued on Page 42, Column 2)

FITTER RESIGNS UA SALES POST; BACH AND FIELD BOOSTED

By DALE POLLOCK

As expected, United Artists has made some top-level changes in its executive hierarchy. Steven Bach and David M. Field have been upped to senior v.p. status for worldwide production while Al Fitter (as predicted here last week) has resigned his post as senior v.p. and domestic sales chief, effective Jan. 11.

UA officials were denying the rupture between Fitter and UA prexy and chief exec officer Andy Albeck all the way through the weekend, but official confirmation of the split came yesterday. Fitter is understood to

(Continued on Page 42, Column 3)

Catholic Conference Lobbying Against Radio Deregulation

Washington, Jan. 7 — The U.S. Catholic Conference has joined the ranks of organizations lobbying against the Federal Communications Commission's proposed deregulation of the radio industry.

The Catholic Conference is urging Americans to file comments against the proposal with arguments that broadcast policy would be dominated by sponsors and not listeners. Comments on the issue are due at the FCC Jan. 25.

The Catholic org argues that the rulemaking is simply a "forerunner to deregulation of television," and that charities and nonprofit organizations will be denied access to radio.

It believes the FCC should hold nationwide field hearings before closing the period for comment on radio deregulation.

NBC To Spend $10 Mil On Spex Aimed At Kids

By MORRIE GELMAN

NBC Entertainment, obviously tuned in to the kidvid polemic in Washington, is making a commitment of at least $10,000,000 to a regular series of 20 kidvid spex to be aired in primetime on an every-other-week basis during the first, second and fourth quarters of 1981.

The series, which will get an umbrella title (but does not have one as yet), is to be wide-ranging and open-ended, encompassing various forms of material from a variety of sources.

In making the announcement of the project yesterday to tv reporters from across the country at a Century Plaza Hotel news conference, NBC Entertainment prexy Mike Weinblatt said

(Continued on Page 40, Column 2)

Pix, People, Pickups

John Gielgud joins cast of "Sphinx," now rolling in Budapest for producer Stanley O'Toole and Orion Pictures, playing an Egyptian shopkeeper.

* * *

Steve Railsback will costar in "Who Fell Asleep" for producers Raymond M. Dryden and Philip Randall. Scott Mansfield directs from his own script.

* * *

Lee Van Cleef will star op-
(Continued on Page 40, Column 4)

Theatremen Considering A Protest Over Effect On B.O. Of Features On Pay-See

By WILL TUSHER

New exhibitor concerns over sharpening pay-cable competition have been triggered by the feverish sales pitches attending the play of Academy Award contending theatrical features on Southern California's three major pay-cable systems — Z, On and SelecTV.

Theatre operators are mulling an organized protest to vent their fear that the practice will cut in on their boxoffice potential in the short run, and that it will inflict permanent audience losses in the long run.

Apparently, subscription tv is no less convinced that the showing of films pushing for Oscars will convert more filmgoers to the pay-tv habit. They have not been coy about selling the advantages of living room features — eliminating parking and baby sitting fees, enjoying the savings represented by eating in rather than prethatre restaurant dining.

Now, for the second successive Academy Award season, they are stressing as an added plus the incentive of seeing most of the Oscar-contending features before they go into general firstrun or post-Oscar rerun release.

"It (the pay-tv screening of Academy Award contenders) is selling subscription television like crazy," was the comment yesterday of Pacific Theatres executive Robert Selig, also a leading figure in Theatres West and Theatre Association of

(Continued on Page 42, Column 4)

RIAA Reports A Big Drop In Numbers Of Platinum Albums

By CYNTHIA KIRK

Although a midyear change in accounting procedures makes exact comparison difficult, the Recording Industry Association of America has reported a 58.8% plunge in the number of platinum certified million-selling LPs in 1979.

In addition to that drop — from 102 platinum albums in 1978 to a mere 42 last year — the number of gold LPs, those selling at least 500,000 tape or vinyl units, fell 41.9%, from 193 to 112.

On the other hand, gold-selling singles pretty much held their own last year — a total of 60 were certified in comparison to last year's 61 — and the num-

(Continued on Page 40, Column 3)

Afghanistan Fallout

RUSSIA COLD-SHOULDERS REQUEST FOR ROUTINE STOCK PIC FOOTAGE

By SID ADILMAN

Toronto, Jan. 7 — Russia appears to be cold-shouldering requests for routine stock film footage following a tough stance taken by western nations over its invasion of Afghanistan.

What started out as cordial negotiations for tourist-type footage of Moscow and Leningrad by producers of the Canadian feature, "Final Assignment," ended up in angry words and a resounding "Nyet" on the night U.S. President Jimmy Carter and Canadian Prime Minister Joe Clark cut off grain sales to the Soviet Union.

The pic, toplining Genevieve Bujold, Michael York, Burgess Meredith and Colleen Dewhurst, and directed by Paul Almond, was filmed in Montreal in November.

But it is set in Russia and centers on a Canadian tv reporter (Bujold) attempting to report on the touchy political situation while on a visit there and trying to smuggle out of the country a six-year-old boy who requires a

(Continued on Page 40, Column 4)

Pertschuk Withdraws From Kidvid Probe

Washington, Jan. 7 — Michael Pertschuk, chairman of the Federal Trade Commission, said today he was withdrawing from participation in a controversial inquiry into kidvid blurbs in hopes that the probe would be permitted to continue.

In what he termed, "a painful decision," Pertschuk said his bowing out of the inquiry would

SUPREME COURT REFUSES TO ORDER CBS FAIRNESS DOCTRINE HEARINGS

Washington, Jan. 7 — The U.S. Supreme Court today refused to force the Federal Communications Commission to conduct Fairness Doctrine proceedings against CBS for allegedly biased reporting of national security issues.

The high bench let stand a lower court ruling that charges against CBS brought by the American Security Council Education Foundation were handled properly by the Commission.

Complaint Filed In 1974

The Foundation filed the Fairness Doctrine complaint against the web in 1974, citing its own study which showed CBS coverage of national security issues was unfairly "dovish."

The FCC rejected the claim because it was not based on a "particular well-defined issue." The D.C. Court of Appeals agreed with the ruling, prompting the Foundation to file with the high court.

In arguing its case, the Foundation said the FCC deliberately avoids handling Fairness Doctrine cases and is more concerned with the burden such cases place on broadcasters.

Arguing against review of the appeals court decision, the government said it would lead to "constant government scrutiny of the day-to-day programming decisions of television journalists."

CBS said the FCC's insistence on a well-defined issue in Fairness Doctrine cases avoids the "kind of broad-ranging, loosely focused governmental supervision of editorial decisions that would obviously stifle the independence of the broadcast press."

Wednesday, August 13, 1986 — *Variety* — FILM REVI[EW]

The Fly
(COLOR)

Gory remake short on believability; b.o. looks good.

A 20th Century Fox release of a Brooksfilms production. Produced by Stuart Cornfeld. Coproducers Marc-Ami Boyman, Kip Ohman. Directed by David Cronenberg. Screenplay, Charles Edward Pogue, Cronenberg, from a story by George Langelaan; camera (Deluxe color), Mark Irwin; editor, Ronald Sanders; music, Howard Shore; production design, Carol Spier; art director, Rolf Harvey; set decorator, Elinor Rose Galbraith; set designer, James Mc Ateer; sound (Dolby stereo), Gerry Humphreys; costumes, Denise Cronenberg; the Fly created and designed by Chris Walas Inc.; assistant director, John Board; casting, Deirdre Bowen. Reviewed at 20th Century Fox screening room, Century City, Calif., Aug. 4, 1986. (MPAA Rating: R.) Running time: **100 MINS.**

Seth Brundle	Jeff Goldblum
Veronica Quaife	Geena Davis
Stathis Borans	John Getz
Tawny	Joy Boushel
Dr. Cheevers	Les Carlson

Hollywood — David Cronenberg's remake of the 1958 horror classic "The Fly" is not for the squeamish, faint-hearted or those prone to motion sickness. All others may find it suitable entertainment.

One does not have to be totally warped to appreciate the film, but it does take a particular sensibility to clude an abortion played for sensationalism, almost devo[id of] human dimensions.

There is no denying, how[ever] that all this is handsomely s[taged] with Chris Walas' design for t[he Fly] never less than visually intrig[uing]. Production design by Carol S[pier], particularly for Goldblum's [green]house lab, is original and app[ropri]ate to the hothouse drama.

Cronenberg contains the a[ction] well in a limited space with a [small] cast. Goldblum carries the a[ction] until the action starts carrying [him] and Davis is a charming pre[sence] until she too becomes second[ary to] the spectacle. John Getz as [her] boyfriend is a curious cha[racter] who never really comes off, [owing] more to the writing than any[thing] in his performance.

Finally, "The Fly" is too tr[ansfixed] by its desire to shock to be tru[ly af]fecting. — *Jagr.*

The Transformers
(ANIMATED-COLOR)

Loud, unintelligible cartoon exercise.

A De Laurentiis Entertainment Group release. Produced by Joe Bacal, Tom Griffin. Executive producers Margaret Loesch, [...]

> ## Geena Davis:
> "Being mentioned for the first time in *Variety* is one of those career-defining moments. When I was a kid, my best friend's mother said, "If a person goes on Johnny Carson, that's IT. They've made it." Being reviewed in *Variety* is like that. Wow, I'm actually in *Variety*! I must be SOMEBODY!
>
> My first review from this most important paper was for *The Fly*, in 1986. I am very proud to be able to say that my performance as the love interest of an insect was favorably looked upon, being referred to as a 'charming presence.' (Until I became '. . . secondary to the spectacle,' of course.) Whatever other comments subsequent roles engendered, I had pulled off being a 'nice girlfriend' in the only review that really mattered."

Hollywood — "Manhunter" is an unpleasantly gripping thriller that rubs one's nose in a sick criminal mentality for two hours. Michael Mann's nerve-jangling style builds up an unhealthy head of [...]

Stephen Lang is outrageously despicable as a scandal sheet writer. Kim Greist, as the hero's wife, has little to do but worry and wait around.

Technical contributions are all of the slickest order. —*Cart.*

Left: January 8, 1980.

months ago amid prophecies of doom, entered the New Year with 4,300,000 homes on the line and a fairly healthy growth curve for both subscribers and advertising revenues."

it proved its merits with coverage of the President Reagan assassination attempt. According to *Daily Variety* on March 31, 1981, CNN's coverage was extensive and nearly around the clock at a time when "the webs were obviously straining to fill the air with fragments of information, some of it embarrassingly wrong. Or as NBC's Bernard Kalb conceded on air, the info fed him kept 'flipping and flopping.'"

John Hinckley's shooting of Ronald Reagan came only four months after Reagan's election, when the November 6, 1980, *Daily* had headlined "Reagan 1st Actor-Turned-President but Showbiz-Politics Ties Numerous," while another headline exulted that "Entertainment Stox in Mkt. Surge Following Reagan Win" ("Wall Street reacted euphorically yesterday to Ronald Reagan's surprising landslide election to the presidency. . . . ")

During the decade, CNN and the other 24-hour news channels that sprang up had plenty to cover.

The 1980–88 Iran-Iraq war provided the channels with plenty of fodder, as did the entire Middle East region. *Daily Variety*, on April 7, 1981, carried a story about a Los Angeles symposium called "The Media in the Middle East," sponsored by the American Professors for Peace in the Middle East.

Jerusalem Post editor Erwin Frenkel criticized coverage as turning Israel into "a media event that has received attention all out of proportion to its international significance," while Douglas Boyd, chairman of the communication department at the University of Delaware, pointed out that *Dallas* is viewed on six of the twelve Arab TV systems and wondered what image is being formed of Americans.

Daily on December 12, 1989, reported that CNN had entered into an unusual arrangement. American Airlines had been carrying in-flight news programs but wanted to excise any coverage of "airplane crashes, airport bombings or attacks by terrorists." In the year since the terrorist bombing

VOL. 207 No. 12   24 Pages   Hollywood, California-90028, Thursday, March 21, 1985   Newspaper Second Class P.O. Entry   50 Cents

MURDOCH'S HAT IN SHOWBIZ RING

Robinson, Allen, Arnold Honored By WG For Work In Films And Television
By DAVE KAUFMAN

Bruce Robinson won a Writers Guild award last night for his screenplay of "The Killing Fields," in the category of screenplay written from another medium (based on Sydney Schanberg's N.Y. Times Magazine article), while Woody Allen won for "Broadway Danny Rose," for a screenplay scripted directly for the screen. "Fields" is a Warner Bros. film, "Rose" is from Orion.

WG West's 37th annual awards, at the BevHilton, also saw honors going to Danny Arnold, the Paddy Chayefsky Laurel Award for tv writing achievement; William Goldman, the Laurel Award for screenwriting achievement; Edmund L. Hartmann, the Morgan Cox Award; Mary C. McCall Jr., the Founders Award; Charles Champlin of the L.A. Times, the Valentine Davies Award.

Arnold, creator, producer and writer of tv's "Barney Miller," was given his award by last year's winner, John Gay. Last annum's Davies winners, Jerry Lawrence and Robert E. Lee, presented the Davies Award, which is for "contributions to the literature of the screen."

McCall, a former Guild prexy, was honored "in recognition of the contributions she has made, through the years, to her Guild and her colleagues . . ." Her daughter, critic Sheila Benson, accepted.

Ed Hume won an award in the original tv drama anthology category for his script of ABC-TV's "The Day After."

In the tv adapted drama anthology category, the winners were Susan Cooper and Hume Cronyn.
(Continued on Page 22, Column 1)

Roger Corman Sets Up Co-Op Distrib'n Org

Roger Corman announced yesterday he has formed a new co-op distribution company to handle his films and those of others willing to share overhead and pay their own print-ad costs.

New outfit is called Concorde Pictures Corp. and Corman said he believes this is the first time a co-op indie distributor has ever been formed.

Though he and his wife Julie are financing Concorde initially and the project envisions handling others' pix as well, Corman said the plan falls within the out-of-court settlement reached last week with New World Pictures.

As part of that pact, Corman agreed not to re-enter the distribution business except with his own films. But in answer to a question at a press conference, Corman assured that New World was aware of the Concorde plan and had no objection.
(Continued on Page 22, Column 1)

KTLA Technicians Vote Strike Okay
By DAVID ROBB

Union technicians at KTLA voted 104-5 Tuesday night to grant their contract negotiators the authority to call a strike in the event ongoing contract talks fail to produce an acceptable agreement.

Current pact between the station and the union — the International Alliance of Theatrical Stage Employes — expires March 31. Col-
(Continued on Page 20, Column 1)

TOMORROW ENT. PLOTS ENTRY INTO PIC AREA
By LAWRENCE COHN

New York, March 20 — Tomorrow Entertainment, the tv programming production outfit, is moving aggressively into the theatrical film arena, with two features going before the cameras this Spring and a third shortly thereafter. Tomorrow president Micky Hyman will be exec producer of the pictures, along with the company's chairman, John Backe, former CBS president.

First up is an action thriller rolling in Atlanta in April titled "Monday, Tuesday, Wednesday." Based on a novel by Robert Houston, pic
(Continued on Page 23, Column 1)

Bill Regulating Sale Of Tickets Draws Criticism
By WILL TUSHER

Provisions calling for registration of customers in a bill to regulate the California ticket-selling industry have drawn heated criticism from computerized ticket companies and many of the clients they serve.

The measure (SB 675), authored by State Sen. Joseph Montoya (D-San Gabriel Valley), would, in part, make it a misdemeanor for any ticket-seller to fail to record the
(Continued on Page 20, Column 3)

BLACK RADIO STATIONS SINGLE OUT WB RECORDS FOR BOYCOTT
By HENRY SCHIPPER

All major black radio stations in Los Angeles, as well as stations in Chicago, New York, Memphis and San Francisco, have rallied behind KACE-FM in its boycott yesterday of Warner Bros. Records over alleged "discriminatory conduct" on the part of the label.

KACE, which indefinitely suspended broadcast of all WB product, has charged the company with "blatant disregard" for black radio, particularly with respect to crossover artists whose records have made it on pop stations.

Joining KACE in the boycott are black stations KJLH and KGFJ, both of which have stopped playing current hits by WB's artists, including cuts by such names as Prince, Madonna, Al Jarreau, The Time and George Benson.

KDAY, L.A.'s other major "urban" station, says it too will kick into the protest, though exact plans have not been finalized.

Reportedly, black stations WBMX in Chicago, WDIA in Memphis, WBLS in New York and KSOL in San Francisco, along with stations in Cleveland and Bakersfield, have also joined in the protest.

While the KACE boycott involves all WB product, including catalog "oldies," the KJLH and KGFJ protests are limited to current WB material. As an added sting, however, latter two stations say they will not report any WB airplay to researchers from Billboard and other publications that compile radio play charts.

Issue involved is the belief among black radio exex that WB — and the industry as a whole — is exploiting inner-city radio as a breeding ground in which to cultivate and launch crossover talent, then turning
(Continued on Page 19, Column 1)

Press Magnate Agrees To Buy Half-Interest In Fox Parent TCF Holdings Inc.
By RAY LOYND

Dramatically expanding his media empire into the Hollywood film business, press magnate Rupert Murdoch has an agreement with Marvin Davis to purchase 50% of TCF Holdings Inc., the parent of 20th Century Fox, for $250,000,000.

Davis and Murdoch, in a joint statement yesterday that caught the industry by surprise, said that Murdoch's News Corporation Ltd. was paying $162,000,000 for a half-interest in TCF and that "in addition, News will advance $88,000,000" to TCF.

The operative word, however, is the combined sum of the two figures — $250,000,000 — because the $88,000,000 is coming to TCF in the form of a loan that is in effect described as an "advance" for tax considerations.

Murdoch, Australian publisher of the New York Post, the Times of London and numerous other newspapers and media enterprises, called the deal "a significant investment for the News Corporation" and underscored "the outstanding leadership of Barry Diller" (Fox chairman and chief exec officer).

Unlike his personal forays into some of his newspaper domains, Murdoch is expected to leave production decisions and the daily running of the studio to Diller.

Immediate impact of the Murdoch purchase will be the pumping of a fresh $132,000,000, through TCF Holdings, into the Fox Film Corp.
(Continued on Page 21, Column 1)

Congress Calls On Showbiz To Fight Drug Use
By DENNIS WHARTON

Washington, March 20 — Congress, which recently became the focal point in an effort to ban beer and wine advertising on tv, today called on the industry to step up efforts to battle all forms of drug abuse.

The hearing, held before a Senate investigations subcommittee, dealt with tv's role in deglamorizing the use of drugs. Sesh included testimony from reps of the three nets; Health & Human Services Secretary Margaret M. Heckler; Gerald McRaney of the CBS series "Simon & Simon"; Susan Kendall Newman of
(Continued on Page 22, Column 3)

Craven Preps 'Flowers,' Sets Other Projects

As "Nightmare On Elm Street" approaches $20,000,000 in grosses (a tidy profit against a budget of $1,700,000), the film's writer-director, Wes Craven, is prepping a May production date for the suspenser "Flowers In The Attic" for Fries Entertainment and New World Pictures.

For Craven, who made his mark with such '70s cult horror pix as "The Last House On The Left" and "The Hills Have Eyes," his forthcoming pic will represent the director's first film without a stalking killer.

Adapted by Craven from the popular novel by V.C. Andrews, the film is budgeted in the $3-4,000,000 range and focuses on the eerie incarceration of two children in a Charles Addams-type house.
(Continued on Page 20, Column 5)

ASCAP Elects New Members To National Board

Songwriters Sammy Cahn, Hal David and Marilyn Bergman have been elected to the American Society of Composers, Authors & Publishers' national board of directors, ASCAP has announced.

The board, consisting of pop music and concert music writers and publishers, is elected by the ASCAP membership to a two-year term. New term begins April 1.

Other pop writers elected were Stanley Adams, Cy Coleman, Sammy Fain, John Green and Arthur Hamilton, all of whom were reelected, along with David and Cahn. Burton Lane and Bergman were voted in for the first time.

Concert scribes reelected were Jacob Druckman, Morton Gould and Elie Siegmeister.

Pop music publishers returning to
(Continued on Page 23, Column 1)

5% REBATE IN ARKANSAS
Contact Joe Glass, Director
Arkansas Motion Picture Office
One Capitol Mall / Little Rock, Arkansas 72201
(501) 371-7676 or (501) 375-4506

Arkansas is a natural

Left: March 21, 1985.

of a Pan Am flight over Lockerbie, Scotland, American Airlines had yanked about 25 percent of broadcast time from *CBS Morning News* airings on flights, and CBS refused to allow the airline to remove segments, so the airline went with CNN instead.

As the decade closed, newsies from all media were working overtime to report on and analyze the turmoil in Panama, China, Poland, and other areas of Eastern Europe.

July 26, 1989, *Weekly*. "A month after the bloody events in Beijing's Tiananmen Square, Taiwan's Central Motion Picture Corp. is prepping a movie on the pro-democracy student movement and its suppression by the mainland Chinese authorities." In the words of Edward Yang, one of Taiwan's best-known directors: "Tiananmen shows nothing has really changed in the ruling mentality."

August 31, 1989. *Daily*: At the Montreal International Film, TV, and Video Market, Adam Zawistowski, general director of Film Polski, talked about the newly elected Solidarity-backed prime minister Tadeusz Mazowiecki replacing the Polish Communist regime.

December 13, 1989, *Weekly*:

> "The current political upheaval in Eastern Europe will be a boon to American major film companies, Walt Disney and Touchstone Pictures' senior v.p. of international marketing Kevin Hyson predicted last week. Disney, whose pics are distributed abroad by Warner Bros. Intl., recently made its first profit-sharing deal in a Communist country with the release in Hungary of 'Cocktail,' which totaled about 400,000 admissions in its first run."

December 22, 1989, *Daily:* Five Americans, including CBS News producer Jon Meyersohn, were abducted in Panama by gunmen loyal to General Manuel Noriega. This occurred as apparent retaliation for the invasion of the country by U.S. troops. The story said gangs loyal to Noriega "clearly see representatives of the American media as prime targets."

On September 25, 1986, in *Daily Variety*, Dave Kaufman noted that newsies weren't the only ones caught up in world events. Kristy McNichol told him that the filming of her CBS telefilm, *Women of Valor*, was shooting in the Philippines when President Ferdinand Marcos was overthrown and Corazon Aquino took over.

And the recession hit a crisis point on October 19, 1987. The following day, *Daily* reported:

> "Wall Street's financial earthquake jolted Hollywood with all the force of the Big One. Shock waves of panic selling market-wide left entertainment issues shuddering beneath a market crash that exceeded 1929s Black Monday. Yesterday's historic collapse of 508.32 points by the Dow Jones Industrials represents a single-day loss of 22.82%—nearly double the percentage pullback 58 years ago."

The 1987 devastation hit with such ferocity that hardly any industry stocks could withstand the tremor. Among those stocks tracked by *Daily Variety*, 102 declined while a mere 3 eked out gains and 8 managed to hold their ground.

But political and economic turmoil were just part of the crises that cable news was covering. On November 20, 1987, *Daily* reported that six U.S. senators had urged the United Nations to respond to a scientific finding that chemicals are causing ozone loss over the Antarctic. They said recent studies showed the hole in the ozone layer was larger than suspected.

Apparently everybody wanted to get into the news act. On April 4, 1989, *Daily Variety* reported, "National Geographic, planning to film in Alaska in June for a short piece about the state's ecological challenges, instead dispatched a three-person crew March 31 to document the Exxon Valdez oil spill disaster."

Right: April 24, 1985.

Following Spread: January 3, 1989; November 15, 1989.

But when the newsies were in high gear, they could bring change. CNN helped America become aware of many homeless Vietnam War vets. In 1988, medical garbage, including hypodermic needles, washed up on the shores of New Jersey. For the first time, Americans seemed to realize that the ocean was not a dumping ground.

And then there was the Soviet Union. On March 13, 1985, *Variety* predicted that the election of Mikhail Gorbachev as Soviet leader would be good for local film business.

("For that matter, anything would be an improvement over the freeze of creative and innovative filmmaking in all the Soviet republics and those Socialist lands that traditionally toe the line when film policies are laid down in the Kremlin.")

Almost a year after Reagan's 1987

"Mr. Gorbachev, tear down this wall" speech in Berlin, Reagan appeared at the National Association of Broadcasters convention and offered a new challenge to the Soviet premier: "Tear down the wall of oppression" so the entire world can enjoy the technological revolution. By November 15, 1989, *Weekly Variety* was reporting, "The sweeping changes that have shaken the foundations of the Berlin Wall are being accompanied by revolutionary changes in East Germany's approach to broadcast news. The country's staid state-run radio and TV operations have been transformed into vanguards of investigative journalism."

The industry was studying the innovations, domestically and overseas, of Ted Turner and Rupert Murdoch. On January 18, 1981, *Daily Variety* carried a story about the bow of Murdoch's Sky Channel, a satellite-to-cable service for ten thousand basic cable subscribers in western England. (It eventually evolved into Sky1.)

But not all the significant changes of the decade were initiated by legislators and technicians. Sometimes artists can pinpoint a problem and offer a solution more clearly than anyone else. While lawmakers were fretting (or pretending to fret) about world events, Bob Geldof and other musicians took action.

After four years without rain, Ethiopia had seen seven to ten million of its people dead or dying due to starvation. A civil war in the country added to the crisis, and there were charges that Ethiopia's Marxist government was using money to purchase weapons from communist countries, rather than to buy food. In 1984, Bob Geldof and Midge Ure created Band Aid. Proceeds from "Do They Know It's Christmas," sung by a congregation of music stars, raised £8 million (about $15 million) to help the Ethiopians.

Harry Belafonte and fund-raiser Ken Kragen followed with an American gathering of music stars, singing "We Are the World," again targeting African relief. The single, released in March 1985, sold an estimated 20 million copies.

On July 13, 1985, Geldof expanded on the concept of these recordings. He gathered musicians for Live Aid, an all-day concert held simultaneously in U.K.'s Wembley Stadium and Philadelphia's John F. Kennedy Stadium, which was satellite-fed to 150 countries and reached an estimated 1.9 billion viewers.

The event raised an estimated £150 million pounds, or more than $280 million.

A month later (August 14, 1985), *Weekly Variety* reported the

Telefilm Boss Axed
(Continued from page 1)

from the beginning, at the government's "pleasure." Appointed by the former liberal government, he is the first art agency boss to be axed by the new government.

During his five years of low-keyed diplomacy, Telefilm staff, annual budget and responsibilities experienced growth that outstripped all other art agencies combined.

Telefilm staff went from about 10 to a current 75 and its budget shot up from $C4,000,000 a year to its present $C65,000,000, which includes $C54,000,000 for the Broadcast Fund, which the government created two years ago and handed to Telefilm to administer. The Broadcast Fund invests in primetime indie tv Canadian content programming.

Expansions

Along with that, Telefilm last year expanded responsibilities to include overall tv and film industry marketing and extended its offices from just Montreal and Toronto to Paris, London, Los Angeles, Vancouver and Halifax.

Before replacing Michael McCade at Telefilm, Lamy, now 50, was head of the National Film Board for five years and for seven years the senior executive at the Canadian Broadcasting Corp. Both are government-owned.

An indie film producer in Montreal prior to becoming a civil servant, he produced several French-track features that include the low-budget "Deux Femmes En Or." It still ranks as Quebec's top French-language domestic grosser.

Rumors he would be dropped for political reasons have circulated in the industry since last November and a month ago Lamy said that he would "like to stay on because I've done a good job."

By Telefilm regulations, its board of directors, who were also appointed by the former government, must hire a successor. But the decision will be made by Federal Communications Minister Marcel Masse and his political aides and then approved by the board whose members themselves are likely to be replaced soon, also for political reasons.

Lamy's last major appearance in the post will be at the Cannes Film Festival as it was for McCade.

DGA After Rights
(Continued from page 174)

"endeavor" to limit the cuts a network elects to make for airing of theatrical films. In the 1987 talks, the DGA will press for guarantees that no theatrical film will be licensed for tv without a stipulation that cuts may not be made to accommodate format or the start of adjacent news programs, but only to conform with standards and practices.

Beatty's concerns over tv editing of "Reds," the Mosk opinion disclosed, prompted Diller to delay execution of the ABC contract for "almost a year" after it was drawn up. Mosk revealed that for more than a year Beatty communicated his concerns to ABC and Paramount. "The evidence was clear," stated Mosk, "that ABC particularly was concerned about what it deemed to be lack of cooperation on the part of Beatty in its efforts to edit the film for television."

Mosk supported Beatty's claim that from the outset he objected to cuts made only to shorten the playing time. Beatty acknowledged that the political nature of "Reds" prompted him to take unusual precautions against gratuitous editing.

In addition to Beatty and Silverstein, other members of the DGS creative rights committee are Milos Forman, Mark Rydell, Jonathan Demme, Sidney Furie, James Goldstone, Arthur Hiller, Lou Antonio, Hy Averback, Jack Cooper, William Crain, Jeffrey Hayden, Jeremy Paul Kagan, Arnold Laven, Alan Myerson, Alex Singer and Paul Stanley.

Midterm Series
(Continued from page 1)

shows. Main reason for the onslaught of new entries was the obvious fact that most of the frosh from last September failed, and the networks sought replacements which would fill the gaps.

But not much of that occurred despite the plethora of new shows, most rejected by the public in the Nielsens. Top-rated new series was "Crazy Like A Fox" on CBS-TV, ranked in a tie for 10th in season numbers.

Beyond that, the pickings are meager. ABC-TV's "Hail To The Chief" rated sixth nationally in its first showing, but dropped sharply later.

All those midseason series made little impact on the numbers game despite the proliferation of shows. In the weekly Nielsens, CBS' "Double Dare" was 31st; ABC's "Mr. Belvedere," 44th; NBC's "Under One Roof," 46th.

NBC's "Half Nelson" rated 52d, CBS' "Detective In The House," 53d; NBC's "Sara," 54th. CBS' "Lucie Arnaz Show" had a dismal 57th; ABC's "Eye To Eye" 63d, same network's "Wildside," 64th; ABC's "Off The Rack" 66th, its "Me & Mom," 68th.

Despite the large turnover, no network could truly point with pride to the numbers of most of its late-starters. ABC's "MacGruder & Loud" is 43d in seasonal numbers; other late beginners are NBC's "Double Trouble," 51st; "Half Nelson," 56th; "Street Hawk" (ABC) 54th; "Moonlighting" (ABC), 61st; "Off The Rack" (ABC) 70th; "Code Name: Foxfire" (NBC) 71st; "Spencer" (NBC) 73d; "Otherworld" (CBS) 92d; "Berrenger's" (NBC) 95th.

Coronet Going Foldo
(Continued from page 1)

ther in this project," Koltai said.

He disparaged the SLS project as it now stands. He said none of the dozen Luxembourgeoise and European financial institutions with shares in SLS had "the slightest experience in television."

By contrast, he said, Coronet was headed by Tom Whitehead, a former chief of the U.S. Office of Telecommunications Policy in the early 1970s and later prime force behind the world's first tv broadcast satellite, the Galaxy, while prexy of Hugh Communications, a subsid of Hughes Aerospace.

In addition, Koltai said, Coronet was backed by the world's biggest cable tv operation, the feevee service Home Box Office.

'Small Hope'

However, Koltai would not say Coronet was irrevocably dead. He said there is only "a very small hope" of a change of conditions in Luxembourg or for a shift to another country with available tv satellite frequency authorizations.

Coronet still holds leverage on the European scene, having placed options on a RCA telecommunications satellite and for a fall 1986 date on the Arianspace launcher.

Coronet maintains it has reserved the only available bird that SLS could use if it wants to compete in a crucial period when France is planning to orbit a direct broadcasting satellite, TDF-1, Turner Broadcasting is seeking to penetrate the European market and other ideas for European-wide satellite operations are afloat.

According to Coronet spokesman Mario Hirsch, a Luxembourger, "SLS officials say they cannot now make decisions on the RCA satellite and the Ariane option that would prejudge future possible developments. SLS is still doing a feasibility study, which is the stage Coronet was at a year ago. It's a big question whether SLS is capable of taking over from us."

DO SOMETHING

When the cry went out to do something about the suffering in Ethiopia, some very concerned school children were among the first to respond.

It wasn't easy. Many were inner city students who had little money to give. Yet they collected over $200,000. And donated it through Save the Children to help the children in Ethiopia.

Wednesday night, April 24, on ABC's "20/20," you'll meet some of these school children. You'll also see how Save the Children is using the money they raised to save lives.

For over 50 years, Save the Children has been among the first to respond

Watch ABC's "20/20" Wed. night April 24* to see how you can help Save the Children bring life and hope to Ethiopian children.

*Check local listing for time and channel.

©1985 SAVE THE CHILDREN FEDERATION, INC.

to human suffering and need. Today in Ethiopia and other drought-stricken countries in Africa, we're providing emergency assistance, medical care and food. But as you'll see on ABC Wednesday night, that's not nearly enough.

The only way to silence the cries of hunger once and for all in suffering African nations is to attack the problem at its roots. With long-term self-help programs in food production, nutrition and education. We've proven these programs work in other countries. They can work here too. But only if *you* do something.

Here's What You Can Do
Save the Children,
African Emergency Fund
50 Wilton Road
Westport, Connecticut 06880
Attn: David L. Guyer, President

☐ I want to help save the children. Here's my tax-deductible contribution for
☐ $25 ☐ $50 ☐ $100
☐ $1,000 ☐ Other:_____

☐ Also, please send information on your worldwide sponsorship programs.

VA 4/24/5

Name_____
Address_____
City_____
State_____ Zip_____

Save the Children®

H'WOOD CLOSE, BUT NO GOLD RING

12 PIX FOR '89
Tri-Star Doubles In-House Prod'n To Hike B.O. Share
By WILL TUSHER

Tri-Star Pictures, which admittedly has nowhere to go but up in domestic boxoffice rankings, is pinning its hopes for a 1989 breakthrough on a quantum leap in in-house production.

Jeff Sagansky, beginning his fifth year as Tri-Star production president, disclosed to *Daily Variety* over the weekend that the company is moving from five in-house productions released in 1988 to more than twice that many, 12, in 1989.

With the majority of product to be filmed in-house, Sagansky reasons, Tri-Star will be less at the mercy of pickups in which it has little or no creative or conceptual input: thus, for the first time in the company's history, it will be largely in control of its own destiny — and fortunes.

He admits to a gut feeling that Tri-Star is overdue for a blockbuster, and he looks for one or more out of six "excellent" 1989 releases to rescue Tri-Star from its estimated 6% market share in 1988, representing a consistent, if not massive slide, from 7.7% in 1986

(Continued on Page 8, Column 3)

Pastor New Prez For CBS/Fox Vid

Rafael Pastor

CBS/Fox Video has recruited Rafael Pastor to take over the post of president, CBS/Fox Video International, replacing Ralston Coffin, who's resigned that post to pursue other interests.

Pastor comes to the homevid joint venture from CBS Inc., where he was recently associate general counsel, handling a variety of business and corporate matters. He's a rare example of a CBS/Fox exec who's been recruited directly out of the CBS half of the joint-venture ownership.

Pastor is assigned to oversee all international operations, including marketing, field sales, administration, operations, credit and finance. The international division operates subsids in the U.K., Germany, Spain, Australia, France and Japan and sub-licenses product into numerous other countries.

Palmieri Attacks Fox' Arguments

U.S. District Court Judge Edmund Palmieri in New York last week rebutted claims by 20th Century Fox that it was wrongfully denied a jury trial in the blockbooking conviction and $500,000 fine the studio is now appealing.

Inability to obtain a jury trial and the doctrine of holding an employer responsible for the actions of employes who allegedly acted on their own initiative — when they broke the law in violation of company policy — are expected to be the major premises of the Fox appeal.

Fox over the weekend confirmed that it has until Feb. 1 to file briefs with the Second Circuit U.S. Court of Appeals in New York. An initial hearing before that tribunal has been scheduled tentatively for the week of March 27.

In a supplementary opinion handed down last Thursday, Palmieri struck out at Fox' argument that lack of a jury trial constitutes grounds for appeal. The issues of a jury trial and employer accountabil-

(Continued on Page 39, Column 1)

Worldvision Names Abrams Sr. Veepee

Elliott Abrams has joined Worldvision Enterprises in the newly created post of senior v.p., acquisitions, with a mandate to make the distributor a significant player in the acquisition of films for worldwide distribution — an area the company has previously eschewed.

Abrams begins today and comes to Worldvision from ITC Entertainment in New York, where he was senior executive v.p. He joined ITC as exec v.p., acquisitions in 1984

(Continued on Page 39, Column 5)

PATRICK GIVEN BUSH'S VOTE TO KEEP FCC GAVEL
By PAUL HARRIS

WASHINGTON — Dennis Patrick will remain as chairman of the Federal Communications Commission "for the foreseeable future" under the Bush administration, a top aide for the president-elect said here last Friday.

This assurance was offered by Chase Untermeyer, assistant for the president-elect for personnel, in response to questions about Patrick's status. Meanwhile, the FCC topper repeated assertions that he has "no intention of leaving at the present time," and that he'll participate in an active Commission agenda that includes "several major broadcast policy reforms."

Patrick's future has been the subject of rampant speculation as a parade of potential appointees to the agency continues to jockey for favor with Bush's transition team. Numerous names have surfaced in connection with the agency's two

(Continued on Page 35, Column 1)

Indies Outpace Major Producers For Tv Season
By DAVE KAUFMAN

Independent tv producers have maintained their edge over major suppliers in Hollywood as a new year begins, the indies retaining their dominance despite the midseason changes and primetime network reshuffling dictated at least in part by the writers strike.

Indies have 27½ hours on primetime at midterm, as compared to 20½ hours from the majors. That compares with 30½ for indies and

(Continued on Page 39, Column 3)

Nugent Enters Pact With Dick Clark Prods.

Tony-winning legit producer Nelle Nugent has entered into an exclusive deal with Dick Clark Prods. to develop and produce tv series and telefilms.

Nugent has been an independent producer at both Walt Disney Prods. and Phoenix Entertainment but has been most active as a producer on Broadway, where her credits include Tony winners "Nicholas Nickleby," "The Elephant Man," "Dracula," "Morning's At Seven" and "Amadeus."

Most recent vidpic credits are CBS-TV's "A Conspiracy Of Love" and "A Fighting Choice" for the Disney Sunday Movie when it was on ABC.

Falls Three Pix Short In '88 Of Release Record; Warners, Cannon Pace Distributors
By LAWRENCE COHN

NEW YORK — New feature films released in the U.S. during 1988 totaled 513, pulling nearly even with 1987's record pace of 515 openings. Frequent leader Warner Bros. encored as most prolific distributor with 25 releases (up from 17 the previous year) while Cannon Releasing led indies with 23 film debuts in America.

Accompanying charts detailing the types and sources of new pix in the marketplace reflect a surprising steadiness in the flow of films, withstanding outside forces such as the October 1987 stock market crash.

The traditional major distributors bounced back with 161 new film releases, almost a 20% increase from last year, and continued their recent movement away from foreign or specialized films with 146 of the 161 titles (over 90%) constituting U.S.-produced fiction features.

The indie distribs collectively exhibited some of the retrenchment caused by difficulties in the financial sector, with a decline of 8% in releases to 352 for the year. The level of indie imports of foreign films was virtually identical with that of 1987, while American-made indie releases dropped by 10% from 1987's peak of 200 titles to 179 for the year. Main portion of that drop was due to De Laurentiis Entertainment Group's absence; DEG released 10 films (including its "Evil Dead 2" through erstwhile Rosebud Releasing) in 1987 but was gone in 1988.

Other steep declines include drops in output from Cannon, New World, Skouras and New Century/Vista, while among foreign film importers, New Yorker and IFEX were considerably less active. Statistically, there were enough new faces (e.g., Avenue Pictures and in-and-out of distribution Kings Road and RAI/Sacis) to keep the level of pix from indie distribs

(Continued on Page 34, Column 1)

COIN FOR PERFORMERS
Sinatra Pushes For New Royalty
By JEAN ROSENBLUTH

Frank Sinatra has signed on to lead a major drive to secure a performance royalty for performers.

As one of the founders of the tentatively titled Performers Rights Society of America, Sinatra is enlisting the aid of several other big-name recording stars and their record companies to get legislation passed that would grant a performance royalty to artists as well as songwriters and their publishers.

Contrary to popular belief, non-songwriter singers and musicians receive no compensation when a recording to which they contributed is played on the radio or on a jukebox.

"If this is going to succeed, the entertainers have to organize, and Frank has agreed to seed the effort," said Robert A. Finkelstein, Sinatra's lawyer and one of the co-founders of the nascent org, which will be nonprofit.

"Frank sent out letters last week to a number of top entertainers, and we've already had meetings with members of Congress. The timetable is now."

Finkelstein said the group has approached all the major labels and several music-industry orgs seeking their support. According to the attorney, the local American Federation of Television & Radio Artists has already agreed to help the effort, and many of the diskeries and the Recording Industry Association of America "have indicated that they are looking favorably upon our proposal."

Long History

The history of efforts to gain a performance royalty for performers is a long and tortuous one. In 1965, most of the major labels began what would ultimately prove to be a fruitless attempt to get such legislation passed.

Eleven years later, when the copyright statute was revised into the Copyright Act of 1976, Congress not only failed to grant performers a

(Continued on Page 8, Column 1)

Extras Guild Posts Another Loss In '88
By DAVID ROBB

Financially troubled Screen Extras Guild continues to bleed red ink but in 1988 managed to cut its annual deficit in half compared to the preceding year.

For fiscal year 1988 (ended Oct. 31), SEG shows a deficit of $120,861. SEG's deficit in 1987 was twice that, or $241,256. Deficit in 1986 was another $232,489. Deficit in 1985 was $20,080.

SEG's income was down $43,370 in 1988 compared to 1987 — from $772,605 in 1987 to $729,235 in

(Continued on Page 39, Column 4)

VARIETY

NEWSPAPER
Second Class P.O. Entry
$2.25

A CAHNERS BUSINESS NEWSPAPER | USPS 656-960 | 02371 | NEW YORK, NOVEMBER 15, 1989 | THE INTERNATIONAL ENTERTAINMENT WEEKLY | $2.75 Canada | £2.25 UK

RUFFLED HARE AIRS RICH BITCH

East German tv shames West with candid Wall coverage

W. German pubcasters victims of inflexible scheduling; once-staid East suddenly critical

By ERNEST GILL

Berlin The sweeping changes that have shaken the foundations of the Berlin Wall are being accompanied by revolutionary changes in East Germany's approach to broadcast news.

The country's staid state-run radio and tv operations have been

---
B.o. bonanza as liberated East Germans go for porn pix ... 11
---

transformed into vanguards of investigative journalism.

The clincher came this weekend when the Wall finally cracked and hundreds of thousands of East Germans streamed into West Germany on an extended spree of shopping, sightseeing and general merry-making.

As news teams in West Germany gaped in bewilderment, East German tv news went live with non-stop coverage of the dramatic events, complete with live interviews with guards as they hacked

The Wall comes tumbling down

away at the Berlin Wall.

West Germany's major public and commercial broadcasters, locked into rigid programming schedules, failed to provide much more than the occasional news

Turn to page 35

Writer of el foldo 'Rapture' lashes out at N.Y. Times' powerful legit critic

By RICHARD HUMMLER

New York The dominant power of The New York Times, a perennial subject of controversy in the U.S. theater community, has gained new relevance this season as Times critic Frank Rich and new second-stringer Laurie Winer have gone on a spree of negative and increasingly biting reviews.

A challenge to Rich, charging that he is "irresponsible" in his refusal to acknowledge the consequences of his reviews within the legit profession, came last week from English playwright David Hare. In a sharply worded and articulately argued Nov. 5 letter to Rich, dispatched after the Times critic declined to meet with him, Hare assailed Rich for what he called a "dishonest" review of Hare's "The Secret Rapture," which folded quickly after Rich's negative notice in the Times.

The text of Hare's letter was released last week by the N.Y. Shakespeare Festival. Hare with-

Critic nixed: The clout of The New York Times and its top legit critic, Frank Rich (left), has aroused the rancor of legit professionals, playwright David Hare (right) included

drew permission for it to be published in VARIETY after a letter of reply from Rich was read to him in London. The playwright touched on the chief points raised in his let-

ter in a telephone interview.

"I think Rich is totally irresponsible in the use of his power. He started out (in 1980) as a fresh and interesting new critic, but he seems to have gotten more bitter and to have less and less regard for the impact of what he writes. I felt it was unforgivable of him to review a play he ostensibly admired in such a way as to make sure it closed.

"There is an unmistakable personal nastiness in what he writes, a series of *ad hominem* attacks that

Turn to page 5

VID BIZ TAKES SOME BIG STEPS IN SELL-THRU, SPONSORS

'Lethal Weapon' only 2d R-rated low-priced vid; 'When Harry Met Sally' to carry a commercial

By TOM BIERBAUM

Hollywood The vid industry moved a couple of important steps down the sell-through and sponsorship roads Nov. 13.

Warner Home Video confirmed it is going the sell-through route on "Lethal Weapon 2" and Nelson Entertainment announced a Diet Sprite sponsorship on the December release of "When Harry Met Sally."

Industry sources say other announcements are believed to be imminent on a mid-February release of Paramount Home Video's "Indiana Jones And The Last Crusade," possibly to be sponsored by one of the Coca-Cola brands, and on a mid-March release of "Honey, I Shrunk The Kids," sponsor as yet unknown. Both are expected to carry a sell-through suggested retail price in the area of $24.95.

All of this comes just as WHV's "Batman" video, a landmark release on both the sell-through and sponsorship fronts, hits vidstore shelves (see story, Page 31).

As is now almost expected on major-title sell-through, reports are starting to come in on some outlets breaking street date on the "Batman" release.

A Warner spokesman said the company received "scattered" reports of stores not waiting till the Nov. 15 release date. The company was trying to pull any tapes offered prior to Nov. 15.

Reports circulating Nov. 14 included word of a Southern California grocery store chain and an east

Turn to page 2

$600-mil NBA web deal in search of winner; big pricetag, bigger risk

By JOHN LIPPMAN

New York The only winners in NBC's record $600-million deal for the new National Basketball Assn. contract appears to be basketball players and league franchise owners.

That is the Monday-morning quarterbacking from analysts and web execs — except NBC execs, of course — who were still shaking their heads at the treble rights fee ponied up by NBC in a fierce battle with CBS for a new NBA contract. ABC, once the Mike Tyson of sports among webs, did not even break bread at the negotiating table.

NBA league players will see their paychecks increase from an average of $750,000 to $1-million, the league concedes, while one web honcho predicts the value of every NBA franchise shot up $20-25-million overnight.

In an ironic twist of reasoning,

Turn to page 4

46

TOP STORIES

Disney peaks again   9
For fifth straight year, Walt Disney Co. sees record income, revenues.

'Batman' bows on vid   31
Pic a potent weapon in sell-through crusade.

Comedy Channel launches   40
About 4-million subscribers set; competing HA! to debut in April.

Resorts Intl. restructures   49
Companies, on way to bankruptcy, propose refinancing.

Tax break on B'way   53
IRS clarifies writeoffs for investors in flop shows.

261

distribution of the $50,000,000 generated by "We Are the World," with $10 million worth of emergency supplies furnished to the eight African nations hit hardest by famine.

The key phrase of a November 15, 1989, article was "revolutionary changes." Sometimes the changes were in terms of consumerism, such as the shift from old Coca-Cola to "New Coke" or "Coke Classic." Reagan's mantra of deregulation meant that there were no time limits on TV commercials, so the thirty-minute-long "infomercial" was born, as were fifteen-second-long blurbs. But many of the era's changes were on a grander scale, involving sexual equality, as well as cultural shifts and major technology changes.

In the 1970s and 1980s, the gay community suffered a series of setbacks, humiliations, and outrages that eventually led to solidarity and power.

While the gay community had been brought together in the 1970s by the Anita Bryant and Harvey Milk crises, AIDS proved even more devastating—and even more uniting.

In the July 23, 1985, issue of *Daily Variety*, Army Archerd's column ran on page two, as usual. It began with a 116-word item saying that Rock Hudson had flown to Paris, to the Institut Pasteur, which "has been very active in research on Acquired Immune Deficiency Syndrome." Archerd concluded with the statement, "Doctors warn that the dread disease (AIDS) is going to reach catastrophic proportions in all communities if a cure is not soon found. . . ."

The item was brief but powerful and was picked up by news outlets

Above: Michael Jackson.

around the world. To many, it was shocking, and the first time that people could put a face to a scary disease, a "gay cancer," that only happened "to other people."

On December 27, 1985, *Daily Variety* ran a story that an industry seminar had attempted to quell misconceptions.

"Many in Hollywood—particularly actors—have become concerned that AIDS may be transmitted during film and TV kissing scenes. The Screen Actors Guild in October went as far as to require producers to notify actors in advance if 'open-mouth kissing' will be required in scenes—this to allow concerned actors to turn down such roles if they so choose."

For years afterward, because families and loved ones of AIDS victims refused to acknowledge the true cause of their deaths, whether from being ashamed or for other reasons, *Variety* ran obits of people who died of "undisclosed causes" or "heart failure." One exception was Broadway director-choreographer Michael Bennett, who was reported as dying of AIDS-related lymphoma. Other unconfirmed but suspected AIDS-related deaths during the 1980s included Peter Allen, Dack Rambo, Anthony Perkins, Liberace, and Freddie Mercury.

On September 17, 1991, *Daily Variety* reported that executives Sid Sheinberg and Barry Diller had asked AIDS Project Los Angeles to establish Hollywood Supports, a program to help Hollywood understand the disease "and send a clear, unmistakable message that AIDS-related discrimination of any kind is simply not allowed."

At the announcement, actor Bruce Davison spoke about the death of actor Brad Davis (1978's *Midnight Express*). In Davis's writings and according to his widow, Susan Bluestein, Davis felt it was necessary to seek medical care under false names, pay for his care out of his own pocket rather than through insurance, and otherwise keep his illness a secret in order to continue his career.

But on the other, gayer hand, *Weekly Variety* on July 18, 1985, chronicled the opening of the musical *La Cage aux Folles*, proclaiming it "the first hit Broadway tuner about a romantic relationship between men." Other gay-related theater pieces of that time included William Hoffman's *As Is* (1985), Robert Chesley's *Night Sweat* (1986), and Larry Kramer's *The Normal Heart* (1985), which directly addressed AIDS, a topic major Hollywood studios avoided until 1993's Oscar-winning *Philadelphia*. One step forward, one step back . . .

There has always been a lot of pop-culture crap, and the 1980s didn't have a higher percentage than previous decades. There was just more available. Cable TV offered a cornucopia of channels filled with forgettable shows, video cassettes offered countless shelves of bad films and TV series for rental, and music videos let mediocre-but-attractive people have their fifteen minutes of fame.

Despite the clutter, a few musical acts stood head and shoulders above

Above: Madonna.

the rest, such as Michael Jackson, Madonna, Prince, David Bowie, and Bruce Springsteen.

Beginning in the 1970s, industry favorite Springsteen wrote and sang about heartland yearnings and heartaches, all with a non-condescending attitude toward blue-collar/Jersey workers. His breakthrough 1984 album, *Born in the U.S.A.*, sold fifteen million copies in the States. Coupled with the United States' hosting of the Olympics in Los Angeles and a sense of general prosperity, Americans were feeling proud of their country for the first time in decades. Interestingly, the album's title song was misinterpreted as a flag-waver and was seized on by politicians and corporations to tout their agendas and products.

An August 8, 1984, *Variety* was ecstatic about Springsteen's four-hour concert. Reviewer Ken (aka Ken Terry) said before the concert started,

> "The crowd exploded in unified shouts of 'Bru-u-uce, Bru-u-uce!' When he appeared, the applause sounded like Niagara Falls. The audience sang along almost all through the first number. . . . Springsteen's legendary rapport with his audience stems from his ability to get them to identify with him and with his story-song characters, and he milked it to the limit on numerous numbers. Audience participation figures greatly in his act."

Also setting off rabid fan reaction was Michael Jackson, whose 1982 *Thriller* spawned seven hit singles and sold an estimated sixty to one hundred million copies in the decades since its release.

Jackson's appeal crossed all boundaries of race, sex, and age. Fannie Hurst's 1933 novel *Imitation of Life*, which was filmed in 1934 and again in 1959, featured a young black woman who tries to pass as white. The 1980s provided a sharp contrast, as middle-class white kids began to dress and speak like the black stars they loved. However, everyone seemed to like Jackson, including parents. Since youngsters are genetically programmed to love music that revolts against their elders, they embraced rap music, which perfectly fit the bill.

Rappers like NWA, Jay-Z, Snoop Dogg, and 2pac/Tupac borrowed from such diverse influences as Blondie, James Brown, Gil Scott-Heron ("The Revolution Will Not Be Televised"), beatnik poetry, and protest songs. Rap performers, mostly black, sang-spoke about their anger at the establishment, and their sexual urges. Parents were horrified, which made the music even more popular.

Also raising parental angst were heavy metal rockers. Ozzy Osbourne, Metallica, and Judas Priest were involved in legal battles as parents blamed them for the suicides of some children. Black Sabbath and Led Zeppelin had paved the way for heavy metal in previous years, but the 1980s saw new life for the genre, with Megadeth, Metallica, Mötley Crüe, Twisted Sister, Anthrax, and Poison benefiting from music videos.

A *Weekly Variety* column of October 8, 1980, addressed a two-day seminar titled "What the Devil's Wrong with Rock Music?" in Pekin, Illinois. Some one thousand people were expected to show up at the First Assembly of God Church to smash records by artists such as Alice Cooper, Black Sabbath, John Denver, and the Bee Gees. Jim and Steve Peters, ministers at Zion Life Center in St. Paul, Minnesota, had taken their anti-rock crusade to about forty cities and explained that "the lyrics, lifestyles and intentions of many rock musicians are perverted, atheistic, homosexual, and push satanism, sex and anti-Biblical schools of thought."

Country was exploding on the music scene. The March 31, 1981, *Daily Variety* quoted a Country Music Association radio survey finding that 2,907 radio stations were programming country music, a 21 percent increase over the previous year. There were

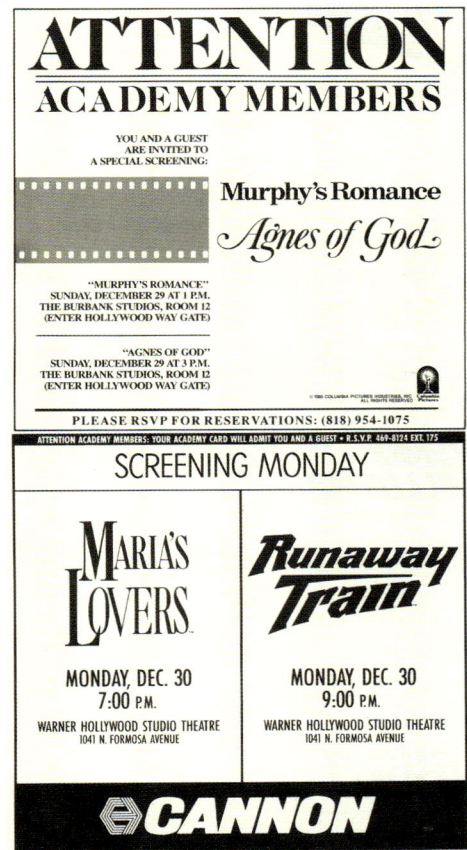

Above: Attention!

Right: 3-D Matt Groening and 2-D Bart Simpson.

Left: Bruce Springsteen.

1,785 full-time country stations in the United States (a 16.3 percent increase from the previous year), "while those carrying country between 12 and 15 hours a day increased by a whopping 54.3% over last year."

It was also a decade of *Rambo*, Arnold Schwarzenegger, Chuck Norris, Jean-Claude van Damme (aka "the Muscles from Brussels"), *Staying Alive* (in which director Stallone transformed John Travolta's body), Hulk Hogan, and *Top Gun* (in which the flying sequences were upstaged by the studly stars' shirtless volleyball game). In other words, it was the decade when straight men discovered the joy of pecs.

Pop-culture snobs fretted over musical and film offerings that are now fondly remembered by those in Generation X, including John Hughes movies, *Dirty Dancing*, *Risky Business*, *Ghostbusters*, *Teenage Mutant Ninja Turtles*, New Kids on the Block, Menudo, and TV's *Saved by the Bell*.

So were the 1980s a cultural wasteland? Iconic TV shows included *Hill Street Blues*, *L.A. Law*, *Cheers*, *Dallas* (with the "Who Shot J.R." episode chalking up a record eighty-three million viewers), *Dynasty*, *The Golden Girls*, *The Simpsons*, and *The Cosby Show*, which had a familiar setup of a sitcom centering upon a family, but with the twist that these were upper-middle-class blacks—in other words, it was traditional and radical at the same time.

PBS and the broadcast networks, inspired by the success of *Roots*, scheduled ambitious miniseries: *Brideshead Revisited* and *Shogun* (1981), *The Jewel in the Crown* (1984), *Winds of War* (1983), and its sequel, *War and Remembrance* (1988).

On the film side, Steven Spielberg followed his *Jaws* phenom with another phenom, *E.T. the Extra-Terrestrial* (1982). In the same year, Martin Scorsese's *Raging Bull* became one of the most admired and influential films of the decade.

The decade featured breakthrough films from Peter Weir, Oliver Stone, Stephen Frears, Ingmar Bergman, and Woody Allen, while theater offered works by Alan Ayckbourn, Alan Bennett, and August Wilson, in addition to the Brit mega-musicals such as *Cats*, *Les Misérables*, *The Phantom of the Opera*, and *Miss Saigon*.

And in the 1980s, *Variety* went through its own revolutionary changes. Ever since its founding in 1905, the paper had been owned and run by the Silverman family. But in 1987, on July 14 (Bastille Day, a day of revolution!), *Daily Variety* reported that *Weekly* and *Daily* were being sold.

The story by Tom Gerard began, "Family-owned *Variety* and *Daily Variety* are being acquired in full by Cahners Publishing Co., a subsidiary of London's publicly traded Reed International PLC."

Cahners, based in Massachusetts, was the U.S. arm of Reed International, described as "a publishing, paper and packaging, manufacturing and transportation conglomerate, with revenues of approximately $3 billion dollars in 1986."

New *Variety* editor Roger Watkins introduced color to the paper. And plans were begun for the use of computers in 1991—very late for a news org, but the previous regime was accustomed to doing things in the way they'd been done in 1905, with cigarette-smoking reporters pounding away at manual typewriters.

The switch was only the beginning of major changes for the news organization—and for the entire entertainment industry—about to experience a major tech revolution in the 1990s.

Orson Welles Dies At L.A. Home, Yul Brynner in N.Y.

Death has once again claimed more than one major showbusiness personality at virtually the same moment. Both Orson Welles and Yul Brynner died yesterday. They appeared together in the long-forgotten Yugoslavian film, "The Battle Of The Neretva," and a friend recalled yesterday that the two men were once stuck in a snowbound taxi for 15 hours while trying to leave the location for Christmas.

Orson Welles

By TODD McCARTHY

Orson Welles, the prodigious creator of "Citizen Kane," "Chimes At Midnight," "The War Of The Worlds" and several landmark stage productions, who spent much of his life living down the fact that he had conquered the worlds of radio, theater and films by the time he was 25, died yesterday at his home in Hollywood. He was 70 years old.

Despite the assortment of health problems that had plagued him for years, Welles had been in robust health of late and had been working vigorously on numerous projects.

The actor-director-writer-orator-

(Continued on Page 2, Column 3)

Yul Brynner

By RICHARD HUMMLER

New York, Oct. 10 — Yul Brynner, legit and film star whose portrayal of the role of the King of Siam in Rodgers & Hammerstein's "The King & I" achieved legendary status, died early this morning in N.Y. Hospital-Cornell Medical Center.

Death resulted from "multiple complications that came as a result of what was originally cancer," according to a statement from his press rep firm, Solters/Roskin/Friedman. Brynner's passport listed him at 65, though various reference books put his age at 70.

The bald, virile actor contracted

(Continued on Page 22, Column 1)

(Continued from Page 1, Column 2)

lung cancer several years ago and underwent treatment at a West German clinic, which enabled him to resume stage performances of "The King & I." The show finished a virtual capacity return engagement on Broadway June 30, grossing a whopping $605,546 in its final week, an alltime single-week Broadway legit boxoffice record.

Few actors in showbiz history became so identified with a single role as was Brynner with the part of the gruff and stubborn 19th century Siamese monarch whose heart and social attitudes are softened by the tempering influence of an English widow hired as a court teacher.

The original stage musical was developed by Rodgers & Hammerstein from the book "Anna And The King Of Siam," by Margaret Landon, as a vehicle for Gertrude Lawrence.

Brynner, a sometime stage actor then working as a director in the early years of live television, impressed the stage-wise authors by auditioning with gypsy folk songs to his guitar accompaniment and was seized as the welcome answer to a knotty casting problem.

"The King & I," with an ironclad Hammerstein libretto and a score brimming with R&H song gems, was a solid Broadway hit in 1951, running three years and 1246 performances. Brynner, who won a 1952 Tony as best supporting actor, stayed with the show throughout the Broadway run and took it on tour, leaving in August 1955.

Oscar, Too

He then went to Hollywood to repeat his role in the 1956 20th Fox film version, costarring with Deborah Kerr (vocally covered by Marni Nixon). Brynner won the Academy Award as best actor and a longrunning career as a screen leading man was launched.

He was born Taidje Khan in Sakhalin, an island north of Japan, to a Mongolian father and a Gypsy mother, who died during his birth. His father, a mining engineer, changed the family name to Brynner. The son spent part of his childhood in China, then moved to France, where he became a cabaret singer and a circus performer.

He worked for some five years with a number of European circuses, performing as an acrobat and trapeze clown, then joined the Theatre des Mathurins as a trainee director.

His first Broadway appearance, as "Youl Bryner," was in the Chekhov Players' production of "Twelfth Night" at the Little Theater, Dec. 2, 1941, for a puny 15-performance run. Returning to England, he appeared in several London productions.

During World War II he worked as a French-speaking radio announcer and commentator for the U.S. Office of War Information. His first major Broadway role was the 1945-46 production of "Lute Song," in which Mary Martin starred.

In 1948 he returned to the U.S. and switched careers by becoming a much-in-demand television director, mainly for CBS.

Fast on the heels of the film release of "King & I" in 1956 came Par's Cecil B. DeMille remake of "The Ten Commandments," in which Brynner played a fierce pharaoh Ramses.

There followed a long string of starring parts in such films as "Anastasia," "The Brothers Karamazov," "The Buccaneer," "The Journey," "The Sound & The Fury" (in which he wore a wig), "Solomon & Sheba," "Once More With Feeling" (an untypical contempo romantic comedy) and "Surprise Package."

In 1960 Brynner was topbilled in the John Sturges Western which has achieved cult status, "The Magnificent Seven." The quality of his films began to diminish in the 1960s, which saw him in such pix as "Taras Bulba," "Flight From Ashiya," "Invitation To A Gunfighter," "The Saboteur," "Cast A Giant Shadow," "Return Of The Seven," "The Long Duel," "Villa Rides," "The Madwoman Of Chailot," and "The File of The Golden Goose."

More programmer-type films followed in the 1970s including "Romance Of A Horsethief," "Adios Sabata," "Catlow" and "Fuzz." In 1973 he played a futuristic gunfighter in the sci-fi "Westworld," later sequeled in "Futureworld" (1976).

Flop Odyssey

In 1975 he returned to legit as the star of a musical version of Homer's "Odyssey," which had a big-grossing national tour, but was a one-night flop on Broadway under the title "Home Sweet Homer."

In 1977 producers Lee Guber and Shelley Gross organized a revival of "The King & I," with Brynner reprising his role and now the unquestioned star and boxoffice magnet of the show.

Brynner took the show to London's Palladium in June 1979, where it was also a huge grosser and played for over a year. He returned to the U.S. touring circuit and generated enormous business everywhere, culminating in the farewell engagement on Broadway last season.

Brynner's financial deal with "King" may have been an alltime legit record. He recevied 50% of the net profits and 15% of the weekly gross receipts, netting him approximately $8,000,000. In all he played the role of the King for 4625 performances.

For the past 13 years he was a member of the U.S. High Commission for Refugees, for whom he made docu films and published a book, "Bring Forth The Children." He was married four times, to Virginia Gilmore, Doris Kleiner, Jacqueline de Croisset and Kathy Lee, a dancer in the "King & I" company, who survives him.

Also survived by four children, Rock, Victoria, Mia and Melody. The funeral service will be private, and a memorial service is being arranged. In lieu of flowers, family suggests any donations be sent to the Yul Brynner Cancer Fund for Children, Memorial-Sloane Kettering Cancer Center, N.Y.

FILM PRODUCTION CHART

(Continued from Page 10, Column 5)

CAM, Ennio Guarnieri; PD, Gianni Quaranta; SND, Roberto Forrest; DISTRIB,Cannon.

PING PONG (Picture Palace/Film Four Intl.) 9/2, London. **David Yip, Lucy Sheen, Robert Lee, Lam Fung, Ric Young, Barbara Yu Ling, Victor Khan, Rex Wei, Hi Ching**
PROD, Malcolm Craddock, Michael Guest; DIR, Po Chih Leong; AD, John O'Connor; SCR, Jerry Liu; CAM, Nic Knowland; ED, David Spiers; PD, Colin Pigott; SET, Bryony Foster; SND, John Midgley; UPM, Annie Rees; CAST, John Hubbard.

THE PINK CHIQUITAS (SC Entertainment Corp., 416-483-0850) 9/15, Toronto. **Frank Stallone, Bruce Pirrie, Liz Edwards, Cindy Valentine, Claudia Udy, Diana Platts, Gerald Isaac, John Hemphill, Don Lake, Laura Robinson**
EXP, Syd Cappe; PROD-CAM, Nick Stiliadis; AP, George Flak, Carl Zittrer; DIR-SCR, Anthony Currie; ART, Danny Addario; SND, Gord Thompson; UPM, Michael Kennedy; P, Prudence Emery; CAST, Karen Hazzard; DISTRIB, Shapiro Entertainment Corp.

POLICE ACADEMY III (WB) 9/1, Toronto. **Bubba Smith, Michael Winslow, David Graf, Art Metrano, Steve Guttenberg, George Gaynes, Debralee Scott, Shawn Wetherly, Tim Kazurinsky, Brian Tochi, Brant Van Hoffman**
PROD, Paul Maslansky; AP, Don West; DIR, Jerry Paris; SCR, Eugene Quintano; CAM, Bob Sadd; ED, Bud Molin; PD, Trevor Williams; ART, Rhiley Fuller; SET, Sean Kirby; COS, Aleida MacDonald; SND, David Lee; UPM Suzanne Lore; P, Howard Brandy; DISTRIB, WB.

POMPEII (Vestron) 9/16, Rome. **Sybil Danning, Donald Pleasence, Stasia Micula, Richard Hill**
EXP, Harry Alan Towers: PROD-DIR, Chuck Vincent; AP-UPM, Per Sjostedt; SCR, Rick Marx.

THE RIGHT HAND MAN (Yarra Man Film Prods.) 10/9, Bathurst, New South Wales. **Rupert Everett, Hugo Weaving, Arthur Dignam, Jennifer Claire, Catherine McClements**
PROD, Steven Grives, Tom Oliver, Basil Appleby; DIR, Di Drew; AD, Phil Rich; SCR, Helen Hodgman; CAM, Peter James; ED, Don Saunders; PD, Neil Angwin; ART, Nic Hepworth; SET, Annette Reid; COS, Graham Purcell; SND, Syd Butterworth; UPM, Renate Wilson; P, Elizabeth Johnson Pty, The Michael Dalling Co.; CAST, Liz Mullinar; DISTRIB, New World.

SID AND NANCY LOVE KILLS (Zenith Prod.) 9/30, London, U.S. **Gary Oldman, Chloe Webb, David Hayman, Drew Schofield, Tony London, Perry Benson, Debby Bishop, Ann Lambton, Kathy Burke, Mark Monero, Michelle Winstanley, Graham Fletcher Cook, Jude Alderson, Sara Sugarman, James Snell**
PROD, Eric Fellner; AP, Peter Jaques; DIR, Alex Cox; AD, Chris Rose; SCR, Alex Cox, Abbe Wood; CAM, Roger Deakins; ED, David Martin; PD, Andrew McAlpine; ART, Caroline Hanania; SET, Joanne Woollard; COS, Cathy Cook; SND, Peter Glossop; P, Sara Keene.

UNDER THE CHERRY MOON (Cavallo/Ruffalo/Fargnoli Prod.) 9/16, Nice, France. **Prince, Jerome Benton, Steven Berkoff, Francesca Annis, Alexandra Stewart, Victor Spinetti, Emmanuelle Sallet, Kristin Scott Thomas**
EXP-PROD, Bob Cavallo, Joe Ruffalo, Steve Fargnoli; AP, Graham Cottle; DIR, Mary Lambert; SCR, Becky Johnston; CAM, Michael Ballhaus; ED, Eva Gardos; PD, Richard Sylbert; COS, Marie-France; DISTRIB, WB.

WHITE DRAGON (Legend Prods./Perspektyva, 871-0474) 9/11, Poland. **Christopher Lloyd, Dee Wallace Stone, Soon-Tech Oh, Christopher Stone, Allison Balson, Luke Askew, Stephan Mara**
EXP, Andre Krakowski, Lloyd Eisenhower; PROD, Alina Szpak, Robert Fleet; DIR, Jerzy Domaradzki; SCR, Robert Fleet; CAM, Vitold Dabal; ART, J, Kosarewicz; COS, Eva Krauze; UPM, Michael Zablocki; P, Hank Gerber.

WINDRIDER (Barron Films) 9/23, Perth, Australia. **Tom Burlinson, Bud Tingwell, Nicole Kidman**
PROD, Paul Barron; DIR, Vince Monton; SCR, Everett de Roche, Bonnie Harris; CAM, Joe Pickering.

YOUNG EINSTEIN (Einstein Entertainment) 9/23, Sydney, Newcastle, Blue Mountains, Australia. **Yahoo Serious, Su Cruickshank, PeeWee Wilson**
PROD Yahoo Serious, David Roach, Warwick Ross; DIR, Yahoo Serious; SCR, Yahoo Serious, David Roach; CAM, Jeff Darling.

THE ZERO BOYS (Omega Pictures/Forminx Corp. Prod., 461-9024) 9/26, Mexico. **Daniel Hirsch, Jared Moses, Crystal Carson, Nicole Rio, T.K. Webb, John Michaels, Elise Turner**
PROD-DIR, Nico Mastorakis; AP, Bob Manning; SCR, Robert Gilliam, Fred C. Perry; PD, Gregory Melton; COS, Richard Abramson, Andrea Phillips; UPM, Virginia Lynch; DISTRIB, Omega.

GLORIA RUSCH
THE TWILIGHT ZONE
CBS • Fri. 8 p.m.
Eat or Be Eaten
Firesign Theatre
Cinemax
Comedy Special
Director: Phil Austin
Oct.: 11, 14, 20, 26, 28, 30
Lee Miller Talent Agency
(213) 469-0077

The Erika Wain Agency
Invites You To Watch
CHRISTOPHER KRIESA
Tonight On
"The Twilight Zone"
8:00 P.M. CBS
Soon To Be Seen In:
"MacGyver" *"Alfred Hitchcock"*

BETTE DAVIS DEAD AT 81

By GERALD PUTZER

Bette Davis, 81, preeminent film actress whose Hollywood career is unsurpassed in its number and range of quality performances, died Oct. 6 of cancer at the American Hospital in Neuilly-sur-Seine, France.

Davis, who had a mastectomy in 1983 as well as a stroke, was en route to her home in West Hollywood. She had been in Spain where she was honored at the San Sebastian Film Festival.

A professional and uncompromising individualist, Davis was intent on putting the best performance she could muster on the screen, and could little suffer those coworkers who weren't so dedicated. She fought often and hard with her longtime studio, Warner Bros., and with Jack Warner in particular, to get the best scriptwriters, directors and costars for her films, thus gaining a reputation for being difficult. Often, those

Turn to page 31

World loved Lucy

Lucille Desiree Ball, known to most as simply "Lucy," and dubbed the First Lady Of Television, is dead at age 77.

At the height of her popularity, her "I Love Lucy" tv sitcom was viewed weekly by a half-billion people, worldwide.

The series changed the way comedy was seen — literally.

Obituary and stories are on Pages 50-52.

John Lennon, 40, One Of Original Beatles, Shot Dead In New York

By FRED KIRBY

John Lennon, 40, a founding member of the Beatles, who revolutionized pop music, was killed outside his New York residence, the Dakota, Monday (8) night.

Mark David Chapman, 25, of Honolulu, whom police described as a "kook," was arrested and charged with murder and possession of a deadly weapon. Police said Lennon was shot in the back after he left his limousine to enter the building. The suspect had apparently been waiting for him.

Fellow Beatle Ringo Starr reportedly enplaned to the U.S. after hearing of the death. George Harrison, another of the quartet, also reportedly in shock, cancelled a recording session. A statement from the office of Paul McCartney, who wrote and sang most of the Beatles clicks with Lennon, expressed regret at the loss.

Lennon only recently returned to recording after a five-year absence with "Double Fantasy," also featuring his wife, Yoko Ono, which is No. 12 on *Variety's* Top Selling LPs & Tapes Chart this week, and "(Just Like) Starting Over," No. eight on the Best-Selling Singles

(Continued on page 99)

Creative Management

The pre-Christmas doldrums are more in evidence than usual this season. One act went screaming to his personal manager asking why he wasn't working.

The manager, surveying the scene, came up with the observation, "Show business is closed this week."

Valenti Gunning For Vid Pirates; Will D.C. Help?

Washington, Dec. 9.

Stiff fines for video pirates will be a legislative concern of the upcoming Congress, a hopeful Motion Picture Assn. of America president Jack Valenti predicted last week.

Valenti took his industry's anti-piracy message to a luncheon gathering of the Federal Communications Bar Assn. in an effort to win the support of this influential constituency for the Congressional fight ahead. An anti-piracy bill was offered in the House late in the term just completed, but was defeated in

1990s

The 1990s were a prelude to the new millennium.

The terrorist bombings in cities ranging from Oklahoma City to Tanzania were a foreshadowing of something even more devastating. Matsushita Electric's purchase of Universal Pictures, at the time the largest buy of a U.S. firm from overseas, was a huge deal, but in the twenty-first century, those kinds of transactions became commonplace. Operation Desert Storm led to the Iraq war; and the excitement of the introduction of the uniting Euro was the calm before the still-divided European storm.

But above all else, news in the 1990s was dominated by the celebrity factor.

A June 12, 1995, *Weekly Variety* story said the broadcast networks' primetime news devoted three times as much coverage to the O.J. Simpson trial as any other news event of the year. The Tyndall Report, which monitors news, concluded that ABC, CBS, and NBC spent 1,592 minutes on the trial, compared to 612 minutes on Haiti (their presidential elections, the U.S. handing over military authority to the United Nations), 418 minutes on Oklahoma City bombings (in which 168 people were killed by the terrorist attack), and 318 minutes on the ongoing war between Bosnia and Herzegovina.

It was hard to avoid the Simpson murder case, which the media dubbed "the trial of the century."

The October 4, 1995, *Daily Variety* carried several stories about the aftermath of the "not guilty" decision. One began,

> "Now that he's free, the question for O.J. is: What does he do for an encore? That was the topic du jour in Hollywood Tuesday after Simpson was cleared of charges of murdering ex-wife Nicole Brown and her friend Ron Goldman. . . . The most persistent rumor is that Simpson will hold a pay-per-view cable event as a means to pay off his massive legal tab."

Another reported that jury forewoman Amanda Cooley had already received huge cash offers for an exclusive interview: "According to sources, the highest offers—said to be in excess of $150,000—appeared to be coming from print tabloids."

Right: Not a ploy for Oprah Winfrey to include this in her book club.

L.A. eyes glued to O.J. ride

By JIM BENSON

Sixty-eight percent of all TV sets in Los Angeles were in use Friday night when the extraordinary O.J. Simpson drama, which was played out all day Friday on nationwide TV, culminated with the suicidal fugitive sports hero's surrender at his Brentwood home.

According to preliminary Nielsen overnight ratings results, HUT (homes using TV) levels were 11% higher when the surreal chase scene ended than the previous Friday from 8-9 p.m.

Turn to page 30

O.J. odyssey has L.A. viewers glued to TV

Continued from page 1

ABC, NBC and CBS interrupted regular programming, including NBC's coverage of the NBA Finals, to cover Friday's events in the double-murder case involving the football great.

Every local station as well as ESPN and CNN covered Simpson's tragic odyssey, which became the night's big event at sports bars and dance clubs around the nation.

Viewers were transfixed as seven L.A. TV station helicopters joined law enforcement officials in their pursuit of the well-known suspect and his former teammate and best friend, Al Cowlings.

In the pivotal 8-9 hour, KTLA won the race with an 18.3 rating/27 share. The indie had one of the best aerial camera angles of the standoff in Simpson's driveway.

KTLA was followed by KABC-TV (15.0/22), KCBS (12.8/19), KNBC (11.4/17), KTTV (6.6/10), KCAL (4.2/6) and KCOP (1.5/2).

KNBC found itself in the unenviable position of having to alternate between the chase and the critical fifth game of the Knicks-Rockets championship series.

At times during the chase, KNBC blew out portions of the game or relegated it to a small soundless square at the bottom of the screen. When darkness fell and the police put a press blackout on the negotiations, KNBC went back to the game completely until Simpson surrendered.

HUT levels were up significantly throughout the traumatic day's events, which began at 11 a.m. when Simpson failed to appear at his scheduled surrender and, a few hours later, the embarrassing admission by the Los Angeles Police Dept. that he had fled.

It then jumped to what KCBS' Ann Martin incorrectly speculated was a suicide at the scene of the Brentwood double murders, dramatic press conferences with District Attorney Gil Garcetti and Simpson attorney Robert Shapiro and the climactic chase played out on Southern California freeways and roads.

"Nothing small ever happens in Southern California," said KCBS general manager Bill Applegate, whose station broke the story about Simpson's possible involvement in the sensational murder case last Monday. "Everybody, I think, in the entire city, if not the country, was transfixed."

KABC led the ratings race from 11 a.m.-5 p.m., posting a 7.0/19, with KNBC in second with a 6.5/18 and KCBS third with a 5.3/15.

From 5-6 p.m., KABC jumped to a 10.7/22, KNBC scored a 9.7/20 and KCBS finished with an unusually strong 9.3/19.

In the 6-7 p.m. block, KCBS jumped into a first-place tie with KABC, with each station garnering a 10.5/20 and KNBC earning a 10.3/19.

As news of the chase spread, KNBC shot up to a 17.4/19 from 7-8 p.m., with KCBS pulling a 12.8/21 and KABC third with an 11.7/19. Among indies, KCAL led in that hour with a 7.1/11; KTLA scored a 6.5/11.

HUT levels were up 6% from 5-7 p.m., 11% from 7-8 p.m. and 7% from 10-11 p.m. over the previous Friday.

Complaints about excessive TV coverage apparently were rare.

"The normal (viewer) reaction is that people want to go back to their soap operas," said Jeff Wald, news director of KCOP. "But on this story it kept building and building."

Scenes of the chase continued to be replayed.

Simpson was the subject of TV coverage all week in connection with the June 12 murder of his ex-wife, Nicole Brown Simpson, and waiter Ronald Goldman. Simpson was charged with the slayings Friday morning. After his failure to surrender, he and Cowlings were tracked to a white Ford Bronco in Orange County. Their ride ended at Simpson's Brentwood house, 60 miles away.

Southern California has engrossed the nation before with TV reports of riots, earthquakes and fire that destroyed celebrity homes in Malibu. But this was something different.

"This has to be one of the most amazing personal dramas in memory, involving an individual

> 'It doesn't take a novelist to take a look at a story like this … to know why we stayed on the air all day.'
> **KCBS G.M. Bill Applegate**

with worldwide celebrity status, a hero fallen from grace and police in pursuit," Applegate said.

"And played out, naturally in Los Angeles, on the freeways," he added.

Freeway chases may be rare elsewhere, but have become nearly a staple in L.A., where such scenes have become almost routine in recent years. This time, local stations were ready, made proficient by experience.

On Friday, the seven TV helicopters and law enforcement aircraft performed a delicate ballet, sharing air space as Simpson and Cowlings crisscrossed two counties by car.

Stations switched rapidly between outside shots and studio reports.

"It's the capability of live technology that allows us to be live on the ground, in the air, everywhere," Applegate said.

He said he does not think that anything was lost in this unedited, rapid-fire coverage.

"The fact of the matter is the newscasts and newspapers in ensuing days will place the drama in perspective," he said. "Our mission, and what we're so capable of doing, is to provide instantaneous, immediate coverage."

But Wald and Applegate did disagree about the earlier coverage Friday.

While Applegate defended the day's TV coverage, which included erroneous rumors that the murder weapon was from the Warner Bros. "Frogmen" pilot in which Simpson starred, Wald called much of it "a media circus."

"I was embarrassed," Wald said. The stations "had nothing, but they stayed on for one-upsmanship and competitive gain. I come from a school where you go with the facts. … We stayed off the air until we had solid information."

"That's baloney," Applegate snapped. "This is one of the great human dramas, criminal dramas and personal dramas that we've ever seen. It's hard to even dignify that kind of criticism.

"All of us are on the air as long as we've been … because this is a sensational story of magnificent interest to the whole country.

"It doesn't take a novelist to take a look at a story like this — a major sports hero, TV and movie star, accused of hacking to death his ex-wife and friend, who when charged with the crime disappears as a fugitive, only to have the lawyer appear and describe the man as potentially committing suicide — to know why we stayed on the air all day.

"It's a story that Hemingway couldn't write."

The Associated Press contributed to this report.

CLASSIFIEDS

EMPLOYMENT OPPORTUNITIES

PARTICIPATIONS ACCOUNTANT
Seeking responsible, organized and detail-oriented accountant to prepare participation stmts. Some familiarity with contracts, reconciliations and account analyses reqd. Lotus 1-2-3 a must. Windows exp. prefd. Minimum 2 years entertainment exp. Accounting degre prefd. Send resume and salary history to: New World Entertainment, Ltd., Job #799, 1440 S. Sepulveda Blvd., Los Angeles, CA 90025. Fax (310) 444-8183. M/F/EOE. NO PHONE CALLS PLEASE.

SAG PAYMASTER
Burbank entertainment company seeks person with experience in SAG low budget. 4 day work week. Excellent benefits. Send resume with salary requirements to:
Box F-17-H, c/o Daily Variety.

ALL STAR AGENCY
ENTERTAINMENT & CORPORATE
JOBS AVAILABLE
- Recpt., G.O., +General Acctng Clerks-Major Studios
- Legal Secty's-High energy ent. law firms
- Exec. Secty's to Film Producers
- Asst. to Agents-Major talent agencies
Temporary & Permanent / NO FEE
The ENTERTAINMENT AGENCY
310-271-5217
205 South Beverly Drive, Suite 214 Beverly Hills, CA 90212

ASSISTANT/SECRETARY
Video production company is seeking a bright, well organized individual with Mac skills. Must be able to handle a variety of office functions.
Fax resume to 310-556-1658

FULL-TIME DIRECTOR OF ADVERTISING/PUBLICITY/PROMOTIONS
to join existing Creative Services staff within a busy Studio City based Television Distribution/Production Co. Minimum 3 yrs. exp. in TV syndication, advertising, publicity and promotion necessary. Competitive salary & benefits. Fax resume to:
Human Resources Supervisor at
(818) 755-2488

EXECUTIVE ASSISTANT
To provide administrative and secretarial assistance to Sr. V.P. and Sr. Dir. of Business Affrs/Legal dept of television production/distribution co. Type 65 wpm, shorthand 80 wpm, Microsoft Word 4 Windows, WordPerfect and Paradox knowledge helpful. 3 yrs. business affrs/ legal secretarial experience required. Fax resume to Human Resources Supervisor at: **(818) 755-2488**

BUSINESS OPPS.

FORGOT THE NAGRA!
DIDN'T KNOW IT'LL TURN OUT GOOD, OKAY? YOUNG FILMMAKER, FIRST FEATURE, 35MM, NO BUDGET. WHAT WERE THE CHANCES? NOW WE HAVE THIS ROUGH CUT ON VIDEO TO BEGIN DUBBING SOUND ITALIAN STYLE.
LIKE A PEEK? (415) 393-3495 LISBON OKAFOR

LAS VEGAS VIDEO PRODUCTION COMPANY
Strong client base.
Owner retiring.
$185K.
(702) 361-3766

COMM. REAL ESTATE

NIGHT CLUB
Full ABR Facilities
Full Restaurant
Beautiful elegant space available for events showcasing talent, wrap parties, jazz, blues, comedy etc. Details 213/936-6400

DAILY VARIETY

$1.25
WEDNESDAY
OCTOBER 4, 1995

$1.95 OUTSIDE CALIFORNIA

A CAHNERS PUBLICATION ▪ LOS ANGELES, CALIFORNIA ▪ NEWSPAPER SECOND CLASS P.O. ENTRY

Patricof eyeing ICM stake

By JOHN BRODIE and MARTIN PEERS

Venture capitalist Alan Patricof is in talks with International Creative Management to purchase a minority stake in the privately held agency. The deep-pocketed, New York-based financier is chairman of Patricof & Co. Ventures Inc., which manages $2 billion in funds for institutional investors and corporate pensions. Previously, the firm has invested in Apple and America Online.

Patricof's potential stake in ICM is estimated to be in the neighborhood of 25% and comes just four months after investment bank Furman Selz was hired by the

Turn to page 12

INSIDE

2 Fox upgrades screening rooms

Inaugurating a general facilities overhaul, 20th Century Fox is rebuilding its on-the-lot screening rooms.

2 'Beast' best at Ovation noms

"Beauty and the Beast" led the Theatre LA Ovation Award noms, followed by East West Players' "Sweeney Todd."

3 The ape that ate Hollywood

The Time Warner-TBS merger will create a company that dominates Hollywood film production to an unprecedented degree.

CAN O.J. STILL MAKE HAY?
Pay-per-view rumors rampant

By JOE FLINT and JOHN DEMPSEY

Now that he's free, the question for O.J. is: What does he do for an encore?

That was the topic du jour in Hollywood Tuesday after Simpson was cleared of charges of murdering ex-wife Nicole Brown and her friend Ron Goldman.

Among the people at Simpson's house when he returned home Tuesday was Jack Gilardi, his longtime ICM agent. Gilardi, who has been a regular Simpson visitor over the past year, has been barraged with offers from people looking to be part of Simpson's next move.

The most persistent rumor is

The media's role in the trial, Changing Channels, page 15

that Simpson will hold a pay-per-view cable event as a means to pay off his massive legal tab.

While one would think that the odds of such a circus event actually happening are astronomical, that did not stop cable industry

Turn to page 12

TBS MAKES 'SUPER' BUY FROM WBTV

By J. MAX ROBINS

NEW YORK — In his first address to his Turner Broadcasting staff since the announced merger with Time Warner, Ted Turner said Tuesday the company purchased off-network rights to Warner Bros. TV's "Lois & Clark: The New Adventures of Superman," according to sources.

It was the first acquisition from one of its new siblings, those sources said.

A Turner spokesman declined comment beyond describing the session as "upbeat."

"Lois & Clark," which generated interest from several cable networks, including Lifetime, the Family Channel, USA Network and E! Entertainment TV, will be available to run on a Turner cable web in September 1997, unless ABC grants permission for an earlier run. According to industry sources, despite Time Warner being family, Turner paid a full-market value of an estimated $275,000 per episode.

Turner mentioned the purchase of the third-year drama series in the context of explaining various

Turn to page 13

NUMBERS

Savoy's stock price
Down 28%

In the two weeks since the indie announced it is shifting its attention from movies to television, its stock has been on the slide. Story, page 4.

SONY CLASSICS BUYS FEST DUO

By GREG EVANS

NEW YORK — Two notable film fest travelers — Pedro Almodovar's "The Flower of My Secret" and Todd Solondz's "Welcome to the Dollhouse" — have landed at Sony Pictures Classics.

SPC's acquisition of North American rights to "Flower" comes just a week before the film gets its Gotham premiere at the New York Film Festival on Oct. 13. The pact reunites Almodovar with SPC co-presidents Tom Bernard, Michael Barker and Marcie Bloom. While at Orion Classics, the three execs distributed the Spanish filmmaker's 1988 breakthrough film, "Women on the Verge of a Nervous Breakdown."

Bloom said the SPC execs expressed interest in the film during

Turn to page 13

Tabs tab O.J. forewoman

By JIM BENSON

Even before O.J. Simpson was found not guilty of murder Tuesday morning, huge cash offers for interviews reportedly had started arriving at the home of trial juror forewoman Amanda Cooley — an apparent violation of court orders that prohibited press contact with jurors.

According to sources, the highest offers — said to be in excess of $150,000 — appeared to be coming from print tabloids.

Cooley's daughter, Yolanda, put out the word to TV shows calling the South-Central Los Angeles home Tuesday for interviews that they would have to stand in line. Over the past two

Turn to page 12

ABC, NBC duke it out as Big 3 lose viewers

By TOM BIERBAUM

ABC maintained a solid households lead in the second week of the new fall season, but NBC equaled the Alphabet network in the important adults 18-49 race and looks primed for a strong challenge this season in the key demographics.

Three-network viewing, meanwhile, was down 6 share points from Sept. 25-Oct. 1 compared with the corresponding week a year earlier, due at least in part to a siphoning away of viewers during closing arguments in the O.J. Simpson murder trial.

After two weeks of the new season, the top two webs look evenly matched on a weekly basis, particularly when sports (ABC's considerable Monday football boost and NBC's big Friday baseball drain) are taken out of the mix. NBC's strength, especially in key demos, is dangerously concentrated on Thursdays, but if that's an NBC vulnerability, it's one the competition has yet to exploit.

Last week, virtually every

Turn to page 8

Tune injury derails 'Alley'

By JEREMY GERARD

NEW YORK — Song-and-dance man Tommy Tune broke his foot Sunday during an evening performance of "Busker Alley" in Tampa, Fla., in the middle of the musical's final pre-Broadway stand. The accident sent an already shaky venture into a tailspin from which it may not recover.

The injury, which producer Barry Weissler said Tuesday will keep the star in a cast and on crutches for at least six weeks, effectively shutters a $5 million show dogged for years by drawn-out arbitration, bad publicity and a grueling, transcontinental tryout tour that began in April. A closing notice was posted

Turn to page 5

275

Most news pundits lamented checkbook journalism but admitted that viewers liked scandal more than "hard" news. Even mainstream papers followed the "if it bleeds, it leads" philosophy that seemed to be working on the evening news.

Showmanship has always been a part of the politics, and rulers as disparate as Franklin D. Roosevelt and Benito Mussolini knew to use new media to carry their messages to the masses. In the 1990s, *Daily Variety* concluded that showbiz and politics were now indistinguishable.

The August 12, 1996, *Daily* carried coverage of the Republican convention. It was the first time *Variety* had sent correspondents to any political convention. The story led with the arrival of Bob Dole in San Diego, standing on the bow of a ship while the "official Dole-Kemp skydiving jump team" flew overhead and a rock band played "Soul Man," with new lyrics about "Dole Man."

According to the report,

"the Republican National Committee estimates 30,000 people here for the convention, including 1,990 delegates, 1,990 alternates, 8,000 volunteers—and 15,000 members of the media. In other words, half the people here are with some news organization, so in theory every attendee can have his or her very own media person."

However,

"the mere mention of the word 'media' drew scattered boos at Sunday's seaside rally for presumptive Republican nominee Bob Dole and his just-announced running mate Jack Kemp, but the GOP is trying to make journalists feel welcome. Each attendee here received a canvas goodie bag that included Dole raisins, a Nicholas-Applegate Mutual Fund T-shirt and a 'Limited Convention Edition' of Kraft Macaroni and Cheese mix with elephant-shaped pasta."

AMY FISHER: MY STORY
NBC, Mon. Dec. 28, 9 p.m.

A presentation of KLM and Spectacor Films in association with Michael Jaffe Films. Executive producers, Michael Jaffe and Alfred Kelman. Producers, Howard Braunstein and Phil Levitan. Co-producers, Christine Lynch, John Danylkiw. Director, Bradford May. Writer, Phil Pennington. Photography, Bradford May; music, Fred Mollin. 120 MIN.
With: Ed Marinaro, Noelle Parker, Boyd Kestner, Pierette Grace, Lawrence Dane, Kate Lynch, Kathleen Lasky.

CASUALTIES OF LOVE: THE 'LONG ISLAND LOLITA' STORY
CBS, Sun. Jan. 3, 9 p.m.

A presentation of Diane Sokolow Prods. in association with TriStar Television. Executive producer, Diane Sokolow. Producers, John Herzfeld, Vahan Moosekian. Director, John Herzfeld. Writer, John Herzfeld. Photography, Karl Walter Lindenlaub; music, David Frank. 120 MIN.
With: Alyssa Milano, Jack Scalia, Phyllis Lyons, Leo Rossi, Lawrence Tierney, Jack Kehler, Anne De Salvo.

BEYOND CONTROL: THE AMY FISHER STORY
ABC, Sun. Jan. 3, 9 p.m.

A presentation of the Andrew Adelson Co. in association with ABC Prods. Executive producer, Andrew Adelson. Producer, George W. Perkins. Director, Andy Tennant. Writer, Janet Brownell. Photography, Glen MacPherson; music, Michael Hoenig. 120 MIN.
With: Drew Barrymore, Anthony John Denison, Harley Jane Kozak, Tom Mason, Laurie Paton, Ken Pogue, Linda Darlow, Gabe Khouth, Garry Davey, Dwight McFee, Philip Granger.

It's easy to see why the story of "Long Island Lolita" Amy Fisher would appeal to TV producers — it's lurid as all-get-out, and the principals are physically attractive and in the right demo range. Three movies on such a strong subject might not be too many under some circumstances, but in this case, it's at least two too many.

The facts of the story have been continual fodder for TV and print tabloids since early last year: Fisher, 17, shot and perhaps permanently injured the wife of 38-year-old body-and-fender man Joey Buttafuoco.

Points of dispute include whether the shooting was (as Fisher claims) accidental, and whether Buttafuoco, with whom (as he denies) she was having a long-time affair, prompted Fisher not only to the attempted murder, but to prostitution for pin money.

Fisher pled guilty to a reduced charge, and was sentenced to a 5-to-15-year prison sentence.

NBC's "Amy Fisher: My Story" was filmed with the cooperation of Fisher and secondary character Paul Makely. CBS's "Casualties of Love: The 'Long Island Lolita' Story" paid for exclusive rights to the Buttafuocos' version, and ABC's "Beyond Control: The Amy Fisher Story" was drawn from journalists' accounts and court records.

The problem with this trio of films is that none of them is especially compelling. The involvement of the principals can be held responsible for pussyfooting on "Amy Fisher: My Story" and "Casualties of Love," but the failure of the "Beyond Control" producers to go all-out is more surprising. Ultimately, the choice of ABC and CBS to go head-to-head may work out; chances are that one Amy Fisher movie will be enough for most viewers.

"Amy Fisher: My Story," may be the best, depending on the audience's willingness to accept Buttafuoco as a manipulator and Fisher as a not-too-innocent victim. Relative unknown Noelle Parker is believable as Amy and Ed Marinaro is an appropriately (for this version) slimy Buttafuoco.

Both the ABC and CBS versions acknowledge the role of TV tabloids in promulgating the story, with "A Current Affair" and "Hard Copy" playing significant roles. New York Post reporter Amy Pagnozzi, played by Harley Jane Kojak, is a secondary lead in "Beyond Control."

Between the ABC and CBS versions, "Casualties of Love" may be the better choice, despite the Buttafuocos' involvement. It's surprisingly hard on Joey without acknowledging any wrongdoing on his part, and opens with a sequence out of a generic '50s film noir that's worth seeing in its own right.

The bottom line is that the acting and direction in both films are of approximately equal quality (with Drew Barrymore and Alyssa Milano okay as Fisher, and Anthony John Denison and Jack Scalia fine as their Joeys).
— *Todd Everett*

STAR TREK: DEEP SPACE NINE
Syndicated

A presentation of Paramount Pictures. Exec producers, Rick Berman, Michael Piller. Producer, Peter Lauritson. Supervising producer, David Livingston. Director, David Carson. Writer, Piller, from a story by Berman, Piller. Creators, Berman, Piller. Photography, Marvin Rush; visual-effects producer, Robert Legato; music, Dennis McCarthy, Jay Chattaway. 90 MIN.
With: Avery Brooks, Rene Auberjonois, Siddig El Fadil, Terry Farrell, Cirroc Lofton, Colm Meaney, Armin Shimerman, Nana Visitor, Patrick Stewart, John Carter, Camille Saviolla.

"Star Trek: The Next Generation" beat some pretty steep odds to become one of the true hits of the syndication marketplace, and now "Star Trek: Deep Space Nine" lifts off the launch pad, facing even steeper odds of its own.

Like "Next Generation," "Nine" is markedly more cerebral and more affably low-key than most of what makes it in the sci-fi and action categories.

But "Nine" faces an important additional handicap. It's missing one of the key stars that so helped the previous "Trek" series deliver its punch — the starship Enterprise itself.

So it's probably no coincidence that this introductory episode shows the "Nine" crew converting their space station into a starship so they can go off and shoot it out with the bad-guy aliens. Such fodder always worked in the earlier "Trek" series, and it may in fact work better than anything the "Nine" writers can be expected to dream up week in and week out for their space-station setting.

But so what if "Deep Space Nine" is not, like the first two "Trek" shows, a "Wagon Train to the Stars?" This latest "Trek" need not be any more limited by its space-station setting than, say, "Gunsmoke" was by its Dodge City setting.

And perhaps "Gunsmoke"-like durability is in store for "Nine" if producers, advertisers and the audience are willing to take the time to get to know a new crew and a new kind of "Trek" story.

"Nine's" Marshal Dillon role (Commander Sisko) goes to Avery Brooks, who delivers the requisite intensity and range, though there's a laid-back nature to the performance that sometimes slows things down. Director David Carson could strive for crisper deliveries all around.

The liveliest turn comes with Nana Visitor as Sisko's second-in-command, Major Kira. Also helping shake the show out of a sometimes lethargic pace are Armin Shimerman as the crafty alien Quark; Siddig El Fadil as the gung-ho doctor; Colm Meaney as Chief O'Brien (transplanted from the "Next Generation"); and a sneering Rene Auberjonois as an alien shape-shifter.

The mission of the "Deep Space Nine" team is to aid a ravaged world called Bajor after the quick exit of its conquerors, the despotic Cardassian race. Creators Rick Berman and Michael Piller have wisely created many links to the "Next Generation" mythology, ensuring heavy sampling by that loyal audience.

This episode, for example, includes a guest shot by "Next Generation's" Patrick Stewart.

The script is a mixed bag, too complex and ambitious at times but generally admirable in its mix of deft characterization, old-fashioned space opera and sophisticated sci-fi concepts.

This 90-minute opener gives Brooks the chance to shine, as Sisko's duties force him to come to terms with personal tragedy.

Fans of the beautiful-looking "Next Generation" series will be pleased that "Deep Space Nine's" visuals are as good as anything on TV. — *Tom Bierbaum*

News Corp. offers $3 mil to Lewinsky

By JENNY HONTZ

Rupert Murdoch's News Corp. is offering former White House intern Monica Lewinsky $3 million for a multimedia tell-all package expected to include a primetime Fox interview special and a HarperCollins book deal, sources said late Wednesday.

Reps for Lewinsky could not be reached, and News Corp. had no comment. However, insiders say serious talks have been ongoing for some time, and the point person for the negoti-

Turn to page 24

Lewinsky

Previous Spread: If the coverage fits . . .

Above: Nice package.

Left: Dueling TV movies.

The "scattered boos" for the media was not an unusual reaction. For many conventioneers, there ceased to be a difference between respectable news organizations and tabloid paparazzi. And a year later, they would continue to be inexorably linked and jointly blamed for Princess Diana's death.

The September 8, 1997, *Weekly Variety* read,

> "Industryites estimate a global audience of 2.5 billion for the Sept. 6 funeral of Diana, Princess of Wales, with much of the world using British coverage. Only the BBC and Independent Television News [the news provider to ITV and Channel 4] were permitted to broadcast the service inside Westminster Abbey."

The issue carried reports from and about England, France, Hong Kong, South Africa, Germany, and Japan and their extensive coverage. For example,

> "South African Broadcasting Corp. devoted one of its three channels to all-day, all-night live coverage variously from the BBC and CNN and, later, its own correspondent in London. . . . The pubcaster was put to shame, however, by Johannesburg private Radio station 702, which assembled its entire news team within an hour of the story breaking, bringing listeners a mix of eyewitnesses, police, royal-family experts and media analysts."

Only Hong Kong seemed underwhelmed. Television Broadcasts Limited

> "confined itself to 15 minutes on the nightly news following the accident. Within days, the story slipped from the lead position on the news in favor of stories on the stock market and a plane crash in Cambodia."

In a roundup from the United States: "No fewer than seven American TV networks—from broadcasters ABC, NBC and CBS to cablers CNN, MSNBC, Fox News Channel and even arts channel A&E—aired the funeral live despite the predawn start time in many parts of the country, using either their own feed or that of the BBC or ITV. . . . Seemingly every TV station in a major U.S. city dispatched at least one reporter and camera crew to London to soak in Great Britain's sweeping anguish."

And, the story concluded, "The paparazzi were disparaged daily."

The blossoming of twenty-four-hour news channels meant increasing competition. Though people throughout the ages had known about the sexual escapades of folks ranging from Thomas Jefferson to John F. Kennedy, such things weren't discussed in polite society. But at the end of the twentieth century, all bets were off. The tabloidization of the news meant reporters liked to catch people with their pants down. Literally and figuratively.

As such, the news media gave more coverage to the apparent sexual connection between President Bill Clinton and intern Monica Lewinsky than to any piece of legislation.

A September 11, 1998, *Daily Variety* story noted that independent counsel Kenneth Starr's 445-page report to Congress was likely to be released that day:

> "The race is now on among magazine and book publishers over how to handle the hot copy—rumored to be full of sexual detail and implications of perjury that may bring down a president."

Pocket Books, PublicAffairs Books, and Prima Publishing rushed paperback compilations of the report into bookstores.

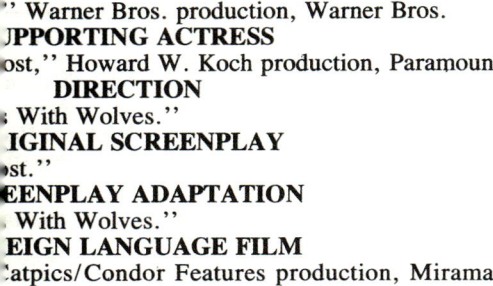

> **Whoopi Goldberg:**
> "One of the first things I did when I first got famous was inconspicuously carry Variety. I could be seen reading Army Archerd, whom I hadn't yet met. People knew I was in the entertainment business when they saw I had a Variety."

Newsies had been under fire since the beginning of the decade. The February 26, 1991, *Daily Variety* reminded readers that the Pentagon had put an official freeze on news from Operation Desert Storm. David Bartlett, president of the D.C.-based Radio-Television News Directors Association told AP it was "Gulf war censorship" and that the Pentagon secrecy "has much more to do with politics and public relations than with genuine military security. Free people fighting for just causes don't need to make war in secret."

While that war was kept under wraps, other forms of violence (or even hints of violence) were grabbing headlines.

In 1992, Ice-T and his group, Body Count, released the rap song "Cop Killer," raising the hackles of parents, teachers, law-enforcement officers, and, of course, legislators, who got a lot of publicity by denouncing the song, the performer, and the group.

The June 25, 1992, *Daily Variety* carried a report saying a national sheriffs' group was urging a boycott of Time Warner, Inc., until the company pulled the song from store shelves. Vice President Dan Quayle spoke to the sheriffs' conference, calling the record "revolting and outrageous" and denounced Time Warner as irresponsible.

Within a few years, store shelves were an endangered species, and Ice-T was appearing as a regular on the NBC series *Law & Order: SVU*.

Still, the "if it bleeds, it leads" philosophy was thriving, on both the news and in dramas. No fewer than three telefilms about Amy Fisher, "the Long Island Lolita," were rushed into production shortly after her trial. An April 11, 1996, a story talked about CBS's and NBC's rival projects inspired by the Unabomber, the terrorist responsible for killing three people and wounding many others during his twenty-year mail-bomb campaign.

The boom in ripped-from-the-headlines dramas that came with the increase of U.S. networks slowed by the end of the decade. On May 20, 1999, about a month after the

Above: Jeremy Irons, Kathy Bates, Whoopi Goldberg, and Joe Pesci.

Right: Terrorists begin to take action against films.

Columbine High School incident, in which two teens shot and killed thirteen people then committed suicide, *Daily* reported that CBS had pulled the plug on a proposed Mafia-related series, *Falcone*.

In the story,

> "CBS Television prexy Leslie Moonves Wednesday admitted that the post-Columbine mood of the country impacted the net's scheduling process and ultimate decision" not to order *Falcone*.

Moonves did not blame TV and movies for a violent society. But he told *Variety*, "Anybody who doesn't pay attention to what's going on and totally says the media has nothing to do with it is an idiot."

In that same issue, the Juvenile Justice Bill, which had been in development for two years in Washington, D.C., underwent some key changes. A story by Christopher Stern reported that the Senate-approved bill

> "started off as an effort to reform the juvenile justice system and ended up becoming the focus of a national debate on whether the media or the gun industry should be blamed for a rash of high school shooting sprees that have plagued the country during the last 25 years."

The hearings

> "provided a stage for politicians to denounce the entertainment industry for allegedly saturating the nation's youth with a flood of violent images in movies, television, video games and the Internet. Republicans led the fight against the entertainment industry, at least in part, to deflect some of the blame away from the gun industry in the wake of the Columbine shootings."

This harkened back to showbiz's worries about its relationship with world violence, first reported in an August 26, 1998, story headlined "H'wood on Alert."

> "The U.S. entertainment industry may be terrorism's newest target following what appears to be the politically motivated bombing of a South African Planet Hollywood restaurant that killed at least one person and injured about 25 others.
>
> "The South African blast follows U.S. retaliatory attacks on suspected terrorist sites in Sudan and Afghanistan, later more than 250 people were killed in the Aug. 7 bombing of American embassies in Kenya and Tanzania. . . . In Hollywood, safety concerns in the wake of mounting Mideast tensions

H'WOOD ON ALERT

South African bomb raises security concerns for biz

By PAUL KARON

The U.S. entertainment industry may be terrorism's newest target following what appears to be the politically motivated bombing of a South African Planet Hollywood restaurant that killed at least one person and injured about 25 others.

The South African blast follows U.S. retaliatory attacks on suspected terrorist sites in Sudan and Afghanistan, after more than 250 people were killed in the Aug. 7 bombing of American embassies in Kenya and Tanzania.

The South African Planet Hollywood site may have been targeted as a symbol of America and the West and because of controversy surrounding Fox's upcoming Bruce Willis film "The Siege."

Willis — a partner in the Planet Hollywood chain with thesps Sylvester Stallone, Arnold Schwarzenegger and Whoopi Goldberg, among others — stars in the film, which depicts a Muslim terrorist group that plans a wave of bombings in New York City.

American Muslims and Arab Americans who have seen trailers of the film have voiced alarm at what they fear is a negative portrayal of Islam.

Radio personality Casey Kasem, a Lebanese American and a Druze Muslim, decried the portrayal of Arabs and Muslims in

Turn to page 19

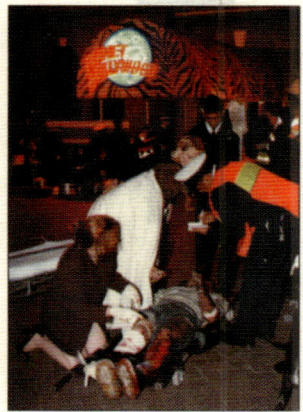

AP photo
Rescue workers aid injured patrons after a bomb ripped through the Cape Town Planet Hollywood Tuesday.

have prompted the Walt Disney Co. to 'redouble' security at its theme parks around the world. In addition, a series of stage shows scheduled for Aug 30–Sept. 1 in the city of Dubai in the United Arab Emirates, has been canceled. . . ."

The story quotes Dr. Laura Drake, a professor and Middle East specialist at American University in Washington, D.C., as saying, "Negative stereotypes of Arabs in films and television, combined with the perception of a strong Jewish influence in the entertainment industry, contributes to an anti-Hollywood sentiment among Islamic fundamentalists."

"Wealthy Islamic leader Osama bin Laden, who U.S. authorities believe to be behind the embassy attacks, has issued a global call for aggression against Americans, but it is not clear if the South African group was affiliated with bin Laden's Intl. Islamic Front for Jihad Against the Jews and Crusaders."

Executives in the film and TV industry, who'd been following certain business models for decades, were forced to be introspective about content—and about fundamental business changes. One major shift was international, the other technological.

On March 15, 1993, *Daily Variety* saluted MCA chairman Lew Wasserman: "Who else can lay claim to having transacted the largest acquisition of an American company by an offshore corporation?" That would be Japanese electronic giant Matsushita, which bought Universal Pictures in 1990; the December 3 *Weekly Variety* ran the headline, in Japanese, "Let the Buyer Beware."

As Peter Bart wrote on March 15, 1993, Wasserman attended every meeting possible of the Motion

All dressed up and no place to go: News anchorwomen (clockwise from above) Diane Sawyer (ABC), Jane Pauley (NBC) and Connie Chung (CBS), and up-and-comers Paula Zahn (CBS) and Deborah Norville (NBC)

NETWORKS DRAGGING FEMME ANCHORS

Though the webs are paying them highly, the proper niche is posing a problem

By ELIZABETH GUIDER

New York They are three of America's most prominent network news anchors and earn over $5-million a year among them.

All are experienced, credible and familiar.

One hosts a Saturday-night news magazine placed third in the ratings. Another co-hosts a magazine show, also third-placed, also yet to find its niche. The third has no show at all.

They are Connie Chung, Diane Sawyer and Jane Pauley. It seems the three networks have no idea what to do with them.

Although female anchors are now highly visible and increasingly credible onscreen, they still have problems going beyond the role of fill-in or sidekick.

Some industry observers believe if networks don't bite the bullet and elevate one of the current frontliners to No. 1 anchor soon, viewers will wait another generation to see a female newscaster.

"Timing is crucial here," says veteran newscaster and ex-anchor Linda Ellerbee. "If an opening (for co-anchoring the evening news) doesn't materialize in the next year or two, the veteran women could be passed over for the next generation of hopefuls," she added.

Sawyer (ABC), Chung (CBS) and Pauley (NBC) currently are substituting for the three male anchors and a handful of others work as fill-ins or weekend anchors — Carole Simpson (ABC) Susan Spenser (CBS), Mary Alice Williams (NBC) — or are earning marks as high-profile reporters in the field — Leslie Stahl (CBS), Rita Braver (CBS) and Andrea Mitchell (NBC). Most of these are pushing 40.

Meanwhile at the networks some younger women are being put on a fast track so as to be moved up, thinks Steve Ridge, a v.p./news consultant for Frank Magid Associates. Already Deborah Norville at NBC and Paula Zahn, last week plucked from ABC by CBS, are two candidates being primed for bigger things.

Turn to page 4

ROME: LA DOLCE VITA MEETS THE BOTTOM LINE 55

VARIETY

THE INTERNATIONAL ENTERTAINMENT WEEKLY ■ DEC. 3, 1990

A CAHNERS BUSINESS NEWSPAPER
USPS 656-960
02371

NEWSPAPER 2ND CLASS P.O. ENTRY
$2.50
$2.95 CAN./£2.25 U.K.

買収者よ、ご用心を！

What Hollywood isn't telling MCA's new owners

PETER BART

NEW YORK The financial seers are telling Akio Tanii of Matsushita that he made a great deal in acquiring MCA at $66 a share, but there are also things they're not telling him. Indeed, both in Hollywood and on Wall Street some serious questions are being uttered about the deal and what it portends — questions the shogun of Matsushita would do well to ponder.

■ The most basic question: Does Akio Tanii really understand what he's got himself into? His meandering responses to press queries about creative controls and the Israeli boycott would suggest that the Japanese leader thinks of MCA as just another product line, like Panasonic. If so, he may be sorely mistaken.

MCA is, on one level, a cultural asset — the sort of enterprise which the governments of France or, indeed, Japan, would not allow to be sold to a foreign corporation. In acquiring MCA,
Turn to page 8

Japanese giant bucks overspending trend

By PAUL NOGLOWS and CHARLES FLEMING

NEW YORK Matsushita's purchase of MCA for $6.6 billion is the priciest foreign acquisition ever of a U.S. media and entertainment company. But unlike most other foreign buys of U.S. media, Wall Street experts seem to think this time the purchase price is more in line with the company's actual value.

When Sony Corp. last year bought Columbia Pictures for $5 billion, and then had to spend an additional $800 million to secure the talents of Peter Guber and Jon Peters, observers concluded that the Japanese company had substantially overpaid to acquire the studio.

"The general consensus is that Sony paid a very full price for Columbia," says entertainment analyst Harold Vogel of Merrill Lynch. "Especially if you factor in that Columbia was not functioning at full speed and had to be revved up and Sony had to acquire Guber-Peters Entertainment, which raised the cost significantly."

The same was true with Sony's $2 billion purchase of CBS Records in 1987. "They were pioneering buying into the American marketplace," says Harley Neuman, senior manager of the entertainment division of Deloitte & Touche. "They had to come in high and hard to get the deal done."

Analysts value the MCA deal in the $69 to $71 per share range (any ultimate sale of WWOR-TV will push the price toward the higher end). "Based upon the industry's long-held perception that MCA would sell in the $80 to
Turn to page 98

BIG BROTHER IS (STILL) WATCHING EURO TV

LONDON Television in Europe may be getting more competitive and commercially oriented, but politicians of all persuasions are still pulling strings.

As private tv proliferates across the Continent and direct

A VARIETY GLOBAL SURVEY

government control of the airwaves diminishes, political influence on broadcasting nonetheless remains pervasive.

In some countries, privatization may mean more politics, not less. And for those building media and broadcasting empires, it clearly helps to have friends in high places.

A VARIETY survey found:

■ Political power over broadcasting is wielded most blatantly in Italy and Spain, where politics colors newscasts and determines who gets the top jobs at pubcasters and, to some degree, which programs are produced or acquired.

■ The tv business in Germany appears fairly apolitical, a careful balance between the pubcasters ARD and ZDF, and burgeoning private webs SAT I and RTL Plus. Yet one well-connected German producer says politics comes into play at both federal
Turn to page 101

SWEEPS STEEP WEBS IN WOES

By J. MAX ROBINS

NEW YORK There were no real winners in the November sweeps. The first-place network, NBC, was really the biggest loser, taking a severe ratings dive from last year. The only network that gained ground, CBS, finished last among the Big Three. And even the upstart Fox lost some of those young viewers that has made it Madison Avenue's darling.

NBC may have won its sixth sweeps period in a row, but the victory was sapped by a 13% rating shortfall from last year.
Turn to page 102

Great Scott! Hot vid vanishes

By MAX ALEXANDER

NEW YORK Just when the video industry thought they had it all figured out, along came "The Rocky Horror Picture Show."

Retailers, rackjobbers and industry sources say the camp classic from CBS/Fox is generating feverish consumer sales even though it's priced as a rental title at $89.98. Most sell-through vids check out at $20 to $25.

Trouble is, there aren't a lot of "Horror" cassettes out there — a little more than 300,000 is the going estimate. That's near the high end for a rental title — translating into millions of dollars in revenue — but low for a sell-through hit, which can move millions of units.

One source figures close to half of all "Horror" tapes have been snatched up by consumers. Reports are now circulating of desperate "Horror" fans renting the tape at vidstores, then "losing" it and paying the store $89.98.

CBS/Fox correctly predicted that "Rocky Horror's" wacky
Turn to page 102

INSIDE

■ Will crix miss Xmas pix?
3

Vids vie for Santa's bucks
19

The sweeps, city-by-city
30

FILM 3 | TV 21 | INTERNATIONAL 47 | REVIEWS 78 | LEGIT 85 | FINANCE 99

DAILY VARIETY

LOS ANGELES, CALIFORNIA ▪ NEWSPAPER

$1.75
TUESDAY
MARCH 3, 1998
$2.50 OUTSIDE CALIFORNIA
PERIODICALS POSTAGE PAID

Braun in Disney TV top post

By JENNY HONTZ

Walt Disney Studios on Monday confirmed that Brillstein-Grey Entertainment president Lloyd Braun has been named to the top TV post at the company — a decision that is being viewed as an attempt to better integrate the production company with the network it owns, ABC.

After playing with several different titles on Monday, Disney finally named Braun, 39, to the newly created post of chairman of Buena Vista TV Prods., which will be the umbrella group encompassing Walt Disney Network TV and Touchstone TV.

Braun's appointment, reporting to Walt Disney Studios chairman Joe Roth, was anticipated (*Daily Variety*, March 2). He will oversee all network primetime development and production, specials and movies of the week.

Turn to page 58

INSIDE

4 **'Dance' step**
Sundance Channel lands major carriage deals with Century and Time Warner cable systems.

6 **Souped up**
New Line TV taps Tom Campbell as senior VP in a bid to beef up its Hollywood profile.

8 **Chips ahoy**
The FCC is set to OK the TV content code, clearing the way for V-chips in sets by 1999.

$1 BIL, & STILL NO ICEBERG
'Titanic' steams to all-time global earnings record

By LEONARD KLADY

After breaking an endless series of box office records, "Titanic" this week crossed over the ultimate threshhold: To no one's surprise, it became the first film to pass $1 billion in worldwide theatrical B.O.

The film docked in Sunday with a combined domestic and international gross of $1,002,706,625. Of that amount, $427 million was generated from North American screens, while overseas it's chalked up $575.7 million.

Domestically, the James Cameron-helmed pic still trails "Star Wars," which has raked in $461 million, but it has taken home every other record. Last week, its overseas tally made it the all-time biggest film overseas and the biggest film worldwide (which encompasses domestic and international). The previous record holder in both those races was "Jurassic Park," with $556 million overseas and $357 million domestically.

Given its steadily titanic B.O. since its Dec. 19 bow, the pic was headed to smash through the billion-dollar mark this week. However, the weekend tally put the pic over that threshold a few days earlier than expected.

One of the remarkable things

Cameron

about the success of "Titanic" is that it defies so many formulas and truisms about what makes a film popular.

For one thing, it harkens back to a type of popular entertainment that hasn't been particularly potent in decades: the epic romance. The biggest hits since the 1970s have been action,

Turn to page 54

Homevideo sales, rentals down for '97

By ADAM SANDLER

Purchases of homevideos in 1997 were off by 10% over the 1996 tallies, while rentals dropped 3% during the year, according to a year-end summary released Monday by vid industry research and consulting outfit Alexander & Associates.

The drop in sales was most prominent among the family fare vids, while the rental marketplace was sustained by the vid release of blockbuster films made available primarily in the fourth quarter.

Vid purchases accounted for 657.3 million units in 1997, compared with 735 million units in 1996, a 78 million unit decline.

The dollar value of the vid sales market checked in at $9.3 billion, a $1 billion drop over the $10.38 billion tally registered in 1996; rentals reached $4.1 billion, a slight drop from the $4.23 billion logged in 1996. Total consumer purchases of the top 10 titles fell by 32 million units over the top 10 vids in the market during 1996.

The drop in sales marks the first year of negative growth for the market, though the declines were

Turn to page 46

One voice for Diller's nets

By JOHN DEMPSEY

NEW YORK — Barry Diller has engineered his first major move as head of USA Networks, consolidating the programming, marketing and promotion of the four cable networks in his portfolio: USA, Sci-Fi Channel, Home Shopping Network and America's Store.

"This is the first big initiative coming out of the new company," said Doug Holloway, executive VP of distribution and affiliate relations for USA and Sci-Fi, who'll add Home Shopping and America's Store to his responsibilities.

Turn to page 46

Graham gets 'Committed'

By CHRIS PETRIKIN

Graham

After skating to acclaim as porn star Rollergirl in "Boogie Nights," Heather Graham is set to topline "Committed," an indie feature directed by "Manny & Lo" helmer Lisa Krueger.

Turn to page 55

for your consideration
BEST PICTURE
Produced by Uberto Pasolini
BEST DIRECTOR
Peter Cattaneo
BEST ORIGINAL SCREENPLAY
Simon Beaufoy

"ENCHANTINGLY FUNNY. Director Peter Cattaneo and writer Simon Beaufoy turn these guys into a most endearing dirty half dozen."
— David Ansen, NEWSWEEK

THE FULL MONTY
Now Showing In Select Theatres

Previous Spread: *Variety* explores women in the media and international markets.

Left: March 3, 1998.

Picture Association of America, the org of the major studios:

> ". . . and on many occasions it's been Wasserman who has held together this often quarrelsome, mismatched group. When talk turns to labor negotiations, political relations or similar topics, industry leaders still reflexively turn to Wasserman."

He was the peacemaker and the elder statesman—and trendsetter, since his James Stewart deal in the 1950s, and his Matsushita deal was a prelude to revolving doors affixed to the executive offices of every Hollywood studio for the next twenty years.

Feature films, TV, and other entertainments were slowly growing in foreign markets.

Oh, and then the Internet happened. As the August 10, 1995, *Daily Variety* reported,

> "The Internet received a stunning vote of confidence Wednesday on Wall Street, as investors mobbed the first public stock offering of Netscape Communications Corp. Initially priced at $28 a share, the stock opened at $71 and climbed as high as $74.50 before settling down to $58.25, a jump of 108%. Netscape's Navigator software is used by about 75% of computer users to plug into the Internet's World Wide Web, the audio-visual arena where many Hollywood studios and entertainment companies recently have installed popular interactive promotional sites."

The following month, columnist Katherine Stalter pointed out that the studios and TV networks had entered "cyberspace" to promote their works.

> "Now the Internet is home to MGM/UA's Lion's Den, a World Wide Web site launched to promote rental and sell-through home video releases. The first releases to be featured on the site are the restored classic 'Doctor Zhivago,' 'Rob Roy' and 'The Outer Limits.'" The site also carried "a comprehensive directory of MGM/UA homevideo titles that can be sorted by title, genre and year."

At the time, this seemed like a real novelty, but home video hit its stride in the 1990s. Only a decade earlier, on February 15, 1984, *Weekly Variety* had been impressed that the *Jane Fonda's Workout* video held an all-time sales record of 270,000 units. By 1991, the September 4 *Daily* reported, "the Fonda fitness titles collectively have sold more than 6 million units to date." And on March 14, 1995, reporter Adam Sandler (no, not *that* Adam Sandler) reported in *Daily* that Disney's *The Lion King* had sold an estimated twenty million copies in its first week. It had taken *Snow White and the Seven Dwarfs* four weeks to hit that mark, while *Jurassic Park* took five months to hit fifteen million. Another game changer was the invention and adoption of the DVD. A *Daily* story on October 31, 1997, correctly predicted that

> "retailers say 1997 is the year DVD will finally become the 'must-have' product for our homes, profoundly affecting virtually every aspect of home entertainment. . . . Clearly, DVD will have a major impact on Hollywood, as people buy new copies of movies they already have on video, but the impact of the new system could run deeper than face value."

A chart that day (October 31, 1997) noted the DVD's debut seven months earlier and projected 1.4

million players would be sold in the first two years; that was miles ahead of the 230,000 VCR players and 243,000 CD players sold in their first two years.

People were spending a lot of time in front of their televisions: *Seinfeld*'s farewell episode drew 76.3 million viewers, "ranking it sixth all-time among entertainment broadcasts," behind the last *M*A*S*H* episode (106 million), the "Who Shot J.R." episode of *Dallas* (83.6 million), the last *Cheers* (80.4 million), *The Day After* (77.4 million), and *Roots*, "Part 7" (76.7 million).

In the April 23, 2001, *Weekly Variety*, Melissa Grego projected that *Seinfeld* would earn an estimated $2 billion in syndication, and that NBC's *Friends* (1994–2004) looked likely to make $1.5 billion.

In the music industry, *Daily* on May 7, 1999, ran an AP story announcing the Academy of Country Music's naming of Garth Brooks as entertainer of the decade. Brooks chalked up 68 million album sales, beating The Beatles and Elvis Presley. In 1992, Nirvana, whose lead force Kurt Cobain offered "Smells like Teen Spirit," marked the start of grunge rock. There were key works from Radiohead, U2, Smashing Pumpkins, Mariah Carey, Janet Jackson, R.E.M., Billy Ray Cyrus, George Michael, the Spice Girls, Hanson, Whitney Houston, Faith Hill, and boy bands such as Backstreet Boys, N*Sync, and Take That.

Margaret Cho marked a TV breakthrough in 1994 in *All-American Girl*, as the first person to ever star in an American sitcom featuring a completely Asian or Asian American cast. ABC cast her in the successful tradition of basing a weekly half-hour show on the persona of various stand-up comics, starting in the earliest days of TV with Burns and Allen and Jack Benny and continuing with Redd Foxx (*Sanford and Son*, 1972), Bob Newhart (*The Bob Newhart Show*, 1972; *Newhart*, 1982; and *Bob*, 1992), Bill Cosby (*The Cosby Show*, 1984), Roseanne Barr (*Roseanne*, 1988), Jerry Seinfeld (*Seinfeld*, 1989), Tim Allen (*Home Improvement*, 1991), Mark Curry (*Hangin' with Mr. Cooper*, 1992), Drew Carey (*The Drew Carey Show*, 1995), Ray Romano (*Everybody Loves Raymond*, 1996), and Steve Harvey (*The Steve Harvey Show*, 1996).

But *All-American Girl* lasted for only nineteen episodes before ABC pulled the plug. Cho's battles with the network over content, her appearance, and her performance became fodder for her stand-up act. Since then, no U.S. sitcom has featured an Asian cast, bringing us to a grand total of one in more than sixty years.

ABC had another flap on its hands when Ellen DeGeneres, stand-up performer and star of its sitcom *Ellen*, announced that she was a lesbian and, soon after that, her character announced that she was a lesbian, too. An April 30, 1997, review of that episode read that this realization by a character who'd thought she was straight was a milestone. The episode was carrying the torch "for a new open-mindedness in primetime," with the review acknowledging DeGeneres's career risks and applauded the humorous handling of the topic.

> **Right**: Umm . . .

The following year, NBC debuted *Will & Grace*, featuring four characters, two of whom are gay men. The show was a huge hit, running eight seasons.

Jurassic Park spawned yet another 1990s revolution. The June 14, 1993, review in *Weekly Variety* of the film, directed by Steven Spielberg and based on the novel by Michael Crichton, read, "Spielberg and his team of special effects aces have put something on the screen that people have never seen before." The CGI (computer-generated imagery) technology that created the dinosaurs enabled creatives around the world to depict worlds, explosions, beasties, and eventually humans in ways never before attempted, forever changing the virtual, metaphorical, and physical landscape of filmmaking.

In 1997, James Cameron directed *Titanic*, and showed the world some of the possibilities of CGI and reminded us that any success, especially a mega-success, is nothing without a story. Some critics, including *Variety*'s, were underwhelmed with the script. *Variety*'s reviewer wondered whether distributor 20th Century-Fox "can come anywhere nearer to break-even in the rest of the world," since the film was so far over budget and behind schedule that its cost was estimated at over $200 million.

But don't worry, audiences ate it up. As Don Groves reported from Sydney on September 11, 1998, Cameron's film was the first to pass $1 billion, with $600 million domestically and that same amount overseas. At that point, the film was still active in its thirty-eighth

America's Families Deserve Better!

Robert Iger, President
Capital Cities/ABC

Michael Eisner, Chairman
The Walt Disney Company

Jamie Tarses, President
ABC Entertainment

Ellen DeGeneres, Dava Savel, Mark Driscoll, Vic Kaplan, Matt Goldman, Jan Nash
Producers of *Ellen*

Dear Mr. Iger, Mr. Eisner, Ms. Tarses, Ms. DeGeneres, Ms. Savel, Mr. Driscoll, Mr. Kaplan, Mr. Goldman, and Ms. Nash:

The much-ballyhooed April 30 "coming out" episode of the show *Ellen* is insulting to millions of American families who once looked to Disney as a beacon of family entertainment. This transparent PR move to revive the show's sagging ratings -- by slowly leaking information throughout the season that Ellen DeGeneres' character might reveal herself to be a lesbian -- is also a blatant attempt by Disney, ABC, and *Ellen* to promote homosexuality to America's families.

Disney is employing one of the industry's oldest PR tricks by inviting high-powered stars, including Oprah Winfrey, Demi Moore, Laura Dern, k.d. lang, Melissa Etheridge, and Billy Bob Thornton, to join *Ellen*'s "coming out" party.

Moreover, Disney is insisting on airing this episode even though a vast majority of Ellen's own viewers are appalled. According to a recent TV Guide *survey, a full 63 percent of Americans who are familiar with the show have stated that they will tune out that night.*

So why have Disney, ABC, and *Ellen* decided to continue this three-ring circus? Could it be Disney and ABC just don't care what American families think? Could it be ABC didn't mean it when it told many of our nation's leaders it would air more family-friendly programming? What else could account for this insult, this slap in the face to America's families?

Now the ABC network has refused to run an ad by the pro-gay Human Rights Campaign during the episode because it doesn't accept "controversial issue advertising." This is hypocritical. The entire episode *is* a controversial issue advertisement.

The big-top act could be expected of Ellen DeGeneres, who has allowed herself to become a pawn of a political movement. But shame on Disney, and shame on ABC. American families deserve better.

L. Brent Bozell III, Chairman
Media Research Center

Pat Robertson, Chairman
CBN, Inc.

Gary Bauer, President
Family Research Council

Michael A. Ferguson, Executive Director
The Catholic Campaign for America

J. C. Willke, M.D., President
Life Issues Institute

Phyllis Schlafly, President
Eagle Forum

Chris Gersten, Director
Center for Jewish and Christian Values

Dr. Balint Vaszonyi

Gary Jarmin, Legislative Director
Christian Voice

Rev. Donald E. Wildmon
American Family Association

Paul Weyrich, President
Free Congress Foundation

Chuck Colson, Founder and Chairman
Prison Fellowship

Rabbi Daniel Lapin, President
Toward Tradition

Dr. Carl Herbster, President
American Association of Christian Schools

Jay Parker, President
Lincoln Institute for Research & Education

The Honorable Howard Phillips, Chairman
The Conservative Caucus, Inc.

Rev. Jerry Falwell

William A. Donohue, President
Catholic League for Religious and Civil Rights

The Honorable Morton C. Blackwell, Chairman
Conservative Leadership PAC

Rabbi Yechiel Eckstein, President
International Fellowship of Christians and Jews

Carolyn Parlato, President
Institute for Republican Women

Robert Cahill, Chairman
Morality in Media

Beverly LaHaye, Chairman
Concerned Women for America

Reed Irvine, Chairman
Accuracy in Media, Inc.

Peter Flaherty, President
National Legal and Policy Center

The Honorable Holland J. Coors

Marlin Maddoux, President
USA Radio Network

Beverly Danielson, Trustee
Media Research Center

Dr. Robert Grant, President
American Freedom Coalition

The Honorable James Miller III

Oliver North, Founder
Freedom Alliance

Sara Hardman, State Chairman
Christian Coalition of California

Stuart Epperson, Chairman
Salem Communications Corp.

For more information contact:
Media Research Center
113 S. West Street, 2nd Floor
Alexandria, VA 22314
(703) 683-9733 ■ www.mediaresearch.org

The Media Research Center is a 501 (c)(3) research and education foundation

week of release and went on to earn $1.8 billion and break records with its soundtrack album, home-video sales, and merchandising.

But, once again, the 1990s proved a prelude, as *Titanic*'s astonishing record was broken by another Cameron film, *Avatar*, in 2009.

Aside from *Jurassic Park* and *Titanic*, the decade gave us Pixar's first feature film, the computer-animated *Toy Story* (1995), which earned $362 million worldwide and spawned a company that dominated feature-film animation for years to come.

One horror film perfectly captured the decade: *Scream* (1996), from writer Matt Williamson and director Wes Craven. The film offered the basic thrills of a good scary movie but with the ironic detachment that permeated every aspect of the decade. It was created for a generation that had grown up with TV and had seen every horror movie possible on video. The endangered youngsters of *Scream* were perfect representations of the audience. They were so familiar with the staples of the genre that they laughed at the idea of going into a dark room alone.

Other horror films flirted with the supernatural, such as the 1994 *Interview with the Vampire* (based on Anne Rice's influential book), the 1992 *Bram Stoker's Dracula*, and the 1998 *Bride of Chucky*. But in general, the suspense and scares came from the weirdness of human beings: Best Picture winner *The Silence of the Lambs* (1991), *Cape Fear* (1991), *Seven* (1995), *I Know What You Did Last Summer* (1997), and *The Sixth Sense* (1999), to mention a few.

The decade ended with a different kind of horror: tech nightmares. A *Daily Variety* story on October 11, 1999, said production would be poky at the end of the year, partly due to the usual holiday slowdown—and partly because everyone wanted to avoid the predicted meltdown at midnight on 01/01/2000. There was a possibility the computers couldn't process this radical date change; as one production exec was quoted as saying, "the effect of Y2K is unknown," and nobody wanted to leave things to chance.

Spoiler alert: the Y2K disaster didn't happen.

Or, as the January 3, 2000, *Daily Weekly* headlined, it was the "Yawn of a New Era":

"The much-feared arrival of Y2K provoked more moderation than madness and a worldwide sigh of relief as chaos failed to manifest itself anywhere on the planet."

With the dawn of a new millennium, was the world slouching toward Bethlehem, as Yeats described the pending apocalypse, or just heading into the dawn of a more exciting time?

"Exciting" might not be the right word, but the twenty-first century proved to be more eventful and intense than anyone had anticipated.

H'W'D PLANS Y2K HOLIDAY

By CLAUDE BRODESSER

The world may be prepping for the party of the millennium, but the dawn of the new century promises to be unusually quiet for the film business.

Although pic and TV productions routinely all but come to a standstill around the year-end holidays, some studios, like DreamWorks and Disney, are shuttering for an extra week. Warner Bros. has canceled all production from mid-December until well after the holidays. And all pic makers, whether studio or independent, seem

Turn to page 17

Above: Hollywood stockpiles water and cash.

Right: June 15, 1993.

Following Spread: And one director to rule them all.

DAILY VARIETY

90 CENTS
TUESDAY
JUNE 15, 1993

A CAHNERS PUBLICATION ■ LOS ANGELES, CALIFORNIA ■ NEWSPAPER SECOND CLASS P.O. ENTRY

Downside to reality: ad rates

BY BRIAN LOWRY

Those perplexed to see so many seemingly successful reality series kept off prime time schedules next fall need only see an estimate of network advertising rates to understand why.

A monthly report distributed to Nielsen subscribers, providing the cost of 30-second commercials for more than 100 prime time series, underscores the lack of enthusiasm for the reality genre on Madison Avenue as well as the sharp drop-off in rates commanded by shows that skew heavily toward an older audience.

An illustration of the latter case would be CBS' "Murder, She Wrote," ranked fourth for the season among all prime time programs in terms of its average rat-

Turn to page 41

NUMBERS

30 seconds on 'Roseanne' $279,000

The most expensive time on TV is during Mrs. Tom Arnold's show. At the other end of the blurb spectrum, a half-minute on "Sightings" costs $32,000.

'JURASSIC' REX RECORDS
DNA means dinosaur numbers astronomical

BY LEONARD KLADY

The numbers are staggering. Universal's "Jurassic Park" grossed $50,159,460 from 2,404 playdates in its opening weekend. The film posted averages of $20,865.

The appropriate word is not "huge" or "boffo" or "gigantic" or even "dinosaurian." It is simply "biggest."

"Jurassic" is the biggest opening-weekend gross ever. It had the biggest preview revenues, and Saturday generated the biggest single-day gross with $18 million. And many, many theaters had their biggest box office earnings ever, to establish new individual house records.

It's all very nice, even if the new apex is not comparable to a Bob Beamon long jump record that stood for more than two decades. The Spielberg picture probably needed to do in the neighborhood of $60 million to keep the next blockbuster at bay for more than a few years. In all likelihood, some film will come along in the next few years to knock the reigning champ among openers off its perch.

Which is not to suggest that it's time to close the record books on the prehysteric picture.

Challenges still to come include the fastest picture to reach a $100 million domestic gross and, of course, the biggest grossing film of all time.

Yes, there's a tremendous sense of energy from the possibilities a giant smash on the order of "Jurassic Park" can expand the marketplace. Only time will tell. And no, it is not the height of film art.

If indeed there are palpable benefits to be earned off of "Jurassic"

Turn to page 10

INSIDE

4 Riot-minded
Anna Deavere Smith illuminates the restive state of the city in "Twilight: Los Angeles, 1992."

5 They'll be making 'Mary'
Ned and Nancy Tanen will produce and Stephen Frears will direct "Mary Reilly" after Tim Burton & co. exit the Jekyll/Hyde love story.

5 Rights to 'Life'
Republic Pictures claims it owns rights that give it control of "It's a Wonderful Life."

30 O'seas Report
Anticipated arrival of Pierre Heros caps off Studio Canal Plus reorganization and Alasdair Waddell abruptly quits as Lumiere chief.

WHITE MALE PENS STILL BUSIEST
Study finds H'wood lags in hiring minority, female writers

BY KATHLEEN O'STEEN

A new five-year study about writer employment in Hollywood shows that the industry is not making any great strides in terms of overcoming racism, sexism and ageism.

Among the companies that made little or no progress in hiring minority or female writers: ABC, NBC, MGM's film division and Orion. Warner Bros. TV made increases in minority hirings but fell behind in female hirings.

"We're not making progress," noted Samantha Shad, chairman of the Women's Committee of the Writers Guild of America West. "We can't really say that it's progress when women are still only making 75¢ on the dollar in earnings compared to white males."

Hispanic media watchdog org targets four L.A. TV stations, page 5.

(That figure compares to 62¢ five years ago.)

The WGAW-commissioned report comes on the heels of a recent Screen Actors Guild earnings report that showed women consistently earned less than their male counterparts. Of the $1 billion that SAG members earned last year, only one third was earned by women.

In terms of the number of women writers being hired, there has been little growth over the past 20 years. As of 1991, women accounted for 22%-25% of those employed in television and 16%-17% of those working in film. Yet women have consistently accounted for 20%-25% of the industry's workforce in the last two decades.

Minorities fared a little better in earnings, making a median 79¢ on the dollar, as compared to 54¢ in 1987, but the number of minorities being hired falls far below that of women.

As of 1991, working minority

Turn to page 42

Madonna

MADONNA'S MAVERICK IN ABC PACT

BY BRIAN LOWRY

Madonna's Maverick Television Co. has entered into a wide-ranging arrangement with the ABC network and ABC Prods. to develop and produce all forms of television, including series, longform programming and specials.

ABC eschewed specifics but said that it's committed to several projects, beginning with a four-hour miniseries biography, "Madonna: The Early Years." Plans for that production had leaked out earlier but turn out to be part of a larger relationship.

Turn to page 36

Cosby NBC bid seen unlikely

BY J. MAX ROBINS

NEW YORK — Wall Streets savants dismissed reports Monday that Bill Cosby is mounting another attempt to buy NBC, saying odds of such a deal are about as good as David Letterman moving to ABC to anchor "Nightline."

A report in Monday's Wall Street Journal said Cosby was working with investment banker

Turn to page 6

Par pickups batting 1.000

BY BRIAN LOWRY

Paramount Network TV has completed a near-perfect pilot-to-series ratio on its 1993-94 development crop with confirmation of pickups on sitcoms "Sister, Sister" from ABC and "Big Wave Dave's" from CBS.

The deals mean the studio has essentially gone six-for-six in turning pilots into series. That batting average has become increasingly important to suppliers, whose concerns about costs have made them more aware of the percentage of what they sell vs. what they develop, in contrast to the scattershot approach sometimes pursued in the past.

A seventh Paramount project remains in development at Fox

Turn to page 8

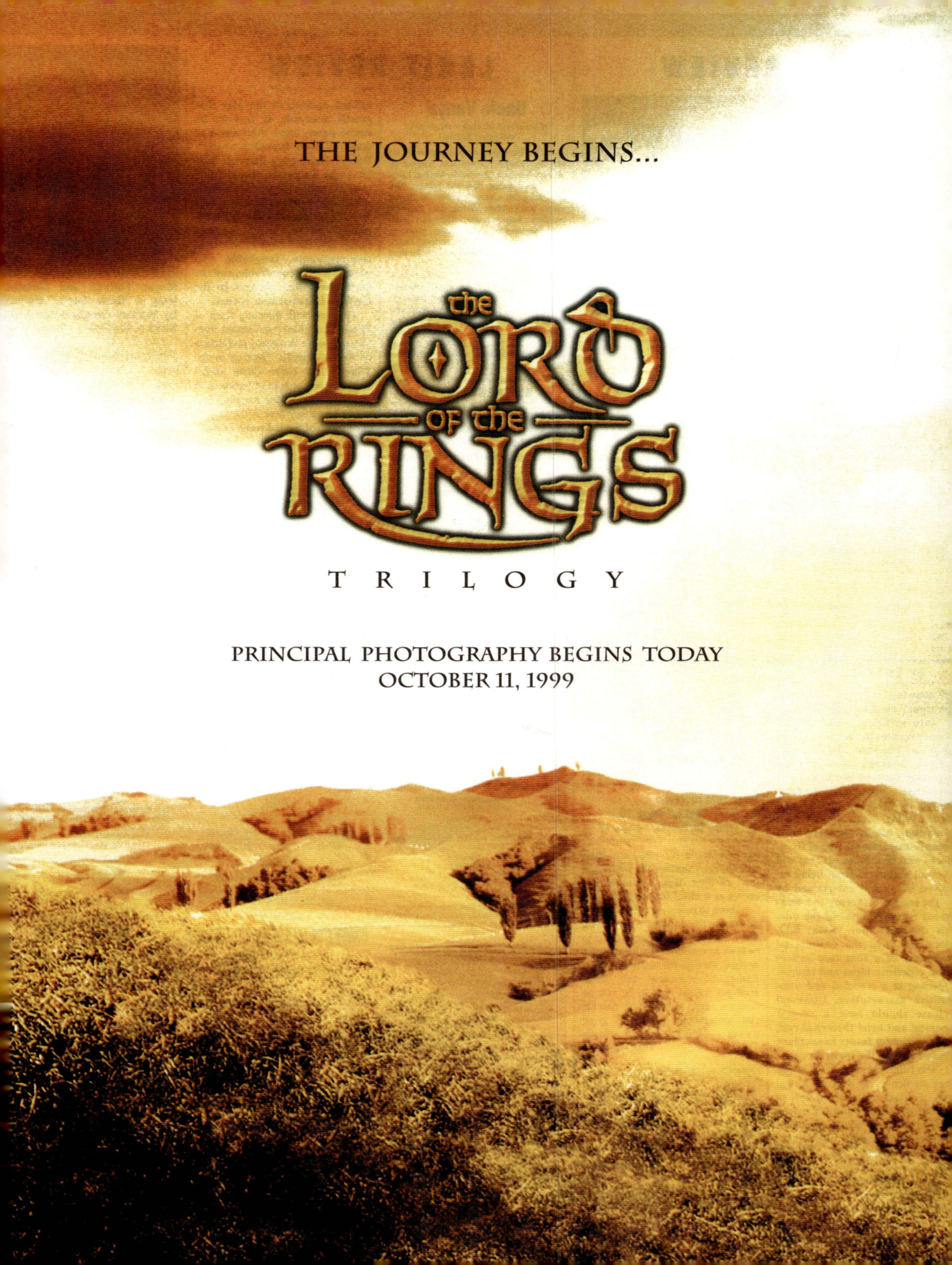

OBITUARIES

AKIRA KUROSAWA

Akira Kurosawa, the internationally acclaimed Japanese film director, died Sept. 6 in Tokyo of a stroke. He was 88.

His landmark films, especially "The Seven Samurai," "Rashomon" and "Ikiru," were popular the world over and influenced a generation of filmmakers, including George Lucas, Francis Coppola, Martin Scorsese and Steven Spielberg.

Considered the most Western of Asian directors, Kurosawa was honored by the Academy of Motion Picture Arts and Sciences with a lifetime achievement award in 1990, and two of his films, "Rashomon" and "Dersu Uzala," won Oscars for best foreign film. He was also nominated as best director in 1985 for "Ran" and received the Directors Guild of America's Jubilee Award in 1986.

There was an immediate outpouring of grief in Japan and around the world upon the news of his death. And officials at the Venice International Film Festival, where "Rashomon" won the Golden Lion in 1951, are planning a special showing of that movie.

The director greatly influenced postwar cinema, particularly in the United States, beginning in 1951 with the release of "Rashomon," a story about the ambiguity of truth and Kurosawa's first international hit. The film was remade as "The Outrage" by director Martin Ritt.

Other Kurosawa films were also remade. "The Seven Samurai" inspired the American Western "The Magnificent Seven," which boosted the career of Steve McQueen. And Sergio Leone reimagined "Yojimbo" as the spaghetti Western "A Fistful of Dollars," which gained Clint Eastwood stardom.

Kurosawa's historical spectacle "The Hidden Fortress" was credited by Lucas as an important source for "Star Wars."

Conversely, Kurosawa's Eastern formalism and stylistic structure were heavily leavened with Western influences. "The Seven Samurai" was shaped by the moral conflicts that dominated the American Westerns of John Ford, to whom Kurosawa frequently paid homage. Frank Capra was another of Kurosawa's favorite directors.

Kurosawa's masterful adaptations of Shakespeare include "Throne of Blood" (Macbeth) and "Ran" (King Lear). Both films preserved the integrity of Shakespeare's tragedy and at the same time honored the tradition of the warrior in Japanese legend.

AKIRA KUROSAWA

Kurosawa eventually fell out of favor in his native Japan, partly because of his increasing fascination with expressionism. But he always had critics at home, those who complained that his films were too Western.

Thanks largely to his American filmmaking champions and other foreign revenue sources, Kurosawa was always able to raise financing for his often expensive (by Japanese standards), lavishly produced films.

Kurosawa was born in Tokyo on March 23, 1910, the son of a solider who took pride in his northern samurai ancestry.

A struggling young painter, Kurosawa happened upon filmmaking by accident. "I saw a newspaper advertisement. PCL, which later became Toho Studios, wanted an assistant director."

After five years as an assistant director and script writer, Kurosawa directed "Sugata Sanshiro" about a judo champion. Its popularity spawned a sequel. But censorship restrictions, as well as the rigid traditions of cinema storytelling in Japan, hampered his progress up until the end of World War II. It wasn't until "Drunken Angel" in 1948, the first of 16 films with actor Toshiro Mifune, that Kurosawa "finally discovered myself," as he told critic Donald Richie, a Japanese cinema authority and longtime friend.

Kurosawa's popularity in Japan broadened to the international arena with "Rashomon," which recounts the murder of a nobleman and the rape of his wife as told by four conflicting witnesses. The film won the Lion D'Or at the Venice Film Festival and became the first Japanese film to achieve arthouse success in the U.S.

With the end of the American occupation of Japan and the release of "Ikiru" (To Live), Kurosawa embarked on a creatively and commercially fecund period, in which he produced such masterpieces as "The Seven Samurai," "Throne of Blood," "The Lower Depths," "The Hidden Fortress," "The Bad Sleep Well," "Yojimbo," "Sanjuro," "High and Low" and "The Red Beard."

In a partnership with several other leading Japanese filmmakers, he created a production company called The Four Musketeers but directed only one film, "Dodeskaden" in 1969, under the banner. It was his first film in color and a commercial disappointment. Its failure, health problems and the shift in Japanese cinema to slicker, more commercial fare led him to attempt suicide in 1971.

After a four-year hiatus, Kurosawa returned with the Oscar-winning (and Russian-financed) "Dersu Uzala," made on location in the Soviet Union. The invitation by Mosofilm, he admits, saved him from "a dark moment."

At the behest of Coppola and Lucas, Alan Ladd Jr., then head of 20th Century Fox, invested $1.5 million in "Kagemusha," which in 1980 became one of Japan's highest-grossing films and won the Palme D'Or in Cannes. It was followed by the enormously successful "Ran," a $10 million French-Japanese co-production. The film earned Kurosawa his only Academy Award nomination for best director.

"Ran" was followed by a number of increasingly meditative, beautifully studied but dramatically unsatisfying films, such as "Dreams" (in which Martin Scorsese made a cameo appearance as Van Gogh), "Rhapsody in August" (featuring Richard Gere) and "Madadayo." Though not entirely successful, the spate of films represented the octogenarian's most productive period since the 1960s.

Kurosawa was married to a former movie actress and has a son, Hiroshi, who is a film producer.
—*Richard Natale and Jon Herskovitz*

LEO PENN

Leo Penn, an Emmy-winning television director and actor, died Sept. 5 of cancer in Los Angeles. He was 77.

Father of actor-director Sean, Penn won his Emmy in 1973 for directing a two-hour episode of "Columbo" called "Any Port in a Storm."

Best known for directing more than 400 hours of primetime television, his numerous credits include "I Spy," "Matlock," "St. Elsewhere," "Magnum P.I." and "Diagnosis Murder."

In addition to his work in television, Penn directed two feature films, "A Man Called Adam" (1966), starring Sammy Davis Jr. and Cicely Tyson, and "Judgment in Berlin" (1988), starring Martin Sheen.

Penn began his career as an actor on stage and in film. He met the woman he would marry, Eileen Ryan, when the two had leading roles for the 1950s Broadway production of "The Iceman Cometh." He appeared in several other plays including "Cat on a Hot Tin Roof" and "Of Mice and Men."

Penn also had a contract with Paramount, the result of his appearance in a college play. He had been studying drama at UCLA.

Beginning in the late 1940s, Penn was blacklisted from Hollywood for a decade, after attending meetings of actors sympathetic to the trade union and speaking out in support of the Hollywood Ten.

He made a living during those years by working as an actor in television, which was less influenced by the Hollywood studios at the time.

After returning to films in 1959 as an actor in "The Story on Page One," Penn decided that he wanted to pursue directing and got a job on the new television series "Ben Casey."

From there he went on to direct for several television series including "Little House on the Prairie," The Bionic Woman," "Hart to Hart," "Cagney and Lacey," "Remington Steele," and "In the Heat of the Night."

In recent years, Penn returned to acting, appearing with his wife in the 1995 film "Crossing Guard," which was directed by son Sean. His latest performance was in the 1997 play "Remembrance," which Sean produced at the Odyssey Theater in West Los Angeles.

He is survived by his wife and three sons. His other sons are Michael, a singer-songwriter, and Chris, an actor.

MARYANNE KASICA-SCHEFF

MaryAnne Kasica-Scheff, a television writer whose work included "Magnum P.I." and "Murder She Wrote," died Sept. 5 in Los Angeles of a brain tumor. She was 58.

Kasica-Scheff entered the entertainment business as an actress, performing in summer stock productions and working with such actors as Tallulah Bankhead, Estelle Winwood and Paul Ford.

In 1966 she moved into the production realm and was named executive director of the Friends of Lincoln Center.

Kasica-Scheff's interest in Wall Street next landed her a position as one of the few women stockbrokers in New York. Originally pursuing an MBA at Cal State University, Los Angeles, she earned an M.A. in drama in 1972. This degree led to her return to acting, and she appeared in TV shows including "Marcus Welby M.D."

After writing several one-act plays to use as audition material, including a piece that won the UCLA Playwright's Award in 1975, and co-authoring the book "The Pushbutton Telephone," Kasica-Scheff began a writing

American film icon Stewart dies at 89

By RICHARD NATALE

James Stewart, who was once described as "unusually usual" and who was a star for 60 years due to that Everyman quality, died Wednesday at his Beverly Hills home at the age of 89.

Stewart's affability, his oft-imitated halting speech pattern, and tall, lanky posture went through three distinct phases in Hollywood. The first was in the '30s when he rose slowly up the ranks from supporting player to leading man in sophisticated comedies like "Made for Each Other" and "Mr. Smith Goes to Washington," culminating in his best actor Oscar for "The Philadelphia Story" in 1940.

After World War II, he adapted his persona to more mature, troubled characters in such film classics as "It's a Wonderful Life," "Broken Arrow," "Vertigo" and "Anatomy of a Murder."

Finally, he continued to work in the '60s and after, often in frothy family comedies and in TV, but became less known for his work than his presence; he was an eminence gris, the

Turn to page 20

More coverage:
- Army Archerd, page 4
- An appreciation, page 21

James Stewart in 1954's "Rear Window," one of his most successful outings for helmer Alfred Hitchcock.

SCREEN LEGEND STEWART DIES AT 89

Continued from page 1

revered and sometimes indulged (as when he read his own poetry on "The Tonight Show") spirit of Old Hollywood folksiness.

Stewart was the 1980 recipient of the American Film Institute's Lifetime Achievement Award; in saluting his former colleague, director Frank Capra said there are few performers capable of making the craft disappear to the extent that "all that's left is the person on the screen." Pointing to Stewart he added, "that tall stringbean … he's one of them."

While never a great actor in the classic sense, he was a great screen presence, capable of wrapping his persona around any given role and commanding audience empathy.

Stewart was born in Indiana, Pa., on May 20, 1908, the son of a hardware store owner. After attending Princeton as an architecture major, he was invited by another alumnus, Joshua Logan, to join the Logan University Players — at first to play the accordion, but eventually to take on bit parts with other former schoolmates, including Margaret Sullavan and Henry Fonda, who remained a lifelong friend.

Bit by the acting bug, he moved to New York, where Fonda was one of his roommates. He was steadily employed in small theatrical roles, breaking through in 1934 in "Yellow Jack," his performance earning assessments such as "simple, sensitive and true," by the New York World Telegram reviewer Robert Garland.

Future gossip columnist Hedda Hopper saw him in his next play, "Divided by Three," and touted him to MGM's casting department. Under contract, he made his film debut in the 1935 "Murder Man" and made eight films in the next year.

The gangly, at times awkward, actor made his first big impact with the unlikely assignment of introducing Cole Porter's "Easy to Love" in the 1936 "Born to Dance" opposite Eleanor Powell.

But as was true of many contract players of the day, he had to work outside MGM before his full potential was recognized by the studio toppers (who were so wrong about Stewart that they cast him as a villain in "After the Thin Man").

The actor began to hit his stride in 1938 when he starred in RKO's "Vivacious Lady" opposite Ginger Rogers and the first of his Capra films, "You Can't Take it With You" at Columbia.

Full-fledged stardom came the following year in another Col pic, Capra's "Mr. Smith Goes to Washington" (which secured Stewart his first Academy Award nomination) and Universal's hit Western comedy "Destry Rides Again" with Marlene Dietrich.

In 1940, back at MGM, he starred in the screen version of Philip Barry's "The Philadelphia Story," in which he was encircled by the creme de la creme team of Katharine Hepburn and Cary Grant under the smooth directorial hand of George Cukor. Stewart took home the Oscar for the pic.

His boyish charm and graceful demeanor attracted directors such as Frank Capra, Ernst Lubitsch and George Stevens during that period. Stewart epitomized an ideal vision of middle-American manhood, combining innocence, sincerity and moral integrity, prized virtues that would be swept away by cynicism and disillusionment following the nation's involvement in the war.

While the U.S. was preparing for the war effort, Stewart and his pal Fonda did a magic act for the USO. When he tried to volunteer for service, he was told he was too thin. He altered his diet and gained weight.

With 400 hours of civilian flying time behind him, he was assigned to the Air Force base at Moffet Field. He rose quickly from mechanic to second lieutenant to lieutenant colonel. After flying bombing missions over Germany from his base in England, Stewart was awarded the Air Force Medal, Distinguished Flying Cross with Oak Leaf Cluster and the Croix de Guerre. He eventually rose to the Air Force rank of brigadier general.

After flying 25 missions over Germany as commander of the Eighth Air Force bomber squadron, Stewart adapted to the post-war world, reinventing his persona. Instead of resigning with MGM, he joined Liberty Prods., a brief partnership between Capra and George Stevens.

The 1946 "It's a Wonderful Life" was the dark side of the Capra vision and Stewart's years of war experience contributed in a chiaroscuro performance that was so harrowing and real in some sections (although not without some Capra-corn elements) that audiences turned away. Still, Stewart nabbed his third Oscar nom. After the pic's copyright elapsed, it came to be appreciated on TV as a Christmas classic, and the pic became probably his most acclaimed and well-known effort.

In 1949 he married Gloria Hatrick MacLean; two years later, they had twin daughters Kelly and Judith. When asked what the most important accomplishment of his life was, Stewart said, "marrying my wife. She's made my life more exciting and interesting and meaningful than I ever thought it could be and she's kept that up."

In 1950 he starred in "Harvey," one of his few post-war comedies (which earned him a fourth Oscar bid), and "Winchester 73." The latter pic marked the first of Stewart's string of violent and psychologically complex Westerns and thrillers for, respectively, directors Anthony Mann and Alfred Hitchcock.

The new Westerns were gritty, brutal, unsparing; they showed a Stewart capable of ferocity. "Winchester 73" and Delmer Daves' "Broken Arrow," also in 1950, did more than revive Stewart's career: They made him a rich man.

Under the counsel of his agents Lew Wasserman and Leland Hayward, he opted for a percentage of profits in lieu of salary. Though the tactic had been popular in the silent era, it disappeared under the studio system, and increased exponentially the power and earning capability of movie stars and their agents.

One of his more successful '50s films, "The Glenn Miller Story," netted Stewart more than $1 million — about 50% of the movie's profits.

Stewart also brought luster to Cecil B. DeMille's best-pic Oscar winner "The Greatest Show on Earth." Although he had first teamed with Hitchcock in the stilted 1948 "Rope," Stewart later starred in two of the suspense master's finest films, 1954's "Rear Window" and 1958 "Vertigo" as well as a '56 remake of "The Man Who Knew Too Much."

By 1955 his star was shining at its brightest, as he was the biggest box office attraction in the U.S. However, one of his personal favorites, Billy Wilder's 1957 "The Spirit of St. Louis," was curiously unpopular, but the actor capped the decade by winning the New York Film Critics award for Otto Preminger's "Anatomy of a Murder," the 1959 pic that marked his fifth Academy Award nomination.

In the '60s, studio mogul Jack Warner learned of Ronald Reagan's presidential aspirations and acutely remarked, "No. Jimmy Stewart for president. Ronald Reagan for best friend."

Had Stewart decided to enter politics, it is easy to imagine that the life-long conservative Republican would have had no trouble being elected chief executive. Or that it might have been considered a step down from his perch as one of Hollywood's most likable and popular stars.

Although he continued to star in films until the late 1970s, rarely at a rate of more than two a year, his last great performance was arguably in John Ford's 1962 classic "The Man Who Shot Liberty Valance," opposite John Wayne.

After starring in several of Ford's later films and the Western "Shenandoah" in the mid-'60s, his last starring role was in the 1971 drama "Fool's Parade," for which he collected his then standard $250,000 fee and 10% of the gross. When the film failed, he went into semi-retirement, making guest appearances in films and reviving "Harvey" onstage in New York and London.

He starred in "The Jimmy Stewart Show," an NBC sitcom that ran for one season in 1971. His 1973 vidpic "Hawkins on Murder" served as a pilot to his law drama series, which ran for the 1973-74 season on CBS. He also appeared in other occasional TV longforms, like the 1983 "Right of Way" with Bette Davis and the 1989 "North and South, Book II." In 1991, he provided a voice for the animated "An American Tail: Fievel Goes West."

Aside from his five Oscar nominations, in 1985 he was voted an honorary Oscar for the body of his work and the Medal of Freedom from President Reagan.

His wife died Feb. 16, 1994, after 44 years of marriage. Stewart is survived by a stepson, Michael McLean, and daughters Judy Merrill and Kelly Harcourt.

(Timothy M. Gray contributed to this report.)

IT'S A WONDERFUL CAREER: Stewart flexed his psychological thriller muscles in yet another Hitchcock pic, "The Man Who Knew Too Much" with co-star Doris Day in 1956 above; became a Christmas favorite as George Bailey in 1946's "It's a Wonderful Life," directed by Frank Capra and co-starring Donna Reed, above right; and personified political idealism in Capra's 1939 pic "Mr. Smith Goes to Washington."

> Director Frank Capra said Stewart was one of few performers capable of making the craft disappear to the extent that 'all that's left is the person on the screen.'

2000s

The early years of the new millennium could be called the ADD era, although by the time I'm writing this, in 2012, attention deficit is no longer regarded as a disorder but a way of life.

One hundred years earlier, the average consumer experienced only a few hours of entertainment a week. By the twenty-first century, however, most people had access to entertainment 24/7, which they could enjoy in theaters, stadiums, and clubs as well as on TV, laptops, cell phones, and iPads. They now have social networking sites like Facebook and could absorb info from websites like Google and YouTube. They can send messages via email, text, or Twitter, while simultaneously doing any of the other above activities (or even during a meal or conversation). Given all of this, it's not surprising the public has ADD, because—wait, sorry, what were we talking about?

In the first few years of the decade, people would describe themselves as multitasking, basically bragging/complaining that they were doing several chores simultaneously. But as the economy collapsed in 2008, layoffs were rampant and companies asked their remaining employees to assume the duties of their fallen brethren. In general, people were either unemployed or overworked. So the word "multitasking" wasn't used so much. People increased workloads and just did what was necessary to survive.

The decade's political unrest—sometimes peaceful, sometimes violent—was often interconnected with the technological and economic changes.

The decade's most notable day, if perhaps the most notable day in generations, was, of course, September 11, 2001. America and the world were stunned by the more than three thousand dead or injured, the damage to the Pentagon, and the collapse of New York City's World Trade Center's Twin Towers. On September 12, *Daily Variety* devoted much of its space to the reactions throughout New York City and the world. Showbizzers had the same concerns as others around the globe: the long-range effects on everyday security and the economy and worries about whether people could ever feel safe again. As David Davis, senior vice president at an investment firm, told *Variety*, "The world changes forever starting today." He was right.

Right: September 12, 2001.

$2.95 NEWSPAPER
**WEDNESDAY
SEPTEMBER 12, 2001**
VARIETY.COM

LOS ANGELES ■ NEW YORK

THE MOURNING AFTER

A 'silent shock' hits New York

By JILL GOLDSMITH and DADE HAYES

Struggling to comprehend the events of Tuesday, Gotham-based industryites described scenes of devastation and chaos that defy belief.

And as ash swirled and debris fell like an eerie snow, the bigger picture became clear: The glittering nexus of global media and business lay in tatters, along with New York's famously irrepressible pride.

"The city is in an extraordinary state of silent shock," said USA Films distrib prexy Jack Foley, his voice rough with emotion.

"Amid all of the chaos there was a gentleness. As people got on the train, no one was pushing, no one was shoving. Everything felt so silent, so somber. I haven't felt like this since the Cuban Missile Crisis."

Even those who weren't in the immediate area caught glimpses of the tragedy — sights they will never forget.

From an upper-story office, Viacom spokesman Carl Folta saw the second plane hit. "We could see it crystal clear from midtown," he said. "We didn't believe what we were seeing. It smashed into the side of the second tower."

Pamela McClintock, *Daily Variety*'s Washington correspondent who was on assignment in New York, watched from 26th Street as the second plane hit.

"At the corner of 6th Avenue, a large group of people were gathered, facing downtown. I thought there

Turn to page 19

■ News nets abandoned their competitive ways on Tuesday in order to cover the largest terrorist attack on U.S. soil. **Page 4**

■ Network programmers struggled with the short- and long-term impact the terrorist attacks will have on primetime skeds and the upcoming fall season. **Page 5**

■ David Angell, the exec producer of "Frasier" and news commentator Barbara Olson were among those who lost their lives in Tuesday's plane crashes. **Page 5**

■ Plotlines of a couple of high-profile Hollywood pics may be too horribly close to the reality of Tuesday's tragic events. **Page 6**

■ Sunday's 53rd annual Emmy Awards have been postponed indefinitely and Tuesday's Latin Grammys were canceled. **Page 6**

■ The nation's capital became a ghost town and several key hearings on media issues have been tabled indefinitely. **Page 9**

■ Most cable nets canceled sports and entertainment programming in favor of nonstop news. Execs canceled a Gotham confab. **Page 17**

■ Security planning becomes the top priority for new AMPAS prexy Frank Pierson. **Page 4**

Showbiz is rocked by real life

It was the day the world stopped. The real world and the play world.

In the real world, casualties from terrorist bombings were estimated at more than 10,000, and the almost nonchalant hijackings of four airliners exposed the vulnerability of aviation security. In fact, all of America was suddenly looking unprotected.

In the play world, events ranging from the Latin Grammys to the Emmys to the Broadway theater to baseball games were abruptly shuttered. Even many movie theaters closed for the day.

On Tuesday, studios quickly moved to postpone the openings of "Big Trouble" and "Collateral Damage," due to their content. Networks canceled airings of explosion-heavy pics like "The Peacemaker" and "Independence Day"; networks axed promos for terrorist-themed shows "24" and "The Agency."

Production was halted on various

Turn to page 19

Global economy jolted in terrorist attacks

By CARL DiORIO

A plunging dollar and hammered overseas stocks suggest congloms of all stripes — and even the world economy — could get pummeled by fallout from Tuesday's terrorist attacks.

"The world changes forever starting today," said David Davis, senior VP and analyst at investment firm Houlihan, Lokey, Howard & Zukin in Los Angeles. "There will be a major economic impact starting when the stock market reopens. This could be what triggers a real recession."

Even the one-day impact on the entertainment business was dramatic, with most companies shutting operations through Hollywood and elsewhere. Disney closed its theme parks in California and Florida, as did Vivendi Universal.

Wall Street effectively closed, with no trading conducted on U.S. stock exchanges Tuesday and a decision made to keep the markets closed today. The terrorist attacks Stateside also ricocheted to indexes worldwide. Stock markets in the U.K. and France logged the biggest declines since the world market crash of October 1987. Germany's main exchange, the Dax, lost 9% in late-day trading. And Japan's Nikkei index fell more than 400 points in midday trading in Tokyo on Wednesday, dipping below 10,000 for the first time since 1984.

Many entertainment conglom shares are listed on exchanges abroad as well as on Wall Street; Euro-listed shares in NBC parent General Electric slid $2.81, or 7%, to $36.54 on Tuesday.

International investors feared the terrorist attacks could escalate and get "totally out of control," said Ian MacFarlane of the Friends Ivory & Sime investment firm in London.

Martin Bayntun of Gartmore Investment Management in London suggested that the attacks make recession in the U.S. "more likely" by undermining consumer confidence.

There was no clear way to predict the impact of the attacks on individual stocks nor certainly the effect on future bottom lines.

Traditionally, news networks see ratings skyrocket in times of crisis and that tends to help corporate parents. But as most broadcast and cable webs are now part of much bigger

Turn to page 19

Can the doodads deliver?	Brave 'New World'		Planning ahead
The new tech advances are impressive, but can gizmos recapture the magic of showbiz? **PAGE 5**	With its year-end lineup, New Line again reminds that it's a maverick studio. **PAGE 8**		The new TV season is in its infancy, but the webs are aggressively planning midseason shifts. **PAGE 15**

Variety

Reed Business Information

100 YEARS

VARIETY.COM ■ THE INTERNATIONAL ENTERTAINMENT WEEKLY ■ OCTOBER 24 - 30, 2005

ROCKIN' IN IRAQ

Locals embrace escapist fare as TV biz rises from ashes

By ALI JAAFAR
BAGHDAD

Like other viewers around the globe, Iraqi TV auds love their reality shows — but with a couple of unique twists.

In the local home-improvement series, the chipper hosts don't merely redecorate a kitchen: They rebuild a war-torn home from the ground up. And contestants on the local version of "American Idol" are so eager for their moment of fame that they risk their lives to get to the Baghdad studio.

As the Western media focus on the uncertain results of last week's national elections, there's one story that has flown below the radar: The success of the Iraqi TV business.

Since the April 2003 ouster of Saddam Hussein, the area has seen the birth of 30 TV stations, the same number of radio stations and an estimated 180 newspapers.

The quality of the programming may be uneven, but Iraq's new media moguls have one thing in their favor: When your audience is afraid to go outside, it's good for ratings.

The immediate goals are prestige and entertainment. Entrepreneurs want to reach the people without government interference or propaganda. It's a boom town and folks are moving in.

Western advertisers like Saatchi + Saatchi and BBDO see the potential, representing accounts like Pepsi and Nokia.

So does the U.S. government, which has established its own TV station. Along with reality are soaps and chatshows — and Hollywood films from an unlikely source: Uday Hussein's personal video collection.

To date, each of Iraq's 18 provinces, including each ethnic community from the Kurds to the Assyrians to every political party, boasts its own local TV channel, with a further dozen Iraqi satcasters beaming out a heady mix of Western-friendly entertainment.

"There is hardly a house without a satellite dish and there is hardly a neighborhood without some kind of local broadcasting," Leith Kubba, spokesman for Iraqi premier Ibrahim Al-Jaafari, tells *Variety*.

The impact on Iraqi culture and politics has been noticeable. While heavily controlled state media and cultural institutions previously pushed pro-Hussein propaganda, the order of the day now is unprecedented freedom of expression.

Satellite dishes were prohibited under Hussein. But some 7 million were sold in the 12 months after his fall. It is a sweet irony that the imprisoned dictator is one of the few Iraqis not to benefit — he is denied a TV in his cell.

Key to the rise in this new phenomenon has been the continued violence in Baghdad and other Iraqi cities. Unable

Turn to page 41

> 'The public wants to see something other than bombs and blood.'
> — Jean-Claude Boulos of satcaster Al-Sumariyah

Most Iraqi homes have a satellite dish; 30 stations have bowed in two years.

The local version of "American Idol" attracts 60% of the Iraqi TV audience.

Newspaper USPS 659-960 02731

$6.95/C$11.00/£5.00/€8.50/A$15.00

294 *VARIETY*

Left: October 30, 2005.

One of the most immediate and specific concerns was about the images of violence that had, until then, been pervasive in news and entertainment. Once entertaining, they suddenly seemed horrifying.

In the September 13 *Daily Variety*, a story referred to showbiz employees returning to work in a "decidedly somber mood." But that wasn't the only thing people were feeling. *Daily* ran the headline "Daze of Our Lives" along with a photo of the burning Twin Towers. Many readers were offended. The staffers who wrote and approved the headline, perhaps still reeling from the terrorist attack and not thinking of the repercussions resulting from such irreverent wording, were unprepared for the onslaught of calls, letters, and emails from readers. Some screamed their objections to the unintentional suggestion that the events were a mere soap opera, but one angry caller summed up his reaction by spitting, "That headline is CLEVER, and this is no time to be clever!"

Though some in showbiz predicted a sharp cutback in on-screen violence, that moratorium only lasted a short time. Within a few years, Hollywood resumed its standard high quota of crashes, explosions, and murders.

A decade after the terrorist attacks, *Variety*'s senior critics Peter Debruge and Justin Chang analyzed post-9/11 films, such as *United 93* and *World Trade Center* (both 2006), as well as films that reflected the new mindset, such as *The Dark Knight* (2008) and the *Harry Potter* series (2008). In the August 22, 2011, *Weekly Variety*, Debruge said,

> "Not since Watergate has a single incident had such a powerful impact on pop culture. Nixon's disgrace shook our faith in government, resulting in decades of entertainment in which corrupt politicians loomed large. In our response to Osama bin Laden, patriotism was the first and strongest reaction, serving to bring the nation together."

But the United States was hardly the only target of terrorist bombings in the first years of the millennium. Bali, Madrid, London, and Mumbai all suffered their share of violence.

The upheavals didn't always involve terrorists. On November 11, 2005, *Daily Variety* reported on the "riot-besieged suburbs" of Paris, then in its thirteenth day, with more than 4,700 cars having been torched and with curfews ordered as Gallic youth protested "racism, unemployment and police brutality."

As China readied itself for the 2008 Olympic Games in Beijing, Steven Spielberg led a quieter protest, quitting as artistic adviser over China's support for the Sudanese government in the Darfur crisis. China also, cracked down on Tibetan protesters, resulting in deaths and "Free Tibet" campaigners following the Olympic torch throughout its tour of the United States and Europe.

After eight years and billions of dollars in preparation, Beijing was ready for the Olympics, but the Chinese government was dealing with "an outpouring of protests, violence and even deaths in the past few months." Reporter Clifford Coonan wrote that many in China were puzzled by the negativity, describing their excitement:

> "People here are wildly enthusiastic about the Aug. 8–24 event. They see the rites as recognition of China's growth into the world's fourth-largest economy and its increasingly important role on the world's stage. All this growth in one generation fills them with pride."

For established news organizations, the public's growing interest in international events was hampered by recession-imposed news-bureau cutbacks and increased competition from influential news organizations like Al Jazeera and Japan's NHK. But they still maintained their advantage, thanks to easy-to-use HD equipment, and modern tools like Skype, which allowed for fast and efficient on-the-scene reporting.

A March 14, 2011, *Daily Variety* story on the front page said U.S. news orgs were pushed to the limit, having to shift quickly from covering the earthquakes in Haiti and New Zealand to splitting their resources between the civil war in Libya and the earthquake and tsunami in Japan and, shortly thereafter, the Arab Spring uprising, which had been foreshadowed by the region's filmmakers, such as Ahmed Abdallah, whose 2010 *Microphone* was an eye-opening look at the underground hip-hop and multimedia arts scene in Alexandria, Egypt.

In 2011, Nick Vivarelli wrote about *18 Days*, an omnibus film shown at the Cannes Film Festival in which ten directors looked at the recent Egypt revolt against Hosni Mubarak's thirty-year regime. The pic included a short by Abdallah, "about a young man who watches the revolution unfold via Facebook and the Internet, barely leaving his apartment." Revolutionaries, politicians, and the international community both within and without the Middle East and North Africa could now stay connected via social media as their dictators toppled and their worlds were turned upside down.

At Cannes, activist-actress Angelina Jolie was asked to comment on the death of Osama bin Laden. She politely declined, saying it's a serious topic worth discussing, but a press conference for *Kung Fu Panda 2* was probably not the appropriate place.

When Muammar Gadhafi died, *Daily Variety* carried a front-page story on October 21, 2011. Though the editors declined to carry a gruesome news-wire photo, the image was a remarkable one. His body, lifeless and bloody, was surrounded by a dozen people all taking photos with their mobile phones. It's as if Brutus and Cassius had wanted to celebrate the moment of Caesar's death with posts to their Facebook pages.

The millennium had begun with rah-rah enthusiasm for new technology. Amazon.com, Craigslist, Yahoo!, MSN, eBay, and Google may have been founded in the 1990s, but they hit their strides in the twenty-first century.

The February 1, 2000, *Daily Variety* carried Phil Gallo's review of the Super Bowl ads, in which computer companies—mostly dot-com start-ups that wanted to establish their brand—accounted for twenty-five of the game's eighty-two commercials, compared to only six for film companies.

The soon-to-burst dot-com bubble was exemplified by AOL's January 11, 2001, purchase of Time Warner. At the time, this move signaled a new world: the new-media company bought the old-media one, not the other way around. But amazement was short-lived and stock plummeted. Ted Turner, Time Warner's largest individual shareholder, lost an estimated $7 billion, while other lowlier workers lost huge chunks of their retirement fund. Time Warner's Gerald Levin, once hailed as a visionary for his negotiation of the deal, quickly became the villain in this story.

And as quickly as they emerged, virtually all of the showbiz dot-coms were either quietly folded into other companies or completely disappeared within a few years.

The new technology wreaked havoc on the entire music industry, due in part to Napster, a peer-to-peer website in which users shared songs for free. Unlike the Betamax decision, the music industry was not concerned with a solution to monetize this new technology. They just wanted to shut it down. In 2000, Napster was hit by a series of suits over copyright infringement by record companies and artists. Though Napster shut down in 2001, the music industry was never able to recover from the digital assault. The September 10, 2003, *Daily Variety* reported that the top five music labels, Universal Music Group, Warner Music Group, BMG, EMI, and Sony Music, accounted for 75 percent of the $32 billion global recorded music market, and global record sales continued to fall.

And yet, in 2002, *Weekly Variety* observed that the vidgame biz had posted an all-time sales record of $9.4

Right: June 5, 2011.

VARIETY.COM • THE INTERNATIONAL ENTERTAINMENT WEEKLY • MAY 30 - JUNE 5, 2011

New York: new rules, new indies

By GREGG GOLDSTEIN

Reports of the death of New York independent filmmaking have been greatly exaggerated.

Jolted by startups like Celine Rattray and Trudie Styler's Maven Pictures, suddenly adventurous financiers, record-high state tax credits, lower budgets, revamped business models and reopened distrib pocketbooks, indie film producers are experiencing a renaissance.

Yes, outfits like New Line Cinema and Rattray's former shingle Mandalay Vision are still being consolidated into their parent companies' Los Angeles homes. Producers' fees are lower, and overhead deals are nearly impossible to find. But as they make painful adjustments to post-recession realities, emerging producers are adapting, finding funds and having their first big breakthroughs.

"The old model of how an independent producer grows has changed a lot, and new producers are navigating new territory," says producer and Filmmaker Magazine editor Scott Macaulay. "Making a first-time film for $2.5 million wasn't a crazy idea, but now a number of people say you should make it for $600,000 or $300,000. New technologies and digital projection at festivals have allowed budgets to come down."

The first big ray of hope came
See **NEW YORK** *page 5*

Borderline got a jolt of coin from the sale of "Martha Marcy May Marlene."

Egyptian actor Amr Waked joined anti-government demonstrators in Cairo during the protests that brought down Hosni Mubarak.

RALLY POINT

Arab Spring opens screen doors

By NICK VIVARELLI
ROME

The Arab Spring, which spread from Tunisia and Egypt, to Libya and beyond, has unleashed the biggest political upheaval the region has seen in more than half a century.

Some say that these forces of social change will also lead to a burst of filmmaking fervor and prompt a systemic shakeup of the Arab world's film industry.

Hints of such a revolution were in the air at the 64th Cannes Film Festival. Just six months after young Tunisian vendor Mohamed Bouazizi set himself on fire in the impoverished town of Sidi Bouzid, sparking the social media and Internet phenom that prompted historic changes, several pics about the so-called Revolution 2.0, which has been trying to turn dictatorships into democracies, were unspooling along the Croisette.

Riding the crest of this wave, former StudioCanal CEO Frederic Sichler and his Middle Eastern partners used the fest as the launching pad for Arab world sales company Pacha Pictures, the first outfit dedicated to selling and promoting works by Arab auteurs internationally.

"Across the Middle East there is an explosion of desire to say things in a different way," Sichler tells *Variety*. Major changes are on the way in terms of what will be said (in movies), and how (it will be said)."

Sichler, who has teamed with some of Egypt's most exciting young talent and various industryites from the region, sees a possible analogy between the changes starting to take place within the film industries in several Arab countries and what happened in Hollywood in the 1970s, when new works by helmers like Francis Ford Coppola, Martin
See **ARAB SPRING** *page 27*

Scandals juicy, but market dry

By TATIANA SIEGEL

Major studios have banished the R-rated erotic thriller from their slates. Bigscreen and smallscreen producers are largely ignoring the tawdry sex scandals that hog the headlines. And A-list nudity is so yesteryear.

As Hollywood's appetite for the salacious has waned to that of a celibate monk, it begs the question: Does sex still sell?

> **Gossip biz thrives on insider trading.**
> **BART Page 2**

The scandals du jour involving Arnold Schwarzenegger and IMF chief Dominique Strauss-Kahn are being met by industryites with a tepid response. Projects that Schwarzenegger had lined up to revive his Hollywood career have dried up as well.

While procedurals such as the "Law & Order" and "CSI" franchises often adopt storylines from newspaper headlines, the infidelities of Tiger Woods (numerous mistresses and call girls), former New York governor Eliot Spitzer (prostitutes) and former South Carolina governor Mark Sanford (a mistress) — to
See **SCANDALS** *page 27*

inside

FILM France, Belgium, Luxembourg toonmakers form Euro cel bloc. **Page 4**
TV Oprah may yet learn that the syndication biz wasn't so bad. **Page 8**
V PLUS Producers fan out to worldwide locations. **Begins after page 14**
BOOKS *Variety* staffers examine the biz with a trio of tomes. **Page 26**
VPAGE "First Class" dash; trial by "Wolf"; all aboard Tassler train **Page 28**

billion in 2001, a number that topped the annual domestic feature film box office gross ($8 billion) for the first time. Then, in 2003, DVD sales also, for the first time, passed box office.

But early in the '00s, the industry was still bullish. The June 11, 2003, *Daily Variety* quoted PricewaterhouseCoopers' Global Entertainment and Media Outlook report, which predicted that the total consumption of films (at box office and subsequent outlets) would grow from $31.7 billion in 2002 to just under $44 billion by 2007. The forecast noted the change in release patterns: in 1998, only eight films opened on more than three thousand screens; by 2002, that number had soared to thirty-two films.

Other box office numbers were also jumping. The 1997 *Titanic* was the first film to earn more than $1 billion at the global box office. In 2011 alone, there were three films hitting that milestone: the eighth *Harry Potter* film, the third *Transformers*, and the fourth *Pirates of the Caribbean*. That trio meant a grand total of ten films had passed $1 billion, seven of them sequels, including the Peter Jackson epic *The Lord of the Rings: Return of the King* (2003), Pixar's *Toy Story 3* (2010), and Christopher Nolan's *The Dark Knight* (2008).

The only non-sequels among the ten were the Tim Burton–directed *Alice in Wonderland* (2010) and the two films at the top of the list, both by James Cameron: *Avatar* (2009), the 3-D adventure that earned a jaw-dropping $2.7 billion, and *Titanic*, at $1.8 billion.

As for that old reliable gauge of horror films, the twenty-first century saw a lot of English-language remakes of Asian fright fests, including *The Ring* (2002; based on the 1998 *Ringu*). There were also clever-gruesome U.S. films such as *Hostel* (2005) and *Saw* (2004); interestingly, technology was central to many of these pics.

One of the biggest hits was the 2007 *Paranormal Activity*, which provided fright onscreen and scary insights behind the scenes; on January 4, 2010, *Variety* estimated the pic's production budget at $11,000 while its marketing budget was $20 million.

Since the film earned nearly $200 million worldwide, it was a terrific investment (on top of the $350,000 paid for the rights by DreamWorks). But the discrepancy between production and marketing expenditures pointed up both the rising costs and the growing importance of marketing in a media-saturated world. That same article said that 60 percent to 70 percent of a pic's marketing budget went to old media TV and radio; only 4 percent went to consumer newspapers, which helped explain why so many consumer papers were in debt or shutting down.

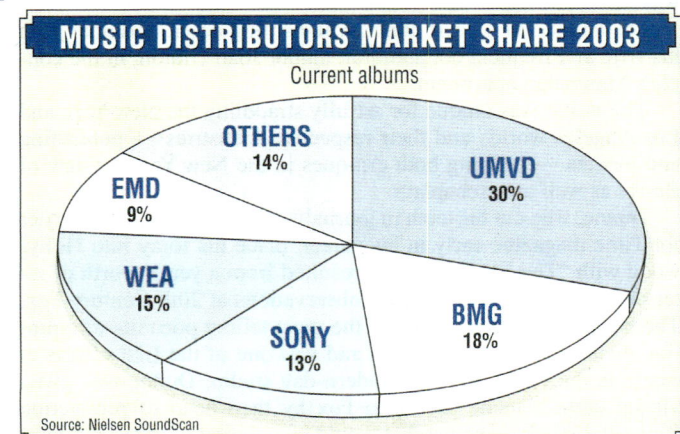

Music biz fails to hit higher notes in 2003

By PHIL GALLO

Despite a 21% increase in sales of recorded music during the Christmas week, overall music sales last year fell 3.6% from 2002, marking a third consecutive down year for the beleaguered industry. Sales of CD albums, which constitute 96% of the market, were down 13.7 million in 2003 to 635.8 million from 649.5 million.

The overall music business was down eight-tenths of a percent for units sold, 687 million in 2003 vs. 693 million in 2002.

Business was bolstered by 19.2 million digital downloads purchased since July. That figure is almost double the number of physical singles purchased; latter category was down 4%. *Turn to page 15*

Above: The music industry begins to struggle.

BY JOSEF ADALIAN

During the first season of her Comedy Central series, Sarah Silverman's small-screen alter ego experimented with lesbianism, gave shelter to a homeless man in an attempt to win a humanitarian award, overdosed on cough medicine and slept with God.

Parents Television Council founder Brent Bozell had a (predictable) hissy fit, but viewers responded positively: Comedy Central renewed "The Sarah Silverman Program" for a second season soon after it premiered.

Penning a rave review, People magazine's Tom Gliatto perhaps said it best: "It feels wrong. And I love it, love it, love it."

Much like Silverman herself, the series — about a narcissistic woman (Silverman), her lesbian sister and her two gay slacker neighbors — seems genetically engineered to offend just about everyone. But Silverman, a stand-up vet who'd previously had short stints on "SNL" and Fox's "Greg the Bunny," says that's sort of the point.

"She's sweet (even though) she's

Sarah Silverman:
"When I was a teenager in New Hampshire I got a subscription to *Variety* for my birthday. I pored over it every week (I got the weekly) and loved it. I didn't understand any of it—at all—but I loved it."

FUNNIEST EPISODE: "Not Without My Daughter," in which Silverman decides [...] can enter [...] to avenge [...] pageant.

[...] Silverman, [...] that's [...] after [...] mean, I'm [...] who's going [...] he going to steal the moon?'"

just terrible," Silverman says. "I [...] to call (it) arrogant ignorance."

After being wooed by Comedy Central, Silverman says she looked to the opening and closing scenes of her 2006 concert film, "Jesus is Magic," for inspiration when creating the series. Those segments featured Silverman sitting around, kibbitzing with her friends, then breaking into song.

"I liked how it felt very real and small, and then went into a musical number," she says. "I wanted to do something like that."

The success of the series forced Silverman to make some changes to her career plans.

"I wanted to be in movies, but I'm getting to do my dream with this show," she says. "Why would I rather play someone else's sassy friend?

Marketers were now heavily focused on social media. It was a decade of self-empowerment. There is an old sarcastic phrase: "Everybody's a critic." In the twenty-first century, that came to be a reality, as MySpace, then Facebook, provided an outlet for everyone's opinions. People were now tweeting their reactions to movies and TV shows as they were watching them.

The twenty-first century was all about branding. As *Variety* pointed out on April 22, 2009, 65 percent of Broadway tickets were bought by tourists, who wanted to know, well in advance of seeing a performance, exactly what they were going to get for their $100. Film versions of popular Broadway shows were seen as valuable marketing tools: the box office for Broadway's *Chicago*, *Mamma Mia!*, and *The Phantom of the Opera* all climbed after their respective film adaptations were released. (This was in sharp contrast to decades past. Frank Capra filmed his version of *Arsenic and Old Lace* in 1941, but Warner Bros. was contractually obligated to delay its release until 1944, when the play closed.) New productions such as *Wicked* and *Spider-Man: Turn Off the Dark* worked to establish their brands, so they could lure tourists to Broadway and then set up traveling companies and overseas franchises.

The film biz was also into branding. The success of the film *Pirates of the Caribbean* (2003) led others to develop films based on titles that were just as recognizable, like *Transformers* (2007), *G.I. Joe* (2009), and *Battleship* (2012). Other movies were based on self-help books, such as *How to Be Single*, in development in 2012, and *He's Just Not That into You* (2009). Why? Because the titles were familiar, making them easy to market to moviegoers.

Music stars including Britney Spears, Christina Aguilera, Beyoncé, Sean "P. Diddy" Combs, Jay-Z, Damon Dash, 50 Cent, Snoop Dogg, Ludacris, Kanye West, Lady Gaga, and Will.i.am established merchandise empires (clothing, colognes, whatever) that capitalized on their names. *Variety*'s June 28, 2011, look at Paris Hilton's empire

DAILY Variety

Reed Business Information

LOS ANGELES ■ WEDNESDAY, NOVEMBER 5, 2008 ■ VARIETY.COM

INSIDE

On a streak
Fox made it two straight weeks atop the primetime demo leaderboard.
Page 5

"House"

A cavalcade of kudos
Variety editor Timothy M. Gray bows a weekly column chronicling the eternal oddities of awards season.
Page 6

VARIETY.COM

Law & Order
The season 18 premiere of "Law & Order" finds the venerable franchise in its shakiest state in recent memory, with marginal chemistry among its latest cast configuration.

V PLUS

AFM
AFM Screening Guide
Your guide to what's playing and when in Santa Monica.
Begins after page 30

★★ ELECTION 2008 ★★

OBAMARAMA

Victory reps a major shift

By TED JOHNSON

President-elect Barack Obama's victory — watched throughout the world and hailed as a turning point in the direction of the country — marked a generational shift on a number of levels, from the way that campaigns raise money, to the engagement of hundreds of thousands of new and younger voters.

But his entire candidacy and campaign also signaled a sea change in politicians' use of the media.

Beyond Tuesday's historic vote that puts the first African-American in the White House, Obama changed things in the way he galvanized his base of supporters. His image is that of someone who's in touch with people. A big part of that was tapping into popular culture beyond the news media, as he connected with audiences on latenight talkshows, "Entertainment Tonight" and "Access Hollywood" and, before his campaign even began, "The Oprah Winfrey Show."

A 30-minute Obama infomercial that ran last week combined campaign propaganda with the messaging techniques of "Extreme Home Makeover." More than any other candidate, he harnessed the power of the Internet. Using sophisticated means of branding and advertising, he cast himself as an agent of change, literally representing a new movement in politics that seeks to unite the country and address a mountain of challenges.

Never before have media and entertainment been so emotionally invested in a candidate.

It's debatable whether Obama will cozy up to showbiz in the way that JFK and Bill Clinton did. Hollywood and its businesses don't seem a top priority to him. But that's OK with Hollywood. Like many other Americans, showbiz people liked his message and embraced Obamamania which — though mocked by the candidate's rivals — spoke to a desire to turn the page on the Bush years. Those in the industry felt like many other Americans that the country is on the wrong track.

"There are many who won't agree with every decision or policy I make as president, and we know that government can't solve every problem," Obama told supporters gathered in Chicago's Grant Park. "But I will always be honest with you about the challenges we face."

Hollywood made its bet on his
Turn to page 54

President-elect Barack Obama delivers his acceptance speech Tuesday night at Chicago's Grant Park, in his home state of Illinois.

The results, the reactions, the watch-parties and all the events are covered in depth at Variety.com.

Confab tackles indie agita

By PATRICK FRATER

Going in to the American Film Market, which starts today, the mood of most folk is somewhere between somber and grim.

But some leading execs appear to believe that troubles in the independent sector and the global financial crisis are creating opportunities.

Former Miramax Intl. co-chief Stuart Ford is expanding his IM Global company, a sales and distribution outfit with big-budget genre movie leanings, to cover specialty films — in part because he believes the retreat of the studios from this sector has gone too far.

Other execs using the AFM as a launchpad for specialty film sales shingles include former Weinstein Co. sales chief Glen Basner's FilmNation, Guy East and Peter Naish's Exclusive Film Distribution (a new sales division of pre-existing HS Media that handles Hammer Films and Spitfire titles) and Icon Entertainment, whose international sales and distribution businesses have been taken over by former Polygram topper Stewart Till.
Turn to page 56

Ford
More AFM news, page 8

Thesps count to '13'

By MICHAEL FLEMING

Mickey Rourke, Ray Winstone, Jason Statham, Sam Riley, 50 Cent and Ray Liotta will star in "13," an English-language remake of the 2005 French pic "13 Tzameti."

That psychological thriller won the grand jury prize for world cinema at the Sundance Film Festival.

Gela Babluani, who wrote and directed the original, has penned the script and will direct a film that begins production in New York on Nov. 20.

Riley ("Control") plays the title character, a young man who stumbles into an underground competition where the wealthy gamble on human beings in a Russian Roulette-like competition.
Turn to page 56

"13 Tzameti"

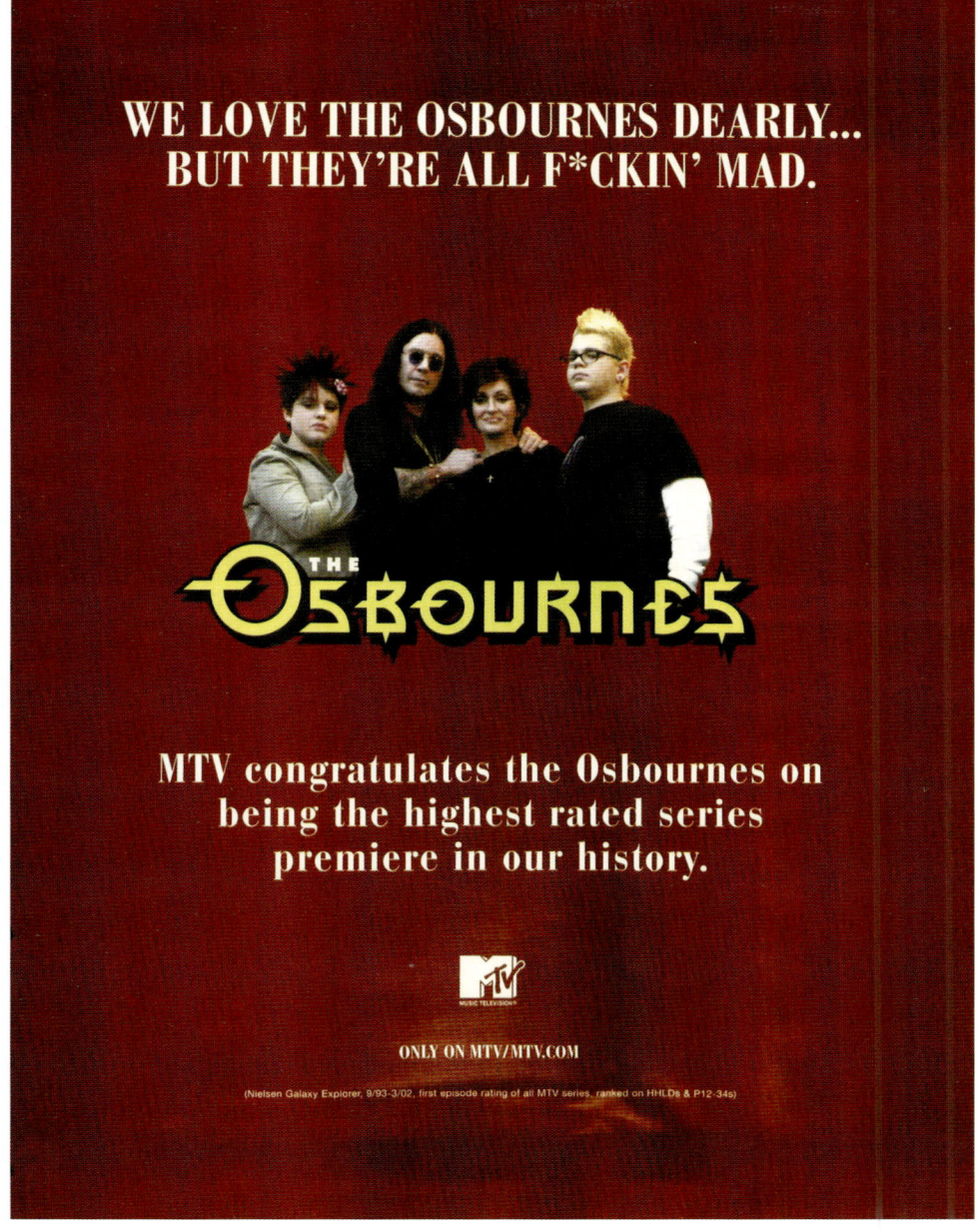

Left: November 5, 2008.

Above: Just your typical family.

estimated that her line of products, including thirty Paris Hilton stores, her clothing lines, and fragrances, had earned more than $1.3 billion since 2004.

Interestingly, Hilton's former step-great-grandmother, Zsa Zsa Gabor, the Hungarian beauty queen who was a frequent guest when talk shows were rising in the 1950s, was one of the first people able to monetize being famous for being famous.

Though the *American Family* of the 1970s and the *Real World* of the 1990s paved the way for reality TV, a tipping point came in 2002 when MTV premiered *The Osbournes*, a ten-episode series starring heavy-metal rocker Ozzy Osbourne, his wife Sharon, and children, Kelly and Jack. The series was irresistible: a lovable-bumbling dad, the take-charge sassy mom, and two rebellious but loving teens. It was a classic sitcom setup, with the difference that these were real people.

The May 3, 2002, *Daily Variety* reported that the family had received $200,000 for the first ten episodes, but only two months after it became "basic cable's most watched series," MTV renewed a deal with them estimated to be worth $20 million. The show spawned numerous imitators, featuring celebrities who wanted to open up their lives for the cameras and, in the process, get money and revitalize their careers, including Whitney Houston and Bobby Brown, Hulk Hogan, Gene Simmons, and David Hasselhoff.

So with all these changes, was life improving in the new millennium?

Minorities still have a long way yet to go, but they had come a long way, baby. On October 27, 2008, *Weekly Variety* casually referred to Will Smith as "the world's biggest box office star," based on his long string of box office hits. A month after that, America elected Barack Obama as its first African American president.

Halle Berry and Denzel Washington won Best Actress and Actor Oscars for their 2001 films, at a ceremony that Whoopi Goldberg—an Oscar-winning actress, producer, author, and talk-show star—hosted for the fourth time. In 2011, James Earl Jones and Oprah Winfrey won two of the three Governors Awards given by the Academy of Motion Picture Arts and Sciences, and in 2012, Octavia Spencer won an Oscar for her supporting role as a maid in 1960s Alabama in *The Help*. Shonda Rimes became one of the most successful and powerful women working in television. Jennifer Lopez, Christina Aguilera, America Ferrara, Salma Hayek, Gael Garcia Bernal, Antonio Banderas, Enrique Iglesias, and many others proved ethnic background mattered less to the public than ever. Ricky Martin deserves a special mention for maintaining his popularity both as a Hispanic and as openly gay. In the LGBT world, two of the biggest names in daytime talk shows were Rosie

Right: February 21, 2010.

O'Donnell and Ellen Degeneres. While many music stars had talked about their gayness, including Elton John, Melissa Etheridge, George Michael, Michael Stipe, k.d. lang, and Boy George, it was rarer for actors. But Ian McKellen opened a lot of doors, and Neil Patrick Harris virtually kicked them down, starring as a heterosexual lothario on CBS' *How I Met Your Mother*, hosting awards shows on the broadcast networks, and starring in 2011's family-targeted *The Smurfs* movie, which earned more than half a billion dollars at the international box office.

Disneyland in Anaheim, which had once refused admittance to anyone with long hair or a bad attitude, began welcoming visitors for "Gay Days," grassroots movements spearheaded by various gay organizations. While the park insists that such days aren't official, park officials do not discourage them.

Three of the five directors nominated for Oscars in 2002 were openly gay men. And in June 9, 2003, *Weekly Variety* profiled such showbiz executives as Fox TV's Joe Earley, who had successfully navigated the system to pioneer gay adoption of children.

Meanwhile, in 2011, the same year the military revoked the "Don't Ask, Don't Tell" policy, no fewer than six states legalized gay marriage, allowing celebrities as varied as Isaac Mizrahi, Wanda Sykes, and David Hyde Pierce to marry.

Another reason for cautious optimism: was ageism on the wane? The September 30, 2011, *Daily Variety* crowed that *Duets 2*, from eighty-five-year-old Tony Bennett, was the week's top-selling album. Other notables from the 1960s, including icons such as Barbra Streisand, Cher, Bob Dylan, Aretha Franklin, the Rolling Stones, Neil Young, Shirley Bassey, Tom Jones, Julie Christie, and Dustin Hoffman, as well as properties like *Dr. Who* and *Star Trek*, were still going strong.

And another reason for optimism: charity. On June 27, 2006, Jill Goldsmith reported in *Daily Variety* that Bill Gates and Warren Buffett "made philanthropy history by pooling their wealth to deliver some $60 billion for global health and education." At the 2007 Cannes Film Festival, Martin Scorsese announced the World Cinema Foundation, a counterpart to the Scorsese-driven Film Foundation, whose mission would be to preserve international film archives. Though the organizations have saved hundreds of films, there are many, many more in need of repair and, especially after the economic downturn of 2008, many of the copyright owners have not allocated enough money to restoration.

Under new president Neil Stiles and new publisher Brian Gott, *Variety*, in 2008–9, jumped into philanthropy in a big way, with its "Power Of" events (Power of Youth, Power of Comedy, etc.), raising $4.5 million for charity in just a few years.

Sounds like only good things in the twenty-first century, right? Well, the new millennium offered many reasons for concern as well.

Terrorism, global violence, bigotry, and wars seemed to increase. Overpopulation was a growing dilemma, literally.

After Lew Wasserman had overseen the sale of Universal to an overseas

VARIETY.COM • THE INTERNATIONAL ENTERTAINMENT WEEKLY • FEBRUARY 15-21, 2010

IN TUNE WITH BEING OUT

Legit world re-tailors its marketing to post-gay era

By GORDON COX

Gay characters in legit works have gone through several distinct phases.

After centuries of invisibility, they moved centerstage in then-shocking works like "Tea and Sympathy" and "Cat on a Hot Tin Roof." Then there were out-and-proud pieces like "Torch Song Trilogy" and "Angels in America" (subtitled "A Gay Fantasia on National Themes"), in which characters grappled with their sexual identity but often came to positive conclusions.

Now a slew of plays are opening in New York that mark a post-gay era — productions in which the lead characters may be gay, but deal with central conflicts that can have nothing to do with sexual roles. And these works are being marketed to straight and gay audiences alike.

The heightened national debate over gay rights, including California's Prop. 8 battle and the rethinking of the military's Don't Ask Don't Tell policy, provides a background and a timeliness to these projects, even as the shows themselves rarely bring such issues explicitly to the fore.

"Next Fall," which opens March 11 at the Helen Hayes Theater, represents a case study of a major shift.

"It's not a gay love story," says Richard Willis, a lead producer of "Next Fall" along with Barbara Manocherian. "It's a love story. And by the way, they're gay."

Among the legit offerings lining up this spring in Gotham for commercial runs, or showing strong potential for commercial transfer:

■ The Off Broadway staging of hit London play "The Pride," a gay-identity story that timeshifts between 1958 and 2008, is earning strong buzz ahead of the Feb. 16 opening of its nonprofit run from MCC Theater. With a couple of commercial producers already in the mix, it's generally acknowledged that the show, starring Hugh Dancy and Ben Whishaw, will likely head to Broadway if press reception and theater availability open the way.

■ A tuner about a couple of WWII soldiers who fall in love, "Yank!" will open Feb. 24 in a co-production between nonprofit York Theater and a commercial team that's not at all closeted about its aim to take the show to the Main Stem.

■ "The Temperamentals," a chronicle of pre-Stonewall gay activists starring Thomas Jay Ryan and Michael Urie ("Ugly Betty"), opens Feb. 28 at New World Stages in a commercial Off Broadway run that follows two earlier hit engagements.

And, for a little perspective, New York auds will also get the second revival in six years of musical comedy "La Cage aux Folles" — replete with drag performers, gay anthems and straight marriage — as well as a revival of Mart Crowley's landmark play about a bitchy gay birthday party, "The Boys in the Band," in a production from nonprofit the Transport Group.

As they pitch these shows to the broadest possible audience, marketers and creatives are treading a careful line between playing up a production's universal themes and avoiding the appearance of trying to hide its gay elements.

For instance, the "Next Fall" poster and print ad features a simple red leaf with the decidedly un-sensational tagline "We love who we love." Nowhere does the ad reveal that the romance at the center of the show is between two men.

"It's a challenge," says Stacy Shane, one of the producers of "The Temperamentals." "The gay element is central, but how do you tell ticketbuyers the play applies to everyone, gay or straight?"

Producers of "Next Fall" and "Temperamentals" reported nicely mixed crowds at prior incarnations of their shows. They are further emboldened by the fact that current auds seem more open to spotting universal elements in a same-sex romance.

Gay activists have seen cautious signs of optimism, ranging from the popularity of "Brokeback Mountain" and "Will and Grace," to multiple gay cast members on reality shows and the enduring success of Ellen DeGeneres on daytime TV.

Polls show that even if one-third of Americans are against legalizing same-sex marriage, a majority support some sort of legal recognition for gay couples. A recent survey showed 57% of the public believes gays should be allowed to serve openly in the military.

For the new crop of gay plays, marketing and publicity must balance a progressive approach — underscoring broad-appeal themes by treating the

Turn to page 34

inside

BART Handing out pinkslips is no way to keep the biz in the black. **Page 2**
FILM Will a shortage of screens create a clash of 3D titans? **Page 6**
MUSIC San Fran's Noise Pop fest wraps music, film into a tight package. **Page 14**
TV Viewers love big events, but are the auds borrowed or true blue? **Page 15**
V PLUS With a majority of first-time acting noms, Oscars have fresh vibe; Irish Film and TV Awards honor Eire's talent. **Begins after page 18**

DAILY VARIETY

LOS ANGELES ■ MONDAY, FEBRUARY 26, 2007 ■ VARIETY.COM

OSCAR THROWS A MARTY PARTY

What a long, strange kudo trip it's been

By DAVE McNARY

If anyone told you they "knew" "The Departed" was going to win the top Oscar, don't believe them.

The 2007 awards season wound up being the most unpredictable within memory, as no film truly dominated as the front-runner.

Instead, awards season trackers found themselves frustrated in making viable predictions throughout the months leading up to Sunday night's Oscar ceremonies.

Indeed, each of the five nominated films had gathered enough trophies to merit consideration as the winner of the final prize, thanks to the strange roller-coaster that the season became.

How baffling was it? Warner Bros. and Martin Scorsese weren't campaigning for "The Departed"; "Little Miss Sunshine" had a non-awards release in mid-summer plus the scruffiness of an indie made for $7.5 million; the bleakness and audacious

Turn to page 35

The Oscars

On the red carpet, page 31
Al Gore, 'Labyrinth' win big, page 32
Scorsese's wait is over, page 32
Backstage notes, 34-35
Winners list, page 36

Picture
The Departed

Director
Martin Scorsese

Actor
Forest Whitaker

Actress
Helen Mirren

Supporting Actor
Alan Arkin

Supporting Actress
Jennifer Hudson

Original Screenplay
Little Miss Sunshine

Adapted Screenplay
The Departed

'Departed,' Scorsese are golden

By PHIL GALLO

A violent streak impressed Oscar on Sunday night as "The Departed" snatched the best pic trophy and won Martin Scorsese his first Oscar.

"The Departed" won four awards, including adapted screenplay, at the 79th annual Academy Awards ceremonies held at the Kodak Theater in Hollywood.

The big winner was, of course, "Departed's" director Scorsese, whose nomination this year was his sixth for directing and eighth overall. Scorsese has been directing films for more than 40 years although he didn't receive a nom until 1980's "Raging Bull."

"Could you double check the envelope?" he asked, after taking the podium to receive his statuette and saying "thank you" a dozen times.

"I just want to say, too, that so many people over the years have been wishing this for me," he said. "Strangers. You know, I went walking

Turn to page 36

The Night Before

Moonlight magic
The fifth annual Night Before soiree at the Beverly Hills Hotel brought out the starriest of stars and executives aplenty. **PAGES 28-29**

At the show...

By TIMOTHY M. GRAY

Three types of people watch the Oscar show: Grumpy TV critics working on deadline; film fans watching at home; and attendees at the Kodak Theater. The first group is guaranteed to gripe; second group, maybe. But for a newcomer to the live event, it's an eye-opening experience: The whoop-de-doo hoopla makes every aspect of the show a lot more fun. The Oscarcast is a richer, glitzier version of the high school prom, but with Federico Fellini and Cecil B. DeMille as the heads of the planning committee. It seems clear that the best way to ensure maximum audience enjoyment is for the Academy of Motion Picture Arts & Sciences and ABC to figure out how to fit 800 million people in the Kodak Theater.

The daylong event kicks off with the drive to Hollywood & Highland. The city of Los Angeles deserves thanks for providing such memorable background extras, since the sidewalks are filled with hundreds of refugees from "The Day of the Locust." Some take photos; others wave to every limo, apparently assuming that if

Turn to page 31

Reviews

Host Ellen DeGeneres tried to get auds in the mood with a musical opening.

...and at home

By BRIAN LOWRY

The most prominent award shows have been undergoing a kind of collective nervous breakdown, wondering what concessions to decorum must be undertaken to stem declining ratings and stand out amid the kudocast glut and "American Idol" era. Against that backdrop, this year's Academy Awards ultimately proved a stately if unspectacular-bordering-on-dull affair, with host Ellen DeGeneres' traditional shtick feeling a trifle small for the industry's biggest stage. As is so often true, the show also exhibited a peculiar sense of time management — rushing through certain promising elements and awkwardly lingering on others.

Oscars LXXIX, to cast the 79th edition in Super Bowl-like grandeur, did start on an elegant note, showcasing the nominees in a taped segment and then panning the room to find them all standing, basking in the warm adulation of their peers. It was a feeling, alas, that couldn't and didn't last.

At times, the Oscarcast vaguely resembled a middle-aged guy trying to squeeze into hipster clothes.

Turn to page 31

Left: February 26, 2007.

Following Spread: June 15, 2003; September 5, 2004.

concern, the studio went through five owners in a little over twenty years: Matsushita, Seagrams, Vivendi, General Electric, and Comcast. Manufacturers of hardware and of software (i.e., the entertainment industry) were looking for the Next Big Thing to buoy their quarterly earnings as DVD sales began to decline. But as technology evolved too quickly for anyone to catch, no Big Thing appeared.

Daily Variety on May 30, 2007, cited the fact that "only 9% of TV writers are minorities, an under-representation that has actually gotten 1 percentage point worse since the last report issued in 2005," according to a study by Writers Guild of America, West.

National Hispanic Media Coalition director Alex Nogales said,

"The hard reality is that if you get the number of shows that portray people of color, the number doesn't come even close to equaling the 32% of the national population that is not white."

The 2011 epidemic films *Rise of the Planet of the Apes* and *Contagion* (with the tagline "Don't talk to anyone. Don't touch anyone.") premiered as the world continued to deal with E. Coli, ebola, AIDS, avian flu, West Nile virus, and SARS, along with old standbys like polio, smallpox, and malaria.

Good times.

EYE'S ISLE BET PAYS
'Survivor' climbs to new highs, boosts 'Brother'

By RICK KISSELL

Island fever continues to be this summer's epidemic of choice, as CBS' "Survivor" added another million viewers Wednesday and surged to new highs in key demo categories.

The 10th week of the adventure-reality series averaged 27.18 million viewers and an 11.9/36 adults 18-49 rating, according to Nielsen, repping gains of 4% over previous series bests set a week earlier. Seg built in its final half-hour by a best-yet 18% in viewers (29.46 million vs. 24.90) and by 21% in young adults (10.8 to 13.1).

'Brother-ly' boost

"Survivor" also served as a more compatible lead-in for the net's similarly themed "Big Brother," which delivered its best numbers since its premiere July 5.

"Brother" averaged 16.92 million viewers and an adults 18-49 rating of 8.0/22 from 9 to 10, retaining 67% of its "Survivor" demo lead-in. It's a hold that's considerably better than the 45% CBS had been seeing in the hour with movies and other series programming but, not surprisingly, it's far from the 93% "Brother" delivered with its much hyped premiere.

"Brother" dropped by a respectable 6% in its second half-hour (from 8.2 to 7.7) and won at 9:30 in the demo by 11 shares over reruns of NBC's "West Wing" and ABC's "Spin City."

CBS moved the hourlong "live" edition of "Big Brother" to Wednesday from Thursday in hopes of boosting the series, which has been a solid, but not sensational, ratings performer with its multiple weekly airings. While Wednesday's hour enabled more people to catch up with the goings-on of the sequestered housemates, it remains to be seen if this translates into ratings spikes on other nights.

What is clear, now more than ever, is that in the CBS reality family, "Survivor" is the real big brother.

USA original series falter at the start

By JOHN DEMPSEY

NEW YORK — USA Network's original series, which are key ingredients in the channel's strategy to rebound from the loss in late September of its high-rated World Wrestling Federation weekly slamfests, are off to a shaky start in the Nielsens.

Despite heavy promotion, USA's two Wednesday-night hours, "Cover Me" at 9 and "The Huntress" at 10, which kicked off with new episodes on July 26 do no better than

Ad helmer Pytka sits out the strike

By DAVE McNARY

Joe Pytka, the industry's most honored commercials director, has decided to sit out the actors' strike against advertisers.

While most directors specializing in shooting ads have contin-

Obradors

Jacqueline short-lived NB Hector Elizon drama "Tortill by Ang Lee's Woman," is cu is repped by T Writers and A at Bloom, Dek

Sasha Ale recently wrapped "All Over the Guy" for producer Don Roos, has been cast as James Van Der Beek's new love interest on "Dawson's Creek." She is repped by Stacy Boniello at the Firm and Endeavor.

Terrence Howard ("Big Momma's House") has been added to the cast of "All That Glitters." Pic, which is currently lensing, will be distributed domestically by Fox and internationally by

Alexander

of Noah Dearborn." Poitier's "Brickmaker" character must cope with the loss of his wife and the obsolescence of his job before finding redemption by becoming a role model to an equally lost 13-year-old.

"Noah Dearborn" was a big ratings draw for CBS in May 1999, winning its time period among adults 18 to 49 (6.2/16), 25-54 (7.9/18) and

de Klerk" and "To Sir With Love II." On film, the Academy Award-winning actor most recently appeared in 1997's "The Jackal."

Ronnie Clemmer, Bill Pace and Joseph Nasser will exec produce "The Last Brickmaker" for Longbow Prods. and Nasser Entertainment. Poitier is repped by CAA.

> ## Mark Burnett:
> "When I first opened an issue of *Variety*, I could tell immediately that this was a trade for insiders . . . or those that wanted to be insiders. I thought that aspect was brilliant. For me, *Variety* has always been a place that I can go to quickly get a rundown of what's going on in all corners of this business. My most memorable *Variety* moment was when I saw the headline about the ratings on the Season 1 finale of 'Survivor.' It was that finale that Richard Hatch won and Sue Hawk gave her incredible "Rats and Snakes" speech. The headline said CBS had set a summer record with 'Survivor' ratings. We averaged a reported 51.69 million viewers that night, with over 72 million tuning in during some portion of that first finale, making it at that point the most watched summer series of all time. That moment was completely surreal."

LIFE

Gay showbizzers adopt family ties

Partners navigate obstacles to parenthood

By GINNY CHIEN

IT ISN'T ALWAYS A PICNIC: *Gay industryites can bond with other families at events hosted by L.A.'s Gay & Lesbian Center.*

Joe Earley is used to exercising control during critical situations. But in the past two years, the senior VP of corporate communications for Fox Broadcasting has had to relinquish the reins for a very important matter in his life: adopting a child.

For industry players who are accustomed to calling the shots, the restrictive, rule-laden process of adoption leads to many a sleepless night.

And when the adoptive parents are gay, like Earley, the path to becoming a family can be even bumpier.

From navigating the maze of nebulous mandates that govern gay adoption to finding a match with a birth mother, the prospective parents' patience and fortitude are constantly put to the test.

"So much of it was out of our hands," Earley says, "so when everything was finalized, it really hit us — no more deadlines, no more paperwork, no more wondering if someone filed the necessary documents."

Under the guidance of the Kinship Center, a nonprofit organization that offers family services, Earley and his partner of 14 years, Adrian Alvarez, finalized the adoption of a 3½-year-old girl in April. The toddler, previously in foster care, now calls Earley "Daddy" and Alvarez "Papi."

While they chose a child in the state system, other couples tap into international and private sources to avoid governmental red tape.

But even then, roadblocks exist.

China now restricts some adoptions, after realizing that many who turn to the country for children are gay, and the U.S. government bans adoptions from Cambodia to prevent the sale of babies. With private adoptions, there's always the fear that birth mothers will chose a heterosexual couple over a gay couple.

Jonathan Murray, co-founder of Bunim/Murray Prods. ("The Real World," "Road Rules"), and partner Harvey Reese elected to go the private route. They toiled for a year alongside an attorney to bring home son Dylan, who's now 4.

"It took about nine months until we finally hooked up with Dylan's birth mom, and boy, we were anxious by that point," says Murray, who has been with Reese for 11 years. "We were just like, 'When is this going to happen? Is it going to happen?'"

Earley, Murray and their partners were able to adopt their children as couples, but some gay men and lesbians are not so lucky.

Florida still has legislation that bans adoption by anyone who's gay (though it's currently being challenged). Most other states make decisions on a case-by-case basis, since the federal government does not dictate adoption law.

Problems can arise when one half of the unmarried couple wants to adopt the child of their partner.

Commonly referred to as a "second-parent adoption," the trying process often requires the would-be parent to justify and prove how they have a connection to a child they've felt to be their own all along.

But getting lost in the muddle of legalities is risky, says Joan Garry, exec director of GLAAD, who adopted partner Eileen Opatut's three biological children 10 years ago. She stresses that it's important not to lose sight of the fundamental purpose of adoption — establishing a legal tie to the child.

Without a binding document, the caregiver does not legally have rights over the child, even if he or she has been bandaging scrapes and taking temperatures since birth. Without that second adoption, only one person can sign off on report cards or make decisions in emergency situations.

There's no question that kids are going to be in gay or lesbian households," Garry says, "so enabling a parent to adopt is all about their best interest. It's really that simple."

Gay families say they face the same challenges as any nuclear clan, such as worrying about how to raise a well-adjusted child and finding ways to juggle demanding careers with personal lives.

Murray's and Reese's son Dylan often plays with other adopted kids at family events hosted by the Los Angeles Gay & Lesbian Center.

The org's most popular get-together, Family Day in the Park, typically draws around 150 people, including dozens of producers, editors and other industryites.

Hilary Rosen, chairman-CEO of the Recording Industry Assn. of America, announced a few months ago that she's leaving her powerful post at the end of the year to devote more time to her young children. She and longtime partner Elizabeth Birch, exec director of the Human Rights Council, adopted newborn twins in 1999.

At the time, Rosen and Birch were targets of the Family Research Council, a right-wing religious org that loudly contested the adoption. The group claimed the couple would deprive the children of "a normal family life."

But with the number of "Leave It to Beaver" families diminishing, that kind of opposition doesn't carry the currency it used to, says Rebecca Isaacs, interim exec director of the L.A. Gay & Lesbian Center.

Moreover, schools are starting to take the lead in demonstrating to kids that the makeup of a traditional household is changing. The movie library at Crossroads Elementary School in Santa Monica — a popular choice among showbiz parents — includes "That's a Family," a doc about family diversity shown every year through third grade.

"A lot of kids today are from single-parent homes," Early says. "Some people have divorced parents. Or maybe they have a disability. The key in all of these situations is to grow up without shame, to be open and honest from the beginning."

FAMILY VACATION: *Jonathan Murray, left, and Harvey Reese relax with son Dylan.*

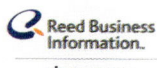
Reed Business Information.

$6.95
C$11.00/£5.00
€8.50/A$15.00
NEWSPAPER
USPS 656-960 02371

Variety

Supplement

Film Fest Guide 2004

WWW.VARIETY.COM ■ THE INTERNATIONAL ENTERTAINMENT WEEKLY ■ AUGUST 30-SEPTEMBER 5, 2004

Film remakes? Don't play it again, Sam p.4

Distribs brace for changes in rules of pic buying p.8

TV nets holding tight for tight race this fall p.15

Brit legit sings an uptempo September song p.35

SUBSCRIBERS
Full access to Variety.com is included in your subscription.
Go to Variety.com/register

$6.95US $11.00CAN

STAR WARS

In the beginning, there was Mary Pickford. Fans wanted to know: What was she *really* like? (Yes, she could toss back a few, but that's another story.)

Now the media is awash in celebrities. There are real celebs (think Tom Hanks) and machine-tooled celebs (Paris Hilton), yet they all converge in the glitter gulch.

And the public can't get enough of them.

The explosion of channels and celeb-driven publications has fueled this apparently insatiable appetite. The success of People, "Entertainment Tonight" and E! has fostered a veritable celeb circus. Even the most unlikely of niche channels like Court TV is now committed to star-gazing.

This means publicists have more range to tout their clients — but less control over how they will be exploited. It also has given birth to a new stratum of celebs whose only talent is making money off being famous.

The Olsen twins and Courtney Love may not be Oscar contenders, but they are chart-toppers in the fame game.

This week, *Variety* examines the impact (both positive and negative) of these star wars on the entertainment biz.

MAGS
Print biz: new star pluckers
By MICHAEL LEARMONTH

Charlie Chaplin appeared on the cover of Time in 1925. Marilyn Monroe graced the cover of Life 10 times, and People magazine put Mia Farrow biting coquettishly on a pearl necklace on its first cover in 1974. But what began as an occasional diet of celebrity in American magazines has evolved into commercial co-dependency.

InStyle pioneered the modern notion that celebs can drive a fashion magazine; the booming crop of weeklies proved that

Turn to page 40

TUBE
TV embraces glut of glitter
By DENISE MARTIN

Among musical pop tarts, Jessica Simpson is a distant third behind Britney Spears and Christina Aguilera, so, by anyone's standards, her 15 minutes of fame should be up.

Instead, her MTV reality show "Newlyweds" (with husband Nick Lachey) is a hit, her latest album has sold 2.4 million copies, and she's hawking everything from make-up to buffalo wings. (Still, mag covers featuring her face have flopped, hinting that the clock is indeed ticking.)

Auds are thirsting for the fizz of pop culture, and the tarter the taste the more they like it. Taking their cue from E! and VH1, numerous cablers are expanding their niches by adding celeb shows in the hopes of luring younger viewers.

Turn to page 40

FLACKS
PR reps battle success excess
By GABRIEL SNYDER

In the celebrity infotainment complex, what's a publicist to do?

Time was when the biggest media-relations decision was choosing between Leno and Letterman, Vanity Fair and GQ. A photo shoot and a few goofy questions later, the job was done.

But there's been an explosion of outlets that want to delve into topics once confined to supermarket tabloids. As a result, the celebrity publicist's job has become

Turn to page 41

REAL CELEBS
- 24 covers — Jennifer Aniston
- 22 — Jennifer Lopez
- 8 — Jesus
- 8 — Mel Gibson

Top 300 consumer mags in past 12 months, as compiled by Source Interlink's Cover Analyzer

QUASI CELEBS
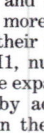
- 19 covers — Jessica Simpson
- 18 — Olsen Twins

- 8 — Paris Hilton
- 6 — Bachelorette Trista

307

THE GREAT COMMUNICATOR DIES AT 93

Continued from page 1

such a high executive office in the Golden State without years in politics.

Whenever actors would get too serious about their causes, the popular retort was: "Calm down. There's only one actor who ever changed history and that was John Wilkes Booth."

After Reagan's electoral wins, that joke was put to bed. No actor before or since has had such long-range political influence on the world.

But even in his acting days, Reagan had been an activist. He served as president of the Screen Actors Guild 1947-52 and 1959-60, a tenure fraught with controversy over possible conflicts of interest with his then-employer, MCA. It was also during this period that Reagan's political leanings switched from liberal to conservative.

Professional and poised

Aside from a few notable performances, such as those in "King's Row" and "The Killers," Reagan's 55 films consisted mostly of B-level assignments at Warner Bros. Contrary to legend, he did sometimes get the girl, but he rarely outshone his co-stars (who sometimes included Errol Flynn and Bette Davis).

He was professional and poised during his career in television as host of "General Electric Theater" and "Death Valley Days," making him a household name and a high-priced ticket on the lecture circuit as a GE spokesman.

Writing in Film Comment, critic Richard Schickel said that as a film actor, Reagan "lacked the art to transform himself through art. For Reagan, lacking the gift of transcendence, acting could only provide an extension of reality, not an escape from it."

But film and TV stardom was merely a prelude for what is regarded, even by his detractors, as one of the most successful political careers in the second half of the 20th century.

Ronald Wilson Reagan was born in Tampico, Ill., to John Edward and Nelle Reagan. His father, an itinerant shoe salesman, was a heavy drinker, which, Reagan wrote in his autobiography, left him with a lifelong aversion to alcohol.

After moving through various towns in Illinois, the Reagan family (which included another son, Neil) settled in Dixon. At Dixon High School, Reagan got his first taste of acting, which continued at Eureka College. He won an award at Northwestern U.'s annual one-act play festival for his role in Edna St. Vincent Millay's "Aria da Capo."

During the Depression, Franklin Roosevelt became his political hero. FDR demonstrated his warmth and ease at the microphone during the famous "Fireside Chats"; Reagan emulated this style, a talent that would later serve him well.

His vocal abilities landed him a job at WOC, a small radio station that broadcast the U. of Iowa football games. When WOC was merged with the larger WHO, Reagan's voice was heard announcing Chicago Cubs games.

While covering Cubs' spring training on Catalina Island, Reagan met talent agent Bill Meikeljohn, who referred him to Warner Bros. casting director Max Arnow. A screen test resulted in a $200-a-week seven-year contract at WB.

After his divorce from Jane Wyman, Reagan married Nancy Davis, with whom he starred in "Hellcats of the Navy."

His first assignment was a lead in the B-movie "Love Is on the Air," in which he played a radio announcer. A number of forgettable supporting roles followed until "Brother Rat," the film on which he met actress Jane Wyman, whom he married in 1940 at Kirk o' Heather in Forest Lawn.

"Rat" was stolen by a rising actor named Eddie Albert, but the studio liked Reagan enough to miscast him as the fey best friend to Bette Davis in "Dark Victory."

As the "Gipper" (George Gipp) in "Knute Rockne, All-American," Reagan gave one of his favorite performances in a supporting role.

From then on he was a leading man, though second leads mostly. He also gave a memorable performance in 1942's "King's Row" as a small-town playboy whose legs are needlessly amputated by a sadistic surgeon. A line he uttered in the film later became the title of his autobiography: "Where's the Rest of Me?"

Military man

"King's Row" was Reagan's greatest success as an actor, and it might have propelled him to greater stardom, but WWII intervened. He entered the Army as a second lieutenant, but because of nearsightedness he was transferred to the motion picture unit of the Air Corps, where he made training films.

He made several films during the war, including his most financially successful project, Irving Berlin's "This Is the Army," in 1943, but after that year he didn't have another picture out until 1947, and his shot at real stardom had passed.

According to legend, Reagan was briefly considered for the role of Rick in "Casablanca," but evidence is scanty and some film historians say he was really up for the role of Victor Laszlo, eventually played by Paul Henreid.

His agent Lew Wasserman renegotiated his contract to $3,500 a week (up from $1,650) after the war. But even though he appeared in high-profile projects like "Voice of the Turtle" and "The Hasty Heart," Warners was more than happy to let him out of his contract so he could freelance.

Television had appeared on the horizon, and the studios, which had lost the right to own their own theaters, were scrambling to trim expenses. During those years he appeared in such forgettable films as "Bedtime for Bonzo" and "Cattle Queen of Montana."

It was during this period that Reagan's political career began.

As president of SAG, he joined other celebrities in a crusade against alleged Communist infiltration of Hollywood and served as a friendly witness before the House Un-American Activities Committee, though he did not name names.

In 1948, Wyman divorced Reagan, in part because of his growing political involvement and because, she later said, she couldn't bear to watch "King's Row" one more time. Wyman is barely mentioned in his autobiography, although they were married for eight years and had two children, Maureen and an adopted son, Michael.

Shortly after divorcing Wyman, Reagan married aspiring actress Nancy Davis (they co-starred in a regrettable movie called "Hellcats of the Navy" in 1957), with whom he had two children Patti (Davis) and Ronald Reagan Jr. In a controversial move, SAG granted MCA the right to produce for television and promote its agency talent in its productions. There were allegations of kickbacks to Reagan, who was then president of SAG, but they were never proved.

In 1952, after a disastrous try at performing in Las Vegas, Reagan was hired by Wasserman to host "General Electric Theater." He also traveled extensively for GE, giving speeches as part of the company's public relations program. The GE connection forged his later commitment to the interests of big business.

After "GE Theater" went off the air, Reagan hosted "Death Valley Days" for three years.

During his final single-year tenure as SAG president from

Reagan, here with Marilyn Monroe, was a favorite on the lecture circuit.

1959-60, Reagan led the union in a five-week strike over residuals. Screen actors got a pension, health and welfare plan (radio and TV actors already had these benefits) and residuals for films made after 1960. They lost any residuals for pre-1948 films (which were regularly shown on TV and later on homevideo), and the producers paid a lump sum to SAG for films made between 1948-60.

SAG prexy Melissa Gilbert issued the following statement:

"Ronald Reagan presided over Screen Actors Guild at one of the most challenging moments in our union's history, as the rise of television significantly impacted the compensation and working conditions for the nation's screen actors. Under his tenure, SAG grew significantly in size and influence as the guild tackled issues ranging from runaway production to fair compensation to unity in an increasingly complex industry — all issues that remain timely to working actors today.

"It can be said that Ronald Reagan got his start in politics at Screen Actors Guild. ... He devoted years of his life to advancing the wages, benefits and working conditions of his fellow actors. He leaves behind an enduring legacy to this industry, as he does to the country as a whole. Our thoughts and prayers are with his family today."

In 1962, Reagan switched to the Republican Party, ending once and for all what he referred to as his

TALENT AND TURMOIL

Star's death stirs frenzy
By PAT SAPERSTEIN

Michael Jackson's death was much like his life — a circus of rabid fans, family, opportunists and media members, who were in a frenzy Thursday trying to confirm yet another rumor about one of the strangest and most high-flying celebrity lives on record.

On Thursday afternoon, a crowd gathered at UCLA Medical Center soon after word spread that the self-declared "King of Pop" had been rushed there from his Bel-Air home. The Los Angeles Fire Dept. responded to a call that he was not breathing.

Website TMZ reported his death around 2:30 p.m. PT, igniting a media frenzy.

Michael Jackson was prepping comeback concerts when he died Thursday at 50.

The rise and fall of Jackson was one of those only-in-America stories of a hugely talented child who became one of the world's most recognized and respected talents — followed by an adulthood of lofty plans, lawsuits, financial crises, plastic surgery, health scares and salacious gossip. Through all the hardships, a loyal core of fans remained faithful, while others fell away (or walked away in dismay).

In the 1980s, he was the center of a little empire: He had hit records, concert appearances, a thriving publishing company and big, big plans. By the time he died,

Turn to page 18

Biz ventures hit and miss
By CYNTHIA LITTLETON

In a life lived mostly in the spotlight, Michael Jackson pursued a wide range of showbiz ventures, some quixotic, some quite lucrative.

He had a reputation for announcing grandiose plans — he was going to play Peter Pan on the bigscreen, he was going to spearhead a theme park in India, he was going to produce a slate of movies for Sony Pictures — that never came to fruition.

His most recent initiative was a series of comeback concerts in London that were to have begun July 8. But that 50-date stand at London's O2

Turn to page 17

Crowds gather at UCLA Medical Center Thursday afternoon.

Fans find ways to mourn Gloved One

By JUSTIN KROLL and ANDREW STEWART

Thursday afternoon and evening, Michael Jackson's fans gathered together to mourn his death and celebrate his life in Hollywood, Westwood and various other spots around town.

But worldwide, the Internet and Twitter became the collective grieving ground for millions who wanted to find news about Jackson or express their feelings. Spikes in traffic were huge, slowing down servers, according to numerous press reports.

Motorists in L.A. could hear various Jackson songs on other drivers' car radios, since plenty of stations devoted airtime to the performer.

In Westwood, dozens gathered outside of the Ronald Reagan UCLA Medical Center. Some supporters brought flowers, looking for a place to lay them, while many others brought out cameras and phones to record the event. One group wired a laptop with speakers and sang along with Jackson's "Billie Jean."

Mourners at the star of another "Michael Jackson" pay tribute. Singer Michael Jackson's star was off-limits Thursday.

Family members and friends of Jackson's also arrived at the hospital, including Elizabeth Taylor and the star's brother, Jermaine Jackson.

Shortly after 6 p.m., Jermaine Jackson held a brief press conference. He said the cause of death had yet to be determined. Then he asked everyone to give the family room to grieve.

In Hollywood, fans' sentiments may have been sincere, even if their sense of location was a bit askew. Jackson's star is in front of the Chinese Theater but was off-limits Thursday afternoon and evening because of Universal's "Bruno" premiere.

The Hollywood Chamber of Commerce directed mourners to the Jacksons' family star on Vine Street. But a few folks came up with an alternative and left flowers on the star of radio host Michael Jackson, the Brit who is considered the father of talkradio in Los Angeles.

NEW 'MASTERPIECE' MINIS

Continued from page 2

Jonathan Pryce, Tim Curry and Tom Hiddleston ("Wallender").

Heidi Thomas, writer of the original adaptation, will pen the sequel.

"The 39 Steps" stars Rupert Penry Jones ("MI-5") in the lead role originated onscreen by Robert Donat in 1935. In addition, WGBH nabbed "Sharpe's Peril" and "Sharpe's Challenge," each consisting of two 90-minute parts starring Sean Bean and shot entirely in India.

BBC and WGBH are also teaming on the 90-minute "Framed," an adaptation of Frank Cottrell Boyce's children's novel, and the two-part "Small Island," based on Andrea Levy's 2004 novel about an ambitious Jamaican woman in post-WWII London. Naomie Harris ("Pirates of the Caribbean") will star in the latter.

LONG, WILD SHOWBIZ RIDE

Continued from page 1

Arena appeared troubled beginning in May, when it was announced that the first four performances would be pushed back. The three nights that were to begin the "This Is It" concert run were rescheduled for the tail end of his stint, which would have pushed the run into the first week of March. All of those concerts at the 15,000-seat facility were sold out, except the four rescheduled dates in March; ticket prices started at $81.

Jackson's most successful biz venture, beyond his own album sales, was his investment in music publishing rights, most notably the Beatles' catalog, which he purchased for about $48 million in 1985. He sold 50% of that catalog to Sony in 1995, and in recent years he was understood to have sold more of his remaining stake in order to support his opulent life style.

Jackson struggled for credibility in showbiz circles in his later years amid reports of increasingly eccentric behavior and allegations of child molestation. The "King of Pop" moniker that he earned in his heyday became a punchline as he struggled to muster respectable sales for his greatest-hits compilations and his last Epic Records release, 2001's "Invincible."

In February 1994, on the heels of the first eruption of child molestation allegations, Jackson and his family members mounted the NBC TV special "Jackson Family Honors." It was billed as the start of an annual event to honor entertainers and others for charitable and humanitarian works. But the reports, tabloid and otherwise, about his alleged bedroom encounters with a 13-year-old boy at Neverland put a dark cloud over the event, and there was never a second installment. In its review of the spesh, the New York Times noted that "it scored a 10 on the bizarre meter."

During AFM in 2002, Jackson announced a deal to invest $15 million-$20 million in Mark Damon's MDP Worldwide Entertainment. The agreement was to have given Jackson equity in MDP and create the Neverland Pictures banner, in partnership with Indian producer Raju Sharad Patel. It's unclear if any pics were produced through that banner.

More recently, Jackson faced a slew of lawsuits and legal actions, on everything from back pay for Neverland Ranch workers to prospective business partners and concert promoters to his former publicist who claimed he owed her a share of business deals she helped negotiate. The flurry of litigation during the past decade offered mounting evidence that Jackson was in dire financial straits and living beyond his means in luxury hotels around the world and traveling on private jets.

Foreclosure proceedings began in 2007 on his famed Neverland Ranch near Santa Barbara, which in its heyday sported an amusement park, a private zoo and other amenities. Jackson, who owed more than $24 million on the 2,700-acre property he purchased in 1988, ultimately worked out a deal with an investment firm, Colony Capital, that allowed him to retain a small ownership interest in Neverland, though he no longer lived there.

Just this month, he was hit with a lawsuit filed by a New Jersey promoter who claimed to have a deal with Jackson for a reunion concert with his brothers this summer. The suit filed by Allgood Entertainment claimed Jackson's London stand violated the exclusivity terms of his deal for the reunion gig.

In April, Jackson got into a legal scuffle with auction house Julien's, which was to have held a sale of more than 1,400 items of Jackson's from Neverland. At the last minute Jackson sued to block the auction, saying that Julien's had reneged on a promise to let him approve the list of items before the sale began. The sides eventually reached a compromise to hold an "exhibition" rather than a sale of the items, which was held over a two-week period at the BevHilton.

The array of items on display reinforced a sense of the fairy-tale world that Jackson crafted for himself at Neverland — complete with floor-to-ceiling portraits of himself in monarch garb.

(Steve Chagollan contributed to this report.)

Nets scramble to air two tributes

By MICHAEL SCHNEIDER

As Michael Jackson's death was confirmed late Thursday afternoon, the networks scrambled to put together last-minute news specials.

Just 90 minutes before primetime was set to begin on the East Coast, ABC, NBC and CBS quickly yanked repeats off their skeds in order to run Jackson specials out of their news departments.

ABC and NBC had already raced to slate 10 p.m. specials on the passing of "Charlie's Angels" star Farrah Fawcett; with Jackson's death, the nets were forced to block out another hour of programming to deal with the news.

Execs at both nets had caught wind early this week that Fawcett was near the end of her life, and by the night before her death, ABC had already slated a Thursday-night special, "Farrah Fawcett: Her Life, Her Loves, Her Legacy."

Following the Jackson news, ABC then also scheduled news special "The Life and Death of Michael Jackson" at 9 p.m.

Barbara Walters introduced the two-hour block, while Martin Bashir — who was behind the famed 2003 documentary "Living With Michael Jackson" — anchored the Jackson tribute. Walters returned to anchor the Fawcett special at 10.

"The news division is very well positioned to crash on a major story like this," said ABC News spokesman Jeffrey Schneider. Over at NBC, the Peacock decided on Thursday to preempt its 10 p.m. hour for a Fawcett special, postponing an episode of "The Listener" until next week. With the Jackson news, Peacock then yanked its 9 p.m. repeats and package a two-hour "Dateline NBC" devoted to news of both deaths.

CBS, meanwhile, preempted its 10 p.m. "Mentalist" repeat (which moved to 8 p.m.) with its own Jackson special — also titled "The Life and Death of Michael Jackson."

"Early Show" anchor Harry Smith hosted the special with "The Insider's" Lara Spencer; the death of Fawcett was also discussed.

Finally, on Fox, judge Nigel Lythgoe paid tribute to Fawcett, Jackson and even Ed McMahon during the live "So You Think You Can Dance" results show.

Meanwhile, MTV preempted its programming to do something it almost never does anymore (outside of the early morning): air musicvideos. Jackson concert footage and videos were being telecast on the cabler during the 7 p.m. hour on the East Coast. (MTV's West Coast feed, however, was still stuck airing other programming.)

According to MTV, the channel and its sisters MTV2, MTV Tres and MTVU went on with Jackson videos around 6:30 p.m. ET; MTV was also breaking in with MTV News segments featuring personality Sway. The cabler also went live at 9 p.m. ET with a one-hour special about Jackson, featuring videos and celebrity/musician reactions.

The Future

And what will the future be—for the entertainment industry, for the world at large, and even for *Variety*?

Things have radically changed since *Variety* began, but, as the song says, "The fundamental things apply / As time goes by."

Three things, though, are certain.

First, personal entertainment will get even more sophisticated. Viewing at home (via TV and computer screens) or on the go (via tablets and mobile) will be even easier. So will self-created fare, like the brief films showcased on YouTube.

Second, audiences will always want to leave the house and be entertained in the company of others.

Third, for better or for worse, though human nature will never change, circumstances will. All the conflicts that *Variety* recorded over the past century—prejudice, resistance to change, management and talent wrangling over salaries, censors and politicians lambasting entertainment—will be played out again and again, many times, in the future.

And, regardless of what the next technological innovation may be, content will always be king. In the early twentieth century, theater owners made films to feed their pipeline. When they were forced to choose between production or exhibition, they chose the former. They knew that without quality movies, the theaters would be empty. Over the years, fads like talkers, 3-D, and TV stole the spotlight for a time, but amazement always fades, and decision makers eventually realize that audiences want quality, not novelty.

What will the future look like? It's been depicted endless times in entertainments since the novels of Jules Verne and H. G. Wells and the films of Georges Méliès, including the 1902 *Le voyage dans la lune*. In general, showbiz's crystal-ball gazing during the past century-plus falls into several categories:

1. The future is different. But only a little.

Though the designs are sleeker, things basically look the same, with only a few key differences. In *Sleeper*, pop culture from the 1960s and 1970s has survived, but kitsch is regarded as high art. In *Back to the Future* (1985), aside from flying cars and hoverboards, the time travelers find the future

Right: A vision of the future from the beginning of filmmaking.

landscape extremely familiar (*Jaws 18* is at the multiplex). In *Never Let Me Go* (2010), the world looks virtually identical to today—the change being that clones have been created to harvest body parts for needy humans. *Idiocracy* (2006) shows the long-range result when intelligent people keep eschewing parenthood while knuckleheads breed without a second or intelligent thought, resulting in a world overtaken by people with low IQs. *Children of Men* (2006) addresses breeding as well, but the future isn't particularly sleek looking: people are still hoarding useless objects and living in a cluttered landscape. In the *X-Men* series, it's again breeding, but this time mutants with unusual powers are trying to survive bigots, who prove to be just as plentiful as they are today.

2. Technology reigns.

Filmmakers have always marveled at inventions, which are, occasionally, beneficial. *Fantastic Voyage* (1966) shows medical advances working to help people. In *Armageddon* (1998), engineers help Earth divert a meteoric disaster.

More often, the technology is neutral (or, to use a term from the computer era, agnostic). Works as diverse as *Flash Gordon* (1936/1980), *Buck Rogers* (1939.1979), *Conquest of Space* (1955) and *When Worlds Collide* (1951), *Barbarella* (1968), *Star Wars* (1977), *Alien* (1979), and *Futurama* (1999) depict a world where people just happen to travel to other planets, facing challenges from other life forms, not from machines. There are spaceships and talking computers, but they're just window dressing.

The same is true of robots. Ever since Karel Capek popularized use of the word "robot" in his 1921 futuristic play *R.U.R.*, these humanlike inventions have popped up frequently, usually doing chores for humans in everything from *The Jetsons* (1962) to *Sleeper* (1973) to *Heartbeeps* (1981).

Some technology is useful in battling aliens, as in *The Thing* (1982), *Mars Attacks!* (1996), *Invaders from Mars* (1953), *War of the Worlds* (1953.2005), and *Independence Day* (1996). Sometimes human ingenuity and integrity are just too puny to fight other life forms, as in *Invasion of the Body Snatchers* (1956/1978). And occasionally those outer-space folks are more evolved and remind us about what it means to be human, as in *The Day the Earth Stood Still* (1951/2008), *E.T. the Extra-Terrestrial* (1982), and *The Abyss* (1989).

The *Star Trek* franchise offers a better, barrier-free world in which one doesn't have to be a rich white man to hold a position of authority. And since interplanetary romances occur, audiences assume that LGBT characters are treated with an equal amount of respect and dignity. Other than the many *Star Trek* incarnations, sci-fi doesn't depict much emotional or philosophical progress.

3. Technology reigns, so watch out!

Of course, there is no drama without conflict, but in most works about the future, machines are our allies—until one little mishap wreaks havoc.

The quintessential science-gone-awry work is Stanley Kubrick's 1968 *2001: A Space Odyssey*, in which computer HAL wrests control from humans (who have become more soulless and unemotional than machines). Computers take over and start a nuclear war in the 1970 *Colossus: The Forbin Project*; in the 1977 *Demon Seed*, a super computer impregnates the wife of its inventor.

But often, technology is just a powerful weapon being used by evil humans. The future is a dangerous place in the 1927 Fritz Lang silent film, *Metropolis*, and the 1936 *Things to Come*, written by H. G. Wells. These concerns are echoed in other seminal works including the works adapted from Aldous Huxley's *Brave New World* and George Orwell's *1984*, as well as films including *THX 1138* (1971), *Logan's Run* (1976), and *Minority Report* (2002).

Above: Nichelle Nichols, DeForest Kelley, William Shatner, and Leonard Nimoy in *Star Trek*.

The *Terminator* franchise features a tech yin-yang, with benevolent robots sent from the future to prevent nuclear annihilation, while other bad robots are out to kill the humans.

4. The future is a wasteland.

There are a lot of dystopian films in which Earth has been decimated, usually as the result of a nuclear catastrophe.

The Road Warrior (1981) (aka *Mad Max 2*) and *Blade Runner* (1982) set the tone and the look for dozens of imitations, but all had the same premise: in the future, things look bleak and human behavior is similar to that of our cave-dwelling ancestors. In *Blade Runner*, most "respectable" people seem to have moved to other planets, leaving Earth to lowlifes, renegade replicants, terrible weather, and neon. *Mad Max* and its sequels set the tone for many other films (ranging from 1981's *Escape from New York* to 1995's *Waterworld* to 2008's *Wall-E*).

The Time Machine (1960/2002) takes its protagonist 800,000 years into the future when nuclear devastation has changed the order of things: the world is run by monsterlike Morlocks who enslave the pretty-but-vacant human race, called Eloi. There's a similar post-annihilation role reversal in *Planet of the Apes*, with humans in cages controlled by the apes.

The 1971 *The Andromeda Strain* (based on a novel by Michael Crichton) was the rare film that addressed global health concerns. Eco-awareness grew after Rachel Carson's influential 1962 nonfiction book about pesticides, *Silent Spring*, but these concerns were a subtext in many futurist works, in which the world's oil or water are depleted, people have reverted to feral behavior, etc., etc. There have been only a few films specifically themed to eco-matters, including *Z.P.G.* (1972; meaning "zero population growth"), *Silent Running* (1974), and, of course, *Godzilla vs. the Smog Monster* (1971). (And, lest we forget, monsters like Godzilla and the creature in South Korea's *The Host* [2006] are the result of science gone wrong.)

Soylent Green (1973) makes it clear that Earth's problems are the result of overpopulation, so the powers that be come up with a unique solution to poverty and world hunger. And James Cameron's *Avatar* (2009) carries a very strong eco-message.

And then there are more unusual predictions.

TV's *Battlestar Galactica* (1978) shows a world where humans have invented smarter robots, which in turn create an even smarter generation of robots . . . which in turn means "look out, humans!"

A.I. (2001), from a script by Stanley Kubrick, was not one of the biggest hits for director Steven Spielberg, but it's one of the most radical movies he made—or anyone else ever made, for that matter. It takes the *Battlestar* scenario one step further. The film posits that humans are just one step in an evolutionary chain and will eventually become unnecessary and extinct. In contrast, robots will continue to evolve and will inherit the Earth.

Many different depictions of tomorrowland, but which will be accurate? All of them. And none of them. It's like when a famous actor puts on old-age makeup for a role. And then, in real life, twenty-five years later, the actor has aged, but not in the way that the makeup people had predicted. The young actor, the made-up young actor, and the older actor all look similar, but different.

As for *Variety*, after being available only in print for ninety years, it added a Web presence and then, in the twenty-first century, initiated multiple new methods of getting the news: email alerts, an iPad app that electronically duplicates the layout of the paper, Twitter feeds, etc. As the world was trying to figure out how to harness the myriad of new technologies, *Variety* inaugurated a paywall on its website, meaning that news and analysis are only available to subscribers.

But, as always, content is king. These new tech tools are cool. Very cool. But they're still less important than the fact that *Variety* keeps the industry—and the world—up to date on what's going on.

Variety's goal for the future remains the same as it was in 1905: news and analysis. As has been proven, for more than one hundred years within our pages, the entertainment industry provides unusual but accurate insights into the tastes and daily habits of audiences—and into the world at large.

Variety may or may not be the spice of life, but it's definitely the prism of life.

Right: January 3, 2010.

VARIETY.COM • THE INTERNATIONAL ENTERTAINMENT WEEKLY • DECEMBER 21, 2009 - JANUARY 3, 2010

TEN YEARS OF TUMULT
Seismic shifts will reverberate in next decade

By CYNTHIA LITTLETON

The new millennium began with a sigh of relief about what *didn't* happen: Y2K. But since then, the past decade has offered nonstop action.

In 2000, the iPod had yet to be introduced. Xbox, iTunes, YouTube, Hulu and Facebook didn't exist. Twitter was something young hearts did in spring. High-speed Internet access was found in less than 5% of U.S. homes (today it's about 63%). DVDs were just starting to take off at the expense of VHS while DVRs were just starting to uproot VCRs.

Change is good, but it's also unsettling and exhausting. A survey of the last 10 years offers ample evidence that Hollywood hasn't lived through such a decade of change since at least the 1920s — which also happened to correspond with a roller-coaster of a business cycle and technological advancements that touched every corner of the industry. Once Mickey Mouse whistled in "Steamboat Willie" and Al Jolson crooned in "The Jazz Singer," the town knew it was all over for silent pictures.

Perhaps the single biggest change that showbiz has grappled with this century is the loss of so much of the control it once wielded over the production, distribution and exhibition of filmed entertainment. Consumers have more say in when and how they decide to see a movie or watch a favorite TV show, or forgo those leisure-time traditions entirely for a vidgame or an online pursuit.

It's maddening to many in the biz that ticket buyers and TV watchers are more fickle, simply because there are so many more options, or that a $15,000 horror pic with great Internet buzz can outshine movies with budgets 1,000 times bigger.

The cost of making a movie or TV show used to be an insurmountable barrier to entry for nonpros, but the dawn of YouTube and the high-def digital videocamera changed all that. Just ask "Paranormal Activity" helmer Oren Peli, who was working as a vidgame programmer in San Diego when he decided to invest in a camera and venture into movie-

Over & Out

How did we get to this point? And, more important, where do we go from here?
In the past 10 years, the old rule book was thrown out, with more changes than in any other decade in showbiz history. Every aspect took momentous new turns, and the biz is still grappling with the ramifications.
These lists are not just for fun, and they're not just a backwards glance at a wacky decade. Rather, it's worth remembering how the transformations of the past 10 years have buffeted the biz, because they are cues for the future.

(And for the persnickety, some consider 2001 the start of the new century. But to most of us, Jan. 1, 2000, was the beginning.)

making, on his own terms. For a biz that has traditionally been incredibly insular and pampered by its unique ability to generate riches and exert far-reaching cultural influence, that kind of party-crashing is hard to get used to.

Merger of the millennium

The event that foreshadowed all of this came nine days after New Year's 2000: The $165-billion marriage of AOL and Time Warner wasn't merely going to accelerate the digital revolution and rewrite the rules of media and showbiz. It was going to change lives, AOL chairman Steve Case and Time Warner chief Gerald Levin gushed in announcing the deal Jan. 10, 2000. "We're going to try and make a better world," Levin told PBS' Jim Lehrer.

Well, it certainly changed *their* lives, not to mention the huge dent it put in the retirement accounts and stock options of thousands of Time Warner employees, who bore the brunt of $125 billion in write-downs taken on AOL's value over the past seven years.

The deal is now regarded as the worst corporate marriage in history. But the AOL-Time Warner union did deliver on at least one of its implicit promises: For Hollywood, the decade would be driven largely by the upheaval wrought by the explosion of digital media.

The merger came together at the height of the dot-com bubble, an era that seems almost quaint by comparison with the disruptions of the current moment. Remember Digital Entertainment Network? Flooz.com? Excite@Home? Pop.com? How can you not look back fondly on an era when college-age kids

See **TUMULT** *page 28*

'00	
Jan. 10, 2000:	AOL, Time Warner announce $165 billion merger
Oct. 23, 2001:	Apple launches the iPod
June 11, 2002:	"American Idol" bows on Fox
Oct. 8, 2003:	GE buys Universal from Vivendi
April 23, 2005:	First video uploaded to YouTube
Oct. 12, 2005:	Disney's groundbreaking iTunes licensing pact
Sept. 10, 2007:	"Harry Potter" becomes top-grossing pic franchise
Nov. 5, 2007:	Start of 100-day writers strike
March 9, 2009:	Media stocks hit historic lows as stock market sinks
Dec. 3, 2009:	Comcast buys 51% of NBC Universal
'09	

inside
- **BART** With budgets high and low, studios go for production polarity. **Page 2**
- **FILM** The aughts brought otherworldly heroes and other people's money. **Page 6**
- **TECH** An intricate guide shows how "Avatar" rethought moviemaking. **Page 12**
- **TV** Broadcast networks endured decade of devices and diversions. **Page 15**
- **LEGIT** Strikes and strife in the '00s didn't stop the song and dance. **Page 25**

Photo Credits

Front cover: Christian Kober/Robert Harding World Imagery/Getty Images

Back cover: The Artist: Peter Iovino

Page 5: The Muppets Take Manhattan (c) 1984 TriStar Pictures, Inc. All Rights Reserved. Courtesy of TriStar Pictures.

Page 6: Cary Grant: Hulton Archive/Getty Images

Page 9: Courtesy of Martin Scorsese

Page 24: Four Follies: Hulton Archive/Getty Images

Page 26: Sarah Bernhardt: W. and D. Downey/Getty Images

Page 27: The Follies: Hulton Archive/Getty Images

Pages 28 and 29: The Birth of a Nation: Hulton Archive/Getty Images

Page 31: P.T. Barnum and Commodore Nutt: Hulton Archive/Getty Images

Page 32: Tarzan of the Apes: Frederic Lewis/Getty Images

Page 34: Vaudeville Theatre: Hulton Archive/Getty Images

Page 35: The Dolly Sisters: General Photographic Agency/Getty Images

Page 38: United Artists: Topical Press Agency/Getty Images

Page 43: Flappers: Hulton Archive/Getty Images

Page 45: Clara Bow: Hulton Archive/Getty Images

Page 46: Joan Crawford: John Kobal Foundation/Getty Images; Harold Lloyd: Hulton Archive/Getty Images

Page 47: Buster Keaton: Hulton Archive/Getty Images

Page 48: The Hunchback of Notre Dame: Michael Ochs Archives/Getty Images

Page 49: The Jazz Singer: Archive Photos/Getty Images

Page 50: The Sheik: Hulton Archive/Getty Images

Page 53: Cleopatra: Hulton Archive/Getty Images

Page 54: Josephine Baker: Hulton Archive/Getty Images

Page 61: Florenz Ziegfeld: Hulton Archive/Getty Images

Page 67: Al Capone: APA/Getty Images; The Public Enemy: Hulton Archive/Getty Images

Page 68: Fred and Adele Astair: Pictorial Parade/Getty Images

Page 69: Fred Astair and Ginger Rogers: Michael Ochs Archives/Getty Images

Page 70: Norma Shearer, Irving Thalberg, and Jack Warner: Hulton Archive/Getty Images

Page 72: Frankenstein: Hulton Archive/Getty Images

Page 75: King Kong: Hulton Archive/Getty Images

Page 77: George and Ira Gershwin: Archive Photos/Getty Images; Cole Porter: Sasha/Getty Images

Page 78: Ingrid Bergman and Cary Grant: Hulton Archive/Getty Images

Page 79: Marlene Dietrich: Eugene Robert Richee/Getty Images

Page 82: Our Gang: Margaret Chute/Getty Images; Shirley Temple: Hulton Archive/Getty Images

Page 83: Bugs Bunny: Apic/Getty Images

Page 84: Laurel and Hardy: Fox Photos/Getty Images

Page 86: Mae West: Hulton Archive/Getty Images

Page 90: The Wizard of Oz: Silver Screen Collection/Getty Images

Page 92: Bessie Smith: Michael Ochs Archives/Getty Images

Page 93: Billie Holiday: Charles Peterson/Getty Images

Page 110: Casablanca: Michael Ochs Archives/Getty Images

Page 112: Betty Grable: Hulton Archive/Getty Images

Page 113: Rita Hayworth in Gilda: Hulton Archive/Getty Images

Page 120: Andy Hardy Meets a Debutante: Hulton Archive/Getty Images

Page 128: Gone with the Wind: Silver Screen Collection/Getty Images

Page 133: James Dean: Michael Ochs Archives/Getty Images

Page 135: Charlie Chaplin images: Hulton Archive/Getty Images

Page 138: Lucille Ball and Desi Arnaz in I Love Lucy: Archive Photos/Getty Images

Page 140: Grace Kelly: Pictorial Parade/Getty Images

Page 141: Rin Tin Tin: Hulton Archive/Getty Images

Page 148: Marilyn Monroe: Michael Ochs Archives/Getty Images

Page 150: A Streetcar Named Desire: Hulton Archive/Getty Images

Page 151: Elvis Presley: Michael Ochs Archives/Getty Images

Page 154: Louis Armstrong: Hulton Archive/Getty Images

Page 165: The Sound of Music/ Michael Ochs Archives/Getty Images

Page 169: Debbie Reynolds with Carrie and Todd Fisher: Bruce Bailey/Getty Images

Page 170: Rosemary's Baby: Keystone/Getty Images

Page 172: The Supremes: Michael Ochs Archives/Getty Images

Page 173: The Beatles: Evening Standard/Getty Images

Pages 178 and 179: Guess Who's Coming to Dinner (c) 1967, renewed 1995 Columbia Pictures Industries, Inc. All Rights Reserved. Courtesy of Columbia Pictures

Page 181: I Spy: Archive Photos/Getty Images

Page 182: Ben-Hur: Silver Screen Collection/Getty Images

Page 183: Bob Dylan: Michael Ochs Archives/Getty Images

Sherry Lansing:

"I was the first woman to run a studio at 35. The headline was a picture of me. '20th Century Fox Gets a First Lady.' It was a great headline! A very clever headline and I saved it.

The most distinctive thing thing about *Variety* to me are the headlines. The phrases and the way you play with words. The cleverness is really one of the unique things you have. And Peter Bart's column, waking up every morning and seeing if your name was there. Everything is just so clever."

Page 184: The Jackson 5: Michael Ochs Archives/Getty Images

Page 186: Sidney Poitier: Archive Photos/Getty Images

Page 189: Janis Joplin: RB/Getty Images

Page 190: Walter Cronkite: Hulton Archive/Getty Images

Page 196: Cleopatra: API/Getty Images

Page 199: Clint Eastwood: CBS Photo Archive/Getty Images

Page 205: James Bond: From Russia With Love: Archive Photos/Getty Images

Page 211: Jaws: Michael Ochs Archives/Getty Images

Page 233: Star Wars: Terry O'Neill/Getty Images

Page 237: Gloria Gaynor and The Village People: Michael Ochs Archives/Getty Images

Page 238: Sesame Street: Hulton Archive/Getty Images

Page 242: Donahue: Yvonne Hemsey/Getty Images

Page 244: Saturday Night Live and SCTV: NBC/Getty Images

Page 249: E.T.: The Extra-Terrestrial: Fotos International/Getty Images

Page 251: Dallas: CBS Photo Archive/Getty Images

Page 252: Ted Turner: Archive Photos/Getty Images

Page 263: Michael Jackson: Dave Hogan/Getty Images

Page 265: Madonna: Michael Putland/Getty Images

Page 267: Matt Groening and Bart Simpson: Getty Images

Page 268: Bruce Springsteen: Hulton Archive/Getty Images

Page 273: Oprah Winfrey: Kevin Winter/Getty Images

Page 311: A Trip to the Moon: Hulton Archive/Getty Images

Page 313: Star Trek: CBS Photo Archive/Getty Images

Thanks and Acknowledgments:

This book would not exist without *Variety* publisher Brian Gott and president Neil Stiles, Ellen Goldsmith-Vein and the gang at Gotham Group. I am indebted to all of them. And a huge thanks to the expert Rizzoli team: publisher Charles Miers, copyeditor Elizabeth Smith, and designer Chris McDonnell.

Personal gratitude to Ashley Peter, Joe Earley, Suzanne Fritz, Lea Yardum, Antonello de'Medici and the staff of the Danieli, and to my brother Larry Gray and the rest of my family.

A deep bow to the current staff of *Variety*, and all the past employees and contributors. I learned many things from Thomas M. Pryor and Peter Bart, including the important intersection of showbiz and "reallife" events. Thanks. And I was helped on the book by current staffers Gregg Byrnes, Terry Flores, Sarah Farr, Lisa Ng, John Ross and Brian Sheehan, Joni Ballinger, Malik Simmons and Stanley Atkins—and by Dina Lawrence, Jasmine Curth and the team at Getty Images.

Thanks to Martin Scorsese, for his movies, his film preservation and, of course, the heartfelt and touching introduction to this book. Special kudos, as we say in *Varietyese*, to T. Tara Turk, whose taste, patience, intelligence and good humor were invaluable every step of the way.

And a standing ovation for my editor, Mr. Robb Pearlman, a man of vision, enthusiasm, taste, and a contagious sense of fun.

And to all of you readers, thanks in advance for not complaining. This is not a comprehensive history of entertainment; it's a look at the constant intertwining of politics, sociology and entertainment. We've tried to cover 107 years of showbiz, so if you don't find your faves, forgive us. If it's any consolation, I omitted or underplayed some of my personal favorites (Tim Burton, Julie Christie, Crowded House, Vanessa Redgrave, George Clooney, Jon Stewart, *The Sopranos*, and many, many others).

Ah, well. That's showbiz.

Tim Gray